The Sports Event Management and Marketing Playbook
Third Edition

The Wiley Event Management Series

Series Editor: Dr. Shawn Seungwon Lee

The Sports Event Management and Marketing Playbook

Third Edition

Frank Supovitz
Robert Goldwater

WILEY

VICE PRESIDENT, ACADEMIC PUBLISHING	Amanda Miller
DIRECTOR	Justin Jeffryes
EXECUTIVE EDITOR	Todd Green
SENIOR MANAGING EDITOR	Judy Howarth
PRODUCTION EDITOR	Mahalakshmi Babu
MARKETING MANAGER	Alex Tasic
COVER PHOTO CREDIT	© Csaba Peterdi/Shutterstock

This book was set in 9.5pt/11.5 pt Fairfield LT Std by Straive™.

Founded in 1807, John Wiley & Sons, Inc. has been a valued source of knowledge and understanding for more than 200 years, helping people around the world meet their needs and fulfill their aspirations. Our company is built on a foundation of principles that include responsibility to the communities we serve and where we live and work. In 2008, we launched a Corporate Citizenship Initiative, a global effort to address the environmental, social, economic, and ethical challenges we face in our business. Among the issues we are addressing are carbon impact, paper specifications and procurement, ethical conduct within our business and among our vendors, and community and charitable support. For more information, please visit our website: www.wiley.com/go/citizenship.

ISBN: 978-1-394-22056-4 (Cloth)

Library of Congress Cataloging-in-Publication Data:

Names: Supovitz, Frank, author. | Goldwater, Robert, author.
Title: The sports event management and marketing playbook / Frank Supovitz,
    Robert Goldwater.
Description: Third edition. | Hoboken, NJ : Wiley, [2024] | Series: The
    Wiley event management series | Includes index.
Identifiers: LCCN 2024019690 (print) | LCCN 2024019691 (ebook) | ISBN
    9781394220564 (hardback) | ISBN 9781394220540 (adobe pdf) | ISBN
    9781394220519 (epub)
Subjects: LCSH: Sports—Marketing—Handbooks, manuals, etc. |
    Sports—Economic aspects—Handbooks, manuals, etc. | Sports
    administration—Handbooks, manuals, etc.
Classification: LCC GV716 .S86 2024 (print) | LCC GV716 (ebook) | DDC
    796.06/9—dc23/eng/20240509
LC record available at https://lccn.loc.gov/2024019690
LC ebook record available at https://lccn.loc.gov/2024019691

The inside back cover will contain printing identification and country of origin if omitted from this page. In addition, if the ISBN on the back cover differs from the ISBN on this page, the one on the back cover is correct.
SKY10083452_090324

DEDICATION

This book is dedicated to the memory of
Edwin and Shirley Supovitz,
who encouraged their son to chase his dreams,
and to Catherine, Matt, Amy, Ethan, Jake, Madison, and Alexandra who live within them;
and to the memory of Bob Goldwater,
who introduced the magic of sports events to his ever-grateful son,
and to Colleen Callahan,
who introduced the gift of sharing magical events with her ever-grateful husband.

CONTENTS

Contents   ix

PREFACE

Sports Events Are Something Special

Dr. Joe Goldblatt, Ed.D., FRSA, tells the story of how the late Disneyland executive Robert F. Jani developed the park's tradition of Main Street parades. On opening day, as Walt Disney noticed his guests leaving his new park in the late afternoon, he turned to Jani, then his director of public relations, and asked him to create an attraction to keep people in the park into the night. Jani used the term "special event" to describe his new attraction, and, when asked to define this new term of art, he replied: "I guess it is something that is different from a normal day of living."

Applying Jani's definition, every sports competition could be considered a special event. Competitors vary from race to race; opponents change from game to game; and the outcome of any meet, match, or competition will remain unpredictable whether the event is one of 82 in a season, or a contest held just once a year. The underlying principles of planning, promotion, management, marketing, budgeting, and presentation are similar for organizations that play a full schedule of games and for event organizers who present a single-day event. Although the ***Third Edition*** of ***The Sports Event Management and Marketing Playbook*** provides the best practices applicable for managing everything from one-time annual events to season-long schedules, it is also devoted to the creation, development, management, marketing, production, and execution of sports events that stand out from the weekly team calendar.

Building a foundation to support and execute unique special events is like building an entirely new company or launching a new brand. It starts with creating a product (an event) to meet the wants and needs of potential customers (the participants, audience, and sponsors). The costs of designing, building, and bringing the product to market must be identified; the expected revenue projected; and the final financial results forecasted. Human resources must be applied to create and sell the product, and modifications considered after consumers provide feedback.

Although the management and marketing of sports events require a thorough grounding in traditional business disciplines, they are much more complex than a typical product introduction. To ensure success, event organizers must build alliances in their host community with local government and businesses, the host facility, sponsors and other business partners, media and broadcasters, and a variety of others with a vested interest in the successful outcome of the event.

About This Book

Welcome to Your Playbook

Exacting strategic planning and effective marketing are integral ingredients for success. By themselves, however, they will not ensure victory or create a finished product. Flawless execution of these events is essential to keep audiences excited, viewers tuned in, participants engaged, and sponsors fulfilled. After all, aside from the event's business partners, no one leaves a sports event comparing statistics about how well the marketing plan performed.

Hours and days, weeks and months must be spent attending to the hundreds of management, operations, and production details that are required to execute a seamless event. Although the preparatory process for one sports event can be different from that of another, most of the details on the planning checklist can be applied to a broad range of programs, regardless of size or budget. The **Third Edition** of **The Sports Event Management and Marketing Playbook** helps event organizers to apply the latest and best industry practices to methodically plan, monitor, manage, and evaluate their progress during the entire event-planning process. It offers an organic view of sports event planning and, as a result, is the only book to truly combine the disciplines of sports marketing and event management—as defined by their practitioners—into a single, integrated approach.

New to This Edition

English poet and essayist Samuel Johnson (1709–1784) once wrote: "Knowledge is of two kinds. We know a subject ourselves, or we know where we can find information upon it." The **Third Edition** of **The Sports Event Management and Marketing Playbook** serves as a practical reference handbook that is as relevant and current for grassroots sports organizers as it is for professional event managers, marketers, and promoters. Every step of the planning process for developing, planning, managing, and executing flawless sports events is explored and discussed with the following updated features:

- Helpful **charts** and **figures** ensure that every detail is considered before the gates open and the scoreclock begins its inexorable countdown.
- Illustrative, contemporary **Sideline Stories** include real-life anecdotes from the field that were a favorite feature of previous editions. These stories provide vivid examples of best practices, as well as plays that were proven best to avoid.
- An expanded section of useful **forms**, **sample documents**, and **checklists** can be accessed in the appendices at the end of the text and on a companion website (www.wiley.com/go/supovitz/sportseventplaybook3e), a resource that will be periodically refreshed as information is updated and innovations are introduced.

Organization and Theme

Eventually, like a concert virtuoso's fingers gliding effortlessly across the keyboard at speeds unfathomable and seemingly as reflex, experienced sports event organizers and marketers will come to know much of what it takes to produce spectacular results intuitively. But until you do, keep this volume close. It is as important to recognize what the questions are as it is to know where and how to derive the answers. The **Third Edition** of **The Sports Event Management and Marketing Playbook** has been organized so you can easily access specific areas of importance, as outlined at the start of each chapter, or "play."

Not every play is applicable in every game or in every situation. Proven fail-safe tactics are not always executed in the same order or in the same combinations. Their effective use depends on the progress of the event; some make more sense early in the game, while others at the end. At the stadium, arena, ball field, track, rink, recreation center, parking lot, or street course, victory is achieved by building the right team. Coaches must provide insightful training and instruction to familiarize the participants with the plays to be run, and then turn them loose. Organizers, those who operate, promote, and market events also build and coach a team of planners, managers, and role players, provide guidance on what actions need to be undertaken to achieve them, and then they turn them loose as well. You know you have the right team when the most common belief becomes apparent on the emotional level: losing is not an option, whether leaving the locker room or managing a budget.

Time to Start Planning

"Does thou love life? Then, do not squander time; for that's the stuff life is made of," said American statesman and philosopher Benjamin Franklin. Time and again, the most common reason we encounter for the cancellation or postponement of a sports event is a lack of sufficient planning time. For the audience, sports events seem to unfold spontaneously, much like the nature of sports contests themselves. But for anyone who has ever tried to organize a sports event, it is no news that these programs can take anywhere from a few months to a few years to plan, promote, and execute.

Some events are fixed on the calendar because they depend on existing league schedules, academic calendars, playing seasons, or weather. Other events are more flexible. Either way, start with the most desirable date for your event and work backward. Read Play 1 to determine what you want your event to achieve, and Plays 2 and 3 to understand the costs and financial benefits. Finally, apply the lessons learned in Play 5 to map out all the details that will have to be considered and how long each will take to complete. It is likely that you will find that no matter how distant the event date, the latest advisable time to start planning is now. So let's get going.

Supplemental Offerings

For those of you using this book in a classroom setting, an online **Instructor's Manual** with **Test Bank** accompanies this book and is available to instructors to help them effectively manage their time and to enhance student learning opportunities.

The computerized version of the **Test Bank** has been specifically formatted for **Respondus**, an easy-to-use software program for creating and managing exams that can be printed to paper or published directly to Blackboard, WebCT, Desire2Learn, eCollege, ANGEL, and other eLearning systems. Instructors who adopt this book can download the test bank for free.

A password-protected Wiley Instructor Book Companion website devoted entirely to this book (www.wiley.com/go/supovitz/sportseventplaybook3e) provides access to the online **Instructor's Manual,** all appendices, and the text-specific teaching resources. The **Respondus Test Bank** and **PowerPoint** lecture slides are also available on the website for download.

ACKNOWLEDGMENTS

The *Third Edition* of *The Sports Event Management and Marketing Playbook* would not have been possible without the hundreds of people who helped me to grow as a person, professional, and educator while contributing to and producing sports, entertainment, civic, and corporate events over more than 35 years. Many have helped us directly in the preparation of this book, and countless more have been teachers, counselors, coaches, mentors, collaborators, critics, employers, clients, colleagues, and friends without whom we could not have learned the lessons that Robert and I have tried to share.

First, I would like to thank Robert Goldwater, my co-author on the second and third editions, for his collegial friendship over the years. From our first collaboration at the 1994 NHL All-Star Weekend at Madison Square Garden to Bobby's broad expertise in running venues and delivering world-class customer experiences, his tenure as a sports commission executive, his professional leadership at the International Association of Venue Managers, and his academic leadership at Georgetown University made him a natural partner to work with me on the preparation of this revised volume.

NHL Commissioner Gary Bettman and then-COO Jon Litner enabled me to write the First Edition of *The Sports Event Management and Marketing Playbook* during my 13th season at the National Hockey League. Working with them to passionately promote the great frozen game in the United States, Canada, and internationally was a great honor and incredible fun. Special thanks to former NHL Enterprises executives Steve Ryan and Steve Flatow, who originally persuaded me to transfer my entertainment event experience into the world of professional sports more than three decades ago, and, as a result, set me on the path to the best jobs I have ever had.

I knew from our first meeting that NFL Commissioner Roger Goodell would make an amazing mentor who continues to challenge himself and those around him to constantly grow, excel, and do everything better than before. I always looked forward to his last words before a major NFL event began: "Don't mess this up." I recognize how lucky I was to work for him and then-Executive Vice President of NFL Business Ventures Eric Grubman, as well as for an organization as admired and successful as the National Football League. It provided me with the opportunity to test myself every day while producing events that I hope defined the best that sports events could offer.

More recently, clients who trust us with their brands and fans have enabled me to continue to evolve with the industry since founding Fast Traffic Events & Entertainment in 2014. Special thanks to my long-time friends at Indianapolis Motor Speedway, the Pro Football Hall of Fame, and other premier sports and entertainment brands who have been exceptional partners over the years.

Special thanks to my friends and colleagues Emilia Zarco and Greg Bouris who warmly welcomed me to the faculty of Adelphi University's Sport Management Program. It has been an exciting and fulfilling opportunity to help the next generation of professionals learn and develop.

My family has selflessly loaned me to sports events, leagues, and celebrations over my entire career, and has provided the balance and lasting value in my life. My wife, Catherine, children, Matt, Amy, Ethan, and Jake, and my grandchildren Madison and Alexandra have tolerated the long absences from home and anchor me when the pressure seems insurmountable. Thank you, all, for lovingly granting me some of the precious time we have together to write the third edition of this book.

We hope to see you at the game!

—*Frank Supovitz*

The invitation from my friend Frank to co-author the Second Edition of *The Sports Event Management and Marketing Playbook* was a direct result of my being a faculty member in Georgetown University's Sports Industry Management master's program. I had come to Frank with a few thoughts based on my using the book as required course reading, and he floored me with the flattering offer to collaborate on updating the book. To be able to work together again on a third edition is beyond what I could have imagined.

Since 2008, there has been nothing more satisfying than the interactions I continue to have with the enthusiastic students and alumni, my outstanding sports industry practitioner faculty colleagues, and supportive SIM and School of Continuing Studies staff while teaching at Georgetown. The knowledge shared and the words written in this book have been with them in mind.

No one could be more fortunate than I was to be able to serve 24 years at The World's Most Famous Arena, Madison Square Garden. There are so many indelible memories and priceless lessons from those years and so many extraordinary people who have remained with me as extended family wherever I go. Collectively, they provided the foundation for what I have been able to contribute to this book. My affection for and my gratitude to everyone and every event at the Garden are boundless.

Tim Leiweke convinced me to leave the Garden to help him, Phil Anschutz, and Ed Roski develop and open Staples Center. I would not have the benefit of the exhilarating experiences I continue to draw on from my time in Los Angeles without Tim's personal salesmanship and encouragement or without the exceptional team who came together to launch an arena that has had a remarkable impact on its city and its industry.

While I was the chief executive of the DC Sports and Entertainment Commission, the two board chairmen, John Richardson and Jack Mahoney, were leaders who sought excellence in sports event and venue management, an attribute we hope is stimulated in those who read and use this book.

My consulting firm, The Goldwater Group, has afforded me opportunities to contribute to a gratifying array of clients and projects, often with accomplished partners. Collectively, they have been tremendous sources of applied knowledge and information.

As a long-time member of the International Association of Venue Managers, I have been inspired by many profoundly dedicated executives and special friends in venue management. It is my hope that our book continues to contribute positively to IAVM, as well as to the current and future members of the Event and Venue Marketing Conference, the assembly of energetic and creative marketers on whom sports and entertainment events and venues rely, and to the Sport Leadership and Management majors at my alma mater, Miami University.

Finally, there are four people to whom I wish to express the deepest appreciation.

My dad, Bob. My overflowing passion for sports events and venues and for having a career in our industry was a natural result of the support of and experiences provided by my father, who also was the best journalism teacher and copy editor a young sports writer could possibly have had. He is missed.

I am very proud to be the husband of an exceptional college educator, a devoted sports fan, a thoughtful editor, a remarkably patient and giving individual, and the person with the most extraordinary spirit in the universe, Colleen Callahan.

Alex Greer, a Georgetown Sports Industry Management alum, was our very capable and meticulous assistant for the second edition of the book. His contributions continue to resonate in this third edition. We remain exceedingly grateful for all he did.

And, Frank Supovitz, the most talented and genuinely caring person in the sports event industry. As I have had the privilege to know for more than 30 years and as the world is reminded with every event that receives the singular Supovitz touch, Frank has literally and figuratively written the book on sports event management and marketing. He is, in a word, spectacular, as a professional colleague and as a generous, personal friend.

At its essence, our industry exists and flourishes because of the infinite talent and dedication of the constellation of stellar people who are responsible for presenting live events in worthy venues and welcoming destinations. On every occasion, we are connected through our capacity to create opportunities for someone to take home a priceless souvenir – an enduring memory – from any event. We hope this book serves as a guide to producing unforgettable moments at your event.

—Robert Goldwater

INTRODUCTION

"Good luck is a residue of preparation."
— *Jack Youngblood, Hall of Fame defensive end, Los Angeles Rams*

This section will . . .

- Explore the size and scope of the sports event management and marketing industry.
- Explore the philosophy that sports event management is based on the development of successful partnerships, as demonstrated by the U.S.O. (Understanding Stakeholders' Objectives) Principle.
- Discuss the latest trends in sports event management and marketing.

The Power of Sports Event Marketing

To the more than one billion sports fans worldwide who leap out of their seats when the home team scores with under a minute to go on the clock, who sacrifice sleep for the thrills of sudden death overtime, who check their mobile devices for game updates seemingly every minute, and who can't read, hear, or watch enough about sports from countless media sources and platforms, the grand strategists of sports are the coaches, trainers, and general managers who guide their favorite teams or athletes. The objectives of these leaders are uncompromising and clear—the pursuit of unequaled excellence: a winning score, a championship season, or a record-beating performance. They embrace a philosophy, system, and playbook that put them in the best possible competitive position. They consider the interpersonal chemistry on the roster, performance data, and the best practices of champions, while keeping track of the time and money available to invest in winning. During the game, they act quickly and decisively to capitalize on rapidly unfolding developments and to fend off the competition. Their world is dynamic and exciting. They change the plan when the plan needs changing, substituting plays, re-shuffling the lines, inserting pinch-hitters, or pulling the goaltender. After the crowds have gone and the locker rooms have cleared, they study recordings of the game, uncovering unanticipated flaws in their plans, and learning from the successes of their opponents. And, from season to season, rules are redefined, coaching strategies are resharpened, and new techniques are added to the playbook to improve the team's performance. The on-field product is constantly changing to maximize success, and so, too, is the business of sports and sports events.

The most successful sports event managers and directors—from professional league executives to community Little League volunteers—approach their mission in much the same way. They identify an event's objectives, develop the plan to achieve their goals, and raise the revenues required to realize them. They assemble the best team, monitor costs, and continually assess the progress they are making. They adjust to changing conditions by reading the field for portents of trouble or triumph. And finally, when it's all over, they conduct postmortems to evaluate how to build on their successes, learn from their mistakes, and apply the latest wisdom, techniques, and practices that will help them stay ahead of the competition.

Sports event marketing is big business, by some estimates a $500 billion+ industry that continues to grow and diversify. What makes sports events the world's most compelling entertainment form is the emotional capital the audience—our fans—invest in the outcome. Sports events are the original reality entertainment experiences—unpredictable and involving dramas for which the final resolution defies prediction. The stories are populated with engaging, larger-than-life characters and the stands are filled with enthusiastic fans who cheer and jeer until time expires.

News and sports websites, blogs, streaming services, influencers, and social networks have exploited this hunger for instant results. Sports fans access scores, statistics, replays, real-time play-by-play, and analysis from anywhere on the globe. Social networks not only provide instant bulletins on scores and statistics, but also enhanced, behind-the-scenes content, fan and media reactions to developments on the field, and information that until recently were accessible only to the most well-connected sports and event "insiders." Increasingly, many of these platforms offer fans the opportunity to customize their experiences and voice their own views.

The power of sports events is as personal as it is cultural. It is this emotional investment that attracts live audiences as well as media, sponsors, a variety of stakeholders, and, of course, the athletes themselves. The allure of sports across a wide diversity of cultures is so pervasive and universal that it brings people together who can agree on little else but their rooting interests. Fans demonstrate their tribal affinities by buying jerseys emblazoned with team logos and the names of their favorite players. They devote hours of their leisure time to watching broadcasts and streams of sports events, tracking statistics for their fantasy teams, and gathering intelligence to help improve their wagering success.

Savvy marketers—from the corner drugstore to multi-national corporations—know how audiences react to the action, excitement, grace, and fan interactivity of sports and sports events, and they use this knowledge to their advantage. They appreciate how potential customers are delivered in ready-made, easy-to-classify demographic and attitudinal bundles, because every sport and event has its distinctive target audience. Education, affluence, socioeconomics, technological literacy, geographic distribution, risk tolerance, and consumer spending patterns are among the many variables that can be readily identified among the fans of a particular sport or sports event audience.

Corporations invest heavily in sports events because their customers devote their dollars and emotions just as passionately. Marketers understand that establishing an association between a consumer's loyalties and a company's product can pay enormous dividends. The marketplace is unquestionably immense. In 2019, Statista.com estimated a total attendance of just the top 11 professional sports leagues around the globe at 221 million fans. Add to these impressive numbers the attending fans of organized sports not accounted for in that figure—college sports, minor leagues, auto racing, horse racing, rodeo and bull riding, golf, tennis, bowling, skating, skiing, curling, lacrosse, volleyball, boxing, mixed martial arts, and the broad range of action and e-sports, to name just a few. Then, consider the friends, family, and businesses that support a community's young athletes by attending and sponsoring their events, and it is easy to imagine that perhaps as many as one billion people worldwide may attend a live sporting event in any given year. Factor in those who watch or listen to sports at home or on their personal devices, or from bars and restaurants, and the financial impact of the industry and its influence in our daily lives becomes all the more impressive.

The Evolution of Sports Event Marketing

The sports event business is not just continually growing. It is constantly evolving and responding to changes and advancements in culture, technology, business practices, and fan behavior. When the first edition of *The Sports Event Management and Marketing Playbook* was first published in 2005, social media platforms were just beginning to proliferate and most sports news was still delivered on paper, through over the air broadcast, or by cable. Phones were used almost exclusively to make or receive calls. Photos could only be taken if you had brought your camera along. The first iPhone wouldn't be introduced until two years later. Online fantasy sports platforms were introduced the same year, as was YouTube—the first popular video streaming service. These technological advances, among many others, rapidly and profoundly changed the sports business and how content was delivered to fans.

When the second edition of the *Playbook* was released in 2014, college athletes in the United States were not permitted to enter into any form of commercial relationship without endangering their eligibility to play. Wagering on sports outside of licensed sports books in Las Vegas was illegal. Organized esports leagues were an oddity. Game tickets were pieces of paper, most of them spit out of a noisy, chattering ticket printer. Field signage had to be physically present to be visible on broadcasts.

This 3rd edition of *The Sports Event Management and Marketing Playbook* celebrates nearly 20 years since our book's original publication. In this new iteration, we explore well-proven sports event practices gathered over decades of experience and learning, incorporating new techniques and technologies, and informed by cultural and business changes.

Not so long ago, captive audiences numbering in the tens of thousands faithfully filled ballparks game after game, leaping to their feet as their hometown's star left fielder went diving for line drives heading for the gap. Over the course of a few leisurely hours, fans sat in full view of dozens of billboards that wallpapered the area above and beside the outfield fence, a barrage of LED advertising appeared on ribbon boards surrounding the playing surface, and players endorsed sponsor brands on television commercials. While these practices remain staples of the industry, the costs of doing business have increased, causing sponsors to demand more and obligating sports event organizers to respond and deliver. Changing consumer demographics, spending behavior, media habits have significantly transformed the way we consume sports, and the way marketers reach us through events.

Changes in the sports event marketplace are particularly evident in the discipline of event marketing. As the global economy treads new territory daily, corporate partners are increasingly sensitive to the costs of doing business in the sports arena. They are more vigilant than ever about identifying clear business objectives to guide their participation—and increasingly aggressive about achieving them.

Sports event organizers have to keep a finger on the pulse of the ticket buying public, evaluate economic pressures on corporate sponsors, and keep abreast of merchandising innovations. They must stay current on content consumption habits and trends, new technologies and content delivery systems, day-to-day profit and loss forecasts, the ongoing effectiveness of an event's marketing plan, and a host of other factors. A sports event organizer must simultaneously be an administrator, marketer and promoter, a financial planner and prognosticator. (For this reason, the terms *organizer* and *promoter* will often be used interchangeably in this book.) He or she must remain creative and cost conscious, free thinking yet focused.

There is no question that the strength and appeal of a sports event begins on the playing field, with the athletes and participants whom the fans come to see. But beyond where the action takes place, the execution of a successful sports event is the result of intelligent planning and well-integrated teamwork. The team is composed of a staff of individuals working as a single unit, dedicated to the achievement of the event's objectives. Coached and led by the event director or organizer, the staff is joined by a second unit composed of stakeholders that include the event facility, sponsors, local government and businesses, broadcasters, and other partners. To achieve greatness for the event, these two units combine to form an irresistible wedge, sweeping obstacles aside or navigating around them.

The Sports Event Golden Rule— Understanding Stakeholders' Objectives (U.S.O.)

As you explore the **Third Edition** of **The Sports Event Management and Marketing Playbook**, you will note a recurrent theme, starting with this introduction. To succeed in today's sports event marketplace, you must embrace a "U.S.O." philosophy and truly desire to *Understand Stakeholders' Objectives*. With the increased sophistication and pragmatism of event sponsors, media platforms, facilities, and communities, event organizers are obligated to demonstrate the great advantages of hosting a particular event and the essential contribution each stakeholder's participation can make. A successful sports event is born of a partnership between all of these parties, as well as the athletes who will compete and the fans that will attend. Understanding what each of these entities want and need from an event is paramount in building consensus and moving this partnership forward.

Application of the U.S.O. philosophy finds its way into nearly every major play—or chapter—in this book. The core concept of U.S.O. is perhaps most noticeable in the plays devoted to host cities and venues, sponsors, media, and broadcasters. Keeping these stakeholders engaged and focused on the success of your event requires regular dialogue and ongoing negotiation. As any good negotiator will tell you, reaching agreement is far easier when both sides understand what the other wants from the relationship.

Facilities, such as arenas, stadiums, recreation centers, ice rinks, training centers, racetracks, convention centers, natatoriums, velodromes, golf courses, hotels, and amusement centers exist to host events. As you begin planning your program, you will have to recognize that most of these venues look at sports events as means of producing revenue and generating exposure for themselves. Play 4 will help you to develop an understanding of what sports event facilities want from you and what you can expect from them.

SIDELINE STORY

The Costs and Benefits of Hosting Major Sports Events

Local media and politicians often question the benefits of applying resources, such as city services and facilities, in pursuit of a winning bid to host an event. The economics and value of every event differ greatly and economists use different methodologies to measure the real benefits of hosting sports events. Some conclude that there is no real direct economic advantage to staging sports events, while others point to multiple millions of dollars in local tax revenues, job creation, and promotional benefits that will generate revenues from tourism and future events. Many cities bid time after time to host major sports events, and invest heavily to support them. Few cities that have successfully hosted sports events later determine that they did not contribute sufficiently to their economies or public image or decide not to re-enter the market to compete for future host opportunities.

In 2021, the city of Tokyo, Japan, was projected to have spent more than $8 billion (US) in public-sector funding in support of the Summer Olympic Games, and estimated that hosting the event would provide £1 billion in advertising value alone. This extraordinary level of public support, combined with ticket revenues, sponsorship, and other local revenue streams would help the Games generate a profit. London hosted the Olympics at the right time in its history, as well. Although the region competed to host the event many years before the date of the opening ceremonies, the Olympics also provided an important, timely, and highly visible promotional tool to counteract the damage done to the image of London and the United Kingdom in the wake of widely publicized civil riots that wracked the country less than one year prior to the Games.

Notwithstanding the broad disagreement among economists on the real benefits of sports events to a regional economy, additional anecdotal evidence of their perceived value is evidenced by considering the history of cities that have successfully competed to host the NFL's Super Bowl. In the Super Bowl's first half century, Miami and New Orleans alone represented 20 of the 50 NFL championship games, each having been awarded the right to host the event 10 times during that period. If there was a question about the value of hosting this major North American sports event, one would think it would have been answered long before bidding on a 10th Super Bowl.

Play 4 will also help you to gain insights into the complex, multidimensional reasons why cities, counties, and states compete fiercely to host sports events. Municipal governments know that sports events generate sales tax dollars, hotel occupancy, expenditures on food and beverages, and income taxes, among many other economic benefits. They also appreciate that hosting events can generate positive exposure and interest in the region from other sports and entertainment properties, as well as from business and pleasure travelers. There are a multitude of other reasons why cities spend time, money, and human energy bidding for events through their local sports commissions and convention and visitors' bureaus. Even small, grassroots sports events generate some form of economic and lifestyle impact. Understanding how cities evaluate this impact will help you successfully solicit their support to stage the best and most cost-efficient event possible.

Broadcasters and streaming platforms can simultaneously be revenue generating beneficiaries and risk-taking partners. Their investment, in the form of production expenses, and rights fees paid to the sports organization, is generally at risk. Their product is the event broadcast itself, and they sell advertising to offset those costs and generate profits. A broadcaster or streamer must also promote the event to viewers or listeners, whose very act of consuming their content will justify the rates they will charge for advertising or subscribing. Knowing the great benefits they can bring to an event organizer, and recognizing that their investments can be very high and their ability to generate profits risky, broadcasters can be very demanding. Play 13 will help you to better understand their point of view, the issues that inevitably arise during the broadcast planning process, and the best ways to work with them.

The often-overlooked beneficiaries of sports events are the athletes, participants, and fans. Events may succeed in generating expected revenues, providing great economic impact to the community and meeting the needs of corporate sponsors, yet fail to survive in subsequent years because the organizers forgot that the athletes and the audience must have had a pleasant and rewarding experience during every phase of the event. The excitement should begin from the time they first hear of the event, begin to crescendo when they first arrive, and continue to be appreciated well after they return home. Losing sight of the needs and expectations of the athletes and fans can endanger the long-term success of your events. Don't forget to identify and deliver what they deserve and expect: an outstanding entertainment and performance environment.

Understand what other sports and leisure-time options your fans attend and why. Is your event designed to attract only the sport's loyal, most avid fan base? Is there an opportunity to expand the event's appeal to casual fans or even curious nonfans? Design your marketing plan to communicate how your sports event will deliver value and unforgettable experiences to the audiences you would most like to attract. Remember that sports events are at their most exciting when presented before a full, emotionally charged audience.

Current Trends in Sports Event Management and Marketing

Hockey Hall of Fame legend Wayne Gretzky once explained that the key to his scoring success was not based on where the puck was at any given moment. "I skate to where the puck is going to be," he said. The key to an event's long-term success is dependent on the organizer's ability to understand their market and where it is heading. During recent periods of economic uncertainty, sports event organizers have come under increasing pressure to achieve more with less and provide even greater value for their partners. Sponsors continue to seek ways to increase sales and market share while trying to reduce costs. Some have cut their sports marketing expenditures while others have redirected where and how their sports marketing budgets are used. Many explore how the sports events they support can better leverage their company's expertise, products, and services. A detailed exploration of what sponsors want and need from today's sports event partnerships is included in Plays 6 and 7.

Recognizing current market sensitivities and ensuring that your sports events are being managed and marketed with the application of sound business practices are essential to achieving the objectives of your program. The more complex the event, the longer the timeframe is required for planning. The longer the planning process, the more likely and more often event organizers will have to change planning details midstream—such as ticket prices, participant accommodations, ancillary grassroots events, and facilities—to meet the constantly shifting pressures of the business environment. Anyone who has ever managed any form of budgeting, at home or in business, knows that it is impossible to determine exactly how much money is going to be spent on precisely every product or service six months, one year, or three years in advance. Yet, many large events require two- to four-year planning windows, and most events need more than six months. After you have developed your sports event, continuous evaluation and flexibility in planning and financial reforecasting are vital. This book is peppered with insights, tips, and options that can help you anticipate areas where such changes might be necessary and how to deal with them.

Understanding the economic environment can help sports event organizers project changes in revenue and anticipate expenses for the following year's program. Against the turbulent backdrop of global economics and frequent temperamental swings in financial markets, prudent organizers planning sports events more than one year in advance often embrace the philosophy of zero-based budgeting. This enables sports event organizers to remain nimble over the long term, providing the opportunity to adjust ticket pricing policies, shift strategies for generating sponsor participation, exploit emerging content distribution technologies, and even change the structure of events themselves to remain economically competitive and encourage growth. The combination of a rapidly changing technological environment and unpredictable economic times has necessitated this flexibility. Sports event organizers, perhaps now more than at any time in the past, need to listen to their customers and stakeholders—their fans, sponsors, broadcasters, and other business partners—to understand what they want from their experience and partnership and to serve them better. Those who do not will lose their relevance to the people and organizations that support them with their presence and money.

Understanding the economy and its effect on partners and fans has increasingly been joined by another consideration—the impact on the host region's physical environment. Spectators inevitably leave behind mountains of trash. Tons of paper and raw construction materials are often expended in preparation for an event. Fuel consumption from added motor traffic, air conditioning, and power generation increases the carbon impact on the host region. And, hundreds of pounds of prepared, unserved food are often wasted. Sustainability policies have become more than just the right thing to do. They help build the relationship between a sports event and its host community and, if properly implemented, can leave the region better than if the event had not been held. This, and other community relations initiatives can leave lasting impacts on the causes that resonate with the region. Play 10 will explore how identifying the causes that appeal to the local community and investing time and a portion of the sports event budget can encourage support from the host region.

Providing a comfortable, safe and secure environment for athletes and fans has taken on an increasingly visible role in the design, planning, and operation of sports events and the venues that host them. Although safety has always been of paramount importance for organizers and venue managers both on the playing field and in the stands, planning for and dealing with conditions beyond the scope of your control—the essence of risk management—are issues to be considered early and often. Best practices for crowd control, severe weather planning, disruptive fans, and other potentially threatening conditions are discussed in Play 14.

The advancement and proliferation of new technologies and software for budgeting, event planning, ticketing, marketing and promotion, event production, and guest management functions, among others, have raised the professionalism of special events and increased the productivity of event teams. The impact of technology is no longer simply manifested in the systems the sports event organizer applies to better manage or present an event. Today, fans and participants also bring technology with them. Audiences enjoy sports events in more ways than at any time in history. Fans at events now often supplement content provided by mass media, updating their friends and family over social media networks and on their own blogs in real time. Followers of professional sports want quick access to statistics to play fantasy sports and gain wagering intelligence while the real events are unfolding. Spectators want to review plays on their own mobile devices to relive the magic of a just-experienced athletic moment and to evaluate the referee's call to formulate their own opinion of a ruling. The power and interaction of a fan with the live sports event now rivals broadcast and other media platforms, which have long been the organizer's valued collaborators for raising event exposure and the biggest competitors for live audience attention.

Providing customer service is no longer just about hiring and deploying friendly and knowledgeable staff, the lynchpin of any well-designed service program. It now extends to all interactions with the athlete and fan. Easy mobile ticket purchasing and reselling options, digital parking passes, instant access to the complete event schedule and venue information that informs fans on what to do, where to go, and what to expect are just a few examples of services that are now imperatives. Building the relationship with the fan attending a sports event is a 365-days-a-year, 24-hours-a-day job, and never more deeply than on the day of the event. So now, let's start getting ready for event day!

Defining and Developing Objectives, Strategies, and Tactics

"All winning teams are goal-oriented. Teams like these win consistently because everyone connected with them concentrates on specific objectives . . . nothing will distract them from achieving their aims."

—*Lou Holtz, Former Notre Dame football coach*

This play will help you to:

- Set the primary objectives for your sports event.

- Develop your event's full potential using the P-A-P-E-R Test (promotion, audience, partnerships, environment, and revenue) to identify the many secondary objectives that can be achieved.

- Set strategies to achieve your primary and secondary objectives in the pursuit of greater success.

- Develop the tactics that will apply your strategies to achieve the greatest results.

Introduction

OK, let's stage an event, your boss or client says. They may have a good creative concept of what they want that event to be. It might be a special match, a championship series, skills competition, all-star game, tournament, fan festival, or awards ceremony. Planning and managing events, as you'll discover, can be labor intensive, time consuming, and expensive. So, it's important that for all that effort and money, they can achieve not only the main reason for staging them, but that they can also realize their greatest potential.

Identify the Primary Objective

Start the process with these questions: what do we want our event to accomplish once the audience has gone home and all the bills have been paid? Is the main goal to generate a profit, raise funds for a cause-related charity, or promote a particular sport, league, or lifestyle? Is it meant to expand or enhance business relationships with sponsors, celebrate player accomplishments, or promote other games or events?

Objectives are the answer to the question "WHY"—why are we investing our organization's time and resources to stage the event? Identify a single primary objective, the essential reason for investing your organization's time and resources. Then, inform all of your planning to achieve—at a minimum—this one overarching objective, the one that, if met, would alone qualify the event as a success. Ensure that every member of your event team understands the primary objective, and no matter what you add to the program later, never lose sight of the purest reason beneath. This will help to keep the highest priority in focus for all members of the event organization team. Once you have done so, you can add more features and content to your event to achieve an even wider range of positive outcomes.

Figure 1.1 illustrates examples of the primary objectives for three fictional sports events: an amateur community baseball event, a not-for-profit participatory athletic event, and a professional sports fan festival. Each of the events' organizers has defined a singular goal that is easy to communicate to their respective staffs and stakeholders.

The Powerful Opportunities of Secondary Objectives

The primary objectives for the events in Figure 1.1 are clear, simple, and easily communicable. Those goals will help to guide the creative development and planning processes for each event to ensure they achieve their main purpose. Live sports events, however, can be immensely more powerful and produce even more positive results for the organization. Considering what other, secondary objectives, an event can realize will help give shape to your concept and make it an even more worthwhile investment.

Example 1: Community Youth League All-Star Game

> **Primary Objective:** Give our town's best youth league players a great end-of-season competition that recognizes them for their great performance during the regular season.

Example 2: Road Runners Club Downtown 10K Road Race

> **Primary Objective:** Promote our sport and healthy lifestyles by offering our city's runners a safe, unobstructed downtown road course, and reinforce the excitement of recreational running by encouraging the community to cheer them on.

Example 3: Playoffs Pregame Fan Festival

> **Primary Objective:** Reward and excite loyal fans with an engaging festival preceding the team's first playoff game appearance in three years.

Figure 1.1 Primary Objectives of Three Types of Events

The P-A-P-E-R Test

One way of maximizing an event's potential is by using the P-A-P-E-R Test. This rubric, which stands for *promotion, audience, partnerships, environment,* and *revenue,* is a useful framework that organizers can use to create a more comprehensive list of additional, or secondary, objectives. Consider each of the P-A-P-E-R components listed in Figure 1.2 and the following discussion to develop additional aspirations for your event.

Developing Strategies

Some outcomes will be more valuable and important to you and your organization than others. Some will be more complicated and difficult, and others far easier to achieve. Prioritize your secondary objectives, selecting those that are most important to your organization, and determine what is feasible, efficient, and desirable for you to pursue. Consider your time and financial resources. Go for the goals with the greatest payoffs in whatever time frame is the most relevant, but with the least possible drain on your resources.

Identifying primary and secondary objectives will help you develop the "Strategies" for your event. Strategies are the answer to the question "WHAT"—what do we need to add to our plans to ensure we meet all of these objectives? For example, if we need to generate revenue, perhaps we need to plan to sell tickets, merchandise, and sponsorships. If we want to expand the audience beyond the core fan, we may have to add new event components that will appeal to them, like more entertainment and giveaways, and communicate that there is more value to attending. If we need to sell more sponsorships, we may have to offer partners more value in advertising, hospitality experiences, and branded fan engagement opportunities. As you can see, this exercise of teasing out more of the opportunities that an event might offer begins to shape the content of the program we are planning.

Let's apply the P-A-P-E-R Test to identify secondary opportunities for the three sample events in Figure 1.1. The first is a typical community sports event with little or no budget, and a staff comprised totally of volunteers. Notwithstanding the minimal resources available, the event has the potential to generate excitement and advance the aims of this community organization. Figure 1.3 illustrates how the P-A-P-E-R Test might be applied to this youth league all-star game.

The volunteer chairman of the youth league in Figure 1.3 realizes that a children's all-star game can do so much more for its participants and teams, the community, and their own organization than simply staging a meaningful competition. As a volunteer with limited time and resources, the chairman knows that the game can exist without any of these additional opportunities and achieve its primary objective with a minimum amount of time investment. All he needs is to obtain a permit for the ball field and hire an umpire. To achieve even a small number of these added secondary objectives, the chairman will have to appoint a committee or task force to prioritize which objectives should be pursued, which ones would be nice to achieve, and which are just not worth the effort.

In the case of the Youth League All-Star Game, getting community leaders (audience) to the event will help to impress businesses from the Chamber of Commerce (partnerships) and encourage coverage by the local media (promotion). A full set of bleachers (audience) watching a well-run, spirited youth activity (environment) will also position future league events as worthy of sponsorships from local businesses and grants facilitated by local politicians (revenue).

It is also helpful to develop secondary objectives that address the host organization's overall mission and challenges. The event chairman in this hypothetical case wants to keep registration fees as low as possible, but knows that money is going to be required the following season to replace equipment and maintain a field that tends to flood after even a brief, moderate shower. The all-star game is a perfect opportunity to raise the money required, whether dollar-by-dollar through the sales of hot dogs or raffle tickets to family members in the bleachers, a few hundred dollars at a time through an expanded group of sponsors, through grants from the county, or all three. Staging the all-star game without engaging in all of the extra work may provide just as wonderful an experience for the children participating. But, with some extra effort, the game could also present an outstanding opportunity to improve the experience for players in seasons to come.

Promotion:

What essential message or important information do we want to communicate about the event, our sport, or our organization? Can we use this event to promote other activities, games, or events?

- Can we use this event to build fan interest in my sport or organization before, during, or after event day? By what measure can this increased interest be demonstrated?
- How do we want the event to position our sport in the community, and what kind of legacy should it leave behind?

Audience:

- Who is our target audience for the event, the people who are most likely to participate, attend, or purchase a ticket?
- Beyond the most likely target, what other audiences with similar interests can we attract to increase attendance, interest, and relevance for our event and further our organization's overall objectives?
- Is there an opportunity to win entirely new fans or enthusiasts to our sport by encouraging their attendance?
- Can we reactivate interest among prior fans who have lost interest?

Partnerships:

- Can we use the event to develop, maintain, or strengthen relationships with our organization's partners and supporters (e.g., our fans, athletes, members, donors, sponsors, community leaders, and local government)?
- What kind of experience do we want our athletes and other partners to have? How do we want them to feel about our organization or sport before, during, and after the event?

Environment:

- Who are our competitors, and how should we differentiate our sports organization from theirs, and our event from the programs they present?
- What do we need to communicate about the positive attributes of our sports event that sets it apart from other activities similarly competing for the public's or a potential sponsor's attention?
- Do we need to address a time or economic inconvenience that attendees, participants, or partners may perceive when deciding to attend?
- Do we need to address a preconceived notion about our sport or organization that makes it more difficult to generate attendance or participation?

Revenue:

- How much revenue do we need to generate for the event and/or for the organization?
- Do we want or need to generate a profit?
- How much money can we invest beyond the revenues we expect to achieve our objectives?
- Should our event be associated with a community cause or charity? How much money do we need to generate for them?

Figure 1.2 Key Elements of the P-A-P-E-R Test

Example 1: Community Youth League All-Star Game

- **Primary Objective:** Give our town's best youth league players a great end-of-season competition that recognizes them for their great performance during the regular season.
- **Secondary Objectives:**
  o **P**romotion
    1. Encourage local media to communicate how our youth league is an important component of our community's quality-of-life, providing our children with a safe, supervised activity.
    2. Generate publicity to bring more kids and families to the event to cheer on their friends and relatives.
    3. Use the event to get more parents to register their kids to play in the league next season.
  o **A**udience
    1. Fill the bleachers and standing areas with at least 200 spectators. (The more people who attend, the more importance the media will place on the game.)
    2. Get new kids from the community to the game to encourage registration at the ball field for next season.
    3. Attract more parents to participate as volunteers, coaches, and assistants. Showcase the importance of the game and our league to local leaders (e.g., mayor, city manager, councilmember, state senator, chamber of commerce representatives).
  o **P**artnerships
    1. Strengthen our ties to members of the local chamber of commerce to encourage current team sponsors to renew their relationships, and to identify new prospective team sponsors for next season.
    2. Use these strengthened ties to businesses and town government to solicit donations to improve the antiquated dugout area and improve overall field maintenance.
  o **E**nvironment
    1. Demonstrate that our league is highly organized, motivated, and dedicated to coaching our kids, improving their skills and promoting good sportsmanship.
    2. Demonstrate that our organization places an emphasis on kids having a good time, as an alternative to highly competitive leagues in which winning is more important.
  o **R**evenue
    1. Generate $500 to replace old equipment (e.g., new batting helmets, bases, batting tees) and to help pay for All-Star trophies.
    2. Increase player preregistration for next season by 10 percent.

Figure 1.3 Expanded Community Youth League All-Star Game Objectives

The second fictional event presented in Figure 1.1 is staged by a local running club. This organization has a handful of permanent administrative staff supplemented by a large body of volunteers, event marshals, and municipal employees assigned by the city. The primary objective for the event is consistent with the overall goals for the organization but could also pertain to any of the nearly 30 other running events the club stages each year. Figure 1.4 illustrates how the P-A-P-E-R Test can be applied to allow the Downtown 10K Road Race to stand out uniquely from the rest of the club's calendar.

Example 2: Road Runners Club Downtown 10K Road Race
- **Primary Objective:** To promote our sport and healthy lifestyles by giving our city's runners a safe, unobstructed downtown road course, and to reinforce the excitement of recreational running by encouraging the community to cheer them on from the sidewalks.
- **Secondary Objectives:**
  - **Promotion**
    1. Demonstrate that our sport is a great lifestyle choice for the entire community, providing health and social benefits to all participants regardless of age or income.
    2. Promote our organization as one of the region's top associations of recreational runners.
    3. Encourage spectators to gather to cheer on the runners.
    4. Designate an official radio station in our market that will appeal to our target market and promote both the registration drive prior to the race and spectator attendance on race day.
  - **Audience**
    1. Increase race registration by 33 percent over last year.
    2. Encourage families and friends to "sample" recreational running together for the first time.
    3. Convert those sampling the event into regular recreational runners.
    4. Leverage the on-site excitement of spectators to increase club membership by 15 percent.
    5. Demonstrate the popularity of running and the benefits of our association to potential sponsors of future races and events.
  - **Partnerships**
    1. Strengthen our ties to the city's parks and recreation, police, street, and sanitation departments, whose active cooperation is essential to running races year-round.
    2. Establish a working relationship with the downtown business improvement district, whose objectives include bringing visitors and entertainment seekers to the downtown core during low-traffic weekends and summer evenings.
  - **Environment**
    1. Demonstrate that running is fun, healthy, mentally and emotionally refreshing, accessible, and inexpensive.
    2. Demonstrate that as compared to other sports, running requires little economic investment, is easy to learn, and has few rules.
  - **Revenue**
    1. Generate net proceeds of $50,000 to pay for operational expenses.
    2. Increase club membership and member revenues by 15 percent.

Figure 1.4 Expanded Downtown 10K Road Race Objectives

The executive director of the Downtown Road Runners Club knows that she can use the scenic attractiveness and excitement of running through the downtown area to revitalize one of the organization's annual 10K races, and has set realistic goals to increase membership and race registration. She also recognizes that she can use the event to establish a working relationship with local businesses in the downtown area to achieve mutual objectives—the repositioning of a business district that is exciting in daylight hours five days a week, but sleepy during nonworking hours. Working with the local chamber of commerce, the race can create unique opportunities for area business owners, and, in turn, generate new sponsorship and official supplier opportunities. Area restaurants and retailers can engage in promotions that will convert work-week customers into weekend event spectators and may also support efforts to increase participation as places for recreational runners to pick up their registration materials, application forms, and information. The expansion of the list of secondary objectives also reveals the potential for future short-distance road race events during evening hours to further enhance the vitality of the city after regular business hours.

Identifying and evaluating secondary objectives provides event organizers with a strategic framework upon which to develop tactics and strategies that will transform an event into a dynamic, multifaceted marketing tool for its organizers, sponsors, the local community, and a host of other stakeholders. For example, the Road Runners' desire to increase the number of recreational runners in the community might lead the organization to consider tactics such as having two starting lines. The second, located near the midpoint of the original route, and following in parallel lanes so as not to interfere with competitive runners, might be offered as a course for families with young children so an upcoming generation of runners can feel the thrill of passing the finish line without having to run the entire course. Adding a family component to the race could also serve as a market test to determine whether the club might introduce "family" or "junior" membership tiers to increase membership and annual dues revenues.

To strengthen the club's relationship with the city agencies whose participation is integral to the successful execution of the event, organizers might consider offering the police, fire, streets, and sanitation departments a limited number of free race registrations. These agencies can, in turn, donate these free spots to their widows and orphans organizations, Big Brothers/Big Sisters, or another worthy group, and encourage the media to generate human interest stories that feature the beneficiaries.

The third hypothetical sports event in Figure 1.1 is a playoff pregame fan festival to be held on the street outside a team's home arena. There is great demand and excitement in the community because tickets for the first postseason game have sold out in a single day. Capturing the buzz in the marketplace, in itself, can be a great reason to stage a fan celebration. But, as Figure 1.5 illustrates, the P-A-P-E-R Test can reveal many more opportunities.

The organizers of the Fan Festival in Figure 1.5 have been presented with the opportunity to take advantage of an appearance in the playoffs to achieve the overall marketing, revenue, and organizational goals of the club. With a program of free festivities outside the arena, ticket holders for the game can arrive early and celebrate with the greater community of fans. In addition to the early arriving ticketed fans, the team and its sponsors also want to fill the plaza in front of their arena with thousands of non-ticketed fans to achieve their merchandise and concessions revenue objectives. But they also realize that the resulting traffic and competition for parking could upset their most loyal ticket holders. Working with the city to add buses to the mass transportation schedule prior to and after game time could help to reduce congestion and demonstrate how convenient it can be to get to and from the arena. From the city's point of view, providing extra shuttles would give fans the ability to sample the ease of access the mass transit system can provide.

The team will not want loyal fans who could not get tickets to miss the pregame celebration, or the broadcast. It makes strategic sense, then, to install large video screens on the event site to provide game coverage. Additional Wi-Fi access points can be added inside and outside of the arena to accommodate the higher-than-normal concentration of devices uploading and downloading content to social networks and friends.

The inclusion of civic leaders and elected officials demonstrates the importance of the team and the game to the community. These are not the type of guests who shy away from cameras and microphones, so just their presence can help expand the media coverage of the event beyond sports to news and feature reporting.

Chances are the team will never have a more exciting opportunity to speak directly to as broad an audience. This is the time to present celebrants with the ability to take advantage of special ticket promotions to sell new season tickets or multigame packages for the following season. Capitalizing on the "got to be there" nature of the events, the club could offer purchasers free playoff merchandise with a deposit for a multigame package for the coming year.

Example 3: Playoffs Pregame Fan Festival
- **Primary Objective:** Reward loyal fans with a street festival preceding the team's first playoff game in three years.
- **Secondary Objectives:**
  - **Promotion**
    1. Generate added publicity for the team beyond the usual sports media platforms.
    2. Provide the media with attractive, camera-friendly opportunities to capture the excitement of our team's appearance in the playoffs
    3. Encourage the posting of user-generated content featuring our branding and increase fan engagement on social media platforms.
    4. Demonstrate how the excitement surrounding the team contributes to the community's quality of life for both residents and local businesses.
  - **Audience**
    1. Encourage the early arrival of playoff ticket holders to the arena.
    2. Bring fans who are not ticket holders to the arena plaza to add to the excitement of game day.
    3. Attract casual sports fans to the arena plaza to build their level of interest in our team and sport.
    4. Enable members of the community with limited economic resources the ability to enjoy our playoff celebration to the fullest extent possible.
  - **Partnerships**
    1. Provide our sponsors with an opportunity to market to, and communicate with, both loyal fans and casual fans at a time of heightened interest in the team.
    2. Provide civic leaders with an opportunity to appear before the widest range of their constituents.
    3. Provide our media partners with opportunities to enhance viewership of pregame coverage and attract additional viewers and listeners to the game broadcasts.
    4. Provide our online partners with unique content that drives increased page views.
  - **Environment**
    1. Present a celebration at least as highly regarded as the one staged by our local baseball franchise before its last appearance in a playoff game three years ago.
    2. Demonstrate that the arena district is in a safe and easy-to-reach location.
    3. Demonstrate to the community that our fans are passionate, loyal, and excited, but also well-behaved and good-natured.
  - **Revenue**
    1. Sell standing-room tickets to the game.
    2. Increase season ticket sales and sell multigame plans for next season while excitement for the team is at its zenith.
    3. Renew existing and expired season ticket accounts.
    4. Generate $200,000+ in sponsor sales to cover expenses.
    5. Increase playoff and team merchandise sales by 15 percent over average regular season in-arena sales.
    6. Increase concessions revenues by 10 percent over average regular season in-arena sales.

Figure 1.5 Expanded Playoffs Pregame Fan Festival

SIDELINE STORY

Professional League Drafts

Player drafts for the four major American sports leagues—the NFL, NBA, MLB, and NHL—have become must-see, and increasingly, must-attend events. At their core, they are essentially business meetings during which the leagues identify which member clubs have the right to negotiate contracts with specific amateur or collegiate players. This essential function, enabled by agreement with their respective player associations, is the primary, and most central objective of any Draft. The secondary objectives of making news, promoting a new generation of players to the fans of each team, and engaging fans in an off-season activity have resulted in the draft meetings becoming televised events. In turn, the success of these broadcasts resulted in a new set of secondary objectives—to satisfy fan demand to attend these news-making events in person, and to add revenue opportunity through sponsors wishing to engage with these avid fans. Each of the leagues is at a different stage in the development of the Draft as a live spectator event and an opportunity to build more business benefit for their organizations. However, they leverage the event to fulfill a variety of organizational goals, and however those objectives change over time, it is still, and ever will be, a business meeting for teams to select the next class of players.

Progress from Strategies to Tactics

Now that you've answered the questions "WHY?" and "WHAT?", it's time to tackle the question "HOW?", that is, the *tactics* you will use to achieve your goals. Identifying the tactics—HOW we will fulfill each these opportunities—will help us identify the features, activities, and promotions we will integrate into the program, what costs we will incur, and what revenue we can generate. Ultimately, it will help us formulate a budget, an estimate of our event's financial expectations.

Identifying objectives and developing strategies cost your event nothing but time, creativity, and analytical thought. The tactics that are selected and employed are the things that will cost, and potentially, make you money. To illustrate, when you take a road trip, you know where you want to go (objective), and by consulting a GPS app, you identify what roads you will need to take (strategy). You start spending money once you decide to get in your car and begin paying for gas and tolls to drive there (tactic).

So, before a budget can be drafted, you have to develop your list of objectives and determine the best, most realistic, and most cost-effective strategies that will achieve as many of those goals as possible at the lowest cost. Only then can you design the tactics—the content and marketing plan of the event itself. It is at this stage that you will evaluate whether the tactics you embrace will be too complex, too expensive, or too labor-intense to achieve. Here, you may determine that your event is trying to do too much, and that some lower-priority objectives may need to be sacrificed to benefit some of the more important ones. This evaluation process often continues throughout the budgeting process.

Take a moment to review Figure 1.6, a brief checklist of some general questions you can apply to developing event objectives. You will note how the answers to many of these questions can serve a variety of purposes and achieve multiple aims.

Promotion

- What key messages do I want my promotional plans to communicate? How will I encourage the media to help me achieve the outcomes I want before the event (e.g., advance ticket sales, walk-up attendance, increased viewership), and/or after (e.g., positive media coverage, increased membership, financial contributions)?
- How can I use publicity, promotion, and advertising to get my message out to the people that I want to hear it? What traditional, digital, and social media outlets should we target?
- How can I encourage engagement with fans on social media networks?
- How can I use the event as a publicity and promotional engine for my sports organization before, during, and after the event? What compelling stories can I tell? What can I add to the program to make my event more newsworthy?
- Can I work with local school districts to deliver educational programs, school visits, or field trips to students that promote my message?
- What long-term legacies or benefits can the event leave behind?
- How will we clarify or correct any misconceptions about my sport or organization?
- Can I expect to achieve my objectives with existing staff and resources, or do I need to get more help from outside the organization?

Audience

- How can I keep the event fast-paced, involving, and exciting for the audience?
- How can I make it easy to buy tickets, easy to travel to, and comfortable for spectators?
- What can I do to add value to the event for our existing fans?
- How can I get new people to my event? How can I turn them into fans, boosters, members, or supporters?
- What other events can I create cross-promotions with to build awareness and attendance?
- How can I educate the public about my sport, organization, or event?
- Is the event worthy of a live broadcast or stream? Can I package highlights that fans can stream or post?
- Can I use social media platforms and mobile apps to engage more deeply and more often with fans at the event and beyond?

Partnerships

- How can I use this sports event to increase value to current sponsors by providing an elevated level of service to their guests? Are there opportunities to provide sponsors and their customers with unique access to the event, special hospitality opportunities, exclusive mementos, or other benefits?
- How can I use this event as a showcase for prospective sponsors by exposing them to satisfied partners at the event?
- What exposure opportunities can I offer to partners in pre- and post-event advertising, on-site signage, awards and trophies, entertainment segments, audience promotions, giveaways, sweepstakes, uniform patches and staff attire, or printed and digital materials (e.g., tickets, websites, flyers, posters, information guides, programs, apps)?

Environment

- Is there another event or organization with which I am competing for audience, attention, sponsors, or athletes? How can I set my event apart from the competition?
- Can the event solve or draw positive attention to a pressing issue in the host community?

Figure 1.6 Strategy-to-Tactics Development Checklist

- How is the local community trying to portray itself, and how can our event support those efforts? How can that portrayal benefit my organization, sport, or event?
- What dates and times for the event might fill an entertainment void in the marketplace?

Revenue

- Should we sell admission tickets? How many and for how much? If we are interested in having children attend should there be a reduced children's price? A family package price? Discounted prices available through sponsor promotions? A special price for friends and family of staff and athletes?
- Can I sell merchandise? Will I be selling existing inventory and/or event-specific merchandise? What kind of merchandise and how much—low price points for kids, high price points for premium adult merchandise? Is there a market for high-priced collectibles and memorabilia?
- Can I sell food and/or beverages? What kinds and how much? Hot foods and drinks for outdoor cold weather venues; cold foods and drinks for outdoor hot-weather events? Are there special regional foods that should be among the offerings? Is it appropriate to serve beer at the event and, if so, what will local ordinances permit?
- Can I sell sponsorships? How many, for how much, and to whom? Can I package this sponsorship with similar opportunities at upcoming events? Should I make low-cost packages available for new sponsors who want to test their association with my event or organization? Can I offer multievent or multiyear sponsorship packages? Do I need outside help to design and sell these packages?
- How can I use the event to encourage sales of tickets to other upcoming events? Can I sell those tickets at the event? Should I distribute discount codes or coupons for future events?

Figure 1.6 (Continued)

Sports Events as Business Solutions

With the popularity of sports event marketing as an impactful addition to the marketing mix for corporations of nearly every size, events are frequently born specifically to meet a partner company's marketing objectives. Leading sports event managers are often approached by brands and their agencies to develop a program that achieves the objectives of their partners, such as launching new products, relaunching existing products, increasing sales, and marketing lifestyle programs.

The following Sideline Story demonstrates that a sports event organizer can apply the needs of a sponsor, as well as its own needs, to the creation of a completely new and compelling event concept. It is, therefore, even more important to apply a rubric like the P-A-P-E-R Test to expand the relevance and impact of the program beyond the primary objective of positioning the sponsor's product. The development of additional secondary objectives ensures that the event can be used to achieve multiple benefits for the sponsor and the sports organization, as well as other stakeholders.

SIDELINE STORY

The Labatt/NHL Pick-Up Hockey Marathon

The Labatt Brewing Company, a Toronto-based sponsor, requested that NHL event organizers create a program at the NHL All-Star Weekend that would capture national attention and would embrace key attributes of their Labatt Blue brand of beer, those of genuineness and being "uniquely Canadian." In response, the NHL created the Labatt Blue/NHL All-Star Pick-Up Hockey Marathon. Labatt and the NHL sought the heartiest amateur adult hockey players throughout Canada to qualify to play on one of the two teams that would compete on a frozen rink in front of Toronto City Hall continuously, 24 hours per day, until one side could no longer put a sufficient number of players on the ice. The puck dropped on Monday at 8:00 A.M., and play continued through four days and three nights until approximately 7:30 A.M. on Thursday morning. The event attracted thousands of curiosity seekers, generated hours of national media coverage, and earned a place in the Guinness Book of World Records (which has since been beaten). Though the event clearly met many objectives for the league, this memorable program would never have been developed without the inspiration, challenge, and support of the Labatt Brewing Company.

Post-play Analysis

To realize the full potential of a sports event, it is essential for organizers to develop a comprehensive list of event objectives before creating a budget and devising a business plan. These objectives answer the question "WHY". Identify the primary objective first—the goal the organization feels is essential above all else. Use the P-A-P-E-R Test (promotion, audience, partnerships, environment, and revenue) as a framework to develop a host of secondary objectives that will offer additional benefits for the organizer, sponsors, and other stakeholders.

Developing strategies answers the question "WHAT" and defines what you will do to achieve your objectives. Identifying tactics answers the question "HOW" and helps you to define in detail how those strategies will be actualized.

Coach's Clipboard

1. Your school's football team is in the top third in the standings and may host a regional championship game in three weeks. Use the P-A-P-E-R Test to outline what the game can achieve for the school, the athletic department, and the team. Prioritize these objectives based on their importance, and how feasible they are to achieve given the time remaining before a possible event. What are the implications if the event must be cancelled the week before it is to be staged because the team does not make the playoffs?
2. You are the brand manager of a line of lifestyle clothing with a modest budget for sports marketing. How can you use the P-A-P-E-R Test to identify the best sports events to fit the marketing aims for your product?
3. What tactics can you employ to make the 10K road race in Figure 1.4 more attractive to a potential "B2B" or "business-to-business" sponsor (i.e., a company that has customers that are primarily other companies, rather than individual consumers)?
4. An energy bar sponsor approaches a minor league sports organization, seeking a new event or promotion that will help to position the product as a nutritionally valid meal replacement bar rather than a candy. The potential sponsor wants the event to portray an active lifestyle and instantly recognized as associated with its product. Design an event that achieves these aims and expand this primary objective to serve the needs of the sports organization.

PLAY 2

Identifying Costs

"The lack of money is the root of all evil."

—*George Bernard Shaw, Irish dramatist (1856–1950)*

This play will help you to:

- Develop and manage the expense side of your event's budget.
- Become familiar with the types of costs most common to sports events.
- Understand the dynamics of fixed and variable event expenses.

Introduction

Now that you know what you are trying to achieve and have a concept of what kind of event you would like to stage as your plan to get there, it is time to begin constructing an event budget. Your budget will identify both revenue opportunities and expense items. When completed, it will also serve as the foundation of your event's *profit and loss ("P&L") statement*, a tool that will monitor and forecast overall financial performance expectations throughout the planning process, as well as at the conclusion of your event.

Although revenue generally appears first on most budgets, it is often more practical to start developing a budget from the expense side, so an event organizer can know how much revenue will be needed to support an event and fulfill its objectives. If there are not enough obvious revenue opportunities to cover these expenses, try to develop new ones. If there is still insufficient funding, it's time to go back to your objectives, tactics, and expenses to determine what cost categories can be reduced or eliminated.

Fledgling sports events most frequently fail for the same reasons new businesses often fail—undercapitalization and an underestimation of expenses. Simply put, it will take money to plan, develop, manage, and execute an event, and a fair amount of it will have to be spent before the very first ticket, T-shirt, or sponsorship is sold. Therefore, some investment is almost always required to get a project moving forward. The larger the event, the greater the initial cash outlay is likely to be needed.

A thorough examination of expected and potential costs will be required to ensure that your event's budget is realistic and that your revenue goals will meet or exceed your financial assumptions. You will find that there are seemingly limitless ways to spend money when planning an event. It is essential to know exactly on what, and have some idea of how much, you will have to spend before the invoices start piling up. Use any event budgeting software or widely available spreadsheet programs to chart your expenses and if using the latter, make it a point to use the formula functions that automatically add columns and perform other mathematical tasks so you can easily calculate the effect on the bottom line as you adjust individual budget items.

A worksheet of typical event budget expenses appears in Appendix 1. It provides a comprehensive list of major expense categories suitable for many sports events, though it is by no means complete. Use this table as a guideline while preparing the expense budget of your event but be sure to account for every possible detail that may be unique to your sport and event.

The definitions of many of the expenses in Appendix 1 will be obvious and familiar. The rest of this chapter provides you with more details, as well as some tricks of the trade, hints, and warning signs for expenses that are particular to sports events.

Expenses fall into two broad categories—*fixed costs* and *variable costs*. Fixed costs, as the name implies, remain immutable regardless of how various other factors may change, such as the number of spectators or sponsors. Examples of fixed costs include but are not limited to player and equipment costs and operational expenses, marketing costs, app development, and flat-rate facility rentals. Variable costs, by contrast, are those that increase or decrease as attendance or sales grow or fail to develop. Examples of variable costs include facility rentals based on a percentage of ticket sales, sales taxes, commissions paid on sponsorship sales, and, expenses for venue staffing (i.e., more guest services, custodial, and security personnel are required as attendance grows).

Facility Costs

Because a significant portion of a sports event's costs may be spent on leasing and preparing a site to host the event, it is wise to begin constructing your budget by selecting the venues most suited and affordable for holding your event. If you are restricted to a particular city or community, your choices will likely be limited to one, or perhaps just a few, event-appropriate facilities. If you are flexible on which community is best to host your event, you will, of course, have a wider range of venue options and greater bargaining power that can potentially save thousands of dollars in venue costs. Play 4 provides more details on how the economic benefits of an event may be leveraged to enhance competition between venues and drive down facility costs.

Rent

In most cases, the facility you will use to host your sports event is in the business of making money, or must at least cover its operating costs. That you may have to pay some form of rent or permit fee is probably obvious, but, if you have never leased an arena, stadium, convention center, or other similar facility, you will be amazed at the unexpected additional costs that can burden a budget. Request a *pro forma* copy of the lease agreement for any facility you are thinking of using while you prepare your expense budget. A *pro forma* is essentially a "fill in the blanks" standard lease form that outlines the major points of an organizer's relationship with the facility. Most venues can also provide you with an *Event Promoter Guide*, or a similarly named document, that outlines rules, regulations, fees, ticketing options, and seating charts, and other important information that can help you anticipate the costs of working there. The facility may request some amount of information about the event to help it prepare the most appropriate first-draft lease. The more potentially profitable your event is for a prospective host venue, the more negotiable its management may be with respect to adjusting the terms and prices.

The biggest, most prestigious events can provide sufficient noncash incentives for a city or venue manager to consider hosting an event at a reduced rate or, in some cases, on a rent-free basis. Some incentives that often tip the scale toward reduced-rate rentals include an unusually large number of hotel room-nights the event could generate for a city, unusually strong promotional benefits for a local team, or positive publicity for the host city, among others.

Most sports events are potentially profitable prospects for an arena, stadium, or other public assembly venue, but the rental rate formula is frequently negotiable. It may be paid as a flat sum, a percentage of gross ticket sales, or some combination of a reduced flat fee plus a percentage of sales. If you are relatively confident in your organization's ability to sell tickets or your ticket prices are premium priced, your budget will go further if you can secure the lowest possible flat rate. If, however, your ticket prices are low or you are less confident in your ticket-selling prospects due to the event's past history, its status as a first-time event, or as a result of external factors such as the effects of the economy on attendance, consider negotiating a variable rental fee that is more heavily weighted toward a percentage of sales. The right strategy can help you better manage a tight budget. In most cases, you will probably have to pay some minimum guarantee if the rent will be calculated on a percentage of sales. Remember that facility managers are smart, experienced businesspeople, and they will be vigilant and conscientious about finding ways to maximize their revenue while you are attempting to reduce your event's financial exposure. Work honestly and candidly with the facility representatives during negotiations. Your mutual interests are best served when both sides have realistic expectations and can benefit from each other's success.

The rental rate, as well as other facilities costs, will be covered in the lease agreement for the venue. The lease should be negotiated early in the budgeting process because building costs can make up a sizable portion of your event expenses. When you receive your first copy of the lease agreement, expect that most terms will be written to benefit and protect the facility. Work with an experienced attorney and, if possible, a seasoned industry professional to review all terms of the agreement before signing.

Ticket Sales Deductions - Taxes and Facility Usage Fees

Although deductions from ticket sales revenues are technically costs, they are not listed on our sports event budget worksheet under expenses. They are classified as "negative revenues," because that money is never really received from the box office or ticket sellers. Every dollar of each ticket sold may carry with it payment obligations, probably in the form of taxes, levies, usage charges, or commissions. Although these costs are discussed here, they will appear on the revenue side of the budget worksheet, but as deductions. They are, nonetheless, costs of doing business that need to be properly accounted for when constructing your financial model for the event.

Make sure your lease agreement covers all expected areas in which the event will incur costs charged by the facility or that will be paid to them on behalf of their contractors, labor unions, and public agencies. For example, be sure that all deductions from ticket revenues are unambiguously defined in your contract. Many facilities charge a small per-ticket fee variously known as a "capital replacement fee" or "facility usage fee." This deduction may range from one to several dollars per ticket or as a percentage of the ticket price and may represent an obligation the building must collect on behalf of the local government to cover the financing costs on the facility's construction. As a result, these fees are often non-negotiable. Be sure to determine whether this fee is traditionally charged to the organizer, or whether it is most often passed along to the ticket buyer, added to the face ticket price. As a variable cost, the total impact of this expense on the overall budget will increase or decrease with the tickets actually sold. Events are not charged a usage fee for seats that go unsold, and may or may not be payable on tickets that are issued on a complimentary basis, depending on the facility.

There are several other costs that will vary with ticket sales. As variable costs are not payable before a ticket is sold, these charges are usually deducted by the venue from your ticket revenues before you receive them. The most common deductions are sales and amusement taxes, which are commonly levied by local, state, or provincial governments. As acts of legislation, their rates are normally not negotiable. They will differ widely between municipalities, so analyze the effect of local taxes on your bottom line before you award an event to a host city or facility. Current, applicable tax rates can often be found on the host government's website.

SIDELINE STORY

A Major League Tax Waiver

There have been instances in which state or local legislators consider and agree to pass a bill that waives tax liabilities for specific sports events. Such a waiver was granted to Major League Baseball and the National Football League in the State of Florida that specifically excludes MLB All-Star Games, the World Series, the Super Bowl, and Pro Bowl from being obligated to pay taxes on the sale of event tickets. This waiver extends as well to Formula 1 Grand Prix events, Major League Soccer and FIFA World Cup championships, and other specific events for the purpose of providing additional incentives for those selected organizations to stage these drivers of high economic impact in their state. Such considerations can become politically sensitive and matters of public debate and have the potential to result in public scrutiny for both the host city and event organizer.

It is not safe to simply assume that the prevailing local sales tax rate will be the actual rate you will be charged on ticket sales. In some cases, the rates may be higher because of an added "amusement" or "entertainment" tax, or lower because an amusement tax will apply, but the sales tax will not. Be sure to check with the finance managers of your prospective event venue to determine the actual rate you will be liable for on ticket sales in that locality.

In many states, provinces, and cities, sales and/or admissions taxes may be payable on the value of at least some tickets that are issued on a complimentary basis. Generally, if the tickets are exchanged for some form of valuable consideration, they are subject to taxation. For example, an organizer may be required to provide complimentary tickets as a benefit to companies that provide an event with either cash or with products and services as part of their sponsorship agreements. Even if tickets make up only a small portion of what the sponsor is entitled to as part of the deal, the value of those tickets may be taxable as though you accepted cash for their face value. In most instances, where complimentary tickets are issued as a courtesy to VIP guests, player families, charities, or to the general fan population as a gesture of goodwill, and for which no recompense in any form is received or expected, they are usually free of tax obligations. Event organizers should seek professional advice on whether and how sales or amusement taxes may apply to complimentary tickets in the locality where the event is being held. If the host venue has been the site of a number of similar events, its chief financial officer can usually provide this information.

Ticket Sales Deductions—Commissions

There are a number of other deductions from ticket sales revenues that usually apply, and these are often overlooked during the budgeting process by first-time sports event organizers. Credit card commissions, for example, can erode ticket revenues by as much as 3 percent. When tickets are purchased by credit card, it is the responsibility of the event organizer to pay a fixed percentage of the transaction to the credit card company. If you are working with an established sports or entertainment venue, you will probably be asked to pay credit card commissions to the facility at a blended rate; that is, as a flat fixed percentage of the transaction. This amount is deducted from ticket revenues to cover the commissions paid to the card issuer, plus a handling fee for the facility. If your organization does not already have the capacity to sell tickets directly to fans, it is usually more labor-efficient and cost-effective to take advantage of the venue's existing box office and its agreements with the credit card companies.

Not all tickets will be purchased with a credit card, such as those paid by check on behalf of groups and corporations. If you will be accepting credit cards, it is recommended your budget forecast that *all* patrons will take advantage of this option. This will protect your budget with a small, hidden contingency fund should other expenses rise beyond expectations.

Many sports events, particularly those held in existing sports and entertainment facilities, make use of a third-party online ticketing platform. Most ticket services will collect some "per ticket" and "per order" service fee from the purchaser. What many novice sports event organizers may not realize is that they may be liable for certain transaction fees, as well. The contracts between event venues and their ticket sales provider will vary, but in many cases, you will not be liable for any appreciable service fees for tickets sold through the system at the venue's box office—that is, at the stadium, arena, or other facility in which the event will occur. Usually, you will get the best deal by being included under the existing contract between the venue and the third-party ticket platform. If your event is very large, or if you are not staging your event in a facility with existing ticketing options, and you wish to avail yourself of the additional sales and management opportunities an online ticket platform can provide, you will have to negotiate your own best deal with the ticket service.

Many stadiums and arenas maintain a database of tour and school groups, bus companies, youth organizations, booster clubs, and other avid ticket buyers that make purchases in block quantities, either through an in-house group sales department or an outside agency. Group sales can be a very effective supplemental means to fill your event venue, but the old maxim that "there is no such thing as a free lunch" applies here, too. You will have to pay the group sales agency and any in-house group sales function provided by the venue a pre-agreed commission rate, a service fee per ticket, and/or a flat fee for handling and processing. Because of the large multiples of tickets that can sold through group sales efforts, they are, in most cases, an effective revenue-generating option for event organizers that is generally worth the expense of commissions.

Facility Labor

It takes dozens, and sometimes hundreds, of facility employees to staff a sports event, and you can expect to have to pay for all of them. The most obvious staff requirements include the *front-of-house staff*—the ticket takers, security officers, guest services, and ticket office personnel the public most often encounters, along with their supervisors and managers. These facility employees are usually paid by the hour, with a predetermined minimum number of hours per event, plus an overtime differential before and after certain times of the day (e.g., after midnight or before 7:00 A.M.), on certain days (e.g., Sundays and holidays), or after a specified number of working hours per day. The venue will most often charge you an hourly rate that is marked up from the employee's actual pay rate, "plus benefits" (e.g., the cost of health insurance premiums and/or vacation accruals). You may also be charged an "administrative fee," which is the facility's way of offsetting the costs of scheduling employees, keeping track of their hours, and servicing their payroll. Once you have provided the facility with enough detail to give a good understanding of your event, the management team can provide you with an estimate of what to expect in the way of front-of-house labor costs. Make sure the estimate includes all administrative, payroll, and benefits charges as well.

Your labor costs will surely also include some *back-of-house* building staff, such as electricians, carpenters, riggers, maintenance workers, and event presentation personnel such as stagehands, stage managers, lighting operators, audio technicians, production crews, and operators to support video boards, scoreboards, and other electronic displays. Many facilities are bound by labor union agreements for at least some of those job functions, which will also obligate any lessee. The venue can provide you with the hourly rates for each of these labor categories, from which you can calculate costs based on your load-in (installation), rehearsal/practice, event, and load-out (dismantle) schedule.

The event organizer's obligation to pay for back-of-house staff may also include a "conversion" charge. The facility may have to reconfigure itself from the form or condition it was in the day before loading in your event, and then back again after your event has vacated. For example, if an arena was being leased to host a martial arts competition following an ice hockey game, personnel will be required for the conversion. In order to be in a condition conducive to host the martial arts event, the boards, glass, and netting around the rink would need to be removed and the ice would be covered with floor panels, plywood, and/or carpeting. Additional items such as floor seating, tables, and equipment for scoring might be added, and the center scoreboard adjusted to the appropriate height (also known as its *trim*). After the event, these materials may need to be removed and stored and the venue returned to its original condition. In this case, the cost of the labor required to convert to and from the ice hockey configuration could be charged to the event organizer.

Additional facility expenses worth mentioning are restoration costs, the amount of money required after the event to repair damage and replace broken equipment. Ideally, you want to be faced with no such costs, but you should be prepared for the possibility that venue assets might be damaged during your event and require repair or replacement. It is wise to inspect the host facility before beginning work on your event and make a record of visible damage already in place. If your organization, vendors, participants, or spectators subsequently damage the facility while preparing for, staging, viewing, participating in, or dismantling the event, you may be billed for the cost of restoration. Determine to what extent your insurance coverage will protect you from this potential liability.

Facility costs are not limited only to those just described and are dependent on both the nature of your event and the type of venue in which it is held. The expenses for some items will be charged to the organizer directly by the facility; others may be purchased or rented directly from a third party to help prepare the venue to properly host the event. The checklist in Figure 2.1 will assist you in the process of identifying these types of costs.

Rent
- ☐ Event day(s)
- ☐ Installation, practice/rehearsal, and dismantle days

Venue Labor*
- ☐ Front-of-house staff (e.g., ushers, ticket takers, security/crowd management, box office, and guest services)
- ☐ Back-of-house staff (e.g., stagehands, electricians, carpenters, riggers, and maintenance workers)
- ☐ Public safety personnel (e.g., police, fire, and EMS)
- ☐ Overnight security
- ☐ Event presentation production crews/operators
- ☐ Medical and first aid staff
- ☐ Conversion crew
- ☐ Taxes and/or facility usage fees*
- ☐ Credit card commissions*
- ☐ Group sales and other sales commissions*
- ☐ Event equipment (e.g., scoreboards, goals, nets, benches, walkie-talkies, and intercoms)
- ☐ Crowd control equipment (e.g., barricades, ropes, and stanchions)
- ☐ Catering and hospitality*
- ☐ Merchandise operations
- ☐ Chair and table rentals
- ☐ Pipe and drape dividers
- ☐ Power and utilities*
- ☐ Postevent cleaning
- ☐ Restoration

*Variable costs

Figure 2.1 Typical Sports Event Facility Costs

Player- and Game-Related Expenses

There are few instances in the sports event world in which the participants or players are not recognized for their achievement in some fashion. In grassroots and amateur athletics, this recognition might take the simple form of medals or trophies. For team and individual championships, from professional and collegiate to scholastic and club, banners and wall plaques are hung as permanent reminders of great accomplishment. In professional sports, trophies are increasingly supplemented with more valuable considerations, including expensive championship rings, cars, and/or other gifts, as well as cash awards that might include appearance fees, prizes for outstanding performance, bonuses for achieving certain benchmarks, and a winner's prize pool, among others.

In addition to setting aside funds for prizes, appearance fees, and winner pools, consider whether you will require the services of athletes beyond the actual competition and whether you can include incremental appearances in the compensation or recognition structure for professional or semiprofessional players. Including an athlete meet-and-greet opportunity for fans, or for sponsor guests, can go a long way toward generating new ticket buyers and corporate partners, so it is strongly recommended that event organizers either seek to include an appearance or two within an athlete's understanding of his/her obligations, or put some cash aside to pay for appearances. (Before offering cash or other value to amateur or collegiate athletes, be sure to consult the appropriate league, collegiate, or governing body rules.)

Some organizations combine the participation of marquee athletes with amateur competitors to add star power to an event and pique spectator interest. The New York Road Runners, for instance, invite a roster of elite runners who are paid appearance fees to participate in the New York City Marathon, running side-by-side—at least for the first mile or so—with accountants, lawyers, clerks, businesspeople, and other purely recreational runners. Many pro-am golf tournaments operate under a similar model, where amateur duffers play the sport they love alongside the greats of the links.

For organizers who must offer cash incentives to participating athletes, there is no one right way to design a compensation strategy. Figure 2.2 illustrates how a sample prize pool can be constructed for a two-team sports event that ensures that every player has an incentive to participate and compete. In this example, the event organizer has budgeted a $250,000 prize pool. The organizer can decide to award the entire sum to the winning team, or split the funds available to ensure that everyone goes home rewarded to some degree.

For the purposes of this example, let's assume there are 15 players on each of the two teams, for a total of 30 play-

Appearance fees	$100,000
Winner's prize pool	$100,000
MVP award	$10,000
Supplementary appearance fees	$40,000
Total Player Prize Pool	**$250,000**

Figure 2.2 Sample Prize Pool

ers. The organizer wants to reward each player with a guaranteed minimum fee for participating. Dividing the $100,000 appearance fee pool by all 30 participants provides a $3,333.33 guarantee for every player. In this compensation scheme, a player can triple his or her award to $10,000.00 by playing on the winning squad. This figure is derived by dividing the winner's prize pool of an additional $100,000 among the 15 winning players, adding $6,666.67 to the guaranteed appearance fee. The event's Most Valuable Player (MVP) is awarded an additional prize of $10,000. Presuming the MVP is on the winning team, that player would be paid a grand total of $20,000. Exclusive of additional fees available for supplementary appearances, the total player prize pool has been divided as follows: $3,333 for players on the losing team, $10,000 for players on the winning team, and $20,000 for the MVP (if on the winning squad, or $13,333 if on the losing side).

This prize pool includes funds for supplementary appearance fees, allowing players to be compensated for sponsor or fan meet and greets. For illustrative purposes, let us assume there are 20 such opportunities during this event, each opportunity representing one hour of time beyond the competition itself. Players can earn $2,000 for each hour they agree to participate and may increase their earnings by appearing for more than a single hour. A player on the losing team, then, can increase his/her earnings to more than $5,300 with one additional supplemental appearance.

☐ Accommodations
☐ Appearance fees
☐ Beverages (water/sports drinks) and snacks for locker rooms/benches
☐ Equipment
☐ Equipment managers and trainers
☐ Gifts
☐ Ice
☐ Laundry
☐ Locker room supplies
☐ Meals and per diems
☐ Medical staff, EMTs, ambulance
☐ Officiating fees and expenses
☐ Player guest expenses
☐ Playing surface preparation and maintenance
☐ Playing surface lighting
☐ Prize money and recognition (e.g., trophies, medals, and plaques)
☐ Scoreboards and timing equipment
☐ Temporary construction
☐ Towels
☐ Trainers fees, equipment, and supplies
☐ Transportation, in-bound/out-bound (to/from home airport and airfares)
☐ Transportation, local (to/from airport, hotels, and event sites)
☐ Uniforms, including numbering and lettering

Figure 2.3 Typical Game- and Player-Related Costs

If you are organizing a tournament, determine how you will recognize the winners. Consider how many age and gender brackets your players will be divided and to what level you will recognize performance in each bracket with trophies, medals, or other prizes (e.g., first place only and first through third place). Will you recognize only a select few top achievers or all of the athletes, the coaches, staff, or the organizations they represent? Identify these expenses and capture them in your game- and player-related expense budget. See Figure 2.3 for a checklist of game- and player-related line items to include in your budget, as applicable.

Event Operations Expenses

Event operations expenses include many of the costs that are essential to run the event but have little direct visible impact on the experiences of the audience or the athletes. They would include the costs for staff hired specifically for the event, and the support equipment, systems, and supplies required by the staff members to execute their responsibilities. See Figure 2.4 for the most common event operations expenses.

Most of the expenses listed in Figure 2.4 may be estimated by simply contacting prospective vendors and requesting price quotes. The area of most financial exposure and business concern, however, is the issue of insurance. How much and what type(s) of insurance should be purchased vary with the type of event you are staging, where it is being held, and the kinds of athletes participating (e.g., amateur or professional and their age and training). In today's litigious society and world political climate, recommended coverage and the cost of insurance are climbing at an increasing rate. However, you cannot afford not to have adequate insurance coverage for your sports event and its organizing entities, and it is essential to the financial well-being of your program to get preliminary quotes before you complete the budgeting process. At minimum, some form of liability coverage is required to protect the event, its parent organization, and

☐ Accounting services
☐ Accreditation (e.g., credential badges, ID cards, and lanyards)
☐ Communications services (e.g., phones, data lines, and Wi-Fi connectivity)
☐ Computer equipment and printer/copiers
☐ Gratuities
☐ Insurance
☐ Legal services
☐ Mobile communications equipment (e.g., walkie-talkies and mobile devices)
☐ Office space, hotel meeting rooms, and/or office trailers
☐ Office supplies
☐ Payroll services
☐ Power consumption and generators
☐ Power distribution (the labor to bring power to where it is needed)
☐ Recycling and material recovery
☐ Shipping, trucking, overnight couriers, and postage
☐ Software licenses (existing applications and custom programming)
☐ Staff and volunteer expenses (refreshments, meals or per diems, transportation, parking)
☐ Staff attire
☐ Storage and warehousing
☐ Temporary staff salaries and fees, including event specialists, freelancers, and interns
☐ Vehicle and equipment rentals (e.g., cars, vans, trucks, golf carts, and lifts)
☐ Volunteer program expenses (e.g., recognition, food and beverage, and parking)

Figure 2.4 Typical Sports Event Operations Expenses

its executives, employees, and sponsors. Proof of liability insurance coverage, often in the millions of dollars per occurrence, is a requirement that appears in the leases of most event facilities. Organizers should consult with their legal counsel and insurance broker to determine what additional insurance coverage would be advisable, particularly in regard to audience and athlete safety, the potential for injury, and other risks associated with the event.

Outdoor events may wish to consider acquiring "weather insurance," coverage that will pay benefits to the organizer if the program must be cancelled because of adverse weather conditions. Premiums for this type of coverage can be expensive, and the conditions that are required to trigger the payment of benefits are often extreme. An organizer should carefully analyze the financial exposure of an uninsured weather cancellation or postponement against the expense of purchasing insurance. The greater the potential loss to the organizer, the more attractive weather cancellation insurance may become. Unless an organizer is able to self-finance unrecoverable expenses and refunds to sponsors and ticket holders, coverage merits serious consideration.

Another expensive variation of cancellation insurance is terrorism insurance. This type of policy protects organizers from the financial calamity that might be faced due to a terrorist activity directed at the event, or occurring within a prescribed geographic radius. A more comprehensive discussion of this and other types of insurance coverage and risk management issues can be found in Play 14.

Marketing and Promotion Expenses

You may be planning the best and most compelling sports event ever staged, but unless you have a plan that will get the word out to both participants and the potential audience, you could be faced with a sparsely attended tournament or empty bleachers. You will probably not have designed a complete marketing plan while the budget is being developed, but you will need to set aside funds for advertising, publicity, promotions, website and app development, social media campaigns, and any designers, content creators, or agencies that will help you create and manage them.

The marketing of your event does not end once the program has begun. Postevent coverage is particularly useful in demonstrating the vitality and relevance of your event to community leaders, potential sponsors, future ticket buyers, and other key stakeholders. If your event is particularly newsworthy, you may have to provide facilities and services that will enable the media to cover your event. Relevant areas of importance include a comfortable and unobstructed vantage point from which they may view the event, as well as a weather-protected media working space with access to power, internet connectivity, and other communication services to facilitate the filing of stories directly from the event site. In addition to wireless access, photographers often require high-speed data lines to upload high-quality images. A press conference area for interviewing athletes, coaches, and other key officials is also often a requirement for major events. These areas often include one or more *step-and-repeat* backdrops dotted with event, sponsor, and/or venue logos, microphones with a public address system, tables, chairs, and lighting, and riser platforms for still and video cameras. Media representatives are accustomed to the periodic receipt of official statistics during an event, and, in the case of televised sports events, monitors within view to access replays and live broadcast coverage. Many organizers will also provide the media with access to food or snacks appropriate to the time of day, along with soft drinks, water, and coffee (remember—happy media write happier stories). Draw applicable expense categories from Figure 2.5 as you develop your marketing budget and refer to Play 8 for more details on how to work with and service the media.

☐ Advertising agency fees and expenses (hourly charges for staff time and creative charges)
☐ Branding and logo development
☐ Broadcast/video advertising production
☐ Broadcast/video advertising time
☐ Information services (phone, text response, automated and/or live chat capability)
☐ Kick-off or announcement news conference or event
☐ Media accreditation
☐ Media center/workroom expenses (furnishings, draping, internet connectivity, phone, copier, and television monitors)
☐ Media guide (printed and/or digital)
☐ Media hospitality (meals, refreshments, snacks, and gifts)
☐ Outdoor advertising (creative, production, and rental of billboards and street banners)
☐ Pre-event promotional giveaway items
☐ Press conference area (step-and-repeat backdrop, tables, chairs, sound, lighting, and risers)
☐ Print advertising creative (design)
☐ Print advertising space
☐ Public relations agency fee and expenses
☐ Radio advertising production (i.e., costs of creating the commercial)
☐ Radio advertising time
☐ Social media content production and management
☐ Staff photographer and videographer
☐ Statistician(s)
☐ Website development and management

Figure 2.5 Typical Sports Event Marketing and Promotion Expenses

Sponsor Fulfillment Expenses

Sponsors expect, and are entitled to, a host of contractual benefits and, in many cases, noncontractual "perks" in exchange for their support of your event. Expenses undertaken to service sponsor needs, whether dictated by the contract or provided as added bonuses by the organizer, are called *fulfillment expenses*.

Almost every event sponsorship agreement will include a minimum quantity of site-specific signage positions that display the sponsor's logo, company name, and/or product identification. Unless otherwise defined by the sponsor's contract, the expense of designing, fabricating, installing, and dismantling this signage is usually a cost to the event budget. Event organizers are often obligated to provide a specified number of complimentary tickets, the cost of which (i.e., the revenue that would have been received had they been sold) should also be accounted for in the budget.

Because the content of sponsor packages varies so widely among different types of events and across the industry, there is no rule of thumb governing what percentage of an organizer's sponsor revenues should be set aside to cover fulfillment costs. The revenue-to-expense ratio will differ even among the family of sponsors for a single event. Any expense that results from an obligation made to a sponsor, and that would not have been incurred if that sponsor was not involved, should be included in this budget line. Extra perquisites that you intend to add that add value to a sponsorship but are not contractually required should also be included. Such expenses may include hosting private VIP receptions, advertisements acknowledging the sponsors' support, special gifts, premiums, and presentations, athlete appearances, custom-made staff attire displaying the sponsor's logo, labor for product sampling—the list and variety of these costs can seem endless. Refer to Figure 2.6 for a summary of sponsorship expenses.

By budgeting for sponsor fulfillment costs before a package of benefits is offered to potential sponsors, event organizers will avoid one of the most basic mistakes in event marketing—offering a sponsor package that will cost too much to manage and fulfill compared to the revenue it will generate. Creating sponsorship packages of value to both the organizer and the business partner will be more fully discussed in Plays 6 and 7.

- ☐ Activation (e.g., fan activities, banners and signage, and sponsor promotion expenses)
- ☐ Advertising (e.g., sponsor thank-you ads)
- ☐ Athlete meet-and-greet functions
- ☐ Complimentary tickets
- ☐ Event merchandise
- ☐ Gifts (e.g., event merchandise, collectibles, and premiums)
- ☐ Hospitality (e.g., receptions, pre-event, and event food and beverage costs)
- ☐ Hotel room amenities and gifts
- ☐ Invitations
- ☐ Postevent market research (e.g., sponsorship valuation and Return on Investment (ROI) analysis)
- ☐ Postevent sponsor recognition
- ☐ Press conferences (relating to the sponsorship or sponsor activation)
- ☐ Sales materials (e.g., website design, proposals, research, and writers)
- ☐ Sales presentation expenses (e.g., travel, accommodations, and business meals)
- ☐ VIP concierge services

Figure 2.6 Typical Sponsorship Expenses

Guest Management and Hospitality Expenses

Sports events have become a major hospitality opportunity, not only for the sponsors that support them but also for the organizations that stage them. From tournaments to touring events, championship matches to all-star games, and fan festivals to skills exhibitions, organizers take advantage of the cachet generated by their programs to invite, excite, and attract VIP guests, sponsors, potential future business partners, celebrities, and other influential individuals to their events. Determine early in the planning process how many guests you will be able to accommodate on a complimentary basis and to what degree you will entertain and service them. Although Play 11 explores this area in greater detail, organizers can use the checklist in Figure 2.7 to identify the most common guest management and hospitality expenses.

☐ Commemorative ticket printing
☐ Directional and welcome signage
☐ Guest transportation (e.g., airport pick-ups and shuttle transportation to events)
☐ Hospitality suites
☐ Hotel accommodations
☐ Hotel attrition and cancellation penalties
☐ Information kiosks and printed information guides and maps
☐ Event guest "apps"
☐ Invitation design (printed or digital) and guest management software
☐ Parties and receptions
☐ Pre-event communication
☐ Shipping/deliveries
☐ Welcome gifts and room amenity deliveries

Figure 2.7 Typical Sports Event Guest Management and Hospitality Expenses

Event Presentation Expenses

Many sports events include opening and/or closing ceremonies, pregame festivities, player introductions, and intermission or halftime entertainment programs—ranging from the simple to the spectacular—that require some level of creative, technical, and production support. Stadium and arena keyboard instruments have been providing entertainment atmosphere during stoppages in play for decades. The playback of recorded music designed for specific game situations, and in sports such as figure skating, complement the competition itself. Video boards and other electronic displays entertain and educate fans with visual and audio features including replays and highlights, statistics and scores, and interactive promotions. Specialized lighting and effects are frequently used to excite the crowd, and to celebrate scoring and game-turning plays. Live talent may perform during pregame, deliver anthems, and entertain during halftimes and intermissions. Some sports events are pure entertainment rather than a competition, celebrating a sport with production, entertainment, pageantry, and noncompetitive athlete appearances, such as opening ceremonies, awards dinners, or fan festivals. All of the traditional elements of entertainment event production may be applied to sports events, including those enumerated in the checklist in Figure 2.8, and discussed in more detail in Play 12.

Depending on the nature and scale of the sports event, a team of production specialists may be required to design, plan and stage the entertainment portions of the program. This team might include event producers, stage managers, technical directors, lighting designers, sound engineers, and scriptwriters, to

☐ Anthem performer travel expenses or honorarium
☐ Costumes
☐ Decorations, flags, banners, and bunting
☐ Fan engagement technology (augmented reality (AR), virtual reality (VR), and proprietary participation platforms)
☐ Lighting (e.g., follow spots, theatrical lighting, broadcast lighting)
☐ Music and voice recording
☐ Pregame and intermission performer(s)
☐ Production staff, including electricians, stagehands, and technical staff
☐ Props and prizes
☐ Public address announcer and/or host
☐ Set design and construction
☐ Sound (e.g., playback equipment, public address system, microphones, and mixer)
☐ Special effects (e.g., pyrotechnics, haze, flame effects, and confetti cannons)
☐ Staging and risers
☐ Video/visual elements production
☐ Video screens, camera package, and playback equipment

Figure 2.8 Typical Sports Event Presentation Expenses

name a few. The right team of experts and presentation tools can elevate a simple athletic contest into a sports entertainment vehicle that makes a lasting, positive impression on the fan, the viewer, and the public at large.

Capital Investment and Amortization

Your sports event budget may require the acquisition of physical assets that are included among many of the identified expense categories, but can be stored and reused for future events. These assets might include equipment for the field of play, signage and display hardware, timing equipment, reusable banners, props, staging, video and sound equipment, video monitors, computer and digital equipment, tools, road cases, and more. If you purchase these items for an event that you expect to stage annually, or for a series of events during a single year, the expense may be amortized, or spread out for bookkeeping purposes, over the course of their expected useful lives.

It is often preferable to rent what is needed because capital assets that are purchased, but not used all the time, can create additional annual expenses such as the leasing of storage space, trucking, and refurbishment. But renting the same things over and over again can result in unnecessary costs. If you have the storage space, and are certain these assets can be used again, you can amortize their costs, or spread the cost over multiple events. Of course, all the cash will have to be spent at the time of purchase. But, the event expenses charged against the first year can be reduced as long as you are prepared to carry that same amortized expense forward until the full cost has been completely accounted for. For example, let's say you have to acquire 25 video monitors at $400, and that you have sufficient storage space available to accommodate them after the purchase. While you have to spend the entire sum of $10,000 immediately to take possession of these assets, you expect to use these same monitors for three years before they will need to be replaced. By dividing the total expense by the number of years you will use these assets, and you can charge only one-third, or $3,333, to this year's budget. However, you must remember that you will have also "already spent" the same sum in the budgets for events over the next two years.

There is nothing that says you cannot amortize your assets over a series of events during the same year, or that you have to charge the same percentage to each. Let's say you have to build three interactive

Total expense to build kiosks: $15,000
Annual championships: 3 units used × 1 time per year × 3 years useful life = 9 usages
Fundraising events: 1 unit used × 3 times per year × 3 years useful life = 9 usages
Total usages = 18
Amortized value per kiosk per use = $833.33
Charge to each annual championship = $833.33 × 3 kiosks = $2,500.00
Charge to each fundraising event = $833.33 × 1 kiosk = $833.33

Figure 2.9 Sample Capital Amortization Calculation

information kiosks that cost $5,000 each. You will use all three kiosks at your biggest annual event, and only one at three smaller events. Although you will have to spend $15,000 in cash right now, you can charge each of your event budgets a smaller figure. Figure 2.9 illustrates the calculations for this hypothetical example.

There will be occasions when assets, the expenses for which you have already amortized, do not reach their projected useful life due to accidental damage, wear and tear, or simple malfunction. If the asset must be replaced, you will need to liquidate, or *write off*, the balance of its value—that is, the portion not yet used by future events. From the example in Figure 2.9, if a kiosk becomes unusable after two years (two-thirds of its useful life), the value charged to events in the third year (the remaining third of the total value, or $5,000), may be reallocated among the budgets of the events at which the asset already provided benefit. If the kiosk is replaced, the ability to amortize that new individual asset over a new three-year period begins again. Similarly, if an event is cancelled, or the need for a particular asset in future events is no longer required, the remaining value will have to be liquidated by reallocating the remaining value over one or more of the budgets for events at which the asset was utilized.

If you are acquiring assets for a sports event that will likely occur only once, and that will have no further use at any future events, you will not be able to enjoy the financial advantages of capital amortization. There may also be the need for unique capital items that must be designed, built, or acquired that cannot be rented. The total cost of such assets should be charged to the event budget, even if you have a plan to later sell or otherwise derive some value from salvaging the items. Any value received on the postevent sale of the asset can later be accounted for as miscellaneous revenue.

Miscellaneous Expenses and Contingency Allowances

Wise drivers always fasten their seatbelts before leaving the driveway because they know that accidents can happen without warning. They also know that there is a greater chance they will survive a mishap by simply taking this precaution before leaving the driveway. The unforeseen can also befall a sports event organizer from the moment the budget is drafted, throughout the planning process, and even after an event is long concluded. For this reason, a wise organizer includes a contingency allowance line for unexpected expenses. By buckling this financial seatbelt before work on an event begins, the organizer will vastly improve the budget's, the event's, and his or her own career's probability of survival.

The contingency line in your budget should not be confused or co-mingled with a line for miscellaneous expenses. The miscellaneous expense line is where individual expenditures that are too small to warrant their own budget categories, or odds and ends that do not easily fit a specific budgeted expense line, should be charged. A contingency line, however, exists as an additional safety net, with the hope that it will not be needed in large part, or at all. It is there to be used in an emergency, to cover cost overruns, restoration or replacement costs, or, if all goes according to plan, to contribute to net profits if it is ultimately unneeded.

If possible, set aside a contingency allowance representing an average of 10 percent of the total event budget. Contingencies of 10 percent, or as much as 15 percent, are most important for sports events with relatively modest expense budgets of under $50,000 to ensure sufficient funds are set aside in case of emergency. For larger budgets ($50,000–$250,000 in expenses), it may be safe to lower the contingency to 7.5 percent or less. It is recommended that for the largest budgets ($250,000 and higher), the safety belt not slip below 5 percent but set higher if the budget allows.

Reforecasts

Experienced sports event organizers periodically reforecast their expense estimates after the budget has been finalized, throughout the planning, management, and execution phases leading to event day, and even up until the books close after the event. The worksheet in Appendix 1 provides a partial illustration of the form for a simple sports event reforecast. The original budget spreadsheet is extended to include several additional columns of figures. Immediately beside the approved budget is a column of forecast expenses, the final amount the organizer expects on each budget line at the end of the event. Once finalized, the numbers in the "Budget" on each line are never adjusted. It is the forecast column where expectations on the final amount of each budget line are periodically updated. Next is the column for actual expenses, those costs for which invoices have been received, or contracts have been signed. The actual expense column will help validate the accuracy of the forecast column to its left, showing the money already spent, and, by extension, indicating the amount remaining. Finally, a variance column shows the difference between the original budget and the forecast, line by line.

The reforecasting process enables the organizer to reallocate budgeted funds overestimated in one area to another budget line that may be suffering from cost overages. Throughout the planning and production process, the combined value of forecasted budget overestimates must be matched or exceeded by the subtotal of underestimates for the budget to balance. If it does not, the event organizer must undergo the painful process of cutting expenses. To be effective, forecasting, like the budgeting process itself, must be grounded in realistic expectations. Make sure when you reduce a budget line to make up for a cost overrun in another area that you will be able to reduce the expense in fact, and not simply on paper.

Post-play Analysis

Sports event expenses are many and varied. The major categories of expenses include facilities costs, game- and player-related expenses, event operations, marketing and promotion, sponsor fulfillment, guest management and hospitality, event presentation, miscellaneous expenses, and contingency allowances. Certain costs for the acquisition of assets that may be used over several events and/or several years may be written off, or amortized, over the useful life of those items, allowing event organizers to spread the cost of an asset over several event budgets. Throughout the planning and execution process, event organizers reforecast the financial performance of their budgets to better manage costs and apply savings in some areas to offset cost overruns in others.

Coach's Clipboard

1. Create an expense budget for a new college tournament in the sport of your choice featuring teams from five universities in your region and five from outside the area.

2. A children's hospital asks you to manage a pro-am golf tournament (foursomes composed of both professionals and amateurs) to raise awareness of, and generate revenues for, its facility. How much will you advise the hospital it must invest in order to stage the tournament before revenues begin to be received? How can this initial investment be covered if the hospital is unable to contribute any capital in advance?

3. An annual street hockey tournament for amateur adult teams requires the acquisition of two portable rink boards and flooring systems costing $15,000 each. If the rinks have a useful life of three years, what amount should be allocated to each year's event? If you can use the rink systems more often by organizing similar annual tournaments in two nearby communities, what amount should be allocated to each event per year?

Identifying Revenue Streams

"Never spend your money before you have it."
— *Thomas Jefferson, third president of the United States, 1743–1826*

This play will help you to:

- Develop and manage the revenue side of your event's budget.
- Become familiar with the types of revenues that sports events can generate.
- Set realistic revenue expectations.

Introduction

Few sports events can exist without some form of funding. Successful sports event organizers are not in the habit of investing capital without great confidence that they will be able to recoup it by the time the event has concluded. But, expenses begin to accumulate the moment an event budget is approved, if not before. Be sure you have developed your event's *revenue streams*—the various sources and times of arrival for incoming cash—to ensure you will have money on hand to satisfy your financial obligations.

By defining your event's objectives in detail, you already have an idea of how you want your bottom line to turn out; that is, whether you aim to make money, break even, or spend a predetermined amount as a promotional or fan development investment. You next compile a detailed analysis of what will be required to stage your event and project the level of expenses you expect to encounter. Then, by comparing your desired bottom line against anticipated expenses, you know how much total revenue you will need to generate. The question now is how to go about generating it.

The revenue streams available to a sports event organizer depend on the type of event, the venue in which it will be held, and its net income objectives (i.e., the amount of profit or loss). Is the event the beneficiary of a charitable endeavor, a break-even not-for-profit effort, or a profit-generating enterprise? The reality is that there are far more ways of spending money than making it. Although revenue streams will vary from event to event, Figure 3.1 provides a list of the most common to consider when creating your event budget.

□ Admissions (i.e., ticket sales)
□ Concessions/food and beverage sales
□ Grants and donations
□ Hospitality packages
□ Media rights fees
□ Merchandise sales
□ Parking
□ Programs and journals
□ Sponsorship and advertising
□ Tournament registration or participation fees

Figure 3.1 Typical Sports Event Revenue Streams

Ticket Sales

Admission tickets are probably the oldest and most common income generator for sports events. Today, they remain the lifeblood of most top amateur and professional sports events, commanding prices that range from just a few dollars to multiple thousands for premium events in the best seating locations. Although ticket revenue can account for 50 percent or more of total revenues for a sports event, the value of having fans in the building goes far deeper. A full venue adds value to sponsorships and to an organizer's other business partnerships by exposing sponsor brands to more potential customers. For televised and streamed programs, a large crowd adds prestige and excitement to the event for the viewing audience and demonstrates that there is a market large enough to fill the venue, and, by extension, to reach into the viewers' living rooms.

There is, of course, a more practical, immediate reason why struggling to fill your inventory of spectator space is of paramount importance. The more people at your event, the more revenue you can also generate from the sales of merchandise, food and beverage, and, for those who operate their own facilities, parking.

There are many sports events where it is either impractical or even undesirable to sell tickets to spectators. For example, running events such as 5Ks, 10Ks, and mini-marathons derive much of their revenue from registration fees and sponsorships rather than tickets. Finish line seating or a standing area might be created to accommodate financial contributors, city officials, and partner corporations, but access to such areas is usually by invitation only and not sold to the ticket-buying public. (It is no less important to the perception of an event's success to ensure these areas are filled, as well.) Grassroots sports events, such as those staged by community youth leagues and other not-for-profit organizations, often do not charge for tickets either. In their world, it is frequently more important to draw the greatest number of family and friends possible to cover their expenses with sales of merchandise, refreshments, journal advertising, and low-cost sponsorships purchased by local businesses.

Calculating the Gross Potential

For events that rely on admission income, the first step in projecting ticket revenues is to assess your inventory. If your program is being held in a stadium or arena, chances are good that there is already a seating plan from similar past events, with a section-by-section manifest of the precise number of seats available. As the shape and dimensions of the playing surface for various sports differ, the same facility's seating plan may vary widely by sport. New York's Madison Square Garden, for example, will seat 18,200 for ice hockey, 19,763 for basketball, and even more for boxing. The seating plans for most permanent sports and entertainment facilities feature obvious divisions of attractiveness, most often determined by the relative height of the seating levels, the distance and orientation radiating from the center of playing action (e.g., red line, 50-yard line, and home plate), the physical size and comfort of the seats themselves, and accompanying perquisites such as access to adjoining club lounge areas or other exclusive spaces. These divisions, also known as *price breaks*, provide convenient ways to offer the ticket-buying audience different economic options. Generally, the closer a seat is to the action and the more exclusive the environment, the higher the price you can charge for a ticket.

If you have to provide a seating area where none normally exists—for example, in a convention center, on a field, in a parking lot, or along a city street—you should contact a seat rental company during the budgeting process. The vendor can measure the proposed site to determine the number of seats that can be comfortably installed. If you must install temporary seating for which tickets will be sold, it is essential that a reliable seating plan be created before sales begin. The rental company can also assist with obtaining permits, generating drawings, scheduling inspections, and gaining approvals as required by a local jurisdiction. Precision is especially important if tickets are sold on a reserved seat basis, as opposed to general admission. Reserved seat tickets entitle the purchaser to a specific location defined by a section, row, and seat number. General admission ticket plans, also known as festival seating, allow the purchaser to sit in any location on a first-come, first-served basis.

Temporary seating areas are often designed with natural price breaks, as well. Whether in permanent or temporary locations, it is always a good idea to ensure that price breaks are separated by some obvious landmark or barrier—a different level, sections separated by aisles or rows separated by some concourse or transverse aisle. Otherwise, ticket buyers at the outer edge of the price breaks may be upset that someone sitting just a few feet immediately behind or next to them paid less for those tickets than they did.

Before entering a sum in the budget for ticket revenue, the organizer must first calculate the event's *gross potential*. To derive the gross potential, multiply the number of tickets within each price break by the price you wish to set for each. Figure 3.2 depicts a fictional event with 2,350 seats configured into six price breaks. In this case, because the promoter believes that front-row seats will sell well at a premium price, they have created a special category for just this small number of seats. Promoters who embrace this philosophy should ensure that front-row seats—even without a visible break—actually offer a prestigious, unobstructed view of the event. The sidelines between the audience and the playing surface in some sports, such as football and soccer, can be crammed with officials, trainers, cameramen, photographers, and unengaged players, so unless the seating in the front row is elevated above the shoulders of those individuals, patrons purchasing front-row seats are actually enjoying less of the event than those who are farther away. Professional basketball teams offer courtside seats at which fans pay for the privilege of sitting immediately adjacent to team benches and having their feet literally on the sidelines. In many cases, front-row seating for a live sports event can be so exciting that a price premium of 50 to 100 percent, or more, can be commanded.

Unless your event is a proven property that enjoys a consistent track record of selling out year after year, it is not recommended that the gross potential be the final number placed in the budget as ticket revenue. Project the percentage of your inventory you can expect to sell with a great degree of confidence. A good rule of thumb is 75–85 percent. If you are uncertain of selling at least 75 percent of your gross potential, you may have selected a facility that is too large for your event's audience. If you feel you can safely sell 80 percent of the gross potential, use that number on the ticket revenue line of your event budget. Referring to Figure 3.2, this would mean selling a minimum of 1,880 tickets (2,350 × 0.80) for a projected $52,700 ($65,875 × 0.80). In budgeting for your event, it is a good practice to be as conservative as practical in your

Seating Area	Inventory	Ticket Price	Potential
Front row	150	$50.00	$7,500
Lower seating, mid-arena	750	$35.00	$26,250
Lower seating, end zone	500	$25.00	$12,500
Upper level, mid-arena	500	$25.00	$12,500
Upper level, end zone	350	$17.50	$6,125
Standing room	100	$10.00	$1,000
GROSS POTENTIAL	**2,350**		**$65,875**

Figure 3.2 Calculation of Gross Revenue Potential

estimates; if your calculations can work at the lowest end of this range and still cover your expenses, the chances for greater financial upside increase.

As discussed in Play 2, do not forget to deduct any applicable sales and amusement taxes and facility use fees from the gross potential. As the organizer will never see any of those revenues, which are kept by the municipality and/or venue, they are best deducted here. (There are no taxes or fees payable in this example.)

You will likely be issuing complimentary tickets to special guests, sponsors, and other business partners. If desired, you may also deduct "comps" from your ticket revenue line. We prefer to categorize complimentary tickets as expenses, so we deduct them like any other expense on the opposite side of the P&L statement. Our philosophy is that the issuing of comps is a cost of doing business, as opposed to a missed revenue opportunity. A comp seat is really sold, but instead of accepting cash, the event is deriving some other benefit. Comp tickets are usually provided to sponsors as a benefit of their association, and the event has accounted for a sponsor's cash, product, or service somewhere else in the budget. Part of the cost in fulfilling the sponsorship agreement is providing the ticket and, therefore, it is categorized as an expense. Other comps, for special guests and celebrities, may lend an event more prestige, legitimacy, or increased cooperation from local businesses, suppliers, and municipalities. Therefore, you will find "Complimentary Tickets" listed as an expense item in our event budgets, as opposed to having their value deducted from the "Ticket Revenue" gross potential.

Setting Ticket Prices

Figure 3.2 suggests that seats located in the middle, or along the long axis, of the arena are more desirable than those in the end zone for this event. As a result, there is a price break between mid-arena and end zone seating. This price break is repeated in the upper level of the arena, where upper-end-zone seats are the second-lowest priced ticket. The promoter of this fictional event feels that tickets for the lower-end zone and the upper mid-arena are of similar desirability and has priced both sections the same so fans can select a mid-priced ticket in either section, according to their own preferences. Finally, the facility, with permission from the local fire marshal, has determined that a small number of patrons can be safely accommodated in standing-room locations. The promoter has scaled these tickets at the lowest possible price to increase attendance and economic accessibility for die-hard fans who cannot otherwise afford tickets, or who purchase tickets after all seated sections are sold out. As a general rule, event organizers should never offer standing-room options unless the facility and local fire marshal deem their locations safe.

The next step is to determine how much you should charge for tickets. Setting ticket prices can be very tricky, and mistakes can prove disastrous. If you set prices too high, it might prove difficult to sell your entire inventory of tickets. If you charge too little, you may have insufficient funds with which to pay your expenses, or you will generate a smaller than otherwise possible net profit. The checklist in Figure 3.3 provides some useful questions, tips, and philosophies to be considered when pondering the level to set for ticket prices.

SIDELINE STORY

Is Ticket Scaling Ancient History?

Historians tell us that admission to one of the oldest and most iconic sports facilities—the Roman Colosseum—was totally free. The emperor staged all manner of sporting events, including those infamous gladiator death matches, to maintain his popularity and the political support of the citizenry. Where you sat, however, was a function of class or office, with the commoners occupying the highest, most distant locations, while government officials and visiting dignitaries enjoyed the better views. As many as 50,000 spectators could enjoy each day of competition at the Colosseum, courtesy of the Caesars. Perhaps the original multiuse arena, the Roman Colosseum, which could also be flooded for reenactments of heroic naval battles, remained a dominant sports and entertainment venue for more than 400 years. Its design was also reportedly ahead of its time in terms of fan experience—the Colosseum was designed to be able to empty its entire capacity after an event in a spectator-friendly five minutes.

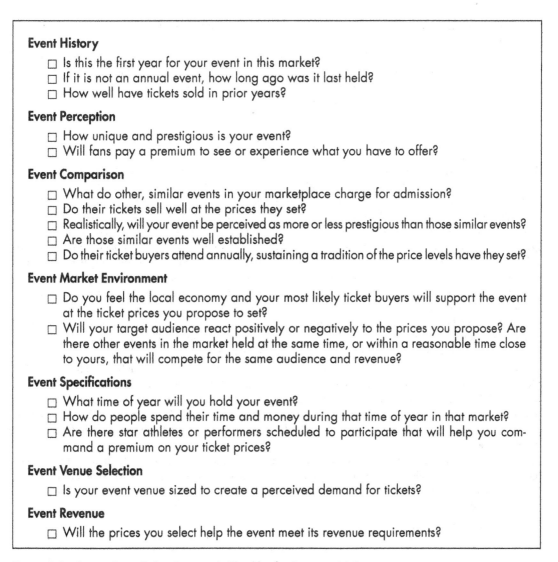

Event History
- [ ] Is this the first year for your event in this market?
- [ ] If it is not an annual event, how long ago was it last held?
- [ ] How well have tickets sold in prior years?

Event Perception
- [ ] How unique and prestigious is your event?
- [ ] Will fans pay a premium to see or experience what you have to offer?

Event Comparison
- [ ] What do other, similar events in your marketplace charge for admission?
- [ ] Do their tickets sell well at the prices they set?
- [ ] Realistically, will your event be perceived as more or less prestigious than those similar events?
- [ ] Are those similar events well established?
- [ ] Do their ticket buyers attend annually, sustaining a tradition of the price levels have they set?

Event Market Environment
- [ ] Do you feel the local economy and your most likely ticket buyers will support the event at the ticket prices you propose to set?
- [ ] Will your target audience react positively or negatively to the prices you propose? Are there other events in the market held at the same time, or within a reasonable time close to yours, that will compete for the same audience and revenue?

Event Specifications
- [ ] What time of year will you hold your event?
- [ ] How do people spend their time and money during that time of year in that market?
- [ ] Are there star athletes or performers scheduled to participate that will help you command a premium on your ticket prices?

Event Venue Selection
- [ ] Is your event venue sized to create a perceived demand for tickets?

Event Revenue
- [ ] Will the prices you select help the event meet its revenue requirements?

Figure 3.3 Sports Event Ticket Pricing: A Checklist for Decision-Making

As part of the event comparison, unless your event is significantly more prestigious (i.e., includes more and better activities, features more marquee athletes, and is a championship event), it is unlikely you will be able to charge more than a less premium event. On the one hand, if your event is breaking into the market, you may want to encourage sales by setting prices a little lower until your program becomes better known and more highly regarded. On the other hand, setting prices too low can also create the impression of the event as a vastly inferior experience compared to similar programs.

The event venue selection process requires strategic thinking. Venues that are too large may communicate the perception that buying tickets will be easy and require no urgency to purchase. It may be more advantageous to sellout in the early years of your event by selecting a venue that offers fewer seats while there is lesser demand. Then, let the perception build over the course of two or three years that those who wait until the day of the event to try to purchase tickets might be out of luck. In subsequent years, you can either select a venue of greater size to accommodate more people, or increase prices while demand is still outpacing supply. There is a secondary reason to limit the number of seats available. It may be preferable for your event to appear sold out at 5,000 seats in a smaller venue, rather than appear two-thirds full with 6,000 fans in a 9,000-seat venue (assuming you can afford to forgo the revenue that can be derived from the extra 1,000 seats). Of course, if you are confident that your event can fill the larger venue, by all means go for it!

You may have to adjust your thinking on prices—or expenses—after plugging all your numbers into your budget. Resist the urge to increase prices to cover expenses unless you are certain that the market will tolerate a higher cost for tickets. Take the time necessary to conduct the due diligence and fully evaluate the answers in the checklist before setting prices.

Pricing for Multiday Events

If your event spans the course of more than a single day, your revenue opportunities and expense liabilities will increase accordingly. Many events, particularly tournaments, are composed of "preliminaries," or early-round matches, or may include events that are subsidiary to the main event. Events that run for several days, perhaps including quarterfinals, semifinals, and final matches, frequently increase their ticket prices with each succeeding round. The premium as competition progresses can be anywhere from 10 to 100 percent of the earlier, preliminary contests. Event organizers often sell tickets as a package that includes all rounds, also known as a "strip," "series" or "subscription," before individual game tickets go on sale to the general public. In this arrangement, the best seats are made available to your best customers, those who will attend the most matches. As a side benefit, it also creates a sense of urgency in the market among those interested only in one or two rounds. There is usually no discount for buying a strip of tickets. To the ticket buyer, the benefit derived is often simply receiving the best seating locations available at their chosen price level. But, if your event is new, and you want to sell tickets more quickly, you can certainly consider a discounted package price, if only to reduce the ticket inventory.

Packaging tickets also helps to fill seats to the "weaker" events, those that might be perceived as less desirable to the public due to the day of the week (in almost all cases, weekends naturally sell better than weekdays), time of day, location, marquee value of the athletes involved, relevance of a particular match or event, and so forth. The fan purchasing the strip often posts tickets they will not be using for sale on a secondary ticketing site such as StubHub, Seat Geek, or Ticket Exchange to help finance their total purchase.

As discussed in Play 2, do not forget to consider the costs of local, state, and federal taxes, facility fees, credit card and group sales commissions, and box office/ticketing service expenses when determining your ticket prices. The higher your ticket prices, the greater the expenses organizers will encounter in many of these variable cost categories.

SIDELINE STORY

Baseball All-Star Game Packages Drive Attendance

When Major League Baseball's (MLB's) All-Star Game was first played at Comiskey Park as part of the mid-summer festivities for the 1933 Chicago World's Fair, few could have foreseen the long-term commercial success of *Chicago Tribune* sports editor Arch Ward's original idea. Watching the likes of Babe Ruth hit the first home run in All-Star Game history, Lou Gehrig protecting first base, and other future Hall of Famers with names like Pie, Lefty, and Gabby at bat and on the same field was novel enough to command enormous attention. More recently, however, MLB's annual showcase of its stars includes far more than just the game, and at varying price points that appeal to a wide range of audiences. Annual activities at the host ballpark include All-Star Workout Day including the extremely popular Home Run Derby and MLB All-Star Saturday featuring the All-Star Futures Game, initially sold to host team season ticket members as a package. Additional programming for the public and available separately includes Play Ball Park, the league's fan festival, a ticketed attraction catering to a family-oriented audience demographic.

Sponsorship and Advertising

Sponsorship is a pervasive, persuasive, and necessary source of funding for sports events at all levels. If organizers had to rely only on ticket sales, the cost of most event tickets would need to be astronomically high to cover the rapidly increasing costs of staging sports events. The support of sponsors, and the ubiquitous manifestations of their participation, is generally accepted by ticket buyers as a natural component of today's event experience. Sidelines, playing surfaces, scoreboards, and time clocks the world over are covered with sponsor advertising messages. In North American professional sports, games are periodically halted for extended stoppages of play to allow broadcasters to air commercials. Video boards showcase replays, features and activities designed both to enhance the fan experience and fulfill sponsor obligations. Uniforms worn by players from Little League baseball to professional soccer teams are emblazoned with the name of the team's primary sponsor. Plays 6 and 7 will explore in detail how sports event organizers can partner with sponsors to their mutual benefit. For budgeting purposes, the event organizer has to assess the degree of relevance and interest a program will have in the corporate community, and the dollars the event might generate. While sponsors evaluate sports events against their own set of objectives and criteria, sponsorship revenue potential for each event will vary depending on factors such as each event's size, scope, audience demographics, visibility, and cultural relevance, to name a few. From grassroots handshake deals of a few hundred dollars to the multimillion-dollar contracts negotiated with the Olympic Games and professional major league sports, the guiding principle is generally the same—the event must deliver opportunities for sponsors increase product sales, brand awareness, and goodwill.

How much should your budget project for sponsorship revenue? Corporate support for mature sports events can be among the most lucrative sources of revenue for event organizers, but also the most labor intense to capture. Success usually lies in a combination of the personal business contacts of the event promoter or their hired agency, past event history, and the ability to design, communicate, and deliver clear, obvious, low-risk opportunities for the companies writing the checks. Set reasonable expectations and attainable revenue goals for your event and get out into the sponsorship marketplace as early as possible, long before you have gone to market with ticket sales (because, among other reasons, top-level sponsors will want recognition in the title or as a presenter of the event and on associated marketing collateral).

Many first-time sports events overestimate their appeal and price their sponsorship packages beyond what a sensible company would spend. Because sponsorship revenues can provide a major source of funding for event planning and operations, overpricing can cause the entire program to fall apart before the first ticket is even sold. It is also far less risky to have the option of altering the size and budget of your event if sponsorship revenue appears to be failing to meet expectations before advertising has begun and tickets have been sold. In the broadest general terms, if you have other sources of revenue, try not to be primarily dependent on corporate support for a first-year sports event. If your objective is to generate a net profit, it is safest to plan to have sponsorship support account for all or most of the expected profit margin, assuming ticket sales and other revenue streams can get you to at least a breakeven position. As your event becomes more established, and its sponsorship track record becomes more predictable, you can start thinking about using more sponsor money to pay for expenses.

Established events, especially those with multiyear sponsorship deals, however, can rely on past history to project sponsorship income. It is a good idea for event organizers with multiyear sponsors to keep a close eye on when those deals expire and take these deadlines into account when preparing their revenue projections. It is also wise to offer sponsorships of differing expiration dates to ensure that not all deals will end during the same year. If sponsors must be renewed or replaced when deals end, it is advantageous not to have all of that marketing opportunity at risk at the same time.

In many cases, sports events require some amount of sponsorship capital to provide the cash flow needed to cover expenses before any other revenues are received. As you prepare the expense side of your budget, identify the costs you will incur early in the planning process, especially before tickets are sold. Unless you have other sources of capital to invest in planning and staging the event, the total of those costs may form your minimum sponsorship revenue requirement. (*Caution*: Remember that using ticket revenues to pay for all of your pre-event expenses is also inherently risky. Cancellation or postponement may require you to have cash on hand to issue immediate refunds to ticket holders, and, eventually, to sponsors.

Event cancellation insurance can protect against some part of this risk, although it is usually the case that an insurance settlement will not be received quickly enough to satisfy ticket holders. See Play 14 for a more complete discussion of event insurance.)

Remember to include a line in your expense budget for "sponsorship fulfillment" whenever you expect to generate sponsor revenues. You should not expect simply to cash a check without providing value to your sponsor, and it will surely take some amount of money to do so. You may have accounted for some of your costs in your "complimentary tickets" line, but there will certainly be more expenses to consider, such as banners and signage, gifts, hospitality, and advertising, among many others. These costs often account for between 25% and as much as 50% of gross sponsorship sales.

Budgeting Value-In-Kind (Barter)

Sponsors and other business partners often ask sports event organizers to accept their products and services in lieu of, or in addition to, cash. This makes good sense to sponsors because it costs them far less to provide your organization with their products or services, even when calculated at a wholesale value, than to pay you in cash. It can also move excess inventory out of their warehouses and, in cases where the products are used in view of the fans at the event, provide them with additional promotional value. This practice is variously known as accepting *value-in-kind* (VIK), barter, or contra. In tight economic times, barter becomes an especially attractive option for business partners.

Accepting VIK is most advantageous to sports event organizers when it offsets an anticipated expense. The partner company provides the required product in partial or total payment for receiving sponsor benefits, and the event organizer acquires these necessary items without expending cash. VIK can also be attractive when the products or services add experiential value for your fans without adding expenses to the budget.

Although no cash changes hands in pure VIK deals, it is wise to account for them as though cash was accepted, and was then used to purchase the products. In other words, if you estimate that your event will encounter $1,000 in gasoline expenses, and a sponsor oil company offers to provide you with $1,000 VIK, forecast the same $1,000 in gasoline expenses and $1,000 in sponsor revenue. In cases where a VIK deal adds value to an event without offsetting budgeted costs, you should "gross up" your budget, adding the retail cost of the product as a new, unbudgeted expense on one side of the ledger, and an unanticipated extra source of revenue on the other side. Even though these "value added" deals may improve the event experience or deliver better operational solutions to the organizer, they may create additional tax liabilities, as the value of a barter deal is often treated the same way as income from cash in many localities. Therefore, accepting VIK for products or services could actually end up costing your budget some unanticipated amount of money in taxes.

Finally, be selective about agreeing to VIK deals. If a potential VIK opportunity would provide you with products or services that neither offset anticipated cash expenses nor add value to the event experience, it is probably not a worthwhile deal. To encourage companies seeking VIK deals to spend a little cash alongside providing their product, you can create a sponsor category for purely VIK partners with fewer or reduced benefits, such as an "official supplier" designation (see Plays 6 and 7), and offer greater benefits and "sponsor" status in return for an added amount of cash.

Prospective sponsors also occasionally offer "activation only" deals in lieu of providing cash or product. Activation can be loosely defined as those activities a partner company undertakes to support its sponsorship beyond the fees and expenses spent directly with the organizer. A pure activation deal may offer attractive advertising and promotional benefits to the event without payment of cash or VIK. A soft-drink distributor, for example, might create a bottle-cap promotion or a quick-service restaurant a tray liner offer, each with a corresponding advertising campaign that would add significant exposure benefits that promote ticket sales for the event. To some extent, these activities could reduce the amount of money originally set aside by the organizer for advertising. However, organizers must weigh these benefits against the fulfillment costs that will still be incurred, recognizing that an activation-only deal does not generally reduce the revenues required from other partners to meet your sponsorship goal (although there may be some savings realized by reducing forecast advertising expenses). Such a deal will also exclude the organizer from making a cash or VIK deal with any competitor of the activation partner. Cash will still be required for most events to remain viable, so an activation-only deal should represent only a portion of the value provided by the event's family of sponsors.

Advertising

Although advertising and on-site marketing rights are usually components of sports event sponsorship deals, smaller sports events may offer non-sponsor companies limited advertising benefits that do not require the larger investments that define more comprehensive sponsor relationships. The ability to sell a limited amount of advertising that does not conflict with the rights of existing event sponsors can provide sports event organizers with an added revenue stream from the corporate community. Assuming you will reserve the best signage positions for sponsors who are paying top dollar, additional scoreboard and venue signage, video board commercials, entrance/exit sampling areas, and other venue-centric advertising positions may be offered on a limited basis to corporate advertisers.

Before committing to specific advertising benefits, be sure to consult your facility lease and venue manager. Your agreement with the event venue may preclude certain forms of added advertising, such as sponsor signage that competes with a venue sponsor, or you may be subject to a fee. In most cases, existing advertising on permanent or programmable signage that had already been sold by the facility may not be covered or obstructed for event-specific signage, so organizers may have to create new positions for advertising, with venue approval.

Advertising on an event's mobile app or website can provide another possible revenue source. Inventory such as sponsored banners on a landing page, tabs, interactive media ads, and other commercially driven content can be both affordable to sponsors and reasonably low in cost to produce.

Event organizers should take care not to offer advertising benefits to a company from an industry category where a larger sponsor relationship might later be available. Closing a sponsorship deal with a soft drink company, for example, after selling an advertising package to its competitor could prove difficult. For this reason, most organizers sell non-sponsor advertising-only packages late in the process, after it appears that sponsorship prospects in those categories have largely dried up.

Merchandise

The process of budgeting revenue from merchandise sales must blend realistic expectations, a familiarity with your audience, and, frankly, your gut instincts. Merchandise first must be designed and purchased from a supplier by the event organizer, incurring costs to develop and create inventory. Then, the organizer hopes to resell these items to consumers with a sufficient profit margin to cover the cost of the goods and all other expenses involved in the transaction (e.g., shipping, labor/commissions, fixtures, supplies [such as shopping bags], taxes, and credit card fees). Thus, the net revenues projected for merchandise sales will be a number that subtracts the "cost of goods sold" from the gross revenues the event organizer expects to realize. It is also important to plan for the significant lead-time, often six to nine months or longer, and related expenses required to produce and to ship merchandise to meet your event date, particularly if it must be imported from a foreign supplier.

Most professional stadium and arena facilities either provide in-house retail merchandising services or have entered into an exclusive partnership with a merchandise concessionaire to provide this capability. The terms of what the in-house retailer will be paid to sell your merchandise is typically negotiated at the same time as the facility lease. Most often, the facility retailer will expect to sell event merchandise on a "consignment" basis; that is, they will sell your items without purchasing them from you first. At the end of the event, the retailer will return the unsold inventory to you, along with payment for the items sold on a previously negotiated price schedule (e.g., 75 percent of the retail price), less agreed-upon deductions (e.g., taxes and credit card commissions). Facilities insist on this type of arrangement because it presents the least amount of risk to them. Creating event-related merchandise is risky for the same reason it is attractive to the fan—it is a souvenir of a specific time, place, and event, and once the event is over, its sales potential drops precipitously. Therefore, not having to purchase event-related merchandise in advance is usually important to third-party retailers. Make sure your estimate of revenues accounts for some amount of "spoilage," the merchandise that will not successfully be resold. Not only will revenues not be received on whatever is left over after the event ends, the cost of having had those items made in the first place will further reduce your net merchandise revenues.

If a sports event has a proven track-record of high merchandise sales results, the organizer has more leverage in negotiating a better deal with the retailer, or one that shifts more of the risk to the merchandiser. In such cases, the organizer can designate "licensees," or exclusive suppliers, from whom the retailer must purchase approved event merchandise. The event may receive royalties on sales from the licensee in addition to the percentage of the merchandiser's sale to the fan. Organizers of major events with a history of high merchandise volume may be able to negotiate a 10–25 percent share of the supplier's sales in cases where the in-house retailer purchases event-specific merchandise directly from a licensee. Event organizers prefer this arrangement because they incur no risk of unsold inventory remaining after the audience has departed.

Local amateur sports events in community-owned facilities often assign their own team of volunteers to sell merchandise on their behalf, accepting only cash, and offering some combination of event-specific and organization-generic items. To minimize the likelihood of being stuck with excess, unsalable merchandise, volunteer organizers should limit their acquisition of event-specific items (such as T-shirts with a date like "the 2025 Columbus Softball Association's July 4th All-Star Game), and weight their inventory with a greater proportion of organization-generic merchandise (e.g., Columbus Softball Association caps). To reduce or eliminate financial risk, grassroots organizations often have their merchandise donated by a local supplier in return for name or logo recognition on the item, or sponsored in part by a local business in exchange for similar recognition.

Regardless of how items are acquired or sold, the most common method of deriving a budget number for merchandise revenue is based on a per capita estimate of sales (also known as a *per cap*). The per cap is the amount of money the event organizer expects to realize in merchandise sales, on average, from each person attending. In professional sports events, the size of the audience is usually used, while grassroots events may also include the participating athletes who would also be likely to buy remembrances of the day. The projected per cap for the event will depend on the product mix being offered and price ranges, as well as a judgment on how desirable the merchandise will be to the fans. Remember—not every spectator will purchase an item, so organizers are advised to think conservatively when projecting the average per cap for their event. To derive a merchandise revenue number for your event budget, simply multiply the per cap by the number of spectators and/or participants expected to attend. Figure 3.4 illustrates an example of how to calculate a merchandise revenue projection utilizing a per cap estimation.

REVENUE CALCULATION

A. "Per cap" estimation	$ 0.75
B. Number of spectators expected	2,500
C. Projected gross revenue (A × B)	$1,875.00
D. Cost of merchandise sold	$950.00
E. Budgeted net merchandise revenue (C–D)	$925.00

Figure 3.4 Sample Sports Event Merchandise Revenue Calculation

The example in Figure 3.4 shows a very conservative per cap. Established sports events can enjoy merchandise per caps in the range of $4.00–$10.00 and even more. Per caps are also dependent on the product mix and the price points of the various items for sale. In order to make a realistic per cap determination, you must have an understanding of your attendees. Will you have an upscale audience that will pay $50.00–$70.00 or more for a jersey or sweatshirt, or is it comprised of families who are more likely to buy a $20.00 T-shirt, a $15.00 cap, an $8.00 plush ball, or a $4.00 key chain? Alternatively, does the audience have a significant representation of kids, whose parents have sent them off to the merchandise stand by themselves with a $10.00 bill for souvenirs? Consider who is likely to be in the stands before determining what kind of merchandise you will offer, how much you need to acquire, and how large a per cap you want to project. Think, too, about whether the merchandiser can accept credit cards. Will attendees who have expected to purchase high-priced items bring enough cash?

While printed programs are in less common use in favor of content delivered online, commemorative hard copy publications remain a special merchandise item from which organizers may derive revenue from both advertising and sales. They are also attractive ways to offer sponsors, broadcasters, and merchandise partners additional value through exposure and special promotions. Advertising on online platforms such as the event website, apps, and social media sites associated with the organizer or event can also generate incremental revenue. Online versions of the event program or limited editions of commemorative content made available as NFTs (*non-fungible tokens*) can also increase merchandise revenue.

Here are some more tips that can help to increase your merchandise sales potential. Consider negotiating a deal with one or more local retailers who will help promote your event by selling your products on consignment (i.e., they only pay you for what they sell and then return what's left over) in advance of game day in their physical or online stores. If your event will be staged in a public space where no retail merchandiser has exclusive rights, you may be able keep costs down by recruiting a body of volunteers or using your own hourly staff to sell your merchandise. For a more professional presentation without the headaches of managing inventory and labor, contract the merchandiser from a nearby arena or stadium, or a large reputable sporting goods store. These vendors may have an interest in servicing your event on a mutually agreeable fee schedule and may also be able to provide points-of-sale kiosks, stands, tables, chairs, and other fixtures to display and sell your merchandise.

Concessions and Food and Beverage Sales

Concession revenues represent the net income from food and beverage items sold to spectators on the event site. As in the case of merchandise sales, virtually all sports stadiums and arenas provide concession services or have entered into an exclusive partnership with a food and beverage concessionaire to provide this capability. In many venues, event organizers will not be able to negotiate to receive any share of food and beverage sales, nor will they be able to vend any of their own products. The concessionaire and the facility often share the income exclusively.

If you are hosting your event in a facility or public space where no such exclusivities exist, you may have the opportunity to benefit from concession revenue and may be able to engage a volunteer staff and provide your own products for sale. For grassroots, not-for-profit, and charitable organizations, this may present an even greater opportunity to generate significant revenues by vending products donated by a retailer, distributor, or manufacturer. Event organizers can negotiate deals with food vendors just as festivals and carnivals do, in which events are guaranteed either a flat fee for each vendor authorized to be at the event site, or some mutually agreeable share of sales. Try to negotiate a 20 to 40 percent share of sales after expenses (such as labor and provisions), keeping in mind that the higher your percentage, the more expensive food prices will likely be for the fans. Think carefully about whether you will achieve greater net sales by taking a 20 percent share on a $6.00 hamburger or a 40 percent share on the same item at $10.00 but selling fewer of them.

If your event is in the position to either vend or arrange for others to sell food and beverage products, the same evaluation process with respect to product mix, price points, and per caps applies as with merchandise. Know your audience, and provide the kinds of refreshments they would enjoy, appropriate to the time of day, the time of year, and the age groups expected to be present. Sports events that promote healthy lifestyles should ensure that healthful refreshment options are also available and should always include a selection of beverages. Making sure that fans stay hydrated, of course, is a key health and safety consideration. Outdoor events, in particular, should offer water and other cold liquid selections in the warm weather months, and hot beverages during the winter.

Broadcasting

A small percentage of sports events are desirable enough for media programmers to devote time to covering them on broadcast, cable, or streaming television platforms (and on radio). An even smaller percentage are so attractive that a broadcaster will agree to pay a rights fee to cover them. As will be covered in Play 13, the broadcast industry, content distribution channels, and technologies have undergone rapid changes. What has remained constant, however, is the dominance of sports as a programming option.

Regardless of how fans access game and event broadcasts, whether on traditional linear television or streamed over the internet to screens ranging from an inch to more than 80 inches, sports remains a live, must-watch-when-it-happens viewing option. And regardless of how that content is consumed, it costs broadcasters, or the organizers themselves, significant money in labor, equipment, talent, and airtime to cover an event. So, broadcasters have to be confident they will be able to sell sufficient advertising to cover their costs, or attract enough viewers to add measurable value to their subscription rates.

Even though relatively few sports events out of the thousands being staged generate broadcast opportunities, not to mention rights fees, the budget line for broadcasting rights is mentioned here so you do not forget to include it if your event is fortunate enough to realize such potential. As in considering sponsor revenues, be sure to check your broadcasting agreement to determine what expenses, if any, you are expected to cover out of your side of the fee. Also, check your facility lease to identify any costs, such as "broadcast origination fees," labor, and utilities that might be payable to the venue, and determine whether the event or the broadcaster will be responsible for them.

On traditional linear and cable television channels, there is another option available to sports event organizers seeking to get their program on the air, known as a *time-buy*. In a time-buy arrangement, an event organizer obtains an agreement with a broadcaster to purchase the airtime, generally costing in the range of tens, or even hundreds, of thousands of dollars on a per-hour basis. The event organizer is then responsible to sell all of the available advertising time to generate the revenues that will cover the cost of the time-buy. Time-buys are generally risky for organizers who undertake them without having corporate sponsors ready to step up and buy the commercials.

The organizer is also likely to be responsible for all of the costs of actually producing the television program for a time-buy. Be sure to identify all of the expenses you will be expected to cover, and all of the advertising revenues that will be required to cover these costs before finalizing an agreement. More details on time-buys and other broadcasting issues may be found in Play 13.

When rights fees and time-buys are not practical or available from linear broadcasters or streaming services, event organizers interested in reaching larger, out-of-venue audiences have a range of additional options. A growing number of social media networks are offering longer-form programming options, with the potential to attract hundreds of millions of viewers monthly and subsequent playbacks annually on their web-based, video-sharing platforms. Programming opportunities cover the gamut of events, from youth and high school sports to food-eating contests and one-of-a-kind stunts to professional sports competition. All of these web-based programming sources are generating impressive, even worldwide, exposure possibilities and increasingly diverse revenue opportunities.

Tournament and Participation Fees

Many grassroots tournaments do not charge admission for spectators, but instead derive their income from registration or entry fees on a per-player or per-team basis. Similarly, non-team sports events such as marathons, races and other individual athletic meets use participation fees to cover expenses. The process of establishing a fee for tournament or race participants is similar to determining ticket prices for a spectator event. Consider what comparable tournaments and races charge participants, the prestige attached to your event, and what other events you are competing against in the marketplace; there may be other relevant factors, as well. Adapt the ticket-pricing checklist in this chapter to help structure your thinking. Tournaments generally have an inventory limit, a maximum number of teams or competitors. Organizers will need to structure their tournament brackets in advance of finalizing their revenue budget to determine how many may be accommodated given the time and facilities available, which, therefore, determines their gross potential for registration fees. Marathons and races have a limited capacity for individual participants that should also be set in advance to control costs and overcrowding. (More than 100,000 runners apply annually to participate in the New York City Marathon, but only 47,000 can be accommodated.)

Most organized amateur competitors are familiar with the concept of paying fees to participate in tournaments. They know that it takes money to rent facilities, provide trophies and recognition, and manage a tournament or race. Although the cost of participant fees can vary from just a few dollars for individuals to hundreds of dollars for teams, the organizer should survey the pricing structure of similar meets with comparable features. For example, do other tournaments offer dormitory housing, meals or refreshments, merchandise, ground transportation, recognition premiums, and other considerations included in the registration fee? Can you provide the same level of experience—or even better?

Grants and Donations

Sports events staged by a not-for-profit organization or that aim to provide a community with significant "quality of life" benefits can apply for and receive grants in the form of cash or services from governmental, quasi-public, corporate foundations, or other charitable entities. Many state, county, and city sports foundations and commissions maintain budgets to assist events that bring economic impact or other benefits to the community or local businesses. Generally, a lengthy application and review process is required, during which the grantor evaluates an event and its organizer according to formalized criteria. If an event meets those criteria, the grantor can determine how much funding it is willing to offer and how the funds may be used to benefit the program. Investigate what organizations exist in your area and/or in your sport whose mission involves supporting and promoting events like the one you are planning. Do not overlook charitable foundations managed by major corporations. They can make funds available to qualifying events from budgets that are totally separate from the sponsorships that are managed by the company's marketing department.

For events that travel or tour from year to year, it is best to apply for grants before the event is awarded to a particular community. Most sports commissions and foundations are charged with the responsibility of attracting events to their area and occasionally offer grants to help them successfully compete against other candidate communities.

Tickets to some sports events are sold in the form of a donation. That is, the proceeds of ticket sales are used to fund a not-for-profit group's operations or generate income for an important humanitarian cause. Targeted e-mail, text, and other direct marketing pieces are often used to sell tickets to a list of people the organizer believes are most likely to support the cause. Organizers of events of this type can increase their charitable impact by including a line on the response card that enables recipients who cannot attend to send a donation in lieu of a ticket purchase (E.g., "No, I cannot attend. Please accept my donation of $___to help support programs for para-athletes.")

Miscellaneous Revenues

In addition to the most common sources of revenue already described, the additional opportunities are as diverse and specific as the types of events the organizers can stage. Areas of revenue potential may include site-specific benefits like parking and valet services, coat and bag checking, the sale of passes to VIP hospitality experiences, admissions to postgame parties or other exclusive-access events, on-site fundraising activities, and raffles and lotteries (e.g., 50/50 tickets), to name just a few.

Balancing the Books

Total up your projected revenues and subtract your estimated expenses (including the ever-important contingency allowance line). Have you met your net income goal? If the first pass at constructing your event's budget falls short of your expectations, welcome to a very large, nonexclusive club. Go back into your expense budget and adjust the numbers so the bottom line meets the event's financial goals. Or, re-examine your ticket prices and other revenue assumptions. Have you been too conservative in projecting revenue or too liberal in projecting expenses? Sharpen your pencil and take another pass at balancing the budget.

SIDELINE STORY

The Super Bowl Tailgate Party

The Super Bowl Tailgate Party, held near the host stadium on the afternoon of the National Football League's (NFL) championship game, is one of corporate America's most prestigious parties. The widely viewed pregame show on the host broadcast network often features live coverage of star musical entertainment and celebrity interviews staged from the Tailgate Party. Because of space and budget constraints, there are a limited number of invited guests, primarily league sponsors and business partners, licensees, broadcasters, alumni, and other partners of the league and its teams. The event is the largest social event on the NFL's calendar and is considered a key networking opportunity for businesses and executives who are closely affiliated with the sport of American football. Corporate business partners are each allotted a specific number of tickets, as defined by their respective sponsor, broadcasting, or licensing agreements.

The popularity of the event has grown over the years to the extent that partners regularly desire significantly more tickets than they are contractually allotted. Although tickets for this exclusive event are not sold publicly, additional party tickets are made available for sale to *partners only* to accommodate the demand and control food and beverage costs, equipment rentals, and décor, and ensure the program remains on budget.

Although proprietary event management software that includes budgeting functionality is widely available, common spreadsheet software programs are also in common use. Remember to set up your spreadsheet with formulas that automatically recalculate totals and subtotals as you make adjustments to the budget so you can see the immediate effect of any single decision on the bottom line.

Figure 3.5 illustrates a small portion of an event budget, specifically the event ticket revenue section. The "Budget" column includes a formula that instantly multiplies the number of tickets in the section by the price per ticket. The subtotal row contains a formula that automatically adds the columns containing the number of tickets per section, and the budget line for each ticket section, respectively. The number in

XYZ SPORTS EVENT
PROJECTED TICKET REVENUES
(Preliminary draft—subject to change)

TICKET REVENUE	#	Price	Budget
Front row	150	$50.00	$7,500.00
Lower seating, mid-arena	750	$35.00	$26,250.00
Lower seating, end zone	500	$25.00	$12,500.00
Upper level, mid-arena	500	$25.00	$12,500.00
Upper level, end zone	350	$17.50	$6,125.00
Standing room	100	$10.00	$1,000.00
Subtotals	2,350		$65,875.00
Ticket Revenue Deductions			
Sales tax (3%)			($1,976.25)
Facility use fee ($1.00/ticket)			($2,350.00)
Net Ticket Revenues			$61,548.75

Figure 3.5   Sports Event Budget Worksheet Sample: Ticket Revenues

TICKET REVENUE	#	Price	Budget
Front row	150	$50.00	$7,500.00
Lower seating, mid-arena	725	$35.00	$25,375.00
Lower seating end zone	500	$25.00	$12,500.00
Upper level, mid-arena	500	$25.00	$12,500.00
Upper level, end zone	350	$19.50	$6,825.00
Standing room	110	$10.00	$1,100.00
Subtotals	2,335		$65,800.00
Ticket Revenue Deductions			
Sales tax (3%)			($1,974.00)
Facility use fee ($1.00/ticket)			($2,335.00)
Net Ticket Revenues		$61,491.00	

Figure 3.6 Sports Event Budget Worksheet Sample: Revised Ticket Revenues

the sales tax cell is a formula that multiplies the budget subtotal by 0.03 (representing 3 percent sales tax), and the number on the facilities usage fee line is derived from a formula multiplying the sum of the ticket inventory lines by $1.00 for each ticket.

Figure 3.6 shows the same spreadsheet segment, with three adjustments subsequently made by the organizer. In this example, 25 lower seating section locations have been removed from inventory (commonly known as "killed" seats) because of obstructed views. The upper-level end zone was increased in price to $19.50, and 10 additional standing-room ticket locations have been approved by the facility. The only changes made by the organizer to the spreadsheet are noted in the three shaded cells. The formulas inserted into each of the cells, as noted in the description of Figure 3.5, have automatically adjusted each cell, line, and column affected by these three revisions. It is a good idea to include a footnote showing the date and time the budget was last revised.

The process of revising the budget must be pursued with the greatest sensitivity and most realistic expectations. Increasing or decreasing budget lines or forecasts do not necessarily cause the actual expenses you will incur to go up or down. Be sure that revising the budget is not simply just the action of moving numbers around to make the budget look better, as tempting as that may be. Make sure that you will actually be able to reduce or avoid the costs you remove from the budget and that you can actually generate the additional revenues you will need before you finalize your spreadsheet.

Reforecasts

Once the budget has been finalized, new information will often show your budget to be less than a totally accurate prediction of actual revenues and expenses. You may discover that some budget lines will be inadequate to cover both the actual expenses already incurred plus those still expected, some may suggest lower than expected revenues, and still others may point to probable areas of cost avoidance or extra cash. You will be better able to manage the finances of your event by reforecasting each budget line regularly. Rather than altering your finalized budget during this process, extend your spreadsheet to include more columns, as illustrated in Figure 3.7.

In this depiction of a partial budget spreadsheet, the organizer has inserted an "Actual" column next to the finalized budget figures, showing the total of invoices received to date applicable to these expense lines. This will help her estimate the values in the next column, the "Forecast" for each line. In this

Expenses	Budget	Actual	Forecast	Variance	Notes
Event Operations					
Temporary staff	15,000	7,500	15,000	0	
Temporary staff expenses	4,500	2,238	4,500	0	
Volunteer staff expenses	3,500	0	3,500	0	
Staff travel expenses	1,000	985	1,500	(500)	
Staff meals or per diem	2,000	540	1,500	500	
Staff wardrobe/uniforms	2,500	1,200	2,500	0	
Site surveys/planning trips	1,500	450	1,000	500	
Pre-event planning meetings	500	200	500	0	
Event location office rent	5,000	2,500	5,000	0	
Event location office equipment	1,000	1,400	3,000	(2,000)	Higher printer/copier costs
Event location office supplies	750	500	750	0	
SUBTOTAL	**37,250**	**17,513**	**38,750**	**(1,500)**	

Figure 3.7   Sample Budget Reforecast (Note: Budget codes should be added to every budget and reforecast for ease of bookkeeping and analysis. See Appendices 1 and 2.)

example, the organizer feels that most areas appear to be on target, but sees that $985, almost all of her original estimate of $1,000 in staff travel expenses, has already been paid. Knowing that she still has a few weeks until the event, she determines that she will be over budget on this line and has forecast an overage of 50 percent, or $500. She similarly sees several areas of potential savings, in staff meals and site surveys, where less money than originally expected has been spent so far. She can see this immediately because the software program she has used to set up her expense budget worksheet displays the values in the "Variance" column that are automatically calculated based on the difference between the budget and the forecast.

As shown in Figure 3.7, her biggest problem area is location office equipment, where a significant overage is predicted. To make her postevent analysis easier, she has inserted a note as to why there was such a large difference between budgeted and forecasted expenses. Her automatic subtotals tell her exactly where she is: $1,500 short of expectations. To stay on track financially, she will have to take cost-savings measures that reduce her forecast in other areas. Again, it is important that she does not simply adjust the numbers, but instead takes actions that will be reflected in the numbers adjusted.

The use of a spreadsheet program provides event organizers with maximum flexibility in designing a form that works best for their projects. Because many of the events the authors produce are held annually, we place some additional columns between the budget item descriptions and the current budget that show final line-item figures from one or more of the previous years' events. That way, we can compare exactly what we spent in each budget line the year before, and the year before that. This is a very useful tool for events that take place in a different city each year, allowing organizers to predict expense increases or decreases from city-to-city, where such items as taxes, labor rates, hotel room rates, airfares, and others can be expected to vary. For example, we would be able to predict intuitively that hotel room rates for an event in Florida in January would be expected to be significantly higher, at the height of their winter tourist season, than an event held at about the same time a year before in St. Louis.

Use a budget form with column headings that work best for you and your event. But, reforecast your budget and analyze your variances as regularly and frequently as you can. Expect surprises but manage their effects by staying on top of your budget at all times and taking the actions necessary to stay on track.

Post-play Analysis

Although there are many ways to generate the revenue needed to fund a sports event, there are not nearly as many as there are ways to spend it (see Appendix 2). Examine your objectives to determine what you must target for your bottom line (a cost of doing business, an investment, break-even, or profit), and find ways to maximize your revenue to get there. Major revenue streams include ticket sales, sponsorship, merchandise, and concessions, among others. Grassroots tournaments and races frequently charge a registration or entry fee to generate revenues instead of ticket sales. Broadcasting and streaming rights fees are generally available only to events of major importance to the viewing public, or to organizers who are willing and able to take on the risk and expense of buying airtime and selling the advertising themselves.

Compare your projected revenues to expenses using a proprietary event management software application or a common spreadsheet program. Design a spreadsheet that works for your event and be sure to include automatic formulas that maximize accuracy and efficiency. Above all, monitor all costs and revenues, and reforecast the financial performance of your events on as regular and frequent a basis as possible.

Coach's Clipboard

1. You would like to improve the food and beverage *per cap* at your basketball tournament from a historical $4.00 to $5.00, a 25 percent increase. How can you achieve this by raising or lowering the prices on existing items at your concessions stands? Are there other ways of increasing the per cap?
2. You are organizing an adult recreational softball tournament for employees of businesses in your area. You want to generate at least $1,000 for a local children's hospital. What revenue streams can you create to meet this objective? What kinds of expenses will reduce your net revenues? Set up a budget for this event on a spreadsheet.
3. Your college alumni association wants to stage a series of games and contests at the campus's recreation facilities on the weekend before classes resume, featuring returning athletes from the school's 10th and 20th reunion classes. Create a financial model for an event that will identify costs and the revenue streams that will be needed, and when, to cover event costs at no risk to the association.
4. You have been asked to organize a youth football skills competition and have been given $2,000 in starting capital to develop the event and recruit participants. How will you use your seed money to generate enough revenue for an event you estimate will ultimately cost $10,000?

Soliciting and Selecting Host Cities and Venues

"If you don't try to win, you might as well hold the Olympics in somebody's backyard."

—*Jesse Owens, American Olympian, 1931–1980*

This play will help you to:

- Understand how cities and venues evaluate the desirability of hosting a sports event and determine how to compete for the opportunity.
- Develop the support and partnership of the host community.
- Negotiate the best deal possible with the venue selected to host your event.

Introduction

Winning sports events begin their path to glory by selecting markets and venues that will actively support and promote the program. A collaborative, enthusiastic host community and a cooperative, engaged host facility can dramatically increase a sports event's chances for success.

In December 2011, "America's Game"—the annual Army–Navy football contest—came to the Washington, D.C., area for the first time in the storied rivalry between the two great military academies. As is often the case with events that come to the nation's capital, cooperative efforts and collaborative strengths among stakeholders in three jurisdictions—the District of Columbia, Maryland, and Virginia—were aligned to create a memorable and successful event. From the bid process that was coordinated by the Greater Washington Sports Alliance, a regional sports commission, to the hospitable lodging and restaurants, primarily in the District and Northern Virginia, to the attentive venue operations and event coordination at FedEx Field, located in Landover, Maryland, the Army–Navy Game were considered an outstanding success in every way. The nation's capital region also positioned itself for future Army–Navy games as well as showcased itself for other high-profile, revenue-generating sports events.

Working with motivated hosts can indeed produce winning results. Sports event managers who take their properties to different cities, either annually or as part of a multistop seasonal tour, know well that organizing successful events is in large part dependent on developing, cultivating, and maintaining a series of strategic and functional partnerships in each market they visit. In order to forge an effective partnership, all parties involved—both hosts and organizers—must acquire an intimate understanding of the wants, needs, and interests of each other.

When savvy sports event organizers set out to find a home for their event, they are careful to evaluate how much they can count on the active support of the local government and various segments of the area's business community. Regional business groups essential to the success of sports events commonly include the hotel and restaurant industries, prominent and influential area media outlets, and the membership of local chambers of commerce and other business groups. Experienced organizers know that except for having to acquire necessary permits and observing community ordinances, managing an event without the active participation of local businesses and government is not possible. There is no question that one is virtually assured of better results by engaging top regional officials and obtaining at least their philosophical investment in the event's success. Soliciting and obtaining their more active involvement can help to achieve even greater success.

Generally, every city or region that seeks to host sports events will sing its own praises and offer glowing platitudes on how uniquely successful an event will be if awarded to its community. It is essential that event organizers get a clear and true sense ahead of time of how a prospective host will embrace a program once the event has been awarded. All too often, ambivalence, attitudes of reduced importance, and even laziness begin to emerge after the deal is finalized. Some sports commissions, for example, are charged only with the responsibility of promoting and selling a city to event organizers. With all respect to the exceptions to the rule, the service provided by many sports commissions disappears once the event is awarded. As their mission is fulfilled, the commissions are already applying their limited resources to promoting their destination to other potential future business prospects. Sports commissions that remain involved to help identify and mobilize local resources are of great value to visiting event organizers and the business community, as their assistance can result in an even larger share of the budget being spent locally.

Although there is no way to guarantee how a community will eventually respond, the best way to engage its leaders' interest and support is to understand what they want to gain by hosting a sports event and then to demonstrate a sensitivity to their needs. Ask community leaders what they envision the event will achieve for their city and respond with a plan that addresses what the event can reasonably deliver and how. Open a dialogue to determine how the community defines success and to provide it with insights on how you do, too. If you want the community to invest in the success of your event, demonstrate your organization's commitment to invest in the success of the community.

What Host Cities Really Want from Sports Events

Sports events may be exciting, involving programs that improve a city's quality of life, but just like most organizers, the local governments, business communities, and venues that host the events are most interested in generating revenue. Cities often undertake financial responsibility for many hidden costs when hosting events, including paying for the extra police, fire, ambulance, and sanitation department members that may be assigned to provide for traffic flow, public safety, and the protection and maintenance of community assets. The local government may have helped to finance the community's sports facilities and may be paying interest on the debt that was incurred on construction or renovation of its arena, stadium, or convention center.

Visiting sports events can help the local government offset these costs in both direct and indirect ways. Events that increase hotel occupancies generate revenue in sales taxes and, in many cities, special hotel taxes. These special taxes are usually acts of local legislation, earmarking the revenue visiting guests generate for specific purposes, such as paying the debt service on airport improvements, a convention center, or other public buildings that attract business to a city or region. Additionally, any event that brings visitors to area hotels also generates sales taxes on the additional meals consumed in restaurants, on rental cars, taxis and rideshare services, on tickets for concurrent entertainment and cultural attractions, and on significant direct spending in the local market on the part of the organizer. The more hotel rooms your event can fill with athletes, staff, guests, and visitors—whether the event budget is paying for them or the guests are reaching into their own pockets is immaterial—the more a city will embrace you and the event you are organizing.

To gauge the interest of a potential host community, the first group to contact is the city's convention and visitors bureau (CVB), an organization dedicated to drawing business meetings, sports and entertainment events, and tourists to its hotel, resort, convention, meeting, and event facilities. The CVB might be sharing office space and/or services with the executive director of a sports commission or may have an account representative on staff who specializes in attracting sports events. These individuals will be able to guide you to the best facilities, hotels, and hospitality sites to accommodate your sports event's needs.

The two factors that most frequently determine the degree to which a city will strive to attract an event, although there are others, are economic impact and its close cousin, hotel room occupancy generated by inbound visitors. CVBs use *room nights* as their unit of measure for hotel occupancy, defined as one room occupied for one night.

Economic Impact

As is their mandate, CVBs and sports commissions will analyze the potential economic impact an event can be expected to generate based on information from the organizer. The results they project will determine how aggressively they will pursue and invest in a sports property. Economic impact is a measure of the dollars that will flow into, or out of, a region solely and specifically because of the presence of a particular event, be it a sports event, a convention, a political action, an act of legislation, or virtually any activity that generates new revenues, or losses, for the local economy.

Economic impact and consumer spending figures provided or circulated by event organizers have come under increasing media scrutiny for years, owing to their seemingly fantastic numbers. A study by the Arizona Host Committee for Super Bowl LVII in Phoenix estimated a regional economic impact of $1.3 billion in 2023, generated from 102,598 out-of-state visitors during the 4 days leading up to and including the game. Estimates from the Los Angeles Host Committee had projected an economic impact of $500 million the year prior, and the Las Vegas committee projected $600 million in 2024.

Methodological differences are likely causes of such wild swings in economic impact estimates. However, it is inarguable that the positive effect of sports events on the local economy can be nevertheless impressive. Published estimates for Major League Baseball's All-Star Game have been pegged at between $50 million in Seattle in 2023, and $30 million for the NHL Winter Classic. In 2024, the NBA All-Star Game brought an estimated $320 million to Indianapolis. But your event doesn't have to be from one of North America's major professional sports to provide the kind of value and economic impact to a city that makes a sports event a highly prized and hotly contested property. The estimated impact of Des Moines, Iowa from the 11-day 57th AAU Junior Olympic Games in 2023 was $69 million, generated by 14,500 participating athletes. The Indiana Sports Corporation projected the 9-day 2024 U.S. Olympic Swimming Trials held at Lucas Oil Stadium in Indianapolis would generate more than $100 million in impact.

Sports Tourism Canada, recognizing the value of being able to evaluate a credible and reliable measure of an event's economic impact, developed a suite of economic assessment tools available on line to its members. By entering estimated values in a series of pull-down questionnaires, local and provincial governments can calculate and compare the impact of various potential events on their region based on a consistent set of criteria, including gross domestic product (the net value added by industries), wages, employment, taxes (e.g., income, sales, and payroll), and a total gross economic impact figure.

The Hawaii Tourism Authority (HTA) has developed a system of generating timely economic impact data from a form distributed to passengers on every airline flight arriving to the Islands. The collected forms provide information on how long arriving visitors will stay, what islands they will visit, and what types of activities they will enjoy while in Hawaii. The survey also asks for the primary reason for visiting Hawaii, and "to attend a sports event" is one of the choices offered. By comparing the data from the travelers indicating they are coming to Hawaii for "a sports event" with the calendar of sports activities scheduled, HTA can extrapolate the incremental number of visitors generated by a specific event, as well as the economic impact by multiplying each traveler by the number of days the visitor will stay.

Estimating your event's economic impact can make it more salable and attractive to a city actively seeking to host sports events. Your organization may be best served by retaining an independent consultant with relevant experience who can be found through searching business-oriented social media platforms, websites, trade publications, and other industry sources, particularly if the objectivity and reliability of your figures is of particular political importance. If the limited resources of your organization require devising a more do-it-yourself estimate of economic impact, you can prepare one using the formula in Figure 4.1 and the instructions that follow.

Instructions for Figure 4.1:
- **Line A:** Examine the event's expense budget and determine, line by line, what portion of each category might be spent in the local market. Exclude expenses that are paid to vendors outside of the region where the event will be held, as well as any overhead costs and payroll for event offices and staff if they are not located in the community hosting the event. If your organization will spend additional funds in the community that are accounted for in areas outside of the event budget, or by other departments within your organization, be sure to include an estimate of their spending as well, and enter the sum of all such expenses on line A.
- **Line B:** Then, calculate the number of hotel rooms that will be occupied by event participants or spectators, but are not already accounted for on line A (i.e., those not paid for by the event budget). Multiply the number of rooms by the average number of nights they will be used to determine the number of room nights your event will generate. Enter this amount on line B.
- **Line C:** Rooms not paid for by the organizer should include estimates for in-bound athletes, spectators, fans, sponsors, vendors, and others whose presence in the community is directly attributable to the event. The local sports commission or CVB will be most interested in the number of room nights generated by the event, whether paid for by the event budget or by other visitors arriving specifically to attend or participate in the event. Enter the average hotel room rate per night, plus occupancy and sales taxes, gratuities, and any other fees on line C.

A. Direct spending by organizer in market _____
B. Participant/audience room nights _____
C. Participant/audience hotel room rate _____
D. Participant/audience hotel spending (B × C) _____
E. # Participants/audience _____
F. # Days in market _____
G. Per diem spending estimate per participant/audience _____
H. Participant/audience per diem spending (E × F × G) _____
I. Direct spending by sponsors/partners in market _____
J. Other estimated spending _____
K. SUBTOTAL (A + D + H + I + J) _____
L. Economic multiplier   2.25
M. Total Estimated Economic Impact (K × L) _____

Figure 4.1 Preparation of an Economic Impact Analysis for Sports Events

- **Line D:** Multiply line B by line C and enter the result on line D.
- **Line E:** Estimate the number of participants and spectators coming from outside the community and enter this figure on line E. As this number refers to individuals, rather than traveling parties, this number should be greater than the number of hotel rooms you expect the event to fill.
- **Line F:** Estimate the average number of days, and fractions thereof, that you expect participants and spectators to be in town for the events and enter on line F. Spectators from within the community are excluded from this number because most economists feel that the amount they spend on an event in their own market represents money they would have spent on other activities in the area anyway, and, therefore, they generate no additional economic impact.
- **Line G:** Then, enter an estimated "per diem" number on line G. A per diem is the average daily amount you expect the participants and spectators to spend in the area on meals, refreshments, entertainment, and personal items such as laundry and other services. This amount will vary widely based on the demographics of your participating athletes, target audience, and the cost of living in the city in which the event is held. To get an idea of reasonable per diem rates in various communities in the United States and beyond, several government websites maintain this information for recompensing their employees and vendors, including the General Services Administration website for domestic rates, and the US State Department website for rates in cities outside of the United States. Although these figures should be considered minimums if your guests are paying for all of their meals and expenses, the actual per diem rates for participants may be lower if the event provides a number of meals or receptions that have already been included in line A. You may also add to or subtract from the per diem rate if you feel it does not adequately reflect the actual expenses you expect your inbound participants or spectators to encounter (e.g., a more upscale audience is very likely to spend more than an average federal employee on meals and entertainment).
- **Line H:** Multiply lines E, F, and G and enter the result on line H.
- **Line I:** An event's sponsors, licensees, merchandisers, broadcast rights holders, vendors, and other stakeholders may host meals or receptions, purchase gifts, or stage events for their own guests during your event. Even though the event organizer does not manage these events or purchases, they are a direct result of the event being staged in that market, and, therefore, may be included in the economic impact analysis. Estimate the direct spending within the community of your various partners in each expense area, including staff who may need to be housed, the additional guests they may attract to hotels, and the direct spending on the ancillary events they may host. Enter your best judgment on line I.
- **Line J:** There may be any number of other spending categories specific to your audience, the marketplace, or event. For example, sports events held in resort or vacation destinations often result in extended hotel stays by attendees, greens and/or activities fees, skiing and other recreational expenses, attraction admission fees, and non-event-specific souvenir purchases, to name a few. These, plus other estimated expenses for participants and spectators such as local ground transportation (e.g., car services and mass transportation, car rentals, gasoline, tolls, and parking), local retail purchases, and any other reasonably conceivable spending, should be inserted on line J.
- **Line K:** Add the expenses estimated on lines A, D, H, I, and J and enter the sum on line K. This subtotal yields an estimate of the direct economic impact generated by your event.
- **Line L:** Many economists consider the overall economic impact of an event to be greater than the sum of direct spending. It is believed that every dollar spent as described above stimulates the local economy and causes each new dollar to be spent again within the community, and more than once, so the final impact can actually be between 2.25 and 2.50 times greater than the direct spending total.
- **Line M:** Applying the more conservative economic multiplier number, multiply the subtotal on line K by 2.25 and enter the result on line M. This quantity is the gross economic impact of your program, a key figure sought after by host cities when considering whether or not to host a sports event.

Room Nights and Other Factors

The importance of the hotel room nights generated by sports events has already been discussed as a component of the event's overall economic impact. For CVBs, this is often the key determinant, as room nights are the life-blood of their most influential and vocal members, the hotel industry. In the accommodations business, the quantity of room nights generated by an event is like a fossil record left behind by an organizer. Past host hotels and CVBs share intelligence with potential future event hosts, so the truthfulness of an organizer's estimates will affect how the community will judge the reliability of every assertion that follows. Therefore, event organizers should be candid—and careful—with the numbers they project during the bidding process.

Potential host cities may also combine their thirst for room nights and economic impact with other business, political, quality-of-life, and/or promotional motivations in the pursuit of certain sports events. An event's timeframe may fit what convention and visitors bureaus call an "opportunity period," times of the year when hotel occupancy is otherwise low. A market may also wish to demonstrate to organizers of larger events its ability to host and handle smaller, but relevant, visible, and well-regarded sports events. City leaders may believe that media coverage of the event will help promote their city as a tourist destination or invest extra city services to benefit the event to attract future corporate meetings, incentives, and conventions held by companies associated with the program. A particular sport may be very strong on the grassroots level in a region, and its ubiquity in the marketplace perceived as a portent for an event's likely success (thus generating a greater economic impact and publicity for the region).

Employing what is known as the USO Principle—understanding stakeholders' objectives—brings event organizers and host cities together. Organizers are best served when they understand what a host city wants and expects from its involvement in a sports event. Don't be shy about trading a demonstrated willingness to assist a community in achieving its objectives in return for the city's understanding and support of your own. Ask the sports commission, CVB, the office of the mayor, and other governmental officials what they would want your event to do for their community and constituents. Talk to local chambers of commerce and business associations to learn what the area's leaders of industry might hope to gain from the event. And, consult with one or more public relations agencies on what past events have proved successful, and why. Gain insights on why others might have gone wrong. By hearing the community's side of the story, you will at minimum make them feel invested and listened to, like an event insider. At best, you will be able to design the event and its supporting promotions to help them achieve objectives they would be less likely to accomplish without your coming to town, gaining their support in return.

Figure 4.2 summarizes some of the most common reasons communities seek to host sports events, many of which have already been discussed. As the figure demonstrates, there are many motivations, ranging from the altruistic to the political, and the relative importance of each may differ from city to city, based on local priorities. Remember that any number of them may be operating at the same time.

- To generate hotel room occupancy
- To stimulate the local economy (i.e., generate economic impact)
- To generate tax revenues
- To showcase new sports, athletic or other public assembly facilities to the community, media, potential corporate sponsors, and organizers of other potential events
- To attract larger, or more newsworthy, events to their venues or community
- To showcase the community or region to potential future visitors
- To attract professional teams and athletes to their premier venues
- To position themselves as leaders among neighboring (sometimes rival) communities
- To revitalize an economically disadvantaged or newly developed part of the community
- To present a positive quality-of-life program to the community
- To present a high-profile event in a critical election year
- To demonstrate the need for improved sports/public assembly facilities

Figure 4.2   Common Reasons Why Communities Host Sports Events

What Sports Events Really Want from Host Cities

Successful sports event organizers know that achieving their objectives is far easier with the support of local government and their constituent businesses, trade organizations, and citizens than without them. It is certainly possible to stage an event in an ambivalent or even antagonistic marketplace, although doing so foreshadows the possibility of great tribulations and rough roads ahead. For this reason, it is strongly suggested that event organizers get a clear understanding of the degree and nature of a community's support, and to have as many relationships formalized in writing with letters of agreement and/or contracts as possible during the romance period before an event is awarded. While it is usually counterproductive and detrimental to an organizer's reputation to pursue legal remedies should a city government or business group renege on promises made during early discussions, it is less likely that they will, knowing that their assertions are in writing and their own reputations are on the line. Having these assurances in writing greatly reduces the potential of later misunderstandings.

Naturally, event organizers will, and should, attempt to manage their budgets by avoiding, or at least reducing, whatever costs they can. Sometimes, the community can provide services, equipment, or other forms of support on either a governmental or business level that will help organizers spend their budget money more efficiently and enable them to expand and improve their event without avoidable or debilitating drains on expenses.

Soliciting Bids with a Request for Proposal

Sports event organizers owe to themselves and prospective hosts a clear description of an event's needs, specific requirements, and expectations from the start. This allows organizers to eliminate less serious contenders and permits the most interested communities to make the best impression. If a community knows how an organizer will make a decision, it can communicate the salient benefits of awarding the event to its city and can incorporate relevant commitments into the strongest possible expression of interest. The most effective way for organizers to begin the process of identifying the ideal host for a sports event is to generate a thoughtful and comprehensive bid document, or *request for proposal* (RFP). RFPs are also frequently used to qualify vendors who wish to bid on supplying or contributing products or services.

An effective RFP is not just an outline of the organizer's expectations. It is also a sales and marketing piece. Through this important document, the event organizer is formally asking the prospective host community to participate in ensuring the success of the program. The preparation of a winning bid will require significant time and energy investments on the part of the community, so it is wise to present an event in the most thorough and enthusiastic, but genuine, terms. To illustrate, a sample RFP for a fictional event titled the "Big Street Sports Tournament" may be found in Appendix 3. The components of this hypothetical RFP are based on the generalized format illustrated in Figure 4.3 and followed with additional description.

I. Introduction
II. Event description (including history and impacts)
III. Event schedule
IV. Role of the event organizer
V. Role of the host city
VI. Definition of the ideal event site (including requirements of the event)
VII. Benefits to the host city
VIII. Sponsors and marketing rights
IX. Response format

Figure 4.3 Sports Event Request for Proposal Components

SIDELINE STORY

The Super Bowl Rotation

If there is any single indicator that host cities do indeed benefit greatly from the public exposure and economic impact generated by major events, one has only to look at the first 60 years of Super Bowl history. Just three regions—Miami, New Orleans, and Los Angeles/Pasadena—account for 30 Super Bowls between them, half of every AFC-NFC championship game ever played. If events of this magnitude were not enormously beneficial to their host communities, it is difficult to conceive why these three perennial hosts haven't yet stopped bidding on Super Bowls.

The NFL changed its bidding procedures in 2015 from a process that invited any qualified NFL city interested in submitting a bid to host to a more strategic one that enables the league to return more often to fan-favorite warm weather locations. The league sets a rotation of target host cities in place, but the local host community still must adhere to the bid specifications for hosting a Super Bowl to be confirmed. Nontraditional Super Bowl host cities may be considered for a one-time opportunity when new weather-friendly or domed stadiums are introduced or for other reasons the NFL may choose.

When the bid process was open to any NFL city, communities competed aggressively to attract the votes of league owners, an expensive and labor-intensive endeavor. New York/New Jersey hosted the first Super Bowl played outdoors in a winter weather environment in 2014. Indianapolis hosted in their new stadium in 2012 after losing the bid for the year prior. Another nontraditional market, Detroit, Michigan, has hosted the Super Bowl twice, once in 1982 and again for the 40th game in 2006. "The genesis of hosting a game was the enormous commitment of one of the NFL's original team owners, William Clay Ford, to move the team from Pontiac, Michigan, to downtown Detroit. This move and investment into the league was pivotal in securing the region's second Super Bowl," recalls then-Detroit Super Bowl Host Committee president Susan Sherer. "The vision for both the bid and the host team was to '*change the conversation about Detroit.*' So while the host committee was faithful to the obligations of the bid, we took great care to be sure everything we invested in would tie into this vision." Billionaire industrialist Roger Penske, well-known in the world of auto racing, chaired the host committee and provided much of the vision along with Sherer of how Super Bowl could transform the public's perception of Detroit. As a result of the Super Bowl being awarded to the city, $150 million was raised by the city from a wide range of sources to improve the city's downtown infrastructure in time for the massive influx of media and business leaders for the event. A week-long outdoor winter festival called "Motown Winter Blast" in the downtown area was created to accommodate Michiganders and inbound fans alike. And, the host committee, like Indianapolis several years later, provided outstanding hospitality to all who visited to enjoy the Super Bowl.

Did all that hard work change the conversation about Detroit? Consider these quotes from national media reports: "I have to admit it, I was dreading going to Detroit. I thought it would be too cold and be a miserable place to host a Super Bowl. Man, was I wrong, Detroit freaking ROCKS!" (*Sports Illustrated*). "I come in praise of Detroit. That's right. I like Detroit, I love Detroit. I could live here. Really" (*The Boston Globe*).

By the time Indianapolis joined the Super Bowl club of host cities, praise in print and on broadcast media was joined by reporters and visitors in social network media in short bursts no less warm and glowing for this traditionally cold winter city: "Indy you get an 11 out of 10. Best collective effort by any city hosting any sporting event I've attended" (*Mike Tirico, ESPN*). "Adios Indy. You crushed it. Congratulations" (*Rich Eisen, NFL Network*). Yes, hosting a major event can, indeed, change the conversation about a city or region.

The event RFP should begin with an "Introduction" that describes the event in general terms and communicates some of the advantages of hosting the event to the interested community. This introduction should focus on engaging prospective bidders by presenting a compelling overview of the event.

Include the most exciting elements and distinctive features that can be anticipated, the size and type of audience that can be expected, the profile of the participating athletes, and its history, prestige, and/or prospects for the future.

The next section, the "Event Description," should describe the event in more detail. Provide estimates for the number of in-bound athletes, guests, and fans, based on historical performance, if available. Define whether the event will be ticketed or free and open to the public. If the event has a history of being held in other communities, their identities should be disclosed. The prospective host will almost certainly want to research the experiences of, and impact on, past host cities. This research can be conducted via search engines, media accounts, and other third parties without several interested cities inundating a single contact individual with requests for information. It is best to provide individual contacts for past references only upon request for two reasons—first, so that only serious contenders, those who take the time to call you to seek this information, will impose on your past contacts, and, second, so you know which cities are doing their due diligence and will most likely submit a bid. Resist the urge to overdramatize, embellish, or exaggerate past history in your RFP, as cities commonly share intelligence on events and you will want to protect the reputation of your organization, as well as your own, by providing truthful, candid, and accurate information. Include a paragraph at the end of the Event Description section that describes how the prospective host should respond, the deadline for submissions, and a personal contact at your organization to whom questions may be directed.

The "Event Schedule" section that follows may contain as many details as the organizer feels comfortable providing. At a minimum, it should define a target date for the event, and when athletes, guests, and fans can be expected to arrive in and depart from the community. Operating hours, ancillary social and hospitality events (parties, receptions, and fan events), and other details, if available, should also be included in this section.

The next section, the "Role of the Event Organizer," should list all responsibilities, both operational and financial, of the organization requesting proposals. Try to be as comprehensive as possible, as inadvertent omissions may be perceived as areas of responsibility that will fall to the community. It is also a good idea

SIDELINE STORY

Hometown Hosts—World-Class Event

The partnership between host cities and sports events can run so deep that it is hard to conceive of them ever moving elsewhere. The city of Williamsport, Pennsylvania (27,754 population 2020 census), is the birthplace of Little League Baseball and arguably the most popular grassroots sports event in the United States. What started as a statewide tournament in 1947 has grown to the 20-team Little League Baseball World Series, annually drawing an attendance of more than 450,000 live spectators as well as millions of broadcast and streaming viewers. Tickets to the event are free.

Spectators eight times outnumber the combined local population of Williamsport and the neighboring host borough of South Williamsport. "Both communities roll out the red carpet for the Little League World Series," says Little League Baseball president Stephen Keener. "We are very fortunate to conduct a premier sports championship event in a smalltown atmosphere. It really is what gives this event its charm." The entire region mobilizes for event day. Fire, police, security, and media emergency personnel of both communities assist with the operation of the event. The Chamber of Commerce's Tourism Department assists with housing, transportation, and the other needs of inbound visitors, and hosts a hospitality day for corporate partners at the Williamsport Country Club. In the case of the Little League Baseball World Series, the hometown values of the organizer and community are truly as one—their objectives are simply well-deserved pride and service to America's youth.

to provide background information and qualifications of the event organizer within this section to reinforce the legitimacy of the program and the experience and reliability of its management.

If the event is supported by sponsors that have already secured exclusive rights to the program, it is essential that the organizer provides their identities in the RFP. This will let the prospective host city know that these sponsor categories are already reserved and may not be offered to competitors in the marketplace. As sponsors can be continually added, you may list these in a separate or an accompanying attachment (as an addendum) to the RFP and specifically note that this list may be updated periodically.

Host communities should play a prominent and meaningful role in ensuring the success of sports events. The section entitled "Role of the Host City" should provide the details those preparing proposals will need to determine their community's ability to accommodate and successfully compete for the event. It is likely that the individual or group formally applying for the event will know its community far better than the event organizer. The familiarity with facilities, past history of similar events, city ordinances, and other market-specific data can provide the essential information that can make the selection process faster, more efficient, and less expensive for everyone involved.

As this is the section that will outline the minimum requirements for a successful bid, the organizer should provide and request as much detailed information as possible. Although the response to an RFP can take any form, it is helpful to include a questionnaire at the end of the document that can be used by the reviewer as a uniform executive summary. This will make it easier to review and compare the first round of submissions. The majority of the bid requirements will often be found in the host city section and may include requests for detailed information including event site commitments or recommendations, venue floor plans and seating diagrams, hotel and local office space recommendations, proposed local media promotional partners and other venue and community marketing assets, signage requirements, equipment and services available from the host city, sources of volunteer staffing, and other topics of interest.

It is not uncommon for sports event organizers to request letters of support from various governmental officials, such as a mayor, governor, senators, congresspeople, or county commissioners, as well as representatives of the local sports commission, convention and visitors bureau, chamber of commerce, and other essential city partners and civic leaders. These letters will ensure that the highest offices and prominent stakeholders in the region are aware of their constituents' interest and are committed to a successful event in their jurisdiction.

Another important inclusion is background information about the key individuals with whom the event organizer can expect to interact during the planning and presentation of the event. These important contacts may be part of a local organizing committee (LOC), the management staff of the venue or another entity that will have responsibilities for the event. The relevant experience these people have in staging events can be a key factor in evaluating a candidate city's response to an RFP.

Since the availability of an appropriate event site is one of the most important factors when evaluating a bid submission, it is recommended that a section be included in the RFP that defines "The Ideal Event Site." This section should outline the minimum requirements and dimensions of the event site, seating configurations, locker room and other support areas, and the dates that are required by the organizer for loading in, setting up, conducting the event, and loading out. Any other requirement, definition, or disclosure specific to the event site, such as requests for information regarding signage restrictions, sponsor exclusivities, merchandise sales, availability and costs for power, lights, water or other necessities, or maximum rental fees and other costs, should also be included here.

Now that you have outlined what the community must do for you, it is time to let the community know what you can do for them in the "Benefits to the Host City" section. Your ability to deliver benefits to the city in exchange for the city's interest and participation in hosting your event is the first indication that you will approach your relationship in a spirit of partnership. Outline all of the rights the community will enjoy as your partner, including the use of event marks, pre-event promotional exposure, on-site exposure, and special, exclusive opportunities, events, access, and marketing rights available only to the host city. If the host has the ability to sell local sponsorships, all of the specifics including categories available for sale, pricing (if available), and the formula for revenue sharing between the organizer and the city, should be outlined in this section.

Distributing Your RFP

One copy of the RFP should be sent to the senior decision-maker in the communities under consideration, most often the top official at the local convention and visitors bureau, sports commission and/or the desired venue. Additional copies may also be sent to other stakeholders in the community upon that decision-maker's request. If information about your event is best disseminated to a wide range of communities, the Sports Events and Tourism Association (Sports ETA) is an outstanding resource of target organizations in more than 225 cities across the United States. The Sports ETA website offers a comprehensive roster of member organizations and key contacts and offers a range of services and resources to event organizers. Information can be found at sportseta.org.

Among other resources for intelligence on potential host cities and the event industry, as well as posting information on events seeking proposals, is *SportsTravel Magazine* (www.sportstravelmagazine.com). This publication also hosts an annual networking, conference, and expo event called TEAMS (Travel, Events, and Management in Sports).

Every RFP should contain a realistic deadline date for the submission and acceptance of proposals. Depending on the amount of information requested by the organizer, giving interested cities 60 to 90 days after receipt of the RFP is generally reasonable for small- to medium-sized events. The more work that is required of prospective cities (e.g., soliciting and holding hotel rooms and event venues, and confirming points of agreement that may require acts of legislation), the more time should be allowed for their responses. Some major events may require six months to a year of proposal preparation. As part of the RFP response process, many event organizers often choose to schedule a required or optional video conference or meeting to answer questions from, or to highlight key information to interested parties. A summary of the topics discussed may be distributed to all participants on the call or to everyone who received the RFP.

Seeking the right home for your event is like finding the right home for your family. It is a process best not rushed. Permit sufficient time for the community preparing the bid, as well as for analysis and evaluation after submission. Be sure to be as specific as possible in your request for all of the information you will require so that you are equipped to make the best decision for your event.

Evaluating Responses to RFPs

Once the deadline for response has passed, it is time to begin evaluating and comparing the proposals you have received. Read and analyze each submission carefully and list salient points of comparison, the pros and cons offered by each city. You can set up another spreadsheet to help compare responses to the questionnaire at a glance (see the example in Appendix 4). Contrast the opportunities of each market, such as the size of the population, the size of the business base (the most likely universe of potential sponsors), and the degree of interest in your sport that might be expected of residents in the local community. Compare the event-related facilities that are available, and the costs of doing business in each market. Consider the convenience and accessibility of each city to the athletes or participants who will travel to compete there. Review the letters of commitment included in each response and evaluate the depth of support that each community will apply to your event in the form of facilities, services, labor, and equipment. Study the event management experience of the key contacts with whom you might be working. If your event will be located outdoors, examine weather records for the targeted event dates in each region. If you are selling tickets, compare household income levels, amusement and sales tax rates, and other factors that might detract from gross revenues. Remember that the prices of tickets that would be deemed reasonable could vary greatly between the bidding cities. Analyze the gross potential in each city based on the proposed venue, expected tickets sales, and the ticket prices likely to be set market by market. Don't forget to deduct applicable taxes and facility usage fees.

The most important question included on your RFP response form is: "We agree to the bid specifications outlined in this request for proposal: Yes or no." If the answer is yes, you can generally bank on an interested city following through. If the answer is no, be sure respondents provide a complete and detailed list of any exceptions they wish to make to the bid specifications. Sometimes, these exceptions are minor, or are legally required by local ordinances, and might be worth overlooking if the rest of the

- Availability of best facilities to stage the event
- Favorable rates on facility rentals, labor, and services in the local market
- Active support of the organizer's objectives by local government, businesses, and media
- Services and support beyond the minimum requirements of the RFP
- Demonstrable community experience in hosting successful sports events of similar size, scope, and structure
- Financial incentives or cost savings offered by local government, the facility, and local businesses beyond those required by the RFP
- No, or affordable, taxes on event revenues
- A natural local affinity, or fan base, for the sport

Figure 4.4 Common Reasons Why Communities Are Chosen to Host Sports Events

bid is particularly strong. Other times, they are so significant that no further consideration of the bid is required and the city may be eliminated from contention. Agreeing to bid specifications, presuming they are reasonable, is certainly a major factor in a positive response to a host city proposal, but it is by no means the sole determinant. Figure 4.4 lists some of the most common reasons why cities are chosen by organizers to host sports events, the relative importance of each being dependent on the event's objectives and business model.

Some RFPs issued by event organizers require a bid fee that must accompany the submission of a proposal, or a host fee upon being awarded the event. Bid fees are relatively rare, and more commonly required for large, prestigious, and high-exposure events. They are sometimes necessary to offset the organizer's costs of having one or more event managers travel into the market to survey the proposed event sites, and to meet with prospective hosts, officials, and sponsors. Bid fees are not recommended for smaller or less-known events, as sports commissions and CVBs are reluctant to invest their money chasing after an unknown quantity or a program that does not generate significant impact or exposure. Few events are awarded without a physical inspection of event facilities and other important resources such as hotels, convention centers, and other city infrastructure. If your event has not required a bid fee, select only the top two or three most attractive proposals and consider visiting only those communities for a full evaluation. It is not unusual, nor unseemly, to request that the host city cover the cost of hotels and ground transportation during the site visit. Chances are the CVB will be able to secure complimentary accommodations to defray the costs of your survey.

If you represent an event with a successful track record, or a totally new event that offers exceptionally good value for a prospective host city, you may encounter two or more responses that meet your minimum bid specifications exactly and are equally attractive on every other level. All other things being equal, it is both acceptable and common practice to re-approach the two "finalists" with the response that their proposals are being viewed favorably and that an opportunity exists for them to offer additional incentives that further strengthen their respective bids. Rather than being forced to make an arbitrary decision between two or more equally competitive cities, the organizer can encourage prospective hosts to contribute more creativity and benefits to the event as a demonstration of their interest and commitment, and to find points of differentiation between them.

Despite the best of intentions on the part of prospective event sites, only one is typically selected to play host to an event. Cities and venues failing to be chosen have every right to inquire as to where their proposal fell short. Figure 4.5 lists some of the most common factors contributing to a city's elimination from the bidding process. Surprisingly, the most often encountered is an inability or unwillingness to meet the minimum requirements of the RFP. This does not mean that cities must adhere with blind obedience to the minimum requirements. Some RFPs may be more demanding than their prestige, economic impact, exposure potential, or other attendant benefits might warrant. Host cities should certainly evaluate the bid specifications of an RFP before simply agreeing to everything an event organizer requests. Prestigious,

- Failure to meet the minimum requirements of the RFP when bids from other competing cities agree to them
- Superior incentives offered by competing cities beyond the minimum requirements of the RFP
- Inadequate or poorly located event facilities
- Inadequate, inappropriate, or high-priced accommodations
- Excessive facility rental fees
- Comparatively high tax rates on ticket sales
- Comparatively high costs of doing business (e.g., hotel room rates and labor rates)
- Local political opposition to the event
- Restrictions placed on the organizer regarding event sponsor recognition
- Lack of sufficient event management experience

Figure 4.5 Most Common Reasons Communities Are Eliminated from the Bidding Process

high-profile events can demand and receive more from a bidding city, and prospective hosts risk losing the opportunity to win the award by falling short of the minimum requirements. Newer and less-prestigious events or event organizations may issue RFPs that are perfectly reasonable and well-scaled for the benefits they offer prospective hosts, but reasonability is always in the eyes of the beholder. Organizers may simply be testing the marketplace to see what cities will offer the best deal, even if the "minimum" requirements are not met by any that ultimately submit responses. Event organizers might still consider prospective host cities submitting proposals that do not meet the minimum specifications, particularly if no other community offers a superior deal. But, cities that do not submit proposals at all can be assured that they will be passed over. As hockey great Wayne Gretzky once said, "You will miss 100 percent of the shots you never take."

This is an appropriate point to offer some advice to prospective host cities—take your best shot and offer the deal that fits both the economic reality of your community and the importance of the event to your civic objectives. If the opportunity to stage a highly desirable event presents itself and the bid specifications are appropriate to its attractiveness, by all means submit your best effort. However, if an event of lesser importance to the community comes knocking with unreasonable expectations but still offers great opportunities (and does not charge a bid fee), you lose nothing but time by putting your best foot forward, even if it means falling a little short of the minimum bid specifications.

Once a host city has been selected, there may be great interest on the part of both parties to announce the award. It is wise to resist the temptation to circulate this information to both the media and the public until some form of formal agreement is reached between the organizer and the host entity, as well as with any essential stakeholder whose participation is considered vital. These may include the actual event venue, hotels, and/or other local resources without which the deal would fall apart. A letter agreement or contract as detailed as possible should be drafted and signed to confirm what the host has agreed to provide, as well as any important deadline dates covering the disposition of any areas not yet confirmed. Failure to meet certain deadline dates might force unfavorable or unacceptable changes to the program, or risk its viability in that market. Therefore, the organizer should include a stipulation allowing cancellation or postponement if the host parties fail to meet their obligations as outlined in the agreement. Frequently, the initial letter agreement with the host entity is relatively brief, and attaches the RFP and the proposal response form as appendices. In these cases, the letter usually states that each requirement of the RFP is material to the agreement, unless modified by the contract. Any additional points not addressed by the RFP, but agreed to between the parties during the evaluation process, should also be included. Without completing this important extra step, entities that were essential to the success of the bid can subsequently back away from promises they might have made before the announcement, and any leverage the organizer once had would vaporize as soon as the award became a matter of public record.

SIDELINE STORY

A Trip Back to the Drawing Board Yields Success

Indianapolis's highly successful turn at hosting Super Bowl XLVI in 2012 was a result of the city's second attempt to win the bid, after competing for the 2011 game. "Participating in the NFL bid application process for the 2011 Super Bowl was an opportunity to learn the process and understand the bid requirements and host city qualifications," said Allison Melangton, then-president and CEO of the 2012 Indianapolis Super Bowl Host Committee. The unsuccessful 2011 bid application process was a learning experience, so when the team regrouped to work on the bid for the 2012 Super Bowl, more time was available to work on the concepts and guarantees of the bid versus answering the technical questions of the bid. The significant difference in the XLV and the XLVI bids was the addition of a unique and very impactful local partnership."

"Whenever Indianapolis has hosted a major sporting event, we've tried to ensure that we used the event as a catalyst for the greater good—leaving a lasting benefit or legacy from the event. For the 2012 bid, the Host Committee proposed an aggressive Legacy initiative that would partner the Host Committee with organizations and residents of a near downtown neighborhood to help the residents achieve their own vision for the redevelopment of their neighborhood. The neighborhood is known locally as the Near Eastside and it is located adjacent to downtown. Historically, it was a vibrant, working-class neighborhood; however, over the past 40 years it has seen unprecedented decline and disinvestment and has been challenged by pervasive issues related to poverty."

"This partnership resulted in more than $150 million of investment in the effort to turnaround this area. These investments have impacted more than 400 housing units with new builds or rehab, spurred the redevelopment of the neighborhood's traditional business corridor, and led to the building of 27,000 square foot wellness, fitness, and education facility. This facility is on the campus of a public high school strategically located within the Near Eastside neighborhood as a part of the NFL's Youth Education Town program. The Near Eastside is an area with 40,000 residents without a YMCA or a Boys & Girls Club so the new facility on the campus of Arsenal Technical High School was desperately needed. We believe that the presentation of this Legacy Initiative resonated with the NFL ownership and they were anxious to be a partner in a program that would significantly and positively change generations to come in that neighborhood." In the first 10 years of operation, more than 9,300 residents have used the Legacy Center more than 450,000 times.

What Event Venues Really Want from Sports Events

Like event organizers and the cities that pursue them, event venues are most frequently interested in generating revenue. How they generate revenue, and how much they must generate, varies from one venue to the next, and is also dependent upon the ownership and management of the facility.

Event venues are of two general types—those that are privately owned and those that are public facilities. Privately owned event sites are generally in the business of making money. They aggressively pursue sports events that can contribute to their profitability. They, therefore, try to fill every available date on their calendar. The busier the venue, the more potentially lucrative to the event site an organizer must be to schedule its dates there. However, event facilities lose money every day they are empty, so sometimes an event with low profit potential looks better to a venue manager than no event at all. Venue managers sometimes confirm dates for less profitable events late in the process, when it appears nothing more profitable is likely to be scheduled.

Some recreation facilities that operate for public participation allocate time and space to special events for additional revenues and promotional exposure. One ski resort event coordinator notes: "If someone comes to our department proposing holding an event at the mountain, first thing we do is crunch the numbers. Will we make a profit, break even, or lose money?" How an event will affect other regularly scheduled facility operations is another key consideration. "We never want to disrupt or take away a highly used area, or an area that would disturb lodging guests and on-hill skiers or riders," adds the coordinator.

A special subset of privately owned sports facilities is composed of those run by colleges and universities. Some of these venues forgo the opportunity to host outside events completely to comply with the stipulations of their charter or the directives of their board. Others may have criteria other than financial gain that they use in considering whether to host outside events.

Public event facilities operate in a totally different and frequently more flexible marketplace. These venues may include convention centers, fairgrounds, municipal arenas and stadiums, outdoor playing fields, armories, parking lots, streets, or any other event site that are owned by the local community, state, or provincial authority. In some cases, and particularly commonplace in the arena or stadium business, facilities are owned by a local government entity, and a management company is charged with the responsibility to rent space, sell event tickets, and manage its overall business. The contract with the government may charge the management company with the responsibility of generating a minimum amount of revenue or profit. The company's own corporate profitability is often tied to achieving or exceeding this minimum. Facility management companies can be wonderful partners that enthusiastically embrace the philosophy of keeping their venues utilized and filled with spectators, realizing revenues on some combination of rent, ticket sales participation, sponsorships, concessions, merchandise, and parking. They are not obligated to accept a deal with an event organizer that does not meet their corporate objectives, although the government/owner may occasionally exert some pressure to accept an event that may serve the community better than the management company's profit-and-loss profile and offer a slightly less expensive financial deal. Although event facility managers are not generally in the business of promoting or sponsoring the programs staged in their buildings, a contract may obligate them to accept a fixed number of "civic" events per year at the government's direction at no, or at a reduced, rental cost.

Public facilities without an outside management entity may also be motivated by the need to generate revenue to pay down the debt of their construction or to fund day-to-day operations. Alternatively, their mission may simply be to serve their community and may be satisfied with a nominal fee for the usage of space. Others, as is often the case with many convention centers, may be operated by the local CVB or similar entity, and exist primarily to attract the booking of events that generate those "heads in beds" at area hotels. These facilities may trade hotel room night guarantees in the local market for a reduced, or even a waived, rental fee. Still others, including nontraditional event sites such as streets, parking lots, decommissioned airfields, and other unorthodox venues, may be made available by the host city at no cost simply to contribute to the success of the event and the enjoyment of the community.

Negotiating with Sports Event Facilities

If you are a sports event organizer, maintain a realistic image of the prestige your event carries as you negotiate with potential host facilities. A venue's history of presenting high-prestige events can have a significant impact on its ability to attract future events of equal or greater impact and magnitude. Therefore, the more prestigious an event, the more negotiating power accrues to the benefit of the organizer. Remember that the number of events that facilities would consider high-profile or high-prestige lessees is but a small fraction of the marketplace that such venues serve. There are countless other tournaments, meets, matches, and other contests and exhibitions that also have great earning potential, but are not globally significant events. There are also many events with earning potential that are questionable, speculative, or risky that facility managers may decide to avoid.

It will come as no surprise to facility managers that sports event organizers want to get as much as they can for as little as they can spend. Prospective organizers will always seek the best possible rental rates, the highest possible percentage of the gross potential, and the greatest freedom in hiring third-party vendors and labor. Of course, event facilities are best served when they seek precisely the opposite—the highest possible rental rates, the highest percentage of the gross potential for themselves, and the ability to charge for as many additional items, services, and labor charges as they are equipped to provide or arrange.

With the objectives of event organizers and the facilities in which they hold events often at such opposites, negotiations for mutually agreeable terms can be long and arduous. The more prestigious, attractive, and potentially profitable an event appears, the more likely a venue will concede some portion of the rent or share of ticket revenues in favor of concluding a deal with the event organizer. The more speculative the event, or the less familiar the promoter is to the venue, the more likely the facility will demand substantial guarantees against ticket sales and/or other revenues.

On occasion, less familiar, sometimes less-sophisticated promoters, who may be local businesspeople with little or no sports event experience but have a vested interest in a particular event, approach venues for dates. In these cases, the process of booking a venue by such inexperienced promoters tends to be a lengthy one. Facility managers will take an opportunity to get to know the promoter and assess his or her capabilities and resources, will follow up on references, and do credit checks. Sometimes the posting of a nonrefundable deposit helps establish an event organizer's credibility and, in some cases, letters of credit or other forms of security are required. A nonrefundable deposit may represent 50 percent of the rental fee, plus 50 percent of the additional estimated costs for labor, equipment, and other in-house charges. Payment of these obligations in advance provides some degree of proof to the facility that the promoter is sufficiently capitalized and will not run out of money before event day.

It is a standard practice of many venues to require in a license agreement with a promoter that the venue controls the box office and the money on deposit through ticket sales. This serves as financial security for a stadium, arena, or other type of venue against expenses.

Aside from cash deposits, another key determinant that event facilities use to evaluate the bona fides of an unfamiliar event promoter is the latter's ability to secure an acceptable liability insurance policy. Proof of insurance is also proof of insurability. That is, the facility can enjoy some sense of confidence if an event promoter is sufficiently capitalized to be able to purchase coverage under which the venue will be named as an additional insured. To facility managers, sports event organizers who are able to secure an underwriter confident enough to write a sizable liability policy may be sufficiently good risks with whom to enter into a lease.

What Sports Event Organizers Want from Event Facilities

Just as facilities seek to host profitable events managed by reputable, reliable organizers, so do most organizers search for venues that will be interested, involved, and service-oriented partners in achieving success. Promoters want to work with venues that actively participate in ensuring their clients' events achieve their objectives, and hit their attendance and profitability goals.

Smart facility managers know that an established event organizer will stage more events in the future and will want the organizer to consider their house in subsequent years, or for other programs. A venue with a staff that is pleasant, professional, competent, helpful, and involved will earn the loyalty of event organizers, and establish a reputation within their circle of influence and opinion. For example, event directors want to know what to expect with respect to a facility's billable costs with a reasonable degree of accuracy. Hidden or undisclosed charges don't remain hidden for long after an event has concluded, and frequently become subjects of contention during the settlement process.

Presuming the physical characteristics and costs are equal between two facilities, event organizers will look for flexibility in their ability to fulfill sponsorships and in the hiring of vendors and labor. In the facilities business, being forced to work with vendors and labor providers that have exclusive contracts with the venue generally means higher costs to the promoter. Facing no meaningful competition, there is little incentive for contractors enjoying exclusive rights in a facility to negotiate with organizers over rates or prices. Organizers will also look at what labor and equipment are included in the rental rate, and the costs they will have to incur to procure the people and equipment that are not included in the overall deal. They will also favor venues that can help them promote their event through the range of a facility's available resources—including website and media platforms, databases of individual and group sales customers, broadcast programming, marketing and advertising programs, interior and exterior signage and marquees, and publicity and promotional channels. These services may be provided by the venue at a cost, but being able to reach a prequalified group of potential ticket buyers is of great value to sports event promoters.

Evaluating Sports Event Facilities

Many factors contribute to an organizer's final decision on facility selection. Some sports events, such as competitive diving, enjoy few options with respect to the types of facilities that can host a particular event. Venues with a diving pool are the most feasible choices. Other sports event organizers need only file for a permit with their community's parks and recreation department to reserve a pool, ball field, rink, or court. For those in search of a professionally operated events venue, whether a stadium, arena, exhibition hall, hotel ballroom, theatre, or gymnasium, prepare a Facility Selection Survey Form such as the one found in Appendix 6. This document can help you to organize your most pertinent requirements before examining facilities, ensure that no important detail is neglected during your inspection, and assist in the comparison and final evaluation of venues afterwards. Event facilities and how they do business may differ greatly from city to city, or even within the same municipality. Once completed, the form will allow you to compare venues along uniform guidelines. The following paragraphs will describe the process of completing the survey form in detail.

Every event will have some time requirement for loading in (the process of delivering, installing, and setting up and configuring the equipment you need to conduct the event) and loading out (the process of dismantling and removing the organizer's property and rented equipment from the facility). Load-ins can range from a few hours to set up tables, chairs, and decorations for a simple sports awards dinner to a week or more to build sets and tents, install playing surfaces, and decorate an event site for a major fan festival. Even a community ball field hosting a schedule of Little League games needs some turnaround time to remove the banners and equipment belonging to the previous team (load-out), and to install the banners, bench equipment, and bases for the next one (load-in). You will need some understanding of what your event will require in terms of set-up and dismantle time when checking on available dates with a potential host facility to ensure that sufficient time will be available. This is also important because your rental terms may increase as you hold the space for more load-in or load-out time. It is not uncommon for the rental rates on these nonevent days to be offered at a cheaper per-day cost.

Determine whether your load-in and load-out can be accomplished during normal working hours, which can avoid overtime labor costs. Will it be more cost effective to pay for one day less in rent and absorb the overtime to move in and set up overnight? Regardless of cost, an organizer can ill afford to have too little time to set up an event and risk not being ready on event day. Neither can it delay the organizers of the next event from moving in by booking too little time or labor to vacate the premises as scheduled. It is essential that these requirements be carefully evaluated and accurately projected before booking the venue.

Next, it is important to consider the number of tickets that may be sold at various levels of the venue. If the seating plan will define a single price for every ticket or a general admission policy (i.e., nonreserved seats offered on a first-to-arrive, first-to-enjoy basis), your planning will be made easy; your gross potential is calculated simply by multiplying the ticket price by the number of available tickets. Event facilities, however, usually offer the ability to create "price breaks" based on a particular section's orientation or distance from the playing surface, or height off the event floor. While it is not necessary to finalize a ticket price in each price break during the initial site selection survey, the facility manager can provide you with sample price breaks, with the number of available seats per break, even by section and row, for your budget planning purposes. The Facility Site Selection Survey Form provides you with a place to record the name of the section (e.g., lower end zone, lower sidelines, upper level end zone, and concourse sidelines) and the number of tickets available for sale in each area. It also offers planners an area to record whether the facility has any *build-out capability*—that is, whether there are standing-room areas for which tickets may be sold, or other normally unutilized spaces that can be converted to safe, temporary seating, increasing the available inventory—and profit potential—beyond the standard seating manifest. An essential component is learning if the venue uses a ticketing site that will handle the sale of event tickets, can employ dynamic pricing based on purchasing demand, and has a secondary ticketing capability. Knowing these details in advance can help organizers plan for the eventuality of selling out, maximizing revenue, and then expanding the seating to accommodate more potential ticket buyers.

In addition to paying a rental rate to the facility, there may be additional charges against ticket sales, as discussed in Play 2. This information should also be recorded on the survey form, along with information on the merchandising and catering contacts, each of which may be managed by a facility's own staff or by an exclusive concessionaire hired to manage these businesses on behalf of the building. The terms quoted by these entities may be noted here. Any capability offered by the facility to assist in the promotion of ticket sales may be recorded as well.

From city to city, and even from venue to venue within a single community, the cost of labor can vary widely. If not analyzed and adequately planned, facility labor can add considerable burden to an event budget. Organizers of large, complex events should consider hiring or identifying an event operations specialist who can estimate the number of staffing hours that will be required from each type of worker, as listed in the Facility Selection Survey Form. Organizers without this capability can have the facility present an estimate of what will be required if the management is provided with sufficient detail. Regardless, it will be easy to compare hourly rates, fees, and mark-ups between various venues by completing this section. Even small differences in hourly labor rates can prove significant when the total number of staffing hours to load in, stage, and load out an event are tabulated.

Before budgeting estimates for labor, it is important to confirm whether the facility has entered into exclusive relationships with a labor provider. As is true of any vendor whose exclusivity is guaranteed by the facility, the organizer's ability to negotiate what are likely to be inflated rates and fees is severely limited. (As unpleasant as inflated rates can be, we have to understand this stakeholder's objective, as well. The exclusive vendor often pays a percentage of its sales to the facility and must, in turn, charge these higher rates to make a profit.)

Higher labor costs and restrictive work rules do not necessarily indicate that these resources are unionized. Union labor is frequently more skilled and experienced in trade professions and may actually be preferable with respect to a worker's familiarity with the facility and appropriate safety procedures. Riggers and electricians, presuming the minimum crews and work rules required by the union local are not unreasonable (e.g., when time-and-a-half and double overtime rates kick in, break times, meal allowances, minimum number of workers per crew, and minimum number of hours per call), can fall into this category. But, union or nonunion, event organizers need to know all of the charges associated with labor, including the hourly rate, benefit payments (e.g., accruals for health benefits, insurance, vacation, and retirement) charged to the promoter, and any administrative mark-ups imposed by the venue for managing the labor pool. Organizers of large events staged in a right-to-work state (i.e., states in which the event can hire anyone the organizer wants to perform work in certain capacities) and that have the potential to employ many union members to work significant hours preparing for and executing an event, may be able to negotiate a more favorable rate with the business manager of the union local.

Many facilities, particularly those with exclusive labor contracts, charge more per staffing hour than is received by the worker, wages, and benefits combined. The venue may be charging an "administrative fee," a percentage of the labor costs booked through its management, which also represents some degree of profit margin. This practice provides a common revenue stream for the facility and is sometimes negotiable (depending on the overall profit potential of the event in other areas).

There are many sound reasons for a facility to enter into exclusive agreements with merchandisers and concessionaires and, to a lesser extent, labor. The venue usually receives a percentage of merchandise, food, and beverages sold by these external entities, occasionally against an annual guarantee. In addition, the venue takes no risk on the costs of inventory, equipment, or human resources. This is one reason why the costs to ticket buyers for food and merchandise are significantly higher inside the facility than outside. (This is only a contributing factor, of course. Having a monopoly on sales also creates a captive audience of consumers inside the venue.)

The next two sections of the Facility Site Selection Survey Form provide organizers with an area to record observations about some of the physical characteristics of the venue, as well as the equipment that might be available either as part of the lease rate or at some additional cost. Are there sufficient locker and dressing rooms and related spaces and services (such as showers and trainers' rooms) of the size required, and are they in good repair? Are the marshaling areas (back-of-house staging areas that are hidden from the public view used to hold sets, props, equipment, and people before they are needed) sufficient in size and security, safely lit, and easily accessible to the playing surface? Are these spaces filled with storage items belonging to the facility and, if so, will they be cleared by building management without the event incurring additional labor, shipping, or storage costs? Are there accessible lockable and unlocked storage areas that may be used by the organizer, and how far ahead of the event may they be used? Are there score clocks, timing devices, and other equipment required for competition (e.g., nets, boards, baskets, goals, and benches) in the facility's possession that may be used or modified for the event without additional charge, or will the organizer have to purchase or rent and install these items? Are there existing and sufficient facilities for the expected media such as a press box, media seating areas, press conference facilities, workrooms, wireless communication and power access, a press lounge, access to statistical and other event information, and a location for broadcast trucks to park and plug in? How much parking for the public and special guests is located within reasonably close proximity to the facility, and how many complimentary spaces for staff can be included in the rental deal?

Does the facility possess a quantity of tables, chairs, and staging risers that may be used by the organizer, and will they add cost to the budget? Is there office space available for the event management staff? Does the venue have reliable and sufficient Internet and mobile device service for staff and fan use, and are these made available at no charge to the event? (Many venues have exclusive relationships with Internet service and equipment providers.) Does the building have a forklift, scissor lifts, or other equipment for material handling that may be used by the organizer's paid hourly labor during load-in and load-out, or will the use of such equipment incur additional costs? If marshaling or storage areas must be temporarily divided to create additional operational or hospitality facilities, does the building have pipe and drape units to lend or rent, and in what condition are they? Are there crowd control barriers, such as metal barricades, available for the organizer's use, or must they be rented? Many other venue-related questions should be answered in these sections, including those that are specific to a particular sport or event that will be utilizing the facility.

The presence or absence of sponsor exclusivities may figure prominently in evaluating the best venue for a sports event. Most every sports venue has rules on what kinds of event sponsor signage will be permitted and precisely where partners' signs, banners, and branding presence may be exhibited. In most venues, the brand of beverages served (or "poured") is governed by an existing building sponsorship deal, and in the case of products containing alcohol, by the local liquor authority. The issues relating to sponsorship are many and varied and will be discussed in detail later. In the interim, Figure 4.6 provides you with a checklist of some of the sponsor-related questions that should be asked during the site selection process.

- What sponsors have "exclusive rights" to the facility? What do those exclusive rights include?
- Can event sponsors that do not conflict with facility sponsors be recognized on signage on or around the playing surface? Elsewhere in the venue? How may event sponsors that do conflict be recognized?
- Can event sponsors that do not conflict with facility sponsors be recognized on temporary signage in the public concourses, or on the scoreboard and electronic displays? What about event sponsors that do conflict?
- May nonconflicting or conflicting sponsors hand out sponsored premiums or product samples as people enter or leave the facility?
- May nonconflicting or conflicting sponsors set up tables or display kiosks in the public concourse areas?
- May nonconflicting or conflicting sponsors be recognized with announcements on the venue's public address system, on video screens and/or message boards, or on banners either inside or outside the structure? Is there any charge for this?
- Can event sponsor products that conflict with facility sponsors be served or distributed in back-of-house areas such as event offices, marshaling areas, catering spaces, and/or media facilities? (Note: It is common for a facility concessionaire to levy a "corkage fee," that is, a per-serving charge for accepting and serving free products from an event's sponsor in lieu of an organizer having to purchase inventory directly from them. This can sometimes be a negotiated item.)

Figure 4.6 Sponsor Exclusivity Checklist

Finally, examine the facility for areas in which hospitality functions may be staged to entertain VIP guests, athletes, sponsors, and others. Are there restaurants, cafeterias, cafes, or lounges that can be partitioned off for private use while the venue is open to the public? Are there on-site kitchens, or must food preparation facilities be temporarily installed? Are there meeting, conference, or board rooms that are available and can be easily accessible to audience areas that can hold smaller functions? Can part of the exterior grounds be reserved for tented functions or fan events? Is the provision of catering in these areas exclusive to the building concessionaire?

Obviously, the needs of every event and organizer will differ greatly. The Facility Selection Survey Form can be modified to include additional sections for any information that is pertinent to the specific project being planned to ensure that the same questions are asked of every venue under consideration. In this way, the answers may be compared and analyzed fairly and with relative ease.

Selecting a Facility

Usually, awarding a sports event to a city is coincident with the confirmation of a facility in which to hold it. Event organizers will weigh multiple factors in reaching their decision, including the costs of operating the event in each venue surveyed, whether the capacity of the facility is appropriate to the event, the reputation and geographic desirability of the venue (e.g., is the facility one that local ticket buyers would associate with a sports event?), and each party's flexibility with respect to protecting each other's sponsor relationships. Once a tentative decision has been reached, the event organizer will be forwarded a lease, or license agreement, that will list all of the agreed-to terms of the relationship. Because license agreements are considerably detailed, it is not unusual for an array of new issues to emerge that had not been discussed during initial negotiations. This is usually only a minor inconvenience, and these issues are better to surface and be settled during the negotiating process rather than closer to the event. It is almost certain that significant "boilerplate" language—that is, legal requirements for insurance, indemnifications, force majeure conditions (cancellations due to various unforeseen disasters or other conditions that would make moving forward with an event impossible), and other protections for the venue—will not have been previously discussed in detail. It is essential for event promoters to have qualified legal counsel review and propose redrafts of these points to ensure that they are as competently and fully protected as the facility. Although the nature of the license agreement will differ from venue to venue, as well as from event to event, a generalized sample license agreement may be found in Appendix 5.

Once the license agreement has been signed and agreements are substantially in progress with other stakeholders without whom the event could not be staged (e.g., the local convention and visitors bureau and hoteliers), it is usually safe to announce the dates and host location of the event. Depending on the economic, political, and cultural significance of the event to the local community, the parties involved may stage a news conference or simply distribute an announcement via the event and venue's respective websites and social media platforms and by news release to inform the media and, through their various outlets, the public. Now, it is time to begin the production planning process, and building the team required to stage the newly awarded event.

Post-play Analysis

A spirit of partnership between host cities, facilities, and event organizers is essential to success for all involved. It is incumbent upon all parties to develop an understanding of each other's wants and needs to achieve this level of cooperation. Host cities for events that travel or tour are most interested in the economic impact sports events offer, including how much in tax revenues and how many hotel room nights they will generate. They also pursue events for political, cultural, and emotional reasons peculiar to each respective market. Event promoters communicate their wants and needs through the development and dissemination of requests for proposal, documents that identify the minimum requirements for a community's or facility's bid to host an event to achieve success. Event venues are generally interested in generating revenue, while event organizers are searching for the best and most cost-effective site to stage their event. A Facility Selection Survey Form is an effective tool for organizing, comparing, and analyzing information derived from surveys of each interested venue.

Coach's Clipboard

1. You are the organizer of an established and successful running marathon in a mid-size American city. Your organization receives an RFP from a similarly sized community in a neighboring state desirous of reenergizing its existing marathon race, which has lately experienced decreasing participation and mounting financial losses. The RFP is very basic—the city will provide no cash and take no risk. All revenues, expenses, and risk must be borne by the organizer. How can you establish a partnership with the community that lowers your risk while providing the city with what it needs—the execution of a successful marathon event with no outlay of cash?

2. You are the organizer of a regional high school track and field meet for which there are limited facilities in your home city. Assuming the costs of staging the event in your local arena are too expensive, and the winter season during which it is held makes holding an outdoor event inadvisable, what venues in your city that are not traditionally associated with track and field might be investigated and approached to host the event?

3. Create an RFP for a statewide college ice hockey tournament that will attract teams from 16 universities, ideally using two venues in a single city yet to be selected. Include requirements for housing staff, participants, families, and fans within a 20-mile radius, as well as a sports memorabilia collector's show and fan festival envisioned to run concurrently during the tournament. Develop an economic impact estimate for the tournament and show.

4. Respond as the host city to the RFP you created in exercise 3. Your community can only offer one arena in which to hold the tournament and does not have a sufficient number of hotel rooms within the required radius. In what ways can you mitigate these shortcomings and provide additional relevant benefits to the event that will competitively position your hypothetical community to the organizer?

5. The best facility available for your minor league all-star game is sponsored by a soft-drink company that directly competes with one of your most important sponsors. Both your organization and the management of the venue want to stage the event there, but also want to protect their respective sponsor's rights. How can the two parties work to resolve the conflict? (Consider this exercise again after reading Plays 6 and 7.)

Starting the Clock on the Sports Event Planning Process

"Excellence is not a singular act but a habit. You are what you do repeatedly."
—Shaquille O'Neal, NBA All-Star center

This play will help you to:

- Identify and plan for each of the critical tasks required for the management of your event.
- Create planning documents that will ensure your event meet its objectives and deadlines.
- Create the organization you will need to execute your event.

Introduction

Professional and college sports teams prepare themselves for the pursuit of a championship season by opening training camps and conducting exhibition games to identify areas of weakness and take the best advantage of their strengths. But drafting the blueprint for building a winning team does not begin the moment the first player reports to training camp. The coaching staff spends the off-season evaluating players and reviewing scouting reports. Coaches and players study game film to assess the abilities of opponents and scouts search lower-level leagues for untapped talent. Meticulous planning, clear communication, and sufficient time are required to prepare a team for each upcoming contest. For coaches and players, far more time is spent preparing for a game than actually playing it.

As a sports event organizer, you also will spend vastly more time planning than executing your event. So far, you have defined what you want your event to accomplish and what it will cost to achieve your objectives. You have set a strategy on how you will finance the event and determine the optimal place to stage it.

Now, it's time to begin the planning in earnest, and putting the right organization together that will make it all happen. Developing your event management plan will reveal the hundreds of tasks you will need to do ahead of time, in what order you will need to do them, and by when each will need to be accomplished. This will also help you determine how much and what kind of help you will need to get it all done.

The general principles of industrial project management apply equally well to event management. After all, events are complex, detail-laden projects. We first have to identify key management tasks, then analyze those tasks to reveal all of the decisions and activities that must be resolved to complete them, and finally, set a system of deadlines that will keep the project on schedule.

Identify and Analyze Management Tasks

First, organize a list of the primary or fundamental tasks that will need to be accomplished. Figure 5.1 offers a sample of just such a list. To begin the process of identifying the elementary tasks required to manage an event, refer to the tactics you decided to employ to meet your objectives in Play 1. Organize the elementary tasks you will need to complete in the order they must be accomplished. Then, break down each task one by one, identifying all of the steps—smaller tasks, activities, and inputs—required to make them work and succeed.

Set a milestone date, or deadline, for every elementary task. Because the successful execution of these key activities is dependent on "supportive tasks" and "decision points" that must precede each of them, set deadlines for those, as well.

Let's go back to the fictional playoff pre-game fan festival to which we applied the P-A-P-E-R Test in Figure 1.4 and develop some elementary tasks. The primary objective of the event was to reward loyal fans by hosting a street festival preceding the team's first playoff game in three years, with secondary objectives of staging the program for promotional and revenue-generating purposes (see page 18 for the complete description of the event's objectives). Figure 5.1 lists the elementary tasks, in rough sequential order, that will form the basis of a critical dates calendar for this event.

- Create an event budget
- Confirm event location
- Create a schedule of events
- Develop attractions and activities
- Identify staffing needs
- Sell sponsorships
- Create a floor plan
- Create a merchandise area
- Create a ticket sales area for next season
- Identify food and beverage offerings
- Book entertainment
- Invite dignitaries, VIP guests, sponsors, business owners, and other stakeholders
- Invite media to cover the event
- Advertise and promote the event to fans and nonfans
- Recruit, train, and orient staff
- Set up and install the event
- Operate the event
- Disassemble the event
- Document the event for future sponsorship sales efforts
- Evaluate the success of the event

Figure 5.1 Elementary Tasks

Assign Deadlines to Elementary Tasks

It is usually helpful to assign preliminary deadlines, or end dates, first and then add the many supportive tasks and decision points that will be needed to achieve them. Put the elementary tasks in the most logical sequence, starting with the first that will need to be initiated and completed. The tasks listed in Figure 5.1 are presented in approximate chronological order. Then add deadline dates, that is, the date by which each task must be completed, as illustrated in Figure 5.2. The most helpful method for assigning deadline dates, is to start from event day and work your way backward.

Tasks that are to be completed after the event ends, such as "document" and "evaluate the event," have been excluded from the balance of this illustration. It should be noted, however, that some subtasks for the elements that will be completed after the event is over may require some activities that happen before event day. To properly document the event, for example, a photographer or videographer would have to be hired in advance.

Add Start Dates

Many teams in competitive leagues, both amateur and professional, do not clinch a playoff position until near the end of the regular season, just before the start of their playoffs. In our example, let's suppose the team is doing well enough to qualify for the playoffs, but is not yet assured of a

FAN FESTIVAL EVENT DATE: April 15

Elementary Task	End Date
Create an event budget	February 15
Confirm event location	February 28
Create a schedule of events	March 15
Develop attractions and activities	March 27
Identify staffing needs	March 29
Sell sponsorships	March 29
Create a merchandise area	March 31
Create ticket sales area for next season	March 31
Identify food and beverage offerings	March 31
Book entertainment	March 31
Create a floor plan	April 5
Invite dignitaries/guests/sponsors/business owners/stakeholders	April 8
Invite media to cover the event	April 8
Advertise and promote the event to fans and non-fans	April 14
Recruit, train, and orient staff	April 14
Set up and install the event	April 14
Obtain/confirm all permits, approvals, inspections, venue details	April 14
Operate the event	April 15
Disassemble and move out the event	April 16

Figure 5.2 Elementary Tasks with Deadline Dates

postseason berth. The team will want to set deadlines that are as late as possible so the event may be canceled with the least embarrassment possible, and with minimal or no financial exposure. In Figure 5.2, deadlines are set very close to event day to avoid having to pay for most expenses until the playoff picture is closer to resolution. It is suggested for most events, when and where possible, that deadlines should be set earlier than in this example, with extra time built in for the fulfillment of tasks that end up taking longer than expected.

Just because end dates for certain tasks are set late does not mean that planning should also start late on those items. Work on all of these tasks should begin as early as possible, in this case even before the probability of the team's playoff appearance becomes apparent. For this reason, it is strongly suggested that critical dates calendars include start dates as well. Figure 5.3 expands the calendar for our fictional fan festival to include start dates for each elementary task.

Note that in our expanded list of elementary tasks, some action areas that have the same deadline date take longer to plan and execute than others. The value of including a start date to the critical dates calendar allows event organizers to prioritize the order in which tasks with a similar end date should be initiated. In this way, planners will not run out of time to manage a more complex elementary task because it was not started early enough. By maintaining the critical dates calendar on a spreadsheet program or using proprietary event management software, organizers can sort their tasks by either start date or end date.

FAN FESTIVAL EVENT DATE: April 15

Elementary Task	Start Date	End Date
Develop an event budget	December 1	February 15
Confirm event location	November 1	February 28
Create a schedule of events	December 1	March 15
Develop attractions and activities	December 1	March 27
Identify staffing needs	January 1	March 29
Sell sponsorships	January 15	March 29
Create merchandise area	March 1	March 31
Create ticket sales area for next season	March 1	March 31
Identify food and beverage offerings	February 15	March 31
Book entertainment	March 1	March 31
Create floor plan	March 15	April 5
Invite dignitaries/guests/sponsors/business owners/others	March 15	April 8
Invite media to cover the event	March 15	April 8
Advertise and promote the event to fans and non-fans	March 22	April 14
Recruit, train, and orient staff	March 15	April 14
Set up and install the event	April 13	April 14
Obtain/confirm all permits, approvals, inspections, details	March 15	April 14
Operate the event	April 15	April 15
Disassemble and move out event	April 16	April 16

Figure 5.3 Elementary Tasks with Start and End Dates

Keeping Your Project on Track

A critical dates calendar, or production schedule, is an efficient way of organizing all of these tasks into a chronological order that identifies the many paths of work required and validates each deadline against a framework of internal logic and practicality. In other words, by listing all of the primary tasks that must be completed, the event director can assign deadline dates that fit together logically, consistent with all of the deadline dates for other activities that must precede or follow them.

This process, called *critical task analysis,* will ultimately help you determine the optimal dates by which to accomplish specific aspects of the planning process. When complete, the calendar will be comprised of myriad details and deadlines that may appear so comprehensive as to seem daunting. However, the more

SIDELINE STORY

Planning for the Playoffs and Payoffs

The most critical and potentially lucrative part of the season for most professional North American sports leagues are the playoffs, or postseason, leading to a final game or series of games to determine the championship. In addition to their competitive importance to the leagues and teams, the postseason has significant financial benefits, as well. This is the period for a sport's greatest viewership and media coverage, the best attendance at the highest ticket prices, and the greatest potential for merchandise sales. The postseason is as much a celebration for the fans as it is for the team. Fans are more willing to devote time and money to their passion at this time than at any other during the season.

Imagine planning logistics for the playoffs. Twelve of 32 NFL teams discover they are in the first round of postseason (i.e., Wild Card Weekend) with a week to prepare, and only six will host the games. In the case of the NBA, half of the 16 teams that qualify for the postseason will find out that they will need to travel, and to where, to meet their playoff rival with only a few days' notice after their final regular season game. The remaining eight may not have to travel, but they will need to prepare for hosting the first games of the postseason with little time to spare. The leagues, teams, and host facilities must prepare for an influx of inbound media, broadcasters, and operational staff who will require hotels and workspaces, as well as acquiring more merchandise inventory and handling the increased demand for tickets. Clearly, this planning cannot first begin when the team clinches its spot in the playoffs.

The uncertainty of where games will be played is sometimes compounded by flexibility in the postseason game schedule. In the NHL, where every one of the four Stanley Cup playoff rounds is a best-of seven series, there is the possibility of starting later rounds ahead of schedule if all of the games in preceding series end in four or five games. As a result, the league's events department must begin planning for the postseason in the earliest stages of the regular season, identifying hotels in all 32 markets that can accommodate media, hospitality, and operational needs over a long range of dates (over as much as six weeks), and then reducing the number of cities as teams drop from playoff contention. Very often, some hotels will be available for only some of the required dates due to other previously booked commitments, requiring different scenarios based on when games will actually be played. As a result, event planners for the Stanley Cup playoffs create many more plans in advance than they will ever use.

Clubs and their home arenas, for their part, have to plan well ahead of knowing whether they will be hosting postseason games. In this environment of uncertainty, they must ensure they have left themselves sufficient time to plan for game operations, staffing, ticketing, hospitality, event presentation, and promotional fan activities. Consider all the advance planning required and one begins to understand the incredible disappointment of being eliminated from the postseason reaching through every level of the organization.

detail devoted to assigning deadlines to the completion of tasks and subtasks, the more effective the organizer will be in keeping the event planning process on schedule. Start with the end point of each process and when that work must be concluded. Then, work your way back through all of the many steps and decisions that must be taken, or subtasks accomplished, to complete the task.

Let's take the seemingly simple task of inviting VIP guests to attend a sports event. Intuitively, we know that we will have to contact guests and receive responses. However, as Figure 5.4 illustrates, there are more than 20 other decisions that must be made, actions that must be taken, and procedures that must be followed. Every indented entry in the figure denotes a subtask or activity that must be completed before plans for the task above it can be finalized.

Expand Calendar with Supportive Tasks and Decision Points

Now it is time to expand the critical dates calendar by deconstructing each elementary task into its component parts through critical task analysis, as seen in the example provided in Figure 5.4. As you do this, you are likely to discover that many of your original assumptions leave not enough time to accommodate all of the activity and decisions that will be required between the start and end dates. You may also discover that certain supplemental tasks or decision points for one elementary task will need to be completed before the supplemental tasks of one or more other elementary tasks. It is perfectly natural to have to make these adjustments as the calendar is developed and refined.

Elementary Task: Invite VIP Guests to the Event
Process: Invitations sent to VIPs, and RSVPs received
- Design invitations (Key activity):
  - Determine method of distribution (texted, e-mailed, or printed)
  - Allocate budget for design and production
  - Determine time required for design, layout, proofs, production, and delivery
  - Identify and engage designer
  - Finalize event logo for inclusion in the design
  - Identify to which activities the VIPs are being invited
  - Determine by what date invitations must be sent
  - Determine RSVP deadline date:
    - Determine when seating assignments must be made
    - Determine when unclaimed VIP tickets must be released to the public
  - Identify the RSVP mechanism (online, app-based, e-mailed, or mailed):
  - Determine how and where responding guests will receive their tickets (electronic, printed)
  - Determine what information should be included with the invitations (e.g., hotel, transportation, parking, and FAQs)
  - Finalize hotel/transportation contracts and booking process
  - Determine how many VIPs can be accommodated:
    - Allocate complimentary seating for VIPs and remove tickets from public sale
    - Ensure the lost revenue from comp seating can be accommodated in the budget
    - Identify the VIPs who should be invited (e.g., city officials, local businesses, celebrities, athlete families, and media)
  - Determine date by which invitees must receive invitations
  - Identify the time that will be required to assign seating
  - Create event information link for responding guests

Figure 5.4 Critical Task Analysis

Let's look at three elementary tasks from the current series of examples: "develop an event budget," "develop attractions and activities," and "sell sponsorships." Work on planning these key elementary tasks should start early and be developed concurrently. Figure 5.5 partially expands each task into component parts to illustrate.

These three elementary tasks were chosen for illustration because they are closely interrelated. To sell sponsorships, you have to create a package of benefits for the sponsor to buy. To create the benefits package, you will need to know what inventory (e.g., attractions and activities) you will have to sell. To finalize the activities, you will have to sell, you will have to know what they are going to cost. To know what they will cost, you will need to conceptualize what you want, contact potential suppliers, and solicit estimates. To price sponsorships for those activities, you will have to know what they will cost to produce, what overhead costs will also need to be covered, and how much income you are trying to generate overall. You will have to order signage to acknowledge your sponsors. And, to have the signage ready in time, you will have to have a deadline by which sponsorships will need to be finalized. (In real life, few sports event organizers will turn down late-arriving sponsors, even if it means incurring higher expenses and last-minute effort to get the deal done.)

After expanding each elementary task into its component supporting tasks and decision points, begin filling in the start and end dates for each, as illustrated in Figure 5.6. This is the step during which the

---

FAN FESTIVAL EVENT DATE: April 15

Elementary Task	Start Date	End Date
Develop an event budget	December 1	February 15
Identify net income/loss goal		
Estimate total expenses		
Estimate total revenues		
Determine sponsor revenue needs		
First draft budget		
Finalize budget		
Develop attractions and activities	December 1	March 27
Identify attraction areas		
Request and receive cost estimates		
Confirm roster of attractions		
Order signage		
Sell sponsorships	January 15	March 31
Create sponsorship tiers and packages		
Create sponsorship presentations		
Solicit potential sponsor companies		
Finalize sponsors		
Order sponsor signage		
Order other sponsor fulfillment elements		

Figure 5.5 Expanding Elementary Tasks

FAN FESTIVAL EVENT DATE: April 15

Task	Start Date	End Date
~~Develop an event budget~~	~~December 1~~	~~February 15~~
Identify net income/loss goal	December 1	December 8
Budget total expenses	December 1	January 2
Budget total revenues	December 10	January 17
Determine sponsor revenue needs	December 10	January 17
First draft budget	December 15	January 8
Finalize budget	January 8	February 15
~~Develop attractions and activities~~	~~December 1~~	~~March 27~~
Identify attraction areas	December 1	January 2
Request and receive cost estimates	December 15	January 8
Confirm roster of attractions	January 8	February 1
Order and receive signage	April 2	April 10
~~Sell sponsorships~~	~~January 15~~	~~March 31~~
Create sponsorship tiers and packages	January 15	February 1
Create sponsorship presentations	January 15	February 15
Solicit potential sponsor companies	February 15	March 22
Finalize sponsors	March 1	March 31

Figure 5.6 Expanded Critical Dates Calendar (Partial)

event organizer must be particularly vigilant to ensure the calendar is internally consistent. That is, all of the tasks that require other activities to occur either as prerequisites or corequisites have start and end dates that are not contradictory. As a result of this process, it is not unusual for some dates to slide earlier or later to accommodate the need for this consistency. In this example, for instance, the task of ordering signage must slide to a slightly later date than originally anticipated because of the organizer's need to delay committing to costs just in case the team falls out of playoff contention. The later date will also allow the organizer to continue to get new sponsors late in the planning process. The experienced sports event planner in this example did not simply assume that his vendor could meet these later, just-in-time ordering and delivery dates. The vendor had to be made aware, and had to have accepted, the delayed time frame.

Several additional examples of internal consistency may be noticed in Figure 5.6. The organizer must have a pretty good idea of their sponsor revenue needs before presenting the event to potential sponsors and would not be able to confirm the pricing of sponsorship packages until the budget is in substantially complete form. Because of the short time frame to bring the event to the attention of sponsors, the organizer is prepared to begin creating sponsorship opportunities as soon as the first draft budget is completed. Therefore, the creation of sponsorship proposals gets underway as soon as the first draft expense budget is nearing completion. While the organizer waits for the development of the business end of the presentation (e.g., creating and pricing the package), work may begin on the introduction, graphics, and background information. The presentations will then be ready to go to market as soon as the budget and business terms of the sponsorship package are finalized.

To get to this point, the roster of attractions must be confirmed. To ensure the budget contains all of the pertinent information relating to each attraction, vendors must be contacted to begin developing cost estimates. The roster of attractions and the budget are finalized simultaneously. At the same time, sponsors first begin to be approached by the organizer.

Note that the original elementary tasks that were listed may now be removed from the calendar of critical dates. With all of the new detail added to the calendar, the elementary entries are now too broad to be very useful to the planning process and are struck through in the figure for the purpose of illustration. Due to the fine level of detail in a truly functional critical dates calendar, the number of entries is generally very large. The three sample elementary tasks selected from the 17 listed in Figure 5.3 generated 14 expanded entries on their own. Critical date calendars can contain lists of 100 or more tasks for even the simplest sports event. It is wise to add one more column to the spreadsheet to assist the event director in managing the planning process—the assignment of staff to each area of responsibility.

Add Responsibilities

Most sports event organizers must delegate responsibilities to a group of area managers, supervisors, helpers, and workers, whether paid professionals, volunteers, vendor companies, or others. A column has been added to note the individual responsible to complete each task on schedule (See Figure 5.7). Although in this case initials have been used, any desired identifier (e.g., full name, last name, and job title) may appear in this column.

Note that the entries in Figure 5.6 have been re-sorted into chronological order, first by start date, next by end date. Event or project management software programs, or spreadsheets, may be further sorted to generate separate charts of responsibility for each individual listed. This provides the sports event organizer and the managers responsible for each functional area with a useful tool to ensure that workload is allocated realistically and communicated properly.

Remember to include activities that occur *after* an event has been completed. Functions such as dismantling an event, vacating and restoring the event site, finalizing the budget settlement, scheduling postmortem event evaluations, documenting the event for sponsors, and releasing temporary seasonal employees are just a sample of the types of activities that should also be included in the calendar.

FAN FESTIVAL EVENT DATE: April 15

Task	Start Date	End Date	Responsibility
Identify net income/loss goal	December 1	December 8	GT
Budget total expenses	December 1	January 2	EN
Identify attraction areas	December 1	January 2	HR
Budget total revenues	December 10	January 17	GT
Determine sponsor revenue needs	December 10	January 17	GT
First draft budget	December 15	January 8	EN
Request and receive cost estimates	December 15	January 8	HR
Finalize budget	January 8	February 1	GT
Confirm roster of attractions	January 8	February 15	GT
Create sponsorship tiers and packages	January 15	February 1	TD
Create sponsorship presentations	January 15	February 15	FL
Solicit potential sponsor companies	February 15	March 22	TD
Finalize sponsors	March 1	March 31	TD
Order and receive signage	April 2	April 10	KD

Figure 5.7 Calendar of Critical Dates (Partial)

Distribute Critical Dates Calendars

Critical dates calendars are most useful when they are distributed to the entire project team. At minimum, everyone listed in the responsibility column should receive a copy of the calendar. Staff in other areas of the organization with a need to know may be sent links or copies, with confidential or organizationally sensitive information deleted from wider distribution. In this way, staff may direct their questions, comments, and feedback directly to the individual overseeing a particular function, rather than solely to the event director. The question now is: "Who are the people doing all this work, and where are they coming from?"

Build a Support Organization

Whether you plan to use some combination of volunteers, part-time or full-time paid staff, or an event planning or production firm to staff your sports event, a structure needs to be put in place that will define areas of responsibility and accountability for each contributing individual. Many sports organizations staff themselves to stage special events year-round. Others are highly seasonal and retain a small core staff on a permanent, full-time basis, periodically augmented by a larger temporary, in-season workforce. Still others retain help from outside organizations, applying some combination of internal staff with resources such as vendors, independent contractors, temporaries, interns, and freelancers. Because the structure of the event team should be defined by the workload ahead, event organizers frequently build their critical dates calendars early in the planning process to determine what resources, skill sets, and talents will be required and when they must be in place. They can then create an organization plan that applies both internal and external resources for the period required. Before they begin looking at areas of responsibility, however, it is important for the event organization to define levels of authority and determine how decisions will be made.

Define the Decision-Making Process

Begin by identifying the ultimate decision-makers—the individual or body of individuals, who have the authority to set objectives, determine strategies, and approve the spending of money to achieve them. The decision-maker may be an individual, a task force, or a committee, but there must be a structure in place that assigns the right amount of responsibility at each level of the organization and recognition of that structure by all who operate within it.

Frequently, a committee, task force, board of directors, or senior officer of a client organization occupies the top level of the event team. It is particularly helpful to define the role of this individual or group, particularly with respect to what decisions must be presented at that level for consideration and resolution. Defining these jurisdictions and limitations in the earliest stages will help the event director to fully understand the responsibilities and authority he or she may exercise autonomously. Although *autonomy* suggests areas of total control over clearly defined areas, it does not obviate the complete accountability the event director has to the overarching group or organization. It is essential, however, to move the majority of the day-to-day decision-making down below the committee, board, or client organization to give the event team the freedom to quickly respond to the myriad challenges, changes, and opportunities that will present themselves throughout the event planning process. Figure 5.8 is a chart of typical authorities and responsibilities for an event's board of directors (or an organization's chief executive officer, event committee, or client), and the top individual charged with managing the event (in this case, the event director). This chart is for illustrative purposes, as authorities and responsibilities may slide from one category to another, depending on the needs of a specific event or the reporting structure of the sports organization.

In Figure 5.8, a system of checks and balances is in place to empower the event director to make the day-to-day decisions required to manage the event without having to run every question, challenge, or issue past the board of directors. In this example, the event director has the broad authority to make

Management Entity	Authorities and Responsibilities
Board of Directors	Definition of event objectives
	Approval of strategies and tactics
	Approval of event budget
	Approval of host city and venue selection
	Approval of sponsor, supplier, or broadcast and media deals with terms of more than one year
	Hiring and firing of event director
Event Director	Budget development and management
	Strategy and tactic development
	Approval of expenses
	Supplier selection, negotiations, and contract approval
	Sponsor solicitation, negotiations, and contract approval
	Broadcast and media solicitation, negotiation, and contract approval
	Hiring, training, and firing of event staff

Figure 5.8   Decision-Making Authorities and Responsibilities

operational decisions that will keep the event running efficiently. The event director is totally responsible to the board, which serves as the governing authority. As the individual held accountable for both triumphs and failures, the board may remove the director at any time for not meeting the demands and expectations of the position.

The board is in place to define the objectives for the event. The event director is, in turn, responsible to develop the strategies, tactics, and budget required by the event to meet these objectives, although these may require presentation to, and approval by, the board. The event director in this example can approve expenses, but is responsible to inform the board if the budget is expected to experience any significant variance.

This illustration limits the event director's authority to approving sponsor, supplier, or media deals of only a single year's duration or less. This frees the director to manage the business of the most immediate event, enabling them to make a short-term deal without the approval of the higher authority. Having a free hand allows deals to be made that may help an organization respond quickly to emerging challenges such as unexpected budget overruns, supplier or sponsor defaults, unfruitful sponsor contract negotiations, or other previously unanticipated revenue shortfalls. Sometimes, a "fire sale" sponsorship at a below-market rate or a last-minute value-in-kind deal must be struck in order to reduce losses or cover shortfalls. Deals like these are consummated late in the planning process and require the kind of rapid decision-making that board intercession would make challenging.

Create an Organization Chart

Organization charts will differ dramatically from event to event; the chart in Figure 5.9 illustrates a generalized presentation of a hypothetical sports event provided for the purpose of discussion. Boxes most often represent the names and titles of individuals but may also describe specific functions rather than individual staff positions. The position of each job on the chart and how the jobs are joined to those above and below symbolize the hierarchy of their reporting relationships. There are many ways to graphically portray an organization's structure; this is just one common example. Several popular software tools are available to assist in the preparation of professional-appearing charts.

There are three key reasons for taking the time to construct an organization chart for your sports event. The first is to define areas of responsibility and accountability. This will let everyone know what their job is and how they relate to other areas of responsibility in the organization. The second is to streamline decision-making. Construct an organization chart with several management tiers so that each and every issue need not be elevated to the event director for resolution. By limiting the number of staff members reporting only to the event director ("direct reports"), as well as those who report to each of the top managers in charge of each functional area (e.g., operations, guest services, marketing, presentation, etc.), top-level managers can delegate authority and responsibility along clearly defined paths to those on levels below. The third reason is to clearly communicate, both within the organization and outside, how each functional area fits into the event's overall management structure. Distributing the chart to all those represented as well as to key outside contacts ensures that questions and concerns will be directed to the individuals who can best handle them.

The fictional sports event organization in Figure 5.9 divides the management team into seven key functional groups: operations, competition, guest services, presentation, marketing, hospitality, and sponsorship. While the structure of every event team will vary with the nature and needs of the program being managed, it is preferable to limit the number of functional areas reporting directly to a particular position to as few as possible. Although all members of the event team are ultimately responsible to the event director, this top manager has only seven "direct reports," managers who are responsible solely to the director. Functions are grouped beneath each of these managers so that each of them, in turn, has fewer than six key areas for which they are responsible.

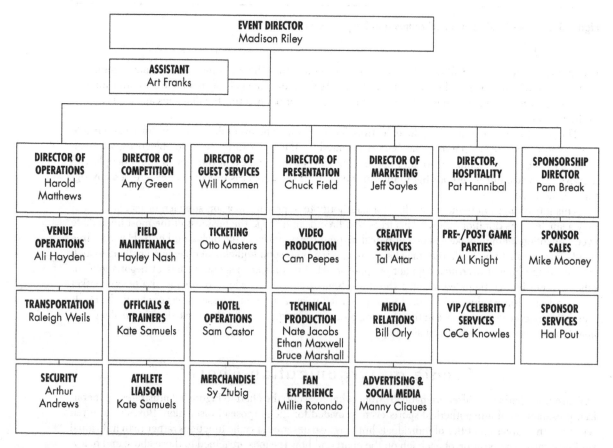

Figure 5.9   Sample Sports Event Organization Chart

Regardless of the vast differences between sports organizations, events apply staff to the management of many common functions. Figure 5.10 lists some of the most frequent with key activities often undertaken by each. To meet an event's specific needs, some might be combined into a single area of responsibility, others more finely subdivided depending on the size, organization, and objectives of the event.

Operations	• Facility/venue management: *space allocation, load-in, installation, dismantle, load-out, front of house staff (security, guest services), locker/dressing rooms, first aid/EMTs* • Credentials • Transportation: *competitor transportation, shipping/receiving* • I.T. & office services • Staff uniforms • Crowd control
Competition	• Tournament/competition scheduling • Athlete management and communication • Competitive equipment • Officiating and judging • Playing field preparation and maintenance • Training facilities, equipment, and personnel • Athlete medical services
Guest Services	• Ticketing • VIP/celebrity invitation process and seating • VIP/athlete gifts • VIP/athlete hospitality • Information app and printed guides • Hotel rooms and space management
Marketing	• Creative services: *logo development, style manual, artwork, digital and printed materials, signage* • Advertising: *social media, website, digital, print, broadcast* • Outdoor: *billboards, banners, posters, marquees* • Promotions: *sponsor cross-promotions, retail promotions* • Publicity: *pre-event, media relations/accreditation, media center operations, photographers* • *Merchandise and programs*
Presentation	• Creative: *runs of show, scripting, music, costumes/wardrobe* • Production management • Talent booking: *announcers, entertainers, rehearsal scheduling* • Stage management • Scoreboard operations • Video production • Technical production: *staging, set construction, lighting, sound, special effects, augmented reality*
Other Functional Areas	• Sponsorship: *business development and sponsor sales and service* • Hospitality and social events: *receptions, parties, spouse programs* • Fan festivals and activities • Broadcasting: *television, streaming, radio* • Business affairs: *accounts payable, accounts receivable, purchasing, legal (i.e., contract negotiations, risk management, and insurance)*

Figure 5.10   Functional Areas for Sports Events

Once you have identified the functional areas that are required for your sports event and you have defined reporting relationships on an organization chart, it is time to begin assigning staff to these various functions, or to search for resources to handle the workload.

Find the Right People

One of the wonderful things about sports events is there is usually no shortage of people who want to help staff them. Grassroots organizations tap family members and friends to create the workforce they need to stage their events. Professional sports teams and their respective leagues are besieged by resumes—not just of those already working in the field but also of sports and event management program students and graduates, career shifters, and job seekers willing to start off as interns or game day staff. The thousands of lesser-connected event organizers in between look to these same pools of experience, talent, and energy to meet their human resources needs.

Sports events staged by established organizations frequently assign full-time employees from other areas of their company to temporarily assist in the management and execution of key annual or one-time programs. To keep costs down, they often supplement their event staff on loan from other departments with temporary "seasonal" employees, individuals hired with defined start and end dates for their employment. Seasonal staff may be retained part time (under 35 hours per week) or full time (35+ hours) and are generally paid hourly or weekly.

Enlist Volunteers

In sheer numbers, there are easily more than enough men, women, boys, and girls who volunteer to help staff and support sports events from the community ball field and the town rink to the campus gymnasium and the downtown arena. Volunteerism is what makes many not-for-profit sports events go, often providing the staffing glue that keeps the event together. Given the passion many feel for their favorite sport, school, community, or team, it is not hard to understand why. The practice of strategically employing well-briefed, enthusiastic volunteers is not restricted to small community grassroots events. Events staged by large amateur sports organizations and even some professional sports businesses also apply the participation of motivated volunteers as short-term and event-day staff for their programs. (Note: The use of unpaid volunteer event staff may be subject to regulation or prohibited by state and local laws. Seek qualified legal advice to fully understand your options.)

Staff for community-oriented grassroots events, from those managing the program to event day helpers, is often entirely composed of volunteers. Some participatory organizations, like running and skating clubs, have hundreds or even thousands of members, many of whom often assist with their association's schedule of events as volunteers. Although volunteers, by definition, are unpaid it is nevertheless recommended that their responsibilities be well defined to minimize confusion and ensure that important tasks do not fail to be accomplished.

When a combination of paid and volunteer staff members works together, volunteers are best suited for positions that require intelligence and people skills, but little training beyond an orientation session or two. Event organizers must recognize that to those attending, volunteers are often indistinguishable from paid staff. As ambassadors for the event organizer and are often the first point of contact for many participants, guests, and fans, volunteers must be selected judiciously and provided with all the information and materials they need to do their jobs. Create a brief bullet-point job description for each volunteer position, as illustrated in Figure 5.11. Consider the personality traits and knowledge they must possess to fulfill these positions, and then identify the resources in your market that can provide a body of motivated, high-performing volunteers.

As may be seen in these examples, volunteer jobs are not usually the most glamorous, but don't underestimate the excitement that sports events generate. Most volunteers understand that they will not be running the show. They know they are providing the muscle and connective tissue that keeps everything together.

Position: Airport Greeter
Description:
- Meet incoming athletes and VIP guests at the airport and direct them to the ground transportation provided
- Assist with the recovery of equipment and luggage from baggage claim and transfer to the guests' transportation
- Offer to answer guests' questions about the event schedule, and dining and entertainment options in the city

Reports To: Event Transportation Dispatcher
Dates/Hours Required: At least two days between Thursday, April 13, and Sunday, April 16, for at least four hours per day as scheduled

Position: Media Host
Description:
- Distribute information to the working press during the event
- Escort athletes to and from the press conference area
- Assist the public relations team in the Media Center during the event

Reports To: Media Relations Manager
Dates/Hours Required: All days between Thursday, April 13, and Sunday, April 16, one hour prior to the start of event to one hour after the end of event

Position: Operations Center Representative
Description:
- Answer e-mails and texts from media requesting event information
- Assist with the distribution of media credentials
- Other office functions, as assigned

Reports To: Office Manager
Dates/Hours Required: At least two days between Thursday, April 13, and Sunday, April 16, for at least four hours per day as assigned

---

Figure 5.11 Sample Sports Event Volunteer Job Descriptions

So, beyond the event staff's circle of friends, where can sports events find these masses of excited and devoted enthusiasts? Many local convention and visitors bureaus and sports commissions maintain databases of local residents who enjoy volunteering for special events and are experienced in dealing with the public, such as airport hosts (see Figure 5.11) and other positions that greet and provide information to incoming visitors. In some cities, the office of the mayor or the department of parks and recreation may maintain similar databases of potential volunteers.

Contact the recreational enthusiasts of your sport for an enthusiastic pool of potential volunteers. In addition, many amateur and professional teams have booster or fan clubs that enjoy supporting sports events. Consider asking to approach their membership even if they are not specifically fans of the same sport as your event. Many fans just enjoy being around a variety of sporting events. Don't overlook the power of *swag*, the exclusive event merchandise most organizers use as a staff uniform. A staff windbreaker, vest, golf shirt or T-shirt and cap can go a long way as an additional motivator.

Is there a university with a sports or event management program in the host community? There are no more motivated prospects for volunteers than those who are looking to make contacts in the sports business while preparing for future careers in this exciting, but hard-to-break-into industry. Contact the dean of the school under which these programs are offered to investigate whether an entire class or individual students can volunteer as part of a field experience. Many schools see great value in offering their students the ability to participate as event staff members. Don't forget to use your own organization's

SIDELINE STORY

The Power of Volunteerism

The NFL's Super Bowl is most often awarded to warm weather cities, allowing fans and business partners to enjoy the festivities in mild weather in leisure-resort locations. Less regularly, cities in colder winter locations with new climate-controlled stadiums are included in the hosting rotation. As Indianapolis prepared to host the Super Bowl in their then-new indoor stadium, the local planners recognized the opportunity to enhance the city's image as a host of major sports happenings. More than 8,000 volunteers were recruited, trained, and managed by the Indianapolis Super Bowl Host Committee to help staff the league's massive inter-active indoor fan festival, and *Super Bowl Village*, the committee's free outdoor street fair. Volunteers also blanketed the streets of downtown Indianapolis, the airport, and area hotels to provide greetings and guidance to fans unfamiliar with the city, as well as to direct fans to Lucas Oil Stadium on Super Bowl Sunday. Distinctively dressed and well-trained, these community ambassadors provided visitors with the "Hoosier Hospitality" experience for which Indianapolis is justifiably famous. Lead volunteers were identified by six-foot-tall flags strapped to their backs and equipped with electronic tablets loaded with maps, schedules, restaurant recommendations, and other information to help showcase their community to the 1.1 million visitors who visited the downtown area during Super Bowl week.

Spirited volunteerism did not end with these frontline representatives of the community. Indianans from across the state contributed by knitting blue and white scarves, each individually different, to protect the volunteers from the cold. Over the course of a year, they generated 13,000 of them—enough to also outfit NFL staff, as well as the participating New England Patriots and New York Giants. Leveraging the power of its volunteer pool, the Indianapolis Host Committee also used the excitement of the upcoming Super Bowl to accelerate the revitalization of the city's Near East Side, promote the donation of breast tissue at a nationally recognized tissue bank, and re-develop a three-block stretch of downtown streetscape into a permanent pedestrian event venue.

social media feeds and website, as well as those of related organizations, to announce the need for paid or volunteer staff, along with basic details of available opportunities. Be sure to include information on how to apply.

There are many instances in which volunteer or temporary paid staff will not meet all of the requirements of an event. Professional expertise not otherwise available within the existing organization may be required to plan, manage, and execute a successful program, and some number of talented freelance staff may need to be retained to achieve the desired result.

Hire Freelancers: Employees and Independent Contractors

Freelance event staff may be retained either as temporary employees or independent contractors. If hired and compensated as employees, the event director may define work hours, set the policies and procedures to be followed, and supervise freelancers as though they were regular full-time employees. Freelancers hired as temporary employees may also be entitled to all of the rights and protections offered to other employees, such as health insurance benefits and overtime pay—except, of course, that their last date of employment is known by both parties at the outset. Executing an employment contract with a freelance employee may not be necessary, although having both parties sign a letter agreement defining compensation, basic work rules, and the date of termination is strongly recommended.

Independent contractors, by contrast, function as one-person vendors. A contract typically documents the relationship containing many of the same terms as the letter agreement used for temporary employees, but because contractors are generally paid a fee upon presentation of an invoice, a payment schedule is usually included. The event manager does not directly supervise the work of an independent contractor, and, unless stipulated by the contract, has no control over what hours the contractor must invest at the event site. Contractors are free to work for more than one client over the course of their term and have the right to hire and fire additional subcontractors at their own expense to assist them in completing their assignment.

Independent contractors are particularly useful for very specialized functions for which the type of expertise exceeds that of the event's staff. Such specialized contractors might include transportation system consultants, presentation directors, tournament competition organizers, construction or production managers, technical directors, and party planners, to name a few. If supervisors hire wisely, they will always search for freelancers that add more firepower to the event team, whether as temporary staff or independent contractors. If the event requires direct and constant supervision by management, retaining the freelancer as a temporary employee will usually be preferable. Be sure to consult an HR specialist, as there are a number of additional procedural and legal differences between the retention of contractors, or freelancers as temporary employees.

If it is determined that a temporary event employee is required, it is strongly suggested that a staff job description be created for each position. The job description should provide greater detail than the version used for volunteers (see Figure 5.11), providing a clear understanding of the position's responsibilities, work rules, and limits of authority.

Use of Agencies

Some companies consider staging sports events even though their business may only be tangentially related to such activities as a sponsor or promotional partner. It may simply make good business sense for the company to own and manage a sports event to further its corporate objectives, or to market a particular product. Event marketing agencies exist for the purpose of assisting such companies. They are advantageous to use as support organizations because they can apply skilled resources toward the client's event marketing objectives. The client company is strongly advised to pursue due diligence into the agency's experience, achievements, and financial health before agreeing to any relationship. Most agencies will work on a fee-plus-expenses basis, and it is the client company's right to request an explanation of all costs.

It is also not unusual for sports event organizations to retain event marketing agencies to assume the management responsibilities of specialized functional areas, such as sponsor sales, advertising, public relations, and group ticket sales, among others. Agencies that assume cost center functions (i.e., those areas that are represented by expenses in the budget) generally work on a fee-plus-expenses basis. Those that are charged with developing profit centers (i.e., those areas represented by revenues in the budget) are usually compensated with a fee or commission based on the amount of revenue they generate for the event.

Manage Your Support Organization

Planning an event and building an event staff are very similar to launching an entirely new company, brand, or product. The organizer defines objectives, strategies, and tactics, a source of capital, and a staff to manage and execute it. The key difference between creating a sports event organization and staffing a startup company is that event teams are designed to be built to meet an event's objectives and then are deconstructed, at least until the next event, when the building process begins anew.

The similarities between an event organization and a startup company include the working environment of long hours and work weeks, multitasking employees who fulfill more than one function, limited finances, and—to those of us who love this business—tremendous excitement. Startups can be confusing places without clearly communicated goals and procedures, and without constant communication between staff members. Event teams can be similarly confusing environments, and with a firm end date soon after the event, places of great anxiety if not properly managed.

Create an Event Staff Manual

Developing and distributing a copy or link to a staff manual or guide with essential information about your event is a vital communications tool. Articulate a statement of your primary and secondary event objectives and, if you are not revealing confidential information, the results of your P-A-P-E-R Test (see Play 1). Your event's managers will not know how to hit the target if they don't know what the target is and how you expect them to reach it. This information will make up the first section of your staff manual. Keep event manuals in electronic form, in a password-controlled website or app, that can be periodically updated and corrected. The manual will serve as the definitive information source to which the event director and staff will refer throughout the planning process, as well as during the event itself.

Add sections to the event staff manual that include the information you feel will be most useful to the team's planning and execution of the event. Most will include a list of contacts, including mobile phone numbers, and e-mail addresses. For ease of use, divide the contact list into four subsections: internal (members of the event team organization), facility, vendors, and external (such as city services contacts). Figure 5.12 provides a list of essential sections common to most event staff manuals. The figure also lists several optional sections that may be included if applicable to your event, or appropriate to the level of employee.

Note that the list of essential sections for the manual includes "policies and procedures." This section is particularly important for event teams that come together on a temporary basis, although it can be of value to virtually every organization. In this area, it is wise to include definitive information on how purchases are to be authorized and made, and how expenses incurred by event staff should be approved and filed for reimbursement. Include links to blank forms such as purchase orders and expense reports, along with instructions on how they should be completed. If travel is required of the employee, include policies

Essential Sections
1. Event Mission and Objectives
2. Contact List
3. Calendar of Critical Dates
4. Emergency Procedures
5. Event Timeline or Schedule
6. Organization Chart
7. Maps and Floor Plans
8. Policies and Procedures

Optional Sections
1. Financial Information
2. Contracts
3. Event Runs of Show and Scripts
4. Facility Information
5. Sponsorship (List of sponsors and summary of benefits)
6. Transportation Plan
7. Travel and Hotel Information
8. FAQs

Figure 5.12   Event Staff Manual Sections

governing reimbursable travel expenses (e.g., preapproval procedures, class of service for air travel, hotel limits, food and beverage per diems). Minimum workdays and hours, codes of conduct, attire guidelines, equal opportunity employment statements, and other administrative information should also be included. In the long run, taking the time to include these explanations in the event staff manual will avoid costly and potentially demoralizing misunderstandings for staff members and your organization.

Schedule Regular Event Staff Meetings

The scheduling of staff meetings is the best way to keep event personnel current and updated to the constant changes of event life. Schedule meetings or video conferences at regular intervals and include them in the critical dates calendar. If possible, set and circulate an agenda a day or two in advance. Meetings tend to become less efficient as the number of attendees increases. Therefore, it is best to keep staff meetings compartmentalized for mid- to large-size events. One meeting unit should include the event director and the directors, managers, or heads of functional areas to share pertinent updates, announce tactical and schedule changes, set policies, discuss challenges, and propose solutions. Each functional head should, in turn, conduct meetings with his or her own direct reports.

Another important meeting should be included on the critical dates calendar—the "tie-down" meeting (also called all-hands, all-agency, or all-department meeting). Usually held just once, one to three weeks ahead of the event, the tie-down meeting includes all event staff, as well as representatives of important stakeholders such as key vendors and freelancers, agencies, operating departments, facility representatives, and broadcasters, among others. The tie-down is best organized as a communications tool to impart information and procedures, and to identify the remaining tasks to be completed. With a potentially large assemblage of many dozens of event personnel, it is best not envisioned as a problem-solving session. Nevertheless, it is inevitable that some issues will be identified during the tie-down meeting as each functional area reports on how they will operate during the event. That is why holding this important session at least a week ahead of the event is so important. The time remaining until event day will give participants the opportunity to solve these late-emerging problems. It is recommended that the larger the event, the earlier the tie-down should be held to provide adequate time to solve the greater number of issues that are bound to surface. Scheduling and conducting follow-up meetings are often necessary and useful.

Now, the event director has a road map and timetable for the many tasks and activities that must be executed to successfully manage and execute the event. Based on these clearly defined plans, he or she can build an organization to undertake the challenge of producing a well-managed, flawlessly executed sports event. Now, let's take the event to market and to start developing a roster of active, engaged sponsors to meet your event's revenue objectives and activate the program's promotional plans.

Post-play Analysis

The framework of the event planning process is compiled into a production schedule, or calendar of critical dates. This schedule lists the essential tasks required to manage and execute the event and includes start dates, end dates, and the individual responsible for each activity. The best way to begin creating the schedule is to break up the tactics and strategies defined by the P-A-P-E-R Test into their component "elementary tasks." These elementary tasks are expanded into all of the supportive tasks and decision points required to meet them and are then sorted into chronological order.

The process of building an event organization begins once the scope of the work is identified by the critical dates calendar. Define the decision-making process and create an organization chart to begin adding muscle to the framework. Regardless of whether the organization will be composed of volunteers, existing staff, temporary staff, freelancers, or some combination, create job descriptions for each position. Be sure to communicate essential information to all staff members through the creation of an event staff manual, website, or app and by holding regularly scheduled staff meetings.

Coach's Clipboard

1. Compile a calendar of critical dates for the community all-star game discussed in Play 1. Create an organization chart and job descriptions for the all-volunteer team you will assemble to manage and execute this event.

2. Create an organization chart to organize, manage, and execute the 10K event discussed in Play 1. How many event-day volunteers do you think you will require? Assuming the event is being held in your community, what specific resources will you employ to fill your requirements?

3. Create a job description for your volunteer director, the individual who will solicit, schedule, and manage all of the event staff referenced in exercise 2. What kinds of job backgrounds and professional skill sets would provide the most qualified candidates for this position?

4. What kinds of information would you include in the volunteer staff manual or website for the positions discussed in Figure 5.11?

PLAY 6

Understanding the Sports Event–Sponsor Relationship

"Champions keep playing until they get it right."
—*Billie Jean King, multiple American tennis champion & founder,*
Women's Tennis Association

This play will help you to:

- Understand how revenue, cost avoidance, and activation generate the value sponsors can provide to sports events.

- Understand how sports events can provide a diverse menu of business solutions to a wide range of sponsors.

- Develop opportunities to strengthen the sports event–sponsor relationship with mutually advantageous activation platforms for consumer and business-to-business companies.

Introduction

Sponsors can provide one of the most important and common revenue streams available to sports event organizers, whether on the amateur, collegiate, or professional level. Not every event can generate revenue from paid tickets, or meaningful profits from merchandise and only the most popular, in-demand sports organizations can secure media willing to pay a rights fee to distribute their events. Revenue from sponsors, however, can be generated for almost any kind of event and for just about any kind of sport. Even if an event's objectives do not include generating a profit, the net cost of an event can be reduced by offering marketing partnerships to sponsor companies.

The *Cambridge Dictionary* offers a simple definition of sponsorship: "money that is given, usually by a company, to support a person, organization, and activity." For our purposes, however, this interpretation is a bit too simplistic. It suggests a one-sided relationship in which a sponsor makes a contribution to an event and expects little or nothing in return.

IEG, a globally recognized sponsorship resource to properties and rights holders, offers a definition in the *IEG Guide to Sponsorship* that begins to refine the notion of sponsorship as a general business practice: a "sponsorship is a cash and/or in-kind fee paid to a property (typically in sports, arts, entertainment, or causes) in return for access to the exploitable commercial potential associated with that property." Here, the concept features a benefit offered to the company that is spending the money—an association with the event. This interpretation, though completely accurate, is purely transactional. The sponsor buys the right to be associated with a sports property in exchange for a fee but it doesn't elaborate as to how those rights are leveraged.

To more fully understand the fundamental dynamics of sports event sponsorship, we offer this more comprehensive definition: *sponsorship is a mutually advantageous, multi-faceted marketing partnership between a property and a brand in which objectives, values, strategies, and tactics are cooperatively coordinated to realize measurable and reciprocal benefits.*

Each component of this definition is important to fully appreciating the power of sports sponsorships. So, let's break it down. Sponsorship is a marketing partnership in which both the property—the sport, team, venue, or event—and the sponsor benefit. It is not a simple transaction, like advertising for instance, in which the property offers an opportunity for exposure in exchange for cash. Rather, a well-crafted sponsorship is a multifaceted relationship that offers a variety of solutions to both partners, who then work closely together to realize their mutual and respective business objectives. The sponsor will define how they will measure success based on their own goals. Is the relationship designed to generate an increase in product sales, new customers, or market share? Is the sponsorship opportunity, instead, designed to introduce or enhance public awareness of a new brand, product line, service, or flavor? How much a sponsor is willing to spend on a particular sponsorship will depend on the value of the benefits offered, expectations on the relationship's return on investment, and how cost-effective it is compared to spending the money on other marketing activities such as advertising, sales promotions, and social media campaigns.

The Evolution of Sports Event Sponsorship

Corporations have long recognized the powerful allure and marketing potential of sports events to highly engaged audiences at the venue and at home (see Figure 6.1). For this reason, signage and advertising at stadiums and arenas and on broadcasts of sports events have been part of the sponsorship portfolio in one form or another for nearly a century. The value of these early sponsorships was primarily evaluated on the basis of tonnage—how many signs, advertisements, and promotions appeared in front of how many people and in how many places? The event organizer would often include event tickets the sponsor could use for the company's important clients as an additional benefit of the association.

The benefits of advertising a company's product at sports events have long been recognized, and still are, because of the simplicity of their measurement and verification. The sports marketer can guarantee exposure of the sponsor's brand to a definable number of fans based on the number of games played, or events staged over the life of an advertisement. The relative attractiveness and cost of an ad vary based on its position. That is, how visible is the ad to how many fans, and how often is it in their field of view?

Exposure of sponsor signage on broadcasts of an event is also measurable based on viewership, the position of a particular sign, and the frequency of its appearance on the screen. These measures are still in common use today as key yardsticks for determining the value of signage at a sports event. Photos from the event distributed on news sites and social media platforms, and in user-generated content, add even more value to the presence of sponsor signage.

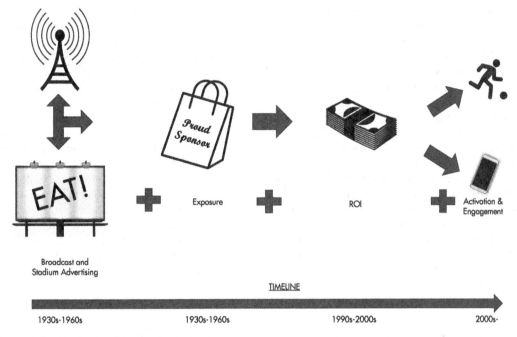

Figure 6.1 Evolution of Sports Sponsorship

Marketers commonly use a "cost per thousand" (CPM) calculation to determine the value of an ad. Simply, the CPM represents the amount of money spent to purchase the ad for every thousand consumers who view it. In general, advertisers look for the lowest, most cost-efficient CPM when evaluating the attractiveness of purchasing a particular exposure opportunity. Online statistics such as page-views, length of stay, and click-throughs to the sponsor's website provide additional measurement metrics.

But, advertising is largely passive in nature. Appropriately, companies next asked themselves: "How effective are these exposure opportunities in developing customers and selling our products?" This essential question led to sponsors seeking and demanding more activation opportunities that better engaged the fan—their customer. While advertising is still a very common, almost universal component in sponsorship packages, the relationship between sports property and sponsors has become increasingly sophisticated, customized, and responsive, and applies new marketing techniques and technologies that offer opportunities tailored to the specific needs of the company. The most impactful of today's sports event sponsorships invest organizers and partner companies in each other's success by immersing fans and sponsor clients in co-branded content at the event site (which still includes signage and advertising), offsite (which still includes retail and product promotion), and online to deliver the desired return on investment for the sponsor and memorable, longer-lasting impressions for the fans.

Although an advertisement's exposure can be objectively measured by its CPM, it is more difficult to quantify its "stickiness," or how well a fan will remember the brand. How effectively will it motivate someone to buy the product, visit the store, or engage online? Because the excitement and emotional involvement of sports events can add to the stickiness of an advertising sign or commercial, some event organizers limit the ability to advertise at their events exclusively to sponsors. It simply adds greater value to sponsorships if the only way to advertise at an event is by becoming a marketing partner.

Sports events are competing for sponsors with other properties and marketing opportunities. To make sense from the sponsor's perspective, a sports event must offer the company more business opportunity than could be purchased for the same amount of money spent on other marketing initiatives. At the same time, from the organizer's point of view, the sponsorship must provide benefits well beyond the costs they will incur to fulfill them. In a real sense, the sponsor and the sports event organizer are investing in each other, and both should expect returns that far outperform a simple cash-for-product (e.g., advertising) transaction.

Thus, although advertising continues to be an important—and sometimes still the central—component in the package of benefits enjoyed by a sponsor, the corporate partner can receive outstanding additional value and more "stickiness" for its message through an increased association with, and investment in, an event. These benefits may include the ability to engage in pre-event promotions that increase the sales of both the sponsor's product and the event's tickets, participation in the event presentation itself, exclusive access to VIP tickets, receptions, parties, and other associated opportunities.

To justify this increased investment, event organizers must design and construct packages of highly attractive and tangible benefits that are available exclusively to sponsors. It is also a quid pro quo for a sponsor's increased investment that it should enjoy exclusivity in the relationship that bars their competitors from participating and associating with the event. The sponsor's ability to promote its products is a valuable and essential ingredient in most sponsorship packages.

As companies have different marketing needs, event organizers must demonstrate flexibility in designing benefit packages individually tailored to a particular sponsor's business objectives. A sponsor that markets a snack food to consumers, for example, may place more value on advertising, sampling, and direct sales opportunities. In contrast, a partner that sells high-priced technology solutions to businesses may place lesser emphasis on advertising and greater value on exclusive access to the best tickets in the house for entertaining prospective clients, meet-and-greet opportunities with the athletes for its dealers and best customers, product demonstration kiosks near premium seating areas, and VIP hospitality opportunities.

What Sports Event Organizers Really Want from Sponsors

Before approaching a potential sponsor, sports event organizers should have a clear understanding of what they themselves want out of the relationship. Most sports events are in the sponsorship business to meet revenue goals. At the same time, sponsors are demanding demonstrable results for their money, so organizers have to invest effort and money to provide an appropriate amount of value for the sponsor. Savvy organizers know that sponsors can bring much more to the event than just cash.

So, what do sports event organizers really want—and need—from their sponsors? Three key things that organizers look for a sponsor to provide are *revenue, cost avoidance,* and *activation.* The first two can have a direct impact on the financial success of an event. The last feature, activation, can have a no less profound effect on an event's success by adding promotional and experiential value for both partners. Forging a sponsor relationship that offers a measure of all three can offer an organizer solutions to event marketing challenges with greater effect than can any alone (Figure 6.2).

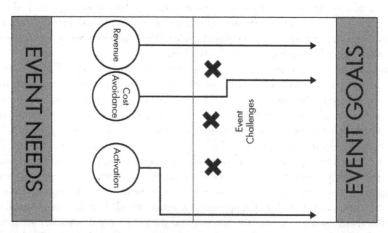

Figure 6.2   What Sports Event Organizers Need from Sponsors

Revenue

Most sports events include sponsorships as part of their business model to generate revenue. Generally, the fewer or more modest the other revenue streams, the more an event will rely on some form of support from sponsors. An event that is free to participants and attendees, for example, often expects the most sizable portion of its revenue budget to be generated from corporate sponsorships.

It is very tempting for sports event organizers to view corporate sponsorship as a gap closer to cover any shortfall in the budget. Event promoters often mistakenly determine how high to set their sponsorship revenue goal by first estimating expenses, then setting a salable ticket price or participation fee, and finally deciding to cover almost all of the difference with sponsor dollars. However, the amount of sponsorship revenue a sports event can generate is not a function of how much expense an organizer needs to cover, but rather, should be based on the event's potential effectiveness in achieving the sponsor's business objectives. There are two essential ingredients to every sponsorship that must overlap: the fans of the sport or event and the sponsor's customers. The greater the overlap, the greater the potential for a mutually advantageous partnership. To this end, the sponsor will first compare the demographics of an event's audience with its own customers to determine whether various characteristics such as age, gender, income, education, and other consumer attributes complement each other. If they match well, the sponsor will then evaluate whether the rights and benefits offered by the event will achieve its marketing goals. Organizers will have to estimate how much money these companies are likely to spend to reach an event's ticket buyers, viewers, or participants, and what the event will have to deliver to its sponsors before finalizing their sponsorship revenue goals.

Cost Avoidance

Many sponsors are attracted to the option of providing products and services in lieu of, or in addition to, cash in payment of their event sponsorship fees, particularly in challenging economic environments. This practice is known variously as *barter, contra,* or *value-in-kind* (VIK). VIK sponsors provide products or services to an event and value them at the retail price an organizer would expect to pay if cash had to be expended to procure them. For the sponsor, this practice has multiple benefits. Obviously, it reduces the cash the company will need to spend in exchange for sponsorship rights. To sponsors, cash represents money that that has already been earned on past sales. Providing VIK, however, moves product inventory out of their warehouses, so sponsors are actually paying for their sponsorship with what amounts to new, *incremental* sales. Additionally, the real cost a sponsor incurs in manufacturing the product may only be 50 percent or less of the retail value provided to the event organizer.

Event organizers should avail themselves of VIK opportunities that provide a level of cost avoidance equal to, or exceeding, the value of a cash sponsorship. Make sure that the products or services received truly reduce your event expenses by at least an amount that equals your income goal had you been paid in cash. Avoid deals that do not decrease a budgeted expense. Ideally, they should be the actual products or services you would require and purchase if the VIK offer was not available.

If quality, quantity, and utility match up with operational and budget requirements, then accepting barter avoids costs, thereby reducing expenses. That can be as good as cash in that it contributes positively to the event's net income. Or, consider a VIK relationship that provides products or services that enhance the fan experience as long as it doesn't add expenses to your budget. Figure 6.3 lists potential barter opportunities commonly sought by corporate sponsors and sports event organizers. As previously discussed, planners are advised to budget for all expenses as though cash is required to acquire these products and services, while pursuing opportunities that VIK arrangements can provide.

Activation

Activation embodies a concept not easily described by a simple synonym. Best put, organizers need sponsors that will invest dollars beyond their sponsorship fee to promote their sports event relationship in ways that build awareness, drive ticket sales, and promote the purchase of merchandise, among other beneficial

Operational Expenses
- Air travel
- Hotel accommodations
- Automobile rentals
- Fuel
- Office space
- Computers and I.T. equipment
- Office supplies
- Electronics (e.g., televisions, cameras, and video equipment)
- Mobile devices and service
- Staff and volunteer wardrobe
- Catering and refreshments (e.g., bottled water and soft drinks)
- Legal, medical, financial, and other professional services
- Construction materials

Direct Event Expenses
- Sport-specific equipment (e.g., balls, bats, gloves, sticks, and motor oil)
- Uniforms, footwear, and performance gear
- Protective gear and equipment
- Timing equipment
- Locker room products
- Athlete participation gifts

Marketing Expenses
- Broadcast advertising time
- Digital and print advertising space
- Outdoor advertising space (e.g., billboards and mass transit advertising)
- Website and app development
- Printing and posters
- Fan giveaways and premiums

Figure 6.3 Typical Sports Event VIK Opportunities

activities (thus, "activation" of their sponsorship). The sponsor can similarly use the event to attract more customers to its brands or increased business through its association with the event. These might include the placement of event-themed advertising, in-store displays, ticket and merchandise giveaways, experiential enhancements at the event, and more. The organizer, as a result, can enjoy the benefits of significant additional exposure through these associated *activations*.

Sponsors apply their own activation strategies to create content that adds value to the events they support while engaging directly with the fan for their own marketing purposes. The traditional "sponsor village," an area set aside at events for sponsors to showcase products in a series of tents, kiosks, or table displays, is increasingly replaced by customized attractions throughout the event site that encourage fan participation. Sponsors have discovered that they can best engage with fans attending a sports event by acknowledging and marketing to their passion—the sport itself. As a result, many companies now sponsor experiential attractions, engaging live content that can make the event better.

Sponsor activation is an essential component of what makes the event–sponsor partnership so powerful because of how effective it is in achieving the objectives of both parties. According to Jim Andrews of IEG, a Chicago-based authority on event sponsorship and the publisher of IEG Sponsorship Report, sponsors generally allocate between $1.40 and $1.90 in activation spending for every dollar they spend on sponsorship fees. For some smaller events, sponsors offer organizers "activation-only" associations, guaranteeing an event valuable advertising and promotion not otherwise available or affordable to the organizer. For the sponsor, this strategy can be an effective way of financing its partnership with an event by incorporating activation plans into their existing marketing budgets. Before an event organizer agrees to an activation-only deal, even if it provides outstanding media value, that organizer should evaluate whether the event's cash revenue goals can be met in other ways.

The ultimate objective of a sponsor's event activation strategies, of course, is to realize its own marketing objectives—winning new customers and selling more products. Event organizers, however, should work cooperatively with sponsors to provide effective platforms for promotional activity that can benefit both the event and its corporate partners.

Commitment to, or Prospect for, Continued Association

Although not as essential as cash or activation campaigns in the short term, it is almost always in the best interest of an organizer to sell the rights to more than a single year of an event as part of a sponsor's package of benefits. A multiyear deal reduces the expense and effort involved in selling every sponsorship annually and provides a degree of financial certainty for one or more succeeding years. (It is actually most beneficial if sponsorship terms for different sponsors are of varying lengths so that expiration dates are staggered over a range of years. In this way, the future of the event will not be endangered by the risk of having a single year in which every sponsorship must be renewed.) From the sponsor's perspective, a multiyear deal can provide the attractive benefit of price protection. The organizer of a successful event would be unable to increase the price of a sponsorship package beyond the terms of the contract for the years covered by the agreement.

The continuity of a sponsor's involvement in an event from year to year builds a stronger and more valuable association between the partners in the minds of the fans. To encourage multiyear support, sponsors can be offered various escape clauses in their agreements. Such provisions may include "the right of first refusal," whereby a sponsor must formally turn down renewal before a deal may be finalized with any other company. Alternatively, sponsors may be protected by a "right of first negotiation." Here, a potential renewal must be negotiated with the sponsor before any other company is even approached. Lastly, the "right to terminate" may be offered, permitting the sponsor or organizer to end the deal after the first event based on predetermined circumstances (e.g., failure of the organizer to reach a defined attendance plateau, or the sponsor to achieve certain sales levels). These inclusions provide the parties with an explicit statement of intent indicating that both intend to continue the association while allowing for an amicable end if the partnership proves to be unsuccessful. See Figure 6.4 for a summary of benefits that organizers seek from sponsors.

- Revenue
- Cost avoidance (value in kind, or VIK)
- Activation
  - o Advertising
  - o Promotions
  - o Publicity
  - o Experiential attractions
- Commitment to, or prospect for a continued association

Figure 6.4 What Sports Event Organizers Really Want from Sponsors

What Sponsors Really Want from Sports Events

Although sponsors have differing motivations for their participation in a sports event and vary as to the value they place on the specific benefits they receive, what they do share is confidence in the strength of sponsorship as a powerful marketing tool. Of course, sponsorships are subject to the same economic, social, and political pressures as any other business activity, experiencing slower growth during turbulent times. They have, however, been proven to be powerful and effective marketing tools because they are complex, multidisciplinary, multisensory, engaging, and, when properly activated, motivational. To attendees and guests, a sports event may be enjoyed as a competitive contest, a live entertainment event, a media broadcast, a social activity, or a meeting place to strengthen business ties. To a sponsor, they can be all of these, plus targeted and high-impact advertising vehicles, promotional platforms, sampling opportunities, sales generators, forums for customer interactivity, and even fundraisers for a company's charitable endeavors.

Figure 6.5 lists some of the most common sponsor benefits that partner companies seek from sports events. The first four—exposure, customer hospitality, sales opportunities, and fundraising for corporate causes—are measurable sponsor benefits that may be derived directly from an event. Every sponsor's needs are different. The organizer should carefully consider how a prospective partner will value each type of benefit in order to design a sponsorship package that will achieve optimal success and return on investment (see Play 7). This is particularly important because prospective sponsors already have their own strategies on how sports events fit into their marketing portfolio and how they will evaluate the opportunities that work best for them.

Associative benefits reinforce the effectiveness of the more direct benefits, and can add considerable intangible value to the relationship between a sponsor and an event. As will be further described in this chapter, the associative benefit of pass-through rights can offer sponsors tangible cost savings, as well as the impression of a strong relationship with an event in the minds of their customers.

Direct Sponsor Benefits

- Exposure
  - In-event advertising
  - Out of venue advertising
  - Social media and other online advertising
  - Product placement
  - Promotions
  - Publicity (media coverage and social media engagements)
- Customer hospitality
  - Event tickets
  - Reception/party invitations
- Sales opportunities
  - Direct on-site, retail, and online sales
  - Product demonstrations
  - Sampling opportunities
  - Database access (e.g., lists of attendees, survey respondents, and mailing lists)
- Fundraising for corporate causes

Associative Benefits

- Exclusivity
- Ownership (*de facto* or perceived)
- Prestige and reputation
- Pass-through rights

Figure 6.5   What Sponsors Really Want from Sports Events

Exposure—Advertising and Promotion

For new and emerging products and companies, exposure is frequently one of the most valuable components of the event sponsorship experience. Most established companies also recognize the value of exposing their brands at sports events to rise above their competitors. Exposure opportunities at sports events abound and are most often manifest in advertising, promotion, and publicity programs, all basic and familiar pillars of the traditional marketing mix.

SIDELINE STORY

Citizens Bank and the New York Roadrunners Club

The New York City market is one of the most competitive in the United States, especially when it comes to financial services companies. To enter this potentially lucrative market, a new competitor must differentiate itself from businesses with brands long-established in the region. Citizens Bank, headquartered in Rhode Island, acquired the locations of two smaller banks in the New York Metropolitan Area, but desired to capture market share from more established financial institutions such as Chase and Citibank. To demonstrate their commitment to the community, Citizens became a major sponsor of the New York Roadrunners Club, the organizers of the New York City Marathon. In addition to becoming a "top tier sponsor" of this nationally recognized race, Citizens Bank became the first-ever title sponsor of the Queens 10K. Citizens Bank branding appeared on signage along the routes of both races, as well as in cheering sections it hosts outside select branches. The bank's vice chair disclosed at the announcement of the partnership that enhanced brand awareness would be the initial measurement used to evaluate the company's return on investment.

Advertising opportunities are among the oldest forms of purchased exposure at sports events. It is widely accepted that repetition of advertising aids in consumer recall. However, some singular advertising opportunities at sports events can make lasting impressions because, in effect, they are repetitive. Even static advertising signage within the audience's field of view may be seen repeatedly and over prolonged periods of time, not only by fans in the stadium, but also those watching on various media. Once a traditional commercial has aired, its impact begins to dissipate. Advertising opportunities at an event, however, can deliver impressions continuously and with varying impact throughout the hours spectators are in the venue. On television, a single advertising location in the event venue comes into and out of view repeatedly throughout the program. Sponsors and their agencies have been measuring this effect for many years. Simply, the number of signage impressions, whether physically present or digitally inserted, can be multiplied by the number of seconds it is visible on the broadcast. This philosophy can be extended, as well, to a live audience. The most valuable advertising location will be in the place that the spectators are looking the most often.

Advertising signage at sports events may be reinforced by other forms of a sponsor's advertising, promotions, and messages during the event. Public address announcements that recognize a partner company or product, accompanied by logos displayed on the video scoreboard provide additional repetition and may aid in spectators' recall of the brand. With the audience already familiar and receptive to a sponsor's message, on-field or in-stand promotions associated with the brand can be all the more effective.

Valuable advertising exposure may also be incorporated on the field of play, on score clocks and timing devices, static or electronic signage bordering the playing surface, at start and finish lines, and behind goals, player benches, dugouts, and penalty boxes. The relative value of each of these positions is, again, determined by the frequency with which signage is in the spectators' or television viewers' active field of vision. During competitive downtime, such as intermissions, and between heats, innings, or sets, special video features and promotions, and on-field fan activities, may be "presented by" a sponsor that is both visually and verbally recognized during the promotion.

SIDELINE STORY

The Opening Puck Drop on Mixed Reality Advertising

In 2022, Chipotle joined forces with Turner Sports, the NHL's Colorado Avalanche and creative agency The Famous Group to present the league's first mixed reality advertisement, staged at an intermission of the Stanley Cup Playoffs. While television viewers prepared for the intermission recap, the in-person audience was directed to watch the arena's video scoreboard. On the broadcast and on the screen, a virtual Chipotle-branded Zamboni towed an enormous burrito bowl onto the live image of the ice. Suddenly, the Zamboni turned to head for the stands as the ice began to shake and then break apart.

A giant hockey-gloved hand emerged from below and pulled the bowl beneath the surface. A few moments later, the glove re-appeared to search the "shattered" surface of the ice for the giant fork that had been knocked off the top of the bowl. This blend of advertising and light-hearted entertainment added to both the fan experience and recall of the sponsor's "Real Food for Real Athletes" message. Thanks to the ad's humorous creativity, it also generated hundreds of thousands of additional impressions through a variety of social media platforms posted by the company, the team, and fans after the game.

A sponsor's exposure benefits can also extend well before and beyond event day, in event advertising and in media purchased by the sponsors themselves to fulfill their activation strategies. Event advertising may acknowledge just a primary, title, or presenting sponsor, or may include a rotating list of other participating companies. Event promotions that help to sell tickets and offer discounts with the purchase of sponsor products can provide both exposure and sales opportunities as direct benefits of sponsorship. Many event organizers also express appreciation for their sponsors' participation in postevent "thank you" ads and posts. This is a particularly effective practice when the ad is placed alongside the postevent editorial coverage of the event.

Online advertising provides sponsors with the opportunity to engage fans by strategically linking to the event's most-visited web pages. Sponsors don't just want to be noticed on the event's website. They want those ad placements to provide links to their own websites, promotions, virtual product demonstrations, and direct sales platforms. The placement of these interactive ads can also be strategic. Restaurants might be most noticed on the webpage that provides directions to the event site, with a click-through to their menu or a special code for savings on the way to or from the event. Banks and financial services companies might enjoy the most targeted exposure by advertising on the page where fans can order event tickets or merchandise, providing a click-through to apply for a new credit card.

Interactive advertising may also be included on event apps to enhance the fan experience. Downloaded before or during an event, apps provide content such as maps and guides, schedule information, competition or tournament rules, athlete and team information, background features, and other content. Advertising on these platforms might connect directly to a sponsor's website, a special offer, or provide information on where to find the sponsor's attraction, sampling, or demonstration area at the event site.

Exposure—Product Placement

One of the most valuable and sought-after sponsorship opportunities is the benefit of product placement. Sponsors attach great importance to the notion that their products, to the exclusion of any competitors, are those that will be used by the sports event organizer or are available to the public at, or through, the event. Food, beverage, and beer sponsors will require their brands be available at every possible sales location in the venue. Apparel manufacturers will likewise insist that their merchandise be available at the event site or affixed with the event's logo. A cap manufacturer will want to see its logo on the event caps worn by athletes during press conferences. Any product category that can be imagined to be useful in preparing for and executing an event is likely to have a product placement provision tied into the sponsorship deal—from airlines, car rentals, and hotels to telecommunications services, computers, and office equipment. In a spirit of partnership, of course, the event organizer can negotiate for preferred pricing on these products and services or accept some portion of an event's requirements as part of a VIK arrangement. Product placement requirements may also involve other manifestations unique to the product category. Examples include soft drink sponsor names on beverage cups and reusable plastic bottles, the use of sponsor vehicles in and around the event venue, and staff wardrobe displaying logos that integrate the event and the manufacturer. On NFL sidelines at the time of this writing, coaches and officials view replays on Microsoft Surface tablets and communicate with the quarterback using sponsor-branded headsets, while Gatorade-branded coolers provide hydration for the players, all of whom wear Nike-branded jerseys.

Sponsors often provide products or services for consumer sweepstakes, promotions, and even awards for the athletes to create excitement and exposure at the event and in publicity generated immediately following. A lucky fan may win an all-expenses-paid trip to a future event provided by an airline and hotel sponsor. The "Most Valuable Player" at the Super Bowl wins a vehicle presented postgame by the NFL's automotive sponsor. These benefits provide sponsors with exposure opportunities that are even more powerful than advertising, serving as an endorsement that demonstrates the event's strong preference for using a particular sponsor's product. The most innovative and compelling of these promotions can also even add entertainment value and media interest in the event.

SIDELINE STORY

KIA's Product Placement Coup

The NBA All-Star Weekend's Slam Dunk Championship has been a fan- and viewer-favorite for many years. NBA players vie for top honors with stylish, gravity-defying acrobatic stunts evaluated by judges and the fans. The 2011 edition of the Sprite Slam Dunk Championship was particularly memorable for the winning basket and for the marketing bonanza that followed. In the final round of the event, Los Angeles Clippers forward Blake Griffin eclipsed runner-up JaVale McGee of the Washington Wizards by successfully jumping over the hood of a silver Kia Optima automobile on his way to the hoop for a spectacular slam dunk.

According to CNBC.com, online car sales marketplace Edmunds.com reported that potential car buyers "were 20 percent more likely to consider a Kia car, and twice as likely to consider the Optima model the day after the broadcast." Not wasting any time, the Korean automobile manufacturer created a television commercial incorporating the stunt immediately after the event. The positive publicity generated by this clever product placement effort continued for several months, culminating with an online auction of the car actually used in the Slam Dunk Championship to benefit "Stand Up to Cancer."

Exposure—Publicity

Sponsors spend millions of dollars each year to generate publicity for their products because they know that media coverage is generally perceived by the public as more objective and credible and holds the public's attention for a longer period of time than a typical advertisement. The most effective way for a company to consistently capitalize on the publicity generated by a sports event is to literally appear within its name, as a *title* or *presenting* sponsor. Title sponsors (also known as naming rights sponsors) are brands whose names appear before or within the identity of a sports event, such as tennis's *BNP Paribas Open*, NASCAR's *Coca-Cola 600*, the NHL's *Discover Winter Classic*, or golf's *FedEx Cup*. Presenting sponsors, companies with identities linked to the end of an event name, such as the *Arnold Palmer Invitational presented by Mastercard*, the *NCAA Men's Final Four presented by Capital One*, and the *TCS New York City Marathon Expo presented by New Balance* (note the latter's combination of a title and presenting sponsor), also hope to increase their public exposure through a close association with the name of the event. Companies that invest heavily in title and presenting sponsorships recognize the publicity value offered by their elevated association, appreciating the likelihood that their brand will be routinely mentioned in news reports and sports articles during the normal coverage of an event. Title and presenting sponsorships command premium sponsorship fees because of the added value of the enhanced public recognition the partner receives. These top-tier sponsors benefit from the inclusion of their identities within event logos and/or word marks, in advertising, on tickets, in information forwarded to participants and guests, and on virtually all printed and digital material generated by the organizer.

Title and presenting sponsorships supported by the sponsor's activation budgets tend to reach deepest into the public consciousness. Sponsors often participate in intriguing and engaging team, player, and fan promotions that capture the imagination and active interest of the media and the public. Significant donations made to a worthy cause as a component of a sports event sponsorship can generate enhanced media interest, as well. Insurance company Liberty Mutual, for example, sponsored a "Million Dollar Game" promotion, offering a hefty financial donation to the charity of choice for qualifying college football teams that competed in a regular season game without a single penalty call. Funds may also be raised as a donated percentage of ticket sales, through silent auctions, via contributions made by fans or viewers and matched by the sponsor, or as a percentage of sponsor product sales during a specified period of time.

Watching an average spectator attempt a difficult athletic feat for an impressive cash prize, such as a "Million Dollar Shot," has been a popular feature of major televised sports events. These sponsored promotions are frequently designed as "insurance prizes" to keep the sponsor's costs within reason. That is, since the odds of someone winning the prize is low (but not zero), the sponsor can purchase an insurance policy to protect against the possibility of having to pay the enormous sum. Several agencies specialize in offering sponsors and organizers insurance prize policies, with premiums ranging from 10 to 50 percent of the prize value, depending on the difficulty of the contest. The insurance agency will require involvement in the setting of contest rules to ensure there is a very good probability that the contestant will fail. The less difficult the test of skill and the greater value of the payoff, the higher the insurance premium will be. Alternatively, the sponsor can self-insure the prize by setting aside the full amount in advance if it desires to better the odds that a contestant will succeed.

SIDELINE STORY

Chick-fil-A's Free Throw Promotion

The 2022–23 season was a great time to be a fan of the NBA's Philadelphia 76ers, and a dangerous time to be a chicken. Thanks to team sponsor Chick-fil-A, if an opponent missed two consecutive free throws in the second half of any game, fans across the city were entitled to redeem a free 6-piece order of chicken nuggets using the sponsor's app. Fans were able to take advantage of this unique "Bricken for Chicken" promotion nine times during the season, consuming more than a half million free nuggets. One game entitled fans to a 12-piece order when the opposing team missed back-to-back free throws an improbable three times in a single game. More than 19,000 fans came to Chick-fil-A locations in the Philadelphia area to claim their prize.

Customer Hospitality

Companies have long regarded sports events as excellent opportunities to extend hospitality and demonstrate appreciation to customers and important clients, dealers, distributors, franchisees, agents, and top salespeople. These benefits enhance relationships between customers and those sponsors providing access to the events, help sponsors turn prospects into customers, and assist companies to close business deals faster. Customer hospitality is of particular importance to companies that transact most of their business with other businesses (commonly known as "B2B" companies). The average monetary value of a business-to-business (B2B) sale by a company to its customer can be significantly greater than that of a sale from a business to a consumer. Therefore, the marketing efforts and dollars B2B companies apply to developing each new customer, and servicing existing ones, are often much greater than those of consumer companies. The experiential aspects of event sponsorship—that is, the ability to host prospects and reward current customers—is of increased importance and often a greater focus on sponsorship activation strategies for B2B companies. Treating special guests with tickets for preferred seating locations, passes to private receptions or invitation-only hospitality suites, the ability to meet the athletes, and other exclusive opportunities can put B2B sponsors at a great advantage over their competition.

Sales Opportunities

Sponsors that have invested significantly in the success of a sports event expect that organizers will provide them with opportunities to offset some of their costs with sales. Most often, these objectives are achieved by engaging in on-site activities such as product demonstrations, sampling, couponing, or giveaways of premium items such as collectibles. Organizers who actively help a sponsor sell more of its products at an event are actually helping themselves. The more business a sponsor can develop at an event, whether through direct sales or as leads to develop new customers, the more likely the company will deem the investment a success and want to continue their partnership.

Sports event venues offer an attractive marketplace for direct sales of some sponsor products, the most common being food, beverages, apparel, and memorabilia. Other products and services may also offer special event-day sales promotions, such as team-associated "affinity" credit cards, or limited-time discounts for online purchases. Recognizing the highly motivated viewing habits of sports fans, streaming services may offer special trial subscriptions or upgrades to fans. Many organizers offer sponsors product demonstration locations and sampling on the facility's public concourses, from kiosks sprinkled through the event site, or special tents or booths in fan festival areas.

Marketers understand that sports events are effective places to reach their customers because attendee demographics are generally predictable and fans are in a highly excited, and therefore receptive, state of mind. The more a sponsor can associate its product with the event through engaging activations, the better it can leverage that excitement and receptivity to influence sales.

SIDELINE STORY

MasterCard's Major League Sponsorship

MasterCard's long-standing relationship with Major League Baseball provides the credit card brand with a wide variety of opportunities to leverage its sponsorship and engage with fans, small businesses, and worthy causes. Marketing partners since 1997, the brand is the presenting sponsor of the MLB All Star Game, a central cornerstone of its "Priceless" campaign. Fans using their credit card for admission to Play Ball Park, the league's fan festival, are permitted to enter an hour early to avoid long lines at the event's most popular attractions. Both partners worked with local businesses to promote the use of MasterCard's "tap to pay" technology at MLB's Food Truck Row. The sponsor also offered a sweepstakes for the "unique experience" of walking the All-Star player red carpet before the pregame festivities, and then getting up close to the players as they arrived from the best spots along the carpet. During the game itself, MasterCard sponsored the "Stand Up to Cancer" audience and player participation promotion featured live in the stadium and on the national broadcast. Through their association with the program since 2010, MasterCard has helped to raise more than $65 million for the cause.

Fundraising for Corporate Causes

Sports events offer outstanding opportunities for doing good beyond the stadium gates. Some socially conscious companies combine their commercial involvement in a sports event with an effort to raise awareness and revenue for important causes and quality-of-life social programs.

Many sports event organizations are themselves not-for-profit associations that exist to promote a particular sport, lifestyle, or quality-of-life benefit. The International Special Olympics, the New York Road Runners Club, the many national governing bodies, Little League, and hundreds of other not-for-profit sports associations are also organizers that stage sports events to promote their movements and messages. Sponsor dollars are required to make their events possible, and most of their business models include raising needed revenues to fund operations, awareness programs, research and development, and other cause-related activities. Some events, like the *AIDS Walk New York*, are activities staged exclusively to achieve philanthropic and social missions, the event providing a compelling backdrop for the worthy cause.

Sponsors understand the enormous public relations benefits of funding cause-related activities. Many reinforce their marketing investments with additional grants from their philanthropic budgets to ensure a sizable return for a charity. In addition to sustaining their good intentions, many corporate supporters still want to take advantage of the rightfully attendant sponsor benefits that are due them as sponsors.

The benefits of being associated with a not-for-profit cause or movement are well understood by event organizers, as well. It is often the charitable aspect of an event that spurs ticket buyers into action and can overcome one of the key components of a ticket-buyer's hesitation—price sensitivity. As long as the cost of admission remains within a range that is not completely unreasonable, members of the ticket-buying public will respond more favorably to an event whose proceeds benefit a charity with which they feel some affinity. Charitable objectives are especially helpful in generating ticket buyers—as well as participants.

Associative Benefits—Exclusivity

With a few exceptions, business partners expect that their financial participation in an event will buy them some level of exclusivity—the ability to promote their company or brand without the presence of their competition. This is not universally true, as in the case of motorsports, in which the participants are individually sponsored by companies that may conflict with the sponsors of the overall event. In most cases, however, exclusivity is highly valued and aggressively protected. Sponsors expect that once they enter into an agreement with a sports event, the organizer will no longer be able to accept revenues from any other company or brand within their defined and protected product category.

SIDELINE STORY

Navigating Sponsor Exclusivity in an Industry-Dominant Market

The NFL's Super Bowl has been played in domed stadiums in the Detroit metropolitan area twice, once in 1982 and again in 2005. As the headquarters city of the three largest American car manufacturers, the local host committee recognized the opportunity to engage the entire industry in the celebration of the Super Bowl's return. As the sponsor of the league and event, General Motors (GM) enjoyed exclusive product placement and promotional benefits, including the NFL's use of Super Bowl-branded Cadillac SUVs as courtesy vehicles for players, coaches, and staff, the awarding of a sponsor vehicle to the game's Most Valuable Player, the use of tickets for sweepstakes and dealer hospitality, and the authorized use of NFL and Super Bowl logos in product advertising. The game was staged at Ford Field, the exclusive naming rights partner of the stadium and the host team. By virtue of their relationship with the stadium, Ford was entitled to use their suite and purchase tickets, but were not permitted to use them in promotions, nor did they have access to any of the NFL's intellectual property (e.g., event names or logos). Chrysler, now Stellantis, had similar access to purchase tickets, but under the same restrictions. All three companies, however, served on the board of the host committee, and provided funding to help support local events celebrating the season's finale mega event.

When a corporate partner enters into an agreement with an event organizer, the contract should define the exact identity being granted sponsorship rights. For example, is it the company being recognized as an official sponsor (e.g., Anheuser-Busch), or a specific brand (e.g., Bud Light)? Because many companies market multiple brands and products, the agreement should also identify the categories of exclusivity protected by the sponsorship. For example, the corporate parent of a soft drink sponsor may also distribute snack foods or own franchises of fast food, or quick-service, restaurants (QSRs). Sponsors often seek to prohibit the event organizer from entering into relationships with companies that compete with their other businesses. Organizers, in turn, often respond by seeking to negotiate a higher sponsorship fee as recompense for the lost opportunities that would be forced by excluding these other business categories from a possible event partnership.

The sponsor's exclusive rights must also be protected in sales promotions, advertising, and other activities that take place before the event or outside of the facility. Organizers are expected to pursue the perpetrators of "ambush marketing" activities, efforts undertaken by competitor companies to give the impression of being associated with an event. Common ambush marketing activities include the unauthorized use of an event's name, logos and images, or the use of terminology and artwork simply suggestive of an association with the event. Illicit techniques include the unauthorized use of event tickets for promotional purposes, the creation and sale of unlicensed merchandise, and advertising that implies a relationship with an event even without using any of the organizer's trademarks. Organizers with the resources to protect themselves and their intellectual property (i.e., logos, trademarks, artwork, etc.), frequently retain legal help to stop ambush marketing activities that infringe on the rights of an event and its sponsors. The most common response is to quickly identify the infringer and to have legal representatives send a "cease and desist" notice. This is a letter from an attorney that outlines the infraction and instructs the ambusher to cease such activities or risk legal action. It is often sufficient to stop blatant trademark infractions. It is important that an attorney handle these communications and to be prepared to take the complaint to the courts if necessary, to demonstrate to sponsors that their promotional rights are being actively protected.

Not all ambush activities are blatant infringements of an organizer's intellectual property rights. Over the years, many non-sponsor companies have identified legal ways to benefit from sports events without participating as a sponsor. Although the authors do not condone such activities, as they do not accrue to the benefit of the event, it is important to understand how some non-sponsors take advantage of these opportunities. For example, non-sponsor companies can stage private parties, receptions, meetings, or customer-oriented programs during the days leading up to and during an event as long as they do not infer a direct relationship and use no intellectual property of the organizer. There is nothing wrong, for instance, for a restaurant to post "Welcome Fans" signage, or for an electronics retailer to offer a special event week sale on televisions so long as they do not use the name, logo, or artwork of the event.

Non-sponsor companies also sometimes seek permits to erect tents for parties, hospitality, or product sampling and demonstrations close to event sites, counting on the greatly increased number of fans and passersby in the area before, during, and after events. It is to the benefit of the organizer and its sponsors to work with the host city on establishing a "clean zone" ordinance that prohibits this publicly visible, opportunistic activity in the immediate area around the event site. Many large cities accustomed to hosting events already have some form of ordinance in existence that can be applied or modified for this purpose. Local ordinances may also limit the degree to which advertising or event signage can be added to temporary structures, or to permanent structures on surfaces not usually used for advertising. Establishing and protecting clean zones can add great value to a sponsorship package.

Billboards and other advertising locations near the event site are rentable by anyone, including companies that are not sponsors. Organizers should be sure to identify billboards that are in clear view of an event site and encourage sponsors to lease them in order to block competitors from these attractive advertising locations. One of the most bedeviling developments facing event organizers is the increasing frequency with which event sponsors and the marketing partners of a host venue are direct competitors. Conflicts between facility signage advertisers and competitive event sponsors are not new. The economically necessary practice of facilities renaming themselves, or sections of their building after one or more major sponsors, however, has created many more noticeable and high-stakes conflicts with event sponsors.

The economic realities of the sports facilities business have resulted in the common practice of selling title sponsorship of new and existing sports venues to a corporate partner. This partnership is highly valuable to both the owner of the venue and the sponsor that buys the right to name it. The sponsor often contributes millions of dollars over the term of its contract to help finance construction or reduce some of the debt incurred during the development of the facility. In return, the sponsor knows that thousands of social media posts, sports reports, and game broadcasts will make regular and frequent reference to the name of the facility. Millions of ticket buyers who enter the building will also be surrounded by the name and logo of the presenting sponsor on signage, tickets, scoreboards, even highway signs directing drivers to its parking lots. There is probably no more positive way for a sponsor to become a household byword than by lending its name to one of a community's most exciting gathering places.

How does this level of ubiquitous corporate identification affect a sports event organizer's ability to protect their own sponsors' rights? Like many relationships, it's complicated. A sports event's existing sponsor that competes with the naming rights partner of a facility will be rightfully concerned that the building sponsor will receive greater publicity exposure than it will. Since the namesake sponsor of a sports event facility will enjoy thousands of incidental references in the media, it correctly presumes that this recognition will provide additional exposure benefits before the fans of all visiting events. A naming rights sponsor knows that its over-arching presence can also effectively discourage competitor companies from entering into agreements with event organizers leasing the venue, further protecting its exclusivity. Naming sponsors, therefore, commonly believe there is often no need to participate as sponsors of teams or events inside their facility.

SIDELINE STORY

Let's Meet at the Game. Where Is That Again?

Sports events organizers can usually count on modern host facilities being maintained in good structural condition. What a stadium or arena might be called on event day, however, can be different from the name on the day the lease was signed. Sports events used to be held in places with romantic names like Boston Garden and Jack Murphy Stadium, the Montreal Forum, and Mile High Stadium. Boston Garden is gone and replaced by a new arena that was called Shawmut Center until just weeks before its opening but changed to Fleet Center named for the northeastern US bank that acquired the original sponsor company. Fleet Center became TD Banknorth Center after those two banks merged, and a few years later, simply TD Garden. Jack Murphy Stadium remains standing, and was renamed Qualcomm Stadium after the wireless chip maker in its hometown of San Diego, California. The stadium was temporarily renamed Snapdragon Stadium to promote Qualcomm's mobile processor in an effort to reach an estimated 30 million television viewers during the 2011 college football bowl season. It has since been replaced with a new stadium of the same name.

The venerated Montreal Forum, built in 1924, could not withstand the growing economic pressures of the sports and entertainment business and was replaced in 1996 by an entirely new facility called the Molson Centre, later renamed the Bell Centre a few short years later. Mile High Stadium was razed and its replacement, Invesco Field at Mile High, created a furor that mobilized both the business and political communities in Denver, Colorado. The controversy was not caused because the old building was destroyed, but because the name of the new stadium was co-branded with a sponsor. Perhaps reflective of the community's sensitivity, for the first three years of the stadium's existence, the *Denver Post* referred to the facility only as Mile High Stadium. Less than a decade later, the stadium was renamed Sports Authority Field at Mile High, after the locally based sporting goods retailer, and later, Empower Field at Mile High.

Miami's football and entertainment facility, opened under the name Joe Robbie Stadium, and may have one of the longest histories of brand identities. In addition to bearing the name of the original owner of the NFL Miami Dolphins, the building has been known as Pro Player Stadium after a now-defunct sporting goods licensee, Dolphins Stadium, Dolphin Stadium, one year as Landshark Stadium, identified with the late musician Jimmy Buffett's beer brand, and Sun Life Stadium just before hosting a Super Bowl, named for a Canadian insurance company. Sun Life has since exited the US market, and the venue is now known as Hard Rock Stadium.

Event organizers should not be surprised if their sponsor values an event less overall at a venue named for one of its direct competitors, and the agreement between the sponsor and organizer may anticipate such circumstances and remedies. The event sponsor may avoid using the program for customer hospitality. They may seek a reduced sponsorship fee or more opportunities away from the event site. For sponsors of televised events, they may push for more on-air visibility and commercial time. Whatever accommodation is made, there is little question that event sponsors will be uncomfortable in buildings with a competitive naming rights partner. It is up to the event organizer to provide additional value to overcome this understandable uneasiness.

Apart from building naming rights arrangements, sports facilities enjoy a large number of other partnerships of varying magnitude, ranging from gate, section, concourse, and club sponsors, to official soft drinks and beers, to advertisers entitled to physical or electronic signage. Some facility sponsors may also pose significant conflicts for event sponsors, especially in the case of soft drinks and other products or services that may have exclusive rights in the building. In most cases, however, event sponsors have become accustomed to sports event facilities that contain pre-existing advertising signage, some of which may conflict with their own.

Many stadium and arena operators have the flexibility to allow organizers to cover, replace, or re-program signage belonging to some of their sponsors on a case-by-case basis, especially if an event of sufficient magnitude and potential profitability requires it. Even in such rare cases, the identity of the facility's naming rights sponsor is usually respected. Beyond prohibiting the obstruction of some existing sponsor signage and displays and insisting on pouring official beverages from their concessions (specifically soft drinks and beer), most facilities will put few restrictions on event organizers. The sponsor that has purchased the naming rights to its building understands that it is in the venue's best interest to encourage organizers to book events there, even those with competing sponsors.

Associative Benefits—Ownership

As may be expected, the greater a sponsor's financial commitment, the more protective it will be about how its company or product will be perceived, even compared with all others that are associated with the event. Sponsors will expect the organizers to protect them from excessive "clutter," a condition in which there are so many sponsors that the impact of their event identification is greatly diminished. To rise above the clutter of their fellow event partners, sponsors strive to develop unique and innovative promotions or to pursue an association with specific event elements they can "own" exclusively. Such elements may include being the presenting sponsor of a championship trophy, an MVP ("most valuable player") award, or some other form of participant recognition. Intermission or halftime entertainment, pregame shows, individual heats, races, or competitions, or in-venue promotions that benefit one or more fans are other components commonly offered to corporate partners that seek to rise above the sponsorship clutter, even if only for a few moments during the program.

Some companies in non-sports industries have taken event ownership to its purest form by developing, owning, and, in some cases, managing sports events themselves. Although the expense of assuming responsibility for all costs and risk is considerable, this strategy provides total control over every aspect of an event's development, management, and execution. Every element of the event may be fashioned to the exact specifications of the corporate owner, to target fans of the precise demographics it seeks, and to maintain a singular focus on its own goals and objectives. They may still provide opportunities for sponsorship and cross-promotions with other brands to help defray some of the costs. The company can customize sponsorship programs for its own business partners that can maximize sales opportunities for both. A soft drink company that owns its own sports event, for instance, might offer an opportunity for participation to a QSR to whom that company itself is a supplier. In this example, promoting the restaurants has the secondary effect of increasing consumption of the company's own products at those locations. As owner of the event, the company can limit consumer-directed activities to promotions that most effectively market its sports property, best enhance its product sales, and control the clutter of too many advertising messages competing for the audience's attention.

SIDELINE STORY

Red Bull as a Sports Event Owner–Sponsor

Red Bull's imaginative lifestyle, music, and sports events bring to life its cutting-edge event ownership strategy to live audiences and viewers on digital and broadcast media worldwide. Many of its sports events are unique to its brand, such as the Red Bull Megaloop, a kite-surfing competition, and Red Bull Campus Clutch esports tour. Many of these events were distributed virally on digital platforms and occasionally incorporate additional sponsors beyond Red Bull.

In 2006, the company purchased the MetroStars, Major League Soccer's (MLS) New York area franchise, and renamed the club the New York Red Bulls, which has attracted other major sponsors such as Honda. Red Bull Media House, the company's media division, covers more than 1,250 sports and cultural events in 160 countries each year, on digital, linear, and print platforms, ensuring that its brand continues to have top-of-mind relevance to the young and active audience that buys its products.

The advantages of corporate event ownership are clear. By controlling every aspect of the program, the corporate owner can ensure its dominance and avoid or manage the effects of multiple sponsor messages and clutter. Smaller-scale, precisely targeted niche events are prime candidates for corporate ownership because of their manageable cost and the simplicity of measuring their effectiveness. Grassroots and community programs involving local amateur athletes offer similarly attractive opportunities for corporate ownership by small local businesses for the same reasons—low costs more easily paid for with incremental sales.

Corporate ownership of large-scale, high-budget events has not become as prevalent for a host of reasons (see "Red Bull" Sideline Story for an exception). The financial and legal liability risks are usually too great for a single company to want to assume. This is why sports event organizers develop opportunities to attract multiple sponsors from a wide range of industries. An athlete's personal endorsement contracts can also prove to be another obstacle to a corporation owning a sports event. Genuine, strategic, and effective partnerships between event organizers and corporate sponsors remain the most common business model standard.

Associative Benefits—Prestige and Reputation

Another intangible benefit sought by sponsors is being associated with an event considered highly attractive by their most valued customers. The prestige and reputation of an event, its participating athletes, and its organizing entity can add significantly to its appeal. The greater the public's interest in an event, the greater the hunger will be for tickets. The greater the demand for tickets, the more desirable the event will be for sponsors to entertain their important business guests. Prestige also adds to the effectiveness of consumer promotions and efforts that increase the likelihood of media coverage.

Pass-through Rights

Some sponsors depend on the advertising or promotional efforts of other companies to bring their products to the consumer, such as retailers, media outlets, and credit card brands, among others. These companies sometimes seek pass-through rights to help make their event partnerships more affordable and efficient. Pass-through rights refer to the transference by a sponsor of some of its event benefits to its suppliers, distributors, retailers, advertisers, or other business partners. Such rights, however, can lead to serious misunderstandings if their limits and restrictions are not clearly defined.

When a sponsor requests the inclusion of pass-through rights, what it really wants is to be able to offer a portion of its contracted entitlements to a third party in exchange for valuable consideration.

An electronics manufacturer, for example, may desire to offer pass-through rights to an electronics retail chain in return for that retailer providing advertising, in-store sales, and preferred aisle placement or point-of-purchase displays featuring their products and a joint association with the sports event.

Media partners are particularly aggressive in pursuing pass-through rights. Being able to offer existing advertisers some limited benefit flowing from their association with an event often helps media sponsors offset their sponsorship fees, whether they are paid in cash or with the value of free advertising space or time. (See Play 8 for a closer look at media relationships.) Event organizers should be judicious and selective in conferring pass-through rights to sponsors. When a third party agrees to an association with an event through a sponsor that passes rights to it, it is effectively removed from the universe of potential sponsors that can be solicited for revenues. After all, why would a company make a large investment to be a sponsor if it can pick and choose only the benefits it absolutely needs, passed through by an existing sponsor at a far lower cost? Perhaps more significantly, this practice could remove an entire category of sponsors from the organizer's list of potential targets. If a quick-service restaurant (QSR) enjoys an association with an event via pass-through rights from a sponsor (a soft drink company, for example), the event organizer would have a very difficult time selling a sponsorship to any other QSR. In addition, the event organizer must protect his or her current sponsors by guarding against the possibility of pass-through rights being offered to an existing partner's competitors. Much as is the case with guarding against ambush marketers, an organizer's vigilance against competitors, regardless of how they may come to associate with an event, is an essential component of what a sponsor pays for.

Pass-through rights, however, can be very advantageous to an event organizer if they provide potential for increased ticket sales, promotions, or exposure opportunities far beyond those otherwise available in the market. In the example just discussed, it may be that no QSR will make the commitment to support the event in cash. Working through the soft drink sponsor, however, the restaurant might agree to undertake promotions involving significant exposure for the event on tray liners, or with in-store posters, on-bag advertising, and app promotions. If the demographics of the event and the restaurant complement each other and there is a low probability of attracting a sponsor in the QSR category, there may be very good reason to accept a pass-through provision in the soft drink company's sponsorship agreement. The limits to which a sponsor will be permitted the right to pass through specific benefits should be clearly defined in its sponsorship agreement. It is also recommended that every proposed third-party relationship be reviewed by the event organizer, and that none be permitted unless specifically approved in advance and in writing by the organizer.

Know Your Sponsors' Needs

Armed with a familiarity of what sponsors generally seek from their sports event partnerships, it is now time to combine the organizer's sponsor revenue objectives with an understanding of what a specific prospective sponsor will want, need, and expect from its investment. As will be explored in Play 7, you will identify the inventory of benefits your event can provide to your partners and try to match those solutions to meeting their needs.

Many event organizers begin by creating standardized packages of benefits for prospective sponsors at a number of different investment levels, assigning the quantity and value of included features corresponding to the size of the proposed fee. Although presenting a package of consistent, predetermined benefits is often a good framework from which to start the sales planning process, every sponsor has different reasons for considering a sponsorship and differing needs. Customizing a benefits package based on intelligence about a prospective sponsor's needs is, therefore, most often a much more effective way to increase their interest and accelerate the closing of a deal.

To successfully customize a sponsorship package with the right components and in the right quantities requires an understanding of a prospective partner's business objectives, its target market, and their marketing strategies. Figure 6.6 provides a useful checklist of questions that can help sports event organizers better understand the businesses of their prospective sponsor partners and the customers they serve.

- Who are the company's customers?
  - Is most of their business with individual consumers (B2C) or with corporate clients (B2B)?
  - If they sell to both businesses and consumers, to whom do they want to direct their event marketing efforts?
  - What are the demographics (i.e., the objective statistical characteristics) of the customers they most want to speak to?
    - Age: Young, middle-aged, or senior citizens?
    - Marital status: Single, married, have children living in their household, or "empty nesters" (i.e., married with grown children living elsewhere)?
    - Disposable income: Modest, average, or appreciable?
    - Education: High school, college, graduate degree?
    - Home ownership: Rent, own, apartment, house?
    - Place of residence: Country, state, city/town?
  - What are the psychographics, or behavioral characteristics, of the company's target customers?
    - In what kinds of sports do they enjoy participating?
    - What kinds of sports events do they most often attend, and how frequently?
    - What kinds of sports do they enjoy watching or streaming on television?
    - How avid are they as fans? How engaged are they with the sport and its athletes or teams?
    - Do they purchase new products and emerging technologies soon after they are introduced ("innovators"), or after most others have adopted ("late majority")?
    - Do they enjoy an active lifestyle? What leisure activities do they pursue?
    - What other kinds of entertainment do they attend or watch?
    - What kind of music do they enjoy?
- What marketing and communications strategies does the sponsor use to appeal to its target customers? How does the company or brand differentiate itself from its competitors?
- Is the company's brand well established or new to the public? Is its market share declining or increasing?
- Does the prospective sponsor have a culture or reputation for innovation and creativity?
- What other sports events does the prospect sponsor?
  - How does it use these events to achieve their objectives?
  - What promotional benefits associated with these events has the company found successful?
- What does the prospective sponsor want to gain from a sports event relationship in general, and from this relationship in particular?
- With what events are their competitors associated? How successful have their competitors been in their event marketing efforts?
- Has the prospective sponsor reduced or eliminated its relationship with other events, and if so, why?
- How will the company evaluate the success of its association?

Figure 6.6 Getting to Know Your Prospective Sponsor and Its Customers

Once in possession of this intelligence, the organizer can determine whether the prospect company is a likely candidate for a sponsorship. Presuming the event presents a good opportunity for the prospect to reach its existing customers, as well as likely new ones, the organizer can be better prepared to design a program that provides solutions of the greatest and most relevant value. What kinds of benefits can the event organizer offer, and in what quantity, to help the sponsor realize its business objectives? Would it be better to load the relationship with more premium-location tickets, trade or consumer advertising, sales promotions, or event promotions with high customer appeal?

- Event tickets
- Moderate capacity, with few exclusive-access opportunities
- Consumer advertising
- Discount promotions
- Collectible giveaways
- Sweepstakes
- Direct sales opportunities
- Product sampling opportunities

Figure 6.7   Typical Sponsor Benefit Features for B2C Companies

- Premium event tickets
- Limited capacity, with greater exclusive access opportunities
- Business, trade, or specialty advertising and publicity
- High-value promotions
- Product demonstration opportunities
- Client hospitality opportunities

Figure 6.8   Typical Sponsor Benefit Features for B2B Companies

How can the event organizer meet the marketing objectives of the sponsor through experiential activation opportunities for fans at the event site? In what way can the event so effectively deliver results that the prospect might consider a relationship of greater scale, such as a title or presenting sponsorship? The organizer can decide to design both a presenting sponsor package as well as a less costly opportunity as options from which a sponsor may choose.

The specific needs of prospective sponsors and the event elements that can best meet their business objectives will vary widely from company to company. As there are fundamental differences between marketing practices most often employed by consumer-oriented businesses (also known as B2C companies) and those that sell their products and services to other businesses (B2B companies), the types of sponsor benefits they seek from their event relationships also tend to be different. Contrast the overall characteristics of the consumer company sponsor package described in Figure 6.7 with the comparable features of a typical B2B sponsor package illustrated in Figure 6.8. Keep in mind that even within these two categories, individual sponsor needs, objectives, and strategies may differ.

Consumer Products (B2C) Company Sponsor Benefits

Consumer products companies are those whose end users are individual customers. They market products they manufacture or sell at retail locations, with costs ranging from just a few cents to thousands of dollars—such as producers of candy bars, beer, mobile telephone carriers, makers of kitchen appliances and home electronics, real estate agencies, and automobile manufacturers. These types of companies commonly use event tickets to entertain their distributors, agents, wholesalers, retailers, and key executives, as well as for prizes in consumer sweepstakes and promotions. Their needs for exclusive access opportunities, such as "meet-and-greet" encounters with athletes and celebrities and passes to receptions and media events, are usually limited in quantity and offered as attractive consumer sweepstakes promotions.

As a marketer of products or services to the public, high-exposure advertising opportunities are usually most beneficial to consumer-oriented companies. These advertising benefits may include public address and scoreboard announcements, commercials aired on the facility's video screen, and display signage in public areas or on the playing surface. Acknowledgments and sponsor logo placement in advertising and social media posts placed by the organizer are also highly desirable elements for B2C companies. Sponsor commercials aired during television or radio coverage, or associated with the online streaming of sports events, is usually a key component of major B2C company sponsorship deals.

The exclusive right to engage in promotional activities directed toward ticket buyers and other consumers is highly attractive to these types of companies. Consumer-oriented promotions may include event merchandise or premium giveaways, ticket and/or travel sweepstakes, or discounts on admission or event merchandise. They may also feature opportunities to offer fans unique participatory activities, ranging from competing in trivia and skills contests to an honorary ceremonial role in the event (e.g., honorary batboy, honorary trainer, dropping of the first puck).

As outstanding opportunities for reaching fans directly, sports events are often activated by consumer products companies as direct sales and sampling opportunities, passing out full- or trial-sized samples or coupons to enjoy discounts at an associated retail location. Consumer product sponsors also frequently distribute premium items such as event posters, visors, or other souvenir items prominently sporting their company or brand logo. Giveaway items are usually distributed to attendees either entering or exiting the facility. Premiums like rally towels, foam fingers, and "thunder sticks" make great experiential elements for fans to utilize while cheering during the event. Most venues prefer giving away products that are not in-game enhancements upon exiting to ensure that samples do not become projectiles or generate trash. "Tabling," the ability to set up a table or kiosk for product sampling, direct sales, or demonstrations, is another form of direct interaction with the fan considered appealing by consumer product companies.

Business-to-Business (B2B) Company Sponsor Benefits

Companies that market their products or services to other businesses (B2B companies) may find many of the same benefits as attractive as B2C companies do, but frequently with different perspectives on their relative importance. The units of sale for B2B marketers are usually significantly higher in price and the purchasing decision-maker often a more highly educated, highly compensated individual—someone who probably could have afforded to purchase a ticket to the event. Therefore, the key attribute that contributes to providing a positive, exciting experience for that decision-making customer is exclusive access, something not available for purchase. This access begins with the best available event tickets. An allotment of premium seats—field level, club level, luxury suites, or a similar location in the event's host venue—is often an absolute requirement.

Exclusive access opportunities for a sponsor's VIP guests that are of even greater value to most B2B companies include "meet-and-greet" receptions—opportunities for a sponsor's guests to interact with athletes, celebrities and other VIPs—attendance at media events, and other behind-the-scenes inclusions that provide great experiential value for business marketers. These are the kinds of exciting experiences a company's clients could not obtain without a prestigious invitation from the B2B sponsor, and, as such, are sometimes considered "must include" components of the deal.

B2B companies may consider the inclusion of consumer advertising benefits extremely attractive, especially those that also market directly to consumers. Few will turn down the opportunity for in-event signage, or public address and video scoreboard acknowledgments, if only to reinforce their association with the event for their own guests in the stands. Many B2B companies also appreciate advertising placed in business or trade publications, on websites, and on feeds frequented by the decision-makers they most often market to.

Some B2B promotions may differ from those offered by consumer marketers in the average value of premiums, prizes, or awards. The sponsor may offer incentive awards, such as all-expense-paid trips to the event, to authorized dealers who reach a new plateau of sales. Premier quality merchandise such as authentic jerseys or leather event jackets may be offered as prizes to top performing sales representatives who achieve significant percentages above their quota, or to retailers who have outperformed expectations. Event tickets and promotional premiums of lesser value may be offered to new clients and existing business relationships. Promotions of reduced value may also provide incentives to clients that operate under ethical compliance regulations limiting what they may accept.

Product sampling opportunities often take the form of product demonstrations in a B2B sponsorship. Products for business clients may be too valuable to distribute for free, and their target market may represent only a small fraction of the total audience. Therefore, rather than marketing to the entire event audience, these sponsors target their invited guest list and other qualified attendees (such as individual purchasers of premium-priced tickets) for demonstrations and direct sales.

There is probably no more attractive opportunity to a B2B sponsor than making exclusive client hospitality options available. Receptions, parties, golf outings, luncheons, dinners, and walk-in hospitality suites provide sponsors with an occasion to interact with clients and future business prospects. As casual entertainment experiences that surround sports events, these insulated environments provide sales opportunities away from the clutter of other sponsors' messages and activities. Invitations to VIP experiences hosted by the event organizer are extremely valuable for client hospitality, although many sponsors will also host their own events for their guests, either at the event site or at a location nearby.

Forearmed with an understanding of how corporate partnerships can work to the advantage of both the sports event and its sponsors and recognizing the highly individualized needs of B2C and B2B marketers, the organizer can begin to formulate a program of benefits that will convert prospective partners into sponsors. Effective marketing starts by identifying these wants and needs, and determining how the power of a sports event can deliver measurable results to satisfy their sales objectives and exceed their business expectations.

Know Your Fans

A successful sponsorship program depends on similarities between an event's fan base and a sponsor's customers. The more alike they are, the more attractive a sponsorship will be to both partners (see Figure 6.9). As demonstrated in Figure 6.6, there are a range of demographic and psychographic, or attitudinal, metrics that marketers use to identify their most likely customers. Event organizers also need to know who their fans are not only to identify target sponsors, but also to develop effective advertising campaigns, design promotions, price and sell tickets, and select merchandise for sale.

Most companies will share basic customer demographics for the asking. As for the organizer, if you don't already have recent empirical data available on who your fans are, it is important to collect and analyze this information before approaching sponsors. You can collect this data at other events you stage, or at the next edition of the one for which you are planning to solicit sponsors. Two common methods are *intercept surveys* and *post-event surveys*. Intercept surveys collect data from fans at the event site. Literally, a staff member, or a market research agency representative, talks to fans at random to ask them questions and gather the responses. Post-event surveys collect data after the fan has left the building. The fan is either

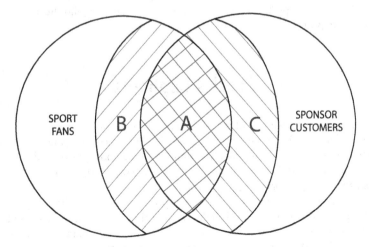

Figure 6.9 The Intersection of Sport Fans and a Sponsor's Customers

given a card with a QR code or is emailed a list of questions soon after the event. Market research agencies can assist with developing the questionnaire, providing staffing, and analyzing the data. Being able to share verifiable information on your fans is essential to attracting great corporate partners.

Figure 6.9 offers a model representing the degree of overlap between a sport event's fans and a potential sponsor's customers. As discussed, the greater the amount of overlap between these two populations (A), the better the prospect of a successful, mutually advantageous partnership between an event and a sponsor. What makes sponsorships even more powerful is their potential to increase the number of new customers among a sport's existing fans (C) through the brand's in-venue event activations. Similarly, the partnership can contribute to building a sport's fanbase, attracting new fans among customers (B) through the brand's out of venue marketing activities.

Post-play Analysis

Like any good partnership, all parties benefit from a well-conceived and well-constructed event sponsorship. Organizers seek relationships with companies that can provide a source of revenue and opportunities to reduce expenses. To stretch an event's promotional budget, organizers seek companies that will reinforce their association with a program of advertising, promotions, and onsite engagement activities and publicity, known as *activation*. They also hope to create alliances that demonstrate a commitment, or at least an intention, to continue their association with the event in future years.

Sponsors can derive a wide range of exposure opportunities from their event partnership, such as advertising at the event site and beyond, product placement, promotions, and media coverage. Sports events offer companies outstanding opportunities for customer hospitality through the provision of event tickets, and access to exclusive experiences such as VIP receptions, parties, and others. They can also provide a platform for direct sales efforts, product demonstrations, and sampling opportunities. Some companies also employ events as fundraising vehicles for corporate philanthropic efforts. Among the attractive intangible properties of sports events sponsorships include category exclusivity, perceived ownership of event elements, an association with an event of prestigious reputation, and the ability to offer pass-through rights to other business partners.

Although the relative importance that each company places on the various elements in a sponsor package varies widely, prospective companies may be divided into two key groups—consumer products (B2C) companies and business-to-business (B2B) marketers. Event organizers begin the process of designing a sponsor package by understanding how their prospective partners market their products or services to their customers, and what a company wants or needs from the relationship to achieve these marketing objectives. To identify likely sponsor prospects, it is important to understand who the sponsor's customers are, and how well they overlap with a sport's fan base.

Coach's Clipboard

1. You are organizing a tournament of regional police department baseball teams with the objective of raising funds for their Widows & Orphans Fund. What kinds of companies would be most likely to be attracted to the event? With projected admissions and donations revenue of $15,000 and operating expenses of $20,000, how can sponsor sales generate $20,000 net to the charity? Consider both cash and VIK sponsorship opportunities.
2. You are the marketing director for a consumer products company that supports esteem-building causes for physically disadvantaged children. Identify an existing sports event or create a new one and explore how the company can help generate needed capital and exposure for the cause. Discuss how this effort can meet your company's marketing needs while supporting this worthy endeavor.

3. A marketer representing a major B2B corporation approaches an event organizer seeking a large block of premium seating, exclusive access, and hospitality opportunities for their upscale clients. The event already has a presenting sponsor under contract that paid more than the B2B company is willing to spend and is receiving less in return than is sought by the marketer. How can the event organizer increase the value of the relationship for the existing sponsor or increase the consideration offered by the B2B company to ensure that all partners are satisfied and treated fairly?

4. You are an event organizer who has enjoyed a long-term relationship with an electronics sponsor, which is set to expire the following year. Renewal negotiations for a new agreement are proceeding reasonably well. The host facility of your next event, however, has announced its new naming rights partner will be a competitive sponsor. How will you manage the relationship with your sponsor to maximize the chances of renewing your agreement successfully?

PLAY 7

Teaming with Sponsors

"Persistence can change failure into extraordinary achievement."
—*Matt Biondi, American Olympic swimming champion, 1965–Present*

This play will help you to:

- Design and customize sponsorship packages.
- Identify the costs and value of providing sponsor benefits.
- Engage in presenting and selling sponsorships.

Introduction

Once a sports event organizer has gathered all of the intelligence possible to gain an understanding of its prospective partner's business, the next step is to develop a sponsor program that will meet the respective needs of all stakeholders—the event organizers, participants, fans, and sponsors. The right program must provide measurable value and business opportunities to the sponsor and help the organizer generate the net revenues their event budget requires.

Scaling and Pricing Sponsorship Packages

What benefits, and in what quantity, should an event organizer include in a prospective sponsor's package? How many tickets, and of what value? What kind of recognition should the company receive in pre-event advertising? How many scoreboard mentions, playing field signs, public address announcements, and in-event logo placements should be offered? What promotional opportunities should be included in its sponsorship package? What presence and prominence will the sponsor enjoy on the event's digital platforms? How much of each of these elements will a sponsor receive relative to other event sponsors?

To sports event organizers, sponsor benefits may be divided into two basic varieties—those that will generate expenses against the event budget and those that also offer value to the relationship but can be provided without the organizer encountering any out-of-pocket expense. Before developing the sponsorship package, organizers should consider the actual expenses of providing the benefits to sponsors.

Development and Fulfillment Costs

Among the most overlooked expenses during the budgeting process are the costs of selling and fulfilling the benefits to which sponsors are entitled. Manufacturers and retailers are quite familiar with the concept of pricing merchandise to cover their "cost of goods sold," or "COGS," plus a margin of profit. Before fixing a price for a product, a manufacturer must identify the cost of materials, labor, and equipment required for its fabrication, as well as for packaging, shipping, advertising, promotion, sales commissions, and other expenses encountered in bringing it to market. An allowance to account for overhead costs, such as rent, staff, equipment, research and development, supplies, utilities, and other expenses not directly associated with the manufacturing, marketing, or distribution processes must also be applied to sell a product for more than it cost the company to produce.

Like retailers, sports event organizers demonstrate an understanding of this concept when they apply a price to merchandise they sell. They account for the cost of acquiring the product, paying the sales staff and cashiers, acquiring the fixtures required for storage and display, allocating a sufficient percentage to cover overhead, and then add a profit margin before attaching the price tag. Sports events fund their operations in a similar manner. All of the expenses expected to create, market, and deliver an event sponsorship must be identified, and a profit margin applied that is sufficient to meet the net revenue expectations from those relationships.

The expenses incurred in selling a sponsorship, or development costs, include sales commissions, sales materials, travel and entertainment expenses, and market research. Obviously, these costs do not provide any value to the sponsor. They do, however, help the event organizer secure business partners and, therefore, should be factored into the "cost of goods sold" when setting sponsorship goals and pricing packages.

The expenses that represent the actual out-of-pocket expenses that an event organizer will incur to provide the benefits to which the sponsor is entitled are called *fulfillment costs*. An event organizer can expect to spend approximately 25%, and in some cases up to 50% of gross sponsorship revenue to deliver these benefits. Some of the most common development and fulfillment expenses encountered by sports event organizers are summarized in Figure 7.1.

Development Costs
- Sales commissions
- Sales expenses
  - Travel and accommodations
  - Business meals
  - Business entertainment (e.g., event tickets and hospitality during sales process)
  - Gifts and merchandise
  - Presentation materials
- Market research

Fulfillment Costs
- Complimentary tickets
- Event signage and displays
- Event guide, website, and in-app advertising
- Pre-event advertising
- VIP hospitality
- Sponsor gifts
- Sampling and giveaways
- Discounting and couponing

Figure 7.1   Common Sports Event Sponsorship Development and Fulfillment Costs

Development Costs

■ Sales Commissions

Experienced event organizers may be consummate experts at planning, managing, and executing events, and perhaps even be outstanding promoters and marketers. They are often less adroit or have limited time available to invest in cultivating sponsors to meet their revenue expectations. Their relationships with corporate event marketing decision-makers may also be limited.

This is why sports event organizers often seek professional help from agencies and individuals who specialize in event marketing and maintain close working relationships with contacts in a wide range of potential sponsor companies. There are a large number and variety of event marketing agencies to be found in *Sports Market Place Directory*, a comprehensive reference volume of contacts within sports and sports-related organizations available from Grey House Publishing Inc. (www.greyhouse.com). For detailed and timely intelligence on event marketing agencies and news about their current activities, outstanding resources also include *Sports Business Journal, Sports Business Daily, Sportico, Front Office Sports*, and *IEG Sponsorship Report*.

An event marketing agency can become the organizer's most important ambassador to the business community. As such, organizers are well advised to interview and check the references for agencies under consideration to evaluate whether they have represented similar properties, the degree of their past successes, their assessment of the revenue potential for the event, and their cost schedules before making a final selection. Once an agency or individual is chosen, they will typically be the exclusive representative of the event to potential sponsors, so conducting thorough due diligence on their reputation, follow-through, experience, and contacts is essential.

Agencies are usually paid a percentage of the gross sponsorship fees they generate. In a well-functioning partnership, the organizer and the agency invest in each other's success. The organizer trusts that the agency is working diligently to recruit the sponsors that are needed, and the marketing agency invests considerable time and energy to generate revenue to benefit the event. It is, therefore, common for the agency to also require a monthly retainer as guaranteed income, often structured as a "draw against commission."

If both the agency and the sponsors it develops continue to be associated with the event in future years, the agency generally continues to receive commissions on an agreed-to schedule. The agency is usually entitled to this percentage of future fees resulting from its sales activities even if its own relationship with the organizer expires. In such cases, the agreement will often determine the period of time during which the commissions will remain payable to the marketer, and at what rate of compensation.

Most event marketing agencies prefer representing established, proven properties with high profit potential. Agencies are less drawn to events where sponsorship revenue expectations are low or set unrealistically high. Events with limited geographic appeal are also generally attractive only to entrepreneurial local event marketing agencies because the revenues, and, therefore, the profits they can generate, are concomitantly limited. For events of modest impact, small budget, or geographically limited impact, retaining an event marketing agency may not be preferred or practical. In such cases, event organizers often reach out through local chambers of commerce or create a business advisory group composed of influential individuals from the community with a desire to see the event succeed. Involving local business leaders can help to leverage established relationships within the community, provide introductions to other receptive business executives, and solicit advice on how to best approach them.

■ Sales Expenses

The agreement negotiated with the event marketing agency should also define the reimbursable direct expenses related to the agency's sales activities. Organizers may incur many of the same expenses whether they retain an agency to sell sponsorships, or do it themselves. These may include travel and accommodations to meet with prospective sponsors, the preparation of sales materials, including graphics, artist renderings, videos, and leave-behind materials, gifts, and shipping, among others.

Market Research

Many event organizers conduct post-event market research to measure ticket-buyer demographics, psychographics, buying behavior, price sensitivities, and fan's perceptions of the quality of the event experience. As discussed in Play 6, these same research programs can also be applied to gauge the effectiveness of sponsorships, advertising, and promotional programs. Responses may be compiled by personal interviews during the event, or from questionnaires that are provided to exiting fans or delivered to them after the event by mail e-mail, or text. Common questions include asking fans for their recollections of which sponsors supported the event, whether they visited various sponsored activities, and if they participated in sponsor activation opportunities. The results can help organizers improve future events, validate the program's value to participating sponsors, demonstrate its appeal to prospective partners, and collect valuable data about attendees that can be used for future outreach.

Fulfillment Costs

Complimentary Tickets

As discussed in Play 3, complimentary tickets (*comps*) are free to neither the organizer nor the sponsor. To the event organizer, tickets they could have otherwise sold represent a lost revenue opportunity. Because complimentary tickets issued to a sponsor reduce the cash received from the ticket revenues that were anticipated by an event's gross potential, they actually "cost" the event budget the amount of their face value. Likewise, a sponsor should regard the market price of complimentary tickets as value received for its cash payment or value-in-kind (VIK) contributions to the event. For these reasons, it is common for sports event organizers to consider the value of complimentary tickets provided to sponsors as a fulfillment expense.

Complimentary tickets are central components of most sponsorship packages, but they should be used judiciously. Organizers want to fill the event venue with fans for the electric atmosphere that full houses provide, as well as for ancillary revenues such as merchandise, concessions, and parking. When provided to business partners in too large a supply, however, there is a tendency for a portion to go unused on event day. On top of the organizer realizing no sales of merchandise, concessions, or other financial benefit from an unused ticket, the event budget has paid for the ticket as a fulfillment cost. Provide the tickets that sponsors feel they need, but resist the urge to provide too many tickets for them to be able to effectively use for their own purposes. Have an understanding of how sponsors would intend to distribute their allotment of complimentary tickets. Would they employ them to bring their own important guests to the event, use them in consumer promotions as sweepstakes prizes, or both? Providing comps that will be used for a sponsor's VIPs most often require better-quality, higher-priced tickets than those that will be used as consumer giveaways.

Signage and Displays

The exposure that companies receive in connection with their event sponsorship may include temporary signage on the playing surface or within otherwise conspicuous view of the fans. Corporate identification may be applied directly on the walls, floors, boards, fencing, or structural surfaces of the host facility. Signage opportunities may also include banners located within and outside the event venue, on street poles, at headquarters hotels, and at area bars, restaurants, and attractions. The costs of designing, constructing, painting, printing, and installing signage with corporate identification, and any required rental for space to display them, that would not have been incurred had a sponsor not been given those opportunities as part of its package would also be considered fulfillment expenses. If street banners promoting the event, for example, would have been created and installed with or without a sponsor included, the expense should be accounted for in the event budget and their cost would not be considered a cost of fulfillment.

Signage mounted on temporary structures installed specifically for the event may also be included as opportunities for exposure. As a general rule, if the structure to which the signage is attached would be installed with or without the need to recognize a sponsor (e.g., signage displayed on speakers, lighting trusses, or camera scaffolds), only the signage itself and not the cost of the structure on which it is supported should be considered a fulfillment expense. However, if the structure is installed strictly to meet the obligations of a sponsorship agreement, the costs of rent or fabrication, installation, and dismantling the structure would be accounted for as fulfillment expenses.

Video screens and electronic message displays on scoreboards or other information displays around the venue can provide high-impact opportunities to expose and recognize a sponsor's association with the event. The costs of creating artwork for the video screens and programming for the electronic message displays should also be included as fulfillment expenses. The actual operation of these features, if they are also used for informational or entertainment purposes during the event such as gameplay coverage, replays, the posting of statistics, and the airing of highlights, would not be included in the calculation of fulfillment costs.

Keep in mind that an overabundance of corporate logos and sponsor marketing messages can create undesirable visual clutter and confusion. Some event marketers believe that "less can be more"—the fewer the sponsor logos that are present at any one location, the more impact each will have. There are a host of techniques that event organizers and venues use to maximize the impact of sponsor signage at sports events:

- *Gate sponsorships.*   Name and theme the different entrance plazas and/or gates for a single sponsor each. Use the sponsor logo's dominant colors in the décor and lighting design for those areas.
- *Quadrant, concourse, or walkway sponsorships.*   Name and theme sections of seating, concourses, or walkways for one sponsor each.
- *Electronic signage dominance.*   Display only one sponsor at a time on video message boards, scoreboards, and/or on virtual signage inserted on the broadcast, and rotate sponsors at regular intervals. This is particularly impactful in venues that possess electronic signs surrounding most, or all, of the seating bowl.

■ Program Advertising

Organizers who publish and market commemorative programs and guides in printed or digital formats often include advertising opportunities in their sponsor packages. To reduce financial risk, some organizers license the rights to a publisher that absorbs the costs of designing, writing, producing, and marketing in exchange for a percentage of sales. The publisher is typically entitled to sell advertising space to help defray their costs. To control fulfillment costs, event organizers who license their publishing rights should negotiate a discounted rate for the purchase of any advertising they purchase to fulfill their sponsorship agreements.

Organizers can also *up-sell* advertising in order to generate additional revenues. For example, a sponsor entitled to a certain sized ad may wish to increase the size of its space, or desire a more prominent position. The difference between the rate for what the sponsor is already entitled to and the price for an ad that better meets its desires may be charged back to the partner.

It is also recommended that one complimentary ad be reserved by the organizer to thank all of the event's sponsors. The inclusion of partner names and logos in a "thank-you ad" will add incremental value to each sponsor's existing exposure benefits while vividly demonstrating the organizer's appreciation.

■ Pre-event Advertising

Event organizers place advertising in a wide variety of digital, printed, and broadcast media to promote ticket sales, attendance, or increase the viewing audience, and often include identification of one or more major sponsors. Sponsorship agreements may also include obligations for an organizer to place a certain amount of advertising with the specific objective of acknowledging a company's support of an event.

These supplemental ads, which would not have otherwise been purchased, would be considered fulfillment expenses.

Many organizers enter into promotional relationships with media outlets that entitle the event to a quantity of complimentary advertising in return for an agreed-to package of sponsor benefits. In such cases, the organizer trades valuable consideration for the VIK advertising, such as complimentary tickets, signage, and other sponsor benefits which the event absorbs as fulfillment costs.

VIP Hospitality

Access to pre-game receptions, post-event parties, and in-venue hospitality suites has become a sponsorship entitlement of increasing appeal and significance, particularly to B2B companies. This allows the sponsors to enjoy the prestige of providing exclusive access and exceptional experiential value to their own invited guests. Invitations to these highly desirable special-access opportunities are greatly sought-after. As a result, this is an area that event organizers must guardedly protect and keep in short supply. Otherwise, an expansion of the guest list may cause expenses to quickly skyrocket while the value of exclusivity declines.

A sponsor's package of benefits should guarantee a specific number of passes to these receptions and parties to control costs. It should not be surprising, however, when sponsors request more invitations or passes to these limited-access events, especially as the event matures. One or two passes here and there probably won't amount to much added cost to the event budget, although one or two requests often develop into far more significant numbers across the roster of sponsors. If the reception is being hosted in an area where the available space will accommodate more guests, the organizer can establish a "buy-in" price to enable sponsors to purchase supplementary passes for their extra guests at a per-person rate. Sponsors can thereby be provided with the additional access they need, while the organizer protects their event budget from costly overruns. A helpful and equitable formula used to set a buy-in price begins with the base per-person cost of food and beverage as charged by the caterer, plus gratuities, service charges, and applicable taxes. It is also fair to factor in an allowance to cover additional décor, furnishings and overhead costs.

To illustrate, suppose a corporate partner requests an additional 20 party tickets to supplement the 30 to which it is already entitled. The cost of food and beverage, as estimated by the caterer, is $50 per person, plus 18 percent service charge ($9 per person) and 7 percent sales tax ($4.13 on $59), for a subtotal of $63.13 per person. As the event is a stand-up reception, only a small allowance must be added for additional décor and furnishings for which the event organizer in this example adds $6.50 per person, inclusive of taxes. Rounding off, the organizer can set a minimum charge of $70 per additional party pass in this example. The value of establishing this policy becomes more obvious in considering the costs of entertaining even as few as 10 additional guests requested by each of the five event sponsors, a total of 50 unanticipated, unbudgeted VIPs. Using this example, the organizer would otherwise incur up to $3,500 in unbudgeted expenses to add this modest number of extra friends to the guest list. To each sponsor, however, the effective cost would total only $700. Access to an exclusive experience is typically what the sponsors are after, and they are often willing to pay to accommodate their additional guests. Organizers often add a profit margin to the buy-in price to generate additional revenue and/or to discourage partners from purchasing an unreasonably large number of additional tickets. In this way, the organizer can maintain the exclusive intimacy of the hospitality experience, if so desired.

Sponsor Gifts

Sports apparel and collectible merchandise are one of the requisite staples of sports events. Few sporting events fail to offer their special VIP guests a cap, t-shirt, golf shirt, or a gift bag containing a selection of event and sponsor items. Premium collectibles, such as framed and autographed keepsakes, personalized jerseys, and other commemorative merchandise, are also frequently given to key sponsor contacts as gifts and expressions of gratitude. Organizers should be sure to include the costs of these items in their estimate of fulfillment costs even though they may not be included as benefits to which sponsors are contractually entitled.

■ Sampling and Giveaways

Companies are often granted *sampling rights,* the ability to distribute one of their consumer products or a giveaway premium featuring their brand logo to the fans and/or athletes. Sponsors typically provide sample products at no cost, and often also pay for the additional staff required for distribution.

Before granting sampling rights to a sponsor, the organizer should consult his or her facility lease and the host venue's management. Some facilities restrict sampling activities to sponsors of an event that do not compete with their own partners. A concessionaire's agreement with the facility may also preclude sampling of food or beverage items out of a concern that providing these free products would cut into their sales. It should be noted that these regulations might not be immediately apparent in a reading of the facility lease. Many leases contain provisions that obligate the event organizer to adhere to the rules and regulations of the facility. To protect themselves against surprises, sports event organizers should not sign a lease agreement until they have been provided with a copy of those regulations. This is often where restrictions on sponsor activities such as sampling and the display of sponsor signage, as well as the rights of the event site's concessionaires and merchandisers, may be found. The lease may also reveal a charge for the right to sample or distribute sponsor products and limitations or outright prohibitions on product categories that may be sampled.

The staff required to distribute the samples may be provided by the sponsor, the event organizer, or by the facility. Volunteer organizations such as community sports teams, scout troops, and other youth organizations are excellent resources for providing labor for sampling at sports events so long as doing so does not violate building regulations or labor agreements. Another way to minimize the labor costs connected with sampling opportunities is to restrict distribution to the period when the audience is exiting. Ushers and other house staff are usually underutilized at this point and may be redeployed to execute sampling activities at the exits. (This also ensures that the sampling of food or beverage items does not compete with concessions sales.)

Facility and labor restrictions for premium giveaways are often similar to those for sampling. Try to avoid distributing commemorative balls, pucks, sticks, bobbleheads, or other implements upon entry to the host venue as they could become projectiles and interfere with play or cause inadvertent injury to other fans. Printed with event and sponsor logos, these items are great keepsakes, but they should be distributed to fans upon exiting. Promotional items, such as rally towels, cheering cards, t-shirts, caps, and other materials that enhance the participatory nature of the viewing experience may be distributed upon entry. Such objects should be sufficiently light and soft in substance so as not to create a safety hazard if fans cause them to become airborne during an event.

Secure the permission of the host venue before approving a sponsor's planned premium item to ensure that it does not violate house regulations or the facility's agreement with the merchandiser. In addition, try to avoid approving the sponsored distribution of premium items that are similar to merchandise being sold at the event. Free premiums can compete with souvenir sales and lower the "per cap" (see Play 3) for both the event organizer and the merchandiser.

The financial responsibility for purchasing the sponsored giveaway item should be defined by the sponsorship agreement. Some preparation ("prepping") costs may also be required, a factor frequently overlooked by both sponsors and organizers. Posters, for example, must be rolled and bound with elastic bands or inserted into tubes for easy distribution to the fans and to prevent product damage. Plastic bags are often used to package a sample or giveaway item with product information, promotional offers, coupons, or future event information. Prepping the giveaway item can be executed by an outside company or by a pool of volunteers. Also be sure to plan on deploying extra custodial staff to keep concourses, aisles, and other areas clean and trash containers serviced. Discarded giveaway items, wrappers, packaging, and couponing can create slip or trip hazards, debris blowing onto the playing surface, and a generally unpleasing aesthetic environment. Be sure to include these extra labor expenses and any additional refuse and recycling containers needed to support the giveaway in your fulfillment costs, or in the estimate of additional charges to your sponsor.

■ Discounting

Corporate partners often activate their sponsorships by offering consumers added value with the purchase of their products—discounts on the price of event tickets or special event merchandise. Ticket discounting is an extremely effective tool used by sponsors to drive customers into retailers selling their products, or into their own stores. A sponsor's event activation strategy may focus heavily on promoting the availability of ticket discounts. Ticket discount coupons may be incorporated into a product's packaging, on the tray liners of quick service restaurants or attached to "point of purchase" displays promoting the product and the event. The discount program may require customers to scan a code on the product's packaging to purchase tickets at a savings, or key in a numerical code that may be redeemed online.

To maximize the effectiveness of a discount promotion, sponsors may purchase advertising or hang posters in retail locations promoting the value they are offering to their customers. The sponsor enjoys the benefit of being perceived by fans as the customer-friendly source of discount options such as a fixed dollars-off discount, a package price for a family of four, or a "Buy One, Get One Free" opportunity. Sponsor promotions can help encourage improved attendance by limiting the discount to less well-attended weeknights or for afternoons. Tickets sold at a discount should be considered during the budgeting process in the calculation of ticket revenues (see Play 3). To anticipate sponsor needs for discount offers, event organizers should set discount prices even before sponsors are confirmed and estimate the number of tickets that will likely be sold at these reduced prices. Usually, the sponsor will create, design, and execute the advertising, point-of-purchase displays, coupons, and packaging promoting its discount offer. It is highly recommended, however, that all materials relating to the event be reviewed and approved by the organizer to ensure accuracy and creative consistency with other event communications.

Some B2B and consumer companies with high price-point products activate their sponsorships by offering event merchandise and tickets *gratis* to their most important clients or as sales promotions designed to transform qualified prospects into loyal customers. An automobile manufacturer may promote its sponsorship by providing consumers who take a test drive with a voucher redeemable for a pair of complimentary tickets. Or, a mobile services company may offer free event tickets to new customers who subscribe to its latest data plan. In cases like these, the quantity of redeemed tickets (the number of customers who actually exchange their vouchers for the free tickets and attend the event) is impossible for either the sponsor or the organizer to predict and budget for in advance. As such, promotions such as these may be limited to discount tickets "while supplies last."

The Sales Process

A sports event director can be imagined as the coach of a team, focusing the organization's talents and resources on the pursuit of the goal—the sale of an event sponsorship to a corporate partner. The sponsorship team is empowered to make on-field decisions. They must maneuver around shifting obstacles and challenges, a line of defense defined by a prospect's objections, reticence, and apathy. The quarterback may be the staff member or internal department responsible for developing sponsors, a volunteer visiting neighborhood businesses, or an event marketing agency retained to apply its expertise and leverage its contacts. The very best come prepared with an understanding of what specific prospects want from their sports event relationships.

The opening play starts with the creation and presentation of a sponsorship program that lines up a series of benefits designed to provide relevant business solutions to prospective partners. The first appeal to the sponsor prospect may move the ball close to the goal for a long gain, or perhaps at first only a few inches. Deficient intelligence or a poorly conceived presentation may result in a loss of progress. The ever-running time clock creates a sense of urgency. There is only a limited amount of time available to bring the package into the end zone and to a victorious close. The quarterback reads the field and senses the potential areas of penetration. New plays are attempted, strategies adjusted based on intelligence gained and, eventually, the program presented is strong enough to score a touchdown. Or perhaps no matter how strategic or creative, the prospective sponsor is going to disengage and the game will have to be pursued with another, more receptive company. Alternatively, as the time ticks down and the final result appears in doubt, the coach may call for a field goal—a smaller sponsorship package to kickoff the relationship. Just a fraction of the revenue the coach set out to realize might be all that is possible to achieve at this point in the game. But, it may just be enough to help win the campaign.

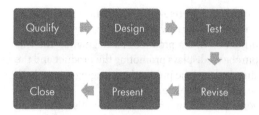

Figure 7.2 Six Steps in the Sponsorship Sales Process

A U.S.O. philosophy, that is, understanding what a potential sponsor wants from their association with a sports event, is the essential unpinning to the sales process. Gaining this intelligence and developing the right set of opportunities to provide the marketing solutions the partner wants is suffused throughout the six-step process of selling sports event sponsorships as described and in Figure 7.2: **(1) qualify, (2) design, (3) test, (4) revise, (5) present,** and **(6) close.**

QUALIFY and Target Sponsor Prospects

Too often, event organizers and marketing agencies present generic presentations featuring a standardized package of sponsor benefits. Sweeping, generous benefits are typical for the highest level—title sponsorship—significant exposure and hospitality opportunities for presenting sponsors, and diminishing levels of signage and ticket allotments for supporting partners. While this structure defines the general hierarchy of sponsor relationships, the specific benefits and opportunities within each level are often customized to provide the best value and results for the partner. Cookie-cutter approaches that offer every prospective partner the same benefits within each level of investment can be far less effective in attracting sponsors. To design the best sponsorship program for any given sponsor brand, the organizer must be familiar with who their customers are and consider how the company prefers to market to them.

Most sports event organizers understand the fan base for their sports and events. The marketing agencies and outside consultants they retain to develop sponsorship revenue require no less familiarity with the brand's customers and the fan-audience. This grounding helps marketing agencies and salespeople better match prospective brands to the event. The event marketer must narrow the list of potential partners to those most likely to consider sponsorship of an event as an effective and cost-efficient marketing solution. Figure 7.3 provides a list of questions that can be used to help refine the roster of qualified

1. What companies or brands appeal to the same customer demographics and lifestyles as the event?
2. What companies or brands sponsor similar or competitive events?
3. What companies compete with the sponsors of these similar events?
4. What companies sponsor events that are also supported by your existing sponsors?
5. What is the event's geographic reach, and does it match the prospect company's marketing strategies (e.g., local, regional, or national)?
6. What companies are launching new products or services that can be promoted by an event marketing partnership?
7. What vendors are doing business with the event organizer that may consider cash or VIK sponsor relationships?
8. What companies support the same charitable or community-based causes as the event?
9. Do the prospective sponsors possess the financial wherewithal to support the event?
10. What is the financial health of the prospective sponsors?

Figure 7.3 Top 10 Qualifiers for Sponsor Prospects

prospective sponsors. The ideal prospect should be one that shares a similar target market with the event, a company with existing or likely customers who are among those expected to either attend or participate. The demographics, lifestyles, interests, values, and habits of an event's guests or attendees should closely approximate those of the prospective sponsor's customers.

SIDELINE STORY

A Youth-Oriented Sports Marketer

Mountain Dew, acquired by Pepsi-Cola in 1964, is a carbonated, caffeinated citrus soft drink brand that has been marketed, in the words of the company's website, toward "young, active, outdoor types." Pepsi reinforces its youthful perception in the marketplace through a major sponsorship of the Dew Tour and Winter Dew Tour festivals of action sports featuring BMX, skateboarding, freeskiing, and other competitions that target young active consumers. Mountain Dew's high level of sponsorship support provides the brand with title identification for the two national tours. It is joined by other marketers seeking youthful, active-lifestyle audiences. Mountain Dew's highly engaging event marketing efforts in social media and on streaming platforms reinforce the image of a brand that appeals to the most creative, talented, and daring of today's young, homegrown athletes.

One of the quickest and easiest ways to get a sense of a company's target market and the types of events they sponsor is to visit the websites and social media pages of the brand and its parent company. A visit to the website of the popular soft drink Mountain Dew, for example, demonstrates the brand's commitment to an active, cutting edge, youth-oriented culture. Many of the sports events they sponsor reflect this lifestyle. The same brand's social network feeds showcase up-to-the-second details about the athletes and events Mountain Dew sponsors, special promotions, and streams of interactive customer commentary.

Other resources for identifying potential sponsors are the websites and social network feeds of events that are similar to, or competitive with, your own. Reach out to these sponsor companies, as well as their competitors, to build your list of prospects. It is also worthwhile to visit the sites of sports, music, community, and cultural events that may appeal to audiences that share the same demographics and lifestyle characteristics as the fans of your sport.

Explore the members of your event's corporate family—any entity with a vested interest in the success of your event—such as your organization's suppliers and service providers. Notwithstanding that many are in business expressly to generate cash by selling their products and services to the event industry, some may see value in reinforcing their partnership with the event organizer to develop additional business. For those sports event organizations that are under the supervision of a board of directors, advisory board, or a group of community and business leaders, a potential sponsor may already be sitting at your conference table. Explore whether companies represented by these involved advisors can take advantage of a more formalized business relationship with the event.

Have you read an article about an exciting new product or service that is being introduced at about the same time as your event? Product launches are usually funded with a temporary infusion of marketing dollars. Most companies, along with their advertising and public relations agencies, are always looking for new and unique ways to spread the word about a new or improved product or service. Sports events can offer new product launches opportunities for sampling, exposure, and promotions that traditional advertising simply cannot match.

If your event is organized by a not-for-profit entity, is a program designed to improve the community's quality of life, or is a revenue generator for a charity, search for companies that support the same kinds of philanthropic endeavors. Check the charity's list of major corporate donors, as well as the supporters of similar charities, to generate more leads. Cause-related marketing—generating funds for a worthy charity—can be a powerful motivator in developing corporate partners. Many companies have two discrete sources of support for events—a marketing budget and a community relations or philanthropy budget. Is the event best positioned as a marketing opportunity, or might it have stronger appeal to a particular sponsor as deserving of charitable support?

Any process of qualifying potential event sponsors should include an analysis of the financial health of partner companies. Does the prospect generate sufficient revenues to consider a sponsorship, and, if so, at what level of participation? If the company is healthy but possesses limited resources, a large cash sponsorship is unlikely. Alternatively, a more modest cash sponsorship package, or some combination of cash and VIK might increase a company's receptivity. What is the state of the industry in which the company does business? If the industry is under economic stress, but the company is a leader in their business, VIK may, again, help to close a deal. What is the company's financial position—it is profitable or losing money? Is it hiring or downsizing? Be knowledgeable about the potential sponsor's corporate health. It is risky to partner with a company under financial stress especially if it may exclude other, healthier companies from considering a sponsorship. Slow payment or default by a distressed partner can cause an event to experience cash flow problems or fall short of its budget expectations.

SIDELINE STORY

The Cryptocurrency Bubble

Emerging industries are often characterized by a mad scramble for consumer awareness by newly formed, competing companies with infusions of start-up capital from investors. Advertising on sports media and sponsorship of sports properties has been a favored tool for jumping ahead of the competition to quickly position brands as leaders in their field. Sports betting companies followed this strategy when wagering was legalized in the United States on the federal level, and sports was a perfect marketing tool given the considerable overlap between fans and potential customers. The cryptocurrency industry emerged as another new entrant in the early 2020s. FTX became the naming rights sponsor of the Miami Heat's arena and was featured on umpire's uniforms when the company became a partner of Major League Baseball. Crypto.com became the naming rights sponsor at Los Angeles' downtown arena and was displayed on Philadelphia 76ers jerseys. Many of these companies became victims of their own success. Overheated demand by cybercurrency markets drove up the cost of sponsorships, and the companies paid inflated prices. Having spent beyond their means on sports sponsorships and other marketing endeavors, some cybercurrency brands folded and others drastically reduced their spending. Skeptical that the sudden emergence of this free-spending, unregulated business could be sustained, some sports marketers predicted the eventual bursting of the cybercurrency bubble. The Louisiana Superdome, for example, rejected a naming-rights offer that was 20% higher from the now-defunct FTX in favor of a deal with Caesar's Entertainment.

DESIGN a Sponsorship Program

It is now time to call for the right play that you, as coach, believe will run your team past the objections, reticence, and apathy of prospective sponsor companies. Sponsor revenue expectations projected during the budgeting process should anticipate the scaling of sponsorships into a range of price categories. As mentioned, the benefits included as marketing solutions for sponsor companies will be customized to meet their needs. In general, however, there is a generalized pyramidal hierarchy of sports event sponsors, as illustrated in Figure 7.4. The model divides available opportunities into four broad levels of participation: (1) title sponsorship, (2) presenting sponsorship, (3) category exclusive sponsors (also frequently called "official" sponsors), and (4) nonexclusive sponsors and official suppliers. A subset

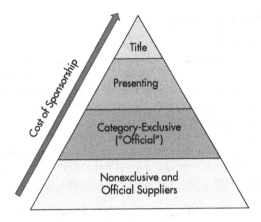

Figure 7.4 Sponsorship Pyramid

of nonexclusive sponsors—donors—may also be available to not-for-profit events and may provide an additional source of revenue for organizers who qualify.

■ Title Sponsorship

The level of greatest corporate support is *title sponsorship,* which, when available, is typically held by a single sponsor. Title sponsors can expect to reap the most valuable business solutions as compared with an event's other corporate partners. What they are paying a premium for is to ensure that their corporate or brand name is uniquely and inseparably connected to the identity of the event. Whether motivated by the desire for maximizing exposure to its product's target market, bragging rights over its competitors, or demonstrating its preeminence in the community, title sponsorship can be a powerful and impactful tool for the corporate partner. A company that purchases a title sponsorship enjoys the singular benefits of appearing in all advertising, press releases and resulting media coverage, web pages, promotions, tickets, signage, and more. Examples of events with title sponsors include the FedEx Cup (PGA), the Famous Idaho Potato Bowl (Boise, ID), and the Pop Tarts Bowl (Orlando, FL), to name just a few.

Naturally, inclusion of the company identity in the event title and its graphic incorporation into the event logo clearly separates the title sponsor from all other partners. Some event organizers consider it important to maintain their own identity within the event title and logo to provide historical context and continuity (e.g., the F1 Lenovo Japanese Grand Prix, the Discover NHL Winter Classic, and the TCS New York City Marathon). The dominant position in the title provides the sponsor with added impact and importance. In cases in which the corporate sponsor's name provides the event's identity in its entirety, the event promoter can attach a significant premium (e.g., the Waste Management Open). In such instances, journalists, as well as other sponsor partners in their own promotional programs, would find it impossible to refer to an event without the title partner's corporate identification.

■ Presenting Sponsorship

In naming rights partnerships, the sponsor's name generally comes first. A presenting sponsorship may also be sold at a premium because their brand is still incorporated into the official name of the event, but the company name is typically secondary to the event title, and preceded with "presented by." (e.g., the NBA Canada Series presented by Bell, the NFL Pro Bowl Games presented by Verizon, the MLB Draft presented by Nike). This type of participation is generally priced at a lower level than title sponsorship because of the relative ease with which journalists and social media posts can ignore the corporate identity. A presenting sponsorship, however, effectively promotes the brand's relationship to the event in all promotions and marketing campaigns undertaken by the event organizer. But, because the identities are so much easier to separate, it is considerably more difficult to insist that an event's other partners feature the presenting sponsor's name in their own advertising or promotional activations.

■ Category Exclusive Sponsors

Title and presenting sponsorships can account for a sizable percentage, or even most, of an event's sponsorship revenue budget. The largest number of sponsor companies and brands, however, are most often found in category-exclusive sponsors, or *official sponsors*. Sponsorships of this type are generally economically accessible to companies at more moderate price levels, and events usually feature more of them. As illustrated in Figure 7.5, the sponsorship hierarchy pyramid combines these essential building blocks to meet revenue and promotional activation goals.

Note that the sponsorships in this area of the pyramid are much greater in number and may even cumulatively account for a greater amount of revenue. Category-exclusive building blocks can include any variety of businesses, as illustrated by examples of industries that commonly sponsor sports events. There is almost limitless opportunity to expand sponsor categories to include companies from many different industries.

Sponsors buy into events to convert the benefits they provide into specific business solutions. What protects them from competitors doing likewise is the exclusivity guaranteed within their category. It is, therefore, essential to define exactly what category is being granted exclusivity. For example, will an automotive company's sponsorship offer exclusivity that covers cars and trucks, or just cars? Will it preclude the event promoter from pursuing a relationship with a rental car company that does not offer their customers the sponsor's vehicles? Is a relationship with a motorcycle manufacturer still be permissible? Does the exclusivity extend to auto parts, prohibiting a deal with an after-market parts manufacturer or retailer? Will an airline partner's sponsorship prevent the organizer from pursuing a relationship with a railroad or bus line? If it is a domestic airline, can the organizer pursue a relationship with an international carrier? Does a deal with a soft drink company cover soda only, or does it provide exclusivities that bar partnerships with other non-alcoholic beverages like juices, water, coffee, tea, milk and dairy drinks, or isotonic sports drinks? Does the soft drink deal permit the promoter to pursue quick-service restaurant (QSR) sponsorships with any chain it desires, or only those that offer that brand?

From the organizer's point of view, it is most advantageous to limit a sponsor's exclusivity to the narrowest extent possible. This would enable the event to attract sponsorships from a greater number of

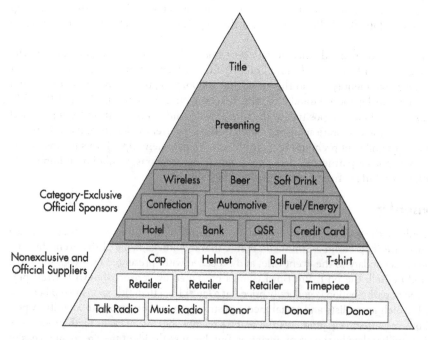

Figure 7.5 Building Blocks of the Sponsorship Pyramid

companies and industries. From the sponsor's standpoint, the broader the definition of exclusivity, the more valuable the partnership can be. Event organizers will often place reasonable limits on areas of exclusivity in the first presentation to prospective sponsors and may negotiate a higher purchase price if additional categories are requested by a sponsor.

Exclusivity granted by a sponsorship does not necessarily mean that the company can use the event to promote every product it sells. The partnership may, instead, define which specific brands may be included. Consider the fictional soft drink company once again: Even if the sponsorship excludes partnerships with any other beverage at the event, what specific brands or varieties can it promote in relation to the event? If not well-defined, a single sponsorship has potential to create a great deal of signage clutter promoting multiple brands from the same company, devaluing the exposure of other, single-brand sponsors. However, as illustrated by the next Sideline Story, if properly priced and creatively designed, a multiple-brand sponsorship can provide a partner with significant impact and activation opportunities.

SIDELINE STORY

Activating Multiple Procter & Gamble Brands

With a diverse portfolio of industry-leading consumer products, Procter & Gamble (P&G) focuses its sports marketing efforts on the promotion of its consumer product brands rather than that of the parent company. Events with a variety of venues, objectives, and target markets provide P&G with discrete, targeted opportunities to promote specific brands with a minimum of clutter and competition.

In 2021, Major League Soccer (MLS) announced a 5-year partnership between the league and P&G that provided opportunities for multiple brands at major North American soccer events. The company's Gillette and Old Spice shaving brands, dental care brands Crest and Oral B, Dawn dishwashing detergent, and Charmin and Bounty paper products were given the rights to activate at the MLS All Star Game and the Leagues Cup (an annual match between MLS and one of Mexico's Liga MX teams), the Campeones Cup (between MLS Cup and Mexican league champions), and the Mexican national soccer team's tour of the United States. Over the course of the 5-year deal, community level activations focus on efforts to support equity and inclusion in the sport. In 2022, MLS and P&G introduced a program effort called *Capitanes del Futuro* to help prepare a new generation of Hispanic youth for entry into the business world hosted at team soccer stadiums and training centers, sponsored by the company's Gillette, Always, Crest, and Oral B brands.

Category-exclusive sponsors desiring to stand out from their corporate peers are frequently attracted to opportunities that imply "ownership" of specific components of an event. With a little creative thought, title or presenting sponsorships of specific event elements may be devised. A trophy or award may be created that bears the sponsor's name, such as the National Football League's "Pepsi Zero Sugar Rookie of the Year." Halftime or intermission entertainment, pregame festivities, and postgame parties often bear the identities of different category-exclusive sponsors. Video or message board programming, event-specific apps, guest services areas and information kiosks, concessions stands, nearly any element of an event may be sponsored by one of the event's corporate partners, providing the sponsor with the sense of ownership it desires.

Some category-exclusive sponsors are less concerned with the ownership of particular event elements than they are with preferential signage locations at the event site, inclusion in advertising, or access to hospitality opportunities. For this reason, event promoters should not feel compelled to include ownership entitlement to specific event elements in every sponsorship pitch. You may be giving away something of little value to a particular sponsor that can help later close a deal with another company that places a greater emphasis on this type of benefit.

Nonexclusive Sponsors and Official Suppliers

For financial, legal, or practical reasons, an organizer may desire to offer certain categories of sponsorship on a nonexclusive basis. For example, some local alcohol ordinances bar beer companies from entering into exclusive sponsorships that prohibit the sale of other brands of beer. For community-based grassroots organizations such as local Little Leagues, it may be practical to allow multiple law firms, dental practices, day camps, pizzerias, or chiropractors to be involved. In such cases, being able to open the event to all local businesses, even those that are competitive with one another, keeps the cost of sponsorships for each community partner at a reasonable level and can help a volunteer organization close many more deals.

Retailers can also be prime candidates for nonexclusive deals. Providing opportunities to sell event merchandise at more than one retailer's locations is often in the best interest of an event organizer. Therefore, designating more than one "official merchandise headquarters" can be a good idea. Unique promotional packages can be developed to make each store's offerings unique and responsive to the specific needs and demographics of their customers. These activities may include scheduling athlete appearances at certain stores or malls, an exclusive early sales period granted to a partner store, or selected items being made available at only one location.

Media partners, more fully discussed in Play 8, are also good targets for nonexclusive relationships. Radio stations with sports talk formats and Top 40 music channels, for instance, may appeal to totally different listener demographics, and, as such, they may not be truly competitive with one another. It is, therefore, often possible to designate more than one "official radio station" based on the broadcasters' formats.

Nonexclusive partnerships are useful for generating last-minute revenues after it has been determined that no company in the category will enter into a more pricey, exclusive relationship. They may also be beneficial for smaller businesses and industries that cannot afford to participate at an exclusive level. That is why official suppliers are often, though not always, nonexclusive. It may be relatively inexpensive for a supplier, such as a sport-specific equipment manufacturer, to provide its products as value-in-kind to the event. The total value simply may not be great enough to warrant granting exclusive rights. Striking a nonexclusive deal, however, may be worthwhile to the supplier for the purposes of promotional exposure, and to the organizer to reduce cash spent for the same items they would have purchased.

For charitable, and other not-for-profit events, a subset of nonexclusive sponsorships—*donors*—may provide additional opportunities to generate revenue. The key distinguishing characteristic between a sponsor and a donor is generally the former's expectation of promotional benefits and rights to use event logos and other intellectual property. Donors, by contrast, simply support the event by *giving* money to the organization staging the event with few expectations of receiving tangible benefits in return. It is common to provide tickets and thank donors for their generosity on event websites, in advertising, and perhaps on signage at the event. But these acknowledgments come at the discretion of the event organizer, often without a defined *quid pro quo*. Donations are simply that, monetary gifts that can come from any socially- or civic-minded person, family, or organization, with no expectation of exclusivity or promotional value. They do, however, often come with the expectation of tax advantages and, as such, are not available to for-profit events or organizers. For not-for-profit organizers, however, they can provide valuable fundraising opportunities to increase the charitable yield.

Create Innovations That Suit Your Event

Although the sponsorship categories described above are among those most commonly encountered, corporate relationships can take many creative forms. Devise new sponsorship concepts to suit your event and organization. For example, an event organizer can establish a partnership in which the sponsor becomes a *guarantor*. Guarantors promise to cover cash shortfalls up to a certain level at the conclusion of the event. This may ensure the organizer generates guaranteed revenues for charitable purposes. The company can fund this guarantee with a grant or agree to purchase a specified number of tickets, buying and using them outright or donating them to deserving recipients such as active military families, first responders, or cancer survivors. Alternatively, guarantors can agree to cover the difference between actual sales and a predefined number of tickets to cover potential losses. A guarantor relationship is best established for events organized by not-for-profit groups or those designed to funnel a significant percentage of their proceeds to charity.

Dynamic Customization

Traditional sponsorship models offer sponsorship tiers defined by price and benefits. As discussed, title sponsors pay the most and receive the greatest opportunities, presenting sponsors pay somewhat less and receive reduced benefits. The level with the greatest number of partners—official, category-exclusive sponsorships—is often divided into multiple levels of varying cost and opportunity, sometimes with familiar hierarchical references (e.g., gold, silver, and bronze, or donor, supporter, patron).

It had been a long-standing practice for sponsorships to be designed with a standardized menu of benefits. A lower-level package (e.g., bronze) would offer the smallest number of complimentary tickets, the least in-venue exposure, and the least frequent inclusion in advertising and promotions. Higher priced packages (e.g., gold) would come with more tickets, more in-venue exposure, and greater presence in advertising.

While this framework is still very common, the benefits to which sponsors are entitled, and in what quantities they are provided, are more often highly customized. That's because the objectives, wants, and needs of the individual prospective sponsor inform which event assets will have the greatest relevance and value to the partner. To meet the needs of some sponsors, tickets in preferred locations and hospitality opportunities are the most important. For others, a greater amount of advertising and exposure opportunities better suit their marketing needs. By matching the inventory of event assets to the business needs of the prospect, the event organizer is no longer selling pre-defined, tiered benefits, but rather, *business solutions* best positioned to meet their partners' needs. Therefore, while the level of sponsorship spending for two partners may be the same, their package of solutions may be quite different. (See Play 6 for a discussion of the differing needs of B2C and B2B partners.)

In order to begin constructing sponsorship packages of customized solutions for prospective partners, identify all of the opportunities your event can offer. Create a master inventory of all the assets that your event can provide or create using a spreadsheet template like the one shown in Figure 7.6. In this example, the event anticipates having up to 8 sponsors in total. The menu of assets is shown in the first column. The second column indicates the number of sponsors that can be offered each type of asset. This illustration suggests that only one sponsor can appear on the tickets, and only one can be included on the credential lanyard. All 8 can be offered complimentary tickets, passes to receptions and parties, and LED signage around the playing field.

The third column shows how much of each asset is available. This hypothetical event can accommodate 12,000 fans. Therefore, the single sponsor that will be shown on the event ticket will be featured on up to 12,000 tickets. There will be 500 credential lanyards that will be used by staff and VIPs printed with the name and logo of one sponsor. There will be 200 street banners printed, but 4 sponsors can be included in the artwork. All 8 may be offered some number of complimentary tickets, so long as the cumulative number does not exceed 200 VIP and 500 general admission tickets. And, so on.

The estimates in the "Value" column should represent the event organizer's best projection of how the prospect company will assess the attractiveness of the sponsorship. Sponsorship agencies and experienced sponsorship sales professionals are particularly adept at calculating the value of a package. If you do not have access to professional assistance, try some of these hints to estimate value:

- Use the prices you would charge to non-sponsors purchasing the same items to derive the value of tickets, advertising, memorabilia, and other easily priced items.
- Apply prevailing advertising rates in the local market to derive estimates for media exposure, advertising and physical signage (compare to rates for outdoor billboards with similar foot traffic).
- Compare the value of hospitality with prices charged for tickets to receptions, dinners, and other events that attract similar guests in your market. A premium may be added if the hospitality is particularly exclusive and available only to "insiders."

Figure 7.6 Sponsorship Asset Inventory Grid for Sample Sports Event

SPONSOR BENEFITS INVENTORY	# SPONSORS	QUANTITY	VALUE PER UNIT	COST PER UNIT	COMMENTS
Featured Partner					
Featured as Naming Rights partner	1		$75,000	$—	Included in event logo, all printed and verbal references
Featured as Presenting partner	1		$50,000	$—	In event logo, all printed and verbal references
In Venue Activation					
Name Recognition on all Tickets	1	12,000	$12,000	$—	Included on electronic and printed tickets
Logo on credential and VIP lanyards	1	500	$500	$—	
Field of Play Signage Locations	3	3	$25,000	$—	One center and two end zone locations
Perimeter LED Signage, camera facing	8	16	$15,000	$—	
Perimeter LED Signage, non-camera facing	8	16	$7,500	$—	
Goal Signage	1	2	$15,000	$—	
Entrance Welcome Banners	1	8	$2,000	$—	For naming or presenting sponsor
Replay sponsor, by quarter	4	32	$10,000	$1,000	Included in replay opening animation
Highlights sponsor, by quarter	4	4	$5,000	$1,000	Included in highlight opening animation
Public Address Announcements/Scoreboard Logo	8	8	$2,000	$—	
Fan Experience Activation/Videoboard	8	8	$4,000	$1,000	For each presenting sponsor of fan experience activations at whistle stoppage
Halftime sponsor	1	1	$6,000	$2,000	
Concourse Tents/Kiosks	8	8	$8,000	$2,000	For sponsor sampling or demo
Concessions Menu Boards	2	24	$8,000	$—	Per 12 locations
Staff shirt logos (security, ushers, event team)	1	150	$7,500	$2,000	Sleeve patch on unis
Press Conference Backdrop Logo	2	2	$10,000	$—	

SPONSOR BENEFITS INVENTORY	# SPONSORS	QUANTITY	VALUE PER UNIT	COST PER UNIT	COMMENTS
Fan Premium Giveaway (on entrance)	1	Up to 12,000	$12,000	$–	Sponsor provides product and distribution
Sampling Giveaway (on exit)	1	Up to 12,000	$12,000	$–	Sponsor provides product and distribution
Seat Cushion Logos	1	12,000	$24,000	$12,000	Provided only if sponsored
Athlete Gift Item	4	60	$6,000	$–	Sponsor provides product
Press Box Giveaway	2	100	$10,000	$–	Sponsor provides product
Out of Venue Advertising/Promotion					
Use of Event Marks in Advertising and Promotion	8		$25,000	$–	All sponsors
Fan App sponsor	1		$12,000	$–	Provided to app presenting partner
Event Street Banners	4	200	$2,000	$–	Installed around venue and downtown
Event Website Banner Ad	4		$1,000	$–	
Event Print Advertising	4		$2,000	$–	Per 1/4 pg+ ad
Event Radio Advertising	4		$1,250	$–	Per 30 secs
Event Television Advertising	4		$2,500	$–	Per 30 secs
Access to Ticket Buyer Database	1		$6,000	$–	One post-event sponsor text opportunity
Hospitality					
Complimentary Tickets, VIP	8	200	$300	$300	Value and cost per ticket
Complimentary Tickets, General	8	500	$75	$75	Value and cost per ticket
Press Conference Passes	4	24	$25	$–	
Athlete Meet and Greet	4	24	$100	$–	
Pregame VIP Reception	8	150	$175	$85	
Postgame Party	8	150	$250	$125	
Autographed Balls	8	64	$200	$20	
Merchandise Gift Bags	8	150	$200	$65	
Other Features					

Figure 7.6 (Continued)

The value of a ticket, for instance, would generally be set at its face price. Having the brand's name or logo prominently featured in an advertisement may be assigned value based on its visibility, and the number of views, viewers, or readers. The value of a party or reception ticket might be what it would have cost the sponsor to treat their own guests to a similar hospitality experience. The value of some assets may require additional calculation, such as the number of views, viewers, and social media posts for a logo on a press conference backdrop, or a field perimeter LED sign.

Value is an important component of the sponsorship package because sponsors will measure the success of their partnership based on several metrics. First, is the sponsorship cost-efficient? Could they have invested less money in other marketing opportunities to achieve the same result? Almost every sponsor will measure their return on investment (ROI) after an event. Did they generate incremental sales and/or receive value in excess of what they paid for their sponsorship? Sponsors often seek value from their event relationship that is 100% to 200% more than the cost.

Fulfillment Costs

The next column in the inventory displays the cost the organizer will encounter to provide each asset to the organizer. It is very helpful to understand the out-of-pocket expenses of a package of sponsorship benefits to ensure the budget accounts for these expenses somewhere. These fulfillment costs may be deducted from gross sponsorship revenues or accounted for as an expense elsewhere in the budget. Since organizers can expect to spend between 25% and as much as 50% of total sponsorship revenues on these expenses, knowing how much fulfillment of a sponsorship package may cost can help set the price you will charge the partner. This is especially useful for packages that are customized with event assets tailored to meet the individual needs of a partner.

There is, of course, a gap between the typical sponsor goal of double or triple in value over their cost of sponsorship vs. the organizer's goal of spending 25% to no more than 50% of sponsor revenue on fulfillment costs. The organizer can close this gap by providing opportunities and assets that the partner values but that do not generate additional costs for the organizer. If perimeter LED signage is to be installed around the playing surface with or without sponsors and the cost for those signage units is captured in the operating budget, including sponsor branding does not generate an incremental cost. Therefore, it may be of great value to the sponsor without adding to the organizer's expenses. Sponsors included in advertising to promote ticket sales, attendance, or viewing similarly offers the partner value without adding new costs for the organizer. Other value-added opportunities that are often offered to sponsors that have little or no incremental cost, or may be accounted for elsewhere in the operating budget include logo or brand name inclusion on electronic or printed tickets and credentials, on staff uniforms, athletic gear and equipment, welcome banners, street banners, concourse video screens, video scoreboard recognition (either as standalone announcements or as animations associated with starting line ups, instant replays, statistics, and trivia), public address announcements, credentials to attend pre- or post-game media conferences, press conference backdrops, athlete/celebrity meet-and-greets, simple fan experience elements like seating upgrades, dance-cams, etc., and concourse sampling, sign-ups, sales or demonstration tables. All of these assets have value to the sponsor but do not cost the organizer much to deliver them.

Many other assets, on the other hand, cost the organizer additional money if they are not accounted for in the operating budget. As mentioned, complimentary tickets have value for the sponsor who receives them, as they would otherwise have to buy them at the face price. But, they represent a lost revenue opportunity for the organizer since they cannot be sold to the public once issued to the sponsor. Passes for parties and receptions generate expenses to the organizer for food and beverage, décor, and entertainment, and can be assigned a per-person cost by dividing the total cost of the party by the number of people attending. The value to the sponsor, however, may be far greater than the per-person fulfillment cost because these are exclusive hospitality opportunities inside the facility that non-sponsors cannot access. Per-person fulfillment costs may also include merchandise and gifts, which again, may have greater value to the sponsor than the cost to the organizer (e.g., the value of the merchandise might be what the organizer is selling these items for at the event, while the cost to the organizer is what they actually purchased these items for wholesale).

Other outstanding opportunities of value that cost the organizer little or nothing to offer may cost the sponsor some of the additional money they set aside for activation (the incremental $1.40–$1.90 referenced in Play 6). For instance, sponsors may be awarded the right to provide a giveaway item that includes their logo, like a cap, t-shirt, ball, puck, bobblehead, or other premium item that fans will enjoy. One sponsor may distribute their giveaway as the fans enter the event, another as fans depart. Typically, the sponsor will purchase the item or pay the organizer to procure it and will either provide staff or cover additional labor if the organizer does not have personnel already on site to do so. A sponsor may also be given an opportunity to distribute samples of their product to fans. This is a great opportunity for a B2C sponsor to introduce fans to a new product, variety, or flavor. Rather than undertaking the cost of providing thousands of product samples to fans in attendance, some sponsor brands may find it valuable and far more cost-effective to provide full-size samples or gifts to VIPs and other sponsor guests, athletes, and/or the media.

Create a similar grid for each individual sponsorship package, including the benefits you are providing and the quantity of each. This will help you calculate both the value and the fulfillment cost for each deal. Be sure to keep a running count of the assets as you commit them to sponsors so those that remain may be applied to sponsorship deals reached later (see Figure 7.7).

TEST the Opportunity

Diligent research, no matter how thorough, cannot uncover all you might need to know for a successful sponsorship pitch. You may not be able to glean from secondary sources many of the new product introductions, promotional campaign launches, and strategic shifts secretly being hatched in the offices and boardrooms of many potential sponsors. The only way to know for certain whether your opportunity is best informed to attract a potential partner is to test your approach before presenting your package of marketing solutions.

When practical, try to schedule a brief meeting or call with your target prospect to gain a better understanding of the company's most immediate needs and objectives. If you have already identified the decision-maker, attempt to speak with that individual directly. If there is a team of decision-makers, you may be able to interview just one. Let them know that you are not scheduling a sales pitch. Rather, that you respect their time and that if and when you return to present details on how your event can provide effective promotional opportunities, it will be on target and worth their time for consideration.

This step may be the most difficult to effectuate, especially for prospects with whom the event organizer has never had a relationship. Busy marketing executives may not accommodate the request if they do not immediately see a benefit to their company. They may also be guarded as to what their objectives truly are to avoid having information leak to their competitors. Offer to sign a confidentiality agreement (also known as a non-disclosure agreement, or NDA) if you sense that this is the case. Unless the event or the organizer has had previous dealings with the marketer, do not expect to receive more than a very modest amount of time from the prospect. Prepare ahead of the first outreach and know what few and focused questions you want to ask. That very first call may be your only opportunity to gain intelligence and test your assumptions. But, showing an interest in focusing your proposal to meet the company's strategies and needs can increase the chances that it will be reviewed when it is received.

If you are afforded a brief phone call, try to limit your questions to the fewest and most revealing possible. Figure 7.8 lists three such questions designed to provide you with relevant intelligence while generating the least resistance.

If your event is held annually, invite potential prospects to attend as your guests before pitching them a sponsorship. You can often discover much about what a company looks for in a sponsorship when you meet a decision-maker in a casual setting and make that person feel like an insider as they walk around the site.

SPONSOR BENEFITS INVENTORY	QUANTITY	VALUE	COST
Featured Partner			
Featured as Naming Rights partner	1	$75,000	$–
In Venue Activation			
Name Recognition on all Tickets	12,000	$12,000	$–
Logo on credential and VIP lanyards	500	$500	$–
Field of Play Signage Locations	1	$25,000	$–
Perimeter LED Signage, camera facing	4	$60,000	$–
Perimeter LED Signage, non-camera facing	2	$15,000	$–
Goal Signage	2	$30,000	$–
Entrance Welcome Banners	8	$16,000	$–
Public Address Announcements/ Scoreboard Logo	4	$8,000	$–
Fan Experience Activation/Videoboard	2	$8,000	$2,000
Concourse Tents/Kiosks	2	$16,000	$4,000
Staff shirt logos (security, ushers, event team)	150	$7,500	$2,000
Press Conference Backdrop Logo	1	$10,000	$–
Fan Premium Giveaway (on entrance)	Up to 12,000	$12,000	$–
Out of Venue Advertising/Promotion			
Use of Event Marks in Advertising and Promotion		$25,000	$–
Event Street Banners	200	$2,000	$–
Event Print Advertising		$8,000	$–
Event Radio Advertising		$50,000	$–
Event Television Advertising		$50,000	$–
Access to Ticket Buyer Database		$6,000	$–
Hospitality			
Complimentary Tickets, VIP	50	$15,000	$15,000
Complimentary Tickets, General	100	$7,500	$7,500
Press Conference Passes	12	$300	$–
Athlete Meet and Greet	12	$1,200	$–
Pregame VIP Reception	50	$8,750	$4,250
Postgame Party	75	$18,750	$9,375
Autographed Balls	20	$4,000	$400
Merchandise Gift Bags	50	$10,000	$3,250
Totals		**$501,500**	**$47,775**

Figure 7.7   Calculating Value and Cost of an Individual Sponsorship

- I notice that your company has sponsored events in the past. What have you tried to achieve with these partnerships?
- How does your company measure the success of these event sponsorships?
- What is your vision of how a perfect sponsorship would help to achieve your company's objectives?

Figure 7.8   Three Sample Test Questions

REVISE the Opportunity

The event promoter has now gathered the intelligence necessary to identify the objectives, needs, and attributes of the prospective sponsor company or brand. Demonstrating responsiveness and flexibility, the promoter must then line up the appropriate opportunities that the event can offer to achieve a partner's goals. Now, it is time to create a customized proposal that will illustrate the value the event can provide to the prospective sponsor, and anticipating objections and answering questions before they can surface.

Taking all questions and feedback into consideration, and adding some creativity, flexibility and intuition, the promoter should tailor the package, incorporating pertinent solutions in response to the additional information provided by the prospect. Reallocate the benefits they value less to beef up those the company finds more appealing. Reinforce every facet of the presentation to maximize its chance for success. Finally, consider whether an upward revision in the sponsorship fee is required to adequately cover any new or expanded fulfillment expenses, or a downward revision to accommodate the company's desire for involvement at a lower level.

PRESENT the Opportunity: The Sponsorship Deck

There are two components to your presentation—the personal, verbal demonstration that a sponsor's marketing wants and needs may be met by your sports event opportunity, and the physical, leave-behind materials that will keep selling after the meeting has concluded. The written presentation is also widely known as a *sponsorship deck*, an easy-to-read restatement of the most important points of the presentation accompanied by relevant illustrations, graphs, and charts.

An effective sponsorship deck demonstrates that the event promoter possesses a basic understanding of the company's event marketing objectives and builds a persuasive case for how sponsoring the event can provide solutions for the company's wants and needs. The deck should contain pertinent and comprehensive information that supports the promoter's arguments, organized in a logical, easy-to-digest format. We prefer to use short paragraphs or bullet points instead of prose. This technique makes it easy for prospects to scan the deck after the presentation for the information they believe is most salient to their evaluation and ultimate decision. If available, be sure to use as many images of past editions of your event that captures the excitement and engagement of fans who attended.

It is essential that sponsorship opportunities be presented in person. There is simply no way to adequately communicate the excitement of your sports event through the mail, e-mail, web links, or even video calls. You can't be certain that your sponsorship proposal, regardless of how well composed, will even be opened or read. Even if it is read, there is no way to respond to questions or counter objections before opinions are formed. Whenever possible, the sponsorship presentation should be delivered during an in-person meeting with the company's event marketing decision-makers. Without the organizer in the room, many prospective sponsors, if they open the deck at all, will look only at the last couple of pages—how much does it cost, and what do we get? Events are not commodities—they are experiences. Without experiencing your presentation, the sponsorship deck will, in fact, become a commodity. Remember that corporate marketing executives are besieged daily by sponsorship pitches. E-mailed proposals can be deleted with a single keystroke. Links may never be accessed. And, mailed proposals do not remain long atop the stacks piled high on their desks; they quickly find their way to the bottom.

The sponsorship deck is an organized, comprehensive summary of the event marketing opportunity, an outline that is presented in the same order as the oral presentation. If a picture is worth a thousand words, a brief, well-edited video, known as a *sizzle reel*, is worth one hundred times that. A video longer than two minutes becomes boring to everyone but the promoter. It should capture not only the excitement of the event, but also the various ways in which sponsors were recognized and how they activated their relationships. One or two brief case studies of sponsorship success with testimonials from existing sponsors can be particularly effective.

If the event is completely new, consider hiring an illustrator to create a series of "artist's renderings" and site plans or maps. It is far easier for the prospect to imagine the scope and scale of the event if they have materials to help them visualize it. Make sure the design of the presentation is as exciting and innovative as the content, and be prepared before you attend the meeting to send a link to it via e-mail immediately after the presentation (unless you are asked to make revisions to it by the sponsor). If you are meeting at the prospect company's location, try to get permission to set up the meeting room at least 30 minutes beforehand. Display enlargements of photos and artist conceptions. Ensure that the computer, display, and connectivity for the presentation are loaded, ready, and in perfect working order before the meeting begins.

Schedule an hour but design your presentation for 20 to 30 minutes. The sponsor prospect may not arrive on time. Even if you are kept waiting for 15 minutes, you want to be able to deliver your entire presentation, and still have a period available for questions and further exploration.

Bring inexpensive gifts of event merchandise to the first meeting, such as t-shirts, caps, and balls or pucks in sufficient quantity to cover each meeting participant. Be careful not to bring anything that has the name or logo of the company's competitor. If you use the company's logo on presentations or premiums, be 100 percent certain it is current and correct. Companies often change their corporate and brand logos in subtle ways without fanfare. A good place to check for logo accuracy is the home page on company's own website.

Remember that the deck has to keep selling after the live presentation is over. Make sure it is persuasive, organized, and comprehensive. Above all, make sure the assumptions and promises in the proposal are realistic and that hyperbole is minimized. Experienced corporate marketers have doubtless sponsored sports events that sounded better than they actually turned out to be, so assume that their hype detectors are turned to "high."

The points of emphasis in sponsorship sales decks are as individually different as the events they represent. Some may be advised to include more in-depth background material on the audience characteristics of the event or its featured sport. Presentations for reorganized or relaunched events may wish to highlight changes in programming, staging, or entertainment value. Some may contain one or a handful of specific sponsorship opportunities, others a menu of opportunities from which the prospect may choose.

Regardless of its ultimate format, there are several basic components of a winning sponsorship presentation (see Figure 7.9), organized in the same sequential, interest-building way in which a good novel unfolds. Capture the prospect's attention with the opening bullet points that, together with your oral presentation, tell one of these simple stories:

1. **Overview**—Capture the tone and significance of the event. Establish the relevance of the event and the credentials of the organizer.
2. **Introduction**—Summarize the opportunities presented by the event and objectives of the presentation. Briefly introduce the demographics of your fans.
3. **The Event**—Present a more complete, but concise, description of the property.
4. **The Opportunity**—Provide details on how the company can get involved.
5. **Next Steps**—Conclude with a call to action.

Figure 7.9 Basic Components of a Winning Sponsorship Sales Deck for Sports Events

"Coming soon is a compelling and unique sports event. This is the story of what makes it compelling and unique, and how savvy sports marketers can realize their goals by being partners. Based on what we have learned about your company's strategies or plans, we believe you can be the next to profit by an association with the event. Here's what you can do to take advantage of a partnership now!"

or

"An event that has provided outstanding results for sponsors and appeals to customers like yours can do the same for your company or brand. The reasons for these proven results are the compelling and unique ways we deeply engage our fans, and the cost-effective marketing opportunities we customize for our sponsors. Here are some of the ways you can leverage our event as an activation platform that will drive similar results for your company. We have some ideas to start with and can work together to develop a host of other opportunities."

The **Overview** of a sponsorship sales presentation should grab the attention of the reader at the outset. Communicate genuine excitement and believable enthusiasm—not hype—in your oral presentation. Establish the attractiveness of the event by portraying its history and its growth in popularity, scale, and scope. Include brief quotes selected from media coverage of past events. Demonstrate a basic understanding of the prospective sponsor's needs, if known, by describing what makes the event engaging, unique, appealing, and a great opportunity for the business partner. Provide a brief statement about the organizer's unique qualifications, and their successes in staging this and other events.

Now that you have the prospect's attention, launch into a meatier **Introduction.** Demonstrate the attractiveness of the event's audience demographics and lifestyle characteristics. Include graphs, charts, and tables that portray the similarities between the typical fan or participant and the company's ideal customer. If this is a first-time event, describe these audience characteristics based on similar events for the same sport(s) in analogous markets. If the event has been held before, disclose the names of other sponsor companies and brands and, if appropriate, provide examples of how their association with the event proved successful to their marketing efforts. Showing a short, fast-paced introductory video of 60 or 90 seconds during this portion can vividly demonstrate the excitement the event will generate. This can transition very smoothly into the next component of the presentation.

In **The Event** section, fully describe the program. Provide a portrayal of what the event is, when it will be held, and where. This is the point in the presentation when all the excitement and warmth of your product—the event—should come shining through. If appropriate, include a facilities map, a schedule of activities, illustrations, photographs, and graphics. Again, be sure to acknowledge and showcase images that feature visible recognition of existing sponsors. Describe the program so the prospect can sense the depth of your commitment to corporate partners. If your description sounds curiously like how you might promote the event to the potential public audience—it should! Although you are selling a corporate partnership and not tickets, you are still selling your event.

The event description must be as captivating and intriguing as possible, because it will lead directly into **The Opportunity**. This is where you will present the series of business solutions, entitlements, and benefits the event can provide to the prospective sponsor. If the promoter has a specific role in mind for a particular prospect, it should be described as an available option in this section. Otherwise, you may offer a series of possible customized packages from which to choose. If you know what the prospect wants from an event marketing partnership, demonstrate how the opportunity can help that company to achieve its marketing objectives. With this information, the company's decision-making process may be vastly simplified. Sponsorship packages that offer companies the right kinds of business solutions can then be evaluated on the basis of price and cost-effectiveness.

We prefer to call the last pages of the sponsorship deck **Next Steps** instead of the "conclusion." A conclusion implies an ending. If the promoter has done his or her job right, the sales process will be just beginning. In this brief summation, the deck should again emphasize the solutions the event can provide. Commit to working with the prospective sponsor to find the right solutions for the company. Be sure to provide a contact name and information for any questions that might arise after the presentation.

A fast-paced, uplifting wrap-up video of 60 to 90 seconds can punctuate your remarks and end the presentation on a high note. After the video, ask for questions and feedback. If questions are not forthcoming, ask a few open-ended questions to get the interchange going. If you were unable to gain input during the "test" phase, this is a great time to get it. Find out if the event, as presented, can meet the company's marketing needs and whether the opportunities outlined in the presentation are on target. If it is not, don't panic. It is rare indeed for a proposal to be so intuitively perfect that it is immediately accepted by the prospective sponsor "as is." Listen carefully to all questions, comments, and objections.

It is likely that a significant number of companies will simply pass on the opportunity outright. With prospects that seem even marginally engaged, ask how the sponsorship's appeal might be strengthened. Try to determine what features they think are essential and which are superfluous to them. Sense what level of involvement the company would be likely to pursue if it did desire to become a partner and explore how the opportunities in the presentation may be better customized for that company's purposes. If you can elicit feedback during the presentation, propose a reasonable time frame for a second, more refined presentation that will better incorporate the prospect's thoughts. If you cannot gain feedback on the spot, propose a date by which you will contact the company for reactions and questions. Then, REVISE the proposal, if necessary, and get ready for your next presentation.

CLOSE the Deal

When you return, revise the overview and introduction sections to communicate what you learned from your last meeting and how you incorporated these insights into an opportunity better focused on the prospect's specific needs. Present the newly fashioned opportunity and, again, ask for questions, comments, and areas of concern. Be prepared to negotiate on the spot if further revisions are requested or required, fortifying areas of importance and reducing assets of less interest. This is why it is so important to be familiar with the fulfillment costs and value of the various elements of all sponsorship deals. This may be your last chance to reach an agreement in principle, so be decisive and *make it count*! Respond immediately with new solutions to the company's challenges.

More fine-tuning of the sponsorship may be required, and negotiations might eventually become complex and protracted. When it appears that a deal is possible, however, propose sending a letter of agreement to the prospect that will officially summarize the areas in accord. Negotiations will certainly continue once the agreement is sent, but this piece of paper may be helpful to keeping the deal on track.

The Decision-Making Process

The decision-making process that a company undertakes to evaluate an event marketing opportunity can be lengthy and arduous for both parties. After investing a significant amount of time and creativity, and crafting what would seem to be the ideal opportunity, the organizer may still find the result to be negative. It is, therefore, important to throw a wide net over the largest number of qualified prospects during the sales process. Don't limit yourself to a single company or brand within the same product category. Approach as many prospects as possible to enhance your chances for success. Waiting for one company at a time to evaluate the opportunity can be a costly mistake.

Present opportunities to targeted prospects as far in advance as possible. Thousands of great potential partnerships wither and die because there was insufficient time available for the sponsor to fully evaluate the program, the company's event marketing budget was already exhausted, or there was not enough time for the sponsor to fully implement an effective activation strategy. It is challenging enough to sell an event sponsorship—don't let insufficient lead time be the reason you are shut out.

How early is early enough? If the program is an annual event, it can be very effective to invite the decision-makers and a guest from targeted companies to attend the next edition as VIPs. Greet them upon arrival and extend treatment befitting an actual partner. Make sure they have access to on-site VIP hospitality functions and provide them with commemorative merchandise. Be sure to also invite the decision-makers of companies that passed on the opportunity if one of their competitors did not join the event partner family. The quality of the event, the hospitality of the promoter, and the longer period of time before decisions must be made for the following year may persuade them to take another look. Try to set up a meeting to explore a partnership opportunity as soon after their attendance as possible.

If it sounds as though you need a year or more to complete the process of securing sponsors, that can be absolutely true, particularly for midsize to large sports events and for deals of significant financial value. Simpler community and grassroots events, presuming their income expectations are reasonable, may be funded in a shorter timeframe. Generally, the lower the cost of the sponsorship and the simpler the benefits, the less time is needed to generate sponsorships. For example, a local Little League all-star game charging a $500 sponsorship fee in return for a banner or two needs only enough time to have the banner designed, printed, and delivered. Events that require advertising or promotional fulfillment activities such as consumer sweepstakes, discount programs, or commemorative giveaways, need more time to develop and fulfill.

The Sponsor's Point of View

Sponsor prospects need time to fully analyze the potential advantages of supporting a sports event marketing opportunity. The evaluation period can take weeks or months, and the greater the degree of involvement and cost, the longer the process can be expected to take. A prospective sponsor will evaluate whether the event will offer the company needed and desirable marketing opportunities and whether its marketing budget can accommodate the associated financial commitment.

In addition to expense, an evaluation of cost-effectiveness will also be of great importance to the sponsor. That is, will spending money on this sports event produce a higher level of product sales than if the same amount was spent on another activity such as advertising, promotion, or even another sports event? The measure often used in this assessment, when product sales are the key performance indicator, is known as the return on investment, or ROI. Simply defined, ROI quantifies the number of additional dollars generated in sales for every dollar spent on the event's marketing fees and activation. If the ROI for an event marketing program can yield better results for the dollar than other components of a product's marketing mix, it will generally be regarded as a good buy by the prospective sponsor.

Of course, the effect on product sales (or brand awareness, or other metric of importance to the sponsor) cannot be accurately projected before the event sponsorship has commenced, only evaluated upon its conclusion. To improve the likelihood of success, savvy marketers measure potential partnerships against the strategies and standards that have yielded them the best results in the past. Figure 7.10 provides a checklist of some of the criteria that sponsors may use to evaluate a new partnership opportunity. Be sure your proposal anticipates the answers to these questions.

Many of these event sponsorship characteristics can be applied equally well to sports events of global significance and to regional and community programs. It all depends on sponsors being able to generate an acceptable return on their investment. A corporate partner wants assurances that the target markets for the event and the customers of its business will be compatible and that a sufficient volume of fans or participants will attend to justify the expense.

Sponsors must also consider the timing of an event. Does the event schedule dovetail with other promotional opportunities (e.g., Fourth of July Sales, holiday shopping, clearances, new product introductions)? Do they already sponsor a sports event that adequately serves their target market at that time of year, making the addition of another program a duplication? Or, does the opportunity fit a time of the year when a marketing program can help a company generate a noticeable spike in sales?

Sports event promoters can provide prospective partners with answers only if they understand the questions. The overarching query will be: "How does this event marketing program offer my business unique and significant opportunity with sufficient and affordable value beyond its intrinsic prestige and attractiveness?"

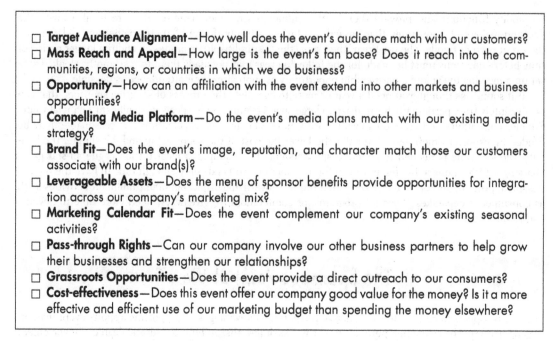

□ **Target Audience Alignment**—How well does the event's audience match with our customers?

□ **Mass Reach and Appeal**—How large is the event's fan base? Does it reach into the communities, regions, or countries in which we do business?

□ **Opportunity**—How can an affiliation with the event extend into other markets and business opportunities?

□ **Compelling Media Platform**—Do the event's media plans match with our existing media strategy?

□ **Brand Fit**—Does the event's image, reputation, and character match those our customers associate with our brand(s)?

□ **Leverageable Assets**—Does the menu of sponsor benefits provide opportunities for integration across our company's marketing mix?

□ **Marketing Calendar Fit**—Does the event complement our company's existing seasonal activities?

□ **Pass-through Rights**—Can our company involve our other business partners to help grow their businesses and strengthen our relationships?

□ **Grassroots Opportunities**—Does the event provide a direct outreach to our consumers?

□ **Cost-effectiveness**—Does this event offer our company good value for the money? Is it a more effective and efficient use of our marketing budget than spending the money elsewhere?

Figure 7.10 Sports Event Sponsorship Evaluation Checklist

How Companies Assess the Value of a Sponsorship

Sports event organizers assign a price to a package of sponsor benefits based on how much it will cost them to fulfill their obligations, plus the net profit required to fund event operations. As previously discussed, organizers may spend between 25% and 50% of sponsorship revenues on fulfillment. Or, put another way, they try to generate a profit margin of 50% to 75% on gross sponsorship sales. Sponsors, for their part, seek to receive double or triple the value for every dollar they spend on their investment. They calculate value based on the market value of the various components. Beyond the numbers, sponsors place great importance on the prestige and reputation of an event, audience loyalty, the number of other event partners vying for attention, and the competitive protection offered by category exclusivity. Most of all, sponsors want to be able to credit their event relationship with a measurable increase in product sales, an increase in market share, increased brand awareness, or other metric that informs their objectives.

Because most businesses have many more active marketing efforts in place than just a single event relationship, the direct effect of a sponsorship on sales is not always easy to quantify. It is easier to attribute an increase in sales for a small neighborhood business supporting a community sports program where anecdotal feedback from customers is personally received. At the opposite extreme, companies with global reach, and spending great sums in support of sports event sponsorships, also hope to experience a noticeable increase in sales and capture market share from their competitors. Sponsorship of sports events with national or international prestige, supplemented with wide-reaching, well-funded activation strategies, can perceptibly influence sales. For the vast majority of companies that fall between the small neighborhood concern and the giant multinational corporation, it is often difficult to attribute an increase in market share to a single sports event sponsorship or to identify the portion of new sales it may have helped to develop. Therefore, it is to the benefit of organizers to devise opportunities that sponsors can use to measurably affect sales attributable to their partnership. These can include direct sales opportunities at the event and discount codes that may be promoted at the event or that are included in the event's marketing efforts. Online visits from the event and click-throughs from the event's app, website, or online advertising to a sponsor's home pages with special offers can provide instant result metrics. Social network postings about the sponsorship can be easily tracked. Any program that adds consumer value to the purchase of a sponsor's product or engagement opportunities before, during, or after the event can provide direct evidence that an event partnership helped to increase a sponsor's sales, enhancing the relationship and strengthening the case for continuing the association.

Evaluation of Marketing Impact and Exposure

Sponsors will calculate the value of sports event partnerships in much the same way event organizers do, though they may evaluate them differently. Although many sports league sponsors conduct their own analysis of value with in-house personnel, companies that spend for sponsorship fees in the six- and seven-figure range often retain an independent evaluation provider before and after the event, or retain the expertise of a sports marketing agency. These companies use a vast database of sophisticated historical data to measure exposure time and value for a sponsor's logo, name, or product seen on various media platforms, on social networks, in advertising, point-of-purchase promotional displays, and presence at the event site. If exposure is among the company's strategic objectives, each such exposure opportunity is assigned a value per impression, multiplied by viewership, circulation, and page views. In some cases, it is multiplied again by a factor representing the length of time each corporate message is exposed.

The analysis of sponsorship value may include other key exposure points, such as the brand's name and/or logo on event tickets, credentials, staff, crew, and athlete uniforms, merchandise, directional and welcome signage, street banners, event site entrance treatments, invitations, posters, and many others. Advertisements associated with direct viewing over various media, ads on the videoboard, and public address announcements provide additional, easily measured value. The results generated by these valuation services will demonstrate that not all signage is created equal. Organizers should ensure that sponsors investing the greatest amount in their event enjoy exposure opportunities that are in the most desirable, visible, and valuable locations.

Finalizing the Deal

The execution of a formal agreement between the sponsor and the event organizer, drafted and reviewed by competent legal counsel, is highly recommended upon conclusion of negotiations. This critical legal document will include the negotiated business points of the deal and various legal protections required by both parties. It is not unusual for attorneys representing the parties to identify dozens of further details that must be defined (e.g., delivery date for tickets, approval processes, restrictions and limitations on promotions, and payment schedules). In addition, there are usually a significant number of necessary legal inclusions relating to insurance, liability, cancellation terms, breach of contract penalties, non-disparagement clauses, and other safeguards that both parties hope never to have to use but are nonetheless necessary. The agreement will also outline how intellectual property rights will be shared (e.g., the permitted usage of the logos and brand names of each party).

Contracts and letter agreements used to finalize sponsorship deals generally remain confidential. Although proprietary and individual to particular event organizers, there are several areas that most sponsorship agreements have in common, as described in Figure 7.11. Many more sections may be added to meet the specific needs of the event and character of the sponsorship deal.

1. Definition of the Event, the Event Organizer, and the Sponsor
   - What corporate entities are entering into the agreement?
   - What event(s) or event element(s) does the agreement cover?
2. Identification of the Sponsor Identity
   - How is the sponsor being identified—by the corporate name or by one or more product or brand names?
3. Sponsor Designation
   - How have the parties agreed to recognize the sponsor in both event and corporate communications (e.g., as part of the event title, presenting sponsor, official sponsor, official supplier, or donor)?
4. Exclusivity
   - What sponsor product category or categories does the agreement include?
   - What kinds of relationships with other companies are made "off limits" to the organizer?
5. Intellectual Property Rights
   - How and in what form may the sponsor use the event's name, logo, or images?
   - How may the event use the sponsor's name and logo?
   - What approval process should be followed for each usage?
6. Territory
   - Over what geographic territory do the sponsor's rights extend (e.g., community, state/province, national, multinational, global)?
   - How is online promotional activity affected by these territorial limitations?
7. Term
   - When does the sponsor partnership begin and end?
8. Renewal Options
   - Under what conditions may the agreement be renewed?
   - Are there exclusive periods of first negotiation or first refusal?
   - Are there any price protections or other incentives offered to returning sponsors?
9. List of Entitlements
   - This list is frequently appended to the agreement as a separate schedule outlining all agreed-to benefits (e.g., tickets, signage, advertising, and hospitality opportunities) in precise detail.
10. Marketing and Promotion Rights
    - What kinds of event-related consumer promotions are the sponsor permitted?
    - How may the sponsor use the event in product advertising, display materials, packaging, or promotions?
    - What digital rights will the sponsor have with respect to the event?
    - Under what conditions is the sponsor entitled to use photographs or video of the event or athletes in its marketing programs?
    - How may event tickets and merchandise be used in consumer sweepstakes and giveaways?
    - Under what conditions, if any, may rights be passed through to the sponsor's other business partners?
11. Consideration
    - The sponsorship fee and schedule of payments, whether in cash or VIK.
    - Fulfillment expenses payable by either the event or sponsor, and any optional add-on benefits.
12. Indemnification and Insurance
    - Under what jurisdiction and procedure will lawsuits proceed stemming from injuries or property damage in connection with the event, sponsor promotions, advertising claims, and other possible causes?
    - To what degree will the organizer protect the sponsor against legal actions by third parties, and vice versa?
    - What minimum types and levels of insurance coverage do the parties require of each other?
13. Cancellation and Default
    - Under what conditions may the agreement be terminated?
    - What are the promoter's obligations, and the sponsor's rights, if the event is canceled or postponed because of conditions not under the control of either party (also known as *force majeure*)?
    - What happens if either the sponsor or the promoter defaults on its obligations?

Figure 7.11   Essential Elements of the Sponsorship Agreement

Now, Service Your Sponsors!

Once you have congratulated your sponsor and the responsible members of your organization on the successful conclusion of negotiations and the execution of your agreement, the work really begins. Too often, it is during the sales and negotiation processes when event organizers devote the most attention to their sponsors. Fulfilling the sponsorship agreement and investing in the sponsor's successful association is a time-consuming but rewarding necessity. It is wise to appoint at least one staff member to serve as an account executive whose key function is to oversee the event's relationship with its sponsors. This individual should be empowered to ensure not only that the spirit and substance of the contract are met, but also that the sponsors feel they are appreciated and integral to the success of the event. Organizers should communicate with them often to share new developments and opportunities, to monitor their success, and to ensure they sense their importance to the event realizing its full potential. Investing the necessary time and effort in helping them achieve their objectives will pay future dividends as the event develops and grows in future years.

Post-play Analysis

The best way to meet the objectives of prospective sponsors is to design a program of event benefits that provides solutions to their business wants and needs. Benefits of sponsorship may include tickets, exclusive-access activities, promotional rights, signage and advertising, among many others. An understanding of what the prospect hopes to achieve through its event association should help an organizer customize an individualized package that contains the most attractive benefits in the right quantities for each sponsor. Organizers should analyze and account for the fulfillment costs of delivering each benefit to ensure that their net sponsor revenue goals remain attainable. Likewise, estimate the value of these components to certify that what you present to a sponsor provides more value than the cost.

Prospective sponsors should be qualified before being considered potential sales targets. Event promoters should create a persuasive sponsorship presentation to prospects that clearly outlines the opportunities available. Get the prospect's reaction to the presentation and make the revisions necessary to close a deal. Formalize the deal with a contract or letter agreement that clearly outlines the obligations of each party, sponsor rights and benefits, and all financial and legal commitments. Understand how the sponsor will evaluate its success post-event and ensure that the results meet or exceed their expectations.

By teaming with sponsors and understanding their wants and needs, event organizers will be better positioned to manage events that will be teeming with sponsors.

Coach's Clipboard

1. A B2B technology company in a mid-size city has never sponsored a sports event in the past. It is not that the company has not been approached before; it has never seen the need. The company employs 1,500 local staff and a network of sales agents across the country to sell its products and services. How can you position participation in your regional gymnastics event as an attractive business solution for the company?

2. You plan to present a B2C prospect with an opportunity to be the title sponsor of a state multi-sport recreational tournament. As a leader in its industry, the company has lesser interest in exposure opportunities than VIP hospitality for its dealers and retailers and fan engagement platforms at the event to enhance customer loyalty. The event site, however, does not offer significant space for sponsor activation or dedicated VIP reception spaces. How can you structure the sponsorship to deliver the appropriate business solutions to the prospect given these limitations of the event site?

3. An event promoter wants to approach a company with a history of spending generously on sponsorships for similar events. The company's contact, however, refuses to provide any meaningful input on the firm's event marketing objectives and asks that all proposals be mailed before an appointment for any live presentation is considered. How should you proceed in preparing a pitch for this prospective sponsor?

4. A sponsor conducts a post-event evaluation, the results of which suggest that the demographics of the event did, in fact, match those of its target market and that the impact of the company's exposure met its expectations. The company's sales, however, showed no meaningful increase. What will you do to encourage the sponsor to return next year?

Maximizing and Servicing the Media Partnership

"I always turn to the sports section first. The sports section records people's accomplishments; the front page nothing but man's failures."
—*U.S. Supreme Court Chief Justice Earl Warren, Sports Illustrated, July 22, 1968*

This play will help you to:

- Understand the opportunities to work with the news-gathering (editorial) and commercial divisions of media organizations to publicize and promote your sports event.
- Encourage media coverage before, during, and after your event.
- Service the needs of the media covering your event on site.

Introduction

The Roman god Janus is most often pictured in profile as a head with two faces. The deity of gates and doors, Janus also represented the concept of new beginnings. (Not coincidentally, this is why the month that bears his name is the first of each new year.) Ancient worshippers believed that one must pass through a gate or door before entering new places and, therefore, the god looks simultaneously in both directions—back into the past and ahead into the future.

To sports event organizers, the media often assume the countenance of Janus. Writers and broadcasters look forward to event day, reporting on preparations and controversies, and speculating on how competition will unfold. They later look back on the results and provide analysis and perspective on the event's successes and outcomes. The media can be an event's best friend or its worst enemy and, like Janus, they can sometimes assume both aspects at the same time. Much like the gods of ancient times,

151

as perceived by their followers, the media can entertain well-directed appeals but cannot be controlled. To understand the delicate relationship between an event and the media, one must first grasp this key stakeholder's business objectives.

The Two Faces of the Media

A media outlet, whether a television network, streaming service, website, newspaper, magazine, radio station, or digital platform, exists for one primary purpose—to transmit information of interest to its specific target audience. Some information and how it is presented—in the form of advertising, promotions, and other marketing ventures—is under the direct control of the event organizer. Typically, the more valuable stream of information—in the form of news coverage and publicity—is under the total control of the media outlet.

The media provide organizers with a resource to publicize and advertise their event, a vital component in the campaign to attract an audience and participants. When coverage of an event is positive, the media can generate the impact, influence, and credibility that advertising alone cannot achieve. Similarly, when the tone of coverage is negative, the impact can likewise be so persuasive that even the most creative advertising and promotional campaigns can have difficulty overcoming the challenge.

To preserve objectivity and journalistic integrity, as well as an attractive platform for advertising and promotion, media outlets most often organize themselves into two separate, semi-autonomous halves: editorial and sales. The editorial half is charged with the responsibility of providing objective informational content by covering news and developing stories and features. This group is typically under the leadership of an editor or producer who, together with his or her writers, correspondents, and columnists, must compile and communicate information that is relevant and interesting to their readers, viewers, or listeners. Event organizers direct their publicity efforts toward this editorial side of the media, disseminating event information as press releases, story ideas, content-sharing, and opportunities for coverage before and during the event itself. Most editors and producers enjoy complete freedom in deciding which stories will be compelling enough to their audience to be written, published, or aired.

In business environments where the press is not financed or controlled by the government, operating a media outlet can be a very expensive proposition. In addition to selling copies, subscriptions, or access, news outlets must sell advertising to cover their costs and generate a profit on their respective platforms. Electronic media such as radio and television also sell advertising to support their operations, or they charge viewers indirectly through carriage agreements with cable operators or streaming services. Digital media producers sell subscriptions to users, access to premium content, valuable collected data, and/or advertising to commercial partners.

This second face of the media business is essential to enable the editorial staff the freedom and funding to pursue their journalistic responsibilities. This is the sales and marketing half of the media partnership, led in the printed media by the publisher and in the electronic and digital media by a sales or marketing executive. Media outlets sell advertising, create and manage promotions, and pursue event-marketing opportunities as vehicles to promote sales, enroll new subscribers and sell additional advertising to event sponsors. Event organizers work with the sales and marketing side of media businesses to purchase advertising, create media partnerships and establish consumer promotions that will drive ticket sales, revenue opportunities, attendance, and viewership.

To preserve the objectivity of reporting, the two halves of the media organization must work independently. In the model media outlet, the presence of a promotional relationship between a sports event and a news-gathering organization will not increase the interest of an editor in providing readers with news coverage. Conversely, its absence or partnership with a competitive media partner will not exclude an event from the editorial assignment calendar. An event–media partnership will neither provide organizers with a warranty against a lack of coverage or negative stories about the event nor encourage glowing reviews afterward. In the eyes of the editor, if the event is newsworthy, it will be covered; if it is well organized and executed, it may be covered positively.

Content publishers, by contrast, see more than just the newsworthiness of sports events. They see unique business opportunities that can generate revenue and increase readership. They view events as attractive vehicles to sell incremental advertising and provide promotional platforms to benefit their business. Some create special pages that add value for readers and profits for the publication through increased circulation (print and digital readership combined) and incremental advertising revenue. The publisher and marketing staff are usually the key decision makers on whether to participate more broadly with an event. In addition to the goal of generating advertising revenues, their objectives may include increasing readership in their core market, expanding total circulation, and attracting users to their digital sites. Magazines with significant and targeted readership are organized along similar lines as daily newspapers. National magazines are difficult to attract as marketing partners, but may be more accessible on the editorial front, assuming the event can generate stories that are nationally relevant. Magazines with a local focus are much more open to working with event organizers as potential marketing partners.

Like magazines, local television stations and network affiliates are good targets for partnership opportunities with sports events. National networks normally provide news stories that are globally or nationally relevant. There is often a similar separation between the news and sports coverage side of their business, as well as the marketing and promotional side that generates the revenue that keeps them both operating. Where television outlets differ is in situations where a network holds the rights to broadcast the event. In such cases, the national broadcaster may engage in promotions that increase awareness for an event for the purpose of increasing viewership of its coverage.

Most business partnerships between sports event organizers and television broadcasters unfold on the local level. On the one hand, the most obvious prospect is the local affiliate of the network that will broadcast coverage of the event. While other stations in the market may be approached if the affiliate decides not to partner, it would be more challenging to convince another television station to promote an event that will be seen on a competitor's channel. On the other hand, if the event is not a broadcast property, nearly any outlet will do. It is best to align the event with the station most watched in the market by the audience you want to attract. Cable television affiliates can be outstanding resources, so don't overlook the local sports networks and news channels.

Radio can also be quite effective in generating local excitement and is frequently the medium most agreeable to considering promotional partnerships. Over-the-air radio is primarily a local medium. Most advertising is sold locally and is usually far less expensive than television advertising, and can also boast a far lower "cost-per-thousand" than newspapers when compared to full-page display advertising. (We compare radio spots to a full-page newspaper ad because they are delivered similarly uncluttered—there is only one radio ad on at a time and there is only one ad on a full page.)

Digital media, particularly social media sites, provide sports events with seemingly limitless opportunities to use an online presence to interact and stay connected with fans. Personalized experiences that resonate with their respective audiences offer abundant and increasing revenue benefits. They are, therefore, most efficient medium for spreading information—and arguably the most dominant—including web-based services, such as social media platforms, news aggregation forums, and media partners' websites.

Online platforms have the distinct advantage over traditional media outlets by having the ability to be updated continuously. The event organizer can offer information and have it disseminated to his or her target market virtually instantly. Conversely, the wide and instantaneous accessibility provided by online media enables them to report time sensitive news to massive audiences, news that may be a tremendous advantage for promotion if the stories are positive (and a burdensome challenge to the event's image if the stories are negative). Web-based media have the power of nearly unlimited reach, so even if the event is locally focused, the event organizer has the potential of reaping benefits on a national, or even a global, scale. Social media sites give the concept of "word-of-mouth" new meaning by allowing individuals, journalists, and fanatics alike to share their thoughts and feelings to possibly millions of other people. Event organizers can leverage social media by curating specialized event pages or feeds, or partnering with popular bloggers—amateur and professional—to provide event content and coverage. Such content can deliver both journalistic information and a branded message to fans and customers.

Perhaps the greatest advantage of web-based media is that it enables direct interaction between the event's organizers and the target audience, especially on social media platforms. This feature creates a more effective touch point than traditional advertising and can build more personal and responsive relationships between prospective customers and event organizers. Positive interactions may serve to benefit the event as these individuals are influenced and, in turn, may relay their experience and interest to many of their own friends on social media platforms. Social media essentially becomes a highly targeted and cost-effective form of free advertising that can stretch an event's limited marketing budget.

What an event organizer hopes media outlets will provide—both as partners and as communicators of news—will differ significantly based on their respective corporate objectives. To understand what one can reasonably expect from the media, an organizer must comprehend what both halves of the media business want and need from a sports event.

What the Editorial Side Really Wants from Sports Events

It is important to recognize that because media outlets are typically bifurcated into independently managed editorial and marketing functions, their wants and needs also diverge along very similar lines. Editors, writers, producers and correspondents are charged with the responsibility of providing a conduit of information to their readers, viewers and listeners, and cover events from perspectives they feel are newsworthy and interesting. To fulfill this mission, the editorial side needs compelling story ideas; accurate information to help support their reporting; good photo, video, or sound bite opportunities to add visual or audio support to their words; and facilities that will help them cover the event and submit their work to the editor or producer (see Figure 8.1).

Whether the sports event is a community tournament or a multinational invitational competition, event organizers must approach the media in a professional manner that demonstrates an understanding of their needs and expectations and represents the organization as competent, authoritative, and knowledgeable. Put another way, sports event organizers should provide no excuse to editors and producers to overlook

---

I. Needs Prior to Event Day
- Compelling story ideas
  - Unusual or compelling stories about participating athletes
  - Interesting historical perspectives on the event and past athletes
  - Significant business stories (e.g., economic benefits, intriguing or innovative partnerships)
- Accurate and comprehensive information
  - Press releases
  - Social media
    - Concise, regular updates
    - Timely and relevant information
  - Media guides
    - Background information
    - Participating team or athlete rosters
    - Event history
    - Official rules and format of competition
    - Official statistics
    - Schedules of events
  - Access to senior event organizer management for interviews
  - A single point of contact for additional information

II. Needs on Event Day
- Appropriate, comfortable working conditions
  - Workstations with clear view of play
  - Timely access to official and accurate statistics, score sheets, athlete background information
  - Clear, unobstructed positions for photographers
  - Availability of required services and technology
  - Access to organizer management, coaches, and athletes at pre- and postevent press conferences

---

Figure 8.1   What the Editorial Side of the Media Needs from Sports Event Organizers

covering the event. Fostering an amateurish impression to the media can seriously damage a sports event's overall marketing plan. Diminishing the perception of an event's importance and credibility in the mind of the editor or producer can jeopardize coverage of the event itself, or worse, generate negative impressions of the event or organizer through instantly available social media. As pre-event media coverage provides the public with a strong first impression of an event and, by extension, reinforces the perceived value of attending, organizers should ensure that every contact and communication with the editorial side is clear, confident, accurate, and appropriate.

Like sports event organizers, editors, reporters, producers, and correspondents must operate within the boundaries of their own limited financial resources. On the editorial side, budget constraints are manifest in the amount of space (newspapers, magazines, and web) or time (radio and television) they may devote to covering an event. The amount of space or time allocated to any story is determined by the editor or producer and is a clear indication of how they view its importance to their readers, viewers, or listeners. Demonstrate the professionalism of the event and its organization and convey the importance of the event to the host community with every media contact. "Space in most newspapers is limited. Some organizers, understandably enthusiastic about their ventures, simply fail to realize that others might not share their enthusiasm," noted former *Los Angeles Times* sports columnist Helene Elliott. "I think the drama and importance must be inherent. The event should be compelling enough on its own that it doesn't need false hype." Maintain frankness and credibility, as well as your reasonable expectations as to the intrinsic newsworthiness of your event.

Like sports event organizers, media also work against immutable deadlines that must be recognized when planning campaigns to generate publicity. Daily print, television, radio, and digital media work on continuous deadlines, while deadlines for inclusion in weekly media may be only a couple of days prior to publication. Social media sites have especially demanding time constraints requiring updates on a minute-to-minute basis as news developments break.

Information, Please

It is up to the sports event organizer to identify the newsworthy opportunities that exist for media coverage throughout the event-planning process and to effectively communicate these possibilities to any combination of editors, writers, columnists, producers, correspondents, and others. A campaign of strategically spaced press announcements should be planned over the days and weeks leading up to the event, during the event itself, and even afterwards to build interest among the media and, by extension, their readership, viewers, or listeners—your actual and potential audience. A sample campaign is presented in Figure 8.2

I. Event Announcement
    a. Event Description, Host City, Venues, and Dates
    b. Logo Introduction
    c. Economic Impact
    d. Charitable Association
    e. What's New
    f. Digital Resources (event website, social media, other digital assets)
II. Announcement of Participating Athletes or Tryouts
III. Major Sponsor Announcements
IV. Human Interest Stories (may be multiple releases)
V. Ticket Sales Information
VI. Credential Application Process
VII. "Hard Hat" Tour Invitation (an opportunity to tour the site during set up)
VIII. Participant Media Introduction
IX. Postevent Announcements
    a. Official Results
    b. Attendance Figures
    c. Amount Raised for Charity

Figure 8.2 Sample Sports Event Press Announcement Schedule

in a generalized, chronologically structured order that will be applicable to many sports events. Organizers may combine any number of these announcements into the same release and schedule additional announcements that are appropriate to their specific event property.

The first communication to the media should, of course, officially announce the event. Even existing events with a long tradition in the host city should plan to release a statement announcing the date(s) and location(s) of the event, ticket sale details and background information such as historical highlights and economic impact estimates, if applicable. A press release distributed to a comprehensive list of media outlets or a news conference for invited media are standard methods to make the first announcement. In addition, before you can communicate this vital information, a digital platform and infrastructure should also be put in place from which you can simultaneously make the announcement. The best way to disseminate this information rapidly to mass audiences is via a robust web presence that includes a customized event site and connectivity with various social media outlets. This will provide a number of avenues for your potential ticket buyers and other targets to access crucial, up-to-the-second event information. If the event is introducing a new logo, it may also be inaugurated at this time to begin the process of building awareness for this refreshed identity. Here, too, an organizer can announce any associated charity that will become the beneficiary of an event, along with information on the contributions the event has provided to charitable organizations in the past.

The first announcement should introduce the media to the event, concisely describing the competition or program of activities. If the property is an established sports event, this description should also include information on what is new and exciting about the upcoming year's edition. Is the competition format different? Are there new activities or attractions planned for existing or new audiences (e.g., children, families, groups, or at-risk youth)? Will there be noted champion teams or players competing? Do not assume that all media are completely familiar with the event or sport, even those with a long tradition in the marketplace. "Event organizers need to provide members of the media with comprehensive background on the event, easy-to-understand chronologies of the event, and comments from participants, where and when applicable," says sportswriter Allan Kreda.

The introductory announcement takes on particular importance for events that were open to bidding by prospective host cities. The first announcement is the organizer's best opportunity to excite the local media, and, through them, the community at large and area businesses. Winning the competition to host an event can be big news but, except for the most major of sports properties, that alone may not be enough information from which to fashion a compelling story. Include additional details on how many other cities competed for the honor, and why the city was selected. Include economic impact data (see Play 4) and the number of hotel room nights event staff, participants, guests, and fans will occupy. If there is a charitable partner or beneficiary of a portion of the event's proceeds, this could be a good opportunity to announce that, as well.

Delivering the Announcement—Press Releases

Distributing press releases via file-sharing, e-mail, digital media, or other means are effective ways of distributing key event information to the media before the event. Most direct communication with media members or partners is likely to be by press release—a concise, well-written missive that provides basic information in convincing, but factual, form. Because press releases are most effective when they are as brief as possible (between one and three double-spaced pages), they cannot provide a full and comprehensive overview of a sports event. That said, a press release should include as many answers to the "who," "what," "where," "why," "when," and "how" details of the event, heralded by an attention-grabbing headline and subheading.

It is essential that the headline and subhead entice the reader to go further. Press releases are marketing and sales documents. To maximize the chances that a release will become a story, it must be compelling, credible, convincing, and free of hype. Above all, preserve your perception of professionalism by ensuring the release is 100 percent error-free, typographically, grammatically, and factually.

Because some media outlets will use the press release as their primary source of information about the event (and might even use portions of the press release as is), it is important to include one or two quotes from reliable and respected authorities. It is appropriate that one or more points of information be provided in the form of a quote from the most senior official of the organization staging the event. A second quote may be included from another important stakeholder, such as a participating star athlete, a key city official, or a representative of the benefiting charity. Don't try to fit every piece of event information into the release, just include those items that provide a complete framework outlining what the program is all about. Writers, reporters, and correspondents may want to incorporate more details, quotes, and information beyond those provided in the press release. Be sure to include a contact name, phone number, and e-mail address either at the top of the first page or at the end of the document. The best stories are almost always generated by writers who look for perspectives that will be unique from those of their colleagues. See Figure 8.3 for a sample press release that officially announces the fictional Big Street Sports Tournament described in the Host City Request for Proposal (RFP) in Appendix 3.

LEDUC SELECTED TO HOST

THIRD ANNUAL BIG STREET SPORTS TOURNAMENT

More than 1,000 Top Amateur Athletes from Across the Nation to Compete against Hometown's Best This Summer

Contact: Dan Sommer
dsommer@mnosports.com
888-000-0000

The City of Leduc has been named as host of one of the nation's fastest-growing street sports festivals and national invitational tournament, the Big Street Sports Tournament, in the summer of 2025. The selection of Leduc as the host city for the Big Street Sports Tournament was announced in a joint statement by the Mayor of Leduc and MNO Sports of Washington, D.C., the promoter of the event.

The Big Street Sports Tournament will bring more than 1,000 top-ranked amateur athletes to compete at Leduc's Civic Sports Complex this July 17 to 21. The visiting athletes will also take on the city's own premier competitors in skateboarding, in-line skating, roller hockey, and BMX bicycle contests for all age, gender, and skill levels, ranging from "8 and Under" to "18 and Older" divisions.

"The Big Street Sports Tournament has found the perfect host in the City of Leduc," said Arthur Andrews, executive director of the event. "Action sports athletes from across the country will enjoy the outstanding hospitality for which the city has become famous." "Leduc has again proven itself to be an active and exciting sports city," said Mayor Angie Arturo. "The Big Street Sports Tournament will attract thousands of families and sports enthusiasts from the local and surrounding communities to watch and enjoy the competitions, as well as to take advantage of a full weekend of great entertainment, interactive activities, and pure fun."

Sports fans and entertainment-seekers will be welcome to attend the event free of charge. In addition to the competitions, visitors will enjoy BMX half-pipe exhibitions, an extreme sports video arcade, "kids-only" clinics and activities, free in-line skating and braking lessons, nonstop musical entertainment, a bicycle tune-up area and obstacle course, a street sports product expo, special guest appearances, food provided by local restaurants, and more.

This will be the third edition of the Big Street Sports Tournament, which has been previously held in Providence, Rhode Island, and Orlando, Florida. An average of more than 30,000 visitors attended the festival and tournament in each city.

The full schedule of events and additional information for the Big Street Sports Tournament will be released at a later date.

Figure 8.3   Sample Sports Event Announcement Press Release

- Compile a list of the appropriate story or assignment editors and producers (e.g., sports, business, entertainment, city desk) to whom you would like to send the release at the host city's major media outlets and ensure that all names, addresses, and titles are current and accurate.
- News has to be new. Make sure that all information is timely, correct, and not previously announced. The press release should be delivered to all outlets on the same date.
- Be sure that every word in the release is used and spelled correctly, and that the body copy is grammatically correct.
- Include one or two brief but meaningful and newsworthy quotes from the highest-ranking organization official. Quotes can underscore why your news is exciting and worthy of coverage.
- Always include a company contact name, number, and e-mail address at either the beginning or end of the release.
- Generating media interest is a marketing and sales process. Be sure to follow up with media representatives who do not contact you directly within a few days after sending the release.
- Make your first effort your best. If the release results in no media interest, do not rewrite and resend it. Move on to preparing the next announcement as scheduled.
- If your release does result in a story, send a brief thank-you note to the editor/producer and writer/correspondent.
- Post the press release on your event website and release details onto the event's social network sites.
- Post links to the stories generated by the media on your event's website and social network sites.

Figure 8.4 Press Release Development Checklist

Some sports event organizers will have the budget available to retain the services of an outside public relations agency to help manage the publicity campaign, write press releases, and coordinate press conferences. Others, with limited financial resources and unable to afford public relations assistance, will be faced with the task of creating and distributing their own releases. Figure 8.4 provides organizers working with restrictive budgets with a brief checklist to consult before distributing the first press release.

Delivering the Announcement—Social Media

Press releases provide a means of formal communication with legitimate media outlets but, given the nature of web journalism, the reach of digital media, and the realities of a 24-hour news cycle, you should also be prepared to offer information through virtual channels. To this extent, social media networks afford the means of mass communication to media members, as well as to thousands of amateur, semiprofessional, and professional bloggers, journalists, and your most avid and engaged fans. These groups may contribute higher speeds of information transmission and potentially great influence among your event's demographics. Although some of these individuals or outlets may not be accredited media, they nonetheless provide targeted outreach and drive the dissemination of information. You may want to distribute links to a version of the official press release directly to the public via a number of social media sites.

Beyond adding efficiency to the process, social media platforms offer the unique opportunity to generate a buzz among consumers. These sites allow events to create customized, interactive profiles enabling fans to converse with each other and with the event organizer. Microblogging sites also provide the ability to drive engagement with and between event guests and help in the spreading of information. The organizer will also get an inside look at what discussion topics are trending and what "followers" are talking about.

In essence, social media serve as a bridge between events, media outlets, and the end users. These platforms can add efficiency and effectiveness to your relationships with the event's media partners, while also decreasing your dependence on the traditional outlets to properly deliver your event's message and excitement. In fact, you can become your own media outlet to a degree. The 24-hour news cycle demands that you play a more active role in disseminating event news and details along with your traditional media partners, though it is still important to cultivate strong relationships with trusted media members to accelerate the consumption of the event's announcements and other critical event information by the public.

Delivering the Announcement—Press Conferences

The first announcement of a sports event and the subsequent issuing of the most meaningful and important event information are often communicated at press, or news, conferences. Although press conferences can be far more effective in generating media attention than simply circulating a press release, they can also be far more involved and expensive. Be reasonable in your expectations. If you truly believe that an announcement is news of genuine significance to the community, it may merit a press conference and may be worth the extra coordination and expense. Will details be revealed that are compelling enough to be worth the time commitment of the media representatives who will attend? It takes far less time for someone to read a press release than to travel to, attend, and return from a press conference. Are the individuals delivering the announcement(s) newsmakers themselves, worthy of including in a report's "sound bites" (brief audio clips) or a personal interview for television or radio reports or in social media posts? Will there be other stakeholders at the press conference who the media may want to interview such as participating athletes, coaches, celebrities, or government representatives? You should be completely confident that staging a press conference is the correct approach for any particular announcement, as meager media attendance suggests to those who did show up that the message delivered was of little importance. There is only one opportunity to do this right. If the announcing press conference is poorly staged, if there are no new or interesting details revealed, or if few media actually attend, the perception of the event in the market can be seriously damaged.

Recognize, too, that attendance at a press conference is a significant time commitment for writers, photographers, and camera crews. News is happening everywhere, and there are only a limited number of personnel and equipment available to cover it all. Make sure the time being dedicated to the press conference will be well spent. Start at the time scheduled and stage it efficiently, no more than 20 minutes, as illustrated in the sample run of show in Figure 8.5.

Consider inviting media and other important stakeholders to view or participate in the press conference remotely. Attendance and coverage can be substantially increased through the access and convenience available through any of the familiar teleconferencing platforms. Simple yet appropriate technology (such as cloud-based software), professional quality equipment (to facilitate video and audio), and staffing (for setup, operation, and troubleshooting) will be required to ensure a professional production for the virtual viewing audience. Flawless delivery will be essential!

Press conferences are announced by circulating a "media advisory" to the same local contacts that were compiled for the distribution of press releases. An advisory is designed to provide enough information to

Time	Item	Duration (mins:secs)
10:00 A.M.	Host Welcome and Press Conference Rundown	1:00
10:01 A.M.	Introduction of VIPs, Special Guests and Tournament Representative	1:00
10:02 A.M.	Announcement of Event by Tournament Representative	3:00
10:05 A.M.	Mayoral Address (introduced by Host)	3:00
10:08 A.M.	Event Description and Details (with video presentation) by Tournament Representative (introduced by Host)	4:00
10:12 A.M.	Questions and Answers (with Tournament Representative)	5:00
10:17 A.M.	Host Wrap-up with Acknowledgments	1:00
10:18 A.M.	Breakout for One-on-One Interviews	

Figure 8.5 Run of Show for a Sports Event Announcement Press Conference

encourage the attendance of media outlets without providing the key details that will be announced at the press conference. It should include a generalized statement describing the subject of the press conference (without inadvertently making the announcement in the advisory), the names of those who will be participating in the announcement, and, of course, where and when the announcement will be made. Again, a contact name, phone number, and e-mail should be provided to enable advisory recipients to request additional information, confirm attendance, or to receive press releases if they cannot attend. Send the advisory a day or two prior to permit assignment editors and producers to schedule a reporter and/or a camera crew to cover the press conference.

Select a venue for the press conference that is convenient to those attending and, if possible, meaningful to the event. Remember that reporters attending the press conference want little more than to hear the announcement, receive the details they need to develop a story, and write their article or broadcast their report. They generally will not want to have to endure lengthy commutes, nor will they desire a sightseeing tour of the event facility. If the host venue is conveniently located, by all means schedule the press conference there. If it is difficult to reach, efforts to generate media attendance may be more successful by staging the press conference at a more centralized location such as a downtown convention center, hotel, city hall, restaurant, or an appropriate local landmark. If held in a facility other than the event venue, try to select a room that will not dwarf the audience. Oversized rooms can give the impression of sparse attendance. If space permits, invite a reasonable number of event staff and local stakeholders to attend. Their presence will improve the appearance of the conference and may even provide additional interview subjects for the media. Press conferences are usually "limited access" events, so inviting a small number of senior-level sponsor executives, business partners, and community leaders can also provide an exciting bonus that demonstrates gratitude for their involvement. But try not to exceed the number of media members with the number of guests. Request that nonmedia guests and staff understand that questions to the participants and interview opportunities are restricted only to members of the media. Also, it is appropriate to make seating assignments to reserve specific locations for expected media.

Some press conferences include a morning breakfast or midday luncheon, or at least snacks, coffee, and soft drinks, to enable the organizer to interact with the media over a longer period of time. Reporters have to eat, too, so this is the one instance when an event of greater duration is acceptable. Once the meal is consumed, though, the clock resumes ticking. Again, make sure the actual presentation is brief and to the point. Try to schedule the announcement on a day and time that does not compete for media attention with other sports or special events being held in the community. Check your local sports and other event calendars to reduce the chance of staging the conference at a time when some other activity can steal attention and media away from the delivery of your message. Avoid scheduling press conferences on a Friday because Saturday readership and viewership are generally weaker than during weekdays or Sundays. Scheduling the start of press conferences for weekday late mornings or early afternoons are usually best for meeting late-afternoon and evening media deadlines.

Ensure that all media members who attend the press conference sign in as they arrive. A well-designed media kit that includes the press release, background information, photos, video content, illustrations of the event site, and other appropriate materials that will help reporters prepare their stories should be prepared and available online. A paper version of the press release also could be given to attendees. Be sure to remember to e-mail a link to the media kit materials immediately after the press conference to media outlets that were in attendance, as well as those who were unable to attend. Providing media members with a small takeaway token such as an event cap, pin, T-shirt, or tote bag is not inappropriate so long as its actual value is minimal.

Select an articulate host or master of ceremonies, preferably from the community such as a sports radio personality or a popular personality who appeals to the same target market as the event. The host should introduce a senior organizer executive to deliver the information that is contained in the announcing press release. This segment should be as brief as possible to enable a guest speaker to be included, such as a city official, community host committee leader, or featured coach or athlete. After the guest speaker's brief remarks, the event executive can continue, providing additional event details. The description of the event can be supported by audio and visual aids. If visual graphics are used to support the presentation, the visual should provide a bright enough picture to be seen clearly without having to turn off the lights in the room and should be part of the online media kit material.

When one or more people are scheduled to have speaking roles, be sure to review each participant's talking points, the broad topics they will address, and the statistics they will use in their remarks. It is best to provide each speaker with a brief written explanation of their role and the subjects they will discuss. Include factual information pertinent to their role to ensure that multiple speakers will not cover the same subjects or, worse, provide the media with contradictory information (e.g., expected attendance, economic impact figures, hotel room occupancies, etc.).

These guidelines are most applicable to the scheduling of pre-event press conferences. During the event itself, press conferences are frequently staged to service attending media with pertinent information, official results, and interviews. Technical requirements and a floor plan for effectively staging press conferences are provided later in this chapter.

The Campaign for Attention

The announcing press conference or release is only the opening salvo in a campaign to maximize media attention. Publicity, by itself, is not a complete marketing plan. It is an essential, but not the sole, component and is reinforced by advertising, promotion, and event marketing campaigns. Audiences presume that news organizations are candid, objective communicators of important news and, therefore, the information they present is often perceived as more credible than the hype of advertising. Organizers need the media to generate stories that will create a sense of believable importance and relevance to their events. In between the first announcement and event day, there may be myriad possibilities to present the media with additional story ideas from a number of different angles or perspectives, as presented in Figure 8.2. Create a schedule of opportunities to "pitch" reporters who had expressed specific interests after the announcing press release or conference. For maximum effect, try to time these efforts to lead up to or coincide with important pre-event milestone dates, such as the first day of ticket sales, the debut of advertising campaigns and promotions, or as player or team registration begins. Other announcements might be timed to generate publicity after the pace of ticket or sponsor sales has ebbed or as the event date approaches and a little extra boost of public awareness is required.

Human Interest Stories

One of the key focal points for pre-event publicity should be the development of stories about the participating athletes. Putting a human face on a sports competition can make an event more interesting to the potential audience and, as a result, appealing to reporters such as Kreda. "To me, the human interest angle always makes a sports event compelling," he observes. "Every event has the ability to produce the unexpected. I go into every sports event realizing that it can provide a drama or situation I've never before encountered." The human perspective on how an athlete prepares for and participates in an event provides the drama Kreda often uses in his reports. "The subtle human stories behind any event are of most interest to me," he adds.

Kreda understands the value of building relationships between his readers, the fans, and the athletes competing in the sports events he covers. The public wants to know who the athletes are, how they came to compete at the event, and why their performance is worthy of the spectators' interest. Roone Arledge, president of ABC Sports from 1968 to 1986, recognized the awesome power of connecting fans to athletes through the use of personal storytelling and revolutionized the way sports events were presented on television. Widely credited as the architect of the now familiar features of today's sports television landscape, Arledge was responsible for the creation of such landmark programming as *ABC's Wide World of Sports* and *Monday Night Football*, and such techniques as slow-motion replay. While supervising production for 10 Olympic Games, he pioneered the practice of integrating in-depth personal features on worldclass athletes with coverage of their competitive performances. To this day, networks apply this programming philosophy as a way of riveting viewers to competitions, establishing powerful emotional bonds that involve the audience beyond simple appreciation of athletic excellence.

SIDELINE STORY

Creating Coverage Creatively

In the mid-1980s, monster truck shows became popular events in arenas throughout the United States. The success of these attractions, whose "stars" were colorful vehicles with giant tires and grandiose monikers that soared off ramps and into the air before landing forcefully and spectacularly on doomed cars and other defenseless objects, caught the attention of booking executives at New York's Madison Square Garden. Originally considered to be an event appealing more to suburban and rural audiences and unlikely to be able to draw large crowds into New York City, the Garden decided to take a chance by booking a show on a February weekend in 1985. Early ticket sales were less than robust. Determined to improve sales in the final days leading up to the event dates, the Garden's public relations department met to brainstorm a "stunt," the kind of high-visibility publicity spectacle the staff often staged to attract the attention of the hard-to-impress New York media.

On an Eighth Avenue sidewalk outside the Garden and the busy Pennsylvania Station train terminal, the media and the public were treated to a fantasy-come-true, the demolition of the city's most ubiquitous vehicle. A "Cab-tastrophe" was staged featuring a monster truck crushing a New York City taxicab. The television and newspaper coverage of the stunt was enormous and the attention helped attract capacity audiences.

Encouraged by the successful weekend, the Garden booked the monster truck show again for a weekend in January 1986. Following its flamboyant publicity stunt for the first event, the Garden's public relations staff had to come up with another tour-de-force exploit, especially since the target audience for the show, young men, would undoubtedly be distracted by the coming weekend's NFL playoff game between the New York Giants and the Chicago Bears.

Rather than ignore a game that sports fans and the media were highly anticipating, the PR team decided to use the Giants-Bears matchup as the theme for another stunt. One of Chicago's most popular players at the time was William Perry, an immense defensive lineman with a mammoth nickname to match his frame, "The Refrigerator." The media found the enthralling image of a monster truck driven by a Giants fan crushing six refrigerators in a quiet Greenwich Village location, Perry Street, in front of number 72, The Refrigerator's uniform, irresistible. The extensive coverage included national as well as the local outlets and was a highlight of an effective campaign to bring crowds to the Garden who wound up enjoying the weekend monster truck show more than the football game, which the Bears won on their way to a Super Bowl title.

Quite often, the trick to pulling off an effective publicity stunt and attracting attention for an event is being creative in finding fresh ways to connect with your audiences. One can only imagine how quickly these events might have gone viral if digital media had been available.

Sports event organizers should harness this power by familiarizing the media with their event's participants and identifying the human-interest stories that may abound. They must identify these opportunities through press releases, advisories, and personally connecting with editors, producers and reporters, either directly or through the efforts of their public relations agency. Athletes need not be Olympians or famous to have engaging or emotional stories to tell, tales of triumphs over tragedy, and courage in the face of personal adversity.

Is there a registration or tryout process for participating teams or athletes? If so, prepare a release or advisory inviting the media to attend, and circulate a press release announcing the final roster of competitors. Are there never-before-told stories about a local participant who has overcome personal challenges to excel on the playing field?

Are there visiting athletes who have unique stories or perspectives on the local community to share? Traveling participants seem to get more fascinating the farther they have had to journey to the event. Will they spend any time sightseeing or learning about the local culture? Is there a contestant who is poised to break a performance record or personal best? Perhaps there are teams seeking to end a particularly long championship drought or athletes focused on extending a winning streak. Don't overlook developing stories from the perspectives of past champions or beloved greats of the sport. The history of a sports event is frequently best communicated in the words of former athletes.

Although sports event organizers and their agencies can encourage the development of human interest stories by circulating press releases, arranging personal interviews are far more effective and usually far more appreciated by the media. Include an offer to set up an interview—in person, by teleconference, by phone, or another available mode—with the individual(s) featured in the release. Reporters will often want interviews to be held one-on-one in an attempt to draw out answers or information that will provide exclusive content or stories that others may overlook. If you expect an unusually large number of media to desire interviews with the subject, a small informal gathering, breakfast, luncheon, or reception may be scheduled with the interview subject and interested reporters. Be prepared to stage brief individual interviews immediately after the larger session. Television news and sports reporters will want to capture the athlete on video to support their stories. Likewise, radio media will want to record sound bites to make their reports more compelling to listeners.

Another convenient interviewing option for the media is to schedule a teleconference meeting. Access to the session can be restricted to invited media with password controls, and later opened to the public on social media platforms for additional publicity value. This option can be the most useful and cost-effective when the interview subject is traveling or lives far from the host city.

Business Stories

The benefits and value that an event can provide to the business community should be promoted to both sports and business media throughout in the campaign. The articles they generate can be particularly useful for attracting local sponsors and promotional partners. Typical minutiae and fun facts may include the number of hotel room nights expected to be sold as a result of the event, the number of staff and volunteers who will work on the program, projected attendance, and even the number of media expected to cover the event. Include historical information about the success of the event in previous years and past host cities.

Sponsor announcements are best directed to business reporters and trade publications and must be relevant to local commerce or the partner's industry. Is the sponsor celebrating a major anniversary of its association with an event? If so, talk about what has made the relationship so valuable to both parties. Perhaps a major sponsor decided to become involved with a sports event because of the cross-promotional potential with other sponsors. Is there is a new or intriguing special promotion that the organizer or sponsor will execute in fulfillment of their partnership?

Is there something new or unique about the sport or organization? Stories can be pitched that discuss the vigor and longevity of the organization, the growth of the sport or the event's popularity, shifts in fan demographics, the advances in equipment, training, and technology associated with the sport, even the success of the organization's leadership.

Creating an Engaging Web Presence

Making fans aware of an event is only half of the battle. Public announcements and stories driven by mass media are great for generating publicity, but driving genuine fan engagement can be the difference between a casually interested individual simply reading about the event and a potential event ticket buyer or attendee. Online media, in particular, provide event organizers an excellent opportunity to develop a relationship with their potential customers and fans well before the event begins. The reach goes beyond any story or advertisement because the event organizer can directly and personally interact with prospective spectators. The power of web-driven influence can have a tremendously positive effect on your event, if used effectively. But when this power is misused or abused, it can have quite the opposite effect. As such, it is important that a strategy is devised to make the event's digital media presence a tool and not a threat to the event's marketing.

The goal of creating a web presence is twofold: to drive excitement among potential event attendees and to start building a relationship with your customers. Driving excitement starts by developing features for the event's website that will encourage fans to link, visit and spend time perusing the site. This content can take many forms, including videos, pictures, exclusive content, and fan-generated multimedia. Media coverage and press releases should also be archived on the site for fan access. Offering rich content serves as a preview to the event, so it is important to deliver material that is representative of the event's product and philosophy and also provides sensory engagement for viewers. Updating the site on a regular basis with information about the event and fresh content will help drive continued, repeat traffic. The cadence of these updates could be as frequent as multiple times a day or might coincide with important dates, such as the beginning of ticket sales, to draw high levels of traffic that may be more easily converted into sales. Content updates should be broadcast across social media platforms and the exchange of the information should be openly encouraged through sharing, reposting, and easy access links.

Building a relationship with fans requires more than simply offering content and informational updates. Sharing news and features is a positive start, but it's only a start. Social media's ubiquitous presence in our society allows even the biggest corporate brands to become "friends" with their consumers. A sports event is no different. It is up to the event organizer to come up with ways to engage fans on a personal level. Posting thoughtful, intimate updates on social networks and microblogging sites will give the event a personality. Create interactive engagement by asking your fans and followers questions. Who is your favorite player? What was the best event you've ever attended, and why? Direct the questions to lead into event-relevant discussion. Include polls and encourage answers. What activity on Friday are you most looking forward to? Another useful tactic is to generate contests that encourage fans to participate in some way for the chance to win a prize. Such contests can be trivia related or may require fans to send in a picture of them participating in the sport, and or attending an event. Request that fans register by signing up or logging in and collect a judicious amount of non-sensitive personal information. This presents an ideal opportunity to capture valuable data, such as e-mail addresses, for later marketing and sales uses. In sum, the goal for creating a web presence is to get potential customers involved and to show them that there are people and personalities behind the title of the event. This will create goodwill and make people feel as though they are part of the event and the brand before they really begin interacting. It is this connection that will compel people to appreciate what the real event is all about.

A word of caution: Social media are extremely influential, and this may not always be a good thing. As a society, we are overwhelmed by the amount of information, content, and requests presented to us on an everyday basis. Be careful not to become part of the clutter by sending too many messages, generating irrelevant updates, or abusing the privilege of your customers' privacy and contact information. Social and other online media can help your organization develop lasting relationships, or insensitive overuse can destroy them twice as fast. Listen to and learn from digital and real-life interactions with your consumers to figure out where the proper balance of engagement lies. In the end, a well-developed and thoughtfully executed online and social media strategy can be the most effective tool in an event organizer's campaign for attention.

Countdown to Event Day

As event day approaches, an organizer's need for media attention can grow exponentially. Publicity over the final few days can help to significantly boost attendance, increase last-minute ticket sales, and, for broadcast events, drive viewer and listener ratings higher. To maximize excitement, pictures best tell the story. Offer the media opportunities to cover preparations as the event moves into its host venue. If the installation of the playing surface or decoration of the event facility can provide good photographs or video footage, be sure to invite the media to capture them. Schedule a media preview or "hard-hat tour" to take interested reporters, photographers, and camera crews through the event site (if there is something to see), or invite them to dry runs, technical run throughs, or tests of important operational systems. If entertainment is a prominent element of the event (e.g., opening and/or closing ceremonies, halftime or intermission acts, special presentations), invite the media to a rehearsal and schedule interviews with the cast or featured performers. For participatory activities, such as at sports festivals, allow the media to preview attractions the day before the public. If a sufficient number of media are expected to cover the event, invite reporters to participate in a low-risk media competition right on the playing surface. Games or skills competitions can be staged between media and athlete alumni, print and digital media against television and radio counterparts, or one media outlet against another. Noncompetitive sports events like 10K runs and other amateur events can even incorporate the participation of media contestants directly into the activity itself. The outlet will not only cover the event as it unfolds from a unique insider's perspective, but it may even generate advance publicity about how its representative is training or otherwise preparing for their participation.

The arrival of teams or athletes may generate additional photo opportunities. Be sure to schedule some media availability time to provide access to the most intriguing participants. Opportunities may be scheduled as press availabilities with a representative handful of participants just before or after a practice, at a welcome reception, during public appearances, or even sightseeing tours of local points of interest. Alternatively, media time can be scheduled in which the participants are scattered throughout a hotel ballroom, on the playing surface, or along a host venue concourse beneath signs displaying their name, enabling reporters to guide themselves to the people they want to interview most. Try to arrange these opportunities at times that will still permit pre-event reporting for last-minute promotion, even if it will appear in the media just an hour or two prior to the competition. Every bit of coverage can be beneficial.

Servicing the Media at the Event Site

As noted in Figure 8.1, media members who cover a sports event expect appropriate, comfortable working conditions and the ability to view the competition from locations conducive to observing, writing, note taking, or uploading. Of equal importance are access to official statistics and score sheets, athlete and event background information, and the ability to avail themselves of facilities and technological services to file stories and broadcast reports in a timely and professional manner. Members of the media also anticipate being granted access to locker rooms, postevent press conference locations, and other areas where athletes and officials may be interviewed and photographed.

Media Guides

A media guide, printed or made available online, can provide all reporters with consistent and authoritative history, facts, athlete information, and statistics. Start with the most basic information—do not assume that the reporters assigned to cover your event are completely familiar with the sport, organization, rules, participants, or the format of the program.

Rosters, line-ups, and the order of competition should be provided to all media as they arrive or, at the latest, before the event begins. Include a detailed event schedule, packages of statistics, past event results, milestones or records, biographical information on the athletes and coaches, and historical background on teams. Competition rules and information on upcoming events also should be available. Many sports event organizers compile all of this information in the form of a media guide that is an immediately accessible through a password-controlled web link or as a printed publication. Media guides are usually completed and published as late as possible to allow for last-minute revisions, which is why digital editions, in addition to being superior for the environment, can be particularly useful for events where changes are frequent and inevitable.

Accreditation

For the purposes of maintaining a safe, exclusive, and professional work environment for the media and to maintain a reasonable level of security for the athletes and others working in nonpublic areas, an accreditation system is strongly recommended. Establishing an accreditation system involves the design and distribution of credentials to authorized personnel that visually identifies the bearer and their affiliation and permits access to non-public areas. The media accreditation plan must be integrated into an overall system that event security and operations personnel will use to control access to all areas of the site restricted to staff, volunteers, vendors, reporters, broadcasters, and other stakeholders.

It is useful for staff to be able to visually identify members of the media to direct them to the facilities set aside for their convenience, as well as for the distribution of press information. The mechanics of setting up a comprehensive event credential system are more fully explored in Play 14, "Managing for the Unexpected." The process of qualifying media who wish to cover an event and using an accreditation system to manage their activities on the event site is more appropriately discussed here.

Distribute an advisory to the target media listed in your press release database that invites media representatives to apply for credentials at least one month prior to the event. Larger and more newsworthy events anticipating a significant media response should circulate this advisory with even more lead time. Include event schedule information and an application requesting the name of the media member(s), their employer, and full contact information. If the event is of the magnitude that media will be traveling to the host city, you may also include information regarding hotel accommodations, airport details, and ground transportation.

In democratic societies, it is the right of the media to cover and report on any event that is open and available to the public. It is similarly the right of any event organizer to limit access to the event site to anyone who does not possess a ticket or credential. Organizers should assess the extent to which they can physically accommodate the media before accepting applications for accreditation. Although it is usually advantageous to maximize an event's opportunities for coverage, the number and nature of media members who should be provided with workspace and professional access, services, and courtesies are completely up to the event organizer and may be limited by the available support space and budget. It is perfectly acceptable to limit the number of credentials to those who can be accommodated safely and effectively. However, it should be kept in mind that competing media outlets within a particular territory (e.g., each of the daily news sites or radio stations in a given market) will demand access that is fair and equal to that provided to their competitors. As a general rule, it is recommended that all bona fide media be accommodated if at all possible. Where the organizer has perhaps a little more leeway in evaluating whether to provide access is with media with small niche readership or viewership or a uncertain relationship to the event audience. If an organizer has not heard of an organization or individual requesting access, it is strongly suggested that the background of the entity or person is checked. Remember that once you provide someone with a credential for access to restricted areas, you also undertake certain liabilities in exposing participants and staff to unfamiliar individuals. Media that cannot be accommodated in limited-access work and press conference facilities or who are unfamiliar to the organizer may be alternatively provided with complimentary tickets without additional access. While it is highly unusual for them to pay for tickets, media members who are not accommodated as above may still attend the event as members of the public and may subsequently write stories without having to apply for and receive credentials.

Be sure to set a deadline for returning completed media credential applications. It is up to the organizer how strictly one will adhere to the deadline, balancing the desire for coverage with the necessity to control access to non-public areas. As a general rule, the organizer is not obligated to admit media to controlled areas if they appear on event day without having applied for credentials. It is, therefore, essential that all media outlets that may cover the event have an opportunity to receive the advisory and application with sufficient time to respond.

The organizer should carefully review applications and respond to approved applicants with information on where, when, and how credentials may be picked up (nonapproved applicants, if any, should also be notified). It is recommended that the physical distribution of credentials be delayed until the day before they are actually needed to enter the venue, or on the event day, to reduce the chance of their being counterfeited and duplicated. Credentials should be worn and visible at all times, particularly in restricted areas. They may take the form of a pressure-sensitive printed sticker (acceptable for limited budget, one-day events), simple laminated cards with a safety-pin back or lanyard to enable it to be worn about the neck (essential for events that are longer than a single day), or a digital identification badge loaded onto a mobile device. An example of an event credential is pictured in Figure 8.6. Note that this example and all credentials should prominently feature the event name and date.

Figure 8.6   Sample Sports Event Media Credential

As previously mentioned, when a sports event organizer provides someone not under the event's direct supervision with access to restricted areas, the organizer assumes a greater level of liability. Therefore, it is recommended that some deterrents to the possible counterfeiting of credentials be considered. For low-budget events, unusual typefaces and multicolor, event-specific artwork can be inexpensive measures, although the widespread availability of software and inexpensive scanners and color printers means that a counterfeiter has only to spend a little time to craft a reasonably close facsimile. The application of small holographic stickers or holographic printing on the credential is another, better measure for organizers of events with greater security concerns. Including unique, scannable bar codes, or printing the credential on special paper with unique weaving are yet other common deterrents to counterfeiting.

The inclusion of a small headshot photo of the media member on the credential is standard practice and strongly suggested for major, high-exposure events. The best and most secure method of using photo identification is to digitally print the image directly onto the credential. For organizers with more modest budgets, the photo can be affixed to the credential and the entire card laminated to discourage counterfeiters from removing the photo and replacing it with another. Request that every person presents a government issued photo ID to confirm the identity of the individual receiving the credential. Companies that specialize in providing accreditation services can be engaged to handle the labor and technical requirements of managing this important function.

If the event security plan is more complex than simply allowing credential-bearers unfettered access to all areas, a color and/or letter code may be included on the face of the credential. This code will provide security personnel with information on the specific areas of access to which the bearer is entitled.

On printed event credentials, such as those being worn with a lanyard, the reverse side of the credential often includes legal disclaimers that transfer the risks of injury during attendance at the event, and as a result of being granted access to restricted areas, to the wearer. The right of the organizer to remove the credential from the bearer for inappropriate behavior should also be included in this language. It is essential that a qualified attorney develop and approve this protective language.

In addition to providing an exclusive, professional work environment for the media and an essential level of security for the event, the accreditation process will also prepare organizers with an understanding of how many media will attend to cover the event. Armed with this information, the organizer can install sufficient media center facilities and seating for the number of writers, broadcasters, and other working media representatives.

Media Center Facilities

As has been discussed, representatives of the media expect comfortable and appropriate working conditions during the event. Most arenas, stadiums, and other regularly utilized sports venues have ready-made press box facilities designed expressly for this purpose. Others offer a selection of multipurpose rooms or empty spaces that can be allocated and outfitted to fulfill various functions based upon a specific event's needs. As you assign spaces to meet your sports event's many requirements, try to keep the facilities that are being set aside for the media in as close proximity to each other as possible. Be sure to post printed, not handwritten, directional signs along the route between the entrance into the venue the media will use and all areas to which they require access, including the media workroom, the event office, press conference location, the media lounge or hospitality area, the press box or other areas designated for the media, and (if the media will have access) athlete locker rooms.

Media Workroom

Media seating at the event should be provided with a clear, unobstructed view of the playing surface whenever possible. Reporters who must "file," or submit their stories to their editor under often tight deadlines, should be provided with "tabletop" seating, that is, seats that are located at tables or countertop working surfaces.

Draped, half-width folding tables can be installed in areas where reporters will be working to provide them with a flat surface for their laptops or other devices. Multiple outlet power bars with surge protection should be run atop or beneath the tabletops to provide writers with access to power for their equipment. Task lighting should be added if the conditions in the area are not conducive to reading statistics and score sheets. Event-day media also require reliable Wi-Fi connectivity for their computers and mobile devices, and a limited number of high-speed data lines to transmit digital photography to editors. It is highly recommended that access to the internet be provided on a system separate from the one used by fans or guests to ensure the media have access with sufficient bandwidth. Other media, such as radio stations for game broadcasts or on-site updates, can be invited to arrange for dedicated service to be installed at their expense. If a code is required to access a Wi-Fi network, post this information visibly. If the event is televised or if an in-house video feed of the action is available, place video monitors within convenient view of the media seating sections, as well as in the media workroom and any spaces set aside as press conference areas.

When the expected media contingent is so large (or the venue is so small) that it is not possible to accommodate all of the media with working space in direct view of the event's proceedings, a secondary media workroom may be constructed elsewhere, such as in a large, open space defined by a curtain wall along the event level of an arena or stadium or outdoors in a tent. All of the requirements set forth for media seating sections—tables, seating, power, Wi-Fi—are equally important in these areas but, for such events, television monitors providing coverage of the event, appropriate heating/air conditioning, and security are absolutely essential.

Members of the media expect and demand instant access to information as the event progresses. If the media are seated in a single area during the event, a separate, localized public address system can be installed to communicate pertinent information exclusively to them. Use the system to announce official results, advise the media on changes in schedule, explain the decisions of judges and referees, update statistics, provide available information on athlete injuries, and communicate postevent press opportunities. Having a media-only public address system is particularly important if an auxiliary media workroom is installed for an overflow of journalists, ensuring that all receive the same information at the same time. In areas where the media tabletops are in public seating areas, the speakers should be sized, placed, and balanced so only the media can hear the announcements that are directed to them. Most importantly, be sure to test all systems—electrical power, technology services, and broadcast feeds—several times before the media arrive to be certain that all are functioning properly.

Media Lounge or Hospitality Area

Keeping the media comfortable is of the utmost importance. Reporters and crews often arrive at the event venue early to grab interviews with arriving athletes and depart late after the event has concluded, postevent press conferences have been held, and their stories have been filed, their reports have been broadcast and their photographs have been uploaded. Provide water, coffee, soft drinks, and snacks throughout the day. Meals appropriate to the time of day can be provided to the media either as an expense to the event or, at a modest charge to cover costs. Most venues with their own in-house caterer or concessionaire require organizers to purchase food, even in backstage areas, only from their service provider, typically an expensive proposition. If the event is able to bring its own food into the facility, an organizer's options become wider. "For a limited budget, grocery stores make sandwich trays," says Toronto-based media consultant David Job of Media Concepts. "Whole fruit and beverages can also be purchased and picked up."

Try to set up the refreshments in an area separate from the workroom if space permits. "Too often, workrooms become social gathering places and noise levels reach points that are distracting to writers who are working on deadline after others may have finished," observes Elliott. "Workrooms are workrooms, period. Set up a separate area, if available, where you have coffee or water and make sure there's a distinction between these areas," she suggests.

To determine what refreshments should be provided, consider what time most of the media will report to the event site and when most will depart. Estimate arrival at least 30 minutes before pre-game player availabilities and departure at least one hour after postevent press conferences to permit them time to complete their work. Do not assume the media will be able to visit concession stands—their job is to cover the competitive event, difficult to do if having to spend time finding a hot dog and soft drink. With this in mind, sandwiches and salads might be provided during lunch hours and a hot entrée can be served if work will take place through normal dinner hours. Soft drinks (if there is a sponsor's brand, serve it), coffee, and light snacks such as pretzels, popcorn, chips, and cookies should always be available. Figure 8.7 provides a handy checklist of media workroom requirements, followed by a real-life example of press box setup protocols from Concacaf's Gold Cup Media Operations Guide in Figure 8.8.

- Seating with tabletops (preferably with unobstructed view of event)
- Multiple power outlets and surge protectors
- Wi-Fi access on a network exclusive to media only
- High-speed data line for photographers
- Cellular network service
- Workspace (task) lighting
- Video monitors
- Small, localized public address system
- Refreshments (preferably in a separate hospitality area)
- Printer
- Schedules, rosters, and line-ups
- Printed material (e.g., press releases, media guides, statistics, event information)

Figure 8.7 Checklist of Media Workroom Requirements

Game Day—Press Box Setup
Three (3) hours prior to first kickoff at each venue, the following must be in place:
  I. Seating chart—hung in elevator, media seating area, and placed on stats table
  II. Placards—one placard placed at each seat signaling name and affiliation of media member
  III. Wireless Internet—check for activation
  IV. Game programs—one game program placed at each media member seat
  V. Game notes—game notes should be placed at each media member seat
  VI. Stats crew—dedicated computer for stats crew connected to printer; headphones to TV trucks; index cards available; flash stats. Concacaf statistics rules will be adhered to.
  VII. TV compound/TV and radio booths—game notes, rosters, and game programs delivered to broadcasters, to be overseen by broadcast liaison. VPO (Venue Press Officer) should nevertheless check in with liaison to make sure TV and radio crews are covered appropriately.
  VIII. In-house feed—broadcast of the game should appear on press box TV monitors as well as be taped in press box. Should it be requested from a media member, the press box supervisor should allow for in-game reviews at halftime and following the end of regulation.
  IX. Catering (press box and photo workroom)—see "Game Day Stadium Needs."

Figure 8.8   Press Box Setup Guidelines (From Concacaf Gold Cup Media Operations Guide)

Media Relations Office

Be sure the media are looked after by knowledgeable staff members or representatives of the event organizer's public relations agency. A media relations office should be located within close proximity of the media workroom to enable reporters access to staff for additional information or special requests. It is recommended that the media relations office be divided into two spaces, one that is separated by closed doors in order to conduct internal, confidential conversations with the event director or other senior managers in the event of a crisis or controversy. It is also helpful to have this quieter separate workspace available to the staff for writing and proofreading press releases without distraction or interruption. A secure storage closet or small room is another necessity.

The office should be staffed at all times the media are at the event site. Additional copies of press releases and other printed materials provided in the workroom should always be available from the office. The phone numbers and e-mail addresses for the media relations office and staff should be posted in the media workroom, as well as at the security office and the media entrance. No reporters, camera crews, or any other member of the media should be admitted to the event site without the knowledge of the media staff. Camera crews should always be escorted by a member of the media relations staff anywhere at the event site.

The media relations office is an essential workspace from which to manage media center operations. Desks or draped and skirted tables with chairs should be installed to provide the staff with a functional workspace. Reliable cellphone service for mobile devices and Wi-Fi capability should be available. At least one television monitor should be installed to follow the progress of the event and other developments.

It is also essential to have convenient and exclusive access to at least one high-speed networked printer with collator, stapler, and a more-than-adequate supply of copy paper along with other needed equipment as determined by the event's media director.

Plans for refreshments or providing meals for the media also should include the media relations staff, who will be working the same long hours as the people they are serving. Don't forget one of the most mundane of details—a carton or two of essential office supplies, including writing implements, folders, paper clips, staplers and staples, writing pads, message pads or Post-its, and any other consumable item that makes any functional office go (see Figure 8.9 for a typical checklist of media office requirements).

- Easy access from media workroom
- Desks or skirted folding tables
- Chairs
- Multiple power outlets and surge protectors
- Laptop computers or tablets
- Wi-Fi access
- Cellular network service
- Workspace lighting
- Television monitor
- High-speed printer with collator and stapler
- Copy paper
- Other equipment as needed
- Office supplies
- Copies of all printed materials
- Secure storage closet or cabinet
- Refreshments

Figure 8.9   Checklist of Media Relations Office Requirements

Press Conference and Interview Facilities

The press conference location provides a focal point for pre- and postevent interviews, the spot for dissemination of any information that is best delivered by a spokesperson throughout the program, and for any interactive exchange between the media and senior organization management. The press conference facility may occupy its own separate room, preferably close to athlete locker rooms and easily accessible from the media workroom. If such space is unavailable, an area can be created in a draped-off, column-free backstage space as conveniently located as practical. Regardless of its location, it should be situated in an area that is inaccessible to the public and as noise- and distraction-free as possible.

A checklist of requirements for a sports event press conference space may be found in Figure 8.10, and a typical layout in Figure 8.11. Set up enough chairs in view of the stage to accommodate the media expected to cover the event. It is acceptable, but not necessary, to provide tabletop surfaces for laptops or writing tablets in the press conference area. The focus of attention in the room is a stage or dais constructed

- Quiet, column-free, limited access space
- Media seating
- Stage riser(s) (preferably skirted)
- Camera/photographer riser
- Skirted tables for stage
- Podium (with optional logo)
- Pipe and drape backdrop (with step-and-repeat banner or drape)
- Public address system with technician
- Table microphones with mic flags for interviewees
- Wireless mics for moderator and interviewer questions
- Lighting for stage wash
- Video camera and monitors
- "Mult" box
- Video presentation equipment (optional)

Figure 8.10   Press Conference Requirements Checklist

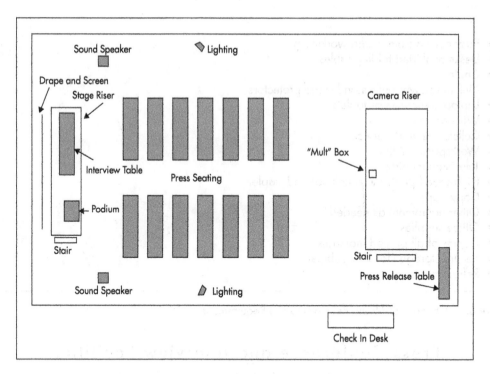

Figure 8.11 Sports Event Press Conference Room Layout

of riser platforms, commonly available through the event venue, at many hotels and convention centers, or through audiovisual rental agencies. Plan to design a stage that is only as large as required to accommodate the number of participants envisioned. Most stage riser platforms are available in 4-foot by 8-foot sections, and at heights generally ranging from 18 inches to up to 36 inches. If the interview subjects will most often be standing at a podium, risers that are 18 inches or 24 inches high are sufficient, raising the participants so they may be easily seen by all media in attendance without seeming to overpower the room. If, instead, the subject(s) will be seated at draped tables, the risers should be set at a minimum of 24 inches in height. For the most professional appearance, the legs of the stage riser should be skirted. It is not uncommon to set the press conference stage with both a podium and draped tables to accommodate a host, or enable the organizer the flexibility to quickly schedule multiple participant interview opportunities and statements without additional, last-minute setup. The podium should be in good, clean condition, and include a top shelf for speaker notes and water bottles. If one is available, an event logo should be centered facing the audience on the top portion of the podium, professionally printed on a lightweight board (and affixed in a way to not damage the podium) to maximize exposure on any video footage used from the press conference. *Mic flags*, small plastic tiles imprinted with the event or event organizer's logo, can also be attached to the microphones on the podium and interview tables to increase visibility.

The microphones should be connected to a high-quality public address system with sufficient speaker cabinets to provide clear, uniformly distributed sound throughout the media seating section. It is strongly recommended that the press conference audio system be installed and operated by a qualified audiovisual equipment supplier that will have a technician remain on-site at all times the area may be in use. Be sure that all systems are periodically tested before the media arrive, as well as immediately before any press conference begins.

Drape the wall behind the stage with a dark, nonshiny background. "Pipe and drape" units, fabric panels suspended on a frame of sturdy metal frames, are commonly available from many event facilities and rental companies in royal blue, navy blue, and black. Blue drapes look best in photographs and video. A step-and-repeat banner with logos of the event, presenting sponsor, and sometimes the venue are commonly set up in front of the drape, behind the participants.

A "camera riser" may be positioned behind the media seating area, centered at the opposite side of the room from podium and sufficiently large to accommodate the number of video and still photographers expected. It should be set at an equal height to the stage risers to enable camerapeople to shoot over the heads of the seated reporters. While most media who cover sports events will be equipped with lenses that will capture the close-ups they need from the back of the room, it is also acceptable to place the media riser closer to the stage so long as those making use of it will not obstruct the view of those seated.

An audio *mult box* should be available and located on or adjacent to the camera riser. A mult box is a small, briefcase-sized unit that distributes the sound directly from the press conference's public address system to any plugged-in television camera, radio line, and audio recording device. This unit is essential to providing the media with top-quality, interference-free sound from the press conference microphones. If your event venue does not own one, a unit can be inexpensively rented.

Press conference areas should be lit for television coverage. The organizer's audiovisual supplier should be asked to light the stage with a "wash" (an even distribution) of television-friendly light. Lighting should be focused on the speaker standing at the podium and/or at the speakers sitting at the tables and never face directly into the eyes of the participants. Rather, they should be hung from a position 8- to 10-feet high, or on lighting "trees" (free-standing poles topped with lighting instruments) and placed at 45-degree angles to the stage's center on either side of the room. Whether hung or placed atop trees, lighting must come from two different positions to eliminate the harsh shadows that can distort or under-expose resulting photographs and footage. If a large contingent of media is expected, the organizer may be well advised to install television monitors at regular intervals in locations distant from the stage and fed by a camera on the riser. The same feed can be sent to the video monitors in the media workroom to enable those in the process of writing their stories to cover the press conference, as well.

If the press conference requires the presentation of event highlights or another video segment, large television monitors are essential. A large screen or monitor may also be installed to the side of the stage riser, if needed. The organizer's audiovisual supplier can provide the necessary equipment to professionally present video elements. An event representative should work with the technician to ensure cues to run the video are smoothly handled.

Questions from the media can be captured by wireless mics passed into the audience by event staff members. At least two mics are recommended, assigned to staff on either side of the room for quick deployment. As these mics will also be tied into the press conference sound system, the questions will be easier to hear within the room and through the recording devices plugged into the mult box.

Depending on the situation, many postevent press conferences are broadcast live on television and/or streamed on websites, making the quality of all production elements associated with the press conference even more important for all concerned.

A Note about Talking to the Media

It is essential to appoint a key contact to serve as a spokesperson for the sports event organizer throughout the event planning process, right up through event day and beyond. All media inquiries and requests for interviews should be funneled through this single individual who can then schedule other event staff, athletes, and other stakeholders to speak with those who are covering. Be sure that all event staff and volunteers know the identity and responsibilities of this main contact and refer all media inquiries to this person. No staff should provide interviews or insights to reporters before this essential step is taken to ensure that the event organizer speaks with a consistent tone and viewpoint, and always provides accurate information. This will also alert the organizer's management of any controversies that may be brewing in relation to the event, its sponsors, and other key stakeholders, as well as to any circulating rumors or potential crises on the horizon. The contact will screen and set up interview requests, determining the ideal and most appropriate individual to provide the media with the information they require.

The media having a single point of contact is a necessary first step to the management of event information, but controlling the message delivered to the media requires full understanding and cooperation from every member of the event staff. Given the speed at which information is transmitted, it is important that everyone on the event team is educated on the use of social media, specifically any policies that are in place governing how or if information is permitted to be shared and by whom. While taking an active role in social media is important in engaging and informing your guests and customers, delivering the wrong message, bad information, or an inappropriate tone can be devastating to your event. The event organizer should inform his or her staff of the issues that mismanaged social media can create, and clear guidelines shared on how they may use social media leading up to and during the event.

Media Coverage and Media Partners

Although journalists' livelihoods ultimately depend on the financial health and business performance of the media entity for which they work, this face of Janus sees not the business and marketing needs of the employer. Conversely, the editorial staff will neither expect nor demand that any benefits be accorded them as a result of a media partnership between their employer and an event. Journalistic ethics would preclude any such expectation. Although great sensitivity needs to be exercised, it is possible for organizers to demonstrate such appreciation for the partnership. For instance, one might provide a media partner with exclusive story ideas and supporting information for advance publicity purposes (although it is unethical to withhold this information from other outlets if they request it). An organizer can also provide media partners with accreditation for a quantity of reporters and photojournalists in excess of what is offered to other outlets and can designate preferential locations from which they can cover the event.

It is essential to ensure that other media outlets covering the event feel no less accommodated in preparing their coverage. Although some feature story ideas and information may be shared with a media partner's editorial staff, it should come as no surprise that after a story appears in one media outlet, it may no longer be considered news, or newsworthy, by others. Every media outlet wants to be the first to release a story, and it may seem accommodating on the part of the event organizer to provide information to its media partner(s) first (something to which the media partner will rarely say no). However, it is important that all media in the market feel accommodated, appreciated, and integral to the day's activities in the event's press room. Therefore, if an organizer feels compelled to break a story first to the event's media partner, the selection and timing of the story should provide the greatest benefit to the organizer's promotional plans, with the least effect on the attitude of the rest of the media. Consequently, writers, reporters, and broadcasters will not feel that the organizer is withholding information from them and serving the media partner preferentially. In most cases, it is best to treat everyone on the editorial side of the media partnership equally.

Post-play Analysis

Sports event organizers need the media to help publicize an event from the moment it is introduced, throughout the planning process, and after event day. A campaign of key, newsworthy event announcements and milestones should be scheduled to promote the event at strategic times, such as prior to the first day of ticket sales or participant registration, and with increasing frequency as event day approaches.

The editorial side of the media needs access to reliable and comprehensive information, statistics, and background to enable them to generate accurate stories. Event organizers must identify opportunities for human interest and business stories to further enhance pre-event coverage. During the event, the media require access to even more information, as well as comfortable working facilities in nonpublic areas that will help them file and broadcast their stories on a timely basis. Refreshments and meals should be offered at appropriate times of the day for events that require the continuing presence of the media. Visual access to the field of play and free access to the event site are essential elements for providing a positive environment for the media. The media also require access to services and technology to enable them to do their work and to press conference facilities for important announcements and interview opportunities.

Coach's Clipboard

1. Create a publicity campaign for the fictional 10K run in Play 1, including a schedule of key announcement dates. Where should you hold the announcing press conference? What kinds of human interest and business stories will you propose to the media, and how? Where will you place the media office, workroom, hospitality area, and press conference area for this outdoor event?

2. Consider the hypothetical playoff fan festival in Play 1. How will the publicity campaign for this event differ from the 10K run above? What kind of pre-event stories might be generated for this event? How should this be managed, given the possibility that the team might not make the playoffs?

3. Write an announcing press release for the playoff fan festival above. When should this announcement be made, and what should it include? How can you keep interest high on your event website and on social media networks?

4. In what unique ways would you use social media networks as pre-event engagement opportunities for the 10K run? How can you utilize these networks during the event to provide enhanced coverage to the families and friends of the participants, and opportunities for your business partners?

PLAY 9

Activating the Sports Event Marketing Plan

"Study the rules so that you won't beat yourself by not knowing something."
—*Babe Didrickson Zaharias, six-time Associated Press Woman Athlete of the Year between 1931 and 1954*

This play will help you to:

- Develop a marketing plan for your event to best suit your resources and needs, using a combination of advertising, publicity, promotion, event marketing, direct sales, and social media.

- Discover how media partnerships can help advance a sports event's marketing objectives.

- Understand why and how media partners use sports events to meet their business objectives.

Introduction

To get their products into the hands of consumers, corporations develop and activate marketing strategies, applying tactics that include a combination of publicity, advertising, promotion, direct sales, event marketing, and social media campaigns. To the sports event organizer, the event is the product and the consumers may be ticket buyers, attendees, corporate partners, the media, and even participating athletes. Like companies that sell goods to consumers, sports event organizers must be more than just managers and manufacturers. They must also be marketers and promoters, employing various forms of media and other mass communications devices to "sell" their event to the public.

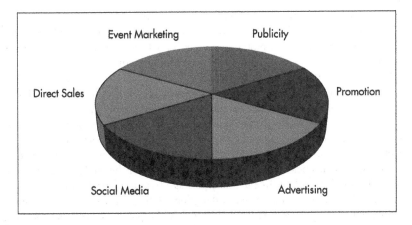

Figure 9.1 The Sports Event Marketing Plan Wheel

The marketing plan fashioned to promote a sports event comprises the same tools as are used by consumer companies in varying degrees, as illustrated in Figure 9.1. The proportion of each event's resources that will be dedicated to various components of the marketing plan will vary widely by location and the type of event, and are totally at the discretion of the organizer.

Play 8 described in detail the infrastructure that is required to service the editorial side of the media and energize an effective publicity campaign. The core attributes of the news media industry, journalistic integrity, and a responsibility to report on reality in objective terms, have little impact on the essential truth that a media outlet is also a business, an entity that has to generate revenue in excess of expenses to remain in business. Although some revenues flow from subscriptions and single-copy sales, most of the revenue that maintains print media businesses, including in their digital editions, is through the sale of advertising space. Much the same holds true for television, radio, and the Internet. Most of the income for commercial stations and websites flows from advertising time or space, although many sports television channels generate revenue through affiliate fees (fees per subscriber charged to cable companies and other pay-TV operators) and online streaming in addition to receiving advertising revenue.

What Media Partners Want from a Sports Event Relationship

Viewed in its most simplified form, advertising rates are predicated on both the number and the demographic quality of a media outlet's readers, viewers, or users. Therefore, any opportunity that can increase readership or viewer or listener ratings, increase usage, or generate measurable incremental advertising, is highly desirable to the owner, publisher, or general manager of a media concern. A marketing partnership with the right sports event can present many such powerful possibilities to print, broadcast and digital media businesses.

"Sports marketing offers newspapers the ability to become a part of a local event that typically appeals to families, youth, and ethnic markets," observed Sheri Wish, while serving as the director of advertising, new business development, multimedia, and sports for the *Los Angeles Times*. "These can be somewhat different than the typical core newspaper reader, offering branding and circulation opportunities to passionate fans and crossing income, race and geographical issues in the marketplace." Executives at broadcast and digital media entities share similar views. They agree that opportunities provided through effective sports marketing can expand their audience, positively contribute to their community, and increase revenue. As previously discussed, event participants, attendees, and viewers can be defined along demographic and lifestyle characteristics and, by taking advantage of an association with a sports event, a media outlet can reach into new markets comprised of loyal, passionate, and motivated fans. In order to effectively reach them, though, the media outlet must promote its association with the event, and provide fans with value not found elsewhere, including expanded coverage, special features, timely, exclusive, and, in some cases, live content, and relevant advertising and promotions.

In well-served markets, local media, including newspapers in print and online forms, radio stations, television outlets, and websites, also view themselves as ambassadors of the community, businesses in a unique position to help promote the vigor and vitality of their readership, viewers, listeners, or user area. There is no hint of conflict of interest or imperiled journalistic integrity because they will still cover news as news, whether it is favorable or reflects poorly on the condition of the local market. Marketing activity that promotes their community, however, is good for area businesses and increases the relevance of the media outlet as an effective place to spend advertising dollars. The outlet is free to participate as a booster of local commerce while the editorial side reports on the news in a community. After all, working behind the scenes to promote economic growth and an improved quality of life directly helps the media's business. An invigorated market can encourage advertisers to move into the community or seek to do more business there. More business can mean more jobs, more jobs can mean more growth, and more growth means a larger universe of readers, viewers, and users. In the long term, attracting more positive attention to their community through sports event marketing efforts is simply a sound strategy for media entities, and, since such efforts are undertaken without the direct involvement of the editorial staff, there is no risk of jeopardizing the company's objective journalistic standards.

Publishers, programming, and digital media executives also know that the excitement that sports events bring to a community can rub off on the companies that take an active role. The media are where potential event attendees and viewers naturally go for information, so establishing a strong, recognizable association with a sports event in the minds of the consumer can generate powerful results for both the media outlet and its advertisers. Readership, listeners, viewers, and users are the gold standard upon which the media's currency—advertising rates—is based, and sports events can provide outlets with outstanding promotional opportunities that can make a partnership both worthwhile and profitable. Sports events are particularly valuable properties with which to be associated for digital media services, as fans will return frequently to the featured event pages, often several times in a single day or even during a single website visit, for the latest exclusive content, event schedule updates, and other detailed event information. Beyond the sheer quantity of visits or page views, the repetition of promotional messages on these pages when fans return adds incremental value to the advertiser.

Media outlets that become media sponsors can be afforded every benefit befitting their level of participation without endangering the objectivity of their editorial coverage. The greater the media company's financial involvement, whether provided in cash or as VIK, the more promotional exclusivities the organizer can offer. For example, a sufficiently robust partnership can enable a media outlet to be the sole source for reader, listener, viewer, or user benefits such as ticket giveaways, sweepstakes, contests, and discounts. At the same time, the division of news media into mutually exclusive editorial and marketing functions helps to protect a sports event from being ignored by nonpartner media due to promotional relationships with competitors. In a perfect world, media partnerships should not jeopardize basic editorial event coverage that will be provided by other outlets.

A formal marketing partnership with a sports event can offer a media outlet many of the same featured benefits that other sponsors enjoy, including: signage at the event, the ability on site for an online service to promote enrollment for free or paid subscription accounts, a newspaper to link digitally to or distribute printed copies of special sections created for the event (sampling) or for a radio or television station to stage a live broadcast with popular on-air personalities (promotional presence), visibility associated with an in-event element (event presentation/fan activity), and the capability of providing special hospitality opportunities for customers or advertisers. As discussed in Play 6, media partners also seek the ability to offer pass-through rights to advertisers, using event benefits to add exceptional value to their existing marketing efforts to sell more space or time. Running a media outlet is an expensive proposition, so it is reasonable to presume that the decision of whether to pursue a marketing partnership with a sports event will be based on the economics of the deal—can the company enjoy direct financial benefits from an association with an event or develop new revenue opportunities as a direct or indirect result of the partnership? Figure 9.2 provides a summary of some of the many reasons media companies seek partnerships with sports events.

- Revenue generation
- Advertising
  - Directly from the sports event organizer
  - From sports event sponsors
  - Incremental advertising opportunities from nonsponsors
- Promotion
  - To increase circulation (readers, listeners, viewers, or users)
  - To increase the subscriber base
  - To expand into new markets
  - To promote new writers, talent, shows, or online services
  - To provide access to exclusive, original content
- Event activation
  - Event site signage
  - Event promotional presence
  - Event presentation/fan activity element(s)
  - Inclusion in event advertising
  - Engagement with fans/readers via social media outlets
- Category exclusivity
- Sampling opportunities
- Exclusive hospitality opportunities for advertisers
- Pass-through rights

Figure 9.2   What the Media Want from Sports Events as a Marketing and Promotional Partner

What Sports Event Organizers Want from a Media Partner

Experienced promoters know that an event will never reach its full potential through publicity efforts alone. The role of the media-event partnership is to enable both parties to exert more control over the message they want to communicate, control that even the best publicity campaign, and resulting press coverage, cannot fully provide. Typically, the message the organizer wishes to convey is a call to action: "Please attend, purchase tickets, and/or tune in to this exciting event." The message the media partner wishes to communicate will vary based on its corporate objectives, but, at its core, it is a reminder of reliance: "Keep reading or watching this space. We will provide you with news and information on events and other happenings and content that are of interest to you, as well as with outstanding value (e.g., ticket discounts and other offers) that will more than compensate you for your attention."

Media outlets are no less mercenary about event partnerships than are event organizers, who also evaluate media partnerships from an economic point of view. Simply put, event organizers must also be event promoters to attract an audience and recognize that media outlets are the key suppliers of the advertising space and commercial time they will need to market their properties. Establishing a partnership with one or more media outlets can offer significant event sponsor benefits in exchange for advertising on a VIK, combined VIK and cash, or a preferred-rate basis. This can help drive marketing costs down for the promoter or expand the budgeted advertising and promotion plan to achieve greater results than just spending cash can do.

In addition to the ability to realize savings on advertising the event, organizers may direct the incremental advertising they must place to satisfy sponsor fulfillment obligations to their media partners. In addition, sponsors also perceive value in placing the advertising that activates their associated promotional campaigns with the websites, platforms, newspapers, or stations that support the event, adding increased presence, credibility, and relevance to the media outlet's users, readers, listeners, or viewers (presuming this audience also complements the sponsor's own target market).

Many media outlets, particularly online and print media, maintain a database of account holders or subscribers. This information may be comprised of e-mail, text, and I.P. (Internet protocol) addresses only, or contain more robust data including zip codes or mailing addresses, and demographics such as age, household income, and special interests. Event organizers want access to account holder databases to promote ticket sales to the most likely buyers. These databases may have an extremely large and diverse membership and may need to be filtered so they reach the most qualified account holders. They will be closely guarded by the media outlet, and your offer may have to be sent directly by partner to protect the privacy of its account holders. Nevertheless, using media partners' subscriber databases to help boost ticket sales can be a very important element of your marketing plan and you should make every reasonable attempt to come to an agreement to use them. Although the event's ticket holder database will not typically be nearly as large as theirs, media outlet partners may request this courtesy in return to help their own marketing efforts.

Media outlets represent the most consistent and continuous source of information about the past successes and failures of other sports events held in the marketplace. Event sponsors come and go, but the media in a given community are considered a constant—they are reliably on hand to cover events and report on them. The members of media organizations almost always have observations as well. Archival information, that is, articles and blogs written, photos and videos posted, and accounts broadcast about past events as they unfolded, only tell part of the story. Editors and writers, producers and correspondents can share their unvarnished perspectives on what made past events work in their city, or not achieve their full potential. Although these points of view usually do not often find their way into the published record, as they do not represent objective reporting but opinions, they are no less valid. While they might represent pure opinion, their perspectives and points of comparison are based on experience, and, therefore, worthy of serious consideration. Members of the editorial staff are usually not shy about sharing their event encounters. Usually being limited to reporting only substantiated facts, many media executives and journalists actually appreciate being able share their personal views. Expect and welcome a wide-ranging conversation—from how the competition was perceived by the press, to treatment of the media on site, to consumer reaction to the organizer, to the value of the event to the community. Be a sponge! These are the guardians through which information and perspective on sports events are filtered and communicated to the public. Few resources will be able to provide better, unbiased feedback. (For the same reason, be sure to speak with these same stakeholders after your event is over—the quantity of intelligence you can gain about your own event can be incredibly revealing!)

Members of the media outlet's marketing staff are equally excellent sources of intelligence regarding past events in their community. Their expertise in advertising and promotion can provide added perspective from a marketing point of view on where events succeeded and fell short in capturing attention and establishing relevance. This is particularly useful for organizers who are staging an existing event that is new to a particular community. Listen and learn from the mistakes or miscalculations that others have made. Potential ticket buyers and event attendees in different markets do not necessarily follow the same patterns or behaviors and may respond positively to certain advertising or promotional activities in one town and negatively to the same marketing endeavors in another.

Experienced marketing professionals from media outlets, like their editorial counterparts, can help organizers decode what has worked best in their community, although their agenda may be totally different. They are in the business of selling advertising space or time and an event organizer with marketing needs—and a budget—can be an attractive prospective client. They also recognize that broader promotional campaigns to enhance revenue potential for their newspaper, station, or website can be designed around an event, its sponsors, and its business partners because of the potential to generate even more advertising income from these event stakeholders. This part of the media business is focused on sales, so organizers should not be surprised when a meeting scheduled to explore the marketplace takes on a very positive and enthusiastic tone and then morphs into an equally enthusiastic sales pitch for advertising space or time. Figure 9.3 provides a list of what sports event organizers expect from media partners.

- Advertising space or commercial time devoted to promotion of the event
- Access to subscriber database
- Intelligence regarding local market sensitivities and perspectives
- Preferred rates for advertising purchased for sponsor fulfillment purposes
- Promotions designed to promote ticket sales, increase attendance, encourage broadcast viewership, and/or drive traffic to digital platforms
- Expanded pre- and event-day coverage to encourage a perception of increased importance
- Provision of added value to attendees (i.e., sampling)
- Co-promotion and fan engagement through partners' social media platforms

Figure 9.3 What Sports Event Organizers Want from Media Partners

Selecting Media Partners

Organizers should concentrate their quest for information and insights, and ultimately their event marketing campaigns, on media outlets whose demographics and lifestyles most closely match the target market of the event. Radio stations and audio streaming apps are so easily segmented based on their programming formats (e.g., news, talk, sports, top 40/pop, urban, rock, soft rock, country, ethnic, easy listening) that the fit between event audience and listener can be almost intuitive. Magazines, websites, and podcasts are similarly segmented among obvious populations and interest niches. Newspapers, on the other hand, are more limited in easily identifying demographic fits and their readers are often defined more along geographic lines. Their demographic segmentation may instead be delineated by what sections and stories their readers access (e.g., news, sports, entertainment/arts, editorial, opinion), and whether they read them in print or online.

Every outlet under consideration will have a marketing information kit available in print and/or online upon request that presents the demographics and lifestyles of its readers, listeners, viewers, or users, the size of the market, and, in many cases, consumer spending behavior. Based on this information and the demographics of an event's target audience, the organizer can select the most suitable media outlets to approach as prospective event partners. What does a partnership between an event and the media really mean, and what various forms can it take? As discussed, a media outlet can legitimately assume the role of an event sponsor, although the decision to do so will usually have no bearing on the quality and tone of event coverage. However, if properly developed and managed, the partnership will probably affect the quantity, depth, and diversity of coverage. In exchange for enjoying all of the benefits normally accorded to a sponsor, plus others that uniquely meet its specific wants and needs, the media partner may provide the event with advertising space or time, a vehicle for promotional activities, cash, or some combination of all three.

Exclusivity Versus Nonexclusivity

The notion of forging a traditional sponsor relationship with a media partner should be, by now, familiar territory. It is important to recognize, though, that the provision of advertising by a media outlet without the exchange of cash is no more cost-free to the outlet than complimentary tickets are to the event organizer. Just as "free" tickets represent lost revenue potential to the event organizer, "free" advertising represents lost revenue potential to the outlet. Media outlets, therefore, expect significant value in exchange for their most attractive and marketable asset—access to potential ticket buyers or attendees through their respective platforms. If sufficient advertising opportunity is provided, the organizer can designate an outlet the "official online partner," "official newspaper," "official radio station," or provide some other similar partner identification that implies category exclusivity. It is important, though, that sponsorship agreements with "official" media partners do not prohibit the organizer from purchasing advertising from competitor outlets. The pace of ticket sales or other market conditions may require the organizer to place advertising on more than one website, newspaper, radio station, or television channel, and restricting marketing efforts solely to a single media partner can later prove debilitating. It is very likely that official print and broadcast media partners will want to also be designated as official online media partners, as most of these traditional outlets also publish digital editions. A media partner will often seek to protect its investment in an event by insisting on a provision in the sponsorship agreement guaranteeing that advertising placed with competitor media be met with an equal or greater amount of paid advertising with "the official" outlet.

There are instances when providing category exclusivity to a media outlet makes less sense because the value of advertising, cash, and other assets offered to the organizer is just not sufficient to warrant a sponsorship. In addition, sometimes realizing an event's sales and marketing objectives require having the ability to communicate with equal force among a broader variety of readers, listeners, viewers, or users than a single outlet can provide. In such cases, organizers can seek to patch together a number of smaller, nonexclusive promotional relationships with a series of media entities. This scenario is most often found in the form of a promotional partnership in which limited benefits are provided to a media organization in return for similarly limited VIK advertising, deeply discounted advertising rates, or outlet-specific promotions. The promotional partner may receive a quantity of tickets and event merchandise for use in sweepstakes or advertiser incentives, limited rights to use the event or organizer's logo, and perhaps some reduced level of on-site presence at the event.

The most effective method of signing a series of complementary nonexclusive media partners is to grant each some exclusivity with respect to one or more event elements. A media partner targeting families or children might be the only outlet permitted to promote a special family ticket package, or authorized to create an event-related educational or skills development program. These rights might include a sweepstakes geared to the specific interests of the outlet's audience, such as an opportunity to attend a special kids-only clinic coached by a star player, alumnus, or celebrity, or exposure at an on-site attraction geared for families with young children. This approach of segmenting media partners by offering them limited exclusivities provides the event organizer with the option to award others promotional rights to elements more suited to their specific target market. For example, a music radio station could be granted rights to a sweepstakes for a ticket giveaway that includes passes to an exclusive winners-only post-game party. A sports talk station partnered with the same event might conduct a promotion that rewards winners with a behind-the-scenes tour, plus an athlete meet-and-greet session, and a visit to the play-by-play booth during the event, all elements of greater intrigue to the hardcore fan.

The strategy of pursuing nonexclusive media partners is most common in the highly segmented radio industry. In a given market, a significant segment of the population listens to the radio at some time in the day, although only one or two stations in a given day. Meanwhile, there are dozens from which to choose in a variety of programming formats. While there is little audience crossover between formats, there is enormous competition between stations that appeal to the same tastes. Therefore, best success will be enjoyed when pursuing radio partnerships that are exclusive within the same programming format (e.g., only one sports talk station, one pop/rock station, one Spanish-language station).

Ownership of stations in the radio industry has also consolidated to a great degree. A sports event organizer might be able to forge a deal with a single company that owns a variety of radio stations within the same community, providing a wide range of partners in various formats and great value to both parties. Figure 9.4 lists the partner stations with the key listener characteristics that, when combined,

Station	Format	Demographics
Station 1	Classic Rock	Men 25–54
Station 2	Contemporary Hit Radio (CHR)	Young Men and Women
Station 3	Sports Talk	Hardcore Sports Fans
Station 4	Alternative Rock	Men 18–34

Figure 9.4 Example of a Nonexclusive Radio Partnership

saturated the market with a series of advertising campaigns and promotions specifically appealing to the tastes and interests of targeted listeners. An event ticket giveaway was staged in association with the sports talk station as the prize of most intense interest among loyal sports fans. Promotion of the event's family-oriented outdoor fan festival received more emphasis on the two stations with formats most appealing to men and women likely to have young families, while a concert starring a popular rock star that was connected to the event was more heavily promoted by the station with a contemporary hit rock (CHR) format.

Nonexclusive media partnerships are much more difficult to achieve in the print sector than in radio. In the remaining markets where there is more than one daily newspaper in a given community, they are almost certain to be highly competitive with one another for readership, advertising dollars, and, yes, even attractive promotional relationships with sports events. In cities where only one newspaper monopolizes the available print and online readership, receptivity to participating as a sponsor or promotional partner will vary with the nature of the outlet's marketing objectives, community relations strategies, and its assessment of the event's attractiveness as a platform to achieve its aims. Some will immediately grasp the promotional opportunities and business solutions an official association with a sports event will offer. Others will desire involvement simply as active supporters of quality-of-life-enhancing events in their community. Still others, knowing they face no competition in their marketplace for an event's advertising dollars, will perceive no value in investing or participating as a media partner. Television can offer opportunities for nonexclusive media partnerships, though on a more limited basis than radio. Unlike radio, there is a great deal of crossover in television audiences. That is, members of the same target market will change channels frequently to view or stream the shows, movies, or events that most interest them at the time that they air, or, much to the chagrin of both broadcasters and advertisers, record their favorite programming for later viewing irrespective of where and how they can be seen. Nevertheless, sports events remain appointment viewing at the time they are broadcast and, therefore, continue to be powerful programming for broadcasters. Even nontelevised sports events can be compelling local opportunities for coverage and sponsor support because of their ability to generate interesting and topical content of relevance to the local community. Sports events can usually segment their television partnerships into two generally noncompetitive halves—an exclusive "over the air" broadcast or cable partner and an exclusive streaming sports partner. Of course, if the event is televised, it is most likely that the only promotional partnership possible will likely be with the channel serving as host broadcaster and the distribution services that provide it (e.g., cable, satellite, online streaming service).

U.S. cable sports giant ESPN has established itself as a brand on multiple platforms—television, radio, and online—cementing a presence in key markets around the country through dozens of local sports talk radio stations that feature a combination of national and local personalities and programming. Although they are local radio affiliates, the well-known and highly regarded ESPN brand can add substantial value to an event and offers the potential of stretching local news into stories with national reach. Event broadcasts, news coverage, results and statistics, and exclusive content can be accessed nationwide on mobile devices with ESPN's app, extending the reach digitally. While it has major competitors nationally, such as FOX Sports, with their own programming and loyal audiences, ESPN provides one prime example of how the lines between television, radio, and online content have blurred, making it difficult to unbundle exclusivities across these electronic media platforms.

Recognizing that broadcast and print media partners often have their own online platforms, the Internet can offer many mutually advantageous media opportunities for the same event, both on an exclusive and nonexclusive basis. To the benefit of the media partner, the event website can feature a range of highly visible options such as a banner advertisement across the top or bottom of a home page and interactive content including information, contests, trivia, video, and features, all of which can be sponsored. Event and sponsor messages can also be extended to friends and followers on a combination of social networks.

The exclusivity an online media partner may seek can be better defined by the nature of the content the organizer can provide, features that can only be found on a particular online sponsor's website and nowhere else. In other words, it is advantageous to have a presence for the event on as many online sites as possible, and, since it is nearly impossible to withhold online rights from an existing print, television, or radio partner, the key to developing additional online partnerships beyond the sites of these more traditional media partners is to find a way to provide each with content that is exclusive to them.

Sports Event Promotions

Sponsors often activate their event relationships with consumer promotions that can support both the corporate objectives of their brand and enhance the success of the event. Most consumer promotions are supported with advertising in various media placed and purchased by the sponsor. Promotions offered by the media in support of their own partnership with a sports event takes the outlet out of the role of the middleman and puts it in control of event marketing programs that can benefit its objectives directly. Media marketers put great value on event promotions that can generate a database of readers, listeners, viewers, or users. For this reason, media promotions are commonly manifest in sweepstakes that require entrants to register by e-mail, text, or scanning a web link. The possibility of winning sports event tickets, experiences, merchandise, and memorabilia are strong incentives for the public to take the time and trouble to submit an entry that will later be compiled into a database for the partner's subsequent direct marketing campaigns. While the number of entries received is a good indicator of the effectiveness of the promotion, the outlet's ultimate, underlying objective will be to use this database to increase subscription sales, webpage or social media site views, or ratings.

A promotion that drives visitors to an outlet's website can be a strong selling point for a media partnership. As discussed, most traditional media outlets also maintain a website that provides visitors with important news and programming information (editorial side) and sells incremental online opportunities to their existing advertisers (marketing side). To set the highest possible rates and create the best value for their online advertisers, media outlets must generate the greatest possible number of "unique visitors" (individuals visiting the site) and "page views" (how many different pages on the site an individual downloads or clicks during their visit). Event organizers and their media partners will realize the best success when they design their online event promotions with these objectives in mind. Don't forget to include links to the event's public website in the media's online materials. If tickets are required for attendance, be sure to also include a link directly to the site where visitors can purchase their tickets to the event online.

From the sports event organizer's perspective, the most effective promotions, whether placed in the media by other sponsors or as the direct product of a partnership between the event and a media outlet, should be designed as tools to sell tickets or build an audience. Sponsor promotions, while clearly helpful to the organizer's sales and marketing efforts even if simply as additional exposure opportunities, are primarily designed to promote and sell the sponsor's brand through its association with the event. If the media partner is granted pass-through rights to leverage its event promotion, the marketing message will be subdivided among the various objectives of a potentially great number of partners. Promotions that result from the simple partnership between the media outlet and the event, with no other participating third party, can, therefore, be the most effective in building an audience.

One other important benefit a promotion can provide is data collection, a highly coveted prize for event organizers and sponsors alike. Any promotion that can include large numbers of participants providing their names and contact information can translate into a treasure trove of potential new customers. "One of the essentials we have for measuring ROI in a sponsorship relationship is how well we are able to collect consumer information," said Shana Gritsavage, formerly Under Armour's director of global events. "We don't consider a promotion with an event a complete success without data mining. Even one new email address is an opportunity. When we look at sponsorship activation, we look to generate hundreds and even thousands of them."

Organizers, sponsors, and media partners can be as creative as they wish in constructing promotions. It is important, however, for the organizer not to lose sight of the key message he or she wishes to communicate or the desired call to action the organizer wishes to precipitate. Identify what you want the reader,

Sales

- Discount offers
- Specially priced family packages
- Multiple-day admission packages
- Premium giveaways
- Bounce-back coupons

Key Messages: Value and Urgency

Awareness Building

- Ticket giveaways
- Merchandise giveaways
- Sports trivia contests
- Essay contests
- Social media engagement promotions or contests
- Press box or press conference access prizes
- Guest columnist or color commentator contest
- Athlete "meet-and-greet" opportunities
- School field trips
- Newspapers in Education (NIE) outreach programs

Key Messages: Inform and Excite

Tune-In

- "Watch and win" sweepstakes (i.e., tune in to see if you're a winner!)
- Insurance prize contests (e.g., million-dollar shots)

Key Message: Appointment Viewing

Figure 9.5 Fulfilling the Sales, Awareness, and Tune-In (S.A.T.) Objectives of Sports Event Promotions

listener, viewer, or user to do, and what value you are prepared to provide to reward them for doing it. Promotions, whether offered by corporate sponsors or media partners, can be divided into the three general categories as illustrated in Figure 9.5, categorized by the key objectives the program seeks to achieve. Tactics employed to fulfill the easy-to-remember "S.A.T." objectives of sports event promotions are those designed to increase sales (S), build awareness (A), and for events covered on radio, television, or digital streaming service, encourage tune-in (T).

Sales Promotions

The most common promotions designed to generate sales feature cost-saving ticket discount offers. (*Note:* In order to maintain sound financial control over the event's revenue budget, an allotment of promotionally priced tickets should have already been included in the calculation of the gross potential—see Play 3.) Coupons entitling the bearer to dollars off ticket purchases may appear in print advertisements, on stand-alone retail displays (also known as "POP," or point-of-purchase promotions), on sponsor product packaging, or on a partner's website for disseminating special codes for online ticket purchases or downloading and printing coupons for physical redemption. To increase the rate of coupon redemption, that is, the number of sales ultimately generated from the promotion, include a web address or telephone number and code that will enable purchasers to conveniently access the discount through online ticket services. The importance of being able to offer consumers a mechanism to take advantage of an offer immediately cannot be underestimated. Try to ensure that as few steps and as little time as possible are needed between receipt of the discount offer and the actual purchasing transaction to enhance the effectiveness of the promotion.

Ticket discount promotions can be designed to achieve any of a number of specialized objectives. Place the fewest possible restrictions on redeeming coupons, except for prohibiting the use of multiple discounts on the same transaction, to increase overall attendance objectives. Alternatively, sales promotions can build attendance for less well-attended periods during multiday events by restricting discounts to weaker midweek dates or preliminary rounds only, or deepening the cost savings for these harder-to-fill dates. A coupon expiration date set before opening day can be applied to the offer if the objective is to increase the urgency to purchase tickets in advance. Another variation is a "family package" promotion, a multiticket deal that offers a specific number of admissions (typically four or more) at a lower combined price than if purchased separately without a coupon. Package promotions can be particularly powerful tools, as they can also increase the average number of tickets sold per transaction.

Whether a cost-savings coupon or a package deal, it is recommended that all discounts be identified as a courtesy made available through a sponsor or media outlet, and not as an offer provided directly by the sports event organizer. Discounting through a sponsor offer is a practice generally accepted even by ticket buyers who failed to participate in the promotion. Discounting offered directly by the organizer can cause customers who purchased tickets at full price to feel unfairly treated and to seek partial refunds. Also, try to time the introduction of the discount offer for a date *at least* a few weeks after the sale of event tickets begins. Promotions that result in a discount ticket being purchased by the same guest who would have otherwise purchased a full-priced ticket make little financial sense. Let the first weeks of ticket sales maximize the yield of full-priced tickets to the fans who want the best seats and add the discount promotions to the marketing mix later, when the rate of ticket sales can be expected to slow and fewer potential incremental ticket buyers need an incentive to purchase.

Promotions designed to increase sales can also include the offer of a premium item with every ticket, or with some minimum number of tickets purchased. These offers can create added value for the ticket buyer and may, again, be designed to achieve any number of specific objectives. Advertising in advance that all ticket buyers will receive a valuable premium upon entry to the event (e.g., a bobblehead figure, commemorative patch, pin, ball) can generate greater overall sales. Events on a more modest budget sometimes offer premiums to a limited number of attendees, such as only to fans who download a special offer from a sponsor's website, or to the first 1,000 to arrive. In addition to saving money on premiums, the latter technique encourages early arrivals to the venue, which has the secondary operational benefit of spreading the flow of incoming guests, as well as increasing pre-event food and beverage sales. To encourage advance ticket sales, the premium item or a coupon redeemable for the premium at the event site can be e-mailed to those who purchase tickets before event day. The cost of the premium can be paid for by a sponsor or promotional partner, directly by the organizer as a marketing or sponsor fulfillment expense, or split between a partner and the organizer. The key to the success of any premium promotion is to ensure that this opportunity is communicated in advance to potential ticket buyers through advertising and other effective marketing platforms so it has the intended effect of increasing ticket sales.

A variation on this type of promotion that is of particular appeal to sponsors is the opportunity for ticket buyers to receive a "bounce-back" coupon with each admission. A bounce-back coupon is distributed to attendees at the event site either in digital or printed form or online with advance ticket purchases, and offers a valuable discount or premium item courtesy of a sponsor if redeemed at a specific location. A consumer electronics store can distribute a coupon or a scannable code upon entering the event site that is redeemable at its retail locations for a deep discount or gift item. Bounce-back offers can also be made during the event, offering discounts or premiums at sponsor-designated locations upon presentation of a digital coupon or proof-of-attendance after the event. While such offers may provide exceptional value to an event sponsor and may be worthwhile creating as a cost-free benefit of the relationship, bounce-back offers are rarely advertised in advance and, therefore, do not usually help organizers to sell tickets.

The messages communicated by effective sales promotions are "value" and "urgency." These programs stress value first. By taking advantage of the promotional offer, the ticket buyer or attendee will save money or receive some other valuable incentive such as merchandise, collectible memorabilia, or cost savings on sponsor products or services. To maximize a sales promotion's effectiveness, however, it should also communicate a sense of urgency. The offer should be taken advantage of as soon as possible to ensure that the ticket buyer will be able to fully enjoy it. Expiration dates and a limited number of premium items available only "while supplies last" can help to convey such urgency.

Awareness-Building Promotions

Sales promotions work best when building attendance for events that have some history or familiarity among potential ticket buyers and may be less effective for events that have a lower level of awareness. The key messages for awareness-building promotions are to inform or familiarize the community with the event, and to present salient information in a way that will excite or intrigue them into considering attendance. Although the call to action is *"Look over here at this exciting event!"* rather than *"Get your tickets now!,"* awareness-enhancing promotions can support attendance-building efforts profoundly, if indirectly. The timing of awareness promotions should be coordinated with the publicity and advertising sections of the marketing wheel. Publicity efforts can be very effective in generating awareness, and advertising is most efficient in driving attendance. Awareness promotions, therefore, are best timed for introduction coincident with the kickoff of the event's publicity campaign, or early in the advertising campaign.

Ticket and merchandise giveaways through a random drawing sweepstakes, a contest of knowledge or skill, a radio "call in to win," or a contest requiring fan response on social media sites are among the most popular forms of awareness building programs. To have the intended effect—ultimately promoting the sale of tickets—the mechanism for giving away tickets or other valuable prizes must be associated with communicating the message of ticket availability. To achieve optimal results, the process of registering to win should be surrounded by a campaign that involves the potential entrant in the event and at the same time educates the public about what the event is, and where and when it will happen. Awareness-building promotions help create what event promoters like to call a "buzz" surrounding an event, that is, a palpable level of excitement building in the marketplace.

Giveaways are highly prized by media sponsors and promotional partners, as they reward their viewers, listeners, readers, or users with value, and, if the "buzz" about the event continues to build, can help build their own readership, ratings, or page views. Radio stations are particularly effective partners for giveaways, and many are involved with multiple giveaway promotions simultaneously. For event promoters, radio campaigns are also highly valued because of the large numbers of listeners to whom the offer is communicated, plus the number of times the promotion—and the event—is mentioned on the air. Radio hosts can not only educate their audience about the upcoming event, but their often-enthusiastic delivery can also excite their listeners into entering the contest and ultimately attending the event. Developing a good relationship with the on-air personalities and providing them with the information they need to promote the event is essential to maximizing the effectiveness of a radio promotion and "building the buzz." Consider involving these individuals in the event itself as guest emcees or hosts. Their personal participation in the event is outstanding promotion for both themselves and their station, and almost guarantees frequent, enthusiastic endorsements on the air.

Sports trivia and essay contests are just two of the many varieties of knowledge- and skill-based competitions that can be used as promotional devices. Trivia contests work equally well as print, radio, and Internet promotions and frequently take the form of entry blank activities for print media, "call in to win" activities for radio, and fan voting platforms online. Essay contests, by contrast, are great vehicles for involving students, and are best executed as newspaper, magazine, and website promotions. Entrants can be given a choice of topics or perspectives from which to write an essay of defined length to be judged by a celebrity panel. (To best manage the judging process, it is recommended that essays be limited in length; approximately 500 words is a reasonable standard.) As campaigns co-promoted with print or Internet media partners, contests such as these serve to supplement the event's schedule of paid or VIK advertising. As a radio or broadcast promotion, they can fulfill this same purpose, but are additionally effective as awareness- and excitement-generating vehicles. The excitement of the contestants who participate live as well as the enthusiasm of the broadcast hosts can vividly help to convey the event's relevance to the listening audience.

As stand-alone promotions, or as prizes for winning essay entrants, behind-the-scenes access opportunities are rewards with a high level of perceived value. These limited-access possibilities can include a backstage tour, a visit to the press box, attendance at a post-event press conference, or the ability to serve as a guest columnist, among others. (It is recommended that if the winner is designated a "guest columnist," the qualifying essay or column be posted on a website or elsewhere online to be sensitive to the newspaper's journalistic integrity.) Meet-and-greet opportunities with athletes before the event, at practices, or during warm-ups can also be particularly attractive prizes.

Effective promotions geared to younger audiences can include school field trips to the event site during nonpublic hours for tours, practices, or a formal educational presentation. These opportunities must be arranged with school districts well in advance to be considered for the academic calendar. Most districts are budgeted for a limited number of trips per year, sometimes only one or two, so the event promoter should contact local educators perhaps as much as a year in advance. Working with a newspaper or online news partner, event organizers can also gain entry into the classroom by developing and circulating academically relevant materials featuring the event as a theme. This, too, is a lengthy, as well as potentially expensive, process, and should be created in partnership with the local board of education. Be certain the schools will accept this material on behalf of their students before spending the time and money to create it. If the program must be sponsored in order to exist, be sure to understand the restrictions the school district or board will place on how sponsors may be recognized, if at all, and what kinds of sponsors might be prohibited. A less expensive and more widely accepted option is to investigate whether a local daily newspaper participates in the Newspapers in Education (NIE) program. An association with this well-established and highly respected program can further reinforce the legitimacy and relevance of the event to the local community.

SIDELINE STORY

Newspapers in Education

In the 1930s, New York City public school teachers, wanting to expand social studies curricula to include daily lessons on current events, approached the *New York Times* to regularly bundle and deliver newspapers for classroom instruction. From these humble roots grew Newspapers in Education (NIE), a program coordinated by the World Association of Newspapers with approximately 700 newspapers in more than 40 different countries. Thousands of schools in the United States offer the NIE program to students from kindergarten to 12th grade through their local newspaper. Publishers have the flexibility to design the NIE program content for their own purposes, but all are designed to expose children to newspapers as a powerful and reliable source of information on current events. This flexibility enables newspapers to feature stories, background information, games, and photographs of events they sponsor or promote in the special NIE supplements they periodically publish. With sports so prominently featured in newspapers every day, providing information on upcoming sports events is directly on-strategy for a print partner's NIE program. Sports event organizers who want to expose their program to children and their families, have sufficient lead time, and can demonstrate the relevance and appeal of their event to this important audience, should investigate whether their town newspaper offers an NIE program in local schools, and do everything possible to be included. Interested event organizers can explore more details on the NIE program at the NIE Online website.

Social media platforms provide excellent outlets for fan engagement. These sites offer a number of benefits over the aforementioned media sources in terms of reach and financial consideration. Social media platforms are often free to use and offer features that allow direct interaction with fans. Promotions such as those outlined in this section can be conducted easily and cheaply with the potential to reach large numbers of fans quickly. For example, an event organizer or sponsor can run a contest requiring users to respond to a question or post with a clever comment or picture in return for a prize. The event organizer will then review the responses and choose a winner. Promotions of this kind can garner a great degree of exposure and sometimes thousands of responses, building hype for the event by incentivizing fans to participate even before the event begins.

Utilizing social media can serve to benefit both the event promoter and the event's media partners (see Figure 9.6). Conducting contests and promotions through social media outlets offers the benefit of contact information collection, instantly, with one simple interaction. This information is valuable for short- and long-term use for the event and its partners. It can be stored in a database for future use when developing and promoting similar events. As will be further explored later in this chapter, the event organizer and his or her partners will better understand their fans and what they are thinking by utilizing this information and, therefore, will be better able to serve their fans' needs and desires at future events.

Social Networks

- Build an event or brand profile with general information and space for fan interaction.
- Collect consumer data such as contact information and preferences to use for future events and marketing.
- Engage fans by asking open-ended questions, serving polls, or requesting action.
- Deliver media-rich content including videos, images, and links back to the official event/brand website.
- Offer updates about the event/brand on a regular basis.
- Create contests or promotions to drive traffic and "likes" to the profile page.
- Share links to news and media promoting your event and brand.
- Encourage sharing between fans and other consumers by incorporating share buttons on the official website and other sponsors' pages.
- Sell goods or tickets to the event on the profile page or via links—especially effective for exclusive pre-sales.

Professional Networks

- Create a buzz among industry professionals by creating a profile and/or event specific page.
- Create job postings and recruit potential event volunteers and/or employees.
- Keep industry professionals up to date and informed on the latest news about the event and brand.
- Encourage sharing between industry professionals by incorporating share buttons on the official website and other sponsors' pages.
- Collect consumer data such as contact information and preferences to use for future events and marketing.
- Deliver media-rich content including videos, images, and links back to the official event/brand website.
- Share links to news and media promoting your event and brand.

Microblogging Sites

- Provide up-to-the-second information about the event to keep followers informed.
- Though abbreviations are commonly used due to character/space restrictions, be sure to deliver messages with proper grammar and spelling when possible.
- Write messages in a way that conveys the personality of your event or brand.
- Write updates on a daily (or more frequent) basis.
- Encourage followers to share content with others and across social networks.
- Create interactive contests and promotions to engage fans and influence actions such as posting event/brand relevant pictures, videos, or posts.
- Deliver media-rich content including videos, images, and links back to the official event/brand website.
- Share links to news and media promoting your event and brand.

Mobile-Based Networks

- Encourage "check-ins" and offer rewards for participation.
- Collect data on consumer behavior such as number of check-ins to specific locations.
- Capture customer contact data upon once they check in to the event.
- Create customized, branded content such as a badge or video that can be unlocked only upon checking in.
- Communicate and interact with customers while they are checked in to the event.

Figure 9.6   Social Media Platforms and Their Effective Marketing Uses

Tune-in Promotions

For televised sports events and the sponsors that support them by purchasing advertising time on the broadcasts, building viewer ratings can be as important as drawing a live audience. Ratings are based on the number of viewers who tune into the broadcast live. (Audiences who record the program for later viewing or download it from the Internet are not factored into television ratings.) Marketing campaigns designed to increase television ratings seek to create "appointment viewing," a desire on the part of the audience to attend the event via television at the time of its original broadcast.

For the most popular of sports programs, events can be relevant and compelling enough by their very nature to generate appointment viewing. The most obvious examples include the National Football League's astronomically rated Super Bowl and the biennial Summer and Winter Olympic Games. But, even these premier mega-events strive to maximize ratings, ever vigilant against even the most modest slide in viewing popularity. In this way, broadcasters can keep their advertising rates high enough to justify the rights fees they pay to the sports event organizer. (For a detailed discussion on the event organizer-broadcasting relationship, see Play 13.) Most events, however, do not approach the perceived relevancy of a mega-event like the Olympics, the Super Bowl, or of many league and international championship games, and need a variety of compelling reasons for the audience to tune in, essential to any continued viability of the program as a broadcasting property.

Among the most popular tune-in devices are sponsored "watch and win" promotions that require viewers to respond to some form of prompt during the live broadcast to win prizes. To be effective, the activity must be promoted, advertised, and publicized well in advance of the event. Typically, the more valuable the prize is the more compelling the reason to tune in and wait for the cue to participate. A sponsor might distribute game cards or advertisements with a serial number, phrase, or other code, along with the instruction to watch for an announcement of the winning variable during the event broadcast. A promotion requiring fans to use their tablets or mobile devices to text a code, quiz answer, or vote for their favorite player, team, or other option to a certain number can be effective on the broadcast, as well as at the venue itself. A similar tune-in scheme requires viewers to register in advance through an e-mailed, mailed, or Internet entry form, or advertisement, and then to tune-in for instructions on how the winner must claim his or her prize during the broadcast.

Another promotional device that enjoys periodic popularity is the "insurance prize" contest. This type of promotion qualifies a sweepstakes winner to compete in a contest of skill for a prize so impressive and valuable that the very fact that an average member of the public—someone just like the viewer—can win is a sufficiently compelling reason for appointment viewing. Although the value of the prize can range from $100,000 to $1,000,000, the event budget need not set aside such a prohibitive sum to cover the possibility of having to pay an extremely lucky contestant. The organizer can contact an insurance broker to purchase a special policy that will pay the contestant should he/she win. The premium for the prize can range from 10 to 50 percent of the payout, depending on the insurance company's assessment of the odds of winning. Insurance companies, being in the business of keeping more money in premiums than they pay in claims, will absolutely require input into the contest rules and procedures. Once these requirements are incorporated into the rules, the odds will, of course, dramatically favor the insurance company. That said, the possibility of a fellow fan winning a fantastic prize, however unlikely, can create another exciting reason to watch an event.

Many events also encourage fan interaction via social media during television or online broadcasts. During the broadcast, hashtags (identifying subject-matter markers) and handles (individualized name markers) may flash on the screen indicating to fans a means for sending their thoughts and questions to the event organizers or partners. Other integrations may encourage fans to share on other social media outlets the content that they are enjoying. Social media integration can be a powerful tool to mobilize fans, both physically and cognitively. In addition, the benefits of employing social media as a tune-in technique include greater viewership, stronger fan connections, and more valuable sponsorship packages from media partners.

This phenomenon of social media integration goes beyond the conventional means of "tuning in" to a broadcast. Events are integrating social media presence into the event itself. During the event, fans may be asked to engage in real-time interaction through means of social media platforms. Select fans' responses will then be displayed at the event, perhaps on a venue's video boards, for other fans to see. Sometimes these interactions are part of a contest or promotions, while other times the event may request fan engagement simply to drive activity. People tend to respond to such requests from event organizers during the event for the prospect of momentary recognition among their peers. Even without formal calls-to-action, fans may react and respond to hashtags and handles that are placed around the event space like sponsor signage. Utilizing in-event social networking tools can be an effective way to add an interactive layer to your events and extend the tune-in effect to the live event.

Effective Sports Event Advertising

Regardless of how talented a sports event's public relations/communications staff might be, no matter how well connected an agency, the ultimate control over what and how much pre-event publicity an event will receive is under the complete control of story editors and producers who have no other agenda than presenting newsworthy content to their audiences. While sponsor and media partner promotions provide opportunities to better control the marketing message, the objectives of those campaigns are formed from a composite of event organizer and sponsor partner needs. The event organizer will often have a singularly important objective that a promotion, because of its compromised agenda, is less well equipped to achieve. If an organizer, for instance, wants to inform the public that event tickets are about to go on sale, simply circulating a press release is relying upon the hope that editors will deem such information newsworthy. (Most will not.) Creating a promotion at this early date diverts attention away from the most important fact—tickets are going on sale—and may detract from full-priced ticket sales during the time they are most likely. The only way to be absolutely certain that the message gets through to the greatest possible audience is to place advertising in targeted print, broadcast, online, and/or other media, either on a paid or VIK basis.

By all means, infuse your advertising with creativity and style, but do not sacrifice the effective communication of essential information in favor of originality for its own sake. The purpose of effective sports event advertising is to incite a reaction, most often the sale of tickets. Provide all the information and motivation that is necessary for the readers, viewers, or users to want to buy their tickets, and direct them to the most convenient way to make their purchase—immediately. The checklist in Figure 9.7 provides guidelines on what information is absolutely essential to include in effective event advertising, as well as additional elements that can be added to enhance the event's position as a "must see" entertainment opportunity.

Essential:
- o Identify the event by name and logo (if available).
- o Include the day, date, time, and location.
- o Make an obvious call to action (e.g., buy tickets now, make plans to attend, watch the event on television).
- o Include a website, link and/or phone number to assist the public in reacting in the desired way (e.g., purchasing tickets or gaining more information).
- o Include copy points that describe compelling event features to encourage reaction to the call.
- o Post event and action photo(s) or footage.
- o Integrate social media outlets and encourage fan participation.

Additional Elements for Consideration:
- o Highlight the names and/or likenesses of featured athletes (be sure to secure the athlete's permission to use).
- o Include player and fan testimonials.
- o Recognize sponsors with appropriate prominence.
- o Include quotes from coverage of past events.

Figure 9.7 Checklist for Designing Sports Event Advertisements

Identifying the name of the event and displaying the logo and essential data like the date, time, and location may seem obvious, but this information is nonetheless critical to include. Be sure to use the day of the week in addition to the date when advertising one-day events to provide absolute clarity to the reader, viewer, or user.

Do not neglect including an obvious call to action. That is, what do you want to tell the reader, listener, viewer, or user to do? If the advertisement is designed to inform the public that tickets are now on sale, say so explicitly and make it easy for them to purchase or order them. Include an easy-to-remember website address, link, and/or phone number so they can order tickets immediately or to gather the information they need to make a purchasing decision. Regardless of the call to action, provide all of the information required to enable the public to react as desired.

Advertisements for sports festivals and demonstration events in which the competitive elements represent more than one sport, involve sports or athletes that are unfamiliar to the public, or are only part of a broader series of attractions should include a brief list or description of compelling features to promote attendance. Descriptions should be short, imperative sentence fragments beginning with verbs that emphasize some form of interactivity with the event. Include only the best sales points, and those that are perceived as necessary to position the event as an exciting way to spend the fan's day or dollar. Use words like those in Figure 9.8 to influence your target audience into taking your desired course of action.

As influential as these commands might be, nothing is more persuasive than exhilarating photographs and action-laden video footage. Communicate the excitement of your event with one or more still images that bring life to your print advertisements. A single dynamic photograph is best for most applications, but multifaceted festivals might be better served with three or four smaller images to more fully represent the broad variety of activities to experience. Try to ensure that your images and copy points complement one another. Use images that communicate a specific story, message, or feeling to the reader or viewer. Post a gallery of still photos and video highlights in online advertising and on websites. The more times a user clicks to explore new images and footage, the more likely you have a hot prospect for tickets sales and attendance.

Be certain you have the rights to use whatever image(s) you select. Unless you own the images outright from a previous edition of your event, the photographer or the photographer's agency must provide permission and will commonly require payment for such use. In addition, any participant or audience member who may appear in the photograph or footage must also provide consent to appear. The permission of athletes and other participants is often secured in advance with a waiver that provides such written consent, or, in the case of more notable personalities, should be included in their appearance agreement. The consent of members of the audience whose images might be incidentally included in future advertising is obviously much more difficult. It is strongly suggested that legal language be included with all event tickets and credentials that includes a statement that using the ticket and attending the event infers permission

---

Add these influential words to your starting line-up of descriptive copy points:
- See. . .!
- Experience. . .!
- Enjoy. . .!
- Watch. . .!
- Meet. . .!
- Join. . .!
- Win. . .!
- Save. . .!
- Get. . .! (or Receive. . .!)
- Hear. . .!
- Play. . .!
- Try. . .!
- Cheer. . .!

Figure 9.8 Starting Line-up of Sports Event Advertising Copy Point Influencers

for their image to be used in advertising, promotion, and other marketing applications. Free events that do not use tickets should post similar permission language in conspicuous positions in the venue, such as at all event entrances, to protect against future claims for illegal use of a fan's image. (It is not a bad idea to post this disclaimer even when it is also included on or with the ticket.) Finally, individual audience members interviewed on camera or photographed during an event may be asked to sign permission forms at the time they are recorded for future possible use. Regardless of how audience image permissions are sought, be sure to utilize the services of an experienced attorney to provide the protection required.

What if the sports event is brand new or no images from prior editions are readily available? If it is impractical or too expensive to stage photography simulating the event, consider using an action image of a participating athlete from another appearance. The same permissions, and perhaps additional ones, will be required and some features of the photograph may require some alteration to disassociate it from the other event (specifically, avoid images displaying the logos, uniform designs, or other intellectual property of other event organizers or sponsors). Failing the availability of this option, the databases of stock photography agencies can be searched to identify and acquire the rights to use a suitable image. Many of the best databases are available online, including thumbnail-sized images, to help speed and simplify the selection process. Using original artwork or graphic images from online sources at varying costs can also be considered.

Television commercials and video clips used online should be well edited, exciting, and fast paced. Avoid subtleties and creative elements that overwhelm the ad's essential information. Employ the same action words to describe the event's compelling features and attractions, enthusiastically delivered by a professional announcer or featured athlete. Use up-tempo music to add excitement to the delivery. The rights to use popular music in commercials (known as "sync" or "synchronization rights") can be very expensive. Less expensive stock music is available through most video editing houses. Promoters will need the same permissions for video and film as are required for still photography and may be able to secure stock footage in a similar way as stock photography. Remember that the information presented in television advertisements is less "sticky" than print ads—you cannot physically retain a television or radio ad for future reference. While it must be memorable, it cannot be expected to impart as much information as a print or online ad. Promoting an easy-to-remember website address for more information can help. Refer to Figure 9.9 for more tips on creating your event's television commercial and online highlight clips, as well as special information specific to advertising in print, radio, and outdoor, or billboard, advertising.

Organizers may be obligated to recognize their sponsors in event advertising. For title or presenting sponsors, integrated recognition within the event name and logo is always expected. Promoters may also have included similar rights for other, or perhaps all, official sponsors to help in their sales efforts. If the family of sponsors is broad and lengthy, some contractual definition to their rights of recognition in event advertising is required to avoid having to fulfill sponsor obligations at the cost of excessively cluttering advertising creative. For example, the sponsor agreement can define the size of the ads in which the sponsor will be recognized (e.g., title and presenting sponsor logos in all ads, official sponsor logos in full- and three-quarter page ads only and listed by name in type in all others). The promoter can also schedule ads so a rotation of logos or sponsor names can be established in which each official sponsor is equally recognized over the course of the entire campaign, but not all sponsors in every ad. This practice is very useful in minimizing clutter and actually increases the recognition of a sponsor's brand when it appears in the company of a lesser number of other partners. All or a designated level of sponsors can have visibility on an event's website.

The right advertising campaign will be as unique as the event it is designed to promote. Evaluate whether the headlines or copy points should use terminology most familiar to passionate fans of the sport, and whether using these colloquialisms is the most effective way to reach the particular audience an advertisement is targeting. Sport-specific terminology could intimidate or turn off the more casual fans and ticket buyers and may be best used in niche publications or on web pages and social media sites that appeal more directly to the sport's most avid audiences. Existing sports events, such as festivals and demonstrations that target a general, entertainment-seeking audience, may include quotes from news coverage of previous editions, a common practice in the motion picture and live entertainment businesses. It is important that the quotes are from sources that will be perceived as credible by the audience. (One creative variation is using quotes from past attendees.) Quotes can also be used to reinforce the legitimacy of a relatively lesser-known competitive event. Consider soliciting quotes and permission to use them from media, athletes, and other participants that enhance the perception of the event's importance.

Print Advertising

- Advertise in the newspapers and magazines that your target audience is most likely to read.
- Place advertising in the part of the newspaper your target audience is most likely to read (e.g., sports section, entertainment/calendar section, community section). Try to avoid less expensive "run-of-paper" (ROP) ads that will appear in whatever location the newspaper has available space.
- Don't count on one placement of an ad being all you will need to achieve your marketing aims.
- Integrate the timing of promotional advertising placed on behalf of sponsors into the overall advertising campaign.
- Keep the design simple and eye catching.
- Use still action photographs reflective of the event's excitement. (Be sure to clear the rights to an athlete's image from both the photographer and the athlete.)
- Remember that print advertisements are excellent reference tools for the readers. They may clip it out of the paper to retain the information they need, so include as much as possible without cluttering the ad.
- Be sure to include a website or code that can be scanned (e.g., QR code) to provide the reader with easy access to further information, content, and ticket ordering capabilities.
- Don't overlook weekly special interest newspapers and magazines such as community papers, local entertainment weeklies, parent publications, and sports-oriented publications.

Radio

- Run ads on stations and programs and at the times of day ("day parts") your target audience is most likely to be listening. As with print advertising, try to avoid a "run-of-station" schedule.
- Include an easy-to-remember website address and phone number for ticket purchases and further information.
- Engage a station's on-air personality to record reading the script with enthusiasm! (You may not be able to use this recording on other radio stations, though.)
- Use upbeat music under the voiceover that captures the excitement of the event.

Television

- Select television programming and special-interest channels and networks that your target audience is most likely to be watching at the time they are originally broadcast. (Programs likely to be recorded may be viewed after the usefulness of the call to action has expired, or may not be viewed at all during playback.)
- Include a screen graphic during the last five seconds of the ad with the event name and logo, day, date, time, location, and an easy-to-remember website and/or phone number for ticket purchases and further information.
- Use footage from previous events that show action, excitement, and fan reactions.
- Include images for which you have obtained rights from both the athletes and the owner of the footage.

Event Website

- Present all key information about the event, including how to purchase tickets and the schedule of activities, in a clear, visible, simple manner.
- Include an easy-to-find link that directs the user to an opportunity to transact a ticket purchase on every page. If the text is lengthy and greater than a full-screen image, include the link on at least the top and bottom of the page.
- Use photos and/or video to their full eye-catching, attention-grabbing effectiveness. Include galleries of multiple images and video clips.
- Provide venue information including seating and parking diagrams, maps, and directions for transportation options.
- Refresh the information and feature content regularly to keep users up to date and to encourage repeat traffic to the website.

Figure 9.9 Sports Event Advertising Tips

Event Social Media
- Present time-sensitive information about the event, including changes to the schedule of activities or updates for fan safety, in an easy-to-read, real-time format.
- Post photos and/or video of fans and their live engagement with past events or pre-event engagements to encourage interest.
- Provide general event and venue information from the event website with easy access to redirect for more in-depth information.
- Create contests, promotions, and polls that encourage fan involvement and response.
- Feature content that keeps fans aware of event-related news and to encourage their reciprocal interaction on the site before, during, and after the event.
- Highlight positive fan interactions on the site to express appreciation and inspire further fan communication and loyalty.

Outdoor (Billboards)
- Keep the artwork simple and readable, and avoid subtleties. Design the billboards with the understanding that people might drive by them at high speeds, so the copy points should be few, but large.
- Ensure an easy-to-remember event information and/or ticket purchase website address is one of the dominant elements of the billboard. Phone or text numbers may be added if they are also easy to recall.
- Don't try to cram so much information on a billboard that it becomes cluttered.
- Remember that billboards are excellent tools for generating awareness for an event, and less effective as ticket sales generators.

Figure 9.9 (Continued)

Event Marketing

Sponsors employ sports event marketing campaigns to promote their products, so why can't event organizers do the same to sell theirs? Strategically scheduled mini-events that provide a taste of the big event to come can excite the public, encourage the purchase of tickets, and generate added publicity coverage. Schedule a fan participatory competition coincident with the campaign to sell tickets or encourage viewership, one that will foster an appreciation for the talents of the athletes featured in the main event. Create an exhibit on the history of the sport being featured, placed in a popular downtown destination. Consider creating a public opportunity out of, or beside, an already scheduled media event. Or, create events that will excite crowds already present in high-traffic areas at high-traffic times of day, as illustrated by the Pro Bowl marketing campaign Sideline Story.

Rights to these ancillary event marketing activities may be included in sponsor packages to provide additional value to prospective partners or can provide promoters with additional inventory they can up-sell to existing sponsors. Be sure that these sponsorships provide incremental revenues beyond those required for funding the main event. Event marketing programs should be anticipated in the expense budget, funded by new sponsors or supported with incremental dollars from existing ones.

Are there other events, sports and nonsports alike, being staged in the host city that attract a similar target audience? Consider staging a mini-event or a promotional attraction on their event site to capitalize on the audience they already spend money to draw. Interactive activities—appearances, autograph sessions and photo opportunities with athletes, batting cages, football tosses, slapshot booths, fan skills or trivia contests, to name just a few—are most effective in creating excitement. A promotional takeaway item with the event date, location, key details and ticket ordering information is highly recommended. Be creative and pick an item that itself represents the sport or event, but, if cost is an issue, the items need not be a permanent keepsake, such as a refrigerator magnet or key chain. After all, from

SIDELINE STORY

The Pro Bowl Event Marketing Campaign

For 30 continuous years, the Pro Bowl, the NFL's all-star game, was played at Hawaii's Aloha Stadium, drawing approximately half of the 50,000 fans at the game from the US mainland. The game was dependent on the engagement of the local community to sell the remaining tickets and the support of the local government and businesses to energize the market to welcome fans, players, and business partners arriving for the event. Of particular importance was the sale of remaining tickets in the local market during the week leading up to the main event. To generate excitement, encourage pre-event media coverage, and promote walk-up ticket sales, the *Pro Bowl Block Party* was staged on Waikiki's Kalakaua Avenue, the main thoroughfare through the resort area, the night before the game. This section of Honolulu is typically busy with tourists and young locals visiting the area's most active nightspots. A half dozen temporary stages presented contemporary, jazz, and Hawaiian music, sports talk, cheerleader performances, and official merchandise tents and food vendors dotted the six-block length of the event. More than 70,000 tourists, fans, and residents filled the streets for this one-night extravaganza, becoming one of the state's best-attended festivals.

Earlier the same day, *'Ohana* (Family) *Day*, a free, public NFL player practice at the stadium enabled fans to see the players close up and hear interviews from the on-field host. (Fans could very conveniently buy Pro Bowl tickets at the stadium box office when they arrived or departed *'Ohana Day*.) These events, among others, not only generated incremental merchandise and ticket sales, but also created an air of celebration and excitement throughout the Honolulu market. Reflective of the mix of in-state and visiting fans, a combination of national and local business partners ranging from Hawaiian Airlines to Anheuser-Busch sponsored stages at the *Block Party* and promotions at *'Ohana Day* as components of their overall Pro Bowl event activation strategies.

While the Pro Bowl is no longer played in Hawaii and the NFL has shifted its format away from a traditional All Star Game, the years of multi-faceted activities conducted to promote the Pro Bowl as a destination event stand as a superior example of effective sports event marketing.

a marketing perspective, the usefulness of the item expires when the main event is over. The premiums and the activity can be fully or partially funded by a sponsor, especially if the partner is common to the host event. Additional elements, such as sampling, can also be included, pending the permission of the host organizer. Try having a supply of tickets available and a mechanism to accept payment, if possible and permitted.

Are there parades, street festivals, civic gatherings, special holiday revelries, ethnic celebrations, or other activities in the host city that bring large numbers of people together? Consider contacting the organizers of these events to create a presence at these festive occasions, presuming the demographics of the audience complements your target market. Fitting into the cultural fabric of the host city, even if it is the home city of the event organizer, is essential and explored in detail in Play 10.

Social Media

As is abundantly apparent in the foregoing discussions on the more traditional components of the marketing wheel, it can be argued that social network media is as much a subset of publicity, advertising, promotion, and even direct sales, as it is a discrete slice. In many ways, social media marketing does share attributes of these other marketing tools, but the dynamics and characteristics of these digital forums suggest applying a further and separate focus to use them to their full marketing potential. A social media campaign is similar to publicity because event organizers can disseminate information about themselves and their events to their most engaged fans, but different because the fans can respond or react—not just to the organizer, but also through conversation with every other fan with whom the organizer engages as well as their own circle of family and friends. It is also similar to advertising because the promoter can provide information directly to users without the middleman of editors or journalists selecting whether, or how much, to provide to their readers or viewers. But, it is also different because organizers have to actively develop the "friends" and "followers" who will read their social media entries. As has been illustrated, the social networks can be used to support promotions and promote sales with links to transactional ticket purchase sites.

To restrict our consideration of how to leverage the social media networks as simply an extension of traditional marketing would be overlooking the full potential of how they may be used to support the organizer's efforts. We view social media networks not as an outward-facing marketing tool, but as a two-way conversation directly between the organizer and any number of friends and followers. Because the fan is free to react publicly to the promoter's message, it is essential that the promoter monitor and respond to the fan's excitement, questions, or concerns. Assign a staff member to monitor the social networks, and watch the nature of fan conversation. Is it supportive or derisive? Are fans asking questions and getting accurate answers? Are they sharing bad information? Are rumors emerging, or are fans complaining about inconveniences? Once posted by users on the social networks, comments become facts if not promptly corrected by the organizer.

There is no marketing tool that can create the depth and intimacy of engagement with your fans as social media. Create accounts on the most popular social networks and provide fans with the latest official information. Slowly drip insider tips onto the sites to keep them relevant and visited often. Read all user posts and if they ask questions, answer them and encourage your fans to engage further by attending the event and posting their observations while the event is underway. Post behind-the-scenes photos as preparations for the event advance and ask fans to post their own images while on site and after the event has concluded. Keep the site active all year for annual events and give fans a reason to check back regularly.

Post-play Analysis

An effective marketing plan cannot rely on pre-event publicity alone. Additional tools, including advertising, promotions, and event marketing, must be employed to achieve your event's marketing objectives. Establishing business partnerships with media outlets can help to maximize exposure for an event at a greatly reduced cost. Newspapers and other print media open to participating as partners generally insist on exclusive relationships. Multiple radio, television, and online partnerships can be designed, with exclusivity protected by programming format or content elements. Promotions can be created with media partners and sponsors that encourage ticket sales or build attendance, generate awareness of the event, or increase ratings for broadcast events. Ensure that event advertising has a clear message, with an obvious and compelling call to action. Apply best practices to social media network marketing. This tool incorporates many of the benefits of advertising, publicity, and promotion, but also provides a platform for direct and instantaneous two-way communication with your fans that can generate awareness, excitement, sales, and engagement like no traditional marketing medium.

Coach's Clipboard

1. Create an advertising campaign for the 10K run described in Play 1. Include an introductory ad to solicit participants, and another designed to appear the day before the event to encourage the attendance of spectators. How many times and when should each ad run? Write a 30-second radio spot to complement the print campaign.

2. At what other kinds of sports and nonsports events could the organizers of the 10K run stage event marketing activities to maximize spectator attendance? What kinds of activities should they stage, and what kinds of premiums could they distribute to help build attendance on event day?

3. How could the 10K run organizer reach into avid and casual running fans using the social media networks to generate participants? In what other ways can social media assist the organizer in creating excitement in the marketplace before, during, and after the event?

PLAY 10

Engaging the Community

"Individual commitment to a group effort—that is what makes a team work, a company work, a society work, a civilization work."

—Vince Lombardi, Hall of Fame NFL coach, 1913–1970

This play will help you to:

- Understand the motivations and apprehensions that influence a community's engagement in sports events.

- Develop programs that benefit and strengthen ties with the host community, including environmental and business development opportunities.

- Invest and involve the host community in the success of your event.

Introduction

Too often, sports event organizers overlook the many resources available in communities that are justifiably proud of the events they stage or host. A talented organizer with sufficient resources can present and promote an event without the active engagement of local government, businesses, and civic organizations. However, ignoring the role the community can play is to ignore the greater impact that can be achieved with the mobilization of these local resources and the greater benefits an event can provide to the region that plays host. Some of the same sports event organizers who are aggressive about pursuing sponsorship revenue in the community fail to notice the vast human resources and valuable services often available simply for the asking.

Programs that showcase the talents and athletic prowess of family, friends, and neighbors can be incredibly appealing to elected officials and local governmental agencies. After all, both the "stars" of the event and the people who come to see them compete are members of their voting constituencies. Local politicians strive to represent happy, vibrant communities, and any event that can improve the quality of life in their jurisdiction—within reasonable cost—is almost always welcomed enthusiastically. By extension, the governmental agencies required to support a sports event—police, fire, sanitation, streets, parks and recreation, and others—apply themselves with equal vigor as long as their participation is kept within acceptable limits. Although they, too, may cooperate in a selfless, community-minded spirit, the agencies' supervisors also know that their annual budgets are often voted on by the politicians who support the event and those they represent.

By the same token, the larger the event and the greater its impact on local infrastructure and municipal services, the more likely that some sectors of the community will come to view it as less desirable, bothersome, or even intrusive. It would be overstating the case to suggest that amateur and professional sports events that draw participants and spectators from an area wider than the local market can develop a love–hate relationship with their host communities. It is true, however, that some constituencies have more to gain from their presence and others perhaps arguably have a bit more to lose. By all means, sports event organizers should accentuate the positive and beneficial aspects of their programs through various marketing and publicity efforts, as well as participate in companion projects that can improve the local quality of life and enhance the health of the local business community. At the same time, they must recognize the areas of potentially negative impact, realizing that communities are composed of a wide variety of individuals and businesses, each legitimately affected by a sports event in their own unique ways (see Figure 10.1).

Local governments seek and support sports events for a host of emotional, practical, and economic reasons. These may include instilling community pride and elevating the self-image and the reputation of their municipality. The availability of entertainment and recreational options improves the perception of the community's quality of life and keeps its citizens within their hometown borders more often, spending money with local businesses and generating incremental tax revenues. Municipalities are not only competing for spending within their city limits but also for state, provincial, and federal grants designated for building, refurbishing, and maintaining recreational and entertainment facilities. An established history as an active focal point for sports and other entertainment events can portray a community as a vibrant, vital hub of economic and tourism activity that is worthy of further funding and development. Finally, do not underestimate the value of bragging rights. Beyond purely economic competitiveness, politicians, city officials, and even area residents simply like to portray themselves as being from a place that is superior to that of their neighbors.

Reasons They Like Them	Reasons They Dislike Them
Community pride	Congestion
Quality of life	Crowds
Self-image	Traffic
Promotion of city to the outside world	Noise
Competitiveness with rival communities	Interference with normal business
Showcase of local talent	Security (fear/incidents of unruly behavior)
Business opportunities	Setting of precedents (apprehension of future events)
Retail sales	Pollution and litter
Hospitality and accommodations	Political opposition from disenfranchised neighborhoods
New business	Expenditure of taxpayer funds in support of events
Future events	Wear and tear of existing facilities
Tax revenues	
Grants for capital improvements	
Existing facility utilization	

Figure 10.1 How Communities React to Sports Events

As explored in Play 4, sports events can generate economic impact across a wide spectrum of businesses, including restaurants, hotels, retailers, ground transportation operators, and other services. The more people an event can attract to a host city, even if only for a day, the greater its impact on the business community and, by extension, the greater the latter's support for the program. Keeping the host community's citizens in town raises the excitement level of the event, but also encourages their money to be spent with local merchants rather than outside the city limits. This helps spike tax revenues for the city and may help fund future capital improvements not just for event facilities, but also for infrastructure the community citizenry uses in their everyday lives, such as roads, parks, and public spaces. In addition, successful sports events help attract more sports and entertainment events, keeping facilities well utilized and developing an increased flow of consumer spending and tax revenues for the future.

The presence and proportionate importance of each of these motivators varies from city to city, and even from one elected administration to the next. What is almost as sure is that at least some constituents will be less enthused about the presence of a sports event, though the magnitude of their dissatisfaction and the degree of their ability to obstruct or otherwise affect its planning will differ. Residents living near event venues may be concerned about how both human and vehicular traffic, noise, and potentially boisterous fan behavior may affect their homes and neighborhoods. Businesses may be concerned about the added difficulties their employees may encounter in reaching their offices, and some retailers about the obstacles their customers could face due to heavy traffic, road closures, or detours.

In almost every community, there are likely to be some number of disenfranchised neighborhoods composed of economically distressed families, underemployed workers, and at-risk youth. Cities and developers often place sports facilities in or on the fringe of these areas, taking advantage of initially lower land values and, in some cases, fostering hopes of revitalizing an area to invite more businesses, more jobs, and improved housing. The residents of these neighborhoods may be profoundly affected by sports events staged in immediate proximity to their homes and businesses, suffering from the realities of game-day noise and congestion, and, if the event is economically exclusionary, on an emotional level, as well.

Many of these issues will be lurking beneath the surface and may become apparent suddenly and without warning in local media reports or from various members of local government as a result of discussions held behind closed doors, in town and city council meetings. Events staged by organizers from outside the community and those that attract participants and spectators from beyond the city limits are particularly susceptible to political criticism and local skepticism. An experienced sports event organizer will identify, acknowledge, and address these challenges early in the planning process to minimize any real or perceived negative impact on the community, demonstrating a sensitivity to the issues facing potentially affected businesses and residents.

Identifying the Gatekeepers

The most effective way of identifying these concerns before they surface is to engage local government officials, business organizations, and community leaders early in the planning process. Forge a genuine and functional partnership based on open communication and acknowledgement of each party's respective agenda. Step 1 is to identify the *gatekeepers*, the influencers whose opinion and leadership help build consensus in the community. The value of finding and building relationships with a community's gatekeepers is illustrated in the next Sideline Story; although it comes not from sports but from the world of civic celebrations, and is a tale several decades old, it is no less relevant and reflective of the influence of gatekeepers and the importance of their role.

Various sectors of the community can throw obstacles in the path of staging a well-conceived sports event, interfering with any number of its logistical component parts, such as venue selection, transportation, parking, or even event marketing and promotion. Gatekeepers are community business or political leaders who can help identify local sensitivities to a sports event before they surface publicly and can help to ease or even eliminate possible areas of frustration for everyone involved. It is important to note that the onus is not on simply finding ways to develop community acceptance of the sports event organizer's plans. It is also up to the organizer to incorporate the intimate intelligence provided by the gatekeepers into plans that will well serve the local area and its residents with significant benefits to hosting the event with a minimum of inconvenience and with no diminution of any measures required for public safety.

As important as gatekeepers are for intelligence, organizers should recognize that they are also advocates for the citizens and businesses in their jurisdiction. They will know what kinds of marketing and community relations programs will work in their city and what will be received tepidly or negatively. They can advise the organizer whether to ignore an obstacle, work around it, or involve the source of potential criticism more closely in the early stages of planning. They can help identify the true needs of both local residents and industry and show how best to integrate them into the event for the gain of all involved. Figure 10.2 lists some of the most common gatekeepers of the community and where they can be found.

SIDELINE STORY
The Influence of the Gatekeeper

Playbook author Frank Supovitz recollects that the Radio City Music Hall Productions event team commonly referred to this gatekeeper as "Dr. No."

The insidious Dr. No was a Philadelphia Police Department senior officer assigned to serve as the liaison to the "We The People" Parade, the nationally televised celebration of the United States Constitution's bicentennial, of which Supovitz was associate producer. One of the largest parades ever staged, the event featured 25,000 marchers and dozens of parade floats, including hand-built, horse-drawn recreations of those constructed for the original Grand Federal Procession of 1787. Perhaps to a greater degree than any other special event, parades depend heavily on the cooperative and integrated efforts of dozens of city agencies and hundreds of city employees. Without the active participation of the police and the departments with oversight of streets and sanitation, it is hard to imagine how a parade might ever hope to occur.

"Whether Dr. No understood the significance of this national celebration to the tourism and economic development efforts of the City of Philadelphia to this day remains unknown," recalls Supovitz. "What was evident is that he was a skillful master of yielding the powerful word that became his alias and employed it liberally as the answer to nearly every inquiry or request." For the record, it should be stated that the authority and expertise of the local police and fire departments, among other government agencies charged with the responsibility of security and public safety, should generally go unchallenged. These professionals know their city, understand their mission, and are charged with the uniquely weighty burden of protecting the public. This is a partnership where the rationally exercised authority of the law should be unquestioned.

"There did come a time, however, that it became apparent that Dr. No's use of his chief weapon had less to do with public safety and more to do with an abhorrence of personal inconvenience and ambivalence toward the event. His refusal to suggest alternatives, make recommendations, or provide feedback that defined the limits to which he was prepared to agree further supported this perception. This is a very unusual occurrence when dealing with our heroes in blue," Supovitz notes. It also became apparent that no operations plan submitted to him would ever be approved, thus seriously endangering the viability of the event and the city's ability to exploit it for its own purposes.

"Dr. No unwittingly taught me the value of identifying a gatekeeper." In this case, the keys to the gate were in the possession of an influential deputy mayor who served as City Hall's direct liaison to the We The People 200 Committee, the event's organizer. "Our encounters with Dr. No were related to this committee member during a hastily called meeting scheduled to review the operational plans for the parade. Within a day, Dr. No was reassigned, probably as much to his relief as ours, and a new event liaison, whose mantra was more akin to 'Let's figure this out together,' appeared." Working more closely as partners, with an understanding and respect for each other's needs and responsibilities, the parade drew an estimated four million people to Center City Philadelphia to celebrate this landmark date in the nation's history.

City Officials
- Mayor and/or city manager
- Deputy mayor
- Communications director
- Marketing director
- City council president and representatives (for impacted districts)
- Executive director, convention and visitors bureau
- Police commissioner or chief of police
- Fire commissioner
- Parks and recreation/other event oversight departments and agencies (i.e., sanitation, emergency medical, traffic/transportation, transit, permits, and special events)

Business Development Organizations
- Convention and visitors bureau
- Chamber(s) of commerce
- Business improvement districts or business partnerships
- Downtown or merchants associations
- Restaurant associations

Civic Groups
- Rotary International
- Kiwanis
- Masonic Lodge
- American Legion and Veterans of Foreign Wars
- Labor union(s)
- Religious group(s)

Sports Organizations
- Amateur sports federations
- Academic sports organizations
- Grassroots and recreational sports leagues
- Sports and entertainment commission

Figure 10.2 The Gatekeepers of the Community

The larger a sports event and the greater the impact it will have on a community's normal operations, the more essential it is to identify one or more highly placed gatekeepers as early in the planning process as possible, perhaps even during the event bidding phase. The local sports commission or the convention and visitors bureau, whose constituencies may have already demonstrated their commitment to the success of the event, can help organizers identify and contact the gatekeepers most important to the tasks and challenges at hand. Certainly, a contact in the office of the mayor or city manager, perhaps the city's own chief executive, may be able to provide the highest of level of active leadership and personal oversight. Members of city council, or similar community body that represents the geographical areas most affected by the event, are also essential partners in order to gain the support of the municipality and the citizens living in its environs.

The interest and support of city hall is particularly important to sports events that are not held in the same location each year. Finding out that the community is not behind an event on the highest levels after it has been awarded can be a major disappointment and perhaps even a mortal blow to its eventual success. With this in mind, it is recommended that a letter of support from the appropriate senior local official, such as the mayor, city manager, county supervisor, or board chairperson, be required for inclusion as part of the request for proposal (RFP) response. It is important to recognize and respect that city officials are responsible first and foremost to their voting constituents, both residents and business owners. The event's benefits to the community must be genuine and measurable to encourage the involvement of top elected officials. This is especially true during an election year, when officials assume a more political mien, pushing through programs that provide great and obvious benefits to their communities or pulling away from almost any program with a hint of controversy.

If possible, arrange a meeting with the highest city official possible before the event is awarded or announced. Prepare an oral presentation of no more than 10 to 15 minutes—that will likely be all the time he or she has—outlining the event and its benefits to the community. (That official may already be aware of the program as a result of the bidding process.) Because such busy administrators will want to ask questions of specific pertinence to them within this brief timeframe, expect to be interrupted frequently. Emphasize your most important points—how the sports event will serve their city, its residents, and businesses—within the first few minutes. Additional information, descriptions, and illustrations may be left behind in a written summary or electronic pdf document. The idea is to communicate sufficiently and succinctly with these officials so they are prepared with answers for their constituents' questions and can represent to their community that they have ongoing, constructive, and direct dialogue with the organizer. At the end of the presentation, offer to answer any remaining questions and, in return, request that the official provide a main liaison through whom all questions and requests to and from their office should be channeled. This may also be a good time to further engage city hall with an offer for the mayor and/or an appropriate councilperson to participate as a featured speaker in the announcement press conference or other upcoming media opportunity.

Failing the ability to successfully arrange a meeting with key local government officials, sometimes simply inviting these senior civic gatekeepers to participate in the sports event in a significant and meaningful way can help to open doors. The next Sideline Story illustrates this point.

SIDELINE STORY

Hockey Hall of Fame Grand Opening

Three days of festivities were scheduled when the Hockey Hall of Fame was due to open in the historic Bank of Montreal building at the busy northwest corner of Front and Yonge Streets in downtown Toronto, Ontario. Among the many and varied celebrations planned included a televised unveiling of the "Honoured Members Wall," the etched glass monument upon which the names of inductees to the Hall were enshrined, a procession of the then-90 living members to the new facility in open-air convertibles, and the "world's largest face-off," a photo opportunity in which the honorees would pose holding hockey sticks in the broad crossroads, forming an arc around a giant commemorative puck. Two street closures were required to execute the event. First, Front Street would have to be closed to accommodate the parade of convertibles. A few minutes later, Yonge Street, one of the city's busiest north-south thoroughfares, would need to be closed to set up and execute the face-off photo opportunity.

At that time, jurisdiction for each of these intersecting streets was under the control of two different government entities—the City of Toronto and Metro Toronto (the latter was a multicity regional government which has since merged with the City). Because of this circumstance, permits were required from each of the two administrations to stage an event in the intersection, but one refused to rule on the application for many weeks and reasons unknown, greatly delaying planning for the event. When Canada's then-Governor-General Ray Hnatyshyn accepted an invitation to ride in the lead car for the procession and pose with the hockey greats in the face-off, however, the permits were hurried through to approval.

Chambers of Commerce and Merchants Associations

Other important gatekeepers are the senior executives representing various sectors of the business community, some of whom may perceive an event as an opportunity and others as an obstacle to their enterprises. The local chamber of commerce represents the interests of area businesses and is responsible for attracting new companies and jobs to the community. Chambers often organize member breakfasts, luncheons, and other regular live and virtual meetings and regularly communicate through newsletters and other digital media methods to impart news, share ideas, and present information on emerging promotional opportunities. Make it a point to meet with the chamber's executive director and marketing director to introduce them to the event and its potential impact on local business. Explore with them the many opportunities—as sponsors, promotional partners, or simply as supporters—for area businesses. Request whether the chamber would consider entertaining a presentation about the event to its membership at an upcoming gathering. Leave plenty of time for questions and answers, be ready to direct attendees to your website for more details, and be prepared to liberally exchange contacts with attendees. Invite feedback and be open to new ideas—you never know where a dynamic and new promotional concept will come from (see Figure 10.3). If being able to speak at a membership event is not available, request the ability to be introduced to the membership through the chamber's newsletter, website, social media, or mailings.

Some groups of neighborhood businesses have more intensive, specific, and localized needs than a chamber of commerce with a citywide constituency. Local not-for-profit organizations with names that contain phrases like "business improvement district (BID)," "downtown association," "merchants association," and "business partnership," among others, concentrate their development efforts on just a handful of streets or blocks. If an event is scheduled within their area of influence, these local merchants could be among the most interested in exploiting the event to further their own business objectives. They will also be the most concerned about whether the event will create unwanted inconvenience, confusion, congestion, noise, and litter during their operating hours. Marketing and promotional programs undertaken with businesses located near sports event venues can be particularly effective, as both their employees and their

---

- Provide opportunities for official sponsorship. Consider adding a less-expensive tier designed expressly for local businesses at national or regional events.
- Provide opportunities for local businesses to serve as contractors or subcontractors for the event. Consider launching or supporting an existing local business development program for small businesses and certified minority- and woman-owned business enterprises (MWBEs).
- Place posters or window cards in retailer windows.
- Conduct a window-decorating contest—participating retailers can win tickets and prizes for decorating their windows (or having children do so) with the sports event's theme.
- Request that businesses post welcome greetings to fans and athletes on company-owned electronic message signs and marquees.
- Offer advance event ticket purchase opportunities to member businesses and their employees.
- Encourage sports-event-themed menus at area restaurants and pubs.
- Consider developing cross-promotions with local attractions.
- Supply lapel pins or buttons with the event's name or slogan to be worn by employees of local businesses prior to and during event days.
- Arrange for event promotion or welcome banners to be hung on streetlight poles along major thoroughfares in the city.

Figure 10.3 Involving Local Businesses

customers are accustomed to traveling to, and spending time on, those few blocks. Creating a promotional incentive to buy tickets specifically for customers and employees of businesses with close proximity to the host facility, perhaps using an exclusive access code on an event or venue's website, can help establish goodwill and support for the event.

Making opportunities for local businesses to provide goods and services in support of a sports event provides direct economic benefit to the community and can often realize cost efficiencies for the organizer, as well. After all, the cost of shipping supplies and equipment and transporting service providers can be wasteful if equally good materials and people are available right there in the local community. Regional business associations, as well as the host facility, are excellent resources for identifying qualified vendors and contractors from the community. The local government may also maintain a list of certified MWBEs—minority and woman-owned business enterprises—that can likely benefit greatly from an association (i.e., contracts) with the event.

SIDELINE STORY

The Super Bowl Business Connect Program

The Super Bowl drives significant economic impact when the National Football League's championship game and its associated events unfold in a host city. To ensure that every segment of the community has a meaningful chance to participate from a business perspective, the local host organization and NFL offer enrollment to certified MWBEs (minority- and woman-owned business enterprises) in the NFL's Business Connect Program. The cornerstone of the program is a searchable vendor database that is made available to contractors, league sponsors, broadcasters, hotels, and other event organizers, as well as all league departments. This database helps procurers find qualified local suppliers and its use is required by the league's agreements with Super Bowl key contractors, which must provide periodic reports on their utilization of local MWBEs.

On any given year, approximately 250 MWBEs qualify for the Business Connect Program. With such a large number of participants, it is made clear that not everyone, not even a majority, will actually receive a contract for the Super Bowl. The program, however, offers significant additional value to enrolling businesses. Several workshops are held throughout the year to help companies better prepare for competing on a larger scale through professional development forums, and learn how to read and respond to requests for proposal (RFPs).

Restaurants

Not everyone views the crowds generated by sports events as a negative. A particular group of businesses that welcomes congestion, at least in the form of foot traffic, is restaurants and taverns. Ask the host city's convention and visitors bureau (CVB) to identify a key contact at the local restaurant association. Try to meet with the owners or managers of area eateries and bars to create mutually beneficial cross-promotions that will drive ticket holders into restaurants and their patrons to the event. Does your event offer an app, post a downloadable information guide, or publish a similar resource for guests, participants, volunteers, or staff? List participating restaurants that agree to offer dining discounts (e.g., 15 percent off the bill, a free appetizer, or complimentary beverage) to fans and athletes upon presentation of an electronic ticket or a printed ticket stub, credential, or coupon. The organizer can further enhance the promotion in the venue with some combination of signage, public address announcements, and messages on video boards or electronic displays during the event, adding even more value to the relationship for participating restaurants.

In exchange for the organizer's promotion, these establishments may also decorate their own spaces in an event-oriented motif, hang event posters, offer event-themed menu items, or help promote the program by offering their regular diners coupons redeemable for ticket or merchandise discounts during the month leading up to the event. To maximize exposure for the event at area restaurants, the organizer may agree to provide digital artwork for the establishments to include on daily menus and welcome banners. A simple one-page permission agreement, drafted by an attorney, that defines how the restaurant may use the event logo (or other graphic material) is strongly recommended for this purpose. The agreement can provide the establishment with the right to use the logo for its own promotional purposes or for decorative uses, presuming an existing sponsorship agreement with another restaurant or chain does not preclude cross-promotions. To protect existing or future event sponsors, it is also suggested that the agreement prohibit the restaurant from including any third-party name or logo on banners or printed materials that feature the event name or logo. For example, a banner displaying the phrase, "Bob's Restaurant Welcomes the Big Street Sports Tournament," would be completely acceptable under such an agreement, while the same greeting from "Bob's Restaurant and Barley's Beer" would be expressly forbidden. In addition, the restaurant should not be permitted to pass through sponsorship rights for any event promotion to a third party, whether paid or unpaid, without written permission from the organizer. Agree on a reasonable expiration date for the promotion, and make sure it is recognized in this simple agreement, as well as on downloadable or printed coupons and any other promotional materials or signage.

Area Attractions and Events

Events that draw tourists and one-day visitors to a community can be highly desirable to an area's sightseeing and cultural attractions, including local landmarks, amusement parks, museums, theaters, and natural wonders. Cross-promotions similar to those described for restaurants and bars may be pursued with these area attractions. The simplest way of reaching out to attractions will be through the local CVB, whose membership roster will include the operating entities of the city's most significant points of interest. Develop programs with high-volume attractions that appeal to similar audience demographics as your sports event. Concentrate on those that can promote the event or a promotional offer to the most residents and one-day visitors during the weeks leading up to event day. In exchange, the attractions should offer admission discounts to the sports event's fans, guests, participants, volunteers, and staff during the period immediately surrounding the program, most often a few days immediately before and after the event. Attraction offers may be communicated at the event site, but are at their most effective when promoted in advance of the planned arrival of inbound guests on apps, websites, social media, and printed materials. As a result of these available opportunities, travelers may determine to extend their stay in the host city to take best advantage of the entertainment, cultural enrichment, and cost savings they can enjoy.

Consider designing promotions with professional and amateur sports teams in the host city, particularly those with crossover appeal to the sports event's target audience. Offer discounts on advance event ticket purchases to the loyal fans of major and minor league organizations, and participants in youth and adult recreational leagues. Send event posters to local recreation centers, park information centers, fitness centers, rinks, and other sports-oriented facilities. Promote group ticket packages to teams and associations that use these venues regularly and include a scannable link, website, e-mail address, and/or telephone number for additional information. Some organizers offer not-for-profit groups such as junior leagues, scouts, hospitals, and other charitable institutions the ability to purchase a block of tickets at a discounted rate for resale to their membership at full price as a fundraiser. (*Hint*: These discounted tickets will show a full price on their face. They should be coded so that, in the unlikely necessity of having to provide a refund, box office personnel will know the tickets were sold at a discount. It is further recommended that if refunds of fundraising tickets are determined to be necessary, they be transacted between the charity and the box office rather than with individual ticket holders.)

Be sure to identify the other events and celebrations being held in the host city during the time when most of your pre-event marketing activities are being planned. Sports and cultural events, festivals, civic and holiday celebrations, parades, fairs, and expositions can provide excellent platforms for additional cross-promotions and publicity. Staffing exhibits demonstrations, information kiosks, and hospitality tents, or providing a printed flyer that can be distributed at these events can help to raise awareness for your program. In addition, attendees of conventions, trade shows, and special interest shows that attract out-of-town delegates are always looking for extracurricular activities during their visit. Concentrate promotional efforts on those that are scheduled during or around the same week as your sports event as a great source for additional attendees.

Welcoming Often-overlooked Neighbors

Often-overlooked opportunities to build an event's relevance and popularity may be available in neighborhoods that are, simply, habitually forgotten by other organizers. Disadvantaged families and at-risk youth may be found in every city, and frequently in the shadow of sports facilities. Extending a welcoming hand to these sometimes-unnoticed segments of the marketplace at sports events can provide an array of benefits, foremost among them, just doing good in the community. Activities designed specifically for the disadvantaged can further a host city's own objectives for promoting inclusiveness, can develop positive public relations and new fans for an event, and can diversify the sport's fan base, to name just a few.

Providing special access or programming for the residents of lower-income neighborhoods and those most impacted by the event (i.e., residents living or working closest to the venue) can also help to gain the support of the community and its elected representatives. Organizers can offer exclusive athlete meet-and-greet opportunities, a special luncheon or barbeque with sports personalities, sports clinics, pre- or postevent access to the playing field, or even a number of unsold tickets on a complimentary basis to help improve the lives of those not fortunate enough to have economic access to event tickets or for those who might be inconvenienced the most by event activities. Hosting or sponsoring programs such as these, beyond their purely philanthropic effect, adds immeasurable value to the main event in the eyes of city government and the community at large.

Consider, too, the impact that can be enjoyed by all parties by involving the participation of groups serving physically and intellectually challenged individuals. Area recreational organizations, charities, hospitals, and schools can assist sports event organizers in identifying these groups and their specific special needs. Organizers may discover active local associations providing recreational programs to Special Olympians and Para-athletes who can be included either as participants or as guest spectators. Incorporating these inspirational athletes into the program can significantly add to the quality of a sports event. If this option is not within the scope of the program, consider offering special clinics or workshops conducted by featured competitors, or showcasing their skills during a pregame or intermission demonstration. Finally, many sports organizations and organizers invite military veterans to attend their events as guests and schedule special opportunities to acknowledge them for their service during the event.

Impacting the Local Environment

"You go home after your event is over. We have to live here."

This is a comment we often hear when managing events away from our home cities. Sometimes, it is offered as an admonition to be aware of the region's political or other sensitivities while planning an event, sometimes about the inconveniences that local residents face during the program. It is equally applicable to the notion that events can impact the local physical environment in both positive or negative ways. There is no question that applying sustainable environmental practices is the right thing to do for the host region and our planet. It is also true that recycling, reuse, and recovery programs are vivid and public demonstrations of a sports event's sensitivity to the community. When you go home after your event is over, leave the environment at least no worse off than when you arrived, just as though you actually were going to continue living there.

Are you using wood, plastic, cardboard, fabric, or metal products in temporary construction, décor, or signage? Work with the local sanitation agency or an environmental services firm to recover those materials for recycling after the event to keep them out of the general waste stream. Allow fans, staff, and athletes to participate by providing recycling containers in offices, locker rooms, and event spaces. Replace disposable plastic water bottles for staff, crew, and participants with reusable water bottles with a sponsor or event logo on them. These keepsakes can be filled from water stations and coolers placed around the site. Collect and donate unused office supplies to a school or hospital rather than throwing them away when the event is over. If permitted, recover prepared, unserved food and beverages for a local food pantry. There are dozens of opportunities large and small to leave a positive impact on the host community, and numerous sites and sources detailing best sustainable event practices.

Focusing and Managing Community Enthusiasm

Almost immediately after a city or neighborhood has been named the host for a prominent sports event, a swell of community pride can cause leaders and influential citizens to seek outlets for their enthusiasm. Each believes that he or she has a role to play, a contribution to make, and insightful ideas that need to be realized. Word can quickly spread of plans for fundraising dinners, public rallies and parades, concerts and clinics, pickup games, and corporate challenges. As unbelievable as it may sound, the actual sports event organizer is frequently among the last to know about these preparations.

SIDELINE STORY

NFL Green—The Super Bowl Environmental Program

On-site construction for the National Football League's annual Super Bowl begins about a month before the game, broadening the capabilities of a state-of-the-art American football stadium to include facilities for 30 international broadcasts and workspaces for more than 5,000 visiting media. The stadium also becomes a theatrical venue for the year's most technically and operationally complex 12-minute entertainment extravaganzas, the Super Bowl Halftime Show, and its immediate surroundings a center for world-class hospitality at the 10,000-guest NFL Tailgate Party and 5,000 guests attending through the NFL On Location sports travel program. The stadium and all of the functional areas required to accommodate these activities are enveloped by a high-security perimeter featuring two-and-a-half miles of fencing covered with decorative fabric, punctuated by tents containing more than 130 airport terminal-quality magnetometers to process more than 90,000 fans, workers, and participants. The amount of recyclable and reusable material generated by four weeks of construction is quite significant, so much so that the NFL hired environmental consultants Jack and Susan Groh to oversee the reclamation project. The Grohs work with NFL departments, broadcasters, contractors, and others to recycle plywood, cardboard shipping boxes, miles of fence fabric, hundreds of street banners and way-finding signage, metals, plastics—anything that can be removed from the waste stream and reused. Wallets, shopping bags, and other items have been made of Super Bowl fence wrap material. More than 90,000 pounds of prepared, but unserved, food is recovered from parties held throughout the host city and sent to local food pantries to help feed the hungry.

NFL Green goes still further. A sports equipment reclamation project collects truckloads of outgrown sports gear representing all sports and provides these used items to children in needy neighborhoods, a carbon mitigation program and e-waste recycling. The program now extends to other major league events, including the NFL Draft and Pro Bowl.

What can your event do to leave a positive environmental legacy in your community?

Dynamic, involved, and enthusiastic boosters of the community begin to formulate ambitious plans to exploit the event for largely positive and selfless purposes. Those allowed to expand and develop unchecked and without the active involvement of the organizer can drain human and financial resources away from the main event, creating a muddle of mixed marketing messages to fans and potential sponsors. If poorly realized, these additional community activities can even taint the core sports event in the eyes of some segments of the marketplace. Simply put, the more active, interested, and involved a community, the more likely there will be a tendency to want to do too much.

It is in the best interest of the event organizer to channel this enthusiasm, not curb or obstruct it. Consider yourself lucky when the community gets so behind an event that it begins to mobilize spontaneously to support and take best advantage of it. A community's ambivalence, in contrast, can make the road to event success much tougher. Reach out and communicate with these fervent and excited souls. Validate the community's desire to become involved and provide focus for their efforts. Demonstrate your USO (understanding stakeholders' objectives) sensitivities—show that you appreciate and support the community's desires and help them understand yours. Channel its members' energy so they are working in support of the actual objectives of both the community and the sports event, rather than what they think those objectives should be. Help organize key local supporters into an advisory board to provide you with counsel and insights into the needs of the community. Or, engage the most driven and energetic individuals into task forces, organizing, or host committees.

Advisory Boards

If it is early in the planning process, organizers can form an advisory board comprised of influential businesspeople, community leaders, and other individuals whose expertise, contacts, and familiarity with the host city can prove invaluable to event operations. Forming an advisory board creates a legitimate, official group of counselors to the event organization who can be relied on for helpful advice and insightful recommendations, perspectives on the community, and past event history. Embracing and engaging these leaders can serve to preempt any unauthorized ad hoc group, no matter how well intentioned, from pursuing a separate agenda in the name of the event. Advisory boards are also useful when the event and its organizing entity have little recognition in the community or among potential sponsors. When it is vital to establish the legitimacy of the event and its organizer, the composition of the advisory board is of more significance than merely managing and monitoring community activities. Members selected should be well regarded as individuals whose presence will immediately reinforce the importance and benefits of the sports event to the community—leaders who are trusted and respected by local government, residents, businesses, and sport. In short, the event advisory board is an organized collection of gatekeepers.

When approaching the people targeted for membership on the event's advisory board, be sure their reputations in the community are beyond reproach. The host city's sports commission can provide insights into potential candidates who are necessary to protect the event's own reputation by association. Be sure the role of the advisory board is well understood by those who are requested to serve. It is a body of experts to give *advice*, not direction, and to provide *recommendations,* not requirements. When an organizer believes the formation of an advisory board would be beneficial to the smooth management and operation of an event, contact potential members as soon as possible after confirmation of the host city. Explain the significance of the event to the local community and the reason for soliciting the recipient's participation. If you don't get an immediate response, allow approximately two weeks to pass before making calls to follow up on each invitee's level of interest. A sample solicitation outlining the roles and responsibilities of an advisory board member appears in Figure 10.4.

It is important to note that the advisory board invitation makes no reference to empowering members to make policy decisions or provide any form of service to the event other than attendance at a monthly update meeting. On the surface, the advisory board will serve as a source of wisdom, but its members' time investment and active engagement can provide influence when needed.

Organizing and Host Committees

Organizing and host committees differ from advisory boards in that, at their most effective, they are groups of individuals dedicated to providing time, work, and expertise on specific functions supporting an event (organizing committee) or fulfilling the city's responsibilities as host (host committee). An organizing committee should be directly responsible to the event organizer, while a host committee may report to a host agency such as the local sports commission or CVB. To use each to the best advantage, organizing and host committees should function as fully integrated extensions of the event team.

Properly managed, organizing and host committees can contribute significantly to the overall event organization. At least one senior member of the sports event management team should attend every meeting of each committee to ensure the objectives of these primarily volunteer bodies and those of the overall event remain well coordinated. Unmanaged, organizing and host committees can run amok. A presence

Dear (Insert Addressee Name Here):

As you may know, Township Village has been named the host city of the upcoming Major Stick Sports Tournament, an event that will attract 500 visiting athletes and up to 2,000 spectators to Civic Gymnasium. The Major Stick Sports Tournament is in its 12th year, and Township Village has committed to making next February's event the very best ever. The tournament will provide area hotels with a beneficial mid-winter boost, and local businesses with a unique opportunity to meaningfully enhance their first quarter marketing campaigns. The event will also generate needed funds for the Civic Gymnasium renovation project scheduled for next summer.

The Major Stick Sports Tournament requested recommendations from the Township Village Sports Commission for potential candidates to the Major Stick Sports Tournament Advisory Board. I am pleased to cordially invite you to be a member of the advisory board. Members will assist us in ensuring the success of the community's participation in the event. The board will convene for a brief virtual or live breakfast meeting once monthly through next February to review our plans and progress, and to provide the members' insights, recommendations, and expert opinions on various topics of interest and impact to the people and businesses of Township Village. An agenda and minutes will be circulated to all members approximately three days prior to each meeting which will take place on the first Tuesday of each month.

As an expression of our gratitude, actively participating advisory board members will enjoy attendance and VIP privileges at the Major Stick Sports Tournament with our compliments.

Please indicate your acceptance of this invitation to participate as a valued member of the Major Stick Sports Tournament Advisory Board with your response to our email address. We look forward to the prospect of your involvement in this important event for Township Village.

Yours very truly,
Sports Event Organizer

Please check one:
☐ I accept appointment to the Major Stick Sports Tournament Advisory Board.
☐ I am unable to participate at this time.

Figure 10.4 Sample Advisory Board Solicitation

at committee meetings demonstrates the organizer's collaborative commitment to and oversight for the progress and quality of work being performed by these community participants. It should not be assumed that the responsibilities assigned and undertaken by a local event support organization will be successfully or sufficiently fulfilled without vigilant monitoring and collaboration. The more an event relies on the work product of a committee, the more conscientious the organizer must be in maintaining an awareness of the committee's activities. It must be recognized that all-volunteer committees will require an investment of management time and energy and, later, expressions of appreciation such as event tickets, party invitations, and acknowledgment gifts. Organizing and host committees for major events may even require full-time professional staff and a budget to finance their operations. In such cases, the financial obligation is usually the responsibility of the host city. In addition, as sports event committees must often supplement their budgets by soliciting sponsorships and donations, the organizer must communicate strict guidelines outlining how they may raise funds and from whom, in order to avoid instances in which the organizer and the committee compete for the same needed corporate infusion of funds. Therefore, before forming or requesting the formation of a host or organizing committee, sports event organizers should be completely certain that the need for such support truly warrants its creation.

Identify the roles and responsibilities expected of the group and create an organization plan that defines all reporting relationships. Be sure the sports event organizer is always indicated as the overall authority for the effort, with at least a dotted-line relationship with host committees that report directly to the local government. Although the specific mission of an organizing or host committee will differ from one event to the next, Figure 10.5 lists some of the most common sports event support areas of responsibility for such committees. This should by no means imply that every committee formed must undertake every role listed, or that other appropriate functions cannot be added to the list.

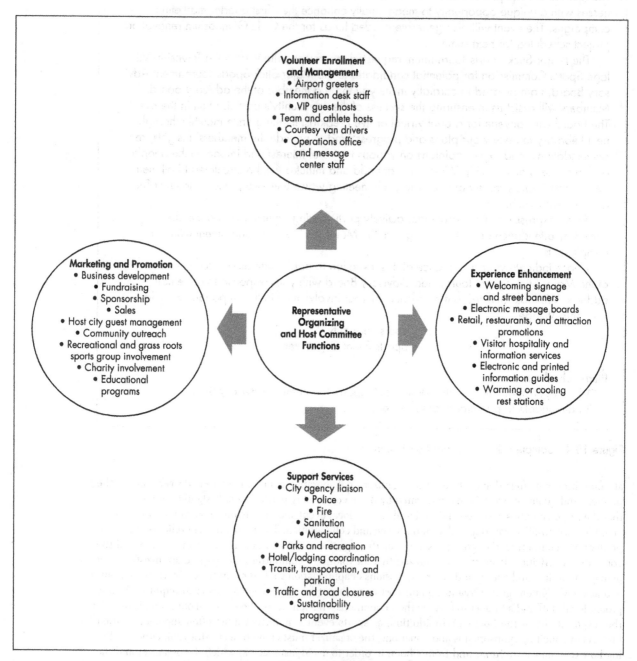

Figure 10.5 Representative Organizing and Host Committee Functions

Notice that each of the functions presented in Figure 10.5 can be assumed directly by event staff that may already be under the organizer's immediate control. Even so, the formation of a committee is an attractive option when the event budget is insufficient to allow the organizer to contract and pay full-time professionals to manage such functions. Also, these support organizations are frequently formed when the scale of the program is so large or so dependent on local resources that some division of labor between an out-of-town organizer and a local body provides significant cost and management efficiencies. In such cases, committees are often staffed with a combination of experienced, paid event professionals and motivated volunteers. Regardless, organizers are well advised to maintain close control over the activities of their supportive committees to ensure they actually provide what they are charged to contribute and with the attention to detail, quality, and timeliness the organizer would expect of his or her own staff.

Host cities should resist the temptation to appoint representatives to the host or organizing committee for the sake of politics or expedience. The best committee is the minimally, efficiently sized committee, and any participant who cannot provide wisdom, work, or experienced perspective to the process will drain precious time and resources, and sap morale from those who will invest their time and talents more fully. A committee chairperson should be appointed, one who enjoys the respect of the community, who can provide leadership and direction, and who can maintain constant communication with both the members and the event organizer. The structure of the membership into functional groups should generally mirror the event organization. The committee chairperson should communicate most consistently with the event director. Subcommittee heads (examples noted in bold type in Figure 10.5) should report their progress to the committee chairperson at regularly scheduled meetings but can also work closely with the event organizer's staff whose operational responsibilities are most similar to their own. Although additional committee members may report to the subcommittee heads, it is recommended that the monthly or semimonthly update meetings be limited to the chairperson and subcommittee heads in the interest of streamlining the meeting agenda and maintaining efficiency. Subcommittee heads should hold subsequent regular sessions with those tasked to work with them, filtering updates down from the last committee meeting and receiving input to present at the next. Committee membership may be composed of city officials, business leaders, and other talented, influential citizens of the community whose common interest lies in the improvement or maintenance of the region's quality of life, and with a proven track record of actively contributing their time, energy, and talents to similar endeavors. The top positions (e.g., the chairperson and subcommittee heads with the greatest responsibilities) should be composed of the highest-level gatekeepers, wherever possible. Figure 10.6 illustrates some of the sources where organizers and host cities can turn for potential organizing committee members.

As discussed earlier, it is often the host city, sports commission, or CVB that will undertake the task of forming a host committee to help execute the specific responsibilities to a sports event without diverting a disproportionate share of city resources from their year-long missions. Thus, it is sometimes difficult to prevent political appointments to the host committee. However, it is important for sports event organizers to make clear to the host city that, to truly support the objectives of both parties, the committee must be well integrated into the event team and must remain in close communication together throughout the planning process.

Local Promoters

When a sports event organizer's offices are located far from the host city, it is sometimes practical to work with a local event promoter to execute specific functions of the event operations and/or marketing plan. Organizers pursuing this option should exercise as much care in the selection of a local promoter as they would in pursuing a candidate for a senior management position with their own company. From the public's perspective, the promoter will be indistinguishable from the organizer. His or her reputation in the community, track record, and management style must complement that of the organizer to ensure that both they and, by inference, the event team will be viewed positively by all stakeholders. Well-connected promoters can be most helpful in marketing and selling event tickets, procuring local labor for event setup, operation,

Position	Resource
Committee Chairperson	Deputy mayor
	City council representative
	Major local real estate owner or developer
	President of local business concern
	General manager of local television or radio station
	Senior partner of local law firm
	Local business personality
Volunteer Enrollment and Management	Sports commission representative
	Convention and visitors bureau representative
	Sports team fan or booster club president
	Community sports program representative
	Community services manager for a local company (preferably a sponsor)
	Representative of an association with a community services mission (e.g., Rotary, Kiwanis, Lions, veterans groups)
Experience Enhancement	Creative director of local advertising agency
	Senior manager of local architectural firm
	Senior manager of an advertising firm
	General manager of local restaurant or attraction
	Senior manager of local chamber of commerce
Support Services	City director of special events
	City director of communications or marketing
	Police department community affairs officer
	Parks and recreation department manager
	Transit authority public affairs manager
	Local hotel general manager
Marketing and Promotion	Sports commission representative
	Convention and visitors bureau representative
	City director of communications or marketing
	Director of development for local charity (when the event benefits the charity)
	Senior manager of local chamber of commerce, business improvement district, or similar group
	Senior account executive of local public relations firm

Figure 10.6 Organizing and Host Committee Resources

dismantling and other logistics, and providing insights into local politics and resources. Promoters may be hired on a fee basis and, if responsible for managing any cost areas, should be provided with a budget that by formal agreement may not be exceeded without the advance written permission of the organizer. If the promoter is solely responsible for the promotion and sale of tickets, then they may also be retained on a flat fee or on a fee-plus-bonus basis for achieving certain levels of paid attendance, or compensated on a commission-per-ticket-sold premise.

Moving Forward

The sports event organization is now in place, and the enthusiasm of the community is focused constructively on building mutually beneficial business opportunities. Advisory boards and committees of gatekeepers and hard-working volunteers are committed to the success of the community and the sports event to which they are about to play host. Costs are under control, marketing plans are in place, and sponsors are being signed. The production schedule shows the time remaining is growing short. Event day is approaching, and there is still much left to do.

Post-play Analysis

Sports events are often staged in a vacuum, with little or no active participation on the part of local government, businesses, or groups that routinely operate in the interest of community service. Many of these sectors of the community recognize that sports events can provide powerful quality-of-life and economic benefits to their region. Organizers who have not engaged the local community on some level may be overlooking a valuable, motivated resource. Organizers should identify the *gatekeepers,* the influential civic, business, and neighborhood leaders who can provide intelligence on the perceptions of the local market and expedite requests to, and approvals by, city agencies and community partners.

Business development groups, such as chambers of commerce, neighborhood business partnerships, restaurant associations, and others, can provide excellent sources of exposure and supportive cross-promotions. Consider how to involve often-overlooked neighbors, such as lower-income communities, disadvantaged youth, and those with special needs, in the event. Be sensitive to the local environment and embrace sustainable event practices to recover, recycle, and redistribute materials that would otherwise enter the waste stream.

Respected members of the community who share an interest in the success of both the sports event and the host city may be organized into an advisory board to provide advice and counsel to the organizer. Task forces composed of local resources, known as organizing and host committees, can provide guidance, work, and accountability to a sports event organizer. The activities and responsibilities of these committees are overseen by a chairperson or executive director and must be continually monitored by the event organizer to ensure completion to desired standards.

Coach's Clipboard

1. Identify the gatekeepers in your local community who can prove helpful in planning and organizing a tournament of visiting youth volleyball teams. What obstacles to staging the tournament could be presented during planning and how would one or more gatekeepers help to advise and overcome them?

2. What organizations would you engage to develop cross-promotions and mutually advantageous exposure opportunities for the event above? How would they help promote the event and what would those business partners expect in return? What costs might be incurred by the event budget in activating these programs?

3. How would you apply best sustainability practices at the volleyball tournament? What materials can be recovered and either recycled or reused? How else can you positively affect the quality of life and the environment before, during, and after the event?

4. How would you reach out to involve lower-income families, at-risk youth, and the physically and intellectually challenged in the event? Presuming entrance to the tournament is free, what value can you provide to these sectors of the community that will enhance their experience and further the objectives of the city and the event?

PLAY 11

Accommodating and Managing Guests

"It is not the critic who counts; not the man who points out how the strong man stumbled, or where the doer of deeds could have done them better. The credit belongs to the man who is actually in the arena."
—*Theodore Roosevelt, 26th President of the United States (1858–1919)*

This play will help you to:

- Develop your event's ticket sales strategy.
- Manage your event's guests and ticket buyers.
- Provide the best and most welcoming experience for your fans.
- Work most efficiently and effectively with host hotels.

Introduction

All the plans are in place; now it's time to manage and execute the event. During this period, event organizers put their production and marketing plans into action. "The devil is in the details," it has been said, and this is never more true than in the planning and execution of sports events. It is here that the needs of the events vary most. Every event requires clear objectives, a budget, a host venue and production schedule, a marketing plan, and the support of sponsors and other promotional and community partners. Some require the organizer to possess an understanding of the dynamics of ticket sales, the basics of broadcasting and other media, and the tenets of technical production. Others require an understanding of the logistical elements of managing participating athletes and incoming guests and fans, still others the fundamentals of working with the hotels that will be engaged to provide event offices, accommodations, and hospitality.

Although the remaining "plays" present specialized subject matter that may be more pertinent to some organizers than to others, a working familiarity with all areas of sports event planning is strongly recommended for all.

Selling Tickets

Sports event organizers should view tickets as monetary instruments. The ticket, whether displayed in electronic form on a digital device or printed on paper, represents value received by the purchaser in exchange for a payment, so steps should be taken to protect the organizer and buyer against the possibility of loss, theft, or counterfeiting by unscrupulous opportunists. For major events, tickets should be generated only as needed by a computerized ticketing service or printed by an experienced, bonded ticket supplier. Tickets with specific seat locations or sections should also be checked for accuracy against the seating manifest, a list of every individual seat as defined by section, row, and seat number. (It is also recommended that the host venue be inspected on a seat-by-seat basis prior to selling tickets to ensure the manifest reflects the current physical reality of the seating configuration.) Until sold, printed tickets should be accurately counted and stored in a secure location such as a bank vault or safe.

With ever-increasing frequency due to technological advances, increased security, and buyer convenience, tickets for sports events are predominantly sold and distributed online. Most often, event organizers use a host venue's ticket sales platform and will utilize a mobile device app or website to provide access to digital ticketing functionality along with venue information, special offers, interactive features, and exclusive content, as will be discussed in this section.

Computer-generated tickets do not exist in physical form until and unless printed and, as such, require anti-theft measures prior to sale. They may be more prone to the possibility of counterfeiting, though. The pervasiveness and quality of design and drawing software and inexpensive color printing can create an illegal market for phony tickets that can endanger the financial viability of an event and may put unsuspecting purchasers at risk of being barred admission when the counterfeits are detected. The most prevalent deterrents to counterfeit tickets, whether hard or electronic, have been the use of barcodes or QR codes on tickets, commonly employed by year-round sports facilities and other venues that use laser scanners to read digital or printed barcodes on tickets at their entrances. Once a unique code has been scanned by a reader device, no other ticket with the same or an invalid code will be permitted admission. Although no anti-counterfeiting measure can be completely effective against sufficiently motivated persons with criminal intent and any ticketing system will have its flaws to overcome, technology has streamlined the ticketing process and has made the process efficient, easy, and reliable for events, venues, and fans.

Ticket Types and Admission Policies

There are two basic types of ticket policies—reserved seating and general admission. Reserved seats guarantee the purchasers specific seat locations. Some sports events, most notably those held in professional sports arenas and stadiums, sell essentially their entire inventory as reserved seat tickets, regardless of price level. General admission (GA) tickets, in contrast, enable the purchasers to occupy any available seat on a first-come, first-served basis. GA tickets may be scaled like reserved seat tickets (see Play 3), with different prices for access to specific sections or levels. They are also sold for events during which the audience moves around the site or views the event from standing locations rather than occupying a seat. Because GA tickets only guarantee admittance, and not necessarily a specific spot from which to enjoy the program, managers of facilities hosting sports events that utilize this policy should be prepared for the formation of queues before the doors open, as audiences holding these tickets arrive early to claim the best possible seats or viewing locations. Some events offer both reserved and GA sections, providing for those who prefer the convenience of having a specific seat waiting for them when they arrive, usually at a premium price, and enabling others who do not mind planning for an earlier arrival to realize some economies at the sports event. Pursuing a GA seating policy can increase the risk of crowd management challenges, particularly if the organizer expects a potential crush of fans racing for the best seats when the venue's doors first open which could result in injuries. For this reason, general admission ticketing is not recommended for professional or large-scale sports events. Work with your risk management specialist to determine whether this policy will potentially raise your insurance premiums or increase the likelihood of injuries (see Play 14).

When to Begin Selling Tickets

Regardless of the nature of the sports event, whether it is an exhibition game, themed game night, skills competition, track meet, opening ceremonies, fundraising dinner, or a player draft, selling or distributing tickets in advance is an absolute must. Relying primarily on tickets sold as fans arrive on event day, also known as "walk-up" business, can put the organizer at serious financial risk. First, advance sales provide cash flow to cover pre-event expenses and deposits. The funds represented by walk-up ticket sales are not available before the day of the event. Second, advance sales reduce the potentially devastating effects of event-day weather conditions. Attendance is guaranteed by tickets sold in advance if atmospheric conditions threaten, but do not ultimately affect, event-day operations. Fans without tickets, however, have the total freedom to decide whether to attend on event day, based on either a whim and/or concern about impending weather conditions. Advance ticket holders have invested their money and will receive no refund unless the event is completely canceled, so, even if there is a small chance the sports event will go on, they will be far more likely to make the effort to be there.

Creating a sense of urgency is the key to generating advance ticket sales. You want fans to think: "If I do not get my tickets right away. . .

- "I will miss out on attending at all because tickets may be sold out later."
- "I will not get the best seats, which could diminish my enjoyment of the event." (A reserved seat policy must be in place to provide ticket buyers with the availability and choice of best seats.)
- "I won't receive an offered premium item or some opportunity available solely to advance purchasers, or only for a limited time."

The "when" of putting tickets on sale is inextricably linked to the "how" to put tickets on sale. You must have enough time to inform the public about the event and communicate the availability of tickets to potential buyers. Then you have to make it easy and convenient for them to make their purchase. You must leave yourself sufficient time to put the word out, let it permeate around the market, and have enough time remaining for them to order or purchase and receive their tickets. You also must give yourself enough time to react to the marketplace with new sales strategies should your initial marketing campaign produce fewer sales than expected.

A sample ticket sales timeline for a hypothetical event scheduled for mid-June is illustrated in Figure 11.1. Before a single sale can be made, a ticket manifest must be finalized. The manifest lists every possible seat location or ticket number that can be sold, including standing room, accessible seats, and seats identified as having obstructed views. It should also include every location that normally exists, but may ultimately be removed from sale because of total obstruction, removal for the installation of television cameras, scoreboards, other operational elements, or any other possible reason that a seat is not expected to be salable. These are known as "seat kills," and it is, of course, preferable to identify them so they may be

February 1	Inspect facility and finalize ticket manifest
March 1	Past-year ticket buyers, sponsor's customers, staff and volunteers receive offer (via e-mail, website, text, tweet, and/or mail) for advance tickets purchase before general public
March 22	Response deadline for past-year ticket buyers
April 1	Marketing and communication campaign begins to promote public ticket sales
April 15	Public ticket sale begins
May 23	Sponsor ticket promotions and second wave marketing campaign (if necessary) begin
June 15	Event day

Figure 11.1 Sample Ticket Sales Timeline

removed from the manifest of tickets available for public sale well before the first ticket is sold. (Remember that if the tickets for killed seats are included in the event's gross potential, their removal from sale will represent an expense against the budget.) Be ready to have the tickets for killed seat locations available anyway, just in case plans later change (e.g., camera positions are shifted) and those seats, as a consequence, end up unaffected by obstructions. A best guest-service practice to follow is to have a small number of ticket locations not available for sale put aside to address any complaints or to solve thorny issues raised by a purchaser. This will enable staff to relocate a disenchanted ticketholder to a more desirable area.

Note that in the hypothetical example given in Figure 11.1, the primary public campaign begins on April 1, approximately 10 weeks prior to the event. Four weeks before this date, an offer will be made to those listed in a database of past ticket buyers, a sponsor's customers, staff, and volunteers, presumably the most loyal and likely purchasers. This offer can reward your best customers and enhance a valued promotional partnership with an opportunity to purchase preferred seat locations ahead of the public sale date. Communicate urgency by establishing a reasonable deadline for response and leave your ticketing staff sufficient time to process orders between the deadline and the first day of public sales. It is important to keep in mind when this kind of advance accommodation is offered, it is wise not to sell all of the best seats to the presale database. It will be perceived as deceptive and unfair if the only seats available to the very first public ticket buyers are in less than prime locations. A common and fair practice as applied to this sample event would be to divide the tickets available so that at least some portion of the best seats will still be available to the public on April 15.

Just as important as not setting the "on sale" date too late (i.e., too close to the date of the event) is to not promote tickets sales too early. Events with unusually strong demand for tickets, such as the Olympic Games, college and professional championship series (e.g., bowls and tournaments), and major league all-star contests, may not require adherence to this rule. Organizers for these uniquely successful events often make tickets available six, eight, in some cases even 10 months or more in advance. For most sports events, though, it is important to time the initial public sale just right. Identifying exactly when that should be will vary depending on the nature and date of the event. Note that first day of public sales for this hypothetical event is in the early spring (April 15). In this case, the organizer feels that the best time to begin selling a warm-weather event is when potential ticket buyers first start thinking about the imminent approach of warmer weather. Attempting to sell the public a far-off, outdoor, warm weather event in the coldest days of winter, when sports fans are in the midst of enjoying indoor and more rugged outdoor events, may prove to be a wasted effort. The database of past purchasers, though, can be approached by e-mail, social media, and/or direct mail campaigns at an earlier time. Their loyalty to the sport and strong, positive memories of past events make them more likely to be future purchasers and perhaps more motivated to procure their tickets ahead of the public rush. Customers and employees of participating sponsors represent another targeted audience who can be reached and are likely to be responsive to such a promotional benefit in advance. In our hypothetical example, these groups are granted a three-week window to order their tickets in advance. Although past purchasers and sponsor customers may be given more time to respond, if desired, a relatively short advance sale opportunity is recommended, again to increase the sense of urgency. The longer a potential buyer is given to make his or her decision, the more likely the decision will be delayed or, possibly, forgotten completely.

How to Sell Tickets

As previously mentioned, it is essential to make it easy and convenient for potential buyers to purchase their tickets, and to encourage them to act immediately. Today's sports event audiences have become accustomed to purchasing event tickets using any one of several methods, from using the convenience of the Internet to traveling to a venue's box office. If a fan happens to be attending other events held in the same venue, or lives or works nearby, the box office can be an opportune option. However, event attendees are comfortable with using the Internet through desktop, tablets, and mobile devices and such conveniences as the ability to consult seating diagrams to find best available locations at different price levels, to securely use a credit card or an online payment system for ticket purchases, to confirm the purchase by printing or digitally saving tickets to their mobile device, and to obtain up-to-date event information, making the Internet a preferred and convenient ticket-purchasing destination.

A similar procedure is suggested for ticket sales to grassroots and community sports events that will be held in temporary facilities or those that do not maintain a box office. A single, reliably available location with regular business hours should be designated for ticket sales. For example, a local merchant's retail store can be selected and promoted for this purpose. Even if the business owner makes no direct profit from ticket sales, the store traffic created by the sports event purchasers, and resulting incremental sales of the storeowner's retail products, can provide a strong incentive to participate as the event "box office." Additionally, ticket sales may be promoted on banners and posters displayed at the retailer's store, increasing exposure and sales for the sports event to their existing shoppers. This option is highly preferable to selling tickets for community sports events out of someone's home, as inconsistent hours of availability will reduce convenience for the potential buyer.

For events taking place at permanent sports facilities, sports fans routinely expect and demand instant access to tickets at the time they see the first advertisement or read the first announcement, lest their response to the call to action be delayed or forgotten. These venues offer or require use of their computerized ticket services The fees for transactions using these ticketing platforms are typically shared between the seller-organizer and purchaser, and are usually defined in the facility lease agreement (see Play 4).

These powerful services also provide event promoters the ability to offer ticket sales over the Internet from anywhere in the world as well as by telephone and at any remote locations in the host city. It is wise to include the primary information to reach the ticket service in every event advertisement, social media post, promotional coupon, and poster, and to provide links from the event organizer's website directly to the ticket service's sales page.

Event venues provide services at a box office where tickets may be purchased before and on the day of an event and where ticket reservations may be picked up at a "Will Call" window on event day. If tickets are picked up on site, or at the event's offices or another designated location, it is strongly suggested they be transferred to the buyer only after presentation of a government-issued photo identification card such as a driver's license, and a matching signature to guard against possible fraud. Business cards should not be accepted as proof of identification.

Events that will be held in facilities with no permanent box office can attempt to negotiate an agreement with a reputable ticket service to sell their tickets. Alternatively, you can take advantage of independent web ticketing services and software to manage your own electronic database of ticket inventory, provide fans with a convenient on-line mechanism to purchase their tickets, and maintain access to up-to-the-minute sales reports. Organizers in pursuing this option should investigate the software and services that are offered by several companies.

Mobile technology is a familiar and popular method of ticket transmission and access into events. Upon purchasing tickets, customers have their tickets sent to them digitally via e-mail or link. In this instance, the customer has the ability to produce the ticket on his or her mobile device for presentation upon entry into the event. Each digital ticket is marked with a unique registration key or barcode for security and authenticity purposes. For this system to be utilized, an event venue must be properly equipped with compatible software and hardware to allow ticket takers to accurately confirm that the ticket is genuine and has not previously been used. This method has become popular because it provides a convenient transfer of the ticket with the added benefit of secure storage within one's mobile device.

Ticket Brokers and Resellers

Ticket brokers essentially resell tickets they purchase from the organizer, the box office, or from other buyers. The laws governing acceptable business practices of ticket brokers and the maximum fees they may legally charge the public vary widely from one local government to the other. Some may be officially authorized to sell event tickets by the organizer, but many more operate outside any chain of direct responsibility. Many brokers maintain websites that list all of the events for which they offer tickets, procured from a variety of sources. Organizers of successful sports events are constantly amazed at the extravagant prices brokers charge for tickets, particularly once the event is officially sold out. As long as the broker does not use the logo, proprietary artwork, or any other intellectual property of the event, there is usually nothing most organizers can do about what many perceive as overly inflated ticket prices. At the same time, the organizer, having had no direct role in the transaction between the broker and the purchaser, bears no responsibility beyond the face value of the ticket. Therefore, if refunds are necessary for any reason, typically only the face value of the ticket need be recompensed. Brokers are generally honest at least to the extent that the tickets they resell are genuine. There are, however, counterfeiters masquerading as ticket brokers that can perpetrate fraud against both the buyer and organizer. The organizer has no obligation to accept counterfeit tickets obtained from such sources and should encourage those who purchased them to seek the assistance of local law enforcement.

Digital services have created a secure forum for resellers and second-hand buyers to do business. These "secondary ticketing services" maintain their popularity by providing an expedient transaction environment, limiting and, in some cases, guaranteeing against illegal selling practices, and creating a structured marketplace to help set market prices. The entities selling tickets on these digital marketplaces range from single sellers to large-scale brokers. Businesses of this kind provide an open commercial space in return for commissions on sales and small fees charged to the purchaser and/or seller. These services typically do all of the work required in transferring the tickets between parties, as well. In addition, an event can sponsor secondary market sales through its own digital platform in order to take advantage of the revenue it may lose on the second-hand market. This practice is used by major professional leagues and teams, as the digital marketplace has become a more common and trusted consumer ecosystem.

A significant problem, though, is the use of bots by some digital services. As described by *amazon.com*, a bot, which is short for robot, is an automated software application that performs repetitive tasks over a network. It follows specific instructions to imitate human behavior but is faster and more accurate. For example, bots can interact with websites, chat with site visitors, or scan through content. According to the International Association of Venue Managers (IAVM), it was estimated in 2023 that bots accounted for some 40% of the traffic during first days of tickets sales for many major and special events, creating obstacles for the general public to have full access to event tickets. In addition, some unscrupulous secondary ticketing services have engaged in the fraudulent practice of speculative ticketing by advertising the availability of tickets that they don't actually have. Event organizers, venue operators, and the public benefit by having legitimate exchanges for selling and buying tickets and need to be constantly on alert to such practices.

Distribution of Tickets to Free Sports Events

Many sports events that embrace a free admission policy may still desire to distribute tickets in advance. Tickets serve as convenient reminders of the event's date and time, and can be added to a digital calendar or easily slipped into wallets and displayed under kitchen magnets. The ticket policy for a free sports event is usually best offered on a general admission basis; reserved seats are not recommended. Free tickets are not usually redeemed at the same rate as priced tickets, as the bearer has exchanged no money or other value for their use. Therefore, organizers will often distribute as many as two or three times the number of free tickets as can normally be accommodated at the host facility in hopes of filling it with spectators. This is not possible with reserved seats. It is a near certainty that a reserved seat ticket policy for a free event would result in a significant and noticeable number of empty seats. The exact multiple of free general admission tickets that is advisable to distribute for a given event should be based on past history, the attractiveness of the event to the public, and the experienced opinions of the venue manager, organizer, and other trusted stakeholders.

Regardless of the number distributed, it is strongly suggested that all tickets include a disclaimer to avoid overfilling of the venue, such as: "This ticket is valid for admission on a first-come, first-served basis. The organizer and facility reserve the exclusive right to delay or deny admission based on crowding and concerns for public safety." In order to guard against overcapacity and to offer admission to fans not holding advance tickets if space permits, it is further suggested that tickets include an advisory that requires arrival at the event at least 30 minutes before it begins. Thus, late-arriving ticket holders may be denied entry if absolutely necessary to maintain safe conditions, while permitting the organizer the option of admitting non-ticket-holding fans in the final minutes leading up the event in order to fill empty seats. Depending on the anticipated popularity of the event, be prepared for an early-arriving crowd for any event admitting fans on a first-come, first-served basis, whether paid or free. Set up organized queue lines in advance, and have security and guest services personnel (i.e., people who can provide information and direction, and communicate with the organizer if necessary) arrive sufficiently early to manage any building crowd. If possible, have your facility and staff ready for a slightly earlier gate-opening time than published for the safety and convenience of your fans.

Free tickets may be distributed in all of the same ways that promotional material and discount coupons are provided to the community to encourage ticket sales. Point-of-purchase displays in area stores, website offers, and print-your-own tickets over the Internet are among the particularly effective ways of dispensing free tickets into the marketplace.

Packaging Tickets

Organizers marketing sports events that are held over a series of days should consider creating packages containing tickets for multiple matches. Packages can include admission for the most attractive event day (e.g., the final round of a tournament) and for one or more dates that are expected to be less popular. This practice can increase ticket revenues and encourage improved attendance during times that might otherwise be expected to draw smaller crowds. Consider selling multiday tickets ahead of the public offer for individual ticket sales to create urgency and provide the incentive of better seats for those purchasing packages.

SIDELINE STORY

NFL On Location

Sports travel packagers have offered fans one-stop-shop opportunities to visit host cities and attend sports events for many years. Most packages are offered by companies that have expanded their core businesses by combining two industries—the proven travel package business familiar to most tourists and the burgeoning broker/secondary ticket business.

In 2005, the National Football League introduced NFL On Location, its own branded and internally managed sports travel business. The program, initially established as a business-to-business service, offered packages to companies hosting guests at Super Bowl XL in Detroit's Ford Field, including a hard-to-get game ticket, a four-night hotel stay, a pregame party across the street from the stadium at Comerica Park, merchandise, and other benefits. Package prices were scaled on the basis of seat location, the quality of the hotel room, and other factors, as well as the pricing established by the many other sports travel businesses already in operation and offering packages to the same event. Companies from across the United States purchased in excess of 900 packages, generally in increments of 20 or more per purchase, in NFL On Location's first year of operation.

In the ensuing seasons, fans hearing about NFL On Location wanted access to the same opportunities as corporations, though perhaps only two or four packages at a time. The NFL responded by making a version of the program available for individual sale. Additionally, many companies and fans wanted to be able to shop for their own accommodations, and locally based purchasers did not need hotel rooms. Game-day packages were created to respond to this need, retaining many of the other benefits and inclusions and lowering the overall cost. Within five years, the number of NFL On Location packages sold for the Super Bowl more than quadrupled, and, later, the program provided sports travel packages for several other league events, including the NFL Draft and the NFL International Series games.

NFL On Location was reimagined in 2015 into On Location Experiences, an Endeavor-owned company that now also sells packages to the NCAA Championships, the Olympics, Major League Baseball All Star Game, and Pro Football Hall of Fame Enshrinement Week, among many others, in addition to the Super Bowl. Chances are, your events are smaller or less well-known than the Super Bowl. If you have fans or guests coming from out of town to attend or participate, you have a chance to generate revenues by packaging conveniences with your event tickets. After all, fans have to stay somewhere, eat, park their cars, or take home a remembrance. What can you add to the event ticket that can provide value and convenience to the purchaser, and profit for your organization?

For both one-day and multiple-day events that draw fans from outside the host area, packages may be created that provide value or one-stop shopping for their convenience. Consider a package price that includes a hotel stay in a property participating as a sponsor or marketing partner, a pre-event party, or post-event experience. (It is to the benefit of the hotel to offer event packages through its own database and marketing campaigns, as well, helping to extend the organizer's marketing campaign and filling the property's inventory of guest rooms. Be sure the hotel takes advantage of this opportunity.) Other features such as preferred parking at the host facility, athlete or alumni meet-and-greets, event merchandise, and concession food vouchers can be included as well.

Creating and scaling ticket packages are similar to building sponsorship deals. Be sure that the fulfillment costs (e.g., the cost of tickets, hotel rooms, parties, food, merchandise and other elements) are fully covered by the package price and add a reasonable profit margin for more revenues. For events that do not bring many fans from out of town, packages need not include hotel rooms, of course. Develop an "event-day package" that combines some of other elements mentioned, and others, to create a menu that provides value to the purchaser, and an attractive, compelling and convenient way to enjoy your event.

Losing Sleep 101—What to Do if Tickets Are Not Selling

Your revenue budget is dependent on ticket sales. An engaging series of social media content has been posted, a well-placed advertisement has already appeared in the local newspaper, press releases have been distributed to the media to announce the on-sale date, e-mail offers have been sent to your best customers, and the website highlights all relevant information. Yet, you are frustrated that advance sales are slower than expected. Is it time to start panicking? Use the decision tree in Figure 11.2 to plan your most appropriate response.

Two courses of action—the reduction of seating inventory and the wide distribution of complimentary tickets, also known as "papering the house"—are scenarios that should be employed after all marketing efforts have failed and the time remaining to sell tickets grows short. Complimentary tickets can still have a small positive effect on the net income of the event (or, perhaps due to disappointing sales, slightly reduce the net loss) through sales of merchandise and concessions, but will have the greatest effect on perception and public opinion. Simply put, they serve to make the audience appear larger and the popularity of the event greater. The practice of adjusting the reserved seat sales policy to skip every alternate row in the final days before the event (5c in Figure 11.2) can also make the audience appear larger.

Reduction of Inventory

If a significant amount of tickets is expected to remain unsold, organizers may decide to reduce the quantity of empty seats by closing off less desirable seating sections. This enables the organizer to save a small amount of money on the house staff (e.g., ushers, security, guest services staff, cleaning) who would have to service the area on event day. Guests who have purchased tickets in those locations may be moved to unsold seats in higher priced sections, generally without any complaint from the public.

Events that are broadcast on television are usually seen from one primary direction. Try to fill the areas the television cameras will be facing first. If the event budget permits, cover empty seating sections with fabric or banners containing event artwork or perhaps a sponsor logo to turn a potential eyesore into pleasing décor and/or additional revenue. Better still, if seats are portable, consider physically removing selected rows and/or sections entirely.

Use this decision tree to plan your response to slow ticket sales. This model presumes that ticket prices are set at reasonable levels and are available to the public by convenient means. It also assumes that advertising and publicity campaigns, as well as the ticket sales date, were not set unreasonably early.

1. Is there still enough time left to sell the remaining tickets? *(YES—go to [1a] and [2]; NO—go to [5])*
    [1a.] Did another sports or entertainment event compete for the fans' disposable income the week your ads were placed? *(YES—go to [1d]; NO—go to [1b]*
    [1b.] Was the public preoccupied by a big news story the week tickets went on sale that diverted attention away from the offer? *(YES—go to [1d]; NO—go to [1c]*
    [1c.] Does the current ad have a clear "call to action," communicate urgency to buy, have all pertinent information, and a convenient response mechanism for purchase? *(YES—go to [1d]; NO—go to [1g])*
    [1d.] Is there more than one additional placement of the ad scheduled? *(YES—go to [1e]; NO—go to [1f])*
    [1e.] **Action:** Consider running the ad again, or extending the campaign, and go to [4].
    [1f.] Is the ad placed in print, radio, television, and/or the Internet in places, at times and within programming the event's target audience will be expected to see it? *(YES—go to [2]; NO—go to [1h])*
    [1g.] **Action:** Make adjustments in the ad and buy additional space and/or time, and go to [2].
    [1h.] **Action:** Consider purchasing additional advertising space and/or time in the media most likely to be read, heard, or seen by the event's target market, and go to [2].
2. Have past ticket buyers had time to receive and respond to their advance ticket offer? *(YES— go to [2a]; NO—go to [2b])*
    [2a.] **Action:** Consider making follow up phone calls, a second mailing, and/or additional posts to past ticket buyers. Go to [3].
    [2b.] Don't panic yet! Go to [3].
3. Are sponsor promotions offering discounts on tickets already in the marketplace? *(YES—go to [3a]; NO—go to [3b])*
    [3a.] **Action:** Request increased promotion by media partners, if available. Investigate adding other discount admission partners. Go to [4].
    [3b.] **Action:** Don't panic yet! Consider moving up the introduction of sponsor promotions to an earlier start date. Go to [4].
    [3c.] Have you been actively communicating with fans in the social network media? *(YES— go to [4a]; NO—go to [4b])*
4. Work with International and external partners to develop more promotional opportunities on multiple platforms. Go to [4a].
    [4a.] **Action:** Increase fan engagement activities and publicize new promotional opportunities. Post trivia contests for prizes, and encourage fan conversations with polls and solicit opinions (e.g., who will win and why). Work with sponsors to activate new short-term promotions that build instant excitement (e.g., schedule and announce new athlete appearances at retailers and special last-minute ticket offers). Generate new storylines. Post pictures of arriving athletes, preparations at the host facility. Go to [5].
    [4b.] **Action:** What are you waiting for? Go to [4a], fire up your computer, and get started!
5. Are far more tickets still available than can reasonably be expected to be sold at this point in time? *(YES—go to [5a]; NO—go to [5b])*
    [5a.] **Action:** Consider reducing seating inventory. Close unsold seating or viewing areas in the venue to save on operational costs. Go to [5b].
    [5b.] **Action:** Consider distributing a quantity of complimentary tickets to deserving groups to make the event day audience appear more robust (called "papering the house"—see discussion to follow). Go to [5c].
    [5c.] **Action:** Consider selling tickets, or distributing complimentary tickets, in every alternate row to make the audience appear larger, and then fill in the empty rows if sales subsequently increase. Go to [5d].
    [5d.] **Action:** Review all other expense areas to compensate for the expected shortfall in revenues.

Figure 11.2   Decision Tree: Response to Slow Ticket Sales

"Papering the House"

Papering the house, that is, issuing and distributing complimentary tickets to fill unsold seats, is a last-minute, few-options-remaining strategy to make the event venue appear more full. If widely publicized, it can send a message to the public, and to sponsors, that the event was either not popular enough to support paid ticket sales or that the event could not justify using as big a venue. It can create dissatisfaction among an event's most loyal guests—those who actually spent money to attend. In addition, once the process of papering the house begins and the availability of free tickets becomes publicly known, the event organizer can usually bid farewell to any possibility of significant incremental ticket revenues. So why do it?

If the event organizer is reasonably certain that all possible avenues to generate additional ticket sales have been exhausted, papering the house effectively can provide a number of advantages. Whether having purchased a ticket or attending for free, audience members also purchase merchandise, concession items, and parking. If the organizer benefits from the sales in these areas, some additional income can be generated from the incremental audience. This is particularly important if budget assumptions require a larger audience to achieve merchandise revenue expectations now that the pace of added ticket revenues appears to be slowing.

A large crowd also creates more fan excitement, motivates the athletes, makes sponsors happier, and helps guests feel that they are attending an event of sufficient importance to have warranted their time and interest. Sparse attendance is almost always mentioned in media reporting. If the program is a multiday sports event, papering earlier rounds can generate more widespread and positive word of mouth and additional ticket sales for later dates. Finally, for televised and video-streamed events, nothing says, "This event is unimportant" more effectively than an empty grandstand.

Deciding to paper the house does not automatically solve these problems unless the strategy to distribute tickets is well reasoned and relatively discreet. The event promoter has also to guard against the biggest negative possibility of all: Complimentary tickets are widely distributed and the people who received them still don't show up. Such circumstances say, "Even the people who could have attended for free didn't think it was worth the bother." Unless you are reasonably convinced that papering will generate the audience you need to enhance the overall experience, minimize embarrassment, and increase merchandise and other nonticket revenues, consider other less-risky ways of making empty seats disappear, such as closing off and/or covering seating sections, before committing yourself to this last-ditch effort.

Distribute tickets to groups or through organizations that can be depended on to actually use them. Many communities have programs run through local government agencies that allocate event tickets to low-income and at-risk youth. If you use a ticketing service, the local sales office frequently maintains relationships with special charitable programs that can channel tickets to qualified, dependable, not-for-profit groups. Blocks of tickets can also be distributed to area businesses through the local chamber of commerce and to hospitality industry employees such as hotel and restaurant workers, through the convention and visitors bureau. Distribution of tickets to groups is much more efficient than trying to dispose of tickets one pair at a time. Consider inviting hospital workers, scout groups, and youth organizations. Think of youth leagues and recreational programs focused on the same sport celebrated by the event.

Event vendors may also be able to use tickets for the promotion of their own business objectives. You can host military personnel and their families by working through the public affairs officer at nearby installations, or members of the police, fire, sanitation, and other service workers through the city government or their unions. Try to salvage some positive benefit from the papering effort by selecting one or more of these groups to receive tickets you may not otherwise be able to sell, and issue a press release that turns the donation into a positive publicity story. Again, be sure that the groups to which you make complimentary tickets available will have the time and ability to distribute them to people who will actually use them to avoid creating sections that, although not empty, are only sparsely populated.

Many of the techniques used to reduce inventory can also be applied to papering. If the event is televised, make sure that you concentrate distribution efforts on the side facing the cameras to give the appearance of better attendance. Invite the families of technical crews and talent working on the television production to attend as guests of the organizer. If tickets display reserved seating locations, you can also distribute complimentary tickets in every alternate row.

Marketing Spaces on Tickets

Messaging in e-mails accompanying digital tickets, the backs of printed tickets, and ancillary page space on print-at-home tickets are often used as marketing opportunities, such as displaying presenting sponsor logos and websites, bounce-back coupons, or promotions for merchandise and future events. Perhaps more importantly, these spaces are frequently used for the inclusion of legal language that can cover a multitude of liability issues, including the right to eject the guest for inappropriate behavior, the right to use the purchaser's image in television coverage and future marketing materials, and, increasingly, the acknowledgment that the use of the ticket implies the guest's understanding that attendance at a sports event can possibly result in physical harm in the normal course of competition and presentation. The organizer's legal counsel must assess the need for any messages that should be included in these areas and draft all appropriate language. Computerized ticket services use standard legal language and may not offer as many options to customize these spaces.

Guest Management

The audience of nearly every sports event will include guests who attend at the invitation of the event organizer, host city, and other stakeholders. These invited guests may include sponsors, broadcasters, and other business partners whose agreements define a number of tickets to which they are contractually entitled. They may also include individuals whose invitations serve as expressions of gratitude for noncontractual contributions to the success of an event. Tickets in appropriate seating locations should be removed from the event's inventory to satisfy contractual obligations before the first tickets are sold to the public. Other discretionary requirements for special guests should also be estimated before ticket sales begin. Use Figure 11.3 to avoid overlooking some of your most important guest "audiences."

	Complimentary	For Purchase
Sponsors, contractual		
Sponsors, guests		
Broadcasters, contractual		
Broadcasters, guests		
Host venue		
Promotional partners		
Players/athletes		
Coaches, officials, trainers		
Alumni		
Celebrities		
Host/organizing committee		
Local government officials		
Influential community contacts		
Prospective future partners		
Key vendors		
Organizer executives and staff		
House seats/miscellaneous		

Figure 11.3 Guest Audience Checklist

Note that the figure includes entries for holding both complimentary and tickets "for purchase." High-demand, high-profile, and charity-oriented events frequently invite the majority, or even all, of their guests to purchase their tickets before the public sale. Others invite guests on a complimentary basis to fulfill sponsorship obligations, express gratitude, and extend hospitality to both current and potential future business partners. Often, sponsors and other guests who are invited on a complimentary basis have additional needs, and the organizer will fulfill these extra requests on a "for purchase" basis, if available.

Sponsors and broadcasters often make up the largest percentage of guests. Be sure that every agreement defines an exact number of complimentary tickets each partner is entitled to receive, as well as how many may also be purchased. Review every agreement before tickets go on sale and remove the required number of tickets from inventory. Figure 11.3 also suggests entries for sponsor and broadcaster "guests," that is, key partner contacts to whom the organizer would like to extend additional, personal courtesies without their attendance counting toward the contractually obligated allotment.

Key host city officials who played a direct or indirect role in the success of an event may also be invited to attend, but do not be surprised if they refuse an offer of complimentary tickets. Many local laws prohibit municipal and state employees from accepting gifts in excess of a certain value. As a consequence, you should take no offense when some government employees offer to purchase their tickets, and others simply respond that they are unable to attend. Gifts of event tickets are also excellent expressions of gratitude for host or organizing committee members and influential community contacts who have provided helpful assistance in the planning, marketing, and execution of the event. Don't overlook potential future business partners in the host city. Consider inviting the key marketing executives of both local and national companies headquartered in the area from which future event partnership proposals might be solicited. Finally, has next year's sports event already been awarded to a new host city? Be sure to invite key contacts and gatekeepers from that community to witness event operations first hand and begin to spark their interest, knowledge, and excitement.

Value-in-kind (VIK) deals with vendors and media partners frequently involve the transfer of event tickets, which should also be held back from the manifest prior to public sale. The organizer may additionally wish to invite key vendors that have provided outstanding service or unusual value to the event. Keep a reasonable supply of "house seats"—tickets in good viewing locations—on hand for last-minute requests and invitations. It is wise to reduce this quantity as the event grows closer, periodically returning unused house seat tickets to the inventory available to the public. Be sure to have an acceptance deadline for all guests, whether invited to receive free or purchased tickets, so you have a way to sell or otherwise dispose of tickets held for those who opt not to attend. Feel free to expand the form in Figure 11.3 to include columns that note the number of tickets needed for ancillary events, such as parties, receptions, workshops, clinics, fan festivals, and player practices. The organizer would be best served by maintaining the form on a spreadsheet or, preferably, in a guest management database using appropriate software or in a proprietary database program, as described later in this chapter.

Conflict Seats

Keep some quantity of tickets available on event day as "conflict seats." These tickets are actually used to resolve conflicts, such as reseating guests from areas that may have become unexpectedly obstructed by such elements as lighting towers, trusses, cameras, scoreboards, staging, or decorative props. Tickets for the seats the organizer is able to identify in advance as seats with obstructed views of the playing surface and standing-room tickets, should be sold with their limitations clearly visible on the ticket front at the time of purchase, so conflict seats are not generally used for relocating these guests. Other uses for conflict seats include reseating guests upset by antagonistic neighboring fans, in the rare event guests bearing duplicate tickets for particular seats present themselves, or for any number of discretionary purposes deemed appropriate by the front-of-house staff. Conflict seats are typically not returned to the box office for public sale, as they could be required at any point during the event. The host facility can recommend an adequate number of conflict seats to hold, based on the venue's size and experience.

ADA Seats

Be sure to retain seats for your guests with mobility, visual, auditory, sensory, and other impairments. It is not only the right thing to do. It is the law, as defined by the Americans with Disabilities Act of 1990, and similar legislation in effect in many other countries. All large sports and recreation facilities already have a plan for accommodating "ADA guests" in various locations around their seating areas, and organizers should consult with the host venue's ticketing supervisor to ensure this inventory is properly managed. For small or nontraditional facilities that do not have a plan, it is up to the organizer to ensure that adequate and equal access to seating areas is provided including ramps for mobility impaired guests, where needed, and a selection of locations with unimpaired visibility to the event is provided. If possible, retain a legal consultant specializing in ADA law to help guide you.

Guest Management Systems

A guest management system encompasses more than the simple compiling of an invitation list, sending invitations, and assigning tickets to those who accept the offer. Whether the needs of guests are maintained on index cards, in a loose-leaf notebook, or in an electronic database, organizers must constantly monitor and manage guest needs, right up to event day. Administering the guest management process efficiently is of paramount importance. Money, goodwill, and reputation are at stake when inviting and hosting these influential individuals. Sponsors and business partners expect a flawless sports event experience in recognition of their participation, and the generation of future business may in part depend upon the organizer exhibiting proven guest management skills and capabilities.

The larger the guest list, the more imperative it is to organize the guest management process electronically. This will give the organizer the ability to access information easily, eliminate duplicate invitations and ticket assignments, generate management summaries, and include a more comprehensive record of information for each invited guest, such as portrayed in Figure 11.4.

The guest management database is comprised of records for each person invited. These individuals are frequently divided into "audiences," a categorical description of the type of organization they represent. Typical audience categories include many of those listed in Figure 11.3, but may be expanded or subdivided as the event and its guest list require. If the database is particularly large, the management of individual audiences may be split among event staff members who most often interact with those groups invited to attend (but cross reference all lists of invited guests to avoid duplications).

The guest database is a powerful, permanent record that can also increase future efficiency, serving as the basis for compiling invitation lists for subsequent sports events, as well. For these reasons, it is important to include as much information in each record as possible. Request that invited guests provide the data for the items (or "fields") 2 through 10 to ensure you have the most up-to-date contact information. Track the invitation process in fields 11 through 13. If a follow-up e-mail, phone call, text, or letter is sent because no response was received by the requested deadline, indicate the most recent attempt at communication in item 12. Fields 14 through 18 initially indicate how many tickets are being held, and ultimately provided for the guest, the seat locations assigned, whether they are to be *gratis* or on a paid basis, and whether payment has been received. If tickets to additional events, such as parties or hospitality programs, are to be provided, they should be inserted in item 19. It is recommended that separate fields be assigned for each ancillary event, providing the organizer with the flexibility of inviting each guest to only the activities desired.

Organizers with the ability to utilize digital tickets generally opt to do so for their invited guests. In cases where sports event tickets represent significant monetary value, the organizer might be advised to not mail tickets to the invited guests, but rather, request that they pick up their tickets on site, either at the box office will call window or at an organizer's guest services desk, or, perhaps suggest printing the tickets themselves if the design or paper stock of the ticket is not a priority. Tickets may be lost in transit, and the use of overnight delivery or bonded messenger services can add considerable operational expenses. Guests

1. Audience
2. Name
3. Title
4. Company
5. Address
6. E-mail
7. Phone (office or residence)
8. Mobile phone
9. Fax
10. Assistant name
11. Date invitation sent
12. Date of most recent follow-up
13. Date response (RSVP) received
14. Number of tickets offered
15. Number of tickets provided
16. Comp or purchase
17. Payment information
18. Seat location
19. Ancillary event tickets
20. Date tickets mailed/delivered
21. Pick-up authorization (i.e., who is allowed to pick up the guest's tickets)
22. Transportation
    a. Arrival information (airport, flight, and time)
    b. Departure information
    c. Ground transportation requirements
23. Hotel
24. Hotel room type
25. Other guests in room
26. Credit card/online payment system
27. Gift
28. Invited by
29. Notes

Figure 11.4 Guest Management Database Record Composition

who have received their printed tickets in advance also often arrive at the venue with their tickets still atop their dresser, or left in their hotel rooms. Be sure to have access to the database and vouchers ready at the guest services desk on which to copy the seat locations for guests who arrive without their tickets.

It is also wise to establish a policy regarding who will be permitted to pick up a guest's tickets. It is recommended that guests pick up their tickets personally, upon presentation of valid photo identification such as a driver's license or passport, especially those seated in the very best locations. (Some may give their tickets away to someone unimportant to the organizer, or even sell their tickets, and this becomes much more difficult if the tickets must be picked up on site.) Many important guests, particularly celebrities, local officials, and senior executives, may find it inconvenient or undesirable to pick up tickets themselves. A representative may be identified to the organizer, and authorized in advance and in writing by the guest to receive tickets in his or her place (field 21). This representative should also produce acceptable identification and sign a log or receipt upon delivery.

The guest management database can also assist in the administration of transportation systems (22) and hotel accommodations (23–26), as well as any other special programs or privilege, such as the distribution of gifts to selected guests (27). Any additional information that suits the organizer's purposes may be included in the database such as the name of the staff member who invited the guest (28), and miscellaneous notes of interest (29).

The great power of an electronic guest management database is evident in the organizer's ability to sort information by any individual field. Management reports can be generated identifying only "Players and Athletes," or just those guests requiring hotel rooms, individuals invited on a complimentary basis, or those invited by a particular staff member. In addition to the use of off-the-shelf software options such as electronic spreadsheet and database programs, there are a host of more specialized solutions. These include online event registration services and web-based software, some incorporating modules for the management of guest accommodations, such as those available from several well-regarded programs. These companies primarily service corporate and association events, but some of their services are easily adaptable to small and mid-size sports and recreational events, particularly for the registration of athletes and teams.

Management of Athletes and Players

For most sports experiences, there simply is no event without the athletes. Athletes should be managed like the most important of VIP guests. Make them feel appreciated, and their enthusiasm and excitement, their professionalism in meeting the media and other important guests, and their physical performance will shine through. The players, whether they are a group of 10-year-old track competitors, a team of college footballers, or members of a professional hockey club, are the ultimate ambassadors for their sport and the events in which they compete. They are the attraction the public comes to see and, in most instances, represent everything that is positive and good in sports. Therefore, no discussion on guest management would be complete without including this most important segment of guests—the athletes and their own guests and families. Manage them with the respect and treatment they deserve and they will come prepared to compete with clear and focused minds.

What athletes want most of all is to perform to their highest potential. Try to make the event a memory of a lifetime, if not only for their performance, then also for the experience. Make sure their families feel the admiration as well. Consider staging special events just for them. Allow families to attend practices and provide them with the best viewing areas that can be made available. If appearances at additional sponsor or fan events are part of a player's participation, transport the athlete to the event location in style. Ensure the player arrives early enough to stay on schedule, but not so early that he/she sits around waiting to participate. Make sure there are healthy refreshments available in an attractively decorated, comfortable waiting area ("green room") before the appearance. Try not to schedule too many appearances, or for such lengthy durations, that the athlete tires before the athletic performance itself. Respect any physical routines an athlete must adhere to leading up to the event (e.g., practices, aerobic workouts, weight training) before scheduling other activities.

Sports event organizers who require athletes to make special appearances should also consider hosting a private reception, post-game meal or party, or open a hospitality lounge that is exclusive to players and their families, an oasis from the frantic atmosphere surrounding most events. Use the same guest management system to track the arrivals, departures, hotel, ticketing, and gift needs used for your most important guests. You may even add their uniform and equipment needs, ground transportation requirements, and ancillary event appearances as additional fields in the database.

Communicating with Guests

Communicate with your guests to ensure they have all pertinent event information before they leave home, and once they arrive at the event. Send a confirmation e-mail with preliminary event information after receiving indication of their attendance. Include instructions on how to book rooms at the event's headquarters hotels, information on ground transportation options in the host city, and a hotline number for last-minute changes to arrival plans. Be sure to maintain a web page and/or a mobile "app" that guests can access for up-to-the-minute information on event developments and reprints of pre-event newspaper coverage. Social media platforms and texts to a personal mobile number can be especially effective in delivering time-sensitive messages, as these sites are checked regularly by users and are expected to provide the timeliest information. An event staff member should be dedicated to updating these sites to ensure the most efficient and accurate dissemination of information to guests. Publish a welcome package to be available to the guest upon hotel check-in or when the guest picks up tickets including a convenient digital or printed event information guide containing final activity schedules, event office locations, e-mail addresses and telephone numbers, transportation schedules, dining and entertainment options, and discounts offered by local businesses. Open an information desk in each headquarters hotel lobby. In short, never leave the guest in a position where he/she neither knows the answer to a question nor knows how to be able to get one.

Hotel Management

Sports events that draw participants and guests from outside of the host community are the most likely to have to enter into a relationship with at least one host hotel. Hotels start to make their money on "heads in beds," but those heads also have mouths that eat in their restaurants, drink in their bars, talk over their telephone systems, and work in their business centers. Guests use their computers and tablets utilizing Internet connections in the hotel's sleeping rooms and public areas, attend dinners and parties in their ballrooms, and utilize audiovisual services in conference facilities. Moreover, the hotel's catering department provides meal and refreshment services to all of these functional spaces.

What Hotels Really Want from Events

Most hotels want to attract groups that they know will fill sleeping rooms and generate restaurant and catering revenue. Sports events, like corporate conferences and conventions that can fill up to 70 to 80 percent of their total capacity, are the most welcome if they bring major food and beverage events such as parties and dinners along with them. Hotels rarely offer more than 80 percent of their rooms to a single group to reduce their risk in case of a poor turnout and to ensure they have a supply of guest rooms for what hotels call their "transient" guests—their loyal and frequent business travelers. In addition, many hotels have contractual agreements in place that guarantee a certain number of rooms to airline crews, visiting guests or transferring employees of local corporations, and other organizations year round. The more long-term contracts that a hotel has in place, the lower the percentage of rooms it will be able to make available for the guests and staff of one-time events.

Hotels are, in a sense, in the wagering business. They bet on the success of an event by agreeing to hold a certain number of rooms for the group's use. However, they do not want to commit to holding rooms for an event if the organizer is not equally, and contractually, obligated to use them. To improve their odds of success, hotels routinely investigate an event's *pick-up history*, the number of rooms the organizer has actually used in the past compared to the number that were originally held, by calling previous host cities and properties. A high percentage of actual usage makes an event very desirable and will encourage the hotel to offer an organizer a greater number of rooms. A poor pick-up percentage may cause a hotel to either offer fewer rooms or pass on participating at all. Hotels want event organizers to constantly monitor their expected needs and to advise the hotel as early as possible if they will not require as many rooms as were requested. If a hotel holds rooms for a sports event that do not materialize into occupancy by guests and it cannot subsequently resell them, it will want to be compensated for lost business.

What Events Really Want from Hotels

Organizers are also in the wagering business. They want to ensure their selected hotels will hold the number of rooms they will require to accommodate their athletes, guests, and staff with the least amount of financial risk. They want the best available accommodations at the lowest possible rate, and courteous, attentive service for their guests. The quality of a sports event's selected host hotels reflects directly upon the overall event experience. Athletes and guests who encounter accommodations of poor quality or inferior service will have equally poor memories of their attendance at the event.

Sports event organizers also need places to work. They require hospitality suites to meet and greet their guests, and rooms for meetings, participant registration, ticket distribution, accreditation, transportation dispatching, and information dissemination. If the event is being held in a city distant from their home offices, they will want to convert some hotel meeting rooms into full-service offices, with workspaces that provide reliable Wi-Fi connectivity, and access to equipment such as printers and copiers.

Some sports events require too many rooms to be accommodated in a single hotel. Although guests may be dispersed into multiple host properties, organizers will most often concentrate their functional offices and staff in one "headquarters hotel." When organizers need to use more than one hotel, they prefer them to be adjacent to one another, or within a reasonable walk, to avoid having to allocate funds to shuttle guests and staff between more distant properties. If large numbers of hotels are required, organizers prefer they be located in clusters to similarly minimize shuttle transportation costs.

Unless the event is committed to using a specific property because of a sponsorship agreement, organizers should inspect as many hotels as possible to compare overall quality, rates, service features, and business policies. The local CVB or sports commission can save the organizer's staff significant time by coordinating inspection visits, or "site surveys," of hotel properties that the local representatives believe meet the stated needs of the event, from overall quality to guest room and space availability and the interest of the property in being considered as a host hotel. During the site survey, each of which might average up to two hours, the organizer will have the opportunity to evaluate the hotel on a wide range of criteria, such as those listed in Figure 11.5 and described in the following section.

- Geographic location and proximity to event site(s) and training site(s)
- Overall hotel quality (via independent ratings and visual inspection)
- Suitability of rooms
- Sufficient rooms and suites available on first hold
- Room rates
- Suite rates
- Complimentary room ratio
- Function space availability
- Function space rates
- Technology availability and installation charges
- Business center services
- Shipping and receiving charges
- Room service hours
- Health club facilities and charges
- Room drop charges
- VIP amenities
- Sponsor sensitivities
- Newspaper delivery
- Valet parking availability
- Parking rates
- Hotel channel
- Signage policies
- Supplier exclusivities (e.g., technology, security, rentals, and decorators)
- Space and systems for merchandise sales
- Deposit and payment schedule
- Cancellation policy
- Attrition policy

Figure 11.5   Host Hotel Evaluation Checklist

Evaluating and Negotiating with Hotels

Among the first characteristics to evaluate is the geographic desirability of the hotel's location. Is it adjacent to, or reasonably close enough to, the event site to enable participants and guests easy access? The farther the hotel is from the host venue, the more likely it is that the organizer will need to establish a shuttle transportation system. Transportation systems are most cost efficient when a single bus or van within a fleet may be used for multiple trips. The farther the hotel(s), the fewer round trips each vehicle will be able to make per hour and the greater the number of vehicles that will be needed. Is the hotel in an attractive location within the host city or on the edge of an economically depressed area? When choosing hotels, sometimes it is preferable to sacrifice proximity to the event site for a more pleasant or attractive location.

For many events, another geographic consideration will be proximity between the athletes' hotel and the location of practice facilities. Avoiding lengthy bus or shuttle trips for participants, coaches, and staff to get to and from training locations can be as a high priority for many event organizers as securing the quality practice sites themselves. "There is a balance of many factors in identifying the best possible accommodations for sports events, especially those such as international soccer with so many people who travel great distances," said Jill Fracisco, former deputy general secretary of soccer's Confederation of North, Central American and Caribbean Association Football (CONCACAF) governing body. "In addition to considering the hotel's amenities, the time to transport between a hotel and a stadium and between a hotel and a practice location are among the most important."

Based on both personal visual inspection and ratings of independent hotel evaluation services that can be found in a variety of online and printed publications, is the property of a quality and reputation that will reflect well upon the sports event? What is the age of the hotel, and what is its experience in serving as a host location? How well is the property maintained, and when were the guest rooms, meeting rooms, and public spaces last renovated? Does the hotel offer all of the amenities demanded by the event's guests? Will some audiences of invited guests require a more elegant hotel and others a more value-oriented property? If so, should the group be split in two or more subgroups based on their price and quality sensitivities?

Is the hotel prepared to hold an adequate number of guest rooms, suites, and meeting and reception rooms for the event's guests? Until a hotel has a signed contract for the rooms, it will place them "on hold," a nonbinding agreement to provide the rooms until a specified deadline date for a final contract—unless someone else signs a contract first. The total inventory of all rooms reserved over all pre-event, event, and post-event days is called a *room block*. It is standard practice for a hotel to contact event organizers holding rooms that are not yet contracted if another group expresses interest in contracting over the same period. The hotel usually offers the organizer the opportunity to formally commit to using the rooms in the block before entering into a contract with another party, but will release the hold if the organizer does not agree in a timely manner. It is also standard practice for hotels to put a "second hold" on rooms, which will entitle the second group to automatically claim the rooms should the first decide to release its hold, fail to enter into a contract, or default on a required deposit.

What percentage of the rooms will be paid for directly by the event and what percentage by the guests? Are the rates within an acceptable price range for the purchaser? Few groups pay the standard "rack rate" for sleeping rooms. The more rooms an organizer will commit to using, and the more catered events that will be held at the hotel, the more negotiable the room rate may become. Will suites be required by the event for important sponsor guests, celebrities, athletes, performers, or senior executives, and are a sufficient number or adequately sized and appointed suites available? Hotels routinely offer a number of complimentary rooms for the organizer's use based on the number of rooms actually used. This ratio is somewhat negotiable (suites are often counted as two or more rooms). Try to negotiate an additional room or suite on a complimentary basis for one or more of the organizer's top executives, and a number of free upgrades into higher-priced rooms, subject to availability.

Does the hotel offer an adequate amount of space for the various hospitality events (e.g., dinners, luncheons, parties, award ceremonies, and meetings) the organizer wants to host? Are there sufficient rooms for event office needs over the dates required for setup, pre-event preparation, and the post-event dismantle period? Every hotel has a standard rental rate for its meeting and ballroom spaces, but many will waive these rates if the event commits to a large enough number of guest rooms or a guaranteed amount of catering over the course of its stay. The cost of meeting room rentals can be a considerable, but often an avoidable, expense and can be a strong enough reason to select one hotel over another as a suitable host.

As part of evaluating the suitability of a hotel, it is certainly fair to ask the management if any inconveniences, such as renovation work in any part of the property, a noisy construction project next door, inaccessibility of a dining facility, or road repairs outside the front door, are scheduled or can be anticipated around the dates of your event. Having this information may be an important factor in deciding among different hotels.

A key area to confirm in evaluating a potential host hotel is technology, specifically the availability of and any associated costs relating to these essential services. Is there Wi-Fi connectivity throughout the hotel? Are guests assessed a daily charge for Internet access in their rooms or meeting facilities? Can mobile devices work in all areas or is there limited reception in portions of the hotel? All guests attending an event will have the expectation to be technologically connected on demand so reliable and no-or-low-cost service is required where guests will be staying.

In addition, guests, particularly sponsors and other business partners, will often require access to the hotel business center for many services including computers, scanners, printers, and copiers, as well as for local or overnight shipping. If your needs do not warrant the costs of renting and installing equipment in your meeting room office, try to negotiate preferred rates and extended hours of operation for the business center.

Are there charges for receiving event materials shipped to the hotel and delivered to the meeting rooms? If these charges cannot be negotiated away, will the hotel agree to a flat or maximum daily fee for received packages and faxes? Are there service charges for shipping materials from the hotel as well? Will the hotel permit courier and freight companies to pick up prepaid shipments without a service charge?

Room service hours, where available, should be compared to the times that guests and staff will most likely make use of in-room dining, particularly late hours after nonmeal events have concluded. Hotels will often extend hours at the organizer's request if the property can reasonably expect to profit from this accommodation. Are there high-quality, health-conscious menu items available? Some hotels may offer to provide special late-night, event-themed items and healthy food selections promoted on special in-room menus during the event. Sports events generally attract athletes, fans, and other guests committed to keeping in shape, so access to fitness facilities is also usually expected. Is there a facility located on the property with a sufficient quantity of aerobic and weight-training equipment in good working order, or is there a health club nearby with which the hotel has an access agreement? Is there a charge for using the facilities and, if so, can it be negotiated to enable event guests to enjoy privileges on a complimentary basis? If the facility is not available 24 hours a day, is it open at times that reasonably complement the event schedule? Can extended hours be negotiated?

Organizers may be planning to communicate with their guests by delivering information packets, letters of welcome or newsletters to their rooms. Surprise gifts such as T-shirts, caps, or a basket of sponsor products can await guests upon their arrival or when they return to their rooms after the event. Hotels may charge a fee per delivery for these "room drops" depending on the size or weight of the items to be delivered.

A less-expensive alternative is to staff a guest information desk in the lobby of the hotel. In addition, most hotels will not charge for the distribution of information packets to guests upon check in. The organizer can request that the hotel recognize a certain number of their most important guests with special welcoming amenities, such as a delivery of a themed basket of goodies, a plate of dry snacks, chocolates, fruit, beverages, and/or a souvenir cap, pennant, or T-shirt. Most hotels will agree to offer these hospitable extras to a limited number of the event's guests, as identified by the organizer, at the property's expense. Make sure that the hotel is aware of sponsor sensitivities, so they do not greet sponsor guests with a basket of their competitor's products. Be aware of the hotel's own sponsorship agreements, although most will agree to serve a sports event sponsor's products even if they have existing agreements with a competitor company.

Are valet parking and self-parking options available and, if so, at what cost? Try to secure a number of complimentary parking accommodations for staff vehicles or courtesy vans and in convenient locations if possible. Are there convenient places on the property for bus shuttles to load, off-load, and park?

Is there an available channel on the hotel's in-room television system for the organizer's own programming? Some hotels permit organizers to run footage of past sports event highlights, an infomercial presentation, and/or other entertainment or information to all guest rooms on an open television channel. There is usually a charge for this service.

What are the policies regarding the use of decorative event and directional signage or other branding elements in the hotel lobby, on the building exterior, and in other public spaces? Some hotels will permit freestanding signage that posts event and transportation schedules, and directs guests to various event offices. Will the property permit the organizer to hang festive welcome banners, display trophies, and outfit front desk staff, bell persons, doorpersons, and waitstaff in event caps, golf shirts, or jackets? Some hotels endorse this level of staff participation, while others will restrict staff at most to wearing lapel pins or buttons.

Many organizers look for opportunities to sell official merchandise, such as selected attire and souvenirs, at designed locations away from the event venue. Is such an operation permitted in the hotel? If so, is there suitable and easily accessible space for a merchandise sales location? Can the organizer bring display units or tables or can the hotel provide them? What is the most convenient way for the organizer to accept credit card and online system payments in the hotel and are there any associated costs?

Finally, are there exclusive suppliers that the organizer must use inside the hotel property? At minimum, hotels generally insist on providing all food and beverage and telecommunication/technology services on their campuses. Does the hotel require union electricians to distribute power or to install lighting for parties and hospitality events? Is the organizer obligated to use the in-house audiovisual company, or can an organizer's needs be bid out to others? In-house vendors with the exclusive right to provide these services will almost always be more expensive than those who must compete with companies that can be brought in from the outside. Can the organizer hire an outside security company to protect its guests and assets, or must all security be arranged through the hotel?

Attrition and Cancellation Clauses

Perhaps the most sensitive and financially risky points of negotiation are the hotel's policies on room attrition and cancellation. An attrition penalty is incurred when the number of guest rooms used by an event falls below an agreed-to percentage of the contracted number. Cancellation penalties, of course, are encountered if the organizer cancels the entire agreement after the contract is signed.

As previously noted, the hotel wants to assume the least risk of being left with unused, nonrevenue-producing sleeping rooms, while the organizer wants to take on the least risk in having to pay for them. Hotels will generally refuse to be bound to hold rooms without defining financial penalties for organizers who cancel their agreement or fail to fill all or the vast majority of rooms they contract. Although the penalties may seem unusually onerous, it's a necessary business practice for the hotel. Consider this, sports event organizers: Would you allow another business to hold event tickets indefinitely without paying for them, understanding that even though there is demand for those tickets, there is a chance they would be returned unused and unpaid? Hotels need these safeguards to maintain their business; at the same time, event organizers need to minimize the financial risk of encountering cancellation or attrition penalties.

As a result, hotels will generally pressure organizers to get contracts signed, while organizers will try to delay executing a formal agreement as long as possible. This dynamic is sometimes reversed when an event is of such great regional, national, or international importance that a city expects a large influx of travelers who are not part of the organizer's room block, or when a particular hotel is strongly desired by an organizer due to quality, convenience, or value. In these cases, the organizer will want to protect a room block at a preferred rate, while some hotel managers resist, preferring to fill their rooms with other corporate or individual travelers, presumably at a more lucrative room rate. As surprising as it may sound, some hotels will simply prefer not to participate in sports event group bookings at all, or will hold only small-sized room blocks, because they expect to operate during that time at high percentages of occupancy, and at rates they need not negotiate.

Once a hotel contract is signed, it indicates that both parties are betting on the success of the other. It also means that the organizer is fully aware of the potential financial impact of the prevailing attrition and cancellation clauses. Thus, when it is time to execute the agreement, be sure the event is unlikely to be canceled or postponed, and that you hold only those rooms that you truly believe will be needed. Penalty provisions aside, hotel contracts actually work in the sports event organizer's favor—it typically does not permit the hotel to cancel or reduce the size of the room block. It may, however, allow the organizer to periodically reduce the size of the room block by a specified percentage without penalty on defined deadline dates well in advance of the event.

Be particularly vigilant regarding how cancellation and attrition penalties are calculated. Some will be calculated on the total number of room nights held during the contract period, or on the quantity of rooms contracted for what is called the peak night, the night when the number of a sports event's guests is at its maximum. Some agreements will demand payment not only for the unoccupied rooms, but also for an estimated amount of lost income from food and beverage operations. Organizers should attempt to assume only the risk for the rooms themselves, as lost income from food and beverage operations are simply assumptions that cannot be substantiated. Most attrition penalties are activated when the total room pick-up falls below 80 to 90 percent of the contracted room nights, a percentage which the organizer should attempt to reduce as much as possible during negotiations. Smaller and more up-scale hotels, however, frequently insist on an even greater percentage of pick-up, some as high as 100 percent. These penalties will be assessed during the settlement of the bill after the event.

On the other hand, cancellation penalties are payable immediately upon termination of the contract. The percentage of room revenue for which the organizer is responsible will increase at contractually defined deadline dates, beginning as low as 10 percent of room revenue upon execution the contract, and increasing periodically to higher percentages as the event date approaches, and up to 100 percent if canceled close to event day. Again, the contract proposed by the hotel may suggest that penalties include estimated food and beverage income, which the organizer should attempt to negotiate out of the agreement. If dinner functions, parties, and other hospitality events are included in the contract, some hoteliers will attempt to include some portion of the projected revenue for these functions in the cancellation penalty. Event organizers should resist this inclusion as no expenses are incurred against these events by the hotel until very close to the event (i.e., the hotel does not purchase food or contract labor for the hospitality function until just days before it occurs).

An essential element for the event organizer to include in the contract relating to cancellation and attrition is the notion that, if rooms are released by the organizer and subsequently resold by the hotel to other groups or to the public, the value received for those rooms will be deducted from the organizer's penalty. Requesting this inclusion is reasonable and puts no one at an economic disadvantage, as the hotel suffers no financial hardship if the rooms that were contracted, but unused by the organizer's group, were eventually sold to others. Without this provision, the organizer would remain totally unprotected against attrition, while the hotel would enjoy the benefits of essentially being paid twice for the same room.

Deposits

Like many business agreements, hotel contracts will often include a request for a nonrefundable deposit, perhaps up to 20 percent of the total value of the rooms on hold, upon execution of the contract. If paying this deposit is unavoidable, it can be applied to satisfying the event's "master account," a tally of all charges that will be paid by the organizer during settlement of the bill after the event. The size of the deposit is frequently negotiable if the organizer can produce evidence of an excellent credit history, or if the majority of the room block will be paid for directly by the event's guests.

It is advisable to set up a master account regardless of who is paying for the guest rooms. The organizer can specify which staff or guest rooms should be billed to the master account. It is recommended that organizers authorize only room and tax charges for these rooms so incidentals, such as room service and restaurant charges, shop purchases, Wi-Fi access, minibar, in-room movies, laundry, telephone, and other fees, are paid by the occupants, and selectively reimbursed after a thorough review of their expense reports. Master account charges may also include fees for catered meetings and receptions, technology and event office costs, delivery and room drop charges, business center usage, and other operational expenses.

Managing Hotel Operations for Sports Events

Once the hotel contract is signed, the property's sales department will take a less active role in the event, replaced by convention services and reservations department representatives who will remain in contact with the organizer on a daily basis. The convention services contact will work with the organizer on the assignment and installation of office, hospitality, and reception facilities, and will often coordinate the event organizer's catering needs.

The reservations department will work with the organizer to manage the room block and guest registration. Many organizers prefer to manage the room block by requiring guests to arrange for hotel accommodations through its own staff rather than directly with hotels. This is particularly useful when a number of host hotels are involved. The organizer can assign guests and participants to the hotels that are most appropriate for them, or to distribute the audience among properties that require the greater number of occupied rooms to avoid attrition penalties. It is also the best way to identify which guests have indicated their intention to attend, but who have failed to make reservations. Event staff can contact these individuals to determine their housing needs as the deadline dates to release the sleeping rooms approach.

The organizer will then generate a "rooming list" for the hotels through a guest management database, updating the hotels with changes throughout the pre-event period. Be sure to work with the reservations department to ensure that the rooming list has all of the information the hotel requires, and to determine how best and often to inform the reservation department of the inevitable changes to the list.

If guests are given the responsibility of making reservations directly with the hotel(s), provide them with a code that will identify them as being associated with the event. The hotel can then provide a rooming list to the organizer indicating who has made reservations within the block. It is essential to regularly and vigilantly compare this list against the guest management system to ensure that all event guests staying in the hotel have identified themselves as being part of the block. Those who make reservations in their assigned hotel, but are not identified as event guests, may not be credited to the room block, which could result in the assessment of an otherwise avoidable attrition penalty. Organizers should provide guests with a reservation deadline well ahead of the key date to release rooms as defined in the hotel contract. Fix a response deadline that is at least two weeks ahead of the release date to give event staff the opportunity to contact those who have not yet appeared on a rooming list.

Finally, recognize that it is standard procedure to provide gratuities to hotel employees dedicated to the success of your event. The hotel sales manager can recommend the customary range of cash gratuities that may be offered to the convention services manager, catering managers, bell staff, and others.

Hotels and organizers share the common objective of ensuring that their guests enjoy the best possible sports event experience. The hotel's convention services department will create a detailed summary of important information for the entire hotel staff regarding the event's operations at the property, which the organizer should review for accuracy. The convention services contact will also schedule a "pre-con" (preconvention) meeting a few days before the majority of the event's guests arrive. Among those invited will be key organizer personnel and each of the property's department heads (e.g., housekeeping, security, bell staff, room service, catering, front desk) to ensure a direct and consistent flow of information between the two partners. The pre-con meeting is an excellent forum to express appreciation for the staff's hard work to come, and to surface any questions or concerns about hotel service encountered to date. The hotel will provide organizers with an "event resume," reflecting all of the vital details about their group, including who is authorized to approve charges to the master account, function space room usages, room service hours, VIPs entitled to amenities, special charges, and much more. Be sure to review it in detail: If the event has any policies regarding athletes or other guests (e.g., no autographs), this is the appropriate forum in which to communicate them. Leave the staff feeling excited, appreciated, and committed to success, and the organizer's guests will enjoy their stay as much as the event itself.

Post-play Analysis

Marketing campaigns should focus on selling tickets in advance to enhance attendance and revenues. Utilizing the best combination of affordable and practical media elements for your event, design these campaigns to establish a sense of urgency, but allow enough time for the public to respond. Set a ticket policy—reserved seats or general admission—that best serves the needs of your sports event. If tickets do not sell well, a number of options may be considered to make the event venue appear more full, including the reduction of seating inventory and the distribution of complimentary tickets, also known as *papering the house*. Before sales begin, be sure to remove tickets required for business partners, athletes, and invited guests from those to be sold.

Keep track of all guest needs by establishing a guest management system that works best for your event. This database will indicate whether invitees have accepted their invitation and what tickets they will receive to which activities; it will include arrival information, accommodations assignments, and more. Athletes and event participants can often be managed using the same system, adding special activities, perquisites, and equipment needs as additional fields that are customized just for them.

Communicate with your guests and ensure they conveniently have all pertinent event details, such as activity and transportation schedules, dining and entertainment options, maps, and contact information for key individuals. Consider publishing a guide on a web page, in a mobile device app, and/or as a printed piece that will provide easy access to the essential information required both during their visit as well as ahead of time.

Carefully evaluate hotels under consideration as host and headquarters properties. Negotiate the best contract possible, and hold only the number of rooms you are reasonably comfortable you will use. Financial penalties for using far fewer rooms than contracted, or for canceling a hotel deal, can be significant.

Coach's Clipboard

1. Ticket sales for a national skateboard competition, which were brisk when first put on sale, have slowed dramatically. Approximately 50 percent of the available tickets have been sold, but the budget had estimated 70 percent. With two weeks remaining until the event, what plans should be considered to balance the budget and fill the venue?

2. A regional track and field event is best viewed from a section of existing bleachers that is open to the public. What viewing options can be considered to accommodate the attendance of sponsor guests? How would you begin to design a similar area on a public beach for a surfing competition?

3. Develop a social media plan to support your marketing efforts for one of the events above. How will you keep fans visiting and interacting from the time the event is announced through and including event day? In what ways can you use social media to continue to engage with fans after the event has concluded?

4. Design an event app that will provide fans with the information essential to their game day experience. What should be added for events that bring a majority of attendees from other regions?

5. A beachfront resort hotel would provide excellent accommodations for important guests traveling into the host city for your event, but the director of sales resists negotiating for preferred rates or anything less than 95 percent pick-up before an attrition penalty begins to apply. While guests will be responsible for their own charges, the organizer will remain liable for the unoccupied rooms. The event venue is located 20 minutes away by shuttle bus. What options should you explore to minimize the event's financial exposure?

Presenting Your Event

"Sports is the only entertainment where, no matter how many times you go back, you never know the ending."

—*Neil Simon, American playwright*

This play will help you to:

- Produce an entertaining environment for fans attending your sports event.

- Create the necessary documents required for good presentation planning, including event runs of show, scripts, blocking diagrams, and production schedules.

- Become familiar with the basic tools of sports event presentation.

Introduction

Today's sports event organizers recognize that audiences have certain minimum expectations when they attend a sports event. When people come to watch their favorite athletes, they expect to be able to experience every competitive moment and to share in the emotional excitement. They come to participate vicariously in the players' victories, to express their admiration with displays of appreciation, approval, encouragement, and support through hearty applause and throaty cheers. To enhance their sense of participation and enable them to react with knowledgeable enthusiasm, fans want to be able to visually comprehend, evaluate, and judge the progress of the contest. They want as much information as possible—rosters, official results, statistics, and the other interpretive data that can enhance and enrich their viewing enjoyment. Finally, they want to be entertained. They want to feel like they are personally involved, witnessing something unique and important, perhaps even historic. Regardless of the final score, a sports event must present an experience worthy of the fan's time and entertainment dollar.

It is not coincidental that the basic requirements of the live sports experience, summarized in Figure 12.1, embrace philosophies that are similar to the way an event is presented on television. Sports event broadcasts inject the viewer into the competition, establishing an intimacy between the audience and

To meet the minimum expectations of the audience, sports events must be presented so that fans are . . .
- Able to see the competitors they came to watch
- Able to visually comprehend the progress of the event or competition
- Kept informed of official results and critical information
- Excited and entertained
- Able to remain connected to their friends and family who are not at the event

Figure 12.1　Basic Requirements of Sports Event Presentation

athletes. Cameras erase the distance, capturing the facial expressions that register accomplishment and display disappointment, achievement, or frustration. Announcers are your hosts. They tell the story of the game. They describe the progress of play, provide insightful analysis, and offer opinions on how athletes and coaches can respond to competitive challenges. Replays reverse time to allow announcers and audiences to dissect and evaluate a team's or athlete's performance. Hosts familiarize the viewer with the athletes, provide pertinent background information, present performance statistics, and summarize the event upon conclusion. Pulsating music, colorful graphics, and the skillful direction of camerawork keep viewers engaged, entertained, and glued to their screens even during breaks in the action. On-screen graphics note the quarter, period, or inning, which side possesses the ball, who is at bat, and how much time and how many timeouts remain. An information ticker crawling across the bottom of the screen shows scores of other games, individual player statistics, and news from other sports.

Whether or not they are televised, the most entertaining sports events are those that embrace the same production values, logical flow, and minute-to-minute attention to detail as a well-planned broadcast. Craft the event as though you were planning a live show on the world's largest 360-degree television screen, and then add the extra elements unique to the live entertainment experience that can enliven the athletes, as well as the audience. Give the event a sense of worth and importance by telling stories. Create an environment of excitement from the moment the fans enter the facility (or even before), through pre-event entertainment and ceremonies, and during the competition itself. Remember that audiences experience sports events in a multisensory way. The sounds of a sports event can be as important as the sights in elevating the level of enthusiasm and enhancing the entertainment experience.

To fully capture the active involvement of the fans, the competitive activities at a sports event may require the support of technical systems including lighting, sound amplification, electronic message boards, and video image magnification (IMAG), among others. The same technical support may also be used to captivate the audience with ceremonies and entertainment elements before, between, and after the competitions.

The in-stadium and in-arena entertainment experience is also personal and customizable. Fans need access to fast and reliable mobile device connectivity at the event venue to download statistics, check on scores from other teams and sports, watch key replays from other games, and in some cases, to place wagers. As much as personal technologies separate us, they also bring us together. Fans want to communicate with their friends and families about the events they are watching via text and social networks, check their statistics-driven sports fantasy teams, upload photos taken from their seat, and meet up with other friends attending the game. Having sufficient bandwidth to accommodate internet connectivity has become essential to the entertainment experience at sports event facilities.

Ceremonies and Entertainment Elements

Every event has its own personality, every sport—even new and emerging ones—its own traditions. For some sports events (e.g., football, hockey, basketball), organizers want to get the crowd loud, energized, and excited during competition. For others (e.g., golf, figure skating, tennis), a more conservative

- Pre-event live musical entertainment
- Opening ceremonies
- Introduction or entrance of teams or athletes
- Presentation of colors and national anthems
- Sport-specific ceremony (first pitch, tip off, face-off, and coin flip)
- Recognition of past champions, Hall of Famers, and event alumni
- Appearances and participation by celebrities and dignitaries
- Video highlights, replays, and storytelling features
- Programming during breaks in play
- Halftime or intermission entertainment
- Live musical performances
- Fan participation elements (live, virtual reality, and augmented reality)
- Post-event presentation of awards and trophies

Figure 12.2   Presentation and Ceremonial Elements of Sports Events

atmosphere is more appropriate. In almost every instance, however, opportunities abound for celebrating the featured sport, setting the tone for an event, and making unique, lasting impressions with opening ceremonies and pre-event festivities, intermission entertainment, and postevent finales (see Figure 12.2).

Many sports events, particularly those involving teams of athletes, are presented on large playing surfaces and, in some cases, before sizable audiences. The playing surface, the natural focal point for an event, can also serve as the stage for ceremonial and entertainment segments, as long as they do not negatively affect the quality of the surface for the competition. Regardless of how impressive the entertainment, the actual competition is what the audience has come to see. The safety of the athletes and quality of the surface – whether it is made of grass, artificial turf, ice, wood, dirt, clay, or padded mats is paramount beyond any other consideration.

Physical stresses on the playing surface can be considerable during the progress of a game, match, or meet. Grounds crews are prepared for the normal wear and tear on the playing field, and, in the case of outdoor events, to best care for the surface when adverse weather occurs. They are less able to mitigate damage from heavy vehicles or equipment used during installation of the event or during pregame or halftime presentations, burns from pyrotechnics, or dangerous debris from special effects. Be sure that any entertainment element you plan to incorporate that may affect the field, ice, or court is reviewed and approved by whomever is chiefly responsible for the playing surface.

Pageantry

Most sports events are presented in a 360-degree format, surrounded by an audience that may be dozens to hundreds of feet distant from the action. Because it is difficult to establish an intimacy with the contest from a range of perspectives and distances, most arenas and stadiums utilize large video displays to simulcast play, deliver information, provide replays, and present video features. The extraordinary distances from the audience create a similarly challenging environment in which to entertain audiences before play and during intermissions. Pageantry—colorful, large-format entertainment with an emphasis on music and mass movement, sometimes supported by video, special effects and fan participation, is a popular solution for these reasons.

Pageantry needs clearly audible sound to go with the big visuals. Depending on the size of the facility, it may be difficult to see details clearly from all points, but it should never be hard to hear or understand. In a large sports venue, sound can provide ceremonies and entertainment with the ability to energize an audience to perhaps an even greater extent than the visuals.

Amateur Entertainers

An enormous budget is not required to stage the vibrant and rousing pageantry that can give even home-grown sports programs the feel of a big event. The area's best high school and college marching bands can provide musical entertainment that can energize and inspire the crowd. Dance teams, drill squads and kicklines can perform choreographed sequences that add a rousing visual dimension, either separately or in step with the thunderous presence of the band. For even greater impact, organizers can combine local bands or drill teams into a massed band, or a larger dance line, for an even grander presentation. Add colorful, waving flags of symbolic significance to the event (flags of countries, states or provinces, sports teams, or schools, and customized designs made especially for the program) for great, inexpensive props that can measurably increase the visual excitement on the field. With the exception of custom banners, you don't even have to buy the flags, poles, or holsters. Most items can be rented from a regional flag retailer.

Using existing groups to provide large numbers of amateur performers is a manageable and efficient approach. Groups often come with their own organizational infrastructure; members are used to following the instructions of their coaches, teachers, or the other adult supervisors who routinely coordinate and manage their activities. They also often have an established procedure for relaying information to their members and are familiar with traveling, arriving, and assembling as groups. It is obviously easier to manage four coaches who are each responsible for 25 team members than 100 individual performers. Each participating performer should receive, review, and sign a simple one-page waiver prepared by the event's attorney, protecting the organizer against liability claims in case of injury or accident, and granting permission to use the performer's images in event photography, video coverage, and broadcast.

Treat amateur entertainers with the same respect and consideration as you would extend to those who are being paid to perform. Take frequent breaks and ensure that plenty of water is readily available at all rehearsals, as well as in staging areas, and that restroom facilities are easily accessible. If rehearsals or call times require participants to be on the event site throughout the day, be sure to provide meals or snacks, or provide meal breaks long enough for them to be able to find food elsewhere. The feeding of cast and crew members is a perfect opportunity for a food or restaurant sponsor. It is a best practice to provide food and beverages for cast, crew, and staff members on site when events or rehearsals are located in areas that offer few dining options. Rehearsals cannot usually restart until all cast members have returned, so it only takes a handful of late-returning participants to hold up an entire show.

SIDELINE STORY

The "Greatest Party in College Basketball"

Attending a men's or women's basketball game at Grand Canyon University Arena in Phoenix, Arizona, may be the loudest and most exciting experiences in college sports if you're a fan, or the most unnerving if you're the opponent. In addition to fielding an award-winning dance team and cheer squad, the Thundering Herd Pep Band, and a dunk squad led by their mascot Thunder, the GCU Antelopes (or, known locally as the "Lopes") are supported by the Havocs, who according to their website "strive to be the most spirited, energetic, and disruptive student section in the country. With positive sportsmanship and respect in mind, Havocs create an energetic environment for our fans and an intimidating atmosphere for opponents" across all of their various Division 1 athletic teams.

To help acclimate fans to responding to the exhortations of the Havocs' leaders, the university hosts two major arena events in their 7,000-seat arena. The first, *Lope-A-Palooza*, is a rally featuring all of the school's spirit programs and saluting the athletic and student communities at the very beginning of the fall semester. Approximately one month later, the Havocs host *Midnight Madness* at the arena as a tip off to the basketball season. Students camp out for days on the adjacent quadrangle to ensure they will be first in line for a visually stunning, up-tempo production in the arena featuring the spirit programs, the introduction of the players, and the "Purple Pre-game Party," a high-energy, audience-participatory dance rally to a driving EDM beat that also precedes each game throughout the season.

Celebrity Entertainers

Organizers of major sports events often incorporate entertainment provided by well-known bands and celebrity performers. Artists who appeal to the same target audience as the featured sport can add significant excitement to pre-event, intermission, and even postevent festivities. Their celebrity stature and amplified sound can help bridge the physical distance between the event and the audience while adding tremendous entertainment value to the experience. Some artists will readily agree to appear during sports events with large live and television audiences in order to enjoy exposure for a new album or soon-to-be-released song. The performer's fee is not related to the length of an appearance. To professional performers, the time investment is nearly the same whether they play a single song, or a full 90-minute concert. They still have to travel to the event, participate in a sound check and rehearsal, perform, and then travel on to the next stop. Their fees may be negotiable to some extent, but do not expect costs to be significantly reduced simply due to the brevity of their appearance.

Well-known musical acts are best procured through a national booking agency. You can usually identify the agency from the act's website. For the right price, performers will appear virtually anywhere as long as they are not on hiatus or working on an album. When bands take a break from touring, members disperse, and it is very difficult for their management to reassemble them.

Artists' fees can be very expensive, but that is only the beginning of the costs that can be incurred when booking recognizable talent. Before making an offer, or after receiving notice of the initial asking price, be sure to request a copy of the act's contract and rider. The rider is a list of all of the extra requirements that must be covered by the organizer, including the number of people for whom travel must be provided and at what class of service. The list typically includes members of the act, as well as backup singers and musicians, the manager, the road or tour manager, sound director, lighting director, and often others. Some acts additionally require such personnel as security, hair and make-up artists, and wardrobe supervisors, and their rider will define whether the specific individuals to fulfill these roles must travel with the artist, or may be provided on site by the sports event organizer. The rider will also contain specific information about the act's hotel needs (which will likely include some number of suites at a top-quality property), meals and special dietary requirements, postevent hospitality, and complimentary tickets. Minimum production requirements are typically provided in an accompanying technical rider, specifying staging, audio equipment, lighting, musical instruments (often referred to as *backline*), and other performance needs.

Negotiate the fee and the rider at the same time, as it is the totality of their costs that is important. You may still be able to meet an artist's minimum fee requirements while reducing the expenses of fulfilling the rider, or partially cover the rider costs with a reduction in the fee.

Figure 12.3 illustrates areas that may be negotiated for contracts with professional artists. Remember that most talent contracts and riders are generic documents. Other than including the date, location, the buyer's name, and the length of the performance, they are not generally customized to the needs of a particular show or sports event. As a result, the contracts that organizers receive will generally be applicable to concert performances. Sports events usually feature professional artists in a much more limited way, as an element of a much broader event. As such, the act's tour management may relax a significant portion of the technical requirements, such as the size of the stage, and supporting lighting, sound, and special effects. With fewer technical requirements, the organizer may be able to successfully reduce the number of personnel that must travel with the artist to the event.

The meal requirements that are outlined in the artist's rider can be exhaustive. They not only specify which meals must be covered and for how many individuals, but often identify the exact menu. To simplify event-day logistics, especially in temporary event facilities that are not equipped for fine catering, organizers can propose a flat fee (also known as a *buy-out*) that will enable tour management to provide meals for the artist and themselves.

Most artists will request complimentary tickets to the event for their management, important business clients, and perhaps local members of their fan club. As the event is not a typical concert, the organizer can usually negotiate a reduction.

Put the offers or counteroffers to the agency in writing, but do not be surprised if they do not respond immediately. The agency will have to confer with the artist's management before accepting any reduced fee, and with the act's tour manager to discuss any alterations to the riders. Acts in high demand may

- Talent fees
- Air travel
  - Reduce the number of people traveling
  - Convert a number of first- and business-class airfares to coach
  - Seek to include sponsor-provided (VIK) air tickets
- Hotel
  - Reduce the number of people traveling
  - Reduce the number of suites required
- Meals and snacks
  - Reduce food requirements or pay a flat buy–out figure
- Reduce the number of complimentary tickets
- Technical rider
  - Reduce technical requirements (e.g., stage size, lighting, special effects, and audio) to levels appropriate to event and its host facility

Figure 12.3 Commonly Negotiable Talent Contract and Rider Terms

also deliberately delay in responding in hope that a concert promoter or an event in another location will offer them more money or greater exposure. It is not unusual for popular performers to refrain from accepting the terms of a counterproposal until 90 days before an event, when it becomes apparent that no more lucrative offer from another party is likely. Therefore, be sure that your proposal includes an expiration date for accepting the offer. While it may not inspire a performer's management company to act with any greater speed, it does enable the organizer to approach other alternative acts after the expiration date has passed.

Hosts and Announcers

Sports events frequently require a public address announcer to welcome and communicate with the audience, relay official scores and statistics, and fulfill marketing obligations to sponsors. An announcer with a smooth, professional delivery will capture the attention of the audience and lend an air of importance to both the festivities and the competition. Quite often, the best sources for announcers are local radio and television stations, which can also provide an exposure opportunity for a media partner. To save money on talent fees, an organizer can seek to incorporate the station's provision of an announcer as part of their media sponsorship deal. Make sure the announcer understands the sport and becomes familiar with the pronunciation of each of the participant's names to ensure an authentic and confident presentation.

Some events also involve a host or emcee in addition to the public address announcer. Unlike the unseen announcer, a host has a visible presence and provides a focus of attention when speaking with the audience. A host can interview players, coaches, and dignitaries, conduct fan engagement activities, and deliver scripted remarks for pre-event and intermission festivities. Like a television color commentator, the host can add dimension and drama, information and insights, enthusiasm, and entertainment value to both the pre-event ceremonies and the contest itself.

Production Planning

Planning the presentation and production of sports events is a complex process that often requires the expertise of an event producer or presentation director. This individual is charged with the responsibility of developing the program's creative approach, working with technical specialists to arrange for sound, lighting, staging, and other presentation tools, and, ultimately, overseeing the day-to-day details of event

```
☐ Event Run of Show (ROS)
☐ Script
☐ Production Schedule
☐ Rehearsal Schedule
☐ Contact List
☐ Cast List
☐ Wardrobe List
☐ Props List
☐ Music Play List
☐ Audio Equipment List
☐ Video Elements List
```

Figure 12.4 Essential Event Production Documents

production. Planning starts with the preparation of lists—lots of them—including contact lists, rehearsal schedules, production schedules, cast lists, wardrobe lists, prop lists, audio and music play lists, video lists, and the event run of show (ROS). These documents help the producer to organize their thinking, identify required purchases, and communicate expectations to the participants, production staff, and crew. Developing and maintaining these many lists ensures that no detail is overlooked, and that every facet of the production is communicated to the entire presentation team. Figure 12.4 provides a summary of the most essential production documents, which are explored in detail in the following sections.

Event Runs of Show

The key event presentation tool is called the *run of show (ROS)*, rundown, or cue sheet, a document that outlines the precise details of how an event will unfold. The document is divided into rows that represent *segments* or *items*, with columns containing descriptions of what happens in each segment. A complete sample event rundown appears in Appendix 10, a small portion of which is represented in Figure 12.5 for the convenience of the discussion that follows.

There are a number of software platforms available that can help you develop a run of show similar to the one in the figure. ShoFlo (shoflo.tv), a cloud-based solution, enables an entire production team to see changes in real-time, even while an event is in progress. This customizable platform also provides the option of including scripting within the run of show document. Other software applications organize cue sheets similarly, in a spreadsheet template of rows for each item number and customizable columns for participant cues, as well as audio, video, and other technical cues. Even a generic spreadsheet program like Microsoft Excel, Google Docs, or Apple Numbers can be adapted to create and manage a run of show. User-generated formulas can be inserted into the cells of these commonly available programs to monitor how changes affect the overall timing of the event.

Let's look at a typical run of show. During planning meetings, as well as during the event itself, it is simplest, the most clear, and most expedient to refer to each segment by its assigned item number. Following the item number is the time column, indicating the precise time of day each segment is expected to begin. Every staff member should use devices synchronized to the common digital clock to ensure everyone is using the "official event time". If the event is televised, this is typically the same time used by the broadcaster.

The next column displays the running time (R/T), the amount of time required to complete each segment. In the preceding example, the running time is expressed in the most common form for televised sports events—"hours:minutes:seconds."

The description column outlines activities occurring within each segment. It should be detailed enough to provide a general sense of how the event site will appear to the audience, as well as any details regarding what should be set up during this time period in preparation for the next segment. In this example, the field

ITEM #	TIME	SEGMENT	R/T	DESCRIPTION	AUDIO	VIDEO/SCOREBOARD
1	7:00:00	**House Open**	0:30:00	Audience enters. Lights at opening preset levels. Gobos in corners. Stage managers to get players out of locker rooms at 7:25:00.	P.A. Mic: Welcome & sponsor recognition (Pea Pond Mills, Pete's Pies, Faroff Airlines, Metro Daily News Online) over APB: Welcome mix	Event & sponsor logos in rotation; Welcome. Sponsor logos displayed during recognition (Pea Pond Mills, Pete's Pies, Faroff Airlines, Metro Daily News Online).
2	7:30:00	**Player Warm-ups**	0:20:00	Players enter and warm up on field. Lights on full competition level.	APB: Warm-up mix	Event & sponsor logos displayed in rotation; Welcome.

Figure 12.5 Setting up an Event Run of Show

will be lit at a predetermined level specifically designed to create a desired theatrical effect as the audience enters. During the same segment, a stage manager, one of the individuals responsible for the movement of people and materials on the field, will ensure that players are moved from the locker rooms with ample time to begin their warm-ups as scheduled in Item 2.

Columns for runs of show can be customized for the specific needs of a particular sports event. Organizers can include an "audio" column that will describe what the audience will hear during the segment. As will be made more apparent by referring to the complete ROS in Appendix 10, the audio column will describe whether the sound the audience should hear will come from an audio file server, an audio track on an accompanying video, or a particular microphone.

A column may also be added for "video." If not already present in the venue, presentation directors for events of more modest scale can rent video projectors and screens, LCD video walls, or large-screen HD television screens, as appropriate for the size of their event and whether it is held in daylight, at night, or indoors.

Video screens can be used to simulcast broadcast coverage, or provide images from cameras operated solely for the venue audience. Providing live non-broadcast video coverage to the screens is commonly called "IMAG," or image magnification. Although including IMAG coverage of the event can be expensive, there are few presentation tools that can establish better intimacy and interactivity between the athletes and the fans. Replays and pre-produced video highlights of past events, features on participating athletes, and other specially-produced stories can also add great entertainment value. Animations and still graphics can be designed to display player close-ups, statistics, standings, and trivia. Video screens often include game operations displays, such as score and play clocks, rosters, penalty timers, and other essential play information when separate scoreboards are not available. In such cases, it is best to display game information at all times somewhere prominent on the screen so it remains visible for players and coaches even when replays and other video features are being shown.

Sponsors also value the ability to run commercials and fan experience promotions on the screens. In basic productions, videos may be run directly from a file server, hard drive, or a computer with a high-speed processor. The same column on the ROS can be used to describe the images displayed on the scoreboards or LED message boards (also known as ribbon boards for displays that ring the venue seating areas).

To customize the ROS to the needs of the program, presentation directors can add more columns to the spreadsheet. For example, an additional column may describe the activities of the broadcaster, of particular importance if the presentation director must keep the audience entertained during commercial breaks. It is also a good practice to add an empty column for comments so various production staff can insert notes related to their own responsibilities for each segment.

The ROS must be kept current and distributed to all production personnel with the date and time of revisions noted on all pages. It is most efficient to post the ROS in the cloud so everyone has the most up-to-date version. If the organizer or venue do not have this real-time capability be sure that everyone knows which revision, printed or digital, represents the "final version."

Scripts

The scripts for the public address announcer and/or host are aligned with the run of show. Some organizers include a column for the script on the ROS itself. Others employ a separate document. For the latter, scripts are best prepared with headings that show the corresponding item number from the ROS, as well as the segment description (see sample script page in Figure 12.6). Center the name or role of the individual who will read this portion of the script. If printed, use large, double-spaced type, and underscore or bold the key points of emphasis.

(1) HOUSE OPEN

ANNOUNCER

WELCOME TO THE FIVE COUNTY FOOTBALL TOURNAMENT, PRESENTED BY **PEA POND MILLS.** TODAY'S EXCITING EVENTS ARE ALSO BROUGHT TO YOU BY:

PETE'S PIES. MADE FRESH EACH DAY RIGHT IN PETE'S OWN KITCHEN. VISIT **PETE'S PIES' WEBSITE** AND ENTER THE CODE DISPLAYED ON YOUR TICKET FOR FREE DELIVERY OF YOUR NEXT FRESH FRUIT PIE ORDER. FRESH PIES FROM FRESH PERSPECTIVES, THAT'S PETE'S . . .

AND BY **FAROFF AIRLINES.** FAROFF IS GOING YOUR WAY WITH 15 FLIGHTS DAILY FROM FIVE COUNTY METRO AIRPORT. CONNECTING YOU WITH AMERICA. FOR YOUR NEXT TRIP, THINK FAROFF . . .

AND **METRO-DAILY-NEWS-DOT-COM.** BE SURE TO STOP BY THE DAILY NEWS KIOSK BEHIND SECTION 101 FOR YOUR FREE TEAM POSTER AND A 90-DAY TRIAL OF **METRO DAILY SPORTS ONLINE.** SEE FOR YOURSELF WHY WE'RE RATED #1 FOR FIVE COUNTY AREA SPORTS!

Figure 12.6 Sample Script Page

Scripts that are included in cloud-based ROS software will always provide the announcers with the latest version. For printed scripts, be sure include a footnote with the time and date of the latest revision. Most important, be sure the public address announcer and/or host has an opportunity to review the script—even if not completely finalized—before event day. This will enable them to make their own notes, investigate the proper pronunciations of names, and be familiar enough with the copy to deliver it confidently, enthusiastically, and error-free. Consider providing printed scripts to the announcer in a loose-leaf notebook to allow the insertion of revised pages without having to replace the entire document.

Scripts often include contractually obligated, sponsored fan engagement activities and public address acknowledgments, delivered during the pre-event period, intermissions, and breaks in the action. Throughout a sports event, however, the audience is often waiting expectantly to know what's going on. Identify for the announcer those moments and situations during the competition when it is appropriate to relay non-scripted information to the public. Think of how you watch a sports event on television—the announcers tell you everything you need to know. Why should your paying customers receive any less information? These moments may include scoring information, roster changes, explanations of officials' decisions, important statistics, and records that have been broken. Establish a protocol as to when those announcements may be delivered—during play or only during a break in the action. Video screens are also often used to communicate important information when it is deemed inappropriate or intrusive to the game to announce it over the audio system.

Production Schedule

If the run of show is the key tool for the actual presentation, the production schedule is its analog for the staff responsible for preparing the participants and physical site ahead of the event. The production schedule outlines all of the preparatory activities at the event facility. A sample production schedule is provided for illustrative purposes in Figure 12.7.

**FIVE COUNTY FOOTBALL TOURNAMENT
PRODUCTION SCHEDULE**

(as of Wednesday, August 7 — 12:30 P.M.)

Day/Date/Time	Activity	Location
Friday, September 9		
9:00 A.M.–12:00 P.M.	Wi-Fi and VOIP lines installed	Room 156
1:00 P.M.–6:00 P.M.	Production office equipment delivered	Room 156
Saturday, September 10		
2:00 P.M.–5:00 P.M.	*Calhoun vs. Kennedy H.S.*	Stadium Field
6:00 P.M.–11:00 P.M.	Production office setup	Room 156
Sunday, September 11		
9:00 A.M.	Security begins—Credentials required	All Areas
9:00 A.M.–6:00 P.M.	Banner and signage installation	All Areas
Monday, September 12		
9:00 A.M.	Production office opens	Room 156
9:00 A.M.	Distribute walkie-talkies	Room 156
10:00 A.M.–5:00 P.M.	Clean and set up locker rooms	Rooms 142/4

Figure 12.7 Sample Production Schedule

**FIVE COUNTY FOOTBALL TOURNAMENT
PRODUCTION SCHEDULE**

(as of Wednesday, August 7 — 12:30 P.M.)

Day/Date/Time	Activity	Location
Tuesday, September 13		
9:00 A.M.–5:00 P.M.	Load in and install lighting	Stadium Field
	Load in and install sound	Stadium Field
7:00 P.M.–11:59 P.M.	Focus lighting	Stadium Field
Wednesday, September 14		
9:00 A.M.	Balance sound system	Stadium Field
9:00 A.M.–12:00 P.M.	Paint field markings and 50-yd. line logo	Stadium Field
9:00 A.M.–2:00 P.M.	**NO STAFF OR CREW PERMITTED ON FIELD!**	
9:00 A.M.–3:00 P.M.	Media workroom and lounge setup	Rooms 136/8
6:00 P.M.–11:00 P.M.	Technical rehearsal	Stadium Field
Thursday, September 15		
4:00 P.M.–8:00 P.M.	Ceremony rehearsals	Stadium Field
7:00 P.M.–11:00 P.M.	Equipment trailers arrive	Gate 5
8:00 P.M.–11:00 P.M.	Technical rehearsals	Stadium Field
Friday, September 16		
8:00 A.M.–3:00 P.M.	Team practices and photos *(No stadium audio!)*	Stadium Field
3:00 P.M.–7:00 P.M.	Ceremony rehearsals	Stadium Field
7:00 P.M.–9:00 P.M.	Dress and camera rehearsal	Stadium Field
Saturday, September 17		
6:00 A.M.	Television news trucks arrive	Gate 5
8:00 A.M.–4:00 P.M.	Team practices and photos *(No stadium audio!)*	Stadium Field
4:30 P.M.–5:45 P.M.	Ceremony rehearsals	Stadium Field
6:00 P.M.	**DOORS OPEN**	
7:00 P.M.	Opening ceremonies begin	
Sunday, September 18		
8:00 A.M.–10:00 P.M.	Tournament play	
Monday, September 19		
8:00 A.M.–6:00 P.M.	Load out all equipment and offices	Room 156
6:00 P.M.	All walkie-talkies returned	

Figure 12.7 *(Continued)*

Cast List

Management of the event's noncompetitive participants and performers can be facilitated by a cast list, as illustrated in Figure 12.8. The cast list is a roster of the various individuals or groups, organized by their role or function. The names in each unit appear in the next column, followed by the key contact for each. Note that the marching band in this example is made up of a total of 150 members from two different high school bands. The key contacts in this case are the band directors of the schools.

Also notice that although the flag bearer unit requires 50 participants, three additional drill team members are included in the cast list. These extra individuals are "alternates," cast members who will attend all rehearsals with their units, so that they can easily replace those who drop out of the event due to illness, schedule conflicts, inadequate rehearsal attendance, or poor performance. Alternates are strongly recommended for amateur performing groups for which the number of participants is critical. In this example, there are 50 flag bearers, each holding a flag of one of the United States. To have 49 states represented would be unacceptable; therefore, it is important to include alternates in case a member of the unit fails to attend the event for any reason. The marching band, however, requires no alternates, as missing members may not be as noticeable. (*Note:* Marching bands that perform intricate field formations, as is often the case in football game halftimes, may require alternates to eliminate the possibility of visible gaps in their routines.) Alternates, therefore, serve a very critical function.

The cast list identifies the key contacts for each unit, the person to whom information should be directed for each group in the cast. Data such as the contact's mobile phone number and e-mail address should be included on the list. The final column on the cast list denotes the talent coordinator (TC), an event staff member directly responsible for logistics and communication with specific cast units. Depending on the complexity of the program, the talent coordinator can serve other roles on the event staff as well. For example, the TC responsible for the participation of sponsors in event ceremonies can also serve as the person looking after sponsor-driven functions such as fulfillment and guest management. TCs should attend all rehearsals for their assigned units and serve as the primary conduit of information to the group's key contact. Although a TC can be assigned to more than one group of participants, care should be

---

FIVE COUNTY FOOTBALL TOURNAMENT

Cast Unit (#)	Name(s)	Key Contact	Coordinator
Marching Band (150)	Maxwell High School Band	Ethan Jacobs	Ryan Holzer
	Nathaniel High School Band	Harold Matthews	Ryan Holzer
Flag Bearers (50 + 3)	Andreas High School Drill Team	Catherine Arthur	Tiffany Richards
	McJames High School Drill Team	Jean Shirley	Tiffany Richards
USMC Color Guard (4)	U.S. Marines—Quantico	Capt. Mitch Field	Marc Levine
Army Parachute Team (5)	U.S. Army—Fort Bragg	Lt. Erwin Edwards	Marc Levine
Lieutenant Governor (1)	Lt. Gov. Jill Samuels	Art Frank	Bill Haufreitz
Coin Toss Celebrity (1)	Senator Jackson Litvak	Katerina Daniels	Bill Haufreitz
Anthem Singer (1)	Jill Andrea	Jill Andrea	Bill Haufreitz
Announcer (1)	Rob Roberts	Rob Roberts	Bill Haufreitz
Trophy Presenter (1)	Phil DeBasquette (Sponsor)	Maria Marconi	Bill Haufreitz

Figure 12.8   Cast List

exercised to avoid tasking one TC with groups that may participate simultaneously in sectional rehearsals that are held in separate locations (see "Sectional Rehearsals").

Wardrobe List

A wardrobe list can provide both the presentation director and the cast members with a clear understanding of required items of uniforms or costumes, and who is expected to provide them. The wardrobe list, as illustrated in Figure 12.9, begins with the same units as the cast list, and includes any other groups that may also be visible to the audience. In our example, wardrobe guidelines are specified for the stage managers, stage crew, and camera people with their utilities (people who accompany camera personnel to handle cables so they are neither tangled nor tripped on, or who aims the antenna that transmits images from a wireless camera to its radio receiver). These staff members are often forgotten until they show up at the event site in torn jeans and dirty T-shirts.

It is not unreasonable to require cast, staff and crew to supply wardrobe items that are commonly worn by the general population such as white sneakers, or black or khaki pants, as long as enough time is provided for participants to procure these personal items should they not already possess them. The event should provide items that are not in common usage, those that include event logos or specific designs, or that must match exactly with other members of the same unit. Stage crew, stage management staff, and camera crew are often dressed in dark clothing to hide or visually de-emphasize their appearance.

Wardrobe items provided by the event are best distributed to the cast and alternates on the day before the event, or the day prior to the dress rehearsal. This way, apparel is less likely to be damaged, soiled, or misplaced prior to event day. Be sure to include alternates in the wardrobe order. Cast members who lose or arrive without the proper wardrobe for dress rehearsal or on event day may yet be another reason to have alternates prepared to take their place.

Scheduling Rehearsals

Rehearsals are essential to the smooth operation of any event. Even the most simple and straightforward presentation should be rehearsed to ensure smooth execution. Several different types of rehearsals may be required including sectional rehearsals, technical run-throughs and dress rehearsals, as illustrated in Figure 12.10.

Sectional Rehearsals

Units that perform at sports events ceremonies may have different rehearsal needs based on the complexity or precision of their performance. A marching band that must execute several formations while playing, for example, would require a larger number of rehearsals than, say, the announcer. A series of sectional rehearsals expressly for the marching band and the drill team members integrated into their field formations have been included in the example illustrated in Figure 12.10. In the early stages, it may not be essential for the band to practice on the same exact field on which they will ultimately appear. To enable the technical staff to install the sound, lights, and other equipment needed at the hypothetical event venue, the first sectional rehearsals are scheduled at a nearby high school.

Sectional rehearsals may be conducted with or without sets, staging, or props. It is wise, however, to simulate the position of any staging or obstacles (e.g., location and orientation of field entrances, team benches, lighting towers, added bleachers, risers, or constructed sets) that will be present during the event

FIVE COUNTY FOOTBALL TOURNAMENT

Wardrobe List

Cast (#)	Wardrobe	Provided By
Marching band (150)	Full band uniform	Band director
	Clean white sneakers	Cast member
Flag bearers (50 + 3)	Black slacks	Cast member
	White shirt	Cast member
	Event jersey	Event
USMC color guard (4)	USMC dress uniform	US Marine Corps
Army parachute team (5)	US Army uniform	US Army
Lieutenant governor (1)	Sport jacket	Own wardrobe
	Shirt and slacks	Own wardrobe
Coin toss celebrity (1)	Sport jacket	Cast member
	Shirt and slacks	Cast member
	Event cap	Event
Anthem singer (1)	Blue skirt	Cast member
	White blouse	Cast member
	Red kerchief	Cast member
Announcer (1)	Sport jacket with event patch	Event
	Shirt and slacks	Cast member
Trophy presenter (1)	Sport jacket with event patch	Event
	Shirt and slacks	Cast member
Stage managers (2)	Khaki slacks (no jeans)	Own wardrobe
	Event T-shirt	Event
	Event cap	Event
Stage crew (3)	Black slacks	Own wardrobe
	Black event T-shirt	Event
	Black event cap	Event
	Black sneakers (no stripes)	Event
Camera crew and utilities (6)	Khaki slacks (no jeans)	Own wardrobe
	Event T-shirt	Event
	Event cap	Event

Figure 12.9 Wardrobe List

Five County Football Tournament Rehearsal Schedule				
Day, Date	Time	Location	Rehearsal	Units
Saturday, September 10	9:00 A.M.–12:00 P.M.	Calhoun H.S.	Pre-show sectional	Marching band (150) Flag bearers (50+3)
Sunday, September 11	4:00–6:00 P.M.	Calhoun H.S.	Pre-show sectional	Marching band (150) Flag bearers (50+3)
Monday, September 12	4:00–6:00 P.M.	Calhoun H.S.	Pre-show sectional	Marching band (150) Flag bearers (50+3)
Wednesday, September 14	4:00–6:00 P.M.	Calhoun H.S.	Pre-show sectional	Marching band (150) Flag bearers (50+3)
Thursday, September 15	6:00–11:00 A.M. 4:00–5:30 P.M. 6:00–8:00 P.M.	Five County Stadium Five County Stadium Five County Stadium	Technical rehearsal Announcer rehearsal Pre-show rehearsal	Announcer Marching band (150) Flag bearer (50+3) Announcer Parachute spotter (1)
Friday, September 16	8:00–11:00 P.M. 3:00–4:00 P.M. 4:00–5:00 P.M. 7:00–9:00 P.M.	Five County Stadium Five County Stadium Five County Stadium Five County Stadium	Technical rehearsal Entrance of athletes rehearsal Color guard and celebrity blocking Dress and camera rehearsal	Athlete stand-ins (50) USMC color guard (4) Celebrity stand-ins (3) Marching band (150) Flag bearers (50+3) Announcer Parachute team (5) USMC color guard (4) Celebrity stand-ins (5)
Saturday, September 17	4:30–5:00 P.M. 5:00–5:15 P.M. 5:15–5:45 P.M. 6:00 P.M.	Five County Stadium Five County Stadium Five County Stadium Five County Stadium	Anthem singer rehearsal Celebrity blocking Trophy presentation rehearsal Doors open!	Anthem (1) Lt. governor (1) Coin toss celebrity (1) Trophy presenter (1)

Figure 12.10 Rehearsal Schedule

with traffic cones and construction tape to familiarize the cast with their locations during rehearsals. Later rehearsals should include the actual props, sets, and technical production elements, and, if feasible, are best held in the venue in which the ceremonies will take place.

Blocking

Blocking is the process of identifying entrances, positions, movements, and exits of participants, props, and staging for each element in the ROS. The first blocking run-through need not be done with the actual participants present. Stand-ins are often used for blocking rehearsals of athlete or team introductions, and ceremonies incorporating dignitaries or celebrities. They may be positioned and repositioned until the presentation director (and television director, if appropriate) is satisfied with the ceremony's flow and appearance. If stand-ins have been used, a final blocking run-through should be scheduled with the actual non-athlete participants, if practical.

Blocking will help to identify potential areas of congestion and confusion at ingress and egress points, and can determine the length of time required for participants to move across the court or field. Blocking diagrams, such as those in Figures 12.11(a) through (c), may be drawn and distributed to cast members and staff to illustrate the proper movement of the cast, sets, and props on the field; these are particularly helpful tools for complex ceremonies that involve large numbers of participants. (In this example, a marching band and flag bearers enter the field to perform, at the end of which a color guard and anthem singer enter, deliver their performance, and all exit to clear the field for the game. Note the applicable ROS item numbers in the headings.)

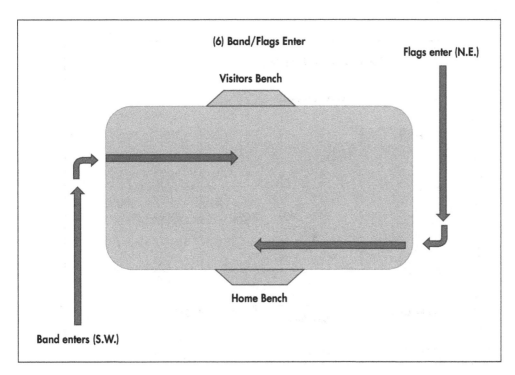

Figure 12.11a Blocking Diagram 1

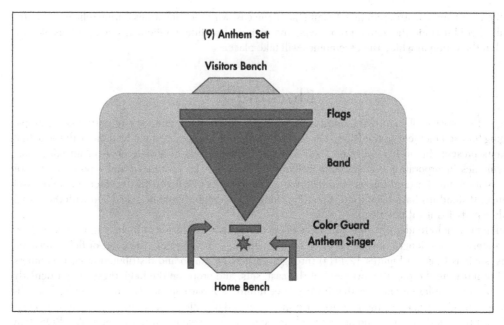

Figure 12.11b   Blocking Diagram 2

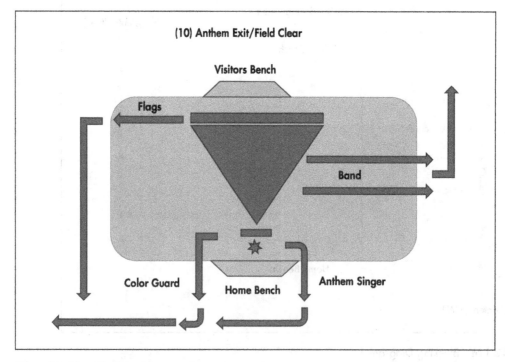

Figure 12.11c   Blocking Diagram 3

SIDELINE STORY

Blocking and Tackling

Blocking sports ceremonies is often an exercise in scheduling and traffic control. Participating athletes and teams always get the right of way. It is essential to manage the entrances on and off the field, court, or rink to ensure that pomp does not interfere with their safe and unhindered access. Will a stage come down the same tunnel through which the players must exit? If there is room on the sidelines, bring the stage through the tunnel during a stoppage in play and temporarily place it in a safe location off the field. Or, if time will permit, wait until the players clear the field before bringing in the stage.

Often, there are a limited number of access points to the playing surface and the competition for time and space can create significant complications. When the National Hockey League's Stanley Cup is awarded at center ice after the deciding game of the best-of-seven series, the crew that deploys carpet runners for dignitaries, the trophy table, and the trophy itself, is standing by in a pre-determined order, along with stage managers and participants, in a tunnel that is frequently the same one that players will use to access their locker rooms. These elements are in place with five minutes remaining in the final period of play, and proceeds quickly through what is typically a narrow one-person-wide door onto the ice when the game is declared officially over. If, with one minute remaining, the game is tied and may be heading for overtime, the elements lined up inside the tunnel have to rapidly move back out of the way and into a holding area so trophy and postgame preparations cannot be seen by teams returning to the locker room. The process of reassembling the postgame ceremony in the tunnel, out of view of the fans and players, is repeated once the players return to the ice to begin the extra period, ready to spring into action at any moment of a sudden death overtime. Consider the frazzled nerves on both sides of that narrow door when a potentially deciding game extends into double or triple overtime.

Technical Rehearsals

The designers and technicians responsible for lighting, sound, video, and special effects need time to program and perfect their event-day presentation. Technical rehearsals are conducted to make sure that all of the equipment functions properly and creates the desired result. This is the time when the presentation director can make adjustments in lighting, sound, video, and other effects before the participants arrive for the rehearsals that will combine the cast with all of the technical elements. As such, technical rehearsals can only be conducted in the actual location where the event will take place. In addition, if the sports event is being held outdoors during any time when the sky is not completely dark, it is best to conduct technical rehearsals at approximately the same time of day as the actual presentation to evaluate the effect of both the intensity and angle of sunlight on presenters, as well as on the visibility of added lighting, video, and other visual effects.

Dress Rehearsal

The final rehearsal is often called the dress rehearsal. This rehearsal should run through the event from start to finish without stopping. This will help the presentation director verify the timings on the rundown and make adjustments as needed. The dress rehearsal should involve every participant in the ceremony, although it is not uncommon to again have dignitaries and celebrities represented by stand-ins. Dress rehearsal is the last, best time to see how the ceremonies will unfold exactly the way the audience will see it on event day. It is final confirmation that the production plan is as accurate as possible. For events that are broadcast on television, it is often also the best opportunity for the broadcast director to conduct their camera rehearsal.

If an event's production is particularly complex, it is strongly recommended that one or more event run-throughs be scheduled before the final rehearsal in "stop-and-go" fashion. These run-throughs of the entire program involve all participants (or stand-ins) and technical departments. The presentation director may stop the rehearsal, request adjustments, provide direction, and restart the segment. Stop-and-go run-throughs should be scheduled to take no less than three times the expected running time of the event to accommodate the many pauses that can be anticipated.

Technical Tools of Sports Event Production

In addition to ceremonies and entertainment at an event, the competition itself will require technical systems such as sound and lights. Fulfilling their most basic objectives, a sound (or audio) system is required for communicating gametime information and the playback of music during stoppages in play. Lighting systems maintain the optimal conditions for safe play and visibility, both live and on television. At minimum, the design of these technical systems must support and never impede competitive activities. These essential functions, often supplemented by the presentation needs of ceremonies and entertainment, are further explored in the following sections.

Staging

Many sports presentations take place directly on the court or field, requiring no special staging at all. On ice, a section of carpet may be provided for the safety of non-playing participants. For event presentation elements that require elevation off the playing surface, and for events that take place in other venues, stage platforms or risers, may be temporarily installed. Putting post-game ceremonies on risers also provides photographers and camera crews with a clearer view over the heads of participants or spectators. Stage risers can be rented in heights as low as six inches or adjusted to be as high as 36 inches. Most rectangular riser units are a standard 4' × 8' in size and can be combined to achieve nearly any total sized platform. Circular stages can also be built, composed of pie-shaped pieces. If more than a few inches high, stages should have safety rails fastened on the back side and a stair unit with handrails for safe and easy access.

Using stages on the playing surface will require the most sensitive considerations. If the stage risers are supported by legs, you must make sure they will not create pits or divots. This can be mitigated by placing bits of plywood or another hardboard material beneath the legs to better distribute the weight of the stage when fully loaded with participants. (Be sure to paint the plywood the same color as the playing surface so it does not stand out—green for grass, white for ice, tan for wood floors, etc.) You must also install it quickly and in such a way as to not damage the surface. Staging may either be hand-carried or rolled out on carts. It is recommended to hand-carry the stage(s) into place if it is not too heavy, large, or dangerous for the crew to do so. If must be rolled into place, be sure the tires are as large as practical and made of rubber—smaller, harder wheels may create greater stresses on the playing surface. Additionally, be sure that wheels are not turned too sharply, which can tear grass and leave skids on wood floors and ice. The same goes for vehicles used in any on-field ceremonies—the combination of sharp turns and weight can cause significant damage, especially to a field made of natural grass.

SIDELINE STORY

Protecting the Players' Turf

Super Bowls are world famous for their halftime shows. Elaborate stages, technical effects, a cast of multitudes, and band gear are set in place during the roughly eight minutes of set-up time while television broadcasters air commercials and recap the action of the game's first half. A crew of hundreds gets everything in place for the 12-minute show, and removal without a trace takes another 7 or 8 minutes.

Until Super Bowl XLIII in 2009, similarly elaborate pre-game entertainment was offered to the audience from the field, sandwiched between player warm-ups and kickoff. To accommodate the installation of the stage, the performances, and the load-out of the show, the time between the end of player warm-ups and kickoff on some years bloated to in excess of 55 minutes. Players could hardly

remain physically prepared for the most important game of the year almost an hour after they completed their warm-ups.

To reduce the amount of time between warm-ups and kickoff and still offer the television audience spectacular pregame entertainment, the featured star performance was relocated at Super Bowl XLIII to a stage at the NFL's Tailgate Party in the stadium parking lot. In this way, player introductions, the anthem performance, the ceremonial coin toss, and other elements requiring far less setup time could be incorporated into the pregame run of show, shortening the time between warm-ups and kickoff to a period similar to a regular season game. A portion of the concert performance in the parking lot is shown live on the stadium screens, or is recorded and played back at another time.

Sound

Sound is one of the most often-overlooked production requirements at sports events. Even many of today's largest professional sports facilities possess permanent installations that are substandard in terms of how well they amplify and distribute sound throughout the venue, or the range of sound they can reproduce. Many use loudspeakers that are well suited to project the range of the human voice but are less suitable for reproducing the wide range of bass and treble tones for playing live or recorded music. If music is integral to the entertainment of the audience, be sure to test any existing permanent systems for the quality of the sound they can provide, using various pieces of music with as wide a range of tones as possible. Orchestral soundtracks and digitally recorded pop tunes can clearly demonstrate the degree of a sound system's versatility.

Also test how well the sound is distributed throughout the audience. Sound reaches spectators in a "line of sight" fashion. That is, if you are in an area where you can see the front of the speakers, then sound should be able to reach your ears without the distortion of first being reflected off another surface. The system should be balanced so the volume and tone of the sound are essentially the same regardless of where a listener sits. A system has an insufficient number of speakers, or is not balanced, when the volume in one area is very loud, but low, distorted, or inaudible in others. Determine whether the sound should be projected onto the playing surface or the benches. If so, additional speakers may be required, as many facility's systems are designed to amplify sound primarily into the audience and not onto the playing surface.

If the existing sound system is not up to required standards, work with a qualified audio designer or rental agency to supplement the number of speakers or add the right kinds of speakers to present clear, distinctive sound. Sometimes, however, it is best to start over and install an entirely new, temporary sound system that will operate independently from the permanent one. Audiophiles are familiar with the two major types of speakers (although there are more)—woofers for low, bass tones, and tweeters for higher pitched sounds. Woofers, are typically housed in larger speaker cabinets to achieve their characteristic deep and resonant tones. Without woofers, music can seem shrill and even irritating. Tweeters are needed to provide the clear, high tones that prevent the sound from seeming muffled. Do not be surprised if your audio company installs what looks like single speaker cabinets. Frequently, both types of speakers, along with those that provide the midrange frequencies, are housed in the same cabinet. Speakers are also often stacked or hung in a long series of cabinets called *line arrays,* to better cover especially tall or wide areas with a uniform level and quality of sound.

Speakers project sound from amplifiers that receive audio signals from a number of sources. The voices of announcers, hosts, and live performers are received from microphones that are either wireless or "hard-wired" (have a cable that plugs to the amplifier). Wireless microphones, also known as RF mics, transmit the sound over a radio frequency. RF microphones can either be handheld, lavaliers that are pinned to a shirt or jersey, or part of a headset. They simplify the staging of an event by allowing the performer to be located anywhere on the stage or playing surface without trailing a microphone cable. It is wise, however, to have back-up mics available (preferably hardwired) in case of a failure of the wireless system or unanticipated interference from another RF source. Note that there are usually many other pieces of electronic equipment at a sports event that will utilize radio frequencies, such as walkie-talkies and gear being used by broadcasters, to name just a few. There may also be RF users outside, but near the venue, such as transportation dispatchers and others. It is, therefore, important that frequencies of all these users are coordinated to ensure the sound system broadcasts the signal from only those sources desired. Many audio services vendors and companies specializing in RF frequency monitoring can provide coordination services before and during your event.

Recorded music at sports events is played back from digital sources ranging from laptops and dedicated audio file servers. Music loaded on a computer server system such as Click Effects and other professional playback or disk jockey programs, offers the great advantage of being able to access any desired piece of music instantaneously from a large library of songs. The software and technology required for music editing and storage of an enormous library of music is relatively inexpensive and widely available even for the home use market. A large number of versatile programs for editing music is available for purchase from software developers and free from some shareware services.

The sound from all audio sources is cabled to a mixing position, a console from which an operator can select which microphones, servers, computers, and other sources are to be turned on and those to be muted. The mix position can also blend the sound received from each source, or channel, to achieve the desired combination of sounds, such as an announcer's microphone and a selection of music in proper balance. The console should be located in or near the audience to allow the operator who is mixing the sound to experience the volume and balance between channels just as the audience does.

One of the characteristics of the sound generated by large-scale pageantry is that may be difficult for participants to hear themselves and the other sounds around them. Figure 12.12 provides a checklist of staging and production helpful hints relating to sound at sports events that will help to reduce performer confusion.

Lighting

Lighting needs can be divided into three major types—competitive necessities, television requirements, and theatrical or ceremonial needs. The organizer's first and most important mission is to ensure that lighting is sufficient for safe play and for the viewing of the competition, with no areas of shadow that can affect the quality of play. (This is, of course, not controllable for outdoor events on sunny days.) Lighting must come from more than a single point in order to avoid the casting of shadows. Further, lighting sources must be elevated so they do not blind the athletes or the audience.

Televised sports events require a more powerful level of lighting for coverage of the competitive events. Most sports event stadiums and arenas that are home to organized professional, semiprofessional, or college sports teams are already equipped with lighting that will serve most television needs. Competitions held in venues that are infrequent sports event hosts, or in temporary outdoor facilities may require added lighting for both competition and television. Companies such as Iowa-based Musco Lighting can provide permanent and temporary rental installations. Their portable systems are often mounted on trucks and are effective at distances of up to 1,000 feet. Temporary units may also be ordered with their own generators and hydraulics to elevate lighting up to 150 feet high. The current industry standard lighting level for high definition broadcasts is 300 foot-candles (approximately 3,230 lux).

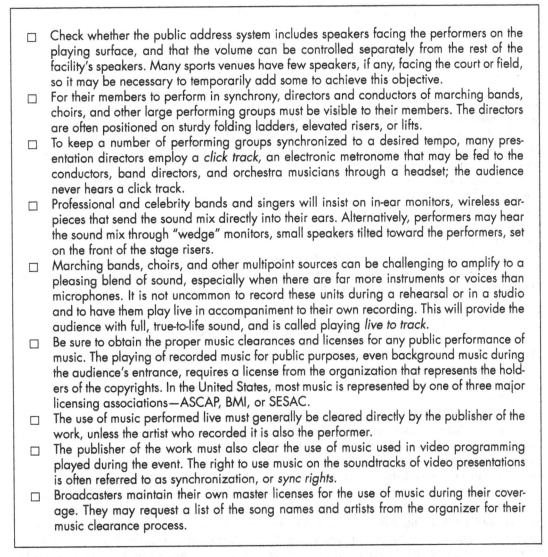

☐ Check whether the public address system includes speakers facing the performers on the playing surface, and that the volume can be controlled separately from the rest of the facility's speakers. Many sports venues have few speakers, if any, facing the court or field, so it may be necessary to temporarily add some to achieve this objective.

☐ For their members to perform in synchrony, directors and conductors of marching bands, choirs, and other large performing groups must be visible to their members. The directors are often positioned on sturdy folding ladders, elevated risers, or lifts.

☐ To keep a number of performing groups synchronized to a desired tempo, many presentation directors employ a *click track*, an electronic metronome that may be fed to the conductors, band directors, and orchestra musicians through a headset; the audience never hears a click track.

☐ Professional and celebrity bands and singers will insist on in-ear monitors, wireless earpieces that send the sound mix directly into their ears. Alternatively, performers may hear the sound mix through "wedge" monitors, small speakers tilted toward the performers, set on the front of the stage risers.

☐ Marching bands, choirs, and other multipoint sources can be challenging to amplify to a pleasing blend of sound, especially when there are far more instruments or voices than microphones. It is not uncommon to record these units during a rehearsal or in a studio and to have them play live in accompaniment to their own recording. This will provide the audience with full, true-to-life sound, and is called playing *live to track*.

☐ Be sure to obtain the proper music clearances and licenses for any public performance of music. The playing of recorded music for public purposes, even background music during the audience's entrance, requires a license from the organization that represents the holders of the copyrights. In the United States, most music is represented by one of three major licensing associations—ASCAP, BMI, or SESAC.

☐ The use of music performed live must generally be cleared directly by the publisher of the work, unless the artist who recorded it is also the performer.

☐ The publisher of the work must also clear the use of music used in video programming played during the event. The right to use music on the soundtracks of video presentations is often referred to as synchronization, or *sync rights*.

☐ Broadcasters maintain their own master licenses for the use of music during their coverage. They may request a list of the song names and artists from the organizer for their music clearance process.

Figure 12.12   Sound Advice: Staging and Production Hints for Sports Events

Various types of lighting instruments and techniques can be applied to the presentation of a sports event, adding theatricality and excitement to opening ceremonies, athlete introductions, entertainment and anthem performances, intermission fan promotions, and more. Before designing the lighting for ceremonies and entertainment, determine how the lighting for competition and television purposes will be controlled. Television lighting, and most competition lighting, is so bright that little in the way of theatrical lighting will be seen unless the competition lights are turned off or dimmed. Many indoor sports venues have converted their lighting technology to LED instruments, which can be turned off temporarily for theatrical purposes and then instantly re-illuminated. The older standard uses lights that, once extinguished, must cool down before they can be relit to full brightness, a period that can take as much as 15 minutes or longer. The event's lighting designer should consult with the facility manager and test the house lighting for this *re-strike time*, the waiting period to restore it to full intensity after being turned off.

Theatrical lighting can be divided into two major types—fixed and movable instruments. Fixed lighting is clamped in a stationary position, focused on a single non-movable location. These may include ellipsoidal spotlights for illuminating a specific area, par lights that provide a large area with a general "wash" of light, up-lights that highlight architectural elements, strobes, and many other specialized stationary instruments. Many have built-in color changing capability or can be colored with a sheet of colored gelatin (also known as a *gel*).

Dozens of stock patterns and custom-built logos can be projected by installing "gobos" on the lighting instrument, stencils that are cut from metal or etched on glass. Glass gobos can be fabricated in a single tone or full color. The effects they can provide can be striking on either fixed or movable lighting systems. Sports event presentation directors can order custom gobos to project the logos of an event, the organizing entity, and sponsors on the playing surface, walls, and other locations throughout and even outside the venue.

Movable lights can create more dynamic and exciting effects than fixed instruments and are further divided into manually operated and computer-controlled instruments. Follow spots are large spotlights that can be moved manually by an operator to follow the action during player introductions and entertainment performances. The use of programmable lighting, however, allows the most exciting effects to be achieved. The beams from a large number of lights may be moved in many directions at once, colors changed, the size and shape of the beams varied, gobos revealed and rotated. Different looks can be preset for the audience's entrance, athlete introductions, ceremonies, anthem performances, video presentations, intermissions, and exits.

The production schedule may have to provide the designer with time to focus fixed lights and to program the complex looks that intelligent lighting can generate. As focusing must be done in darkness, the programming of lighting for events held outdoors must be done at night.

Video and Projectors

As is true of audio, there are two ends to a video system. On one end is the source of the images, such as the live program feed of a broadcast or stream, the event's dedicated non-broadcast cameras, and the playback of recorded content. Like audio, recorded video is generally played from a computer server or hard drive.

On the other end is the medium upon which the images are made visible to the audience. The various sources are cabled to a video switcher that enables an operator to select the images desired and change from one to the next with a desired effect, such as a cut (an instantaneous change from one camera or image to another), dissolve (a gradual fading out of one image as another fades in), or a wipe (an animated transition). In a darkened indoor facility or an outdoor venue at night, video images may be projected on white screens (or even on the playing surface). A projector is positioned either in front of or behind the screen. Rear projection (RP) screens are often preferred to eliminate the chance of shadows from the audience or cast. The disadvantage of rear projection is that it requires space behind the screen for the positioning of the projector so the image is of desired size. This is often referred to as the *throw*, or the distance between the projector and the screen. Rear screen projection is also best when the audience views the screen only from one side—the front. Fans who watch anything projected on an RP screen from behind will see a mirror image.

Many projectors using LCD (liquid crystal display) technology can automatically switch from front screen to rear screen imaging without special lenses, and electronically correct the phenomenon known as *keystoning*, a common form of image distortion caused when the projector lens is not exactly centered on the screen. (A keystoned image may look wider at the top of the screen, for example, than at the bottom, or vice versa.) If projectors are to be used, it is recommended that two projectors be simultaneously focused on each screen if the budget permits. This will provide an important back-up system in case one projector fails. If one does fail, the image will appear to dim rather than go completely dark.

Most major sports and entertainment events use LED screens instead of projectors. Recognizable names like Jumbotron, Diamond Vision, and Daktronics are the standard for scoreboard-mounted screens, as well as for ribbon boards around the perimeter of the playing surface and on structural surfaces of the building. Temporary screen installations can be added of nearly any shape or size. Whether using projectors or LED screens, control equipment is required to show video and recorded content, including switchers, servers, graphics generators, and more. If your venue has existing screens, it is likely to be equipped with the right kind of support gear. For outdoor events, a mobile, truck-mounted screen, complete with an on-board control room, may be rented.

Autocue

Participants who deliver speeches at an event, as well as hosts and emcees who are visible on camera, can be supported with device called an autocue or teleprompter. This equipment is composed of a television monitor supported by a special word-processing program that scrolls through the script as the speaker reads. The autocue is positioned near, or is mounted directly on, a camera lens so the speaker is able to read while appearing to look into the camera. Because users do not have to memorize their script or consult note cards, they will appear more professional, confident, and believable when using an autocue.

Confetti and Streamers

The dropping of confetti and streamers from the roof trusses of indoor facilities at the end of events can provide an inexpensive visual crescendo. For outdoor facilities without overhanging roofs, confetti cannons can be rented to launch colorful, lightweight tissue paper or Mylar high into the air that will flutter slowly back down. Work with your groundskeeper to understand how these effects will affect your playing surface. For instance, because the small pieces of paper or metal can melt into ice, discolor the surface, and create skating hazards, its use is not recommended unless the ice will be removed or scraped down after the event. Confetti can also clog drains used to pull water off of artificial turf and natural grass and should be vacuumed off of playing surfaces as soon as is practical.

SIDELINE STORY

"Doing the Math" Takes on a New Prominence

Sports statistics used to be compiled solely for distribution to the media after a game. Today, fans enjoy sports on many levels, both inside and outside of the event, including sports wagering and fantasy games that require instant access to up-to-the-second statistics. Fans want accurate and definitive information immediately on their devices or by watching information scroll across videoboards and electronic message displays in the venue. This often requires event organizers to retain a legion of statisticians with access to official, verifiable information and in constant communication with officials, media relations, game presentation, and I.T. personnel. Frequently, statisticians are not only monitoring and disseminating data at the stadium in which they are located but are also keeping current with other matches and events to ensure fans in the venue are receiving the broad spectrum of sports statistics that they desire.

Fans also want more than just the scores of out-of-town contests. They want to see replays of notable action from those games, as well. Event presentation teams must be sure to have access to broadcasts or streams of other important matches and key moments from those games to share with the audience during stoppages in play.

Pyrotechnics & Flame Effects

Pyrotechnics, or fireworks, can punctuate an event with spectacular color and heart-stopping sound. Fireworks displays can be designed to last just a few brilliant seconds during athlete introductions, as a celebratory finale after the closing moments of an event, or to provide a visually rich and thunderous pageant of 20 minutes or more, synchronized to a musical soundtrack. In short, fireworks almost always imply a feeling of celebration and importance.

The catalog of aerial pyrotechnic effects is extremely varied, their names often reflective of their visual impact. It is easy to imagine the effects created by Yellow Chrysanthemums, Red Comets, Split Comets, Ring Shells, Stars, and Roman Candles, to name just a few. The size of the shell's burst is determined by the size of the shells—three-inch (diameter) shells are among the smallest and least expensive, larger shells in popular use reaching eight inches, 10 inches, and even 12 inches or more. Shells that create a loud noise upon exploding include a "report charge," although many can be designed to display without this loud bang.

Ground-based fireworks, such as gerbs or pyrotechnic fountains, do not launch shells into the air and, therefore, are the effect of choice for indoor events. The precise position and the height of these effects can be more precisely designed and controlled. Small shells can also be suspended from roof beams on non-flammable cables to provide a controlled indoor "aerial" display. Graphics, such as logos and line art, can be executed in fireworks called set pieces, or pyrographics. These ground-based displays can create a brilliant finale moment, literally burning an event's or sponsor's brand image into the memories of thousands of spectators.

A gas flame projector uses a burner that releases and ignites a flammable natural gas, producing a bright orange flame and a wave of heated air that is perceptible for hundreds of feet. It is important to keep all flames and pyrotechnics effects away from athletes, fans, staff, equipment, and décor that can ignite or be functionally affected by their heat or the byproducts of ignition. Gas effects, which are not technically considered fireworks, usually burn clean, with no visible smoke or debris. Fireworks, however, can leave behind ash, pieces of shell casings, ignition assemblies, chemical salts, and invisible gases that can irritate or injure if they come into contact with the audience, cast members, or athletes. They also create smoke, which can produce additional irritation and partially obscure the playing surface for both live and broadcast spectators. The effects of smoke are particularly noticeable when using pyrotechnics indoors, as it often takes the host facility's ventilation system a noticeable amount of time to remove it.

Pyrotechnics should be designed and fired only by experienced, licensed fireworks companies and technicians. These professionals will be familiar with the safety requirements governing the use of pyrotechnics and gas effects, as recommended by the manufacturer and the American Pyrotechnics Association or other national bodies. They will file for all needed permits (be sure to plan far enough in advance to accommodate for this application process) and arrange for the necessary test firings that are required by local fire marshals. Be prepared to produce certificates of fireproofing for all banners, sets, props, and other materials near the firing and spectator areas, as well as proof of liability insurance. Also make sure that the amount of smoke and debris generated will not interfere with the quality of the playing surface or the comfort and performance of the athletes.

SIDELINE STORY

Mixed Reality Effects

Augmented reality effects are not entirely new. The yellow "first down line" has been a staple of American football broadcasts for more than a quarter century. A few years before its introduction, one broadcast network experimented with glowing hockey pucks that left comet trails proportional to their speed. Since then, mixed reality moments have blended live environments with high-quality graphics and animation to tell stories and activate sponsorships with compelling visuals on broadcasts, as well as on stadium videoboards.

The Famous Group (El Segundo, CA) pioneered mixed reality content at sports events by showing a giant panther statue fixed outside the Carolina Panthers (NFL) stadium coming to life prior to the team's season opener. The giant feline leaps over the wall onto the scoreboard to snatch the opposing team's flag, then prowls over live footage of the field before bellowing a throaty growl. Recognizing the commercial opportunities available by integrating sponsors into the storytelling, the company has also developed proprietary augmented reality software that enables event organizers to focus their cameras on fans and turn them into animated bobbleheads, mascots, and other virtual characters on the stadium screens.

Supovitz's Theory of Event Flow

Like nature, live events abhor a vacuum. When nothing is happening, audiences lose interest and begin thinking about being elsewhere. The broadcast industry is very familiar with the tenuousness of its hold on the audience. There are rarely even a few seconds during which there is a total absence of movement and sound. If there is a gap of just a few moments, viewers know that someone has made a mistake. Take a cue from our broadcasting brethren and *produce live events as though they were television shows.*

The running order and script reveal the visuals and words that will be used to support a sports event, but not necessarily how well they are stitched together. The cueing, or the second-by-second timing of how the event flows from one segment to the next, should be perfected during rehearsals. Be on the lookout for times when absolutely no visual or audio content is being presented during ceremonial elements, as well as during stoppages in the competition. Such a gap might last only a few seconds, but the excitement of the audience and momentum of the event can quickly dissipate during that time and may require great effort to restore.

If an event is to be broadcast, embracing this philosophy will make the live event far easier to translate to the viewing audience. Even if it's not, today's audiences are accustomed to fast-paced, multisensory experiences and constant access to compelling information. Many professional basketball, baseball, football, and hockey teams direct their everyday games in this manner, but this theory suggests that other sports events, including amateur and grassroots programs, can be easily executed in this same way.

To continually engage the audience, have hosts conduct player interviews, play upbeat music, or stage promotions and contests that give away prizes. Start these elements as soon as a pause in the play begins and cease just as the contest resumes. Fulfill sponsor obligations for public address announcements but include a background of appropriate music. (Think of these as your commercials.) Play enlivening and inspirational music as athletes are introduced. Program fan participation activities between matches or during intermissions. Have a band perform, screen music videos, provide replays of highlights from the competition in progress, announce or show statistics. Cue these elements tightly together so as one finishes, the next begins. Don't just make the event as good as if you were watching it on television—make it better.

Sports purists often decry the loss of conversation between members of the audience, and the cultures of some sports require more sedate surroundings. Although producers should design the most appropriate presentation for entertaining their core fans, the notion of tying event elements closely together is no less valid. There should always be something for the audience to do or discover when competition is not in progress, even if the experience is in a location to which the audience has to re-direct its attention. Having activities and entertainment planned elsewhere on the event site is a good alternative for events whose culture frowns on noise where the sport is being played. In such cases, provide activity at corporate hospitality pavilions, public food areas, or at an on-site fan festival.

Some sports events, of course, are already broadcast presentations. Producers who embrace the notion of designing their events as though they were televised shows are well positioned to work side by side with their media counterparts and will be able to balance their needs with the unique requirements of this important medium. See Play 13 to better understand the needs of our broadcasting and streaming stakeholders.

Post-play Analysis

Sports events are entertainment experiences. Audiences want to be able to support their favorite athletes or teams, monitor the progress of play, be kept apprised of important information, and be entertained. Pageantry provided by marching bands, drill teams, kicklines, and other large-format performing units can add significant scale and excitement to pre-event ceremonies and intermission periods, their large-scale visuals and sound filling the often substantial void between the audience and the playing surface.

Sports event presentation directors or producers manage the production by generating important planning documents including an event run of show, production schedule, cast list, wardrobe list, and rehearsal schedule, among others. These essential tools help to organize the myriad details that must be managed while preparing the facility for event day. Consider all of the presentation tools that can help to excite, entertain, and inform the audience including lighting, sound, video, and special effects such as pyrotechnics and mixed reality. The use of each must be designed for maximum effect without affecting play or the quality of the playing surface.

Coach's Clipboard

1. An action sports competition featuring skateboarders, BMX bicyclists, and in-line skaters is scheduled for a local stadium of 5,000 seats. The competitors are composed of participants from the community and invited athletes who traveled from a significant distance. Create brief pre-event, intermission, and post-event ceremonies that will excite the audience and familiarize attendees with the visiting athletes. Include an event run of show and rehearsal schedule in your plan.

2. A statewide high school all-star football game marks 50 years of players advancing to college and professional football greatness. Design and draw blocking diagrams for a pregame and halftime commemoration that salutes the schools and 50 returning alumni.

3. What kinds of technical equipment, both for the competition itself and for presentation purposes, will be required to produce the event described in item 1? Create a production schedule to organize the facility for deliveries, installations, rehearsals, and dismantling of the event.

4. Your sponsors have requested recognition beyond signage at the host venue for the event described in item 1. What exposure opportunities can be offered to partners during opening ceremonies, intermissions, and during the competition itself? How can you use various technical presentation tools to provide unique impact for your top sponsors?

PLAY 13

Working with Broadcasters

"You're never as good as the praise or as bad as the criticism."
—*Gary Bettman, commissioner, National Hockey League*

This play will help you to:

- Understand what broadcasters want, need, and expect from a sports event.
- Explore the options for broadcasting your event.
- Learn how to work harmoniously with broadcast partners.

Introduction

Mass media such as broadcast and cable television, streaming platforms, and radio can offer events the opportunity for broad geographic and demographic exposure. The ability to make an event available to an exponentially larger audience than the live crowd alone can position a sport like no other promotional tool, achieving a degree of instant accessibility and notoriety and, in time, reinforcing its cultural relevance. A sports event broadcast places the event in a superior competitive position, enabling the organizer to attract more and better athletes and teams, and package sponsorships at pricing levels far greater than nontelevised events. Even incidental television exposure can have a significant positive effect on a sponsor's sales. Guarantees of a viewing audience for a company's commercials, signage, and products are major selling points for potential sponsorships. As will be seen, this outstanding and enhanced exposure opportunity can be challenging to achieve, and may be costly.

Although the number of opportunities for the distribution of sports programming has grown in recent years, only a select few events will ever be attractive enough for media companies to invest in covering an event, or for sponsors and advertisers to purchase the commercial time to make the venture financially viable. Even fewer will be so universally appealing that the broadcaster will agree to pay a rights fee to feature matches on one or more of its media platforms. Yet, media rights fees for the most popular leagues, teams, and events in an ever-evolving sports programming landscape continue to increase.

SIDELINE STORY

Sports Television—Where It's Been, Where It's Going

Television's American debut gathered curious crowds to the RCA Pavilion at the 1939 New York World's Fair. A few weeks later, college baseball enjoyed the distinction of being the first sport ever featured on this then-nascent medium. A single camera on the third base line made broadcasting history when it transmitted images from a game between Columbia and Princeton Universities on RCA's experimental television station W2XBS, the forerunner of New York's WNBC. Five years later, a featherweight boxing championship anchored the first network sports broadcast on NBC's *Gillette Cavalcade of Sports*. Neither pugilist Willie Pep nor opponent Chalky Wright could have conceived of themselves as pioneer athletes back in 1944, especially when there were only 7,000 functioning television sets in the United States. But it was apparent even then, in the waning years of World War II, that corporate sponsorship of televised sports events would be necessary to cover the considerable costs of putting them on the air.

Decades later, rights fees would make up the majority of a broadcaster's expenses in covering the largest and most widely viewed sports events. In 1970, networks paid the National Football League $50 million for the right to broadcast their games, and, by 1985, those fees had risen to $450 million. In 1998, the NFL's broadcasting rights were sold in an eight-year package worth $17.6 billion. By 2023, the league's wide ranging rights deals with broadcasters and streaming services were estimated to yield a guaranteed $125.5 billion over a 10-year term.

What Broadcasters Want from Sports Events

Broadcasters are in the business of making money while serving their viewing and/or listening audience. Depending on the platform, they may earn the majority of their revenues by selling commercial time or advertising space, collecting viewer subscriber fees, or being paid by cable and satellite operators. Additional revenue potential is realized by providing various forms of in-program recognition to partners, usually associated with programming elements such as replays, score clock graphics, time-outs and breaks, special features, and virtual signage (superimposed branding that appears to be at the event site, but is visible only to the television audience). In short, the potential to make a profit by televising a sports event is generally the motivation for a broadcaster to desire covering it.

Viewership and Ratings

For most broadcasters, profit potential is driven by how many viewers they can attract to sports event programming. The more viewers they can generate, the more the broadcaster can charge their advertisers or justify their subscriber rates. In the United States, two standards are used to measure the quantity of viewers—Nielsen ratings points and market share. These measures were long employed to measure only those watching an event on over the air broadcast or linear television (that is, distributed by a cable or satellite network). Today's fans, however, consume sports broadcasts using a variety of technologies in addition to linear television, including mobile devices, computer screens, and others. Nielsen Media Research now offers a cross-media measurement platform that accounts for all viewers of a program across all of the ways they might consume it, without duplication of those viewing on multiple devices.

Through a variety of proprietary and open source data collection methods, Nielsen assigns ratings points that represent the number of households that watched a particular program within a specified viewing area. (Nielsen also offers a similar service that calculates ratings for radio broadcasters). In the United States, a nation of an estimated 125 million households, one national Nielsen ratings point is equivalent to one percent of the total, approximately 1.25 million households. Ratings points are also compiled on a market-to-market basis, the value of which varies, depending on the local population. A single local ratings point earned for a broadcast in a city of 2 million households would represent an estimated 20,000 viewing households (1 percent of the market). Ratings for nationally broadcast events are compiled on both national and local levels, the data for which can help disclose to organizers and sponsors which regions are stronger and those that are weaker for a particular sport or event. For example, a sports event with a national rating of 1.7 (2.125 million households) can present a much more impressive rating of 5.8 in a host city of 1 million households (58,000 viewing households), and yet only a 1.1 score in a larger market of 4 million (44,000). Of course, sports events that are shown only in a single market, such as a marathon or a high school game, generate only local ratings.

Nielsen ratings data are often extrapolated into other terms, such as the total number of viewers, unique viewers, and the millions of minutes viewed. These measures help networks, sponsors, and advertisers analyze a program's performance in greater detail. Nielsen can also subdivide ratings across a variety of demographic categories to assist sponsors in better targeting their advertising purchases. Ratings can be tabulated strictly for male viewers of ages 18 to 34, for example, a highly prized market for many sports event advertisers. Low national ratings, however, are not always indicators of weak programming. Depending on the sponsor, national ratings points may be less important than local ratings in their most important geographic markets or exceptionally good viewership among their products' target demographics (such as specific age groups or gender).

Another common reference point used in determining the effectiveness of a program in attracting viewers is a number that represents the *share of market*. The number often quoted as a program's *share* is the percentage of viewers tuned to a particular program out of all viewers watching broadcasts and streams during the same time period. Programs that are scheduled to air late at night may generate only modest ratings (because many households are asleep), but a strong share of market (because a disproportionate percentage of those who are awake are viewing a particular program).

Event organizers can also increase visibility by actively posting highlights on social media platforms and mobile device apps in near-real time. Some organizers also make "second screen" programming available as a complement to the broadcast, featuring streams of specific camera angles, augmented reality environments, and enriched graphics of statistical data.

Commercial Sales Potential

From the broadcaster's perspective, the profit potential of covering a sports event is almost always dependent on the viewership it can be expected to generate. The ability to identify past years' ratings performance among audiences with various demographic characteristics determines how much the broadcaster will be able to charge for commercial time. A more detailed demographic analysis of the ratings also can be used to target companies that want to position themselves before the types of viewers a sports event attracts.

The most likely companies to purchase commercial time on a sports event broadcast are the sponsors that already enjoy a business relationship with the sport or organizer. Many corporate partners will have already planned to "activate" their event sponsorship with the purchase of commercial time. Other companies will have spent their budget assuming that the on-site signage to which they are entitled will already be highly visible during the event broadcast, and that no additional purchase of commercial exposure is necessary. Overall, however, the attractiveness of a sports event to a broadcaster increases with commitments from current event sponsors to purchase commercial time.

The broadcaster will also evaluate whether the program has enough appeal to attract new advertisers that are not already sponsors of the sports event to consider purchasing commercial time. If event sponsors do not elect to participate as advertisers on the program, the broadcaster will want the flexibility to sell the opportunity to any company willing to spend money to reach the event's target audience—including competitors of sponsors. In most cases, sponsor contracts provide exclusivity only at the event site, and not necessarily on the broadcast. However, agreements should guarantee sponsors the right of first refusal on opportunities to purchase commercial time on the broadcast. That is, the organizer's agreement with the broadcaster would obligate them only to present event sponsors with the first opportunity to buy commercial time before offering the same deal to a sponsor's competitors. If the sports event sponsor waives its right to purchase commercials on the broadcast or fails to respond within a certain amount of time, the broadcaster would then be permitted to approach competitor companies. There are many major events that offer broadcast advertising as part of their sponsorship entitlements to preserve their exclusivity. Such packages are generally priced expensively, as they often include the purchase of broadcast advertising as a sponsorship fulfillment item.

Exclusivity

Broadcasters that have invested the considerable capital required to produce the media coverage of a sports event want assurances that their own right to exclusivity is protected. They will vigorously defend their rights against any other mechanism by which a fan can, in whole or in part, visually experience the event. Any simultaneous transmission of the sports event within their viewing territory will detract from their ratings and make it more difficult to sell advertising at the highest possible rates. The presence of radio broadcasters and still photographers are usually not problematic for the broadcaster, but any video cameras, even those desiring to record only pieces of the event for news coverage, can create significant issues for the rights holder. Simply, the broadcaster will want to be the exclusive source of all video footage and highlights for general and sports news broadcasts, and commercial uses. Even the presence of the organizer's own video cameras that are commonly dedicated to recording the event for archival or promotional purposes may be addressed in the agreement between the organizer and the broadcaster to clarify how the footage may be used while preserving broadcast rights holder exclusivity.

SIDELINE STORY

The Conundrum of Mass Public Viewing

There are few opportunities to demonstrate the popularity of a major sports contest more than public viewing events, rallies, and parties. Gatherings of thousands, even tens of thousands, have watched and celebrated national championship games and international competitions with fellow fans in open plazas, on streets, in arenas, and at stadiums across the globe.

Federation Internationale de Football Association, globally known as FIFA, the international governing body of football (soccer), recognized in 2002 that unofficial mass viewing areas showing games on giant television screens were popping up on public plazas in Japan and Korea, hosts of that year's World Cup. For the following edition, held in Germany in 2006, FIFA introduced "Fan Fests," officially designating focal points in each German host city where mass viewing of broadcasts could take place. The notion was expanded further at the 2010 World Cup in South Africa. FIFA added six locations in key international cities—Berlin, Mexico City, Paris, Rio de Janeiro, Rome, and Sydney—and nine South African cities hosting World Cup for Fan Fest viewing events. In 2023, as many as 1.8 million fans watched games and other entertainment at the festival staged in the host city of Doha, Qatar, alone.

Fan festivals and other gatherings for mass viewing are events unto themselves, and require a sufficient budget, meticulous planning, a focus on crowd control and safety, public health and security, adequate facilities (including access to restrooms and drinking water), local government support, a marketing plan, and technical support. They also require the permission of the event organizer and the broadcaster that holds the rights to the match and broadcast.

Event organizers assume a great deal of risk when they create a mass public viewing environment, as excited—or disappointed—crowds can get out of hand. Additionally, for many broadcasters, mass public viewing can be an anathema. Fans who are watching the broadcast in a public location would have otherwise likely watched the event at their own homes. If mass gathering audiences are not factored into viewership figures, ratings may be misleadingly skewed downward by an out-of-home simulcast. Even a handful of fans leaving homes with metered televisions in favor of a public viewing event can generate this decrease and cause broadcasters to miss the ratings they promised advertisers. As a result, some sports event organizers and broadcasters choose to withhold permission for mass public viewing of broadcasts.

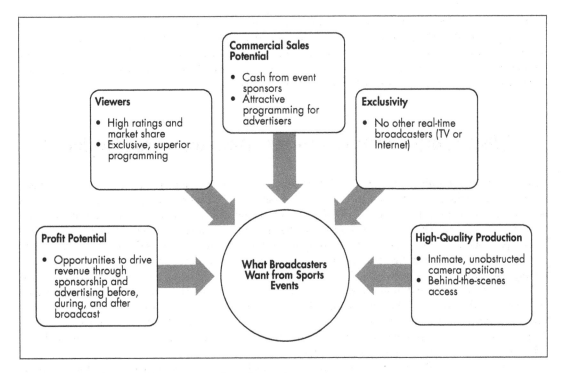

Figure 13.1 What Broadcasters Want from Sports Events

Even when observing broadcast exclusivity, organizers should be open to welcoming video crews from other media outlets. You may, however, be obligated to limit their access to defined areas with no view of the playing surface, such as news conference rooms and other back-of-house areas, to preserve the rights of the host broadcaster. (Enabling media to videotape segments of the competition if there is no host broadcaster is completely at the discretion of the organizer.) Linear and over the air broadcasters may also wish to be protected with respect to any simulcasts of the sports event on streaming platforms, and may wish to include in its agreement the right to simulcast video coverage of the sports event on its own streaming or linear outlets. Some may also wish to provide pre-event coverage on their streaming service before switching to event coverage on their primary distribution channel.

Opportunities to Provide High Production Values

If providing coverage of a sports event represents a viable business proposition, the broadcaster's next objective is to ensure the product it can deliver to viewers is of the best quality possible. Generally speaking, producing coverage of a sports event is an expensive proposition. It requires an enormous expenditure in labor for on-air talent, camera operators, electricians, video editors, sound engineers, graphics designers, statisticians, drivers, and support staff, to name just a few. Cameras and production trucks with video and audio control rooms must be rented and/or moved to the event site, scaffolds or sets for anchor positions and studios built, lighting and audio systems installed, recorded features edited, and host scripts written. With all that effort and expense, broadcast producers want to make sure they can position cameras in locations to cover the event from the best possible perspectives.

Although there are producers who well understand that energized audiences make for compelling broadcast content, broadcast executives sometimes neglect to take into account the quality of the experience for the live audience at the event. Producers want their cameras in the best possible locations, but the cameras themselves may create visual obstructions for those who may have purchased seats immediately behind. For this reason, it is best to know where camera locations may be planned before tickets are put on sale. The seats immediately behind the cameras may be removed from public sale (or "killed"), or made available to the broadcaster to entertain their own complimentary guests. Broadcasters also want access to athletes before the event to conduct interviews and provide behind-the-scenes glimpses of the event. Both are perceived to add great value to the viewing experience. As a general rule, if providing access will not interfere with the operation of the event, the safety or performance of the athletes, or the quality of the viewing experience for the live audience, it is best to grant these rights to the broadcaster. Figure 13.1 summarizes what broadcasters are looking for in sports events.

What Sports Events Organizers Want from Broadcasters

Sports events can provide broadcasters and their viewers with outstanding entertainment. For their part, organizers desire the greatest and broadest exposure possible for their sport (see Figure 13.2). From a brand positioning perspective, this exposure provides legitimacy and validation that the event and its featured sport are relevant enough to merit broadcast coverage and provides them with outstanding opportunities for self-promotion. Broadcast exposure does not come without a potential downside, however. Live events must be compelling enough that the local paying audience will still come to witness the event in person. Simply, purchasing tickets, parking, and refreshments cost money, and fans also encounter inconvenience and costs in traveling to and from the event. Media coverage, by contrast, provides fans with no-, or low-cost access to the event and the convenience of a quality viewing experience without leaving their home. The convenience and economics of consuming a sports event remotely, whether on television or on another device, is yet another reason to ensure that the live, in-venue presentation is even more exciting and provides the greatest experiential value, as discussed in Play 12.

The exposure provided by broadcast coverage also makes an event more relevant and attractive to potential and existing sponsors. The camera-visible positions granted by the organizer for sponsor signage at the venue becomes even more significant: Those with the greatest probability of being seen on the broadcast command higher fees or are included only within premium-priced partner packages. Presuming that sponsorships are priced competitively for the expected number of viewers, broadcast coverage generally makes events far easier and more desirable to sell to potential sponsors.

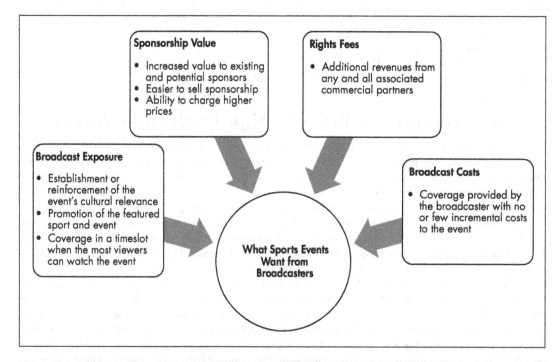

Figure 13.2 What Sports Events Organizers Want from Broadcasters

Broadcaster–Sports Event Business Relationships

In addition to increased sponsorship value derived from greater exposure, sports event organizers hope to profit from rights fees paid by the broadcaster. At the very least, they want to enjoy the remarkable benefits of broader media exposure without experiencing any net increase in their costs. Agreements with broadcasters should define what fees, if any, would be paid to the organizer, and which expenses would be assumed by the broadcaster. These parameters define the four basic relationships between a broadcaster and the sports events they cover, as listed below.

- Fee-based rights holder
- Fee-free rights holder
- Time buy provider
- Owner or co-owner

Event organizers who represent properties with an extremely high perceived value, typically those of global or national importance, often offer broadcasting rights to interested bidders in exchange for a cash payment, or rights fee. A broadcaster that purchases the rights to televise an event (the *rights holder*) expects that the program, by virtue of its expected ratings and viewer demographics, will appeal so strongly to advertisers that it will be able to charge the high rates for commercial time to cover the production costs and the rights fee, and still generate a profit. Needless to say, only the most prestigious sports properties that can command significant rights fees.

Other events may be attractive enough for broadcasters to consider airing but may not be expected to generate sufficient profitability to warrant offering the organizer a rights fee. Some event organizers will, therefore, award the rights to a broadcaster on a no-fee basis to take advantage of the broadened exposure for promotional purposes and the incremental value the broadcast provides to sponsors. (Organizers may also be able to negotiate for a free commercial spot or two in no-fee deals, which can be used for their own advertising, resold to a sponsor, or included in a high-end sponsorship package.) Organizations who are willing to enter into a no-rights-fee relationship in exchange for greater exposure are discovering more opportunities for generating viewers than at any time in the past as broadcasters and streaming services expand their live programming offerings.

If broadcasters pass on covering a sports event in exchange for a rights fee, or even if offered rights-free, other alternatives may still be available. Many organizers negotiate with broadcasters to purchase a timeslot in return for a flat cash payment, and then produce and air their own coverage of a sports event. These productions can air live or may be re-edited into a compressed form for later airing. Entering into a "time buy" relationship releases the broadcaster from all risks of having to generate viewers and selling advertising, placing both responsibilities squarely on the shoulders of the organizer. In return for the purchase of the airtime, the organizer will usually receive all of the available advertising time, perhaps minus one or two spots the broadcaster will hold back for promoting their other programming. The organizer, in turn, can sell the commercial time to sponsors and other advertisers, either independently or through a third-party marketing agency. Alternatively, the value of the commercial time can be included in the fulfillment costs of event sponsorship packages, a benefit perceived to be of great value to business partners.

Obviously, time buys can be dicey propositions. The organizer assumes the significant financial risk of purchasing the airtime, as well as the costs of producing the event for television—basically all of the expenses the broadcasters themselves were not confident enough they would be able to offset themselves. Before committing to a time buy, event organizers are well advised to confirm the timeslot being purchased. The value of commercials that an organizer will be able to sell to sponsors to offset costs will be dependent on the customary advertising rates charged by the broadcaster during the time and day an event will air. Production costs will remain the same whether a program is shown at 1:00 A.M. on an overnight Monday or 8:00 P.M. primetime on a Thursday. The value and attractiveness of the airtime—and the rates that can be set for advertising—will obviously be much greater for the timeslot when more viewers can be expected.

The limiting factor, of course, is the number of viewers that many streaming platforms and niche broadcasters can attract and the advertising rates that organizers can charge sponsors to offset the production. Although production costs will be the same no matter where the program airs, the smaller the potential viewing audience, the less valuable the commercial time will be. Therefore, another important point to negotiate in a time buy agreement is the platform's willingness and ability to promote the telecast or live stream, as the most likely audience for a televised event may be the viewers already watching that channel.

SIDELINE STORY

ESPN'S X Games

In 1995, ESPN, the most popular all-sports cable network in the United States, staged the first Extreme Games across four cities in Rhode Island and Vermont before an estimated 198,000 spectators. This eight-day multidisciplinary tournament included nine competitive action sports such as windsurfing, bungee jumping, and mountain biking. The following year, ESPN announced that a new winter sports festival would be added to the X Games brand. By 1998, the X Games franchise went truly global, the organizers staging an Asian X Games exhibition in Phuket, Thailand, during which winners advanced to the Summer X Games in San Diego. Reports suggest that, at its peak, as many as 275,000 spectators attended the summer games, and more than 80,000 attended the winter edition. More significantly, these various X Games events and qualifiers provided ESPN with hours of programming including direct event coverage, highlights featured on its flagship SportsCenter broadcasts, and incorporation into magazine show features. As both the organizer and rights holder, ESPN asserted total control over the event schedule, invited athletes, featured sports, sponsorships, and staging.

In 2012, more than 20 hours of X Games coverage was broadcast live on multiple channels owned by the rights holder, including ESPN, ESPN2, and ABC in the United States, plus additional live broadcasts in Africa, Asia, Australia, and South America. Additionally, the X Games and Winter X Games provide many opportunities for broad and extended coverage on ESPN's robust digital platforms, media with which the network's technically savvy young audiences are comfortable spending hours consuming sports content. In 2022, after 27 years, majority ownership of the X Games was sold to a private equity firm, with ESPN and ABC continuing as the traditional broadcast rights holder but with the freedom to sell the digital streaming rights to other platforms for even greater exposure and revenue-generating opportunities.

Working with Broadcast Producers

While ESPN and others in the industry own and present their own events, in most cases broadcasters are engaged in the sole business of broadcasting events, not staging them. A close working relationship between the organizer and rights holder, based on a mutual understanding of each other's objectives, is essential to a positive and beneficial outcome for all involved. It has been stated that events should be presented just the way they would be seen on television to keep the live audience energized and engaged. Similarly, broadcasters want to capture the excitement and dynamism of the live event experience, first to attract viewers and ultimately to keep viewers from switching to other programming alternatives or tuning out altogether. "Through my experience, I have found that live event coordination and television producing is in many ways similar," observes Canadian Broadcasting Corporation sports producer Sherali Najak. "In television one of my jobs is to extract the passion and emotion an event can create." If a sports event is televised, the organizer should work closely and cooperatively with the broadcast producer to find ways to help the viewers feel like they are there, and perhaps even wish they were.

If the organizer has done their job well, the live audience will feel the pulse of excitement from the moment they arrive. The event environment is loaded with visual and auditory cues that something special is about to happen, and the audience will react enthusiastically at predictable points in the run of show—when athletes first enter the arena, for example. For live broadcasts, it is essential to coordinate the timing and staging of these key moments with the broadcaster so the production can also take best advantage of them, rather than having viewers watching a commercial when the most climactic live moment happens. In-venue audiences enjoy the sense of participation in an event—let them know when the television audience is joining them at the event, and prompt them to demonstrate their enthusiasm at that very moment with hearty cheers of excitement.

The broadcaster and event presentation director should also remain in communication during the competitions themselves to coordinate when commercial breaks will be taken, preferably during natural stoppages of play. Many sports that are regularly televised in real time have adopted protocols that determine when television breaks can be taken and delay the resumption of play until the at-home audience has returned from commercials. The competitive cultures of others totally preclude stopping play for commercial breaks, and, as a result, the broadcaster must decide whether commercials will air only during intermissions, or during unpredictable but potentially decisive moments in the competition. Some broadcasts feature commercials running side-by-side on screen while coverage of on-field action continues.

Remember that when a sports event is televised, there is no real "backstage." Anything and everything can be captured on television or recorded unless specific instructions regarding access are communicated. Clearly define whether a broadcaster's cameras will have access to the athletes' locker rooms and, if so, during what periods. Can they enter the locker room pre-event to tape interviews? Will they be able to broadcast live from the dressing rooms during intermissions, or will they be limited to a location outside the door? What kind of access will they be permitted postevent? Decorate the nonpublic areas in which cameras will be permitted to shoot with event banners and posters, perhaps with sponsor identification, for additional exposure.

Identify what kinds of production trucks and trailers the broadcaster will require for its coverage of the event and where they will be positioned. The truck contains all of the equipment required for producing the broadcast coverage. The positioning of cameras, existing utilities and cable pathways will often determine its location. Understand how cables will be routed between the truck and the cameras. If they run through public areas, determine whether they must be hung from the ceiling or placed beneath temporary cable ramps to ensure they are not trip hazards for the athletes, fans, or staff.

Speaking from experience, former CBS Sports Executive Vice President, Operations, Engineering, and Production Services Ken Aagaard is familiar with the commonly recurring challenges that need to be anticipated and addressed. "Probably the least understood of the broadcaster's basic needs are setup time, parking, and access to the venue." Producers need the time to install their cameras, cable them to the truck, establish communication with the network, and for the director and his or her crew to rehearse. At the same time, the most experienced producers understand the many competing demands for time and space in the host facility. "Broadcasters least understand the multiple of conflicts the organizer encounters from stadiums, team owners, players, and local organizers," says Aagaard. By appreciating and solving the other's concerns, a smooth and collaborative relationship resulting in the best possible event can be achieved.

Sometimes, to save on costs, the equipment and personnel usually located in the production truck are not at the venue at all, but rather at remote location that may be hundreds of miles away. In these cases, the cameras transmit their images to the remote studio via a high-speed fiber optic network instead of a truck parked on-site. In such cases, the play-by-play talent and analysts are also often located off-site. (This is to ensure that the video and the sound are synchronized.) As an economical alternative to a truck or remote studio often used for basic streaming coverage, a temporary production studio called a "fly pack system" may be installed in a back-of-house room inside the venue. From there, the finished production can be transmitted to the rights holder via satellite or fiber optic network.

Integrating Audience Needs

When dysfunctional relationships develop between sports event organizers and their broadcasting counter-parts, they are often over the lack of the basic understanding that there is really only one audience being served simultaneously by both parties. When a difference of opinion emerges between the live presentation director and a television producer, it is far from unusual to hear this argument surface: "To whom would you rather promote your product—to the few thousand people here or the millions watching on television?" The right answer is: "Both!"

Appealing to both audiences is mutually beneficial and, in fact, finding the proper balance is crucial to creating a vibrant and exciting entertainment environment in the arena and at home. Organizers are responsible for delivering value and an emotional payoff to the loyal fans of their sport to keep them engaged, entertained, and energized to return for future events. These devoted fans are the same people who will later watch coverage of events they cannot attend, so ultimately, even home viewership will ebb if they are neglected. Keeping fans coming back is as much a ratings concern for broadcasters as a financial one for the organizer. Simply, a full event venue also makes for good television. Nothing says, "This event is not important enough for me to spend time watching it," than empty grandstands on television. Provide good reasons for the live audience to keep coming back for future events.

"Nothing will enhance your event more than great television coverage," says former NBC Sports producer Fred Gaudelli. "Understand how you may use TV to benefit whatever event you're organizing. On the flip side, TV should understand that the integrity of the event can't be compromised to make 'better TV.' The common goal we share is for the event to be great. Together we can make that happen for both parties. Understand that if the event fails on either platform (broadcast or at the venue), the event is a failure."

Broadcasters have concerns similar to those faced by live sports event organizers, but with a significant added challenge. They must keep their viewing audience entertained and their interests served at all times to keep them coming back to watch future events. But, their concerns are more immediate and acute with respect to a sports event broadcast. A fan who has already invested the capital, time, and effort to pay for a ticket, given up a day or evening, and traveled to see a sports event live has far greater staying power than those fans watching from outside the venue. The fan in attendance will likely remain at the event a far longer period of time, even if the contest proves disappointing. A fan viewing from home has ready access to a remote control. Broadcast producers must be concerned with attracting and holding their audience on a minute-to-minute basis, lest viewers switch to alternative sports programming or another leisure-time option. Understanding this important stakeholder's key objective is paramount to the future business of the sports event organizer—the most likely potential ticket buyers are those watching the event from outside the venue! Organizers should do everything possible to help media producers keep their coverage interesting, informative, and entertaining. Give them the unique access they need to bring the viewer closer to the athletes and the sport. Make sure they do not miss a second of action. And, work closely with them on developing new camera positions to give viewers fresh perspectives on the coverage of your sport.

Similarly, sports broadcasters should also take note: "Prime viewers are watching the event live!" The most likely viewers for coverage of future sports events are seated in the grandstands. Ensure that your game presentation director brings replays, player features, and interviews to the fans in the building. Fans like to associate with others who are devoted to their favorite sport. Demonstrate your knowledge, respect, and loyalties to the sports they love, and they will devote an allegiance to your coverage and on-air talent, as well.

Glenn Adamo, the NFL's former Vice President of Broadcasting, Production, and Media Operations, and veteran of sports broadcasts ranging from national championships to Olympic competition, is a master at working closely and collaboratively with live sports event producers to achieve mutual objectives. He notes five areas of "Must Dos" for sports event organizers when working with broadcasters (see Figure 13.3).

---

1. Communicate during planning.
2. Integrate timings and other broadcasting needs.
3. Remain flexible.
4. Rehearse together.
5. Communicate during events.

Figure 13.3 Adamo's Top 5 Broadcasting "Must Dos" for Sports Event Organizers

"One Event—One Audience"

Sports event organizers must let the broadcaster know what activities are being planned well before live coverage is scheduled to begin. Pre-event fan activities can provide outstanding recorded footage (known as "B-roll") that can be integrated into event coverage or incorporated into the opening of the broadcast. Make sure the broadcast producer is offered opportunities to send a camera crew and reporter to all press conferences and other media events, which can be excellent opportunities to interview athletes. Engage the broadcast producer in discussions regarding the development of the event run of show so they can plan camera positions, commercial breaks, segment timings, and scripting. Familiarize the producer with every aspect of the event to ensure they can portray the sport with the impact, if not all of the imagery, presented to the live audience. If organizers strive to stage the event with the precision of a broadcast production, both parties can integrate their timings so that each understands what to expect as the event unfolds. "Timing is always underestimated," says the CBC's Najak. "Five seconds of a dead house can be a lifetime on television. It's magical to the viewer when events or introductions happen exactly on cue without a second of silence or hesitation." As Najak, Gaudelli, and Adamo can attest, there may be two productions being presented simultaneously (i.e., broadcast and live), but there is still "One Event—One Audience."

To achieve this unity of purpose, both parties must remain flexible and understanding of each other's objectives throughout the planning process. A segment may need to be moved to provide a broadcaster with time to break for commercials, another may need to be shortened or lengthened to accommodate other requirements and realities. Broadcasters, similarly, should maintain some flexibility to ensure that the event neither loses its focus or momentum for the live audience. "Remember, the event producers have spent days and even weeks planning their execution so it is perfectly timed for their purposes. Asking them to 'scrap' their show for TV will not work," says Adamo. "They can be flexible but need you [broadcasters] to also understand their issues."

In this spirit, accommodating commercial breaks cannot result in a total interruption of activity for the live audience. While the broadcaster is fulfilling its advertiser and sponsor obligations, the organizer can likewise use the opportunity to do the same. But often, the momentum, especially with regard to pre-event entertainment activities, must continue to keep the audience engaged. It is helpful for both the broadcaster and the live presentation director to agree in advance on what segments might be missed by the broadcast production, and over what period of time. Providing broadcasters with an opportunity to review runs of show, scripts, and other presentation plans well in advance gives them the opportunity to create their own production strategy and surface challenges, requests, and requirements during the early stages of planning. By crafting the runs of show in an integrated way, both presentations are more likely to appear seamless.

Camera Rehearsals

There is only one way to test whether these integrated timings will, in fact, work to the benefit of both audiences: rehearse all critical segments together! For example, decisions should be made in advance as to whether the broadcaster will use the event's announcer or its own during athlete introductions, how they will be covered by the cameras, whether hand-held cameras will be temporarily permitted on the playing surface, and at what pace they will progress to accommodate the needs of the broadcast. For the live-event audience, athletes could be announced more rapidly, but if being planned for television, a pace must be determined to allow for smooth direction of the cameras, graphics, and the announcers. Staging a camera rehearsal for segments such as this is by far the best way to establish these parameters. The athletes themselves are rarely available for these essential rehearsals. Use stand-ins to simulate the timing and assist in the blocking of player introductions and other important ceremonial elements (see Play 12) for both the live event and broadcast production. Schedule joint rehearsals far in advance—like the producer of the live sports event, the broadcast producer has many more rehearsals that must be staged during the time leading up to the program.

The camera rehearsal will also establish whether the lighting conditions planned for various segments will be conducive to broadcast coverage. Live presentation directors love to stage events in the dark. Lighting, video projection, and special effects shows are often at their most dramatic when they are executed in a dark environment. For broadcast, however, dark environments are horrendously limiting. The impact of a light show on a television or mobile device screen does not approach the excitement it generates in the facility. As wonderful as they might be for the live audience, light shows are often indecipherable on television, so these theatrical moments are frequently the points during which broadcasters will be doing something else.

Broadcast directors also don't like concentrating on a single shot or subject for a long time. The response of the fans at a sports event and during pre-event introductions is a great visual opportunity for television directors. If the fans are in darkness, the director will have difficulty depicting their enthusiasm. Consider partially lighting fans in selected seating sections during times and segments when the rest of the audience is otherwise in the dark to provide directors with an option to show spirited audience reactions. Broadcasters should also demonstrate what lighting they plan to use during various theatrically illuminated portions of the event. Thousands of dollars in lighting and special effects can be ruined by floodlights used during an unanticipated interview at the edge of the playing surface, or in an anchor position overlooking the field.

State of the art venues are often equipped with LED lighting for the illumination of the playing surface. These types of lights can instantly provide the proper amount of lighting for broadcast purposes at the flick of a switch. Lighting in facilities with older systems may require long warm-up times for their lighting, making it less practical to temporarily shut lights off for pre-event ceremonies. Some can take up to 15 minutes to restore full illumination levels.

The Importance of Communication during the Event

Close and regular communication between the organizer and broadcaster must extend well beyond the planning process. It is also essential to maintain open lines of communication throughout the event and broadcast as they progress in real time. The game presentation director should appoint an individual on staff to maintain contact with the producer in the television truck during the event to address the concerns of the broadcaster, as well as to communicate any timing changes required by either party. Accidents or unforeseen issues happen during events, and aberrations in timing, order of competition, and athlete appearances, to name a few, are to be expected. "If your show, or theirs, goes awry you need to be able to communicate in order to execute the integration without embarrassment," observes Adamo. Install a "PL," a private line phone, headset, or other wired device between the truck and the presentation director, to keep a flow of communications going during all phases of the event. Know when the broadcaster is cutting away to accommodate a commercial, and when broadcast coverage has returned to ensure no part of the action is missed. Communicate judging and referees' decisions so the broadcaster is as well informed as the live audience. Provide game statistics and confirm historical milestones. Make sure the broadcaster has access to all essential information to make the coverage genuine, authoritative, and reliable.

Post-play Analysis

Broadcast coverage of sports events can exponentially increase the size of the audience that witnesses a competition and provide tremendous additional value to event sponsors. To present a viable business opportunity to a broadcaster, sports events must be able to generate revenues in excess of production costs and any rights fees that might be paid to the organizer. As a result, very few events become broadcast properties compared to the total number staged. Alternatively, sports event organizers can invest in a *time buy,* the outright purchase of time from a broadcaster. In exchange for a cash payment, the organizer typically receives the inventory of commercials available during the purchased time period, which can be resold to sponsors or other advertisers. The organizer, however, must pay the costly expenses of production and, in the case of recorded events, the postproduction editing of the event.

Sports event organizers and broadcast producers can create a seamless production by embracing the "One Event—One Audience" concept. The future viability of both the sports event and its broadcast coverage depends on serving the needs of the live and broadcast audiences. Both parties should communicate with each other regarding their plans before the event and exhibit reasonable flexibility to ensure that the needs of both the live program and its broadcaster are met. Rehearse important televised moments with broadcast cameras operating and be prepared to make adjustments to enhance their coverage. Keep the lines of communication open throughout the planning process and establish a real-time communications system during the event broadcast to minimize errors, mistakes, and oversights, and to inform the broadcaster of all pertinent developments.

Coach's Clipboard

1. Both national and regional broadcasters have decided not to take advantage of the opportunity to televise a top-tier skateboarding competition. The event's presenting sponsor is keenly interested in having the program featured on a broadcast or streaming service, but the organizer has no available funds to risk buying the time on the regional sports network that is willing to air it for a price. What can the organizer do to improve the chances of the event being broadcast? What other options exist if broadcast coverage remains elusive?

2. A broadcast producer has been assigned to cover your one-day track and field meet just two weeks before the competition. A pre-event ceremony has been scheduled and publicized to begin at 3:00 P.M., with the first race stepping off at 3:20 P.M. During the first conference call to review the event run of show, the producer indicates that for broadcast purposes, the first race must begin at 3:08 P.M. What options are available to you as the event organizer?

3. A major news event has suddenly preempted live coverage of an organizer's sports event while in progress. What kinds of risks may the organizer be subject to, and what protections should it have in place, to minimize the financial impact?

Managing for the Unexpected

"If they expect us to expect the unexpected, doesn't the unexpected become the expected?"

—*Anonymous*

"The unexpected always happens."

—*Proverb*

This play will help you to:

- Analyze your event's risk exposure and manage those risks.
- Develop security and accreditation plans for your event to protect participants, fans, and property.
- Understand the types of insurance available to protect the organizer from unanticipated crises.
- Develop an emergency response and communications plan.

Introduction

As game day approaches, the countless hours of intense and detailed planning have laid a solid foundation for an entertaining, smooth-running, and rewarding experience for the athletes, fans, sponsors, and staff. Regardless of how simple a sports event may appear to be, rest assured that there will be dozens of unfulfilled details and inadvertent omissions that will come to light in the final days, hours, and minutes, from just about every direction. Some may even become evident as the event itself progresses. It remains the sports event organizer's job to predict, project, and plan for these issues and challenges before they present themselves, and to establish a plan to deal with those that emerge unexpectedly.

Contingency Planning

It is, of course, best to avoid suffering from the impacts of certain risks by anticipating challenges and having a plan to manage them before they actually unfold. The most simple and obvious example is having a medical response capability in case someone gets hurt. You hope your medical team will not have to treat anyone, or transport someone to a hospital, but you have to be prepared in case they must. Contingency planning is much like that on an operational level. You hope you won't have to activate a contingency plan, but you should be prepared in case conditions warrant.

An event's contingency plan is one that guides how an organizer will respond to a potential obstacle to success. Not every challenge rises to the level of a crisis or a threat to health and safety. Some may interfere with the progress of the competitive event, the quality of the experience, or threaten the completion of the program. Contingency planning requires an assessment of what obstacles may impact a successful outcome and anticipates a course of action to solve or manage the problem if they do occur. The most common contingency plan for outdoor programs is how various weather conditions might affect operations. How will the organizer respond if it rains or snows during the event? Will the program proceed, be postponed to another date (and when that might be), or cancelled entirely? Will some components of the event need to be modified? Will the organizer need to move the sponsor hospitality function indoors or under a tent (and when would that decision have to be made)? Will the organizer offer ticket refunds? Weather planning is also appropriate for indoor events. How will the organizer respond if snow, ice, high winds, or flooding makes it dangerous for athletes, staff, or fans to travel to the venue?

The time to develop weather contingency plans is well in advance of the 10-day forecast. There are many decision points and action plans that need adequate time to develop. What other contingencies should the organizer consider during the planning process? It is not possible, of course, to prepare a plan for everything that might be anticipated—you will have to prioritize which "Plan B" contingencies you will put in place. You will also need to be prepared for those problems that will arise that were entirely unexpected. For those issues that can be anticipated, it is wise to have a specific contingency plan or response prepared for the most probable and the most potentially impactful (the B quadrant in Figure 14.1). The potential impact may be manifest as a safety risk, possible property damage, financial loss, legal concerns, a fan experience or brand reputation risk, or any combination of these. This is not to suggest you shouldn't have a plan to cope with highly impactful but less probable possibilities (the A quadrant), or more probable but less impactful circumstances (the D quadrant). These somewhat predictable challenges may still occur and affect the overall success or quality of the event. As for the unexpected, we will explore how to prepare for those eventualities later in this chapter.

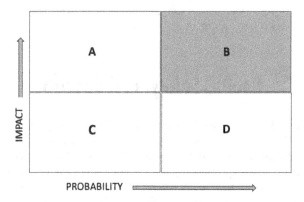

Figure 14.1 Contingency Priority Grid

1. Identify probable areas of risk.
2. Consider the impacts on the event and the organization by these risks.
3. Develop contingency plans to manage potential risks.
4. Identify how to respond to, solve, or manage problems to avoid their advancement into a crisis.
5. Develop crisis management and communications procedures.

Figure 14.2 Risk Management Process

Risk Assessment and Management

Beyond the operational issues that contingency planning is meant to anticipate, every sports event carries elements of risk—and lots of them. Athletes may be injured during competition or by accident off the field of play. A spectator can fall from the bleachers, slip on a wet floor, trip over a cable, or be struck by an errant ball, puck, or bat. A food services vendor can unknowingly serve tainted food, lighting trusses can tip and fall, wind can cause production elements to detach and drop to the ground, a bus or van carrying participants can become involved in a traffic accident. Fireworks can drop smoldering debris on the audience or damage parked cars. In short, absolutely anything can happen and without warning. Although organizers cannot totally eliminate the possibility of an injury or damage during a sports event, they can exercise the good judgment and sensitivity required to evaluate, plan for, and manage risks and reduce the potential of their occurrence. Figure 14.2 outlines the general steps for developing a basic risk management process.

Analyzing Risk Exposure and Possible Outcomes

Identify the many areas in which an event and its participants, spectators, staff, stakeholders, and the organization may be placed at risk. Issues can be separated into three broad categories. The first and most urgent are areas that may affect the *health, safety, and security* of spectators, staff, and participants. Every plan and every contingency should strive to reduce risk to health and safety to the greatest extent possible. Next, consider the *financial and legal* issues that can threaten the ability of the organizer to complete the event. Finally, identify the potentially catastrophic circumstances that can cause the event to be interrupted, postponed, or canceled (see Figure 14.3).

Health, Safety, and Security

The safety and well-being of all who attend a sports event, from participants to spectators to staff, is of paramount importance. With all other considerations treated as secondary, determine whether you, the organizer, and the venue are providing a sufficiently safe environment for the event from the time and point of arrival through departure. Have operational plans created an environment that will encourage fans to arrive extremely early and rush into the facility when the doors first open (such as frequently occurs during a first-come, first-served general admission event)? How far in advance will spectators arrive, and will they begin crowding around the entrances? How early should the facility plan to queue the spectators into orderly lines? Can temporary weather conditions delay the arrival of crowds so they appear at the gates late, and all at once?

A careful and comprehensive evaluation of the areas listed can help sports events manage potential risks that could impact the safety of the public and participants, as well as the financial health of the organizer.

Safety and Security	Financial and Legal Issues	Cancellation Scenarios
Crowd management	Labor disputes	"Acts of God"
Organized queuing of early- or rapidly arriving spectators	Unavailability of labor	• Weather conditions (snow, ice, rain, lightning, wind) that make playing, atte- nding, or traveling to the event inadvisable
Sufficient points of ingress and egress	Picket lines and protests	
Sufficient front-of-house staff for directing and providing information to guests	Legal challenges	
	Court injunctions	
Emergency evacuation plan	Failure to secure required permits or pass inspections	• Flooding
Dissemination of instructions and information to staff and the public	Intellectual property right infringements	• Earthquake
Clearly marked emergency exits	Athlete/participant failure to appear	Power failure
Reassembly area for staff		Structural damage to, or collapse of host facility
Security of athletes and playing surface from spectators	Criminal investigations	
	Civil suits	Irreparable damage to playing surface
Security of assets and property	Public protests and civil disturbances	Toxic waste spills
Lockable storage and office areas to prevent theft of equipment and material	Designation of free speech zones	Catastrophic political or cultural events
Adequate security personnel to safeguard equipment and material	Bankruptcy	Global or national tragedy
Policies regarding banned materials and substances at the event site (weapons, alcohol, bottles, cans, drugs, etc.)	• Organizer • Host facility • Other stakeholders (e.g., ven- dor, sponsor, broadcaster)	Civil unrest Acts of terror
Audience screening upon entrance (e.g., visible inspection, pat downs, magnetometers, wands, bag x-rays or searches)	Refund policies and procedures	War National day(s) of mourning
Inspection of vehicles entering restricted areas		Inability of teams or participants to appear or play for any reason
Policies regarding sales and consumption of alcohol		State of emergency declaration
Accreditation process and system		Inaccessibility of event facility to participants or fans due to road- way or parking area closures
Background checks of staff, freelancers, and volunteers		
Security for entrances to nonpublic areas		
Physical condition of the event venue		
Safety in public areas (e.g., entrances, exits, concourses, seating areas)		
Condition of playing surface (including team benches, dugouts, etc.)		
Condition of backstage and locker room facilities		

Figure 14.3 Managing Sports Event Risk Factors

Parking facilities
Lighting conditions
Accessibility to emergency medical
  personnel and facilities
  • Athletes & staff
  • Fans
Food safety
Presentation elements
Pyrotechnics and other special effects
Safety procedures during darkened
  periods

Figure 14.3 (*Continued*)

How early should the public be admitted to the venue on the day of the event? Will there be sufficient time and staff assistance to ensure that all arrivals can reach their seats within a reasonable period of time? Are trained, informed personnel available to keep crowds moving, to direct spectators, and to answer questions? Is there pre-event entertainment to encourage early-arriving guests to take their seats before the competition, rather than rushing in from the concourses as the event begins? Is there sufficient room for crowds to move through every area safely? Is there a separation between the spectators and the athletes to protect each from the activities or enthusiasms of the other?

Are concessions open to enable fans to purchase refreshments and merchandise while they wait for the event to begin, or to occupy them during breaks in play? Are there sufficient staff and points of purchase to keep waiting times as short as possible and queues arranged to avoid constricting the public concourse? Is alcohol being served only to adults who show the required proof of age? How late into the event will alcohol be served, and are there trained personnel on the concessions staff who can determine whether a spectator's reasonable limit of alcohol consumption has been reached? Are there limits to the amount of alcohol that may be purchased per transaction?

Most permanent event venues maintain a written evacuation plan in case of fire and other extreme conditions, such as storms containing lightning, or credible threats to public safety. Become familiar with the plan and understand under what circumstances they might be activated. What procedures are to be followed if an evacuation does become necessary? How will the public know the best routes to vacate the building? What role does the event's staff play while the facility is being cleared? Who makes key decisions, and by what method will venue or event decision makers meet to consider options and required courses of action?

Is there a way to stop fans from accessing nonpublic areas like the locker rooms or media facilities? Is there a plan to screen those arriving at the venue and to search bags to ensure that no one enters with materials that can intentionally—or accidentally—injure participants and other spectators? Are there prohibited items that fans cannot carry through the entrance checkpoint, and are these items posted online and onsite? Does the screening system create long waiting lines at the doors, or are there adequate personnel and entrances to handle the numbers of spectators expected? Do plans also call for athletes, media, and support staff to be screened and searched?

Does the event's system of designing and distributing credentials discourage the possibility of counterfeiting? Is there a process in place that requires the review and approval of the list of those requesting credentials? Are there different levels of credentials that allow access to the most sensitive areas by only those whose jobs require it? Does the organizer's system of hiring staff, freelancers, and volunteers include some form of background or reference check? Do event staff drivers or vendors providing transportation services have valid and appropriate licenses with acceptable safety records?

Is the event facility in good physical condition, or are there areas that require upgraded lighting or repair? Have temporarily built event venues been designed to permit the flow of people through safe, well-lit areas? Have power, broadcast, and other cables been dressed or covered to minimize the possibility of ensnaring or tripping passersby? Are fences, barricades, lighting towers and other upright structures appropriately secured to keep them from upending in wind? Are there wind load limits for temporary structures that would require closure in threatening weather? How will organizers monitor approaching storms? Are tower and tent guy wires installed so they do not interfere with public access? Are there sufficient refuse receptacles and restroom facilities, and how often will they be serviced? Is there sufficient parking or nearby access to mass transportation systems to accommodate arriving participants and spectators? Are there hard surface walkways or a clear path off the street between the parking areas and the event venue? Are shuttle buses a safer alternative to move spectators to the venue?

Is the playing surface in good condition or are modifications, or renovations required to guard against injuries to athletes and game officials? Are there holes, metal covers, gratings, or depressions in the surface that must be filled, capped, or repaired? Is there a clear, unobstructed path between the locker room or athlete preparation areas and the playing surface? Will there be easy access for athletes, game officials, and spectators to medical personnel, equipment, and supplies, and a system in place to direct help to where it is needed? Is an ambulance on site for transporting the injured or ill to a nearby hospital or clinic? If not, how long will it take for emergency vehicles to reach the event venue in the traffic conditions that will exist at various times on event day?

SIDELINE STORY

Protecting Athletes and Participants

The safety of fans, athletes, and staff is of the highest priority in designing and managing an event venue. A thorough inspection of the entire facility is highly recommended before the event opens its doors to ensure that every potential obstacle to crowd flow, every trip hazard, and any other sources of potential injury are remedied. Organizers should go through the same rigorous process with respect to the playing surface, locker rooms, training facilities, and anyplace athletes will encounter during their time on-site. The playing surface is the athlete's stage, and as such, it must provide the best possible conditions for safety and top-quality performance. There is no tolerance for unsafe conditions on the field:

- The final two periods of an outdoor NBC Network-broadcast outdoor NHL game at Lake Tahoe, Nevada, was postponed for 8 hours due to poor ice conditions that caused players to slip and fall frequently during the first period. Warmer than expected temperatures and the radiant heat from bright sunshine caused the highly anticipated game between the Colorado Avalanche and Las Vegas Golden Knights to be delayed until 9:00 P.M. to allow the ice to be restored to proper gametime conditions. Unfortunately, the broadcast had to be shifted to a less-watched NBC channel and, as it was already dark outside, without the stunning visuals of the lake and snow-capped mountains in the background.

- After the first highly successful Carrier Classic between North Carolina and Michigan State, played on the flightdeck of the USS Carl Vinson aircraft carrier in San Diego, the doubleheader of two college basketball games scheduled to be held on aircraft carriers in Jacksonville, Florida, and Charleston, South Carolina, were cancelled. The courts were deemed too wet to play due to condensation accumulating on the court.

- A Women's Super League soccer game between Chelsea and Liverpool was halted after 6 minutes of play due to a frozen field. Heaters had been used to dry and soften the soil beneath the pitch before the game, but shortly after the game began, the re-hardened surface was considered too risky for the athletes to continue play.

Are there presentation elements that can pose a threat to safety, such as pyrotechnics, flame effects, lasers, or trusses or towers containing lighting and sound equipment? Has the design and installation of all technical elements been supervised by professional, experienced personnel? Are all potentially dangerous special effects located in areas that are of sufficient distance from the public to minimize any possible mishap? Have experienced, licensed riggers installed all equipment that is suspended over the playing surface or spectator viewing areas?

Remedying and Responding to Risk Exposure

Considering the many potential areas of risk exposure and then analyzing the impact of circumstances that could befall a sports event will help organizers develop plans for response. For example, if an unsafe structural condition exists in the facility, it is the responsibility of the organizer to bring it to the attention of the venue management to request or demand its repair. Conditions that are not sufficiently safe or secure should be addressed before they can present clear threats to safety. Another potential area of exposure can be reduced by ensuring a secure environment for the athletes. They should be protected by restricting public access to nonpublic areas.

The answers to other hypothetical challenges require reflection and the application of sound, ethical, and responsible practices. It is impossible to predict how outside events beyond the control of the organizer might affect the safe conduct of the event, or the advisability of opening the doors to the venue at all. These are the kinds of concerns for which insurance was invented.

Financial and Legal Issues

Safety is of the utmost importance, but there are many other areas of risk that can affect the successful delivery of a sports event. Would weak ticket sales or non-payment by a sponsor generate a risk of running out of cash before the event is held? Securing letters of credit from a bank may help. Does the organizer have a written refund policy and procedure for fans to follow if an event is interrupted, postponed, or canceled? Will the organizer be able to access cash quickly if refunds must be made?

Is there a possibility of a strike, lockout, or work slowdown due to labor unrest at the venue or a major supplier? How would the potential of labor actions affect the safe and smooth conduct of the event? Is there a possibility of a picket line or protest being staged outside of the event facility? Have you worked with public safety officials to set aside an area that can be designated as a "free speech zone," a place where protestors can exercise their rights without interfering with the safe conduct of participants and fans?

Has a legal challenge been filed against the event, organizer, host facility, or major sponsor? Is there a claim being levied against any stakeholder associated with the event that could cause the program to be postponed, delayed, or altered in any way? Are all required permits secured or in the process of review? Have all appropriate licenses for the public performance of music, video, or design elements been acquired?

Are any stakeholders, including the organizer, venue, sponsors, vendors, or media partners, in financial distress? Are any of them in imminent danger of ceasing operations? How much cash has been paid in the form of deposits to financially shaky stakeholders, and may, therefore, be at risk of loss? Are there legal actions pending against any stakeholder that has failed to meet past contractual obligations?

Cancellation Scenarios

What circumstances can cause the event to be canceled or postponed? Is the event's successful completion subject to favorable weather conditions? At what minimum and maximum air temperatures may the event proceed? Does an outdoor contest require a dry surface? What extreme precipitation conditions could cause the event to be cancelled or postponed? What effect would electrical storms, accumulating ice, or high wind conditions have on competition? Would decisions be made differently before the event begins versus after fans have arrived and the event was already underway? At what point in the competition is the score considered "official" if it must end early?

What is the likelihood of a weather delay or postponement? How long can the start of the competition be delayed? If the event must be postponed, is an alternate "rain date" identified in the facility lease? Is it practical to move an outdoor contest to an indoor location? What additional costs would the organizer have to bear to hold the event on an alternate date or in an alternate space? What is the financial exposure associated with a total cancellation? In addition to refunding ticket revenues, what portion of sponsorship, broadcast, and other revenues might need to be returned? Is the event venue in a seismically active zone prone to earthquake activity? Does the venue have its own power-generating capability, or would it be subject to the possibility of interruption due to a power outage? Is there adequate illumination in case a daytime event must be delayed until after sunset? Are there local curfew or sound ordinances that require the event to be completed by a specified time?

How would the organizer react to the great unknown of a catastrophic political or cultural event, such as a global or national tragedy, act of terror, the sudden outbreak of war, or an epidemic or pandemic? Would the event continue to be held if a national day of mourning was declared following a tragic circumstance?

SIDELINE STORY

Moving Minnesota

On early Sunday morning, December 12, 2010, a massive and rapid accumulation of snow resulting from a blizzard caused the air-pressure supported dome over the Hubert H. Humphrey Metrodome to tear and collapse, rendering the stadium useless for the game scheduled for later that afternoon, as well as for the remaining game of the NFL Minnesota Vikings' season. An emergency task force of league and team personnel quickly convened by conference call to explore the options—find another football stadium that could be mobilized to host the game against the New York Giants, rescheduled for Monday evening. The Detroit Lions, just hours from opening the stadium doors for their own Sunday afternoon game, began preparations to schedule staff and develop an operations plan for Ford Field to host the game. One day after Minnesotans shoveled away nearly 18 inches of snow from their homes, and while hometown fans watched the contest on national television, more than 40,000 fans were admitted the stadium free of charge to enjoy the game in Detroit.

Simultaneously, work began to relocate the one remaining Vikings home game on the schedule, set for the very next Monday night. The University of Minnesota's open-air TCF Bank Field had already been winterized for the deep cold of the Northern Midwest winter, its field under several feet of accumulated snow from multiple winter storms. All utilities had been shut down for the season. Through a heroic effort led by the school, team, and league, a temporary labor force removed hundreds of truckloads of snow from the stands and field, the stadium was reactivated, game-day staff contacted and confirmed, and the facility readied to host the Vikings' last home game of the season against the Chicago Bears (during which even more snow fell).

Although it is unlikely that such drastic measures will be required for your event, be sure to consider what your weather contingency plans will be — will your event be postponed, moved, or canceled in case of extreme weather? What measures must you take to protect your facilities, equipment, and playing surface should adverse weather be expected?

Liability Insurance

In its most basic form, an insurance policy is a contract issued by a company that agrees to assume the financial risks of unforeseen and unfortunate occurrences in return for a fee (the *premium*). Depending on the amount and type of protections an event organizer chooses to procure and the likelihood of the risks involved, the cost of insurance premiums can represent a significant budget expense.

SIDELINE STORY

Simulating Emergency Reaction and Response

Many large event organizers and public safety agencies stage *tabletop readiness exercises*, simulations designed to test their decision-making processes and preparedness for the unexpected. Senior game-day managers for the NFL's Super Bowl, for example, participate in such an exercise approximately a week before the game. A hired facilitator interviews representatives from most operational areas (e.g., facilities, security, guest management, game operations, law enforcement, fire and medical services) over the course of several weeks to gain a thorough knowledge of every facet of the event, and then tests for weaknesses in the plan by presenting managers with emergency scenarios that must be solved in real time. The half-dozen cases that will be presented by the facilitator over the half-day exercise are kept confidential until they are revealed to the group to ensure that solutions developed by the team generate a response under the pressure of time. Over the years, many solutions developed during these simulated scenarios have resulted in permanent changes to the emergency preparedness plan for the Super Bowl.

The simulation also builds trust between the event management team and the public safety officials overseeing the event by demonstrating how different decisions will be made, and by whom. Oversight on matters of public safety and law enforcement, for instance, is recognized as the responsibility of the government agencies with ultimate authority (e.g., police and fire departments). The event organizer's staff will support their decisions and direction. Decision making on most other operational contingencies, such as postponement or cancellation, belongs to the event organizer. Organizers should define an emergency operations plan, and work with the host venue's management and public safety agencies that have jurisdiction over the event to establish processes for clear decision-making and response. Can your events benefit from a tabletop simulation?

At minimum, event organizers should procure liability insurance to protect themselves from the expenses and legal actions that may result from injuries to spectators, athletes, and staff. Proof of insurance against property damage is also often required by event facilities, sponsors, equipment rental companies, and/or other business partners to help protect their own assets and manage risks.

The amount of liability insurance that should be procured is both a budgetary and business decision based on the event's size and complexity. Most event liability policies should carry minimum protection per occurrence ($2 million is an often suggested amount, although larger events with a higher level of attendance may consider coverage of $5 million to $10 million per occurrence, or even more). Most policies have an aggregate ceiling as well, limiting the total amount of coverage per event to a fixed figure. Just like personal auto, medical, and homeowner's insurance, a deductible will usually apply. That is, the organizer will be responsible to pay the deductible amount to satisfy claims against an event before the policy's protections begin providing the balance.

Check the policy's coverage and exclusions carefully and speak with your legal and insurance agency representatives to determine what additional insurance coverages are advisable. Is special automobile coverage required for personal and rental vehicles? Are alcoholic beverages being served? Liquor liability insurance is strongly advised in such cases. Are checkroom facilities being provided for spectators' coats and bags? Coat check insurance is available to protect against theft or loss of expensive personal property. Is the organizer serving food or selling merchandise? Consider product liability insurance to guard against the risk of inadvertently serving tainted food, or injuries and accidents related to souvenir giveaways and merchandise (miniature bats, balls, sticks, and flags on sticks can hurt bystanders or become missiles). Work closely with an experienced attorney and insurance agency to identify the types and limits of coverage that should be purchased for a particular sports event.

Be sure to procure injury insurance for participating athletes. Some athletic governing organizations require an insurance policy whenever an athletic competition is staged, and some will assist in procuring appropriate coverage. Organizations such as USA Cycling, for example, offer approved event organizers the option to purchase insurance through the governing body's own broker. The event may instead arrange for its own policy independently so long as coverage meets the certain minimum requirements. Coverage is especially recommended for exhibition activities, such as "alumni games," "amateur invitational tournaments," and "celebrity games," among others. Athletes who do not train daily for regular competition are especially susceptible to injury.

Make sure your own vendors are carrying adequate insurance, as well. Legal actions against an uninsured vendor working on the organizer's behalf can cause the supplier to go out of business, leaving the organizer exposed to pay 100 percent of a plaintiff's damages. Vendors can provide proof of coverage upon request, in the form of a *certificate of insurance* (COI) that includes definitions of policy limits and inclusions. Check all of your leases and other contracts for requirements to name the host facility, sponsors, vendors, and other stakeholders as *additional insured* parties. Your insurance company can issue a COI that identifies them as covered by your insurance. In return, your attorney and insurance broker will help you identify which of your business partners should also name your organization as an additional insured. Commonly, these will include an event's host venue, as well as vendors in "high risk" businesses, such as rigging, lighting, and pyrotechnics companies, among others.

Cancellation Insurance

Cancellation insurance is designed to reimburse an organizer for event expenses if the program is unable to proceed or be held at all. Cancellation insurance can be very expensive and may be subject to a number of significant restrictions. Because policies vary, it is wise to work with an experienced broker or agency to shop and compare the coverage available and prices charged by different insurance companies. Cancellation coverage can be used to repay sponsors and ticket buyers, satisfy vendor invoices, and fulfill other financial obligations that will protect the organizer from significant economic damage due to unlikely and unforeseen circumstances. The premium charged is usually a percentage of the total amount covered, which can range from protecting gross receipts to paying the organizer back for unrecoverable expenses. An organizer cannot simply cancel a sports event and expect the insurer to honor a claim. The policy will define specific acceptable reasons why an event may be canceled and losses reimbursed, many of which were described in Figure 14.3.

As programs that may attract large audiences, a sports event may unfortunately be a target for an act of terror. The availability of insurance protection for "certified acts of terrorism" is currently guaranteed in the United States through at least 2027 by the Federal Terrorism Risk Insurance Act (see Figure 14.4 for the

---

FEDERAL TERRORISM RISK INSURANCE ACT OF 2002

Note: This legislation is set to expire in 2027 unless renewed or modified by the US Congress.

Section 102(1)(A): Any act that is certified by the Secretary (of the Treasury), in concurrence with the Secretary of State, and the Attorney General of the United States (i) to be an act of terrorism; (ii) to be a violent act or an act that is dangerous to (I) human life; (II) property; or (III) infrastructure; (iii) to have resulted in damage within the United States, or outside the United States in the case of (I) an air carrier or vessel described in paragraph (5)(B); or (II) the premises of a United States mission; and (iv) to have been committed by an individual or individuals acting on behalf of any foreign person or foreign interest, as part of an effort to coerce the civilian population of the United States or to influence the policy or affect the conduct of the United States Government by coercion.

Figure 14.4 Definition of "Certified Act of Terrorism"

government's definition of certified acts. This legislation was passed as a temporary measure in 2002 but has been re-authorized by the U.S. Congress several times since. The current extension may be renewed or modified again before its current expiration date). For an additional premium, many insurance policies can also offer coverage against "noncertified acts of terrorism," modifications of the Treasury Department's official limitations. Insurers may offer enhanced levels of coverage for noncertified acts that expand the distances of the occurrence from the event venue (e.g., 250 miles), or within a specified time before the start of an event (e.g., seven days). Both time and distance variables are frequently negotiable, but the wider the coverage, the more expensive the premium. The location of the host facility will also be considered when the insurer sets the premium. Generally, sports events held in major cities are considered as more likely targets by insurance companies than those staged in less-populated areas.

Insurance is available to protect against cybersecurity incidents, including data breaches, ransomware attacks, and other incursions that may affect operations or cause an event cancellation. Other protections can also be added to cancellation insurance policies at the organizer's request and expense. Sponsor revenues dependent on television coverage, for instance, can be insured against preemption due to matters of national attention, such as breaking global news stories and tragedies that may disrupt a broadcast. An outbreak of a virulent communicable disease can cause spectators, sponsors, and athletes to reconsider their plans to travel to a sports event, or cause a program to be canceled, postponed, or staged without a live audience, as was often the case during the COVID-19 pandemic.

Weather Insurance

Weather insurance is another type of coverage to carefully consider for outdoor events that can be affected by such meteorological events as rain, snow, temperature, lightning, high wind speeds, or fog. This type of cancellation protection specifies under what circumstances the insurer will honor claims to recover expenses and requires highly specific conditions to activate coverage. Typical measures include how much rain or snow must fall over a certain period, sustained wind speeds or gusts, and trigger levels for extreme temperatures. Specific conditions are negotiable based on how much the organizer is willing to spend. For instance, a policy that will honor claims for events canceled due to rainfall of four inches over two hours immediately before the event will cost less than one that protects against two inches falling during the same period. If it seems more like wagering than the usual process of making a sound business decision, you are not mistaken. Insurers want to improve the odds that they will be able to keep your money and reduce the probability you will collect on a claim. Nevertheless, cancellation coverage is often essential for ticketed and sponsored events to avoid the possibility of financial disaster due to inclement weather. Some sponsors will actually require the organizer to carry cancellation insurance to ensure their marketing investment will be repaid if the event is not successfully executed.

Waivers (Releases)

Waivers, or releases, are simple, often single-page documents designed to provide sports event organizers with limited, but specific, protections from legal actions stemming from a participant's or fan's activities on an event site. Signed waivers are usually requested from individuals who will engage in some participatory aspect of a sports event, such as amateur athletes, performers, volunteer staff, promotion contestants, and fan participants in certain physical demonstrations and activities. An experienced attorney should craft an organizer's waiver that is most appropriate to the type of event and the protections desired. A parent or legal guardian must always sign waivers required from minors. Waivers should include language indemnifying the organizer against claims arising from injuries that result from participation in the event. A participant's receipt of the document infers acceptance that some level of risk is involved and their signature acknowledges that they have taken this into account before participating.

Another common purpose of a participant waiver is to provide agreement that images of the signatory at the event are the property of the organizer. This grants the organizer permission to use a person's image in video footage and photography for live or recorded broadcasts, social media, future digital or printed advertising, and promotions. The participants will not be paid, nor will further permission be required if their images appear in any of these or other materials. Many sports event organizers also post similar consent language on large placards prominently displayed at the host facility's entrances to further reinforce their intention to use audience and/or participants' images in broadcast(s) of the event.

Accident Response

The presence of first aid personnel, such as qualified nurse and medical practitioners, emergency medical technicians (EMTs), and physicians, is essential to protect the safety and well-being of all in attendance. Sports events are inherently risky, especially for participants in athletic competition, but also in some respects for the spectators. It is strongly recommended that wherever possible an ambulance be present or accessible to the event site for the timely transfer of the injured or sick to full-service medical facilities. At minimum, an ambulance service or nearby hospital should be made aware of the event in case of the need for the rapid dispatch of an emergency vehicle. All staff and volunteers should be familiar with the procedure to summon first responders to the scene of an injury or other situation requiring medical attention.

If an accident occurs on the event site, whether involving athletes, spectators, staff, crew, volunteers, or vendors, ensure that affected parties are referred to first aid personnel whether injuries appear to exist or not. An incident form should be filled out to provide complete contact information for the affected party, as well as a description of the injury or situation, the location, and circumstances surrounding the occurrence (see Figure 14.5). If possible, the facts recorded on the report should be reviewed and verified by the injured party. Most permanent event facilities have a standard incident report form. The accuracy and comprehensiveness of this document is essential, as it will certainly play a role of major importance if any legal action is taken later.

Accreditation

Event credentials and the access they provide to non-public areas are neither a right nor a perk to be automatically granted to staff, stakeholders, or important guests. Although they are often perceived as such, credentials serve the primary function of controlling access to areas that require a measure of security or safety. At their most basic, they identify the wearer as an individual who is working in the venue on behalf of the organizer. More importantly, they can help an organizer improve security at an event by prohibiting unauthorized access into sensitive locations such as the area around the playing surface, player benches and sidelines, locker rooms, media facilities, and other places where greater operational control is essential. (see Figure 14.6).

Designing an accreditation process begins by defining which areas of the event facility should be restricted from public access, and how strictly controlled those areas must be. Make copies of the event venue floor plan and separate public areas from those to which access should be limited. Note where checkpoints should be—the points at which credentials must be presented to security personnel for access to restricted areas. Make sure that there are no other ways of entering these restricted areas (i.e., back doors, elevators, and staircases) without first showing a credential at a checkpoint.

The simplest credential system is one in which only a single level of access is indicated—an "All Access" credential. For many events, different levels of access are required to provide even more security for some areas. For example, it may be desirable to limit access to the locker room corridor from all but team staff and a handful of essential event personnel. The area immediately surrounding the playing surface might be off limits to all media except to authorized photographers and television camera operators, requiring a different level of credential and, many times, a more vivid method of display such as a bib or armband.

The general design of all accreditation, regardless of the level of access each type permits, should look essentially the same to enable security personnel to identify bona fide credentials at a quick glance. A best practice is to visually distinguish credentials that provide special access with a headshot photo of the bearer, a band of a color specific to the level of access, and a large letter or number code that can immediately identify its validity to security personnel from a distance of several feet. Post a chart at each checkpoint that identifies for both security staff and credential bearers what color bands and codes are permitted to pass into any adjacent restricted area. As it is wise to consider the egos of credential holders, it is often

(Event, Organizer, or Host Facility Name)

INCIDENT REPORT FORM

Date of Incident:_____

Name of Person Assisted:_____

Home Address:_____

Local Address (if different from above):_____

Phone (Day):_____(Night):_____

E-Mail:_____Gender:_____

This person is _____a guest _____staff member _____volunteer _____event participant _____other (describe:)_____

Emergency Notification Contact & Number:_____

Description of Injury or Complaint:_____

_____

Location of Incident (as detailed as possible):_____

_____

_____

Details of Incident (use back of form if additional space is required):_____

_____

_____

_____

_____

Assistance Provided & Actions Taken:_____

_____

_____

_____

Name of Responding Individual:_____

Signature:_____Date:_____

This form must be submitted to the Event Operations Office as soon as possible following the incident.

Figure 14.5　Sample Incident Report Form

- Identify levels of access.
- Design credential system (anti-counterfeit, photo, color and/or alphanumeric code).
- Confirm display method (i.e., lanyard, clip, lapel pin, bib, and armband).
- Create and communicate application procedures.
- Validate and distribute credentials.
- Manage and enforce accreditation program.

Figure 14.6　Designing an Event Accreditation System

best not to label credentials with access level codes that indicate an obvious hierarchy (e.g., A, B, and C). Working representatives of local police and fire departments in uniform should not require credentials to gain access to event facilities.

Credentials should be designed and printed so they may not be easily counterfeited. The bearer of a credential has more privileged access to an event site than a ticket holder, and a breach of security by someone with bogus credentials can have incredibly serious results. For this reason, it is strongly recommended that credentials include the name and affiliation of the wearer and photo identification that is sealed onto the card in a plastic laminate. Without this measure, it is too easy for the recipient to pass a credential to someone else and for the photo to be replaced. It is also helpful to include design elements such as embossed metallic logos or holograms, or special papers with colored or metal threads that are commonly used as anti-counterfeiting devices.

To further reduce the possibility of counterfeiting, it is recommended that credentials be distributed at the latest possible moment, preferably at the actual event site and on the day before, or on the first day, they are required. Credentials should be prepared by the organizer in advance and picked up in person. A valid government-issued ID card, such as a driver's license or passport, should be presented as proof of identity before the credential is released. Be sure to keep track of all those who have been issued their credential and require a signature beside each name as proof it has been picked up. (We don't want any duplicate credentials floating around!) Credentials should clipped to a lanyard that can be worn around the neck or directly attached to clothing in a plainly visible location at all times the wearer is on site. Some high-security events may require background checks of staff and vendors. This is of particular importance for individuals who will be in proximity to star athletes, celebrities, and dignitaries. A security contractor can assist with performing background checks.

Audience Security

Do your security needs require screening everyone who enters the venue? Should staff and athletes who enter through the loading docks, employee entrances, or the media gate be required to undergo the same security check as the audience? High-volume security checks might include walk-through magnetometers (metal detectors) or electronic wands and bag searches. While these measures can increase the level of security at an event, they can detract from the fan experience and delay the entrance of the audience unless there are sufficient security staff and equipment. Be sure you have enough of both. Such security measures prevent the possibility of criminal activity and may also be required to secure an affordable premium for liability insurance.

The sense of a safe and secure environment is essential for the enjoyment of the audience. Are security staff members within easy reach of all seating areas in case of an altercation? Are crowd management teams properly assigned to prevent or discourage fans from attempting to enter the playing area? Are trained security personnel on the lookout for pickpockets, thieves, and shoplifters? Are they in radio contact, or have another easy way, to summon a supervisor for additional assistance?

Preparing for the Unknown

The risk assessment and management methodologies discussed so far can be very effective in reducing the chances of accidents and emergencies, but they cannot completely eliminate their possibility. Despite planning meticulously, identifying threats, remedying hazards, and instituting best security practices, incidents beyond our control may still occur. Few event organizers finish their careers without encountering something, somewhere, somehow going wrong. It is how they and their team respond to those challenges that matters most.

We have briefly discussed the concept of contingency planning, the notion of having a "Plan B" for the challenges an organizer is most likely to encounter. Being able to switch to an alternate plan that was well thought out in advance takes some of the stress and guesswork out of responding when a challenge does arise. It is, of course, not possible to have a contingency plan for absolutely *everything* that can happen. It is, however, important to plan for how you would respond to *anything* that might happen. That's because problems don't often follow patterns, but solutions often do. How do you plan for anything? The most important steps include transforming your staff into an empowered team, establishing a clear chain of command, ensuring your team can communicate to an event's decision-makers, and developing a crisis communications plan. (A helpful and comprehensive reference for crisis management at events is *What to Do When Things Go Wrong* by Frank Supovitz (McGraw-Hill, 2019).)

Building an Empowered Team

An event staff may be comprised of any combination of an organization's own employees, a venue's temporary workers, and staff provided by a vendor. They are not a team, however, until you establish an environment that encourages collaboration and a shared responsibility to deliver a great event experience for the fans and the athletes. Every individual who works at an event, regardless of their job or who pays them, has an impact on that experience. When staff members understand their role in providing a safe, secure, welcoming, and entertaining environment, they begin to work as a team. Each of these teammates are part of an early-warning system that can identify problems as they arise and before they develop into greater challenges. The familiar saying "if you see something say something" applies perfectly to your team. They should feel empowered to let their supervisor know if they see a problem unfolding. That's everybody's job. Perhaps they see a banner coming loose in the wind, a water leak beginning to dampen floors, trash piling up in a concourse, or a confrontation developing between fans. This doesn't mean they need to try to fix those things (unless that's their specific role). But, if what they see is not elevated to someone who can get the right people involved, the banner and its hardware can pull loose and hurt someone, the water leak can drip down into the locker rooms or power cabinets, the trash can become trip hazards, or the confrontation can become injurious and ruin the experience for others. Teammates should know they are empowered to be an active part of the solution by identifying and reporting problems to their supervisor. In order to do so, they should be aware of how to communicate and to whom.

Establish a Chain of Command

Sports events are fast-moving environments, where unpredictable situations can develop from any quarter. Things happen quickly, and once they are identified, an appropriate and decisive response must be handled rapidly, responsibly, and authoritatively. Establish a chain of command that identifies the decision makers who are empowered to manage defined areas of responsibility. Define the scope and limits to their authority. Every teammate should know who their supervisor is and how to reach them. Some staff members may be issued walkie-talkie radios, others may be reliant on their cell phones to communicate. Every teammate should know how to identify and elevate problems. An easy way to do that is to provide a call-in number, code, or text line on the back of their credential that can be used to report problems.

Determine what kinds of issues should be immediately reported to the most senior members of the event team and identify how those individuals can be reached. The most important document in managing the operations of an event is a contact list—the list of event, venue, and organization staff with accompanying e-mail addresses and phone/text numbers. Ensure that all personnel have the most important event day information stored in their mobile devices. Alternatively, provide a small laminated information card that can be attached to their credential.

A chain of command, in its simplest form, identifies the levels of management and authority. *What to Do When Things Go Wrong* identifies an improvement on that theme—establishing a *Web of Command*. The concept here is that not every problem needs to be elevated to the next, or the highest level of management. Teammates should have the authority to work collaboratively between each other on lower organizational levels to solve lesser problems. In this way, the challenges of the greatest impact or concern—including those that rise to the level of a crisis—can be more quickly solved or managed by the most senior members without a greater volume of smaller problems interfering with their response.

Communications

From operational and risk management perspectives, there is an essential need for information to be exchanged continuously through the chain, or web, of command. Communications systems—two-way radios/walkie-talkies, ClearComs, mobile devices and phones, private line (PL) communicators, and others—provide much of the connective tissue that keeps an event together and running smoothly.

In 1949, United States Air Force Captain Edward A. Murphy, an engineer working at Edwards Air Force Base, inspired the famous and oft-quoted "Murphy's Law"—"If anything can go wrong, it will." Murphy was working on an Air Force project charged with the responsibility of determining how much sudden deceleration a human being might be able to survive in a crash. Inspecting the device that would be used in the experiment, Murphy found it wired incorrectly. When he expressed his annoyance at the technician who installed it, his famous namesake principle was immortalized. Murphy's First Corollary demonstrates how important it is to empower your team to identify challenges for a quick management response: "Left to themselves, things tend to go from bad to worse."

We believe there is another corollary to Murphy's law relating to what is too often the most common source of grief in the execution of special events. That is—"The area with which you cannot communicate is the place where things will inevitably go wrong." Events are living, dynamic organisms where challenges are presented in real time and must be solved before they grow into bigger ones. So, as you plan your event, consider Supovitz's Corollary, expressed in the vernacular of Sun Tzu, the author of *The Art of War*: "You have already lost control where communication does not exist."

You are simply not in control of your event if you do not have a reliable system of communication that will provide instantaneous contact to and from every area where decisions must be made and directions transformed into action. It is sometimes tempting to skimp on walkie talkies and intercoms to reduce costs when, in fact, not being able to communicate with event staff, and them not being able to communicate with their supervisor, can result in the entire budget being wasted on a completely failed event.

Every staff member, volunteer, or participant should know how to reach someone in a position of authority and responsibility. There should likewise be a way to reach each and every individual empowered to execute a job at an event. For event participants, this pathway of communication may be through an area supervisor who can relay messages and information between the event director and the coaches, athletes, officials, or cast members.

The most common devices in use for event site communications are two-way radios, or walkie-talkies, and Clear-com intercom systems. Two-way radios are advantageous because they are wireless, permitting the user mobility throughout the event site. Test the radios well in advance to determine if there are any areas in which transmissions cannot be heard. Such "dead spots" are common in indoor facilities, where radio signals may have difficulty penetrating some concrete walls. Consider working with your radio supplier to install a repeater antenna, a device that essentially receives the transmission, and then rebroadcasts it into harder-to-reach or more distant locations.

Walkie-talkies are radio frequency (RF) devices, as are wireless microphones and remote television cameras. There may be many groups that have independent two-way radios in the same facility, including the production staff, broadcasters, the front-of-house staff, transportation dispatchers, parking lot staff, and even independent entities outside the venue. Work with your radio vendor to "coordinate frequencies," ensuring that the communications channel used by each group does not interfere with any other. Interference between different groups using the same radio frequencies can prove confusing and disastrous. They can also render the pictures and sound from wireless television cameras and microphones useless.

Be sure to provide the right kind of earpieces for your radios. Transmissions that can be heard by the fans can be disturbing. In low-volume areas, an earphone might suffice. A single- or double-headset, one that completely covers the ear(s), might be more advisable in louder locations.

Closed-circuit, wired intercom systems, such as Clear-coms, are commonly used in areas where continuous and simultaneous two-way conversations are required. The limitation of walkie-talkies is that users cannot hear anyone else when they are talking. Clear-coms, however, operate more like telephones. Both parties can hear each other at the same time. Wireless Clear-com packs, the frequencies for which must also be coordinated, are also available for users who require more mobility. A single or double headset is a must for these systems.

Develop a Crisis Communications Plan

A written communications plan should be developed to formalize how the organizer will manage major challenges, and define the method by which staff, participants, media, and the public will receive information during a crisis. The plan should outline the step-by-step process by which a potential crisis will be identified, managed, and communicated (see Figure 14.7).

The organizer will have already completed the first part of this exercise—the identification of potential crises—during the risk assessment process (see Figure 14.2). Identify in writing the ultimate decision maker who will determine whether an event should be canceled, postponed, delayed, or in any way altered. Some organizations require that decisions affecting the financial health or public image of a company be made by the chief executive or board of directors. There may not be time for that formality when a crisis arises quickly. A more rapid response may be required. It is recommended that a single final decision maker be designated in advance, if possible. Also select a second-in-command to take this individual's place if the decision maker is incapacitated, missing, or otherwise unavailable when a crisis arises.

These top-level officials may comprise, at least in part, a Crisis Assessment Task Force, a small, select group of experts who, with the decision maker, will develop or manage the response during an emergency. At minimum, the individuals in charge of security and operations, the event facility, media relations, broadcasting should be included in this group. The function of the task force is to receive information, analyze any developments related to the crisis, and to make recommendations to the decision maker. It is suggested that this group be kept to as small a number as possible to streamline discussion, consultation, and decision making.

Remember that there is usually more than a single decision and response required when managing a crisis. There may be many second-to-second judgments that are necessary as an emergency develops and its impacts become known. Identify a command center where the decision maker and the appointed members of the Crisis Assessment Task Force will report when an emergency condition becomes apparent. This facility should be in a secure area out of public view, but within easy reach by those who will require access. Major events install a command center staffed with representatives from across the event organization during the entire time that fans are in the facility. Having an operational location like this, overlooking the entire venue from the press level, or in a meeting room or trailer equipped with closed circuit television monitors, can help to ensure everyone who can help solve problems are in the same place, able to communicate and collaborate quickly. If possible, install video feeds from security cameras, plenty of electrical outlets, and connectivity for mobile devices and walkie-talkie radios.

The courses of action formulated in the command center may also affect the businesses of important event stakeholders. It may be appropriate to alert some of these stakeholders to the crisis and anticipated responses. If an announcement is determined to be of sufficient importance to communicate to the media, consider whether a limited number of top sponsors and broadcasters should be informed simultaneously or just before, so they have time to prepare their own responses.

If a major emergency emerges, you probably will not have to worry about calling the media to inform them—the media will likely already be calling you. Select a spokesperson to provide them with a consistent source of information and communication. Who that spokesperson should be can depend upon the nature and severity of the crisis. Credibility and authority are key. The greater the potential impact of the crisis, the higher into the organization you may want to reach for the spokesperson. If the media are already on site, convene a news conference and prepare a press release with relevant information for immediate distribution upon completion of the session. If the media are not on site, circulate brief statements and

---

☐ Identify areas of crisis potential.
☐ Identify the decision maker(s) and members of the Crisis Assessment Task Force.
☐ Establish a command center.
☐ Identify critical stakeholders and their representatives.
☐ Develop and evaluate appropriate responses.
☐ Create a media communications plan.

Figure 14.7 Crisis Communications Plan

updates via a press release with a contact name and number for further inquiries. The press contact should not be the spokesperson, but someone who will screen and prioritize calls and schedule interviews for the spokesperson. A news conference may be scheduled at a time and place the media can attend. Identify the cause for concern (e.g., athlete injury, potential cancellation/rescheduling of the event, etc.), and how and when the organizer will respond, as known at that time. The spokesperson should only make truthful, to-the-point statements of fact and offer no speculation. If details regarding the crisis and its response continue to develop and additional information is expected to be provided at a later time, provide the media with an estimated time frame as to when they might be updated.

SIDELINE STORY

The Blackout Bowl

The second half began with a touchdown on the very first play, a kickoff return for 108 yards, tying an NFL record. Ninety-eight seconds into the 3rd quarter, the power in one half of the Mercedes Benz Superdome failed. The lights on the field went dark, radio communications were interrupted, and the league's command center was plunged into darkness. Super Bowl XLVII in New Orleans was abruptly halted before a packed stadium and a television audience of 108 million viewers.

The team in the command center—the event director and representatives from security, law enforcement, stadium operations, broadcasting, public relations, social media, and football operations—immediately began to consider their priorities. Certainly, getting the power restored and the game resumed were among the highest. What was more important, however, was determining whether the stadium was a safe or an unsafe environment. If it was unsafe, an evacuation order would have to be declared. If it was safe, it was important to keep people calm and inside the stadium. The highest priority, then, was to make that determination and inform the more than 70,000 fans what to do. The event team could not let social media or crowd-think incite an uninformed response that could endanger the well-being of the fans.

Within a few moments, the stadium established that a power feeder cable relay had tripped. Security and law enforcement determined that there was no fire, no act of terror, and no cybersecurity breach. The team hastily scribbled a brief script for the public address announcer telling the fans that they should remain in the building and that the game would resume after a brief delay. The sound systems in many stadiums and arenas are equipped with a back-up to provide emergency power for just this kind of life-safety purpose. While the stadium operations team shut down non-essential power drains in the half of the building that was still energized, electrical engineers activated the stadium's back-up feeder cable.

The lights were reilluminated and back to full strength within 24 minutes. The command center team, however, resisted the temptation of re-starting the game without testing every electronic system that might have been affected by the power failure. They checked the score clock, play clocks, coach-to-quarterback radio systems, and the instant replay system, to make sure all were fully functional. Not everything was found to be working. One team's coach-to-quarterback system had to be rebooted before play began again 10 minutes later.

This story illustrates a few important points. Responses should be prioritized. Focus on the most important things first—in this case, as it should always be, protecting the safety of the people in the stadium. Once it was determined that the building was not under threat, it was important to keep the audience informed. Then, the event team could focus on getting the power restored. They did not react to the pressure to resume the game as soon as the lights were re-illuminated. Their response considered whether there could be other consequences of the power failure, like electronic systems being compromised. It was important to make sure that if there was another score, or a controversial play, there was a functioning instant replay system for the officials to consult. If there wasn't, the integrity of the game might have been compromised. Instead, after 34 minutes, the game was back underway. Although conspiracy theorists may still speculate that the blackout was purposely engineered to interrupt the momentum of the team in the lead, the ability to resume with all competitive equipment in perfect operating order ensured that the official result would not be accompanied by an asterisk.

Acknowledging the World Condition

Globally significant circumstances, whether occurring in the host city or miles away, can affect an organizer's plans. In the days following the tragic terror attacks on the World Trade Center and Pentagon in 2001, dozens of amateur, college, and professional sports events were canceled or postponed. As emphasized throughout this book, sports events are very public reflections of our culture and, as such, must sometimes mirror society's moods and expectations. After a respectful pause in the staging of many sports events, both to reflect on the September 11 tragedies and to make necessary adjustments in security procedures, play was resumed, many preceded by "moments of silence." Flags flew at half-staff, black bunting draped the walls of many arenas and stadiums—in later days replaced with patriotic red, white, and blue—and intermission sponsor promotions were replaced by the singing of "God Bless America." As a gathering of human beings with common interests (i.e., fans of a sport or team) and the values shared by all people, a sports event is also expected to provide opportunities for public reflection.

Thankfully, few world events match the horrors of September 2001. But other tragedies of cultural significance can develop at any time. It is important for organizers to demonstrate their own sensitivities, and those of their nation and local community, when such occurrences present themselves. Carefully review all aspects of the event presentation plan—ceremonies, production elements, public address announcements, decorative components, and advertisements—to ensure that no inadvertent lapse of judgment or taste are apparent when such unfortunate circumstances occur.

Applying sensitivity in the wake of a tragedy is simply common sense. It is, on one hand, incumbent upon sports event organizers to entertain their guests and ticket buyers. To do any less would be a disservice to their loyal, paying customers. On the other, difficult times call for a candid assessment of how appropriate a celebration of sport may be in light of the world condition. Here's hoping you never have to make such decisions. But, be prepared to act thoughtfully in case you do.

Tie Down the Details

Another way to prepare for the unexpected is to make sure that staff and stakeholders have a clear understanding of important event details before the actual program takes place. Schedule a "Tie-Down Meeting"—also called a production meeting, an all-hands meeting, or an all-agency meeting, depending on the sport and event—two to five days prior to the event and invite staff and representatives of each functional area and agency (e.g., security, marketing, public relations, insurance, information technologies, parking). The meeting should systematically review the schedule of events, the production schedule, the run of show, athlete and competitive issues, transportation systems, sponsorship fulfillment plans, and of course, communications processes and emergency procedures—any and every detail that should become common knowledge to the event team. During this meeting, the staff should feel free to ask questions, request additional information, and surface issues and challenges. The larger and more complex the event, the farther in advance of event day you will want to schedule the tie-down to permit sufficient time to make adjustments that will address issues that will come to light during the meeting. Be sure to communicate any changes to the plan made after the tie-down meeting. Prepare and distribute the link to an event manual that contains all of the pertinent information and schedules discussed.

Volunteers and event-day staff should have an orientation meeting that is a more condensed version of the tie-down. They, too, should receive the link to appropriate information in an easy-to-access reference document.

Post-Mortems and After-Action Reports

Every event should plan to host some form of post-mortem meeting and/or develop an after-action report soon after the event has concluded. Prepare an agenda that covers major areas of focus, such as the competition itself, the fan experience, security, and staff experience, to name a few. Did the event meet or exceed its primary and secondary objectives? What went well? What could have gone better? If there were significant areas that require improvement, this meeting is a good forum to discuss them. It is recommended that each operational area be represented but try not have too many people attending. We have found that the larger the meeting, somehow the less open people are to sharing their observations. If it is important to hear from multiple people in each functional area, the post-mortem can be divided into several different sessions to keep attendance limited to a smaller number of participants each. You may find that you will hear about more things that can be improved if you keep the meetings relatively modest in size.

Many event organizers follow their post-mortem meetings with a written after-action report that captures the intelligence gained. Having this institutional reference available can be particularly helpful as events move from place to place, or staff changes over the course of time.

Post-play Analysis

Subject all aspects of the event to a thorough risk assessment and management process. Identify areas of risk to athletes, officials, spectators, and staff, as well as financial risks to the organization. Project possible remedies to potential crises flowing from these risks and take actions that will reduce the likelihood of their occurrence. If your event will be held outdoors, be sure to have a weather contingency plan that identifies under what conditions the event might be postponed, canceled, or continue to move forward. Procure liability insurance and, if necessary, event cancellation insurance to reduce the financial burden on the organization in case of accidents, emergencies, and circumstances that could cause the program to be canceled or postponed. Prepare to respond to emergencies by establishing a chain of command and a crisis communications plan.

Be sure to have a system available for communication between the event director and major areas of responsibility. It is impossible to control an event or respond to the unexpected without the ability to communicate. Information is power and its accessibility the best defense against confusion. Schedule a staff tie-down meeting and an orientation for event-day staff and volunteers to review event details and surface conflicts and inaccuracies. Make an event manual available with all pertinent schedules, contacts, and information that may be used as an easy reference tool. Be sure to conduct a post-mortem meeting and write an after-action report soon after the event ends.

Coach's Clipboard

1. A statewide high school football tournament has been moved to a nearby college campus, having outgrown the available facilities in the host community. As three games are scheduled each day, temporary locker rooms have been set up in the gymnasium with drapes separating each of six team dressing areas. An audience of 5,000 is expected, while the full population of college students is living on campus. What security and safety factors should be considered during the three-day tournament?

2. A regional track and field event is scheduled for Sunday morning at your local high school gymnasium. Three days before the event, the national weather service issues a forecast calling for a 50 percent chance of blizzard-like conditions beginning after sundown on Saturday. What courses of action should be considered by the event organizer?

3. You are organizing a marathon race through a major downtown area. Analyze and list the risks you could likely encounter. What kinds of insurance coverage should be secured?

4. Your marathon budget is dependent on having 75 percent of the revenues derived from sponsorships. The presenting sponsor, which was to provide 50 percent of total sponsor revenues, has filed for bankruptcy and will default on its final payment. How will the organizer continue to pay the bills? What steps might have been taken during the event planning process to avoid this crisis?

5. Create a crisis communications plan for the marathon. Who should the Crisis Assessment Task Force include? Where is the best place to locate the command center? How would you respond if threatening weather appeared likely to turn dangerous during the course of the event?

APPENDIX 1

Event Expense Budget Worksheet

ACCT. NO.	EXPENSES	BUDGET	FORECAST	ACTUAL	VARIANCE	COMMENTS
1000	**PLAYER COSTS**					
1001	Player Appearance Fees					
1002	Player Prize Money					
1003	Player Gifts					
1004	Player Travel, Air					
1005	Player Travel, Ground Transfers					
1006	Player Travel, Hotel					
1007	Per Diem					
1008	Player Scheduled Meals					
1009	Player Guest Expenses					
1010	Uniforms & Equipment					
1011	Insurance					
1012	Officials Fees					
1013	Officials, Travel Expenses					
1014	Trainers Fees					
1015	Trainer Expenses					
1016	Medical Staff					
1017	Ambulance					
1018	Player/Athlete Transportation/Parking					
1049	Miscellaneous Player Costs					

ACCT. NO.	EXPENSES	BUDGET	FORECAST	ACTUAL	VARIANCE	COMMENTS
1050	**TICKETING EXPENSES**					
1051	Capital Replacement Fees					
1052	Sales & Amusement Taxes					
1053	Box Office/Ticket Staff Labor					
1054	Ticket Service Fees					
1055	Credit Card Commissions					
1056	Ticket Printing					
1057	Group Sales Commissions					
1058	Ticket Sales Materials, Design					
1059	Ticket Sales Materials, Publish/Printing					
1060	Shipping/Postage					
1099	Miscellaneous Ticketing Expenses					
1100	**FACILITY EXPENSES**					
1101	Facility Rental					
1102	Facility Labor					
1103	Carpenters					
1104	Electricians					
1105	Laborers					
1106	Riggers					
1107	Cleaners					
1108	Groundskeeping Crew					
1109	Ushers & Guest Services					
1110	Ticket Takers/Scanners					
1111	Security					
1112	Front-of-House Supervisors					
1113	Medical/First Aid					
1114	Scoreboard Operator					
1115	P.A. Announcer/Host					
1116	Video & Matrix Crew					
1117	Stagehands					
1118	Spotlights					
1119	Changeover Crew					
1120	Miscellaneous Facility Labor					
1121	Bleachers/Additional Seating					

ACCT. NO.	EXPENSES	BUDGET	FORECAST	ACTUAL	VARIANCE	COMMENTS
1122	Game-Required Equipment					
1123	Rope & Stanchion					
1124	Barricades					
1125	Fencing					
1126	Security Screening Equipment					
1130	Utility Costs					
1131	Generators					
1132	Power Distribution					
1133	Water					
1134	Waste Receptacles & Dumpsters					
1135	Custodial/Cleaners					
1136	Portable Toilet Facilities					
1140	Venue Décor & Wayfinding Signage					
1141	Tenting					
1142	Flooring & Carpeting					
1143	Pipe & Drape					
1199	Miscellaneous Facility Expenses					
1200	**GUEST SERVICES**					
1201	Invitation Design & Publishing/Printing					
1202	Guest Management Expenses					
1203	Guest Transportation					
1204	Guest Gifts					
1205	Guest Hospitality					
1206	Complimentary Tickets					
1207	Event Info Guide App Development					
1208	Offsite Directional Signage & Info Desks					
1250	Hotel Lobby Décor					
1251	Hotel Staff Gratuities					
1253	Hotel Attrition Contingency					
1299	Miscellaneous Guest Services Costs					
1300	**EVENT OPERATIONS**					
1301	Temporary Staff & Interns					
1302	Volunteer Staff Expenses					

ACCT. NO.	EXPENSES	BUDGET	FORECAST	ACTUAL	VARIANCE	COMMENTS
1303	Staff Travel Expenses					
1304	Staff Meals or Per Diem					
1305	Staff Wardrobe/Uniforms					
1306	Site Surveys/Planning Trips					
1307	Pre-Event Planning & Tie-Down Meetings					
1308	Event Location Office Rent					
1309	Event Location Office Furnishings					
1310	Office Equipment Rental					
1313	Office Phone & Wi-Fi Connectivity					
1315	Mobile Phones					
1320	Event Location Office Supplies					
1321	Radios					
1330	Accreditation					
1340	Postage, Messenger, Shipping					
1342	Storage					
1343	Trucking					
1350	Liability Insurance					
1351	Event Cancellation Insurance					
1352	Legal Services					
1360	Police					
1361	Sanitation					
1362	Fire					
1363	Other City Services					
1364	Permits					
1399	Miscellaneous Event Operations Costs					
1500	**MARKETING/PROMOTION**					
1501	Logo Development					
1502	Advertising Agency Fees					
1503	Advertising Agency Expenses					
1504	Advertising, Print					
1505	Advertising, Radio					
1506	Advertising, Digital					
1506	Advertising, Outdoor					
1507	Posters & Handbills					

ACCT. NO.	EXPENSES	BUDGET	FORECAST	ACTUAL	VARIANCE	COMMENTS
1520	Website Design & Management					
1521	Social Media Marketing					
1540	Public Relations Agency Fees					
1541	Public Relations Agency Expenses					
1560	Street Banners, Design & Printing					
1561	Street Banners, Installation					
1562	Airport Signage					
1570	Promotional Items (caps, pins, t-shirts)					
1599	Miscellaneous Marketing Expenses					
1600	**MEDIA EXPENSES**					
1601	Press Conferences					
1602	Media Pre-/Post-Game Meals, Refreshments					
1604	Media Tabletops, Phones, Wi-Fi					
1605	Printers/Copiers					
1606	Media Office Expenses					
1607	Media Office Supplies					
1610	Media Guide					
1611	Photography					
1620	Media Gift					
1699	Miscellaneous Media Expenses					
1700	**SPONSOR FULFILLMENT COSTS**					
1701	Agency Commissions					
1702	Sales Expenses					
1703	Banners & Signage					
1704	Complimentary Tickets					
1705	Sponsor Hospitality					
1710	Sponsor Activation Costs					
1720	Sponsor Gifts and Post-Event Recognition					
1799	Miscellaneous Fulfillment Expenses					
1800	**BROADCASTING**					
1801	Broadcast Expenses					
1802	Airtime Purchase					

ACCT. NO.	EXPENSES	BUDGET	FORECAST	ACTUAL	VARIANCE	COMMENTS
2000	**PRODUCTION COSTS**					
2001	Stage Risers & Platforms					
2002	Set Design					
2003	Set Construction/Rentals					
2005	Lighting					
2006	Audio					
2007	Special Effects & Pyrotechnics					
2007	Props & Flags					
2008	Draping					
2009	Floral					
2030	ClearCom					
2040	Video Production					
2041	LED Screens					
2050	Production Management Fees					
2051	Production Management Expenses					
2052	Production Labor, Installation					
2053	Production Labor, Rehearsal & Event					
2054	Production Labor, Dismantle					
2060	Equipment Rental					
2070	Talent Fees					
2071	Talent Expenses					
2075	Costumes & Wardrobe					
2099	Miscellaneous Production Expenses					
3000	**ASSOCIATED EVENTS & PROGRAMS**					
3001	School/Educational Outreach					
3100	Welcome Party					
3200	Closing Party					
3300	VIP Hospitality					
3400	Spouse Program					
4000	**OTHER EXPENSES & ADJUSTMENTS**					
4100	Amortization of Prior Year Assets					
4200	Deferral of Capital Assets/5yr.					
4300	Deferral of Capital Assets/3yr.					
4400	Contingency					

TOTAL EXPENSES

APPENDIX 2

Event Revenue Budget Worksheet

ACCT. NO.	REVENUES	BUDGET	FORECAST	ACTUAL	VARIANCE	COMMENTS
0010	**ADMISSIONS**					
0011	General Admission Tickets—Price A					
0012	General Admission Tickets—Price B					
0013	General Admission Tickets—Price C					
0014	General Admission Tickets—Promo Price A					
0015	General Admission Tickets—Promo Price B					
0016	General Admission Tickets—Family Deal					
0018	VIP Seating					
0020	Party Area Rental					
0021	Picnic Area Rental					
0029	Miscellaneous Admissions Revenue					
0030	**CONCESSIONS**					
0031	Food & Beverage Sales					
0032	Catering Sales					
0035	Merchandise Sales					
0036	NFT Sales					
0041	Bag Check					
0043	Parking					
0049	Miscellaneous Concessions Revenue					

ACCT. NO.	REVENUES	BUDGET	FORECAST	ACTUAL	VARIANCE	COMMENTS
0050	**SPONSORSHIP**					
0051	Title Sponsorship					
0052	Presenting Sponsorship					
0053	Exclusive Sponsorship					
0054	Non-Exclusive Sponsorship					
0055	Official Suppliers					
0056	Value-In-Kind					
0058	Donors/Donations					
0059	Grants					
0060	Sponsor Activation Revenue					
0061	Advertising—Printed Materials					
0062	Advertising—Signage & Banners					
0063	Advertising—Website					
0064	Advertising—Event App					
0065	Supplemental (buy-in) Hospitality					
0069	Miscellaneous Sponsorship Revenue					
0070	**TOURNAMENT & PARTICIPATION FEES**					
0071	Tournament Fees					
0079	Miscellaneous Participation Fees					
0080	**MEDIA REVENUES**					
0081	Television/Streaming Rights Fees					
0082	Radio/Audio Rights Fees					
0085	Photos/Footage Licensing					
0089	Miscellaneous Media Revenues					
0090	**MISCELLANEOUS**					
0099	Miscellaneous Revenues					

TOTAL REVENUES

APPENDIX 3

Sample Host City Request for Proposal

MNO Sports Events, Inc.

Request for Proposal to Host
The Big Street Sports Tournament
Summer, 2026

MNO Sports
123 S.W. 2nd Avenue
Biggtown, MD 00000
© September 2024

Request for Proposal
The Big Street Sports Tournament

Table of Contents

I. INTRODUCTION

MNO Sports is pleased to offer communities with an active interest in world-class amateur sports events and festivals the opportunity to host a proven, exciting, and crowd-pleasing concept in amateur street sports: **The Big Street Sports Tournament**.

The Big Street Sports Tournament will attract thousands of families and sports enthusiasts from local and surrounding communities free-of-charge, as well as participating amateur street and professional extreme athletes from throughout North America for a full weekend of entertainment, interactive activities, competition, and pure fun, including:

- Age-Bracketed Skateboard Competitions
- BMX Half-Pipe Exhibitions
- In-line Skating Demo Zone
- Roller Hockey Rink
- Street Sports New Product Expo
- "Kids Only" Clinics and Activities
- Bicycle Tune-Up Area and Obstacle Course
- Extreme Sports Video Arcade
- Special Guest Appearances
- Nonstop Musical Entertainment
- Food Concessions
- . . . and more!

The Big Street Sports Tournament will be totally new for 2026 with more to see, more to do, and more to enjoy than ever before! Your city can capitalize on the expanding interest and phenomenal growth in street sports within your community and beyond by participating as the host of this outstanding street sports festival and national invitational tournament.

II. THE BIG STREET SPORTS TOURNAMENT: A New Tradition Continues

The Big Street Sports Tournament enters its 20th year in 2026, combining visually captivating, heart-stopping athletic demonstrations by top street athletes with an invitational tournament matching local amateur players with visiting teams from across the continent in all age, gender, and skill levels ranging from "8 and Under" to "18 and Older" divisions. The tournament draws approximately 1,000 top amateur athletes from all over North America, accompanied by their friends and families. Past host cities include Orlando, FL, Kansas City, MO, Providence, RI, Syracuse, NY, Potomac, MD, and Appleton, WI.

This document has been prepared to provide prospective host cities with comprehensive guidelines and specifications to assist them in the preparation of a proposal to host The Big Street Sports Tournament. For your ease of preparation and to assist us in the evaluation process, a questionnaire is included that, when complete, will form the core of your proposal. The questionnaire must be completed and requested materials attached for successful consideration. You are, however, welcome to include any additional information to the questionnaire that you believe will present your community as the best possible host for The Big Street Sports Tournament.

Please submit your proposal by November 15, 2024, to the address noted on the last page of the questionnaire. Once all proposals have been received, MNO Sports will analyze submissions and evaluate whether site visits will be required prior to final selection of a host city.

If you have any questions regarding this document or the preparation of your proposal, or wish to receive a copy of this document via e-mail, please do not hesitate to contact Nathaniel Jacobs, Vice President, MNO Sports by e-mail at njacobs@mnosports.com.

III. EVENT SCHEDULE

The next available edition of **The Big Street Sports Tournament** will be held on a single weekend in Summer 2026. Potential host cities should select first- and second-choice weekends that are the optimal dates for staging the event in their community.

Most in-bound participants and their guests will arrive on Friday evening. The host city is welcome to provide a hospitality reception sponsored by a local restaurant for arriving players, if desired.

The public is welcome on the event site beginning with the first tournament games at 8:00 a.m. on Saturday. The site will close at 7:00 p.m. Saturday, reopen at 8:00 a.m. Sunday morning and remain open until closing ceremonies conclude at 6:00 p.m. Sunday evening.

Special events and entertainment will be scheduled throughout the weekend at times to be determined.

IV. ROLE OF MNO SPORTS

MNO Sports will work closely with the host city, its designated agencies, and local corporate partners to ensure that **The Big Street Sports Tournament** offers a positive and rewarding program for all visitors, athletes, sponsors, and business partners, while providing a major sports showcase for the host city.

MNO Sports will:

- Design, manage, and produce The Big Street Sports Tournament at its own expense.
- Install, operate, and dismantle all event attractions, equipment, and other elements.
- Work with the local sports commission, convention and visitors bureau, and/or other authority to promote and publicize the event on a national basis.
- Manage the tournament invitation and registration process.
- Work with area hotels to offer attractive, reasonably priced accommodations for visiting athletes, fans, and event staff.
- Promote extended visits to the host city and local points of interest to visiting athletes and their families in their invitations and registration packets, as well as on the event's phone app and website for visiting fans.
- Provide additional benefits to the host city as outlined in Section VII.

V. ROLE OF THE HOST CITY

The host city will play a prominent role in helping to shape the character of **The Big Street Sports Tournament**:

A. EVENT SITE RECOMMENDATIONS

It is an objective of MNO Sports to attract the largest audience possible for the event. The ideal event site will provide a minimum of 75,000 usable* square feet of space in a location demonstrably familiar to the local community as a major event site and/or one that regularly experiences high pedestrian traffic during a weekend or for a featured event.

---

*Required gross square footage may be higher to avoid the presence of street lamps, medians, planters, sewer grates, or other obstructions on the actual playing surfaces.

Up to seven (7) performance and street sports competition areas will be installed on the event site, requiring level footprints of clear, flat, unobstructed blacktop free of potholes, streetlamps, utility poles, planters, sewer grates, and manhole access covers. This space is required to accommodate the playing and demonstration surfaces, team benches, and spectator viewing areas. Competition areas range from the smallest at 30' × 50' to the largest at 110' × 160'.

Preference will be given to event sites that reflect the unique culture and qualities of the host city.

B. EVENT SITE SERVICES

The host city will ensure that the site is delivered in clean condition to the event before the scheduled onset of installation. The city will provide sufficient refuse and recycling containers, provide sanitation services during and after event hours, and will supervise cleaning of the site immediately after the removal of event elements by MNO Sports at no cost to the event.

The host city will schedule sufficient police, fire, and emergency medical service coverage during the event, and during installation and dismantling operations, to protect the health and safety of the public, participants, and event staff. Adequate overnight security staffing by either bonded guards or on-/off-duty police is essential. These requirements will be provided by the host city at no cost to MNO Sports.

C. HOTEL RECOMMENDATIONS

Approximately 350 quality (3-star) and competitively priced hotel rooms will be required on peak nights. A preliminary schedule of room requirements appears below:

	Mon.–Thurs.	Fri.	Sat.	Sun.	Mon.–Tues.
Rooms	10	350	350	350	10

Host hotels will also make available the meeting rooms or function space required for the management of the event during the days listed above at no cost. To be considered as a prospective host hotel, function space should be put on a tentative hold per the following schedule:

Office	Min. Sq. Ft.	Occupancy
Operations Office	1,500 sq. ft.	7 days prior through 2 days following event
Event Storage	1,500	7 days prior through 1 day following event
Gift Bag Distribution	1,500	7 days prior through 1 day following event
Sponsor Hospitality	1,500	1 day prior through final event day

The event headquarters hotel will permit MNO Sports to place welcome and directional signage in the hotel lobby area and on the exterior of the building in mutually agreed locations. The event will be permitted to staff an information desk in the lobby of the hotel within line-of-sight of the guest registration area.

The headquarters hotel(s) will provide a total of 30 complimentary room-nights for pre-event planning trips, the fulfillment of which will be administered by the local convention and visitors bureau (CVB).

During the event and for up to four (4) weeks prior, a discounted "staff rate" will be available to event staff, up to a maximum of 80 room nights.

Hotels will agree to provide the event with a rebate of $10.00 USD per room night occupied by visitors assigned to the event room block during the period listed above, except the discounted staff rate rooms as defined above.

The headquarters hotel will agree to make Wi-Fi access and health facility services available to the management and staff of the event at no cost. The event will look favorably upon hotels offering this policy to all guests in the event's room block.

While the host city should identify facilities interested in being considered as the headquarters hotel after they have reviewed and agreed to these specifications, MNO Sports will negotiate and contract with local hotels directly.

D. PROMOTION AND PUBLICITY

The host city will undertake all efforts to publicize the event in advance to promote attendance. The promotion plan should combine advertising on local television and radio, in local websites, magazines, and newspapers, as well as additional promotion through the installation of street banners, outdoor advertising, and other mechanisms. MNO Sports will consider—but must approve all—proposals for media partnerships (e.g., the naming of one or more media outlets as **"the official television station, radio station, news site, etc. of 'The Big Street Sports Tournament'"**).

Please enclose letters of support and/or interest from media interested in participating as promotional partners for the event with your proposal, including commitments to provide advertising time or space. Host city websites will actively promote and prominently feature the Tournament at least ninety (90) days prior to the event through the last day of the program.

E. WELCOME SIGNAGE

The event will look favorably upon proposals that include welcome signage installed to greet inbound players, sponsors and special guests at airport locations, on street poles in major business districts and near headquarters hotels, and approaching the event site in high-visibility locations or on outdoor advertising billboards. Event sponsor identification may be included, following the guidelines discussed in Section F below. (*Note:* MNO Sports may, at its sole discretion, require inclusion of the event's national presenting or title sponsor(s) of the event in the design of all welcome signage wherever local sponsors are included.)

F. LOCAL SPONSOR PARTNERS

The Event maintains an impressive list of national and regional sponsors entitled to marketing and promotional rights at The Big Street Sports Tournament (see Section VIII for the roster as of the date indicated).

MNO Sports will consider—but must approve—any local sponsors and the package of entitlements proposed by the host city. The sponsors may provide either cash or value-in-kind products or services to the host city to offset the latter's expenses. Notwithstanding the above, MNO Sports maintains its rights to procure local sponsorships or value-in-kind arrangements at its sole discretion.

The host city will retain all revenues from local cash sponsorships from the agreements it generates, providing they are approved in advance by MNO Sports. All costs in fulfilling said sponsorships will be borne by the host city. The event is appreciative of value-in-kind deals provided by the host city that can supply additional value to the event. MNO Sports, however, cannot offer cash payments or commissions to the host city for such donated goods and/or services.

Notwithstanding the above, MNO Sports will not approve local sponsorship deals with companies that, in MNO's sole opinion, are competitive with the event's current or prospective business partners, as listed in Section VIII.

G. HOST CITY FEE

There is no fee required to submit a proposal for consideration as host city of The Big Street Sports Tournament. A $10,000 host city fee will be paid to MNO Sports by the selected host city, due upon execution of a letter agreement between the host city and MNO Sports. This fee is not refundable if the host city subsequently cancels its participation for any reason.

MNO Sports may waive the host city fee if, in its sole opinion, the host city is providing exceptional value in equipment, products, or services that will benefit the event beyond the minimum requirements of this Request for Proposal.

H. VOLUNTEER STAFFING

MNO Sports will provide all management and paid staff for the event. The host city will be required to provide approximately thirty (30) volunteer staff members per event day to work under the direction of MNO Sports for the proper, safe, and efficient operation of the event. The host city should identify how it will assist MNO Sports in the solicitation of volunteer staff. Volunteer staff members will receive an event cap and t-shirt for their use on-site and as a take-home memento. Meals and refreshments appropriate to the time of day will also be available to volunteer staff working full shifts.

I. FOOD VENDOR MANAGEMENT

The host city will be responsible for the identification of licensed, reliable, and experienced food vendors for the event site. MNO Sports will be entitled to a $75 fee per vendor per location. The host city may assess an additional fee to vendors to offset its own expenses.

J. KEY POINT OF CONTACT

The host city should identify a key staff person to serve as a high-level liaison between the local government and the Event Director. This key contact will interact directly with the municipal departments required to successfully stage the event, expedite all local permitting requirements, and ensure that the event complies with all applicable municipal ordinances, where appropriate.

K. AVAILABILITY OF EVENT EQUIPMENT AND SUPPLIES

The host city should identify any event equipment and services it will agree to make available to the event at no cost.

The following items are essential to the operation of the event, and their provision at no cost would significantly improve the chances of a successful bid. Please enter the quantity of items available on the attached questionnaire:

- Folding tables
- Folding chairs
- Staging platforms and/or risers
- Power generators or access to power sources
- Bleachers
- Portalettes
- Golf and utility carts
- Water trucks
- Forklifts
- Dumpsters
- Waste receptacles
- Ice and ice storage
- Tents and canopies
- Shuttle buses between player hotel and event site (may be municipal transit vehicles)

The recommendation of an appropriate, attractive, and highly desirable event site is among the most important considerations in preparing a successful event proposal. As previously discussed, it is a mutual objective to attract the largest local and in-bound audience possible for the event. Therefore, the ideal event site will showcase the unique aspects and culture of the host city, and will possess a combination of many of the following attributes:

- An area in or adjacent to, a normally high pedestrian traffic flow during the operating hours of the event;
- An area in or overlooking a landmark or nationally recognized buildings, scenery, skylines, or natural wonders;
- A flat, smooth, and well-maintained paved surface with sufficient drainage and contiguous space to accommodate the various playing surfaces and entertainment areas, plus safe pedestrian flow through all areas of the event;
- A player equipment drop-off location and visitor access to nearby free or reasonably priced parking and/or mass transportation;
- Visitor and participant access to on-site or nearby restroom facilities (or the ability to install portable restroom facilities provided by the host city at no cost to the event);
- Sufficient weight-load capacities to enable fully laden tractor-trailers to park and off-load at the event site (*Note:* Several decorated trailers will remain on the event site for the duration of the program.);
- Complete and unencumbered access for installation beginning Thursday afternoon at 5:00 p.m. and completion of dismantle by Monday morning at 8:00 a.m.;
- No rental charges, permit fees, or other financial obligation payable by the event to the city and/or private owner of the property;
- No broadcast origination fees or media restrictions for the event of live or taped telecasts or news coverage;
- Permission for the sale of event merchandise to the public with no additional charges levied against gross proceeds except for local and/or state or provincial sales taxes;
- No site-specific sponsor exclusivities that conflict with the business partners of the event as described in Section VIII.

VI. HOST CITY BENEFITS

- **Host City Designation**   The host city will be able to use its designation as **"Host City of the 2026 Big Street Sports Tournament"** in all advertising, promotions, and publicity prior to, during, and one year following the event, each such use subject to the approval of MNO Sports.
- **Use of Marks**   The host city will have the right to incorporate the logo of "The 2026 Big Street Sports Tournament" into all digital and printed advertising and promotional material, as well as in the production and distribution of premium items, such use subject to MNO Sports approval.
- **Promotional Opportunities**   The host city will have the opportunity to utilize the event to promote tourism, or in marketing campaigns undertaken by the local government and its agencies among both participants and visitors. Opportunities may feature the inclusion of a premium item in visiting player gift bags, city attraction and restaurant maps, discount codes and/or product samples delivered at check-in for visiting players, and the inclusion of a special promotional information in the player solicitation package sent to potential participants during the team application process, all such materials and use subject to MNO Sports approval.

The event organizer will promote the host city on **The Big Street Sports Tournament** web page at www.bigstreetsports.com, in banner advertising, pre-event publicity, and broadcast or streaming coverage of the event. All printed and electronic materials designed to promote the event will prominently feature the host city, including press releases, participant applications, and advertising.

- **Event Site Benefits**   The host city will receive significant and prominent recognition at the event site on signage boards located throughout the area and in scheduled public address announcements. The host city will receive a 10′ × 10′ tent on site for its own exhibition purposes for the duration of the event. Alternatively, the host city may utilize its own existing structure for such purposes, which may exceed the 10′ × 10′ footprint, subject to the approval of MNO Sports.

    The host city may enter one athlete or team in each amateur tournament event at no cost. This opportunity may be used for internal or promotional purposes, at the discretion of the host city.

- **Database Access**   MNO Sports will make the database of all tournament participants and MNO Sports-run sweepstakes entrants, if any, available to the host city for postevent marketing purposes, as permitted by law. The event organizer will make two one-hour appearances of five visiting street sports athletes available to the host city during the week of the event, for attendance at a city-run reception, hospital visits, or other opportunity to be mutually agreed upon.

VII. THE BIG STREET SPORTS TOURNAMENT PARTNERS

The Big Street Sports Tournament Partners
(Effective August 30, 2024, and subject to change)

The companies listed here are the national sponsors of The Big Street Sports Tournament and are entitled to exclusive promotional benefits in connection with the event. Additional national event sponsors may be confirmed by MNO Sports at any time without notice. The host city may seek to secure local sponsors in product categories other than those listed below, with the prior approval of MNO Sports:

SOFT DRINK COMPANY
ISOTONIC BEVERAGE COMPANY
BICYCLE COMPANY
IN-LINE SKATE COMPANY
SKATE WHEEL COMPANY
SKATEBOARD COMPANY
SAFETY EQUIPMENT COMPANY
FIRST AID SUPPLIES COMPANY
QUICK SERVICE RESTAURANT COMPANY
MOBILE PHONE COMPANY

Note: In an actual RFP, the real names of sponsor companies would appear above.

VIII. THE BIG STREET SPORTS TOURNAMENT

Request for Proposal Response Form

Prospective host cities are invited to prepare their proposal in any format desired, delivered electronically to Nathaniel Jacobs at njacobs@mnosports.com. A fully completed Request for Proposal Response Form should be included as the first section of the submitted document.

Please submit all applicable forms and accompanying materials by November 15, 2024. Late submissions may not be reviewed or acknowledged.

I. CONTACT INFORMATION:

HOST CITY: _____

APPLYING ENTITY (E.G., CVB, SPORTS COMMISSION):

_____

PRIMARY CONTACT: _____

TITLE: _____

ADDRESS: _____

_____

TELEPHONE: _____ FAX: _____

E-MAIL: _____

Weekend(s) applied for:

1st Choice: _____

2nd Choice: _____

The applying city agrees to all terms as outlined in the bid specifications for **The 2026 Big Street Sports Tournament** _____ YES _____NO

(If "no," please attach a detailed description of exceptions)

Are there other city festivals or events scheduled on the same weekend(s), or on the weekends immediately prior to or following these dates? _____YES_____ NO

(If "yes," please note or attach further information)

II. PROPOSED EVENT SITE

SITE NAME: _____

SITE OWNER: _____

EVENT SITE CONTACT NAME: _____

CONTACT PHONE: _____E-MAIL: _____

Please submit a description of how the proposed event site fulfills the "Ideal Event Site" characteristics described in this RFP (include photos, floorplans, and elevations, as available):

SEATING CAPACITY: _____

TAXES AND FEES ON SALES OF TICKETS: _____

LABOR AND UNION EXCLUSIVITIES: _____

HOURLY LABOR RATES (including benefits and management fees):

Ushers: _____

Security: _____

Electricians: _____

Carpenters: _____

Riggers: _____

CATERING EXCLUSIVITIES: _____

CONCESSIONS EXCLUSIVITIES: _____

MERCHANDISE EXCLUSIVITIES: _____

OTHER RESTRICTIONS: _____

III. HOTEL

Hotels participating in the bidding process must hold space on a first-option basis until the determination of a host city is made. Please complete one hotel form for each property participating in the bid.

HOTEL NAME: _____

TOTAL # ROOMS: _____

TOTAL HELD FOR EVENT ON A FIRST-OPTION BASIS: _____

PROPOSED ROOMRATES:SINGLE:_____DBL/DBL:_____

TAX RATES ON SLEEPING ROOMS: _____

YEAR OF LAST SLEEPING ROOM RENOVATION: _____

YEAR OF LAST PUBLIC/FUNCTION SPACE RENOVATION: _____

If selected, the hotel agrees to provide function space in the quantity, and as described in this RFP
_____YES_____NO

Please attach description of any exceptions or exclusions

HOTEL CONTACT NAME/TITLE: _____

PHONE: _____FAX: _____

E-MAIL: _____

CONTACT SIGNATURE: _____

IV. HOST CITY

CITY SERVICES LIAISON: _____

TITLE AND PHONE: _____

CONVENTION & VISITORS BUREAU CONTACT: _____

TITLE AND PHONE: _____

AVAILABILITY OF EVENT RESOURCES (SEE SECTION V.(K)).

Item	# Available	Comments (e.g., size)
Folding tables	_____	
Folding chairs	_____	
Staging and/or risers	_____	
Power generators/access to power	_____	
Bleachers	_____	
Portalettes	_____	
Golf and utility carts	_____	
Water trucks	_____	
Forklifts	_____	
Dumpsters	_____	
Waste receptacles	_____	
Ice and ice storage	_____	
Tents and canopies	_____	
Shuttle buses	_____	

REGIONAL POPULATION: _____

AVERAGE HOUSEHOLD INCOME: _____

EFFECTIVE STATE AND LOCAL SALES TAXES: _____

ADDITIONAL NON–HOTEL-RELATED TAXES: _____

Proposed Media Partners:

Please enclose letters of interest or support

PRINT: _____

TELEVISION: _____

RADIO: _____

OTHER: _____

SOURCE OF VOLUNTEER POOL: _____

APPENDIX 4

Request for Proposal Evaluation Form

**Sports Organization
Event Name**

Selection Criteria	CITY A	CITY B	CITY C	CITY D
Contact Name and Title	_____	_____	_____	_____
Contact Phone	_____	_____	_____	_____
Contact Email				
Agree to All Bid Specifications (Yes/No)	_____	_____	_____	_____
Exceptions:	_____	_____	_____	_____
	_____	_____	_____	_____
Other Events Scheduled within Time Period	_____	_____	_____	_____
Event Site Information:	_____	_____	_____	_____
Name of Event Site	_____	_____	_____	_____
Location of Event Site	_____	_____	_____	_____
Size or Seating Capacity	_____	_____	_____	_____
Contact Name and Phone	_____	_____	_____	_____
Meets Ideal Event Site Requirements? (Yes/No)	_____	_____	_____	_____
Exceptions:	_____	_____	_____	_____
	_____	_____	_____	_____
Effective Taxes on Ticket Sales	_____	_____	_____	_____
Other Fees on Ticket Sales	_____	_____	_____	_____
Labor and Union Exclusivities	_____	_____	_____	_____

Selection Criteria	CITY A	CITY B	CITY C	CITY D
Hourly Rates (incl. Benefits and Management Fees)	___	___	___	___
Ushers	___	___	___	___
Security	___	___	___	___
Electricians	___	___	___	___
Carpenters	___	___	___	___
Riggers	___	___	___	___
Catering Exclusivity?	___	___	___	___
Merchandise Exclusivity?	___	___	___	___
Concessions Exclusivity?	___	___	___	___

Hotels:

	CITY A	CITY B	CITY C	CITY D
Hotel Name (# Rooms)	___	___	___	___
Overflow Hotel (# Rooms)	___	___	___	___
Room Rates	___	___	___	___
Tax Rate on Sleeping Rooms	___	___	___	___
Will Hotels Meet Minimum Requirements? (Yes/No)	___	___	___	___
Exceptions:	___	___	___	___
	___	___	___	___

Host City:

	CITY A	CITY B	CITY C	CITY D
Will Host City Provide Support Required (Yes/No)	___	___	___	___
Exceptions:	___	___	___	___
	___	___	___	___
Size of Market (Population)	___	___	___	___
Average Household Income	___	___	___	___
State and Local Sales Taxes	___	___	___	___
Letters of Support Included	___	___	___	___
Additional Pertinent Information	___	___	___	___
	___	___	___	___
	___	___	___	___
Evaluator Comments	___	___	___	___

APPENDIX 5

Sample Facility Event License Agreement

This Facility Event License Agreement is provided for illustrative purposes only, and is an abbreviated, representative composite inspired by a variety of actual contracts. This document is not intended for use as a legal instrument. Additional legal details may appear in an actual Facility Event License Agreement. Event organizers and facilities should retain the services of competent and experienced legal counsel for the process of creating, negotiating, and agreeing to any contract, including a Facility Event License Agreement. The words, passages, and figures in italics denote inclusions of details for a fictional event to better illustrate the appearance of a typical Facility Event License Agreement.

* * *

XYZ ENTERTAINMENT CENTER EVENT LICENSE AGREEMENT

This agreement (the "Agreement"), made and entered into on this _____ day of _____, 20 __, by and between *XYZ Sports & Entertainment, Inc.* ("XYZ"), *a Florida* corporation, and hereinafter referred to as **Licensor**, and for the use of *XYZ Center (the "Center")*:

JKL Sports Events, Ltd.
123 S.W. Fifth Avenue
Cityview, FL 30000
954-000-0000 (Tel); 954-000-0001 (Fax)
Harold Matthews, President

Hereinafter referred to as **Licensee**.
The Licensor and Licensee hereby agree as follows:

1. EVENT (the "Event")

Event Name/Description: _____

Move-In/Rehearsal Day(s): _____

Event/Performance Days & Times: _____

Move-Out Day(s): _____

Ticket Prices: _____

Estimated Gross Potential: _____

Move-in, Rehearsal, Event and Move-Out days shall collectively be referred to as the "License Period." Use of *XYZ Center* in excess of the time described herein may result in additional charges to the Licensee.

2. LICENSE FEES

(a) The Licensee agrees to pay to the Licensor the following License Fees (the "License Fees"):
   1. Basic License Fee: *$30,000*
   2. All other fees referenced in this Agreement, including, but not limited to, the Television Origination Fee and Souvenir Merchandise Fee;
   3. All such additional fees, charges, and other amounts payable by the Licensee, including, but not limited to, event staff service charges, food and beverage service charges, ticket sales commissions, cleaning, maintenance, and conversion charges.

(b) The Licensee agrees to pay all taxes levied on the License Fees or as a result of the Licensee's use of the *Center* including, but not limited to, admission taxes, amusement taxes, and sales taxes on the ticket price. The Licensee agrees to pay *$15,000* as a nonrefundable license deposit. The deposit is due and payable upon execution of this Agreement.

(c) The Licensee will be responsible for paying in full the amount of the Licensor's actual costs on settlement in accordance with the provisions herein. The Licensor will, upon request, provide the Licensee with estimates of projected Event costs. Such estimates are reasonable attempts at identifying costs made in good faith by the Licensor based on information provided by the Licensee and are not binding on the Licensor.

(d) The License Fee has been determined based on the Ticket Prices and Estimated Gross Potential as defined above. In the event that the Actual Gross exceeds the Estimated Gross Potential, the License Fee shall increase by *0.5%* for each *1.0%* positive difference between the Estimated Gross Potential and the Actual Gross. Regardless of the Actual Gross, the License Fee will not be decreased.

3. LICENSE AREA

(a) The Licensor hereby agrees to grant to the Licensee the nonexclusive right to occupy and use the following areas (the "Licensed Areas") of the *Center* during the License Period: *the Center seating bowl, concourses, locker rooms, media facilities, and all other non-office spaces in the Center*.

(b) No other areas shall be occupied by the Licensee unless authorized in advance in writing by the Licensor. The Licensor reserves the right to license or use all areas of the *Center* not expressly assigned to the Licensee during the License Period for any purpose whatsoever. The Licensee acknowledges that the *Center* or various parts thereof may or will be used for the installation, hosting, and removal of other activities or events. It may be necessary for the use of the *Center*, including, without limitation, all common areas, to be shared by the Licensee and others as designated by the Licensor. The Licensor shall have the authority to establish the schedule for the use and availability of such services and accommodations.

(c) The Licensee shall use the Licensed Areas solely for the purpose of preparing for and presenting the Event during the License Period. The Licensee will not permit the use of the Licensed Areas or any part thereof for any other Event, business, or purpose.

(d) The Licensor shall have the right to the free access of any and all areas of the *Center* including, but not limited to, the Licensed Areas at all times during the License Period.

4. SERVICES TO BE PROVIDED BY THE LICENSOR

(a) The Licensor shall provide lighting, heating, air conditioning, and water, as installed at the time of this agreement, and at such times and in such amounts as shall be necessary in the Licensor's sole opinion acting reasonably, for the comfortable use and occupancy of the *Center*.

(b) The Licensor will provide equipment, staffing, or services for this Event at its discretion, taking into consideration Event information provided by Licensee and at the Licensee's sole cost. Such staffing and services include, but are not limited to, ushers, ticket takers, guest service hosts, security, police, ticket sellers, conversion crew, cleaning staff, carpenter(s), laborers, electrician(s), riggers, and emergency medical personnel. The Licensor retains the right to determine the appropriate number of personnel necessary to properly staff the *Center* and protect the public. All personnel provided by the Licensor shall remain employees of the Licensor and will be under the Licensor's direct supervision.

(c) All utilities, including, but not limited to, electricity, water, gas, telecommunications, data and Internet service, and other equipment and services needed by the Licensee, must be ordered through the Licensor.

5. EVENT TICKETS

(a) The Licensee acknowledges that the Licensor has an exclusive agreement with *Ticket Service, Inc. ("TS")*, a computerized ticket service company, whereby the Licensor/TS will jointly act as exclusive agents and be responsible for maintaining control over the inventory, distribution, and sale of all tickets for the Event through the Licensor's Box Office and TS outlets, unless otherwise agreed to in writing by the Licensor.

(b) Regardless of whether tickets will be sold on a reserved-seat or general-admission basis, the number of tickets printed shall not exceed the maximum capacity of the *Center*, which the Licensor shall determine in its sole discretion.

(c) The Licensor shall at all times maintain control and direction of the ticket office, ticket personnel, ticket sales, and will call window operations.

(d) The Licensee acknowledges that ticket sales are subject to service charges payable to TS and/or the Licensor in addition to the basic ticket price.

(e) The Licensee shall pay to the Licensor all applicable credit card service charges, based on gross credit card revenues, including applicable taxes, of *three percent (3.0%)*.

(f) Following the Event, the Licensor shall provide to the Licensee a full report of ticket sales by the Licensor/TS for the Event, and prepare the Preliminary Settlement Summary. The Licensor shall then pay to the Licensee the proceeds of all tickets sold by the Licensor/TS, less the following amounts:

   i.   The total of all applicable taxes, service charges, and Facility Usage Fees (the latter will be deducted from gross ticket proceeds at a rate of $0.50 per ticket);

   ii. The total identified by the Licensor as owing pursuant to this Agreement, in accordance with the Preliminary Settlement Summary. To the extent that ticket sales proceeds can be applied in full against the payment obligations of the Licensee to the Licensor hereunder, those obligations shall be deemed to have been satisfied. The Licensee shall submit payment for obligations of the Licensee not so satisfied to the Licensor at the completion of the Event.

(g) The Licensor shall provide to the Licensee a Final Settlement Summary thirty (30) days after the final date of the Event indicating any adjustments due to either party to this Agreement.

6. COMPLIMENTARY TICKETS AND PASSES

The Licensee shall provide to the Licensor *sixty (60)* complimentary tickets for the event, at least fifty percent (50%) of which will be located in prime seating areas, the value of which shall not be included as part of the proceeds from ticket sales.

7. REFUNDS

(a) As a result of cancellation or postponement of the Event, TS and the Licensor shall refund the ticket price of any unused tickets, and may, in accordance with TS and/or the Licensor's policy, refund applicable service charges and/or handling fees at the point of purchase.

(b) In the event that part of the Event is cancelled or postponed, Licensor may in its sole discretion determine what, if any, portion of the ticket price shall be refunded.

(c)   Any amounts forwarded to the Licensee by the Licensor with respect to ticket sales shall be returned immediately to the Licensor after the Event has been cancelled or postponed.

(d)   The Licensor shall retain the right to make ticket refunds for cause or maintaining the public faith. This right shall include, but is not limited to, seats blocked by equipment of the Licensee, its broadcasting partners or sponsors, when exchange for comparable locations is not possible. Refunds will not be made if tickets for such seats were sold clearly marked for sale at a discounted price, and clearly marked as "Obstructed View" seats. If the Event is cancelled, the Licensee shall permit the Licensor to reimburse any amount that ticket holders paid for tickets. The Licensee shall pay the licensor a mutually agreed on ticket handling charge on tickets sold up to the time of cancellation as compensation for the task of refunding tickets to the cancelled Event, except if cancellation was caused by a force majeure, as described in this Agreement.

8. MERCHANDISE AND PROGRAM SALES

(a)   The Licensee or the Licensee's designated agent(s) shall have the exclusive right to provide souvenir merchandise and programs to the Licensor for sale by the Licensor on a consignment basis during the Event on behalf of the Licensee.

(b)   The Licensee shall not sell, authorize, or permit the sale of any souvenir merchandise and/or programs during the License Period within a one (1) mile radius of the outside of the *Center*.

(c)   At the conclusion of the Event, the Licensor shall return all the unsold souvenir merchandise and programs provided by the Licensee or the Licensee's designated agent(s). The Licensor shall retain a commission of 20% of Net Revenues on merchandise and program sales, less all applicable taxes and credit card commissions.

(d)   The numbers and locations of the merchandise sales areas in the *Center* for use of the Licensee or the Licensee's designated agent(s) will be at the sole determination of Licensor.

(e)   Notwithstanding Section 5(a) above, the Licensor retains the exclusive right to operate and maintain its concessions, store, and concourse merchandise kiosks during the Event to sell souvenir merchandise and programs not related to the Event, and without any payment due to the Licensee.

9. ADVERTISING AND SPONSORSHIP

(a)   The Licensor retains the exclusive right to conduct, sell, and retain all revenues from all advertising and promotion whatsoever in and about the *Center* including, without limitation, on the public address system, video screens, main scoreboard, auxiliary scoreboards, LED signage, other electronic and display signage, posters, banners, and promotional displays during the Event and without approval by or payment to the Licensee. The Licensee shall not obstruct or cover any such advertising or promotion.

(b)   The Licensee shall not display or grant to Event sponsor(s) or others any right to display advertising at the *Center* without the prior written consent of the Licensor, and which consent may be withheld for any reason.

(c)   The Licensor consents to and grants the Licensee a limited license to use the logo and name *XYZ Center*, as applicable, in Licensor's approved typeface as the site designation for the Event in advertising and other material promoting the Event. All such usage shall be subject to the Licensor's prior written approval and shall be accompanied by applicable trademark notifications as designated by the Licensor.

(d)   The Licensee shall not permit the distribution of any free samples or promotional merchandise, programs, food, beverages, or printed material of any kind at the *Center* during the Term without the prior written consent of the Licensor, which consent may be withheld in the Licensor's sole discretion.

10. VIDEO AND/OR AUDIO REPRODUCTION

Licensee and Licensor hereby agree that there shall be no electronic media exploitation of the Event whatsoever without the prior written permission of the Licensee. The term "electronic media exploitation" shall be defined as the exploitation of the Event, whether on a live, delayed, or other basis, through any means of signal distribution including, but not limited to: broadcast, cable, satellite, streaming, or pay-per-view television, or over-the-air broadcast or satellite radio.

11. LABOR AGREEMENTS

Licensee shall not perform any work or employ any personnel in connection with the Event except if such work or employment conforms to labor agreements to which the Licensor or its contractors are a party. The Licensor may deny access to the *Center* to any person whose admittance could result in a violation of any such labor agreement.

12. FOOD AND BEVERAGE CATERING SERVICE

The Licensor reserves the exclusive right to provide all food, beverage, and catering service outlets within the *Center* including alcoholic and other beverages, and to retain all revenue derived therefrom.

13. INSURANCE, INDEMNIFICATION, AND DAMAGES

(a)   The Licensee agrees to assume, defend, indemnify, protect, and hold harmless the Licensor, and its affiliates, shareholders, officers, and employees against any and all claims, or causes of action arising or resulting: (i) from the use, occupancy, or licensing of the *Center* by the Licensee, its contractors, subcontractors, exhibitors, or other invitees or persons attending the Event; or (ii) out of any personal injury or property damage occurring in or upon the *Center* due to any contravention of the provisions of the License, the said rules and regulations, or any applicable laws, rules, regulations, or orders of any governmental agency having jurisdiction over the *Center*, or due to any negligence or willful act by the Licensee or those for whom the Licensee is in law responsible.

(b)   The Licensee shall obtain and maintain, at its own cost and expense, for the duration of the License Period, a Comprehensive Public Liability and Property Damage Insurance policy along with the required Workers' Compensation, Automobile Liability and Umbrella Liability coverages. A certificate of insurance shall be provided to the Licensor a minimum of thirty (30) days prior to the starting date of the Event. The Licensee shall name the Licensor and its respective shareholders and officers as additional named insureds on the insurance policy. Such insurance shall be provided by a comprehensive general liability insurance policy including personal injury, contractual liability, cross liability, and occurrence property damage with a combined single limit of at least $5,000,000 for each occurrence.

(c)   The Licensee shall not make any alterations of any kind to the *Center* without the prior written consent of the Licensor, which consent may be withheld in the Licensor's sole discretion. The Licensee agrees that if the *Center* is damaged by the act, default, or negligence of the Licensee, or those persons for whom the Licensee is responsible in law, or any person admitted to the *Center* by the Licensee or Licensee's agents, then the Licensee shall pay to the Licensor upon demand such reasonable sums as shall be necessary to restore the *Center* to its original condition.

14. FORCE MAJEURE

None of the parties shall be in breach of this Agreement if the performance by that party of any of its obligations hereunder is prevented or preempted because of an Act of God, accident, fire, labor dispute, riot or civil commotion, act of public enemy, governmental act, or any other reason beyond the control of that party. In any such event, this License shall terminate and the Licensee and the Licensor shall each only be responsible for their own expenses. The Licensee hereby waives any claim against the Licensor for damages or compensation by reason of such termination.

15. OBSERVANCE OF LAW AND PUBLIC SAFETY

(a)   The Licensee, its employees, agents, and all other persons connected with its use of the *Center* shall comply with all laws, statutes, regulations (including, but not limited to, police and fire and regulations and occupational health and safety regulations), and all requirements of governmental and regulatory bodies.

(b) The Licensee will obtain all necessary permits, licenses, and approvals relating to the use of and the conduct of the Event in the Licensed Areas and provide the Licensor with satisfactory evidence of the licenses and approvals.

(c) The Licensee will obtain at its expense the right to use any patented, trademarked, or copyrighted materials, dramatic rights, or performance rights used in the conduct of the Event.

(d) The Licensee agrees that it shall not use any pyrotechnic devices without the prior written consent of the Licensor, which consent may be withheld in the Licensor's sole discretion. If such consent is granted, the Licensee shall comply with all laws, rules, regulations, criteria, and policies of all federal, state, and municipal authorities or agencies applicable thereto. The Licensee shall deliver all supporting documentation confirming the Licensee's compliance with the above requirements at least fifteen (15) days prior to the first performance of the Event.

(e) The Licensor reserves the right to make announcements in the interest of public safety, to provide safety information to attendees, and, in coordination with Licensee, to announce and otherwise promote upcoming events at the *Center* during the Event.

16. TERMINATION

(a) If the Licensee is adjudicated bankrupt, or adjudged to be insolvent, or a receiver or trustee of the Licensee's property and affairs is appointed, or the Licensee is in default of any of its obligations under this Agreement or pursuant hereto, then this license may at the option of the Licensor be cancelled by delivering to the Licensee notice to that effect.

(b) Upon any termination, the Licensee shall immediately pay to Licensor the License Fees as liquidated damages, together with all costs, losses, expenses, and damages, as determined by the Licensor. Deposits and payments received are nonrefundable in all instances including, but not limited to, a termination.

THE LICENSOR:

XYZ SPORTS & ENTERTAINMENT, INC.

By: _____

    Name: _____

    Title: _____

THE LICENSEE:

JKL SPORTS EVENTS, LTD.

By: _____

    Name: _____

    Title: _____

APPENDIX 6

Facility Selection Survey Form (Simplified)

PROPOSED EVENT: _____

Date(s)/Time(s): _____

Load-in Date(s): _____

Load-out Date(s): _____

FACILITY: _____

Facility Address: _____

_____

Key Contact: _____

Title: _____

Phone: _____

Email: _____

Date Availability for Load-in: _____

Event Date(s): _____

Date Availability for Load-out: _____

Available Seating by Scale/Level: _____

Total Manifest: _____

Manifest by Break: **Section:** _____   Tickets: _____

_____   Tickets: _____

_____   Tickets: _____

_____   Tickets: _____

_____   Tickets: _____

Total ADA Seating Included Above: _____

Temporary Seat/Build-Out Options? _____

RENTAL COSTS/TERMS: _____

Tax Rate on Tickets: _____

Capital Replacement Fees on Tickets: _____ paid by _____

Other Service Fees on Tickets: _____ paid by _____

Credit Card Processing Rate: _____

Other Box Office Fees: _____

Merchandise Contact: _____

Merchandise Sales Exclusivity? _____ Terms: _____

Concessionaire/Caterer Contact: _____

Concessionaire/Caterer Exclusivity? _____

Food/Soft Drink/Beer Exclusivity? _____

Event Promotion Services: _____

HOURLY LABOR RATES:

Electricians: _____ Union: _____

Carpenters: _____ Union: _____

Riggers: _____ Union: _____

Stagehands: _____ Union: _____

Decorators: _____ Union: _____

Security: _____ Union: _____

FOH: _____ Union: _____

Medical: _____

Scoreboard/Video Crew: _____

Estimated Conversion/Cleaning Costs: _____

FACILITY NOTES:

Locker Rooms: _____

Dressing Rooms: _____

Marshaling and Storage Areas: _____

Scoreboard/Videoboard/Other Displays: _____

Media Facilities: _____

Parking Facilities: _____

Concourse Information Displays: _____

Exterior Electronic Signage/Marquees: _____

BROADCASTING NOTES:

Number of Loading Docks: _____

Broadcast Truck Docks or Compound(s): _____

Permanent Camera Positions and Baskets: _____

_____

Broadcast Booths for TV/Streaming/Radio/Other: _____

Broadcast Origination Fees? _____

CONNECTIVITY:

Available Wi-Fi Capability and Available Fiber Optic Capacity: _____

Phone/Internet Vendor: _____

Costs: _____

AVAILABLE EQUIPMENT (quantity/cost):

Tables: _____ Tablecloths: _____

Chairs: _____ Risers: _____

Forklifts: _____ Barriers: _____

Pipe and Drape (lgt/ht/color): _____

Crowd Barriers (lgt/type): _____

Other: _____

_____

_____

SPONSOR EXCLUSIVITIES AND SIGNAGE RESTRICTIONS:

_____

_____

_____

_____

_____

_____

HOSPITALITY OPTIONS: _____

_____

_____

OTHER NOTES: _____

_____

_____

APPENDIX 7

Sample Sports Event Sponsorship Deck

D.E.F. Sports & Entertainment

An Introduction to
SPORTSFEST 2025

A Mid-States Regional Multi-Sport Festival
presented to
Mid-States Car Dealers Association

August 2024

An Introduction to Sportsfest 2025

Table of Contents

I. SportsFest—An Overview

Mid-summer weekends in the Mid-States Region changed forever with the area's first test drive of Sports-Fest in 1998.

SportsFest has annually provided the region's children and their families with an exciting, highly anticipated weekend of wholesome fun and friendly competition enveloped in a festival atmosphere offering great entertainment, fantastic local food, and a midway filled with interactive exhibits, intriguing displays, thrilling rides, and involving activities.

More than just a sports festival, SportsFest is a celebration of our region's diverse cultural heritage, our active lifestyle, and our vibrant business community.

More than 50,000 active, fun-seeking families are expected to **GET INTO IT** by participating in SportsFest 2025, returning to enjoy their favorite sports events, plus a host of new programs, activities, and entertainment.

SportsFest is a favorite location for local media and a magnet for dozens of live remote broadcasts throughout the weekend. The event also generates significant social media interest coverage throughout the Mid-States Region.

SportsFest provides participating businesses with outstanding opportunities to reach a large number of the area's active consumers, introduce new products, host important customers, and demonstrate their support of community recreation programs. The Mid-States Regional Car Dealers Association (**MSCDA**) can drive qualified buyers into its members' showrooms, conduct test drives right on the event site, and explore limitless options for a wide variety of promotional opportunities at the Mid-States Region's most anticipated sports and active lifestyle festival.

The net operating proceeds of SportsFest 2025 will be donated to the Mid-States Region Sports Council for the redevelopment of recreational facilities, the acquisition of new sports equipment, and funding of physical fitness programs for the area's disadvantaged youth.

SportsFest 2025. . .

. . . **GET INTO IT!**

SportsFest was founded by D.E.F. Sports & Entertainment, a Mid-States Region corporation that specializes in the organization and management of sports tournaments and events for youth. D.E.F. Sports & Entertainment is also the producer of the Mid-States Region Invitational and the Grain City Wheat Festival.

II. INTRODUCTION

The appeal of SportsFest has grown steadily since its inaugural model rolled out in 1998. Now in its 26th edition, SportsFest will expand to over 10 acres of the Old Fairgrounds, featuring full tournament competition in nine team and individual sports.

Our goal is to attract more than 60,000 participants in 2025, more than triple the number of attendees of the inaugural year. Preliminary attendance for the recently completed SportsFest 2024 is projected to reach 55,000.

Most recent market research indicates:

94% of attendees intended to return to SportsFest the next year

87% rated their experience at SportsFest good to excellent

74% reported visiting the Hometown Market Midway

62% stated they expected to patronize sponsors of SportsFest

95% attended with other family members or friends

73% said they would return with more or the same number of family members or friends next year

78% of families have school-age children involved in one or more organized sports activities

45% of families have school-age children involved in two or more organized sports activities

Of attendees surveyed:

71% are 18+ years of age

58% are between 18 and 45 years of age

68% have a household income of more than $75,000 per year

84% have completed high school

63% have completed college

Source: Intercept surveys conducted during SportsFest 2023. Additional statistics and background are available upon request.

III. SportsFest 2025—Why Everyone Is "Getting Into It!"

SportsFest 2025 will combine proven fan favorites with attractions and programming that are totally new for its biggest year yet. There will be more to see, more to do, and more to enjoy than ever before! **Admission is free**. Tournament participation requires a registration fee to cover uniform t-shirts and other competition expenses.

This year's schedule includes nine sports tournaments for all age groups:

1. The Plainside Journal Baseball Classic
2. The Pyne Brothers Department Store Softball Tournament
3. The L&M Garden Center Field Hockey Championships*
4. Basketball*
5. Flag Football
6. P.B.F. Shoes Track & Field Meet
7. Shuffleboard*
8. Archery*
9. *Freestyle Skateboarding (New for 2025)**

Plus . . .

- All-age clinics for all nine featured sports
- An expanded 350-seat multivendor food pavilion, presented by FF Supermarkets
- The Hometown Market Midway
- The KMMM-FM Radio Main Stage
- The Angel's Cola Entertainment Band Shell
- Three additional entertainment stages
- The Bob's Burgers Kid Zone
- The Mid-States Region Sports Hall of Fame Traveling Exhibit
- The SportsFest Country Store
- . . .and more!

Includes paralympic competition.

IV. EVENT SCHEDULE

The 2025 edition of SportsFest will be held on the weekend of July 25–27. For our SportsFest partners and their guests, the fun will start right away!

Friday, July 25: 3 P.M. to 10 P.M.

3 P.M. Corporate Challenge   SportsFest sponsor companies may participate in our Corporate Challenge Ironman Tournament at no charge. Each company may register a team of up to 20 participants to vie for Mid-States Region dominance, competing in skills competitions in each of our nine featured sports areas. The event site is open exclusively to all sponsor-company employees and their guests.

5 P.M. Grand Opening   The public is officially welcomed to the event site when our 2025 SportsFest Grand Marshal arrives in a procession of **MSCDA**-provided convertibles to cut the "starting line" ribbon. Guests enjoy entertainment throughout SportsFest as they explore our 10 acres of sports and activity areas.

6 P.M. Mid-States Regional Media Challenge   Reporters and social media influencers compete for bragging rights in skills competitions within each of our nine featured sports areas, streaming live remotes and covering their stories from inside the dugouts and on the sidelines.

7 P.M. Grand Opening BBQ Celebration, presented by Angel's Cola   The Mid-States Region's gastronomical event of the summer! Spread out the picnic blanket as you settle down to enjoy pit barbecue, ribs, chicken, roasted corn and local vegetables, fresh hearth-baked bread, ice cream, and apple pie with thousands of your potential customers, neighbors, friends, and family. While you eat, watch featured musical entertainment on the nearby KMMM-FM Radio Main Stage. Frisbees and beach balls optional!

Saturday, July 26: 8 A.M.–10 P.M.

8 A.M. Let the Fun Begin!   Mid-States Regional athletes of all ages begin competing in nine sports—baseball, softball, field hockey, basketball, flag football, track & field, shuffleboard, archery, and freestyle skateboarding.

Because competitors and their ardent supporters are always hungry, our Food Pavilion, presented by FF Supermarkets, opens with limited breakfast and coffee service at 7 A.M.

9 A.M. All Entertainment and Activity Areas Open   There is truly something for everyone at SportsFest 2025!

Before and after checking out all the sports event action, guests will be able to explore the many products and services offered by our world-class sponsors at the **Hometown Market Midway**. The increasingly popular Midway is an outstanding opportunity for the **MSCDA** and each of our participating companies to meet thousands of SportsFest participants and attendees first hand, to demonstrate innovative models, products, and services, and to develop new customers!

Entertainment will abound at SportsFest 2025 with featured performers at the **KMMM-FM Radio Main Stage** and the **Angel's Cola Band Shell**, as well as **three additional entertainment stages** located throughout the event. Whether your interest is old-time rock and roll, EDM, hip-hop, country western, jazz, pop, blues or bluegrass, SportsFest 2025 has become almost as much a showcase of local musical artists as it is of athletics and regional businesses. Don't be surprised to see your local high school band suddenly march across the Old Fairgrounds to a thundering cadence of drums and horns!

Kids from 5 to 12 are welcome to discover **Bob's Burgers Kid Zone**, a supervised activity center filled with safe play opportunities evocative of each of SportsFest 2025's nine featured sports. Parents can relax with a cup of Bob's famous coffee while their children enjoy either structured games or free play, inflatable bounces, and arts and crafts stations. Each young visitor receives a participant's gold medal, courtesy of Bob's Burgers.

Every area athlete will want to visit the **Mid-States Region Sports Hall of Fame Traveling Exhibit**, an inspirational exploration of the rich sports heritage of our communities. Four generations of trophies, memorabilia, and photographs of great moments in Mid-States sports are sources of great local pride—as are the achievements and memorabilia on display of Mid-States alumni in college and professional athletics throughout the world!

A wide range of delicious food will be available at our multivendor **Food Pavilion, presented by FF Supermarkets**. From burgers and wings to grilled sandwiches and healthful salads, the Pavilion will offer delights to suit the most discriminating palate. Although most SportsFest guests enjoy eating under the sun—or on the run—the dining area under the Pavilion tent has been expanded to accommodate those wishing to consume their meals in the shade and at a more leisurely pace.

Guests will shop for official SportsFest merchandise, local crafts, and take-home confections at the **SportsFest Country Store**. Concessionaires will also be on hand to offer sundries including, batteries, sunscreen, sunglasses, and other items to make the day at SportsFest that much more memorable and enjoyable.

11 A.M. All-Age Clinics Begin   You're never too old and never too young to learn the rules of the game and get pointers from our region's accomplished athletes in all nine featured sports at the Sports Clinic attraction. Forty-minute sports clinics for a range of age groups are offered every hour on the hour until the evening's events at 6 P.M.

1 P.M. Picnic on the Green, presented by Angel's Cola   Bring your blanket for a trip back to a simpler time. Enjoy a five-cent glass of Angel's Cola as the Mid-States All-Star Brass Band plays a tribute to the music of the early 20th century at the Angel's Cola Band Shell. Prizes will be awarded for the best costumes!

6 P.M. Mid-States Region Pasta Cook-off, benefiting Starlight Foundation   Replenish yourself after a full weekend of watching or playing in athletic competition at SportsFest's nowfamous pasta feast! Bring the whole family for heaping bowls of salad, spaghetti, meatballs and sauce, garlic bread, and other treats. Tickets are $10 for adults and $5 for kids, with proceeds benefiting the Mid-States Region chapter of the Starlight Foundation. Save room for dessert!

7 P.M. Mid-States Region Fruit Pie Bake-off, benefiting Youth Sports   Who bakes the best fruit pies in the Mid-States Region? You be the judge, and then destroy the evidence! Proceeds benefit our community's youth recreation programs.

8 P.M. Headline Concert at KMMM-FM Radio Main Stage   A top-name musical artist (to be announced in late Winter 2024) will round out a full day of fun. Past performers have included: *Cheryl Byrd*, *Second Ear*, *Cryptic Message*, and *Two for Holding*.

Sunday, July 27: 9 A.M.–9 P.M.

9 A.M. Let the Fun Continue!   Competition in all nine sports—baseball, softball, field hockey, basketball, flag football, track & field, shuffleboard, archery, and freestyle skateboarding continues.

9 A.M. All Entertainment and Activity Areas Open

11 A.M. All-Age Clinics Begin   Forty-minute sports clinics for various age groups are offered every hour on the hour until 5 p.m., with "elite" clinics available for more seasoned athletes at 1 p.m. and 3 p.m.

7 P.M. SportsFest 2025 Parade of Athletes & Medal Ceremonies   Cheer on all of your SportsFest 2025 neighbors, family and friends. All registered tournament participants are welcome to march to the KMMM-FM Main Stage for a salute to the athletes and the presentation of medals. Everyone who participated in the nine featured competitive tournaments will be recognized.

8 P.M. SportsFest 2025 Ice Cream Social, benefiting the Mid-States Shelter Relax after the pomp and pageantry of the medal ceremonies at the SportsFest Ice Cream Social, a place to greet your friends and meet new ones. The $3.00 sundae buffet, with do-it-yourself toppings, benefits the Mid-States Shelter. Take your sundae to your favorite location at SportsFest for the excitement at 9:00 p.m.!

9 P.M. SportsFest 2025 Grand Finale Fireworks Spectacular Tens of thousands of Mid-States Region citizens and guests will enjoy a spectacular fireworks extravaganza visible for miles around, set to a sports theme soundtrack broadcast on KMMM-FM radio. When the show is over and the smoke clears, you will wonder just how you will be able to wait another full year to see what SportsFest 2026 will have to offer!

Additional special events and entertainment will be scheduled throughout the weekend at times to be determined.

V. HOW THE MSCDA CAN *"GET INTO IT!"*

The **MSCDA** can GET INTO IT in a big way as a title or presenting sponsor of SportsFest 2025, as a tournament sponsor, activity area sponsor, or as a nonexclusive event participant.

SportsFest 2025 can provide the **MSCDA** with outstanding opportunities to feature your new models, offer test drives, raise awareness, promote special sales and financing incentives, and entertain important fleet customers.

In addition, the **MSCDA** can reinforce its position as a major corporate citizen in our community, joining a proud family of sponsors that includes: Angel's Cola, Bob's Burgers, FF Supermarkets, KMMM-FM Radio, L&M Garden Center, P.B.F. Shoes, Pyne Brothers Department Store, the Plainside Journal, Community Bank, Tomvel Ice Cream, Dell's Sports, and a host of official suppliers.

The pages that follow describe just some of the ways the **MSCDA** can **GET INTO IT!**

GOLD MEDAL—TITLE SPONSORSHIP

- SportsFest 2025 will be renamed **MSCDA SportsFest 2025**.
- The **MSCDA** will be integrated into the highly recognizable SportsFest logo and featured in all event site signage, banners, promotional point-of-purchase displays, social media campaigns, advertising, and event merchandise. All event press releases will include acknowledgment of the **MSCDA** as the title sponsor of SportsFest 2025.
- All third-party sponsor promotions authorized by the event organizer will be required to include the **MSCDA** identification in the event name.
- The **MSCDA** will be given the exclusive right to promote itself as the **"Official Car Dealership Association of SportsFest 2025."** All member dealers will be given the exclusive right to promote themselves as **"Members of the Official Car Dealership Association of SportsFest 2025."**
- The **MSCDA** and its member dealers will be granted exclusivity as sponsors of SportsFest 2025 in the automotive sales, service, and after-market parts categories.
- The **MSCDA** will be granted the opportunity to conduct test drives, subject to safety restrictions, in a mutually agreeable area adjacent to the event site. The **MSCDA** will have the right to provide shuttle transportation from the main entrance of StreetFest to the test drive site.
- An **MSCDA** representative will be given the opportunity to participate as a featured speaker in the grand opening ceremonies, as well as during the closing addresses prior to the Fireworks Spectacular.
- An **MSCDA** representative will participate on stage during the Medal Ceremonies on Sunday night.
- The **MSCDA** will be granted a 40' × 40' exhibit area in the Hometown Market Midway. Up to twelve (12) automobiles may be parked around the Midway as static displays, with signage promoting the test drives and dealer promotions.
- The **MSCDA** may additionally select one available tournament area to be recognized as the presenting sponsor. Currently available tournaments include basketball, flag football, shuffleboard, archery, and freestyle skateboarding.

- The **MSCDA** may additionally select one available entertainment activity to be recognized as the presenting sponsor. Currently available entertainment activities include the fireworks spectacular, ice cream social, pasta cook-off, fruit pie bake-off, and the medal ceremonies.
- The **MSCDA** will be granted to right to conduct an exclusive SportsFest 2025 sweepstakes promotion at PlainsideJournal.com (see below).
- The **MSCDA** will have the exclusive right to provide the weekend's grand drawing prize of one-year's use of a brand new car for one lucky winner.
- The **MSCDA** will receive two hundred (200) complimentary tickets to each of the pasta cook-off, the fruit pie bake-off, and the ice cream social.
- The **MSCDA** will receive one (1) complimentary team registration for the **MSCDA** SportsFest Corporate Challenge.
- The **MSCDA** will receive ten (10) complimentary athlete registrations for each of the tournament's nine featured sports.
- The **MSCDA** will have the exclusive use of a 40' × 40' VIP tent for private receptions and entertaining. (Furnishings, food, beverage, entertainment, signage, and decoration are at **MSCDA**'s cost.)
- The **MSCDA** will receive two hundred (200) complimentary daily passes to the SportsFest 2025 VIP Hospitality Tent. A great spot to show your appreciation to your best customers!
- The **MSCDA** will receive twenty (20) backstage passes for the Headline Concert, including a meet-and-greet opportunity with the artist (subject to the artist's contract restrictions). Fifty percent (50%) of these backstage passes must be given away as part of a consumer promotion by the **MSCDA** and its member dealers.
- The **MSCDA** will receive fifty (50) VIP seating passes for the Headline Concert. Guests will be seated on a first-come, first-served basis.
- The **MSCDA** will receive one hundred (100) VIP SportsFest merchandise packs, including a t-shirt, cap, pin, and commemorative poster. Fifty percent (50%) of these merchandise packs must be given away as part of a consumer promotion by the **MSCDA** and its member dealers.

MSCDA SPORTSFEST 2025 TITLE SPONSORSHIP: $150,000

VI. NEXT STEPS

SportsFest 2025 and D.E.F. Sports & Entertainment are excited about the possibility of welcoming the **MSCDA** as our 2025 title sponsor.

The sponsorship opportunities described in this proposal have been prepared to reflect the **MSCDA**'s stated desire to increase the exposure of its member dealerships to area residents and to encourage test drives by potential car purchasers. Additional sponsorship opportunities may be customized to best fit the needs of the **MSCDA**. We look forward to working with you to create a dynamic partnership that will help the **MSCDA** meet its marketing objectives, and exceed its expectations.

Please call:
Jack D'Andrea
Executive Director
SportsFest 2025
1836 Adams Street
Brownsville, MO 00000
Tel: 000-000-0000
Fax: 000-000-0000
Jdandrea@sportsfest.net

APPENDIX 8

Sample Sponsorship Agreement

Note: This sample abbreviated sponsorship agreement is provided for illustrative purposes only. It should not be used as a legal document without the review and advice of competent legal counsel. Additional sections should be added to memorialize any additional elements agreed to during negotiations.

* * *

DATE _____

Corporate Name of Sponsor
Attn: *Contact Name Address*
Re: *Name of Event*

Dear _____:

This letter, when executed by the parties, shall set forth the agreement (the "Agreement") between _____ (the "Company") and _____ (the "Event Organizer"), relating to the Company's sponsorship of _____ (the "Event").

1. DEFINITIONS

As used herein, the following terms shall have the following meanings:
1.1. "Event" shall consist of (*Insert a full description of the event here, including dates, times, and location*)
_____
_____

1.2. The Company acknowledges and agrees that, subject to the Event Organizer's obligations to the Company as set forth herein, the Event Organizer shall have complete creative and operational control over every aspect of the Event.

1.3. "Marks" shall mean the following: (i) the name and logo of the Event, (ii) the name and logo of Event Organizer, (iii) any marks developed after the date of this Agreement that describe elements of the Event or contain the name of the Event.

1.4. "Term" shall mean the period beginning as of the date of this Agreement and ending on (*insert the expiration date of the sponsorship agreement, typically shortly after the last event the sponsor has agreed to support if multiple years*) _____

_____

1.5. "Territory" shall mean (*specifically describe here the geographic boundaries defined by the sponsorship, i.e., the name of the community, state, or broader territory in which the sponsor will have marketing rights to the event*) _____

_____

2. MARKETING RIGHTS

The Event Organizer hereby grants to the Company the following sponsorship rights in connection with the Event in the Territory and during the Term, subject to and in accordance with the terms and conditions set forth in this Agreement:

2.1. The Event shall be referred to as (*insert the official title of the event here, including title or presenting sponsor references, if applicable*) _____. This title shall be used in all promotional, advertising, and other materials prepared by each of the Event Organizer and the Company, in connection with the Event.

2.2. The Company shall have the right to use the Marks in connection with Event-themed advertising and promotional programs in print, online, broadcast and streaming media, at retail locations, and points of purchase in the Territory during the Term at its sole cost and expense. Each such advertising or promotional program shall be subject to the approval of the Event Organizer in its sole discretion.

2.3. The Company shall have the right to distribute product samples or premiums at its own expense using the Marks in the Territory during the Term. Each such product sample or premium prepared for distribution using the Marks must be approved by the Event Organizer in its sole discretion.

2.4. The Company's name and/or logo shall be included in all print, online, social media, and broadcast advertising promoting the Event, including but not limited to press releases concerning the Event; signage placed in various locations throughout the Event listing corporate sponsors of the Event, and on any mobile device applications related to the Event.

2.5. The Company shall be entitled to five (5) public address announcements during the Event, each of no more than twenty (20) seconds duration. The timing and placement in the program of such public address announcements is at the sole discretion of the Event Organizer.

2.6. The Company shall be entitled to two (2) commercial spots each of no more than thirty (30) seconds duration to be displayed during the Event on the scoreboard video screen and approved for use by the Event Organizer in its sole discretion. The timing and placement in the program of such commercial spots is at the sole discretion of the Event Organizer.

3. OTHER BENEFITS

(*Note: Benefits outlined below are for a hypothetical sports event. Include all benefits other than Marketing Rights in this section.*)

The Company shall receive, at no additional cost:

3.1. Number (#) tickets to the Event in the Premium Seating section of the Facility.

3.2. Number (#) tickets to the Event in other sections of the Facility on a best-available basis.

3.3. Number (#) tickets to each of the pregame hospitality suite and the postevent party.

3.4. Number (#) invitations to the VIP athlete meet-and-greet opportunity on the evening prior to the Event.

4. COMPENSATION

In full consideration for the rights granted and agreements made hereunder, the Company shall pay to the Event Organizer a fee equal to $_____ in the aggregate, which shall be payable as follows: $_____ upon execution of this agreement, $_____ on or before _____, and $_____ on or before _____.

5. REPRESENTATIONS, WARRANTIES, AND COVENANTS

The Company shall indemnify and hold harmless the Event Organizer, its owners, directors, governors, officers, employees, agents, successors, and assigns, from and against any claims, demands, causes of action, suits, proceedings, judgments, losses, liabilities, damages, injuries, costs, and expenses arising out of, resulting from, or which, if true, would arise out of or result from, any act or omission of the Company relating to this Agreement; or misrepresentation, breach of warranty, or other breach of any obligation or covenant made by Company in this Agreement. Without limitation of the indemnification hereunder, the Company shall maintain both general liability and product liability insurance, in customary amounts and on reasonable terms, which policies shall include the Event Organizer and its owners, directors, governors, officers, partners, partnerships, principals, employees, agents, successors, and assigns as additional insureds.

6. TERMINATION

6.1. The Event Organizer may terminate this Agreement by written notice to Company should Company fail to make any payment required hereunder when due, or observe or perform any of its other material obligations under this Agreement, in each case if such failure, if curable, is not cured within five (5) business days after receipt by Company of written notice of thereof.

6.2. This Agreement shall terminate automatically if either party files any voluntary, or if there is filed against either party an involuntary, petition in bankruptcy under the Bankruptcy Act.

7. MISCELLANEOUS

The Company shall not assign this Agreement to any person, corporation, or other entity without the prior written consent of the Event Organizer. The Event Organizer shall not assign this Agreement to any person, corporation, or other entity, other than to a parent, subsidiary, or other affiliate, without the prior written consent of the Company. This Agreement and all of the terms and provisions hereof, will be binding upon, and will inure to the benefit of, the parties hereto and their respective successors and permitted assigns.

Please indicate your agreement with the foregoing terms by signing this Agreement. A fully executed copy of this Agreement will be returned to you promptly thereafter.

Sincerely,

Event Organizer

By: _____

Name: _____

Title: _____

ACCEPTED AND AGREED, this _____ day of _____, _____.

The Company

By: _____

Name: _____

Title: _____

APPENDIX 9

Sports Event
Participant Release

This sample participant waiver and release is provided for illustrative purposes only. It should not be used as a legal document without the review and advice of competent legal counsel.

Name ("Participant"): _____

Address: _____

_____

Email: _____

Telephone (Home): _____

Telephone (Mobile): _____

RELEASE FROM LIABILITY.   By freely agreeing to participate in (name of event) (the "Event") as a volunteer, athlete, sports activity participant, or attendee, the "Participant," and if the Participant is younger than 18 years old, his/her parent or guardian, hereby voluntarily agree to release (name of organizer) (the "Sports Event Organizer"), each owner, operator, and management agent of each event facility, each sponsor, agency, vendor, independent contractor, and person, partnership, or corporation engaged by the Sports Event Organizer, and each of their respective parent entities, subsidiaries, stockholders, affiliates, and other related entities, and each officer, director, employee, volunteer, licensor, sponsor, partner, principal, representative, and agent of the Sports Event Organizer and each of the foregoing, and all of the foregoing's respective successors and assigns (collectively, the "Releasees"), from, and waive in respect of each Releasee and covenant not to sue any Releasee for any and all liabilities, losses, damages, costs, expenses, causes of action, suits, and claims of any nature whatsoever (collectively, the "Liabilities") arising from, based on, or relating to personal injury or death to, or damage to or loss of property of, the Participant sustained in connection with the Participant's participation in any activity or event associated with the Event, or travel to or from any of the foregoing activities or events. Such release, discharge, waiver, and covenant not to sue shall include, but not be limited to, any and all such Liabilities caused in whole or in part by the negligence of any Releasee in connection with such Releasee's involvement with the Event.

PARTICIPANT ASSUMES RISK.   The Participant is aware of and understands the inherent risks and dangers of the Event in which he or she will be participating and the potential for injury that exists when participating in the Event, and agrees to assume all risk of and responsibility for personal injury or death to, or damage to or loss of property of, the Participant arising from, or relating to the Participant's participation in the Event. Such assumption of risk includes, but is not limited to, any personal injury or death, or damage to or loss of property caused in whole or in part by the negligence of any Releasee. The Participant understands and agrees that, in the event of any injury to the Participant, none of the Releasees will be responsible for any decisions relating to medical treatment for the Participant or for such treatment itself.

RIGHT OF PUBLICITY.   Participation in the Event shall constitute permission to use the name, likeness, or any other identification of the Participant for advertising, publicity, or any other purposes in connection with the Event or the business of any of the Releasees, in any medium and at any time, in perpetuity, and without compensation to or right of prior review or approval by the Participant or his or her parent or legal guardian (except where prohibited by law). The Participant agrees, for itself and its personal representatives, executors, administrators, heirs, next of kin, successors and assigns, to release and discharge each Releasee from, to waive in respect of each Releasee, and not to sue any Releasee for, any and all Liabilities arising from, based on, or relating to any claim for invasion of privacy, violation of right of publicity, defamation, or appropriation in connection with any such use.

NO OBLIGATION OF RELEASEES.   None of the Releasees shall have, or be deemed to have, any obligation to the Participant hereunder or otherwise in connection with the Event unless set forth in writing signed by the Participant and the Releasee.

MISCELLANEOUS.   This Release shall be governed by and construed in accordance with the laws of _(state or province in which the organizer is incorporated)_____. If any portion of this Release shall be held invalid or unenforceable, the remaining portion hereof shall not be affected thereby and shall remain in full force and effect.

REPRESENTATIONS.   The Participant and his or her parent or legal guardian states that he/ she has had full opportunity to ask any questions regarding the Event that he or she may have, that he or she has read and understands this Release (or that his or her parent or legal guardian has read and understands this Release, and has explained it to the Participant), and that he or she has been given an opportunity to review this Release with anyone he or she chooses, including a lawyer, and has done so to the extent he or she wishes to do so. The Participant further states that he or she is in good physical condition, is physically fit to participate in the Event, and is not subject to any medical condition that poses or may pose any risk of harm or disability to others.

_____   Date: _____
(Signature of Participant)

I am over the age of 18 as of this date: _____Yes _____No
Name of Parent or Guardian (Please Print) if Participant is Under 18:
_____   Date: _____
(Signature of Parent or Guardian)

Emergency Contact Name:_____
Emergency Contact Telephone Number:_____
Emergency Contact Email:_____

Sample Sports Event
Run of Show (Pre-event)

FIVE COUNTY FOOTBALL TOURNAMENT
FINAL GAME RUN OF SHOW
(as of November 28)

#	TIME	SEGMENT	R/T	DESCRIPTION	AUDIO	VIDEO/SCOREBOARD
1	7:00:00	**House Open**	0:30:00	Audience enters. Lights at opening preset levels. Gobos in corners. Stage managers to get players out of locker rooms at 7:25:00.	P.A. Mic: Welcome & sponsor recognition (Pea Pond Mills, Pete's Pies, Faroff Airlines, Metro Daily News Online) over APB: Welcome mix	Event & sponsor logos in rotation; Welcome. Sponsor logos displayed during recognition (Pea Pond Mills, Pete's Pies, Faroff Airlines, Metro Daily News Online).
2	7:30:00	**Player Warm-ups**	0:20:00	Players enter and warm up on field. Lights on full competition level.	APB: Warm-up mix	Event & sponsor logos displayed in rotation; Welcome.
3	7:50:00	**Set Up Opening Ceremonies**	0:10:00	Players leave field. Dim lights to house open level. Crew sets up opening ceremonies riser at 50-yard line. Band, flag bearers, and kick line at position on sidelines at 7:57:00.	APB: Set up mix	Event & sponsor logos in rotation; Welcome. Sponsor logos displayed during recognition.
4	8:00:00	**Five County High Schools All-Star Marching Band**	0:03:30	Lights on full. Massed Five County High Schools All-Star Marching Band, flag bearers, and kick line enter field from sidelines to drum cadence, then perform: "Remember the Titans."	Fade music. Marching Band plays live	"Please Welcome the Five County High Schools All-Star Marching Band!"

(Continued)

#	TIME	SEGMENT	R/T	DESCRIPTION	AUDIO	VIDEO/SCOREBOARD
5	8:03:30	**Host Welcome**	0:01:00	Public address announcer welcomes J.J. Jayson. Jayson walks from sideline to opening ceremonies riser and welcomes audience. Jayson intros Superintendent of Schools Andrew Anderson.	P.A. Mic for Host Introduction; riser mic	"WFMS Host J.J. Jayson"
6	8:04:30	**Superintendent of Schools**	0:02:00	Superintendent Anderson walks from sideline to opening ceremonies riser and speaks from riser mic. Exits to sidelines when finished with remarks.	Riser mic	"Superintendent of Schools Andrew Anderson"
7	8:06:30	**Introduction of the Players**	0:06:00	Jayson returns to mic. Band plays on cue as teams run from sidelines (without helmets!) to their respective 20-yard lines. Jayson introduces each player; players wave.	Riser mic; Marching Band (live)	"The Five County High Schools All-Stars!"
8	8:12:30	**National Anthem**	0:02:00	Jayson introduces Betty Fumbles to sing National Anthem. Fumbles walks from sideline halfway to riser holding wired microphone. Players and singer face band's color guard. Fumbles sings.	Riser mic; Singer mic	"Our National Anthem"
9	8:14:30	**Ready to Go!**	0:02:30	Fumbles exits. Jayson thanks all, departs. Players to proper sidelines. Band, flag bearers, and kick line march off to "On Wisconsin!" Crew removes ceremony riser.	Riser mic; Marching Band (live)	"Welcome to the Five County Football Tournafest!"
10	8:17:00	**KICKOFF!**		Band continues playing until kickoff.	Marching Band (live) until kickoff	"It's Game Time!"

APPENDIX 11

Sample Event Pocket Guide

(or Link)

Mid-Regional Football Championship
Game Day Staff Pocket Guide

Stadium Seating Plan

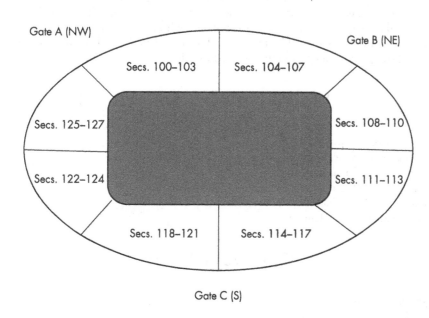

FAN SERVICES LOCATIONS:

First Aid: Gate C

Restrooms: Sections 102, 106, 116, 120, and Gate A

Refreshments: Sections 100, 104, 108, 111, 114, 118, 122

ADA Seating: Sections 101, 106, 115, 120

Guest Services and Box Office/Ticket Conflicts: Gate C

Security Office: Gate B

Emergency and Security Procedures

1. In case of fire or medical emergency, call 911, then contact stadium supervisor or event security on Radio Channel 2 to notify management of all emergencies.
2. In case of weather emergency, your supervisor will instruct you to direct fans to concourses under seating areas. Do not act until directed by your supervisor.
3. To deal with unruly fans, seek assistance from event security (Channel 2).
4. Report suspicious behavior and packages to event security immediately.

Prohibited Items

The following items are not permitted in the stadium at any time: glass bottles, firearms, knives, or weapons of any kind; signs and banners containing offensive language, photographs, or illustrations; backpacks; bags greater than 3 cubic feet; or camera tripods. Fans who wish to take photographs or video footage for their own enjoyment and noncommercial use are welcome to do so from their seats only.

There are no facilities at the event for checking and recovering prohibited and other items.

Fans should leave prohibited items in their parked vehicles.

Walkie-Talkie Channels

- Channel 1: Event Management
- Channel 2: Stadium Security
- Channel 3: Game Management
- Channel 4: Game Presentation
- Channel 5: Food/Merchandise Management
- Channel 6: Spare/Talk Channel

Key Event Times

Doors open: 12:00 noon

Pregame ceremonies begin: 1:15 P.M.

Kickoff: 1:35 P.M.

Approximate end time: 4:30 P.M.

APPENDIX 12

Simple Accreditation Plan

Use these codes on event credentials to enable the security staff to quickly identify those permitted access to various event site areas. Credential colors or additional codes for access to specific zones may be added as required by the event.

Code	Classification	Description
PRE	Pre-event	Access during installation and dismantle only; not valid event day
A	Special access	Permits access for staff to all event areas
AA	All access	Access for staff to all event areas except field
FOH	Front of house	Access to audience areas only
VIP	VIP guest	Access to hospitality; also non-audience areas if escorted by event staff
M	Media	Access to press working areas and photographer risers
P	Participant/Player	Access to locker rooms and field
C	Cast	Access to cast marshaling area
TV	Broadcast	Access to broadcasting facilities and production trucks

APPENDIX 13

Checklist of Public Address Announcements

Ensure you have scripted these public address announcements in advance:

☐ **Emergency Evacuation Procedure (Pre-event)**
  o Describe the safest ways to leave the host facility from seating locations and where to go if notified of a weather emergency, and/or
  o Describe where to go if notified to evacuate the host facility.
  o Sample: *"Your attention, please, ladies and gentlemen. If informed of a weather or other emergency, it may be necessary to interrupt today's game and provide you with instructions to exit your seats for your own safety. In the unlikely event of an evacuation, please follow instructions provided by our staff and calmly leave your seats for shelter in the concourses beneath or proceed to the school gymnasium located outside of Gate C. Please be sure to take a few moments to become familiar with the exit closest to your seat. Thank you for attending today's game and have a great time!"*

☐ **Welcome Announcement**
  o Welcome fans with an announcement designed to elicit a hearty and excited response. Very effective just before broadcasters join the action. One familiar example of such an announcement is: *"Good evening, everyone. Welcome to Madison Square Garden, The World's Most Famous Arena. Tonight, it's the Chicago Bulls against your New York Knicks!"*

☐ **Player/Athlete/Team Introductions**
  o Script these to a format most appropriate to your sport

☐ **Starting Line-Up**

☐ **Game Specific Announcement Formats**
  o Write blank scripts formatted for the various needs of your sport
  o Samples: "_____ penalty on number _____.(name of player), _____ minutes for _____." (e.g., "Wranglers penalty on number 43, Joe James two minutes for holding.") "At the end of the first quarter, the score: (team in the lead) _____, (team behind) _____."

☐ **Fan Behavior Announcements**
  o Many events and venues have an announcement to advise fans of the expectation of appropriate behavior.
  o Samples: *"Ladies and gentlemen, smoking is not permitted inside the arena." "Please be reminded that the use of offensive language or engaging in unruly or disrespectful behavior is prohibited and offenders will be subject to ejection and possible arrest. Everyone's cooperation will be appreciated. Thank you."*

☐ **Emergency Evacuation Alert (Do not incorporate into script; use only if needed)**
- o Instruct fans of an emergency weather condition, repeat instructions on where you want fans to calmly go and what you want them to do, and/or
- o Instruct fans on an emergency condition that requires evacuation, repeat instructions on how you want fans to exit calmly, and where you want them to go.
- o Sample: *"Your attention, please, ladies and gentlemen. We have been advised of lightning (or other condition) in the vicinity. For the safety of our fans and athletes, we ask you to calmly leave the seating area and seek shelter in the concourses beneath (or nearby school, gymnasium, auditorium, etc.) until the weather passes. We hope to resume the game as soon as possible and will provide you with periodic updates.* [NOTE: Make sure you have a way to communicate by public address or another efficient system in the area to which you are sending fans.]

☐ **Emergency Evacuation Updates (These need not be scripted, but should be on your checklist.)**
- o Provide periodic updates on the status of the evacuation; fans will appreciate being well informed and will feel frustrated if they do not know what is going on.
- o Sample: *"Ladies and gentlemen. We have been advised that the weather system over the stadium is expected to move away within the next 20 minutes. For your safety, please remain in a sheltered location. We will update you again in approximately 10 minutes. Thank you for your patience."*

☐ **Emergency Evacuation All-Clear (Do not incorporate into script; use only if needed)**
- o If the event is to continue, advise fans that the weather emergency has ended, and instruct them to return to their seats. Notify them of the approximate time the event will resume.
- o Sample: *"Ladies and gentlemen. The weather system has passed and it is now safe to return to your seats. We expect to resume play in approximately 15 minutes. Please proceed calmly back into the stadium. Thank you for your patience."*

☐ **Sponsor Obligations and Promotional Announcements**
- o For the best impact, try to keep promotional public announcements brief, no more than two sentences long.
- o Samples: *"The [name of event] is brought to you by Ebb Detergent. Look for money-saving coupons for Ebb in today's Metro Daily News Online." "Be sure to take a test drive of the new CarCaro sports utility vehicle in Parking Lot B after the game. Or, bring your ticket stub to your local CarCaro dealer for a special gift expressly for our fans."*
- o Sponsors always welcome mentions over the public address system. Consider including an acknowledgement message for all of your sponsors.
- o Sample: *"The (name of event) wishes to gratefully acknowledge the support of its sponsors: (list each sponsor by company name)."*

☐ **Goodbye Announcement**
- o It is always a good idea to verbally let fans know when the event is officially over, to thank them for attending and to wish them a safe journey.
- o Sample *"The final score of today's game:_____. Thank you for joining us for [name of event] and please arrive home safely."*

APPENDIX 14
Sample Event Day Checklist

Event organizers should create an event day checklist appropriate to their event. This checklist is a representative sample of requirements for a hypothetical event day. Many of these items should be checked or inspected before the day of the event.

Stadium
- [ ] Parking lots staffed and ready to open?
- [ ] Seats or bleachers clean and labeled?
- [ ] Path to ADA guest routes and seating areas inspected and clear?
- [ ] Crowd control queues in place?
- [ ] List of prohibited items posted at parking lot and entrances?
- [ ] Public notice of possible use of images in footage and photos posted at entrances?
- [ ] All entrances and exits clear of obstructions?
- [ ] Refuse and recycling containers deployed?
- [ ] All trash and empty boxes from installation cleared from public areas?
- [ ] Stadium lights on, if required?
- [ ] Décor, signage, and banner installations inspected and secured?
- [ ] Event day staff checked in and assigned to posts?
- [ ] Event day staff briefing conducted?
- [ ] Evacuation contingencies finalized and communicated to staff?
- [ ] Walkie-talkies distributed?
- [ ] Security and fan services staff in place and equipped with pocket guides?
- [ ] Fan activity areas clean, staffed, and ready?
- [ ] Guest Wi-Fi functioning correctly?
- [ ] Restroom facilities clean, stocked, and ready?
- [ ] Event presentation crew, staging, props, equipment ready to go?
- [ ] Performers and participating dignitaries confirmed and marshaled?
- [ ] Public address system and microphones tested and sound checked?
- [ ] Public address script and evacuation information prepared?
- [ ] Video screens functioning properly?
- [ ] Trophies, medals, and other participant recognition on site and ready?
- [ ] Ticket staff ready for last-minute sales and ticket conflict resolution?
- [ ] First aid staff in place and equipped as required?
- [ ] Concessions ready to serve?
- [ ] Hospitality areas ready for VIP guests?
- [ ] Merchandise in place and ready to sell?
- [ ] Staff break areas and refreshments ready for use?
- [ ] Back-up electricians, carpenters, equipment repair personnel in place or on call?
- [ ] Radio frequencies coordinated for wireless devices?

Field
- ☐ Final playing surface inspection conducted by grounds crew?
- ☐ Team bench areas set up properly and stocked with towels, ice, water, isotonic beverages, and other required items?
- ☐ Playing equipment (balls, nets, goalposts, etc.) inspected and flawless?
- ☐ Scoreclocks and scoreboards inspected and functioning properly?
- ☐ Team communication systems, heaters, or cooling fans in place?

Team and Locker Room Requirements
- ☐ Signs on outer doors of locker rooms?
- ☐ Lockers assigned and labeled?
- ☐ Lockers stocked and/or equipped?
- ☐ Uniforms and protective gear ready?
- ☐ Towels and/or ice available?
- ☐ Water and isotonic drinks ready?
- ☐ Showers, sinks, and restroom facilities clean, stocked, and ready?
- ☐ Required training equipment in place?
- ☐ Officials' locker room similarly ready?
- ☐ Emergency medical technicians and ambulances on site?

Media and Broadcast
- ☐ Media work areas and press conference areas inspected and ready?
- ☐ Media meal or refreshments ordered and ready to be served?
- ☐ Media support staff in place and ready to greet and provide service?
- ☐ Power, Wi-Fi, and phone service tested and functioning properly?
- ☐ Official rosters and statistics, and any changes, available for media and broadcasters?
- ☐ Have the staff members synchronized their watches and stopwatches to "truck time"?

Sponsors
- ☐ All sponsor activation areas clean, staffed, and ready for operation?
- ☐ Clean zone around stadium inspected for ordinance violations and ambush activity?
- ☐ Sponsor signage locations inventoried and provided as promised?
- ☐ Sponsor commercial and promotional spots received and ready?
- ☐ Sampling and giveaway items deployed in sufficient quantity to the people who will distribute them?

INDEX